"This readable emolument is a timely reminder of how Merton was shaped by the liturgical year and his own immersion in the monastic offices. It is wonderful to have it available to a new audience."

　　—LAWRENCE S. CUNNINGHAM, author of *Thomas Merton & the Monastic Vision*

"In these conferences, Thomas Merton exhorts his novices to 'absorb the meaning' of the chants they sing and to participate in the liturgy 'with intelligent faith and enlightened love.' The text consists of the notes Merton used to prepare the novices to celebrate various liturgical feasts and seasons. Patrick O'Connell's meticulous scholarship and comprehensive familiarity with Merton's thought is evident throughout his extensive introduction to the book and in the notes he provides to the text."

　　—THERESA SANDOK, former director of the Thomas Merton Center, Bellarmine University

"Introduced with meticulous care by Patrick O'Connell, *Liturgical Feasts and Seasons* is a wonderful opportunity to journey with Merton through the liturgical year as his novices once did—to be guided by Merton not only as a monastic teacher but also as a contemplative teacher for all of us. Merton's explication is at once deep and clear, but also at times strikingly personal and immediate—as much as he illuminates the liturgical seasons and their biblical roots, he connects them to who we are and our own spiritual journeys."

　　—THOMAS DEL PRETE, former president, the International Thomas Merton Society

Liturgical Feasts and Seasons

Novitiate Conferences on Scripture and Liturgy

Thomas Merton. *A Monastic Introduction to Sacred Scripture: Novitiate Conferences on Scripture and Liturgy 1*. Edited with an introduction by Patrick F. O'Connell. Foreword by Bonnie Bowman Thurston. Eugene, OR: Cascade Books, 2020.

Thomas Merton. *Notes on Genesis and Exodus: Novitiate Conferences on Scripture and Liturgy 2*. Edited with an Introduction by Patrick F. O'Connell. Foreword by Pauline A. Viviano. Eugene, OR: Cascade Books, 2021.

Thomas Merton. *Liturgical Feasts and Seasons: Novitiate Conferences on Scripture and Liturgy 3*. Edited with an Introduction by Patrick F. O'Connell. Foreword by Paul Quenon, OCSO. Eugene, OR: Cascade Books, 2022.

Liturgical Feasts and Seasons

Novitiate Conferences on
Scripture and Liturgy 3

Thomas Merton

EDITED WITH AN INTRODUCTION BY
Patrick F. O'Connell

FOREWORD BY
Paul Quenon, OCSO

 CASCADE *Books* · Eugene, Oregon

LITURGICAL FEASTS AND SEASONS
Novitiate Conferences on Scripture and Liturgy 3

Cascade Books
An Imprint of Wipf and Stock Publishers
199 W. 8th Ave., Suite 3
Eugene, OR 97401

www.wipfandstock.com

PAPERBACK ISBN: 978-1-7252-5312-4
HARDCOVER ISBN: 978-1-7252-5313-1
EBOOK ISBN: 978-1-7252-5314-8

Cataloguing-in-Publication data:

Names: Merton, Thomas, 1915–1968, author. | O'Connell, Patrick F., editor and
    introduction. | Quenon, Paul, foreword.
Title: Liturgical feasts and seasons : novitiate conferences on scripture and liturgy
    3. / Thomas Merton; edited and introduction by Patrick F. O'Connell; foreword
    by Paul Quenon.
Description: Eugene, OR: Cascade Books, 2022. | Includes bibliographical refer-
    ences and indexes.
Identifiers: ISBN 978-1-7252-5312-4 (paperback). | ISBN 978-1-7252-5313-1 (hard-
    cover). | ISBN 978-1-7252-5314-8 (ebook).
Subjects: LCSH: Cistercians—Liturgy. | Cistercians—Spiritual life. | Merton,
    Thomas, 1915–1968.
Classification: BX3403 M33 2022 (print). | BX3403 (ebook).

CONTENTS

FOREWORD

For those of us who, as scholastics or novices, were under the instruction of Fr. Louis, a major part was the teachings on the liturgy throughout the seasons. That was comprised of commentaries on the gospels, epistles, orations and antiphons, vigil readings, and hymns. It was conducted as a guided tour through the spiritual climates of Advent, Lent, Easter and on into Ordinary Time. Whenever some major solemnity came looming up on the horizon, we were duly prepared with points given on the central themes and the high notes of the day.

Fr. Louis served well that special pedagogical role which the Greek Church of old called a mystagogue—a term he never applied to himself. Yet, nowhere in Merton's previously published writings can this function so clearly be found as in these conference notes. Traditionally, a mystagogue leads the neophyte through the sacred rites into the mystery of their deeper meaning and power. These notes and reflections are spiritual instruction for newcomers to the monastic life, men who are already liturgically initiated as Christians, but generally are unformed in a contemplative assimilation of the daily liturgy and divine office. These notes go far beyond catechetical instruction, for they take us into one man's lifetime of reflection and seasoned experience of the Church Year.

The perspectives here are broad and full. On the one hand there might be a homely evocation of waking on a frosty Christmas dawn for the Morning Mass: "The atmosphere . . . brisk and purposeful . . . coming down from the dormitory in the atmosphere of mutual encouragement prescribed in the *Rule!*" (32–33). On the other hand there might be found astute references to contemporary theologians, papal encyclicals, quotations from Saint Thomas Aquinas, and even a surprising foray into the Byzantine Rite regarding the Assumption of Mary.

The heart and substance of these novitiate talks were always the liturgy's scriptural passages, which Fr. Louis would read at length. The overall effect for the listener depended on hearing these passages read, and fortunately the readings are provided here in full by the footnotes. Nowhere in all of Merton's writings can one find such an extended demonstration of the hermeneutical approach he took in commenting on Scripture. This was focused intensely on finding the meaning Scripture had for our life in God, and especially on how it might apply to the monastic life of the priests and brothers he was instructing. I would often leave at the end of a conference lifted with the feeling I had nourishment enough to last a week.

Probably many segments of these notes never reached the ears of the novices. Fr. Louis had a way of over-preparing, and then would skip through several pages to get to the points he wanted finally to make. The reader may be the first to have access to the complete content of these notes. On the other hand, much that was said in the conferences was never included in the notes; Fr. Louis was not one to be confined by the written page, and would launch out on what was relevant for the moment.

Now it is for those who take up this volume to continue the spiritual formation it offers, a deeper appreciation of liturgy which is a perpetual source of personal and community renewal. For in Christ, as Merton says, "the cycle of the seasons is something entirely new. It has become a *cycle of salvation*. The year is not just another year; it is the *Year of the Lord*—a year in which the passage of time itself brings us not only the natural renewal of spring and the fruitfulness of an earthly summer, but also the spiritual and interior fruitfulness of grace" (303).

Br. Paul Quenon, OCSO
Abbey of Gethsemani

INTRODUCTION

On August 21, 1957, Thomas Merton wrote to his friend and sometime typist Sr. Thérèse Lentfoehr[1] about a new set of novitiate conferences he was planning to send to her soon.

> One reason why I have been late in starting my letters is that I had to preach the sermon for the feast of St Bernard. I like to prepare sermons but didn't get much chance this time. A brother novice has the notes at the moment but I will send them on to you when I get them back—with the other material I wanted to get you to type. I am so sorry I haven't been able to send this material along yet. It is a collection of conferences on the Liturgical Cycle, given to the novices. I want to go over the ms and make changes and corrections and have been waiting for a chance to do so since May. . . . I was going to try to get the liturgy notes to you by July 16. All I could do was pray for you as fervently as I could at Mass on your wonderful feasts. But the notes will be along soon, if I can get at them.[2]

Sr. Thérèse had typed the mimeographs for the six sets of "Monastic Orientation" notes compiled from Merton's time as master of students at the Abbey of Gethsemani, between 1951 and 1955,[3] and was continuing to help out in this capacity now that Merton was the novice master at the

---

1. For a thorough presentation of this relationship as it developed over the course of two decades (1948–1968), see Nugent, *Thomas Merton and Thérèse Lentfoehr*.

2. Unpublished portion of August 21, 1957, letter from Thomas Merton to Thérèse Lentfoehr, SDS (archives of the Thomas Merton Center [TMC], Bellarmine University, Louisville, Kentucky); for the letter as published, see Merton, *Road to Joy*, 227–29.

3. See Merton's reference to her typing "the *last* series" of these notes in his October 22, 1955 letter to Sr. Thérèse announcing that he has become novice master (Merton, *Road to Joy*, 221); unpublished portions of this letter include further mention of "all this work over the past six years" (TMC archives). The first series of these notes actually predates Merton's appointment as master of students.

monastery, beginning in the fall of 1955. In return, she generally was able to keep the original copies for her extensive collection of Merton materials, which she assiduously preserved and carefully catalogued.[4]

On October 12, 1957, the conferences were finally mailed off: "It is ages since I got permission to send these Liturgy notes to you to be mimeographed," Merton wrote. "I am finally doing so, having renounced the vain ambition of going through every one of them and correcting all that I wanted to. I think they will have to do as they stand. I hope there are no terrible errors, I don't believe there are."[5] On November 10, a brief note accompanied what appears to be the return of some conferences that Sr. Thérèse had already typed and sent:

> I rush this off to you with the notes, which I have gone over rather hurriedly but I am sure everything is fine. I think I have answered all your queries, if not just use your own judgement. I add one messy page I found—on the Exaltation of the Holy Cross. Hard to read but fortunately brief Note that I have spelled out a few words clearly—they are not supposed to be put in twice. I just made them clear for your sake: I hope I made them clear.[6]

Four days later, some additional conferences were sent, and a suggestion made about the organization of the material:

> I enclose a few liturgy conferences that are not in the set I sent before. You can fit them in when you feel like it. Did I mention last time the idea that perhaps we could make two sets of notes, one for the "Time" and another for the "Saints"? That would make the whole business easier to manage. Unless you would want to mimeograph both sides of each sheet. Why not two volumes? It would be simpler.[7]

---

4. The material is now housed in the Rare Book and Manuscript Collection at Butler Library, Columbia University, New York City.

5. Unpublished portion of October 12, 1957, letter from Thomas Merton to Thérèse Lentfoehr, SDS (TMC archives); for the letter as published, see Merton, *Road to Joy*, 229.

6. Unpublished letter of November 10, 1957 from Thomas Merton to Thérèse Lentfoehr, SDS (TMC archives); this letter originally was dated simply "Nov 10," without a year; "[1958]" was subsequently added in pencil, presumably not by Merton, as it is demonstrably erroneous, since by that date the final mimeographed version of the conferences had already been run off.

7. Unpublished letter of November 14, 1957 from Thomas Merton to Thérèse Lentfoehr, SDS (TMC archives).

Apparently the original order had been simply chronological, moving through the liturgical year sequentially and interspersing conferences on the successive celebrations of the liturgical seasons, running from the First Sunday of Advent through the Last Sunday after Pentecost, with those on the feasts of various saints attached to fixed days of the calendar, likewise running from late November through late November, corresponding to the cycle beginning with Advent. The change was made more to accommodate the bulk of the material, which would have been very large for a single mimeographed volume, than to distinguish between the temporal and the sanctoral cycles, but the result was to create a more coherent two-part work, now titled "Liturgical Feasts and Seasons," though the "seasons" section comes first and the feast-day section second.

As 1958 arrived, Merton was still sending along additional material. On January 2 he wrote, "The liturgy notes haven't showed up yet but there is no hurry at all. I am enclosing herewith a couple of pages of extra 'feasts' in longhand, alas."[8] But shortly afterward, Sr. Thérèse had evidently completed typing up the material—not as yet in mimeograph form, but as a regular typescript for Merton to check before she retyped the entire work on stencils,[9] which would then be run off and distributed not only to the novices but to formation directors at other American Cistercian monasteries. On March 27, Merton wrote, "Months ago I got permission to write and send back the Liturgy notes, but everything has conspired to prevent me,"[10] including illness, complications with some of the novices and various other writing tasks. In a postscript he added, "I am sending you some odds and ends for your collection. Nothing here needs to be typed," but then he modifies that assurance: "The St Bernard sermon might however go in with the Liturgy notes for the feasts if you do not have it already. I don't think you have the Epiphany notes either but you may not be able to read them so no matter, they are not important."[11]

8. Unpublished letter of January 2, 1958, from Thomas Merton to Thérèse Lentfoehr, SDS (TMC archives); the "extra" pages are probably the conferences on Sts. Simon & Jude, the Vigil of All Saints and the Feast of All Saints—one page each of handwritten material and the only items other than the single handwritten page on the Exaltation of the Holy Cross, already sent, that were not typed.

9. For Sr. Thérèse's evident previous practice of making a separate typescript for Merton's personal use, see his comment in an unpublished portion of his October 22, 1955, letter: "Oh, and by the way, don't bother to type a special copy of the Sacred Art notes for me—please! The mimeographed copies are amply sufficient."

10. Merton, *Road to Joy*, 229.

11. Unpublished portion of March 27, 1958, letter from Thomas Merton to Thérèse

On April 18 he wrote, "Take your time with the Liturgy notes,"[12] but evidently she had promptly gotten down to work on the final version, which had been completed, bound, and sent by midsummer, as Merton wrote on July 14: "I have not yet thanked you for the Liturgy Notes. The color is just right, and they are much appreciated. We have of course paid the bill for the binding, I did not have to tell you that. You should always send those bills here, they are our responsibility." At the conclusion of the same lengthy letter he expressed his gratitude once again: "I . . . thank you very much. Above all for the Liturgy Notes. I am gradually stopping all this note business so you won't be bothered much longer with it. You have held up nobly, and I feel as usual guilty about burdening you."[13] Though he certainly was far from finished with "all this note business," as most of the dozen different sets of monastic conferences composed during his years as novice master were presented in their final form and reproduced for distribution subsequent to "Liturgical Feasts and Seasons," the rest were all typed up and multigraphed in-house by various novices over the years, so Sr. Thérèse was not in fact burdened with the task of typing them that she had performed so diligently for these notes.

The liturgy materials are unique among the various sets of novitiate conferences in that they were not presented regularly on a weekly (or even biweekly) basis over the course of months or even years as were Merton's classes on various aspects of monastic history and practices.[14] Rather they

---

Lentfoehr, SDS (TMC archives); the sermon is presumably the one he preached the previous August, mentioned in his August 21 letter; the Epiphany conference is probably the conference on Epiphany and Missions, the only item from the "Liturgical Feasts and Seasons" material sent by Merton to Sr. Thérèse that is not extant in the Lentfoehr collection at Columbia. Both these conferences are found in their proper place in the typescript Sr. Thérèse prepared for Merton before typing the stencils for the mimeograph, which may indicate that she already had copies of both at this time.

12. Unpublished portion of April 18, 1958 letter from Thomas Merton to Thérèse Lentfoehr, SDS (TMC archives); for the letter as published, see Merton, *Road to Joy*, 229–30.

13. Unpublished portions of July 14, 1958, letter from Thomas Merton to Thérèse Lentfoehr, SDS (TMC archives); for the letter as published, see Merton, *Road to Joy*, 230–31.

14. See Merton, *Cassian and the Fathers*; Merton, *Pre-Benedictine Monasticism*; Merton, *Introduction to Christian Mysticism*; Merton, *Rule of Saint Benedict*; Merton, *Monastic Observances*; Merton, *Life of the Vows*; Merton, *Charter, Customs,*

would have been given on occasions corresponding to the specific liturgi-cal celebrations being considered. He began the series for Advent 1955, almost immediately after becoming novice master, appending the date November 25, 1955, to "The Opening of the Liturgical Year" (301–9), written as an introduction for what was evidently already projected as a comprehensive set of reflections. On the verso side of the last of the five pages of this original typescript, he jotted down possible topics for "Further Advent Conferences"—including "Sat Dec 3—St John Baptist in Advent Liturgy (Lit of 2nd and 3rd Sundays)" which was indeed written (9–13); "Wed Dec 7 Something for Immac Conception," which probably corresponds to a two-page handwritten "Feast of the Immaculate Con-ception—Some themes from the office" (375–77); an undated, paren-thetical "(The Advent Ember Days + O Antiphons ?)"—both the former (13–15) and the latter (18–24) are included in the conferences; "Sun Dec 18—Cistercian Xmas Sermons—or something on the Incarnation"—the latter presumably the four-page typescript "The Mystery of the Incarna-tion" (24–30), while there is no evidence that the former was composed; "Dec 30. Friday—conf. on Christmas Liturgy" which probably became "The Christmas Liturgy—The 3 Masses" (30–37); a separate section on "Conferences after Christmas" concludes with "Thurs Epiphany Liturgy," which probably became the three-page handwritten "The Office of the Epiphany of Our Lord" (48–51).

There are no further notes of this kind specifying particular dates for conferences, but presumably the bulk of the material for both the temporal and sanctoral cycles was presented during the course of 1956. Evidently the two earliest dated conferences were actually presented before the introduction was completed: the conference on "The Dedica-tion of the Church" (291–95), celebrated at Gethsemani on November 15, is dated "1955" on the typescript; even earlier was the conference on St. Martin of Tours (285–87), a handwritten page dated "Nov. 11 1955." The conference titled "Monastic Peace" (267–71) is specified as "F. of St Luke, 1956"; the handwritten "Notes for the Feast of the Presentation" (of Mary) (295–300) are dated "1956"; "Further Advent Notes" (16–18) are parenthetically dated "1956"—thus belonging to a second year of conferences begun with Advent the year before. The conference on the Feast of St. Benedict (186–89) is dated 1957; as indicated in Merton's

Constitutions; Merton, Cistercian Fathers and Their Monastic Theology; Merton, Me-dieval Cistercian History; Merton, Monastic Introduction to Sacred Scripture; Merton, Notes on Genesis and Exodus.

correspondence with Sr. Thérèse, the sermon for the Feast of St. Bernard (240–43) was apparently given in 1957 (August 20),[15] as well as the conference on the Exaltation of the Holy Cross, celebrated on September 14 (250–51). The brief notes on the Circumcision (47–48) are among the latest materials, since they are found written below jottings that include mention of "1958 Common Work"; evidently the material on Epiphany and Missions (52–54) mentioned in his March 27, 1958, letter (the only material not extant in Merton's own version) also comes from that year. For those feasts that have more than one conference devoted to them, presumably they come from successive years. But since the major part of the material had been sent to Sr. Thérèse by mid-October 1957, it is clear that almost all of the "Liturgical Feasts and Seasons" mimeograph had been composed between November 1955 and that date, with the Epiphany notes of January 1958 evidently being the last conference to be included.

~

The textual development of *Liturgical Feasts and Seasons* is rather more complicated than that of other sets of Merton's monastic conferences. There are five versions of the materials, all of which contribute to some degree to the critical text of the present edition. (For a list of the versions of each of the individual conferences, see Appendix A [381–90].)

The first (designated TMa here), housed in the archives of the Thomas Merton Center at Bellarmine University in Louisville, Kentucky, is composed solely of typescripts and handwritten pages produced by Merton himself and used by him in delivering the conferences to the novices. What is quickly apparent is that this collection includes only part of the materials that eventually were included in the "Liturgical Feasts and Seasons" mimeograph: only twelve of fifty-five items found in Part I and twenty-four of forty-five items found in Part II. The major reason for these gaps becomes apparent when the second version of the material (designated TMb) is examined. It is clear that many of the items found here and missing in TMa were also part of Merton's original reading typescripts, pages which he sent to Sr. Thérèse for retyping, leaving him without copies at the monastery. What is more puzzling is that TMa also

15. It is dated 1958 on the typescript, but this is clearly in error as it is mentioned in Merton's letter of March 27 of that year, long before the feast on August 20, by which time the final mimeograph of the entire set of conferences had been run off.

includes thirty-four items that are not found in the final mimeographed "Liturgical Feasts and Seasons." Some of this material is slight and may have been purposely excluded. One item, for Monday of the Second Week of Lent (346), is actually written on a fragmentary piece of paper and can be assigned to its proper day only by identifying it through its lectionary readings. Some of the material, which was probably assembled in its present form not by Merton himself but at some point well after his death by longtime Merton Center director Robert E. Daggy, is loosely associated at best with the liturgical year, and one item, on the chapter of faults (326–28), is probably included only because it was filed along with material on spiritual direction associated with the Epiphany (321–26), which is itself an early version of the first two parts of "Spiritual Direction in the Monastic Setting," included as an Appendix to the *Monastic Observances* conferences.[16] But it seems likely that many if not most of these items were omitted inadvertently, misplaced, or perhaps forgotten when Merton was assembling the disparate materials to send to Sr. Thérèse. Even some of the relatively short items would fill in gaps in the mimeographed series, such as the notes for Passion Sunday (349–50), the Monday after Easter (353–55), Low Sunday (356–57) and the Third Sunday after Easter (357–59). Given the Marian focus of so much of the material in the final version, which includes conferences on even relatively minor Marian feasts, it seems inconceivable that Merton would have excluded material on the Feast of the Immaculate Conception if it had been readily accessible (no less than three separate conferences on the feast, one of which is quite substantial, are part of TMa [367–77]). Likewise a major discussion of "Jesus in the Lenten Gospels" (333–45) would seem very unlikely to have been left out on purpose. However "The Opening of the Liturgical Year," certainly one of the major pieces of writing in the whole collection, was evidently considered significant enough by Merton to publish it in slightly revised form as an article titled "Time and the Liturgy" in 1956,[17] which is no doubt the reason why it was omitted from the mimeographed text of "Liturgical Feasts and Seasons," despite its singular relevance and

16. See Merton, *Monastic Observances*, 255–61.

17. There are about a dozen minor alterations in this published text, the most extensive being the addition of a single sentence (8) quoting the secret from the ninth Sunday after Pentecost after the sentence: "By the liturgy, while remaining in time, we enter into the great celebration that takes place before the throne of the Lamb in heaven, in eternity" (307). This article was much more heavily revised for its inclusion in Merton, *Seasons of Celebration*, 45–60: see below, pages xlii–xliv.

importance in providing a general orientation to the rest of the material that was originally intended to follow it. All these items uniquely present in TMa, for the sake of completeness even those arguably not originally intended by Merton to form part of the liturgy conferences, are included in the present edition in a section of "Additional Materials" following Parts I and II, rearranged slightly from the order in which they appear in the Merton Center collection, roughly following the liturgical calendar but not separated into temporal and sanctoral cycles.

The second version of the text (TMb), now part of the Lentfoehr collection at the Columbia University Library, begins with a title page handwritten by Merton that reads: "LITURGICAL / *FEASTS* / AND / *SEASONS* / conferences given in the Choir Novitiate / Abbey of Gethsemani." It includes every item found in the final mimeograph except the conference on Epiphany and Missions, which was apparently mislaid by Sr. Thérèse at some point and not filed with the rest of the material. For those items not found in TMa this version carries the primary textual authority. For those items present in both versions, it might seem that the later versions found in TMb would have the greater authority, but a comparison of the two texts reveals that in many cases the TMb version is inferior to that of TMa, particularly for those items in TMa that were handwritten by Merton and were subsequently typed before being sent to Sr. Thérèse. It is evident that these typed copies were not made by Merton himself but presumably by one of the novices, Merton's typical practice for most of his novitiate conferences,[18] because occasionally the typist misreads Merton's difficult handwriting and introduces errors into the TMb text which are then transmitted to Sr. Thérèse's own typescript (designated TL) and subsequently to the mimeograph version. While Merton frequently introduces authorial alterations in the TMb text before it is sent to Sr. Thérèse, more often the differences between the two texts are the result of scribal error. Therefore determining the proper reading for each particular discrepancy is necessary in establishing what Merton actually intended.

18. For the textual witnesses to the other published sets of conferences, see Merton, *Cassian and the Fathers*, liv–lxi; Merton, *Pre-Benedictine Monasticism*, lxii–lxv; Merton, *Introduction to Christian Mysticism*, liii–lv; Merton, *Rule of Saint Benedict*, lvi–lix; Merton, *Monastic Observances*, l–liii; Merton, *Life of the Vows*, lxxiv–lxxviii; Merton, *Charter, Customs, Constitutions*, xvi–xvii, xxii, xxx–xxxi, lvii–lix; Merton, *Cistercian Fathers*, lv–lvii, lxxx–lxxxiii, cviii–cix; Merton, *Medieval Cistercian History*, xv–xx, l–li; Merton, *Monastic Introduction to Sacred Scripture*, xi–xiii; Merton, *Notes on Genesis and Exodus*, lv–lvi.

The third version of the text (designated TMc), now in the archives of the Thomas Merton Center, was apparently a set that Merton had put together for his own use. It has a cover with a pasted label reading: "LITURGY NOTES / (Choir novitiate)" and a handwritten title page reading: "NOTES / ON / THE / LITURGY / ad usum novitiorum chori. / B. M. de Gethsemani."[19] The text consists of eighty-four separate items (plus three duplicates), arranged in a somewhat different order than what would become the final sequence of the conferences, all but two of which are either carbons or ribbon copies identical to the typescripts found in TMb, but lacking the alterations Merton made on many of these typescripts prior to sending them to Sr. Thérèse. Thirteen of the items in TMb are not found in this collection: ten of them (nine handwritten[20] plus the late sermon outline for the Feast of St. Bernard) were evidently sent to Sr. Thérèse subsequent to the original mailing; "Epiphany and Missions" is not included, nor are "Tenth Sunday after Pentecost" and "September Ember Days." (TMb includes a duplicate copy of the former, which may have originally belonged with this set, though there is no second copy of the latter, which immediately follows.) Since all of the items shared by this collection and TMb are present in the latter either in identical or in revised form, TMc does not serve as copy text for any of this material. However, two unique items are present only in the TMc collection: a four-page typescript titled "The Feast of the Annunciation" and a one-page typescript immediately following titled "*Wednesday of the Fourth Week in Lent.*" It seems probable that these two items would have been intended to be included in the set Merton forwarded to Sr. Thérèse to be typed but were inadvertently misplaced either before they were sent or after they arrived. They have therefore been reintegrated into the *Liturgical Feasts and Seasons* text proper—the latter in its original location immediately preceding "Passiontide" and the former inserted into the sanctoral cycle in its appropriate chronological position (March 25) between "Feast of Our Holy Father St. Benedict" (March 21) and "Feast of the Seven Dolors" (Friday in Passion Week). TMc serves as the copy text only for these two conferences.

19. "for the use of the novices of the choir / Our Lady of Gethsemani."

20. "Fourth Sunday {in} Advent"; "*The Prince of Peace*—Christmas Season"; "Sunday within {the} Octave of Christmas"; "Circumcision"; "Twenty-First Sunday after Pentecost"; "Exaltation of the Holy Cross"; "Saints Simon and Jude"; "Vigil of All Saints"; "Feast of All Saints."

The fourth version of the text (TL) is the draft typescript that Sr. Thérèse produced from TMb and sent to Merton to check before making the final mimeograph stencils. She was a careful typist, but introduced occasional new errata due to eyeskip or misreadings for the few handwritten pages included in TMb. On five occasions[21] there was also a misordering of pages that resulted in material from one conference erroneously becoming attached to a totally different conference. It is clear from his letters that the busy Merton did not proofread Sr. Thérèse's typescript carefully, and did not notice these new errata, nor most of those that had been introduced by his typist(s) in TMb and reproduced by Sr. Thérèse. Thus this version contains some further flaws, and in any case would have no textual authority independent of TMb of which it is intended to be an accurate copy. However Merton did introduce a few handwritten alterations on this typescript, often including missing dates of particular feasts in Part II, but occasionally making substantive changes, as when he canceled some of the extensive description of the horarium for Holy Thursday (97, 98; see 419). These alterations made by Merton himself are the only elements in TL that are incorporated into the critical text of this edition (other than the conference on "Epiphany and Missions," which is not present in TMa and no longer extant as part of TMb).

The final version of the text is the mimeograph that Sr. Thérèse also typed, which is virtually identical to TL as altered by Merton's few handwritten additions and excisions. This is of course the only version that would have been read by anyone other than those involved in producing the four previous versions, so it has been the *textus receptus* of "Liturgical Feasts and Seasons" for the relatively few readers within and beyond Gethsemani who might have encountered it at the time it was first made available or subsequently, for example in volume 24 of Merton's *Collected Essays*, the twenty-four-volume bound set of published and unpublished materials assembled at the Abbey of Gethsemani and available both there and at the Thomas Merton Center. It of course has no textual authority of its own, being based completely on the emended version of TL, which is itself dependent on TMb for all but the handful of changes Merton made on the typescript. It does include, however, a Table of Contents preceding each of the two sections, no doubt assembled by Sr. Thérèse but certainly

---

21. The conferences on the Baptism (54–58), Septuagesima (58–61), the Easter Liturgy (113–18), the Seventh Sunday after Pentecost (147–49), the Nativity of John the Baptist (207–12).

accepted by Merton, and therefore included as an integral part of the text in this volume.

Thus the present critical edition of *Liturgical Feasts and Seasons* provides for the first time a text that reflects Merton's actual intentions as they developed, determined by examining each relevant witness to each particular conference, and of course makes available the first opportunity to read those items from TMa that do not appear in the mimeograph. The textual notes in Appendix B appended to this edition thus record both the alterations Merton made in the process of composing the original version of each conference, as found either in TMa or in TMb, the alterations added on the typescript of TL, and lists of those substantive readings selected from each of the two primary witnesses and the variants found in the other text, so that interested readers can both trace the development of Merton's process of composition and determine for themselves whether a particular reading selected is plausibly superior to its alternative.

All substantive additions made to the text, in order to turn elliptical or fragmentary statements into complete sentences, are included in braces, as are the few emendations incorporated directly into the text, so that the reader can always determine exactly what Merton himself wrote. No effort is made to reproduce Merton's rather inconsistent punctuation, paragraphing, abbreviations, and typographical features; a standardized format for these features is established that in the judgment of the editor best represents a synthesis of Merton's own practice and contemporary usage: e.g., all Latin passages are italicized unless specific parts of a longer passage are underlined by Merton, in which case the underlined section of the passage is in roman type; all other passages underlined by Merton are italicized; words in uppercase in the text are printed in small caps; periods and commas are uniformly included within quotation marks; patterns of abbreviation and capitalization, very inconsistent in the copy text, are regularized. All references to primary and secondary sources are cited in the notes. Untranslated Latin passages in the original text are left in Latin but translated by the editor in the notes. Scriptural citations are taken from the Douai–Rheims–Challoner version of the Bible, the edition Merton himself regularly used.

⁓

As for the content of the conferences, there is considerable variation in length, in depth, in focus, and in significance across the 133 different conferences included in the text: fifty-five in Part I, forty-four in Part II, and thirty-four in the Additional Materials section. Of course the conferences date from the period just before the reform of the liturgy that would arise from the Second Vatican Council, so that they have a retrospective quality about them when read now, marked by a different language, a different lectionary, a different liturgical office, even a somewhat different liturgical cycle, with its celebration of the Circumcision on January 1, of the Epiphany on January 6, its commemoration of the Baptism a week later, the pre-Lenten triad of Septuagesima, Sexagesima, and Quinquagesima Sundays, the designation of the Fifth Sunday of Lent as Passion Sunday, even the change of date for some feasts, notably the removal of the Feast of the Visitation from July 2 to May 31. Still, the overall shape of the liturgical cycle remains substantially the same, and Merton's commentary on the meaning of the various feasts retains its pertinence for the insights it provides not only into his own commitment to this central dimension of Christian and monastic life, as well as his understanding of his role as novice master in introducing those in his care to the liturgical patterns and rhythms that would mark their lives in the monastery, but into the perennial meaning of the major, and some minor, events of the Christian narrative of salvation, if not on all the particulars of their celebration.

Part I of *Liturgical Feasts and Seasons* includes some consideration of twenty-five of the fifty-two Sundays of the year, along with a general discussion of "The Meaning of Sunday." Other major feasts not celebrated on Sunday (Circumcision, Epiphany, Baptism, Ascension, Corpus Christi, Sacred Heart), as well as less central commemorations (Ember Days, Rogation Days, Forty Hours) are given due attention. But not surprisingly the two central foci of the Christian mystery occupy the major part of Merton's attention. The first seven conferences are concerned with Advent, followed by four on Christmas. Ten conferences are devoted to Lent and Holy Week, with another five on Easter itself—a total of twenty-six of the fifty-five items in Part I, making up more than half of the actual text—sixty-five of the 113 pages of the mimeograph (thirty and thirty-five pages on Advent/Christmas and Lent/Easter, respectively). A further nine pages (four conferences) are given over to the conclusion of the

Easter season with the Feasts of the Ascension and Pentecost. It is evident then that Merton's emphasis in his instruction to the novices corresponds closely to that of the church itself, as one would expect.

Merton appropriately opens his initial conference, on the First Sunday of Advent (4–6), with comments on the meaning of liturgy itself:

> The liturgy is the expression of the Church's love for God. Hence it is a school of love. It forms our hearts, minds, wills, sensibilities and taste. But this formation is not merely psychological. We are formed by the objective reality of God's love for us, acting upon us in and through the liturgy. This formation gives us a "mind" and "heart" greater than our own. It takes us above and beyond ourselves. We rise to the level of the liturgy, and this makes us greater than we were before. The liturgy elevates us; it broadens our horizons, makes us capable of greater things. Jesus Himself forms our souls as we pray and sing with the liturgy. (4)

The focus here on the educational role of the liturgy is particularly relevant for Merton's audience of aspiring monks in formation. But he takes care immediately not to reduce the liturgy to a matter of subjective feelings and impressions. It is a participation in the expression of the entire church's love for God, and its effects are due to "the objective reality" of divine love, which transforms and elevates mind and heart. He continues by distinguishing between the artificial stimulation of sentimentality, cultivation of emotion for its own sake, and a healthy engagement and integration of affectivity in a mature response to the mysteries of faith celebrated in the liturgical cycle:

> The action of the liturgy on our hearts is meant to be to a great extent felt and sensible, not in the sense that the liturgy should be expected to produce sentimental effects—emotion for its own sake—but it certainly works upon and forms our sensibilities. This is quite evident in the various liturgical seasons—the joy of Easter, for instance, or the compunction and attentive devotion of Lent. Here in Advent, the Church's love for the Redeemer expresses itself mostly in terms of *desire*. The liturgy of Advent forms our minds, hearts and wills with loving, humble desire, a desire which has in past ages burned in the hearts of all the saints. It is a desire which is found in the Heart of God Himself—His love as our Father and Redeemer. (4)

Thus at the very outset of the conferences, Merton sets the tone for all that is to follow. His instruction on the various liturgical feasts, minor and major, is primarily intended to provide his audience with sufficient material for reflection to prompt or encourage a recognition and reception of the divine gifts offered through the Church's own worship, to evoke a desire for union with God in response to God's desire for union with humanity.

Merton will occasionally return in the course of these conferences on the temporal cycle to the significance of liturgy. In his "practical notes" on the Advent liturgy (6–9), he cautions that the liturgy must be distinguished "from the mere seasonal cycle: in {the} dead of winter, near {the} solstice, we think of the coming of life and light" (7). Something more than a simple analogy to natural processes is taking place here (a point that he explores in more detail in his introductory "The Opening of the Liturgical Year"). When he reaches Passiontide (76–88), he emphasizes the crucial importance of active engagement in the liturgical process rather than mere passive observation: "The liturgy cannot be understood by one who has not lived with the Church the Easter mystery. This understanding cannot be gained from books and conferences, even though they may be 'about' the liturgy. These may indeed open to us the way to a more fruitful participation, but *participation itself is the only key to the mystery*" (76). Here he is placing these conferences themselves, along with other sources of liturgical information, in the proper context: they are beneficial only to the extent that they lead to experiential appropriation of the mysteries being celebrated, an appropriation that is not made as an isolated individual but as a member of the ecclesial community of faith. He makes a similar point in his Easter conference on the meaning of the Paschal mystery (113–18): "Like all other graces, the joy of Paschaltide is not something which comes to us automatically and passively, without our having to do anything. The joy is all there in the liturgy, and it is easy to get. Yet we must wish to *deepen* it in ourselves by digging deeper roots of faith into the mystery of the Resurrection" (115).

This does not mean, of course, that the need for intellectual formation is to be minimized. He stresses that meaningful participation depends on clear comprehension: "By actively participating, with intelligent faith and enlightened love, in the ritual mystery of Easter, we are entering deeper into the FACT of our incorporation and divinization in Christ. How {can we} make this more understandable? by realizing {the} meaning of {the} texts and rites" (94). Thus Merton regularly provides bits of information that he believes will assist his charges to appreciate properly whatever feast he is discussing. For example, he points out in

connection with the Feast of the Circumcision that the "mystery" referred to in the office of the day is the Incarnation itself, not the rite of
circumcision, which is "far in {the} background . . . only mentioned in
passing in the gospel." He notes that there is "nothing about 'bloodshedding' *anywhere* in the liturgy; in {the} first nocturn we are fortified by
faith and NOT by circumcision" (47–48). Elsewhere he will occasionally
provide factual explanations and historical information that he considers
necessary to avoid misapprehensions, as when he mentions that the "St.
Mark's Procession" held on that saint's feast day (April 25) actually predates the existence of the feast and is a Christianization of the old pagan
agricultural festival of Robigalia (123–24). His extensive exposition of
"The Meaning of Sunday" (141–47) distinguishes a properly balanced
Christian approach from puritanical rigidity, merely secular relaxation
or a simple transposition of the Jewish Sabbath, drawing on the patristic
tradition of the Lord's Day as both "the first day," celebrating at once the
creation of light, the Resurrection and the descent of the Holy Spirit, and
"the eighth day," the "figure and promise of eternity" (147).

Here as throughout the conferences on the temporal cycle, he
makes reference when appropriate to specifically monastic and Cistercian elements of a particular celebration, pointing out that the increased
amount of free time on a Sunday fosters appreciation of the gift of such
a life: "{Note the} beauty of peace and silence in {the} monastic family
on Sunday, reading together in the garden or scriptorium—{an} image
of heaven; {a} monastic paradise." At the same time he warns against an
unrealistic and artificial understanding of this traditional image: "do not
become attached to the paradise aspect of {the} monastery—remember it
is only to be purchased by the Cross" (146). He identifies the First Sunday
of Lent as "a great monastic day in the liturgy, in so far as monks, above
all, participate in the mystery of Jesus' fast and temptation in the desert"
(72), and goes on to comment on the uniquely Cistercian custom of the
Lenten curtain hung before the presbytery and to remind his listeners
that Psalm 90[91], used as the text for the introit and tract of the Mass,
had been used by St. Bernard for his great series of Lenten sermons, "a
real spiritual directory" (73). Commenting on the Ascension as a "feast of
the contemplative life," Merton notes that the monastic life is to be understood as an "imitation of Christ," who came from the Father and returns
to the Father: "As Jesus came forth from the Father, we leave our own
families and what is our own, like Abraham . . . . By mortification we 'go
out' of our own human nature and our own will. Then we leave the world

and go to the Father, by prayer" (124–25). In discussing Easter, he points
out that the monk's particular way of appropriating the Paschal mystery
is through "the life of our vows: *conversion of manners* makes our life a
paschal life in the Risen Christ" (113). At the same time, like all Christians the monk shares in Christ's risen life "by faith" and "the sacraments"
(113)—vows are not an alternative to but a particular way of living out
the Christian life common to all believers. Reflecting on Jesus as Prince
of Peace, Merton provides an early articulation of the connection of the
monastic vocation with care for the sufferings and struggles of humanity
that will emerge so prominently and powerfully in the final decade of his
life: "*The Messianic Kingdom is to be the Kingdom of Justice and Peace.* . . .
Christians, and especially priests and monks, are to be *peacemakers.* The
peace of Christ must exist in the world *through our efforts*—our efforts to
make peace in community and first of all in our own hearts by sacrifice
of ourselves. {The} monastery {is to be} a 'pattern' for {the} working out
of this—this is {the} meaning of monastic sacrifice" (43–44). Thus these
conferences are not narrowly or exclusively monastic in their focus, but
situate the Cistercian life in the context of the broader worship and witness of the universal church.

This interweaving of the more specifically monastic with the more
generally ecclesial aspects of the liturgy is particularly evident in the fact
that Merton regularly draws both on the readings of the divine office
(not of course unique to monks but characteristically associated with
a life centered on the *opus Dei*) and on the texts used at Mass. Either
separately or in tandem, these constitute the principal focus for most of
the conferences. Often Merton simply surveys pertinent texts in outline
form, interspersing brief quotations from the Latin with interpretative
comments often not much more extensive, as he does for example for the
Third Sunday of Advent, touching successively on the Scripture readings
and the proper of the Mass:

> {the} *epistle* (*Modestia vestra* . . .) {teaches} confidence and peace
> {as} our perfect preparation for Christmas, in spite of trial. *Nihil
> solliciti sitis*: {this is} only possible with heroic faith and prayer—
> prayer and supplication {in an} ardent expression of our needs
> to God, with thanksgiving, {which} adds to confidence {through
> our} recognition of Him and His goodness. {The} *pax Dei* {is}
> not just any peace, but the peace of *God, beyond all feeling* and
> all understanding. (It must come from Him in a way we know
> not, and not just be produced by us. We must *let Him give* what

we need, as He wills and when He wills—He is God.) {We pray} *custodiat* corda—from fluctuations of emotion and doubt, from anxious desires and needs; {*custodiat*} intelligentias—from error, presumption, restless curiosity, etc. (15)

A similar procedure occurs—rather less frequently—with the office readings, but can be found, for example, in the conference on the Feast of the Sacred Heart (138–41) (which also includes a discussion of the readings for Mass):

> *The Office*: {the} second nocturn (not really by St. Bernard) {focuses on} transformation in Jesus:
>
> a) *To dwell in His Heart* (read *John* 15:1–11: "*Manete in me . . .*"); to renounce all other loves; to be sustained by His love alone. This implies sacrifice, but above all trust: "casting all my care on the Heart of the Lord Jesus."
>
> b) *His Heart is a temple in which God is perfectly adored*; hence we ask to be drawn entirely into this mystical sanctuary, so as to praise God perfectly.
>
> c) *To "find" the Heart of Jesus* is at once to "find" our own heart and His (cf. Oriental spirituality: "seeking" and "finding" the heart). The Sacred Heart, King and Center of all hearts, *is the inmost center of our own heart* (because of our Eucharistic communions especially, and the action of the Holy Spirit conforming our heart to His).
>
> d) {He is} the *Way*: there is only one sure way and His Heart teaches us this way to conformity—to experience in ourselves the humility of Jesus. "Learn of Me that I am meek and humble of heart" (antiphon: lauds). (140–41)

Mass and office are both drawn on when considering the Ascension and Pentecost as "*Feasts of Fullness*":

> *Spiritus Domini* replevit *orbem terrarum. Cum* complerentur *dies. Reple tuorum corda fidelium. Reple cordis intima. Repleti sunt omnes Spiritu Sancto.* God Himself comes to dwell within us—the Father, Son and Holy Spirit "remain" in us (gospel: Pentecost). We are not only filled but *purified* (*Spiritus Sancti illustratione emunda*) and fecundated (*tui roris intima aspersione fecundet*). All this begins with the Ascension: *Ascendit ut impleret omnia* (epistle: vigil of {the} Ascension). *Read* {the} epistle of {the} vigil: *Captivam duxit captivitatem.* {This is} His triumph: *He takes us with Him* (see St. Leo, second nocturn): hence our great joy! *Unitam sibi fragilitatis nostrae substantiam*

> *in gloriae tuae dextera collocavit* (communicantes: Ascension);
> *ut nos divinitatis suae tribueret esse participes* (preface: Ascen-
> sion). Here indeed we have the overwhelming fullness of the
> Mystery of Christ!! Our nature *in its weakness* is seated in heav-
> en. In our trials, temptations and sufferings our own humanity
> is enthroned with Jesus, *as long as* we are sharers in His divinity.
> How? by the Holy Spirit. {This is} a sublime and consoling truth.
> Not just our souls and our "interior life" {are} sanctified, but
> *all* is elevated and transformed in Christ; all is heavenly; all is
> divine. Understand why we sing the *Alleluia*, and long for the
> Holy Spirit: our offices, jobs and functions—all are sanctified
> by the Holy Spirit as we come together to form *one body*. "*Ut in
> omnibus glorificetur Deus.*" Read {the} epistle for {the} Sunday
> within {the} Octave {of the Ascension}. (130–31)

Presumably Merton expanded his commentary when actually presenting
this material to the novices, using his written notes as a basic outline providing "talking points" that he could then develop as he would, adjusting
the length to fit the available time frame (normally the allotted half-hour
set aside for novitiate conferences).[22]

Many of the conferences, however, include extensive reflections on
particular texts—in some cases no doubt *more* detailed than the actual
oral presentation would have been. For example, for the Fifth Sunday
after Easter, Merton first takes a single line of a second nocturn reading
from the *De Fide Resurrectionis* of St. Ambrose, "*Resurrexit in eo mundus,
resurrexit in eo coelum, resurrexit in eo terra*" ("In Him the world is raised,
in Him the heaven is raised, in Him the earth is raised"), and develops a
reflection on cosmic renewal already begun in Christ's resurrection and
to be brought to final fulfillment at the parousia:

> As we near the end of Paschal Time and are ready for the con-
> summation of Christ's triumph in the giving of the Holy Spirit,
> our attention is drawn by the liturgy to the *restoration of all
> things* in Christ which is precisely the work of the Spirit. Berdy-
> aev says: "The world has been imprisoned by evil, and it can only
> be delivered by love." It is as a result of man's sin that the world,

---

22. Since all these presentations were made long before Merton's novitiate conferences began to be recorded in late April 1962, there is of course no way to compare
the written text to the oral delivery, as can be done with some of the other sets of
conferences (see Merton, *Cassian and the Fathers*, xlvii–liv; Merton, *Pre-Benedictine
Monasticism*, li–lxi; Merton, *Rule of Saint Benedict*, xlii–xlvi; Merton, *Life of the Vows*,
xlvi–li; Merton, *Cistercian Fathers*, ci–cviii; Merton, *Medieval Cistercian History*, xliii–
l; lxix–lxxiv).

with man himself, is subject to *inertia* and *necessity*, to laws that lead inevitably and inexorably to dissolution and death. Since the fall, all nature tends downwards to nothingness. But with the coming of Christ, the second Adam, love and liberty are once again in the world, and once again creation is ordered not towards inertia, necessity and death, but liberty, creativity and life. Why? because in Christ, God and man become one, and man is elevated above the determinism of nature, above merely natural laws of life and death. The whole world is his kingdom and helps him to serve God; the whole world is elevated with him and ordered with him to a spiritual end. This will be fully apparent only at the last day. (122)

This is followed by a somewhat briefer five-point reflection on St. Augustine's commentary from the third nocturn on John 16:24 ("Ask and you shall receive"), considering what it means to ask in prayer, what is to be sought, and what ("eternal life or the means thereto") is received (122–23).

More extensive commentaries are devoted to key texts and key events in the liturgical cycle, such as the celebrated "O Antiphons" of the Advent office, the "seven great and solemn invocations, the cry of the Church bringing down the Savior from heaven" (18), to each of which is devoted a separate meditation (19–24) following an overview characterizing the antiphons as "contain[ing] the very essence of Advent prayer" and "resum[ing] the whole history of salvation and the gradual manifestation of the Word Incarnate," expressing at once the desire of the patriarchs and prophets for the Messiah, the prayers of Mary and the entire church on earth and in heaven for the final fulfillment of the second coming, the "inarticulate longings" of all people for spiritual illumination, and "the cry of the oppressed, the poor, the downtrodden, the persecuted, all those whom Christ seeks out with preference" (19). The reflection on the respective readings of the three Christmas Masses (30–37) brings out what Merton calls the "theological and contemplative richness" of the various texts, which convey the "tremendously rich and varied" theological significance of the incarnation (31). Comparable in-depth reflections are provided repeatedly throughout these conferences, as for the readings of Passion Sunday, both from the office and the Mass (77–79); for the fourth Isaian Servant Song, given a line-by-line commentary for the Wednesday of Holy Week (88–89); for the prophecies and prayers read at the Vigil of Pentecost (133–36), perhaps especially what Merton calls the "magnificent prophecy" (135) of Baruch 3:9–39, with its emphasis on God as the source of authentic wisdom. In these and similar reflections Merton models for the novices how personal meditative engagement with liturgical texts is an integral dimension of participation in the public prayer of the church, and is ultimately experienced as an essential component of the contemplative dimension of the Christian life and more specifically of the contemplative vocation of the monk.

For Merton, liturgy properly understood and authentically experienced is integral to any life oriented to union with God through Christ. It is the normal and normative way to participate in the paschal mystery celebrated and re-presented at each Eucharist and reflected in the pattern that draws the disciple from Christ's birth through his death and resurrection to the gift of the Holy Spirit that empowers the community of disciples to be signs and instruments of life in Christ, of transformed, transfigured creation, to and for a still-broken world. Merton repeatedly emphasizes the associations of the liturgy with imagery of light, a *via positiva* of word and symbol and gesture complementing the apophatic way of imageless prayer. The two are ultimately not mutually exclusive alternatives but mutually necessary correlatives in a holistic Christian spirituality. "The light that illumines us," Merton declares in reflecting on the Epiphany, the manifestation of the Light of the World in the form of a helpless infant, "is the understanding that darkness is our light, and that we do not have to see; rather that to see is not to see, and not to see is to see" (52). At the very opening of the liturgical year the entrance of the "*Aeterna lux credentium*," the Eternal Light of believers, sets the keynote of Advent (4–5) and culminates in the brightness of the Nativity:

> The mystery of Christmas is a mystery of light. It is *the shining forth of the light of eternity*. The "sanctified day" which shines out upon us is the day of eternity, the *hodie* in which the Son comes forth as the splendor of the Father (epistle and gospel, third Mass). The day is the Child Himself. He Himself is the light. Hence we can see Him at midnight, without any other light than His own. He is the day that dawns *ante luciferum*. All these nuances point to the fact that the feast is one in which we celebrate the spiritual and divine birth of Christ in our hearts as light. (34–35)

It is the light of conversion, which "*purifies and renovates our entire being, so that we are born again with the newborn Christ*" (41), and of contemplation, which "does not strike the intelligence alone, but here illuminates the intimate depths of the spirit, the 'high point' of the soul, the *scintilla animae*, above both will and intelligence . . . and from there it sheds its radiance over all our faculties" (39). This same light is perceived at the Baptism, pattern of "the sacrament of our illumination and incorporation in Him," but only because it "is already a type of His death on the Cross, His victorious struggle with sin and with the evil one" (54). The paradox of light in darkness characterizes not just the Christmas season but the entire cycle of redemption.

> {The} Lenten liturgy . . . realizes again the struggle between light and darkness: darkness in us {is} sin. There is in us a principle opposed to the Light of God. Our self-will crucified Him. There must be struggle: He dies and rises in us (a) sacramentally (baptism and Eucharist); (b) ascetically (prayer and penance prolong the sacramental action of baptism and the Eucharist). Lent prepares for the great fifty-day Feast of Easter. Lent is not the chief reality. Easter is. Lent is the preparation. Don't put the cart before the horse. Light is more important than darkness. (62)

On the Second Sunday of Lent the Transfiguration gospel is read as a reminder that the "light of the Risen Christ will shine in us and 'transfigure' our souls at Easter if we are generous in Lent" (74). This light is paradoxically not obscured but intensified in the events of Holy Week: "*Fulget Crucis Mysterium*"—the mystery of the Cross shines forth: "in this great mystery we see the radiance of the divine light, of pure Truth, of supreme wisdom, the wisdom of God, which is only revealed in mystery, and in one mystery, the mystery of Christ" (82). The liturgical reenactment of this divine illumination of course reaches its height in the celebration of the Easter Vigil, in the "*Lucernarium*—{the} feast of lights" (104), the lighting of "the *new fire* which will become, mystically, the Light of Christ (*Lumen Christi*)" (102), the paschal candle whose "light shines in darkness {as a sign of the} Resurrection" (104). It is this light of the risen and glorified Jesus that is celebrated each Sunday:

> Sunday {is} a *day of light*, {the} "first day" on which light was made, {the} day when Christ, {the} true Light, rose from the tomb (*lumen Christi*) to shine forever. {The} light of grace {shines} in our hearts {on this} day of grace, {this} day on which Jesus comes, the doors being shut, and says, "Peace be to you." {See the} hymns of our Breviary, "*Aeterne Rerum Conditor*" {and} "*Splendor Paternae Gloriae*." *Aeterne Rerum* {speaks of} God disposing and ruling time: {at} cockcrow, the rising sun

> dispels {the} darkness of sin and error, brings courage {and} re-
> pentance, revives our energy {with the} awakening of faith and
> good resolve, {of} hope, {from the} memory of Jesus looking on
> Peter. (This hymn is more a vigil hymn than a Sunday one, how-
> ever.) *Splendor Paternae Gloriae* {is} a lauds hymn, especially
> appropriate for Sunday: "*Lux lucis et fons luminis,*" the true sun,
> pouring the light of the Holy Spirit into our hearts. (144)

The point of all this, of course, is not merely to recognize a pattern of imagery, or to develop an aesthetic appreciation for the liturgy,
but to be illumined, to become enlightened, to pass from darkness into
light, through death to new life in union with the Word made flesh, the
crucified and risen Lord. The liturgy is meaningless ritual unless it is a
participation in the mystery of Christ's incarnation and redemption, unless it is a vehicle for finding one's true identity in Christ, who "became
Incarnate precisely in order to unite us perfectly to Himself and to live in
us. The humanity which God united to Himself, the humanity of Jesus, is
filled with the light and life of God. But when we receive Him, He fills us
with His own light and life and strength and love. The Humanity which
He united to Himself has the power to sanctify and save all mankind, and
it saves them by *contact*, by *union*" (29).

Liturgy for Merton is essentially oriented to contemplation, because
authentic contemplation is participation in divine life in and through and
with and as Christ: "it is no longer I who live but Christ lives in me" (Gal
2:20). He presents the Christmas cycle to the novices as "one of the most
'contemplative' portions of the Church year," and goes on to explain:

> In the Christmas liturgy more plainly than anywhere else, the
> Church teaches us *her* way of contemplation. It is a way sin-
> gularly simple and efficacious. It puts us in the most effective
> possible contact with Jesus Himself, the Way, the Truth and the
> Life. What is contemplation in this connection? *to enter into
> the mystery of the divine Light, through love of the Infant Jesus,
> the Incarnate Word, embraced by faith and charity, and received
> sacramentally into our hearts that He may there transform us into
> sons of God by grace.* (37)

If the Christmas season is contemplative, the Paschal season is in a
sense something "above and beyond even contemplation—we are sharing in the life of the Risen Lord, and anticipating the triumphant life of
heaven which is the life of glory rather than the life of contemplation as
we know it" (37). But this foretaste of participation in Trinitarian life is

made possible only through incorporation in Christ, already effected by baptism, which "is a death and resurrection with Christ, in a liturgical rite, which unites us to Him in the mystery of His 'Pascha' and makes us new men, conformed to Him, clad with His sacred Being as with a white garment—other Christs, anointed with the Holy Spirit" (54), but which must be actualized, realized, in the process of dying and rising with Christ in the concrete circumstances of one's own life. "Our 'pascha'—our passage in mystery from death to life—is *our participation in this sacred mystery*" (83–84). What has objectively taken place in the redemptive events of Christ's submission to and triumph over death, his assumption and transformation of the limitations of the condition of fallen, suffering humanity, is appropriated personally and communally by taking up the Cross and being "crucified with Christ" (Gal 2:19), choosing to renounce the illusion of an autonomous, self-sustaining existence, the primal temptation of Eden, and to embrace the freedom of total dependence on God that is experienced as a death but is the only authentic life: "by sharing in the death and resurrection of Christ, BY PARTICIPATION IN THE ACTION BY WHICH CHRIST REDEEMED MANKIND . . . in the ritual mystery of Easter, we are entering deeper into the FACT of our incorporation and divinization in Christ" (93–94). This paschal transformation is sacramentally re-presented in every Mass, and above all in the "high holy days" of the paschal triduum, revealing and making available in grace-bearing ritual the passage through death to new, unending life that is the heart of the Christian mystery. In beginning his conferences on Passiontide Merton tells the novices:

> [E]ach day we celebrate and share in the Easter mystery in Holy Mass. But it is also necessary that at this culminating point in the liturgical year the whole mystery itself be explicitly set out before us and that we celebrate it in all its fullness and in all its aspects. . . . What we celebrate in the Passion is not the sufferings of Christ but *His victory*. More precisely, we who celebrate His victory declare the glory He has won by His victory over death, and in which He reigns enthroned at the right hand of the Father. We celebrate this glory by living through His struggle and victory over death. But this is done in mystery, and in the fullest imaginable sense by the fact that He Who reigns in glory, *during this celebration, actually dies and rises again in us*. How? spiritually, mystically—by grace; through the sacramental action of the liturgy. {We must} distinguish—it is not a physical participation in the Passion (feelings of suffering do not add to

the celebration), nor is it a moral or psychological participation. *The participation is mystical and sacramental*, through the
action of the liturgy. The liturgy does not work by magic. The
rites and prayers are not incantations. Our *participation* is what
counts. (76–77)

Here is the essence of Merton's understanding of and teaching on the
deepest meaning of liturgy—a way of experiencing, of "living through"
Christ's kenotic, salvific self-gift by accepting its invitation to surrender
oneself in return, a dynamic response that is at once sacramental and
mystical, both visible sign and reality beyond articulation and beyond
comprehension.

∾

The conferences making up Part II, on the sanctoral cycle, are considerably more varied in their tone and in their ways of engaging with the
material; they are necessarily less comprehensive, certainly making no
attempt to touch on all or even most of the saints commemorated in the
Church's calendar. The selection is therefore quite revealing of at least
some of Merton's own predilections, and of what he considered most
important to communicate to the novices. No less than fourteen of the
forty-three conferences in Part II have a Marian connection; eleven have
a specifically Cistercian focus, and another six a wider monastic associa-
tion; four are reflections on five of the apostles (plus St. Paul), with five
more on the New Testament figures of St. Joseph, John the Baptist, Mary
Magdalen, and St. Luke (two conferences); three consider feasts associated with Christ—two of which (the Transfiguration and the Exaltation of
the Holy Cross) might well have been included in Part I, while the third
(the Reception of the Holy Crown of Thorns) has a particular Cistercian
connection; three discuss the Feast of All Saints and one combines the
Feast of St. Michael with that of the Guardian Angels; the only nonscrip-
tural, nonmonastic figure represented in the entire series is St. Lawrence.
    As with the temporal cycle, many of the conferences, particularly
the shorter ones, are closely based on the readings from the office, the
Mass, or both. For example, on the Feast of Sts. Simon and Jude (October 28) Merton provides brief reflections on the gospel of the feast (John
15:17–25)—comparing its tone with John 14:16–24, which features Jude's
question to Christ about the gift of the Spirit; on the first nocturn readings (from the Epistle of Jude); and on the collect found in both Mass

and office. The first two highlight "the theme of the conflict between the Christian and the world, and the idea that even the religious spirit can be, in some cases, only a worldly spirit in disguise" (271). The third, with its striking inversion *"proficiendo celebrare et celebrando proficere"* ("to celebrate by progressing and to progress by celebrating"), illustrates the "intimate connection between spiritual growth and participation in the liturgy" (273) and draws attention to Merton's own perceptiveness and sensitivity to the liturgical texts and their nuances.

Sometimes he selects a particular motif from the readings, as when he focuses on the Visitation as "the feast of the *voice*," drawn from Elizabeth's opening words to Mary, so that the "human voice, in Mary, becomes the instrument by {which} God Himself speaks," and the "wonderfully sweet harmony of *voices*" (215) that characterizes the encounter, including of course the Magnificat, flows out into the liturgy: "The office is '*vox dilecti*,' the voice of God" (216) and makes possible the "union of our *thoughts* and *voices* with His" (215). Other conferences will cover the entire range of liturgical texts, as for the Feast of the Nativity of John the Baptist (207–12), which moves from the vespers antiphon to the collect to the introit of the vigil to the reading from St. Ambrose in the third nocturn to the epistle of the vigil, from Jeremiah, to the epistle of the feast, from Isaiah, to the twelfth responsory to the hymn for lauds to the gospel for the vigil, from Luke—all of which leads in some way up to the recognition of John as the model par excellence for the monk (a connection Merton frequently makes in his writings[23]): "To be a monk is to be a prophet in the sense of one who *knows* and recognizes Jesus in a world that sees Him not" (211–12).

Merton's deep respect and love for the Eastern Church leads him to draw on texts from the Byzantine liturgy in three of the conferences. The imagery of light that runs through much of Part I is naturally evident in the readings for Candlemas Day—the Feast of the Presentation—and Merton reflects on "Christ the true light that enlightens every man coming into the world" (176) and the call to "bear the light of Christ mystically for the glory of the Father" (175) that is symbolically represented in the procession with lighted candles, and then goes on to quote extensively (in his own translations from the French) texts used in the Oriental Church that lyrically celebrate the encounter ("Hypapante") of Simeon with the Christ Child, symbolizing "the meeting of the people of God with the

23. For a discussion of the figure of John the Baptist in Merton's poetry, see O'Connell, "'The First Cistercian and the Greatest Trappist.'"

Divine Bridegroom, the Word made Flesh" (177). After considering the first vespers readings in the Cistercian office for the Assumption, Merton then quotes four substantial excerpts from "some beautiful odes" drawn from the Byzantine "great matins of the Assumption" (235), marked by striking imagery, as in this prayer: "In truth, O Virgin of Virgins, thy Child has placed thee in the holy of holies like a clear torch of immaterial flame, like a golden censer filled with divine fire, like a cup and a scepter, like the tables of the Law written by the finger of God, like the Holy Ark, the table {of} the bread of life" (236–37). The Feast of the Nativity of the Virgin likewise juxtaposes the "solemn, sober, simple, magniloquent, strong, restrained" tone of the Roman liturgy of the feast with the "same themes . . . intoned by the Greek Church with more lyricism and splendor" (246) as illustrated by five relatively brief excerpts, in which Mary is celebrated as "the nuptial chamber of the Light," "the door that brings into the world the Christ, and Him alone," "the bridge of life by [whom] mortal men have found salvation after their fall into hell," concluding that the "Greek liturgy {is} characterized by awe and holy exultation, jubilation before God (*Jubilate Deo*) with adoration and compunction {that} touches {the} deepest springs of the human soul {and} transforms us—yet the Roman liturgy is probably better for every day" (247). Thus Merton seeks to expand the liturgical horizons of his audience to encompass the universal church, without neglecting or minimizing the positive qualities of their own liturgical tradition.

In some of the conferences Merton develops an extensive commentary on the readings, such as that on St. Benedict, which begins with the question:

> What does the office of our Father, St. Benedict, teach us about his spirit? Indeed, it is for this "spirit" that we pray in the collect, and where will we better find out about it than in the other texts, the *proper* texts which make up the office. The Spirit "Whom St. Benedict served" was, of course, the Holy Spirit. But when we speak of the "spirit of St. Benedict" we are speaking of something special and characteristic in his own way of life, willed especially for his monastic family by the Holy Spirit. Let us look particularly at those texts which were written about St. Benedict himself and are not simply applied to him from the Common of Confessors. (186)

He goes on to discuss in detail key texts from the feast: the vespers responsory, which "strikes the keynote of Benedictine sacrifice," from which a

novice might learn not to be "too sensitive and fussy about his own feelings and his own self-respect" and yet that "a little honest sensitivity is
better than the simulated humility which keeps quiet but seeks in devious
ways to get its own back" (186–87); the vespers and vigils hymns that
provide an overview of the saint's life, and the antiphons and responsories of vigils, drawn from Gregory the Great's *Dialogues*, which highlight
his discretion, his spirit of prayer and contemplation, his patience and
charity. Merton concludes that to appreciate Benedict's spirit fully, "we
should return more and more frequently to the *Holy Rule*, which is the
true source of our knowledge of his heart and of his life . . . learning above
all to do that which in few words gives the full picture of St. Benedict: 'To
PREFER ABSOLUTELY NOTHING TO THE LOVE OF CHRIST'" (189).

Some conferences combine attention to the readings of the office
with reflection on sermons from the Cistercian Fathers. For the Feast of
the Immaculate Heart of Mary, Merton moves from consideration of the
readings from St. Bernardine of Siena and Venerable Bede in the lessons
of the second and third nocturns to St. Bernard's sermon *De Aquaeductu*,
in which Mary is depicted as a "reservoir" of grace "poured forth from
Jesus . . . from which an aqueduct brings the waters of life into our souls"
(244). Merton's second conference on the Nativity of Mary begins by
reflecting on the "*simplicity and splendor* of the feast" as found in the
office, which presents Mary as a model of prayer uniting mind, spirit,
and devotion (247), then draws of Guerric of Igny's second sermon for
the feast which develops Guerric's "favorite doctrine of the formation of
Christ in us through the action of Mary" (248). Merton "Cistercianizes"
the Feast of the Dedication of a Church by applying the office and Mass
readings specifically to their own abbey church ("Today is a feast of all
the saints of Gethsemani—visit them in the cemetery, and recognize how
much we owe to them, without being able to know it clearly in this life"
[289]) and drawing on St. Bernard's First Dedication Sermon to complete
his reflections ("When he says this is *your feast*, he means it is not only
the feast of your church, but of your dedication as a living temple to God"
[293]). Occasionally the conference will dispense with the office readings altogether and rely solely on the Cistercian materials: St. Bernard's
sermons on Saints Peter and Paul both as "masters and mediators" (212)
and as sinners who learned compassion from their own experiences of
forgiveness make up the whole of the brief discussion of the shared feast
of the two great saints, and teach the "practicality of St. Bernard and of
Cistercian thought" to the novices, who are "not here to learn merely

rules and exterior practices, or how to sing psalms, etc., or how to get along without responsibility, but truly to *live* in Christ" (213). More extensively, Bernard's two sermons for the Feast of St. Andrew (165–69) present the apostle as a model of the true disciple who follows Jesus even to the Cross, "not the sign of death but of life, not {of} destruction but fructification . . . . not loved for suffering's sake, but for the sake of the grace and union with God which we can reach by loving the Cross . . . . the tree of life . . . planted in the midst of the paradise of the Church" (165). In all these conferences it is evident that Merton seeks to stimulate in the novices a deepened awareness and appreciation of the spiritual resources provided in both the liturgy and the Cistercian tradition, as well as fostering devotion to whatever particular saint is being commemorated.

While the first two conferences on St. Bernard (237–40) both draw on the readings from the office (the third being the sermon mentioned in Merton's August 21, 1957, letter to Sr. Thérèse when the subject of the liturgy notes was first mentioned), and the feast of all the saints of the Order (287–88) does likewise, commentary for the feasts of the other three Cistercian Fathers discussed is largely independent of the liturgy. The conference on St. Robert (199–202) provides a capsule biography followed by a discussion of the ideals of Benedictine commitment that led the first Cistercians to leave Molesme for the New Monastery. The second conference on St. Stephen Harding (218–22) does begin by quoting the collect of the feast, but then draws on the *Exordium Parvum* and the later *Exordium Magnum* to articulate Stephen's vision for Cîteaux and his own efforts to embody that vision in his life and his abbacy. (The first conference on Stephen [216–18] is used to provide "a simple outline of the office of vigils for beginners"—introducing the novices to the structure of the night office as provided in the common of confessors, with no specific references to Stephen himself.) The conference on Ailred (Aelred) of Rievaulx (179–82) likewise draws on Walter Daniel's *Vita* and a sermon on Aelred by Gilbert of Hoyland, rather than liturgical texts, to help the novices to come to "know our Fathers and the way they lived—their attitude, their outlook" and so "to become a monk, by contact with real monks" (179).

This largely nonliturgical approach is also found in the conference on St. Joseph (182–86), though of course Merton includes the relevant passages from Matthew's and Luke's Gospels to present Joseph as the last of the patriarchs, in whom the "characteristics of all the patriarchs merge together and reach a higher fulfillment" (182); but he then goes on to focus on St. Joseph the Worker, who not only looks back to the entire history of Israel but "looks forward also to the innumerable multitude of the poor and the faithful in whom Christ truly lives and suffers and continues His work of the Redemption of the world" (184–85). The conference on St. Thomas (169–74) begins with brief quotations from the common of apostles (169), but develops from the gospel of the vigil (John 15:12–16) the idea of priesthood, specifically monastic priesthood, as friendship with Christ, a special way of sharing in the humility, the trials, the charity, the revelation of truth and the contemplation of Jesus; this spiritual reflection is followed by the more practical outline of the successive stages of orders leading to sacerdotal ordination—an opportunity to provide the choir novices, all of whom would in due course go on to priesthood, concrete information on the process that would take them there—but having nothing specifically to do with the apostle Thomas in particular. Merton thus felt free to use the opportunity provided by these conferences to make available whatever instruction he considered most beneficial for his audience at a given time, rather than following a standard template to be applied in basically the same way for each feast considered.

Along with the specifically Cistercian "flavor" of much of this material, the most prominent aspect of Part II is the attention given to Mary. Though presented in discrete segments rather than as a unified discussion, the Marian instruction found here is the most extensive of any single work of Merton. Ten of the conferences are focused on eight particular Marian feasts—the Annunciation (189–95), the Seven Dolors (195–98), the Visitation (213–16), the Assumption (two conferences [234–35, 235–37]), the Immaculate Heart (243–44), the Nativity (two conferences [244–47, 247–49]), the Holy Name (249–50), and the Presentation (295–300). In addition the conference on Candlemas Day (174–79) as well as that on the Feast of St. Anne (226–28) are of course intimately linked with Mary. The opening conference of Part II, "The Mystery of Mary and the Church" (162–65) has no connection to the liturgical calendar, and four other conferences ("May—Consecration to Our Lady" [202–3]; "Mary in the Passion" [203–7]; "The Rosary and Its Mysteries" [251–57] and a second conference on the Rosary [258–59]) are only loosely linked to the cycle. Merton obviously did not feel constrained, either in presenting or in collecting the conferences, to limit himself to specific feasts, but he also took advantage of the multiplicity of Marian commemorations to explore different aspects of Mary's role in the Christian story, in the life of the church, and in monastic and specifically Cistercian spirituality. As has already been noted, he draws on liturgical readings, including texts from the Byzantine office as well as on the preaching of the Cistercian Fathers, to plumb the significance of the various Marian feasts.

Without in any way underemphasizing the supreme importance of Mary's central role in the incarnation, Merton repeatedly highlights the significance of Mary's participation in the paschal mystery as the culmination of her complete gift of herself to God and God's saving work. In the opening conference of Part II on "The Mystery of Mary and the Church," an apt introduction not just for the Marian conferences but for the entire series on the sanctoral cycle, he points out the twofold vocation of Mary, "who by her *fiat* cooperates in the great work of the Incarnation, who by her compassion on Calvary cooperates in the objective Redemption of man" (162). Here[24] and in later conferences he presents a "high" doctrine of Mary's role in redemption,[25] freely using terms such as "co-redeemer and mediatrix of all grace" (202), subsequently noting that if "the universal mediation of Mary is defined as dogma,"[26] St. Bernard's sermon on the aqueduct will no doubt be cited in the declaration (244); he will cite, without directly endorsing, the opinion of some theologians that Mary's unique share in the objective redemption of humanity, found in her *fiat* making possible the incarnation, might extend as well to understanding "her *fiat* on Calvary" to be "a strict, direct and immediate cooperation with Jesus on the Cross in effecting man's objective redemption" (196). But he is less interested in speculative theology of Mary than in fostering an intimacy of trust and love in which Mary is at once recognized as model of faithful discipleship, participant par excellence in the paschal mystery, and maternal intercessor who at the foot of the Cross received

---

24. "Through Mary, whom Christ willed to have as His collaborator in His great work, all grace is given to the mystical members of Christ" (162); "Each one fills out his little share in the sufferings of Jesus, so that together we form one 'Bride' of Christ, perfectly conformed to Mary the Co-redeemer" (164).

25. Merton will later become more restrained in his Mariology, writing in his journal for January 30, 1965, "I do not agree with the medieval idea of *Mediatrix apud mediatorem* . . . (without prejudice to her motherhood which is a much better statement and truth)" (Merton, *Dancing in the Water of Life*, 197); for an overview of Merton's writing on Mary, see O'Connell, "Mary."

26. Such a possibility was being discussed at this time. In the period leading up to the beginning of the Second Vatican Council, there was an expectation in some quarters that there would be a dogmatic definition at the Council of Mary's role as co-redemptrix: see O'Malley, *Catholic History for Today's Church*, 116.

all humanity as her children. Mary's cooperation in the work of redemption, though unique, is also exemplary, and calls for active, dynamic engagement in the transforming work of Christ, which is the vocation of the church, of which she is the perfect representation:

> All who are called to membership and life in Christ are called, like Mary (but in a less strict sense), to collaborate with Jesus in the work of the Redemption—we "redeem" one another. . . . Hence, though Jesus is our only Savior, He wills that we should all cooperate in our own salvation and in that of others. In this we are all His instruments, Mary principally, but each one of us also in a more remote and partial fashion. THE WHOLE MYSTERY OF MAN'S COLLABORATION WITH CHRIST IN THE WORK OF SALVATION IS THE MYSTERY OF THE CHURCH. MARY IS THE PERFECT TYPE OF THE CHURCH. IN HER PERSONALLY WAS REALIZED ALL THAT THE CHURCH, COLLECTIVELY, MUST BE. BOTH MARY AND THE CHURCH ARE THE BRIDE OF CHRIST. MARY IS AS IT WERE THE MODEL AND CENTER AROUND WHICH THE CHURCH'S LIFE IS BUILT. (163)

Mary is to be regarded not only as exemplary but as efficient cause of this intimate identification with the person and work of Christ: "Mary has as her mission now to form the members of the Mystical Christ after the model of her own perfection" (297). Thus authentic Marian piety, Merton consistently teaches, is always oriented toward deeper union with Jesus, hence "the impossibility of her interfering with the mediatorship of Christ Our Lord" (162). Her love for her Son embraces all humanity, and true devotion to her passes through her to the Source and End of her love.

This is the inner contemplative dynamic of the rosary, as Merton explains in the longest and most circumstantial of the Marian conferences: "seeing, with the *eyes of the heart*, the virtues and dispositions of Mary and of Jesus in the mystery before us" (255), we are drawn into the mutual love of Mother and Son: "we 'experience' each Hail Mary, so to speak, as the breathing of our love, as the rhythmic beating of the heart of love; indeed, in our affection of love, as we say the rosary, the vocal prayers tend to become the united heartbeat of our hearts, the Immaculate Heart of Mary, and the Sacred Heart of Jesus, living and beating in unison" (254). As he leads the novices through the successive mysteries—or successive aspects of what he has previously call the "one great reality" of "the Mystery of Christ in His Church" (162), he shows that it is less a matter of looking at Mary than of looking with and through Mary at her Son. The value of the rosary is that "it takes us directly to Jesus, the Word Incarnate" (253). By "uniting ourselves to her experience of joy, sorrow and glory" (256), Merton explains, we not only affirm belief in the central doctrines of the Christian faith, but "'go forth' to meet the grace of God that is offered to us" (256) by opening ourselves to the transforming power of the mystery they articulate.

Merton reminds the novices throughout these Marian conferences that the mediatorial role of Mary has particular relevance to their way of life. In presenting May as Mary's month, he explains and recommends the traditional Trappist practice of personal consecration to the Blessed Virgin as simply making explicit what is already a constituent dimension of a monastic commitment and as a way to become more openly receptive to the qualities that are essential to living out that commitment:

> Our contemplative life by its very nature is a life of "consecration" to Mary, of more intimate dependence on her, and more perfect participation in her most special virtues of *faith, obedience, purity of heart, love, humility*. However, in order to appreciate this, we should explicitly consecrate ourselves to Mary in the novitiate as a sign of our willingness to persevere. (This consecration should take the place of those private vows which are not to be advised in the novitiate.) Mary will then *take over* and do for us what we cannot do ourselves. Mary wants to obtain for us a share above all in *her humility*, so important for all Christians, vitally important above all for contemplatives. (202–3)

In his conference on the Holy Name of Mary, he concludes his reflections on St. Bernard's Second Homily on the *Missus Est* with the comment: "The whole of our monastic life can be summed up as a trusting love for Our Lady, a love that seeks her face always, that always calls upon her merciful and motherly love" (250). As the sanctoral cycle conferences of Part II had opened with "The Mystery of Mary and the Church," so they conclude with reflections on the late November Feast of Our Lady's Presentation, in which Merton turns for a final time to this theme of "*Maria Regula Monachorum*"—the "Rule," the Model, of monks (295). While making no explicit reference to the apocryphal tradition of Mary's years of childhood service in the temple which the feast commemorates, Merton finds in her virginity, poverty, and total obedience to God's will the true pattern of the vowed life, but even more importantly finds in her a source not only of inspiration but of encouragement and assistance, a channel of grace leading to perseverance, peace, simplicity, and union with God:

> Mary, as the first religious, is the Queen and Mother of each religious. Our vocation is from her; our whole life and perfection depend, in fact, on how closely we reproduce in our own religious life her gift of herself to God. This in turn depends on how close we are to Mary by love and confidence. We have come to the monastery to give ourselves to God. Sooner or later we must find that we cannot truly give ourselves to God without the special help of Mary, and that one of the greatest graces of the religious life is the grace to abandon our life, our body, {our} soul, all our gifts and actions and merits, our past, present and future, into the hands of Our Lady. (295)

In the Catholic tradition the saints function both as models and as intercessors, and Merton leaves his monastic listeners and readers of these liturgical conferences with the assurance that this is preeminently true of the greatest saint of all, and the directive to allow Mary, in both these roles, to provide the necessary guidance for actualizing to its full extent the vitality of their chosen vocation.

～

The "additional material" preserved only in TMa consists more of material belonging to the temporal than to the sanctoral cycle, not surprising in that TMa is represented much more heavily in Part II than in Part I. It is headed by "The Opening of the Liturgical Year" (301–9), the projected introduction to the whole collection. Of the thirty-three remaining items, seven are Advent-related with an additional conference on Christmas; eight are on Lent, with one each on the day after Easter and the Sunday after Easter; Sexagesima and the Third Sunday after Easter are the only other Sundays included (the latter, like Low Sunday, missing from Part I); four conferences are Marian, three of which are on the Immaculate Conception; St. Benedict on the meaning of the Cross and a second conference on St. Bernard's sermons for the dedication of the monastic church have a specifically monastic focus; the only saints' feasts included are brief discussions of St. Mark and St. Thomas Aquinas, with an additional conference on All Saints Day; the other five are connected only tenuously (an Epiphany conference concerned with spiritual direction) or not at all

(Chapter of Faults; Eros and Agape; Thoughts on Grace; Mary and the Priest) to the liturgical cycle.

Of these, clearly the most significant is the initial conference on the opening of the liturgical year, a profound meditation on the meaning of time, both secular and liturgical, that is arguably the most powerful single piece in the entire set of conferences, which, as already noted, Merton considered significant enough to detach from its original context and publish in revised form as a separate article. In his introductory remarks on the drama of fall and redemption, Merton highlights the element of realized eschatology: "We live in the Kingdom of Christ, the new world, consecrated to God, the Messianic Kingdom, the New Jerusalem" (301); but this Kingdom is perceptible only to the eyes of faith, and what has already been definitively established by the resurrection and glorification of Christ will be manifested fully only in the final consummation of all things, Christ's parousia. Therefore sanctification of history, of the time between first and second coming, is not experienced either as an accomplishment of the past nor as a hope for the future but as an ever-renewed present event. "To say that the Redemption is an ever-present spiritual reality is to say that Christ has laid hold upon time and sanctified it, giving it a sacramental character, that is to say, making it an efficacious sign of our union with God in Him. So 'time' is a medium which makes the fact of Redemption present to all men" (302). But of course presence does not automatically translate into awareness. Seen in isolation from the redemption, the cycle of the seasons is at best an ambiguous sign, a witness at once to renewal and to decay, to vitality and to mutability. "For fallen man, the cycle of seasons, the wheel of time itself, is only a spiritual prison. Each new spring brings a temporary hope. Autumn and winter destroy that hope with their ever-returning reminder of death. . . . The cycle of the seasons reminds us, by this perpetual renewal and perpetual death, that death is the end of all. The universe which came into being will some day grow cold, perhaps, and die. What will remain?" (302-3). For contemporary people, estranged from the natural cycle, Merton goes on to say, time has not even this much meaning. "In such a world, man's life is no longer even a seasonal cycle. It is a linear *flight* into nothingness, a flight from reality and from God, without purpose and without objective, except to keep moving, to keep from having to face reality" (303). To appreciate and respond creatively to the redemption of time, one must "first break away from this linear flight into nothingness and recover" (303) an awareness of and participation in the rhythms of natural time, the cycle of the day, the cycle of the year. Only then is it possible to transcend, in the risen Christ, the endless round of recurrence and to discover that it is life, not death, that is the final and definitive culmination of the journey through time. This is the good news of liturgical time: "The Word of God . . . has changed the cycle of the seasons from an imprisonment to a liberation" (303). Every liturgical celebration witnesses to some aspect of this liberation, to the presence of eternity within time. Therefore the liturgical cycle "is a year of *salvation*, but also a year of *enlightenment* and of *transformation*," a source both of "insights into the ways of God . . . and the great transforming force which reshapes our souls and our characters in the likeness of Christ" (304–5). Here is the rationale for Merton's own series of conferences, an effort to bring his novices into contact with the scriptural and ecclesial wisdom that is essential for authentic human and spiritual development. In liturgy we encounter the Christ who has redeemed the time, and in liturgy we are summoned to participate in that work of redemption, to make it accessible in this particular time, in the present. "In the liturgy, then, the Church would have us realize that we meet the same Christ Who went about everywhere doing good, and Who is still present in the midst of us wherever two or three are gathered together in His Name. And we meet Him by sharing in His life and His Redemption. We meet Christ in order to *be* Christ, and with Him save the world" (306). Here, at the very beginning of his decade as novice master, the seeds of Merton's incarnational engagement with the world beyond the monastery can be perceived as rooted in and springing from his understanding of the purpose of the liturgy as a participation in the deepest sense in the *opus Dei*, the saving work of God, made possible because the power of God is made present in the "now" that brings together the once-for-all events of Christ's definitive saving acts and their full realization in the Kingdom of God.

> In every liturgical mystery we have this telescoping of time and eternity, of the universal and the personal, what is common to all ages, what is above and beyond all time, and what is most particular and most immediate to our own time and place where we celebrate the liturgy. Christ in His infinite greatness embraces all things, the divine and the human, the spiritual and the material, the old and the new, the great and the small, and in the liturgy He makes Himself all things to all men and becomes all in all. The works which Christ accomplished in time remain complete, unique and perfect in eternity, and the liturgical

> mysteries make these works present to us each time they are
> celebrated. Not only that, they incorporate us in His mysteries
> and renew their effect in time and in space. By the liturgy, while
> remaining in time, we enter into the great celebration that takes
> place before the throne of the Lamb in heaven, in eternity. The
> liturgical year takes the passage of time and elevates it to the
> level of eternity. (307)

Liturgy is at once the elevation of time into eternity and the bringing of
eternity into time, a participation in the Trinitarian life of love and the
diffusion of that love throughout the world, a sacrament in the truest
sense of the term, both a sign and an instrument of God's redemptive
power transforming the individual, the community, and the cosmos. "It
is the prayer and praise of the Bride of Christ, the Church, and if we
are one with her, then we too will be united, as she is, with the Divine
Bridegroom" (309).

Though none of the other pieces among these additional materials
comes close to matching this introductory reflection in intensity or pro-
fundity, there are certainly other segments that are of comparable quality
to the conferences found in Parts I and II of *Liturgical Feasts and Seasons*.
While relatively brief, the reflections on "*The Mystery of the Cross in the
Rule of St. Benedict*" (347–48) implicitly connect the Feast of St. Benedict,
March 21, with the Lenten season in which it occurs. While the term
"the Cross" never occurs in the Benedictine *Rule*, Merton points out that
Benedict's understanding of the monastery as a "school of the Lord's service" presupposes that the monk is educated by taking up the cross and
following Christ to Calvary, so as to be "*united to Christ in His Passion*"
and so "share His glory" (347), a process that takes place above all in the
various steps of humility described in chapter 7 of the *Rule*. The conference concludes by making an explicit reference to the third responsory
of the night office for the feast, the passage from Gregory the Great's *Life
of Benedict* in which the abbot makes the sign of the cross over the cup
of poisoned wine given him by the rebellious monks of Vicovaro, which
then shatters, leading to the final observation that the "sign of the Cross
{is the} sign of *Life*. The Risen Lord lives in us because He died for us. He
lives in us in proportion as our 'old man' is put to death by His Spirit. For
this we are monks" (348).

The much longer conference on "Jesus in the Lenten Gospels"
(333–45) touches on no less than twenty-seven gospel readings (out of a
possible thirty-two) from Ash Wednesday through the end of the fourth

week of Lent (i.e. the period before Passiontide begins with Passion Sunday at the beginning of the fifth week), generally though not rigidly following the calendar, in some cases limiting himself to brief references, in others providing a detailed exegesis of the pertinent passage. It is the most comprehensive consideration of an extended period in the liturgical cycle found in any single conference (and must actually have taken a number of conference periods to present if done as thoroughly in person as in the text). Merton's purpose is to show how the Lenten gospels provide a thorough and detailed exposition of the identity, character, and teachings of Jesus as a prelude to the culminating events of his life as presented in the two final weeks of Passiontide. He sums up his reflections in a concluding section on *"The personality of Jesus"* by emphasizing the intimacy with all humanity that is at the heart of Christ's life and mission, and by pointing out that Jesus' identification with us must be reciprocated by our identification with him if the relationship is to have its full transforming effect:

> everywhere in the Lenten gospels we find the human traits of the God–Man which are all significant revelations of God in Christ His Son—His tenderness and compassion . . . His simplicity and kindness . . . [His willingness] to share all the conditions and limitations of human nature, to be really one with those whom He has chosen as His brothers. All the warm human traits of Jesus express this great truth, that the love of God has willed to descend among us in our own humanity and dwell among us as one of ourselves, truly our Brother. This is one of the greatest truths which the Gospel teaches about Jesus and this we must learn above all, that His love has sought to identify Him with us, and to be like us in everything, and all He asks is that our faith respond with a simplicity and a totality corresponding to His own. (345)

The three conferences devoted to the immaculate conception (367–73, 373–74, 375–77) presumably date from three successive years, though since none are dated there is no way to be sure which belongs to which year. That presented first in this edition is certainly the most detailed and most fully developed, with an opening that explicitly situates the feast in the context of the liturgical cycle in general and the principal mysteries of Christ in particular:

> the purpose of every liturgical feast is to give glory to God, to praise Him and magnify Him in admiration at what His

mysteries reveal of His infinite goodness. In all the feasts of
Our Lady and of the saints we ultimately magnify and extol the
greatness of God; we contemplate God in them; we praise the
great work of God in them. All the works of grace are manifestations of the mystery of Christ, and Christ Himself is the
great manifestation of the Father. The Immaculate Conception
is most intimately connected with the mystery of our Incarnation and Redemption, and in it we see a peculiar evidence of the
divine goodness and love. (367)

Merton goes on to emphasize that the dogma of the immaculate conception is not intended to set Mary apart from the rest of humanity but to
serve as a *"pledge of our own purification and sanctification by the all-
powerful merits of the Cross of Jesus. The Immaculate Conception is the
first great testimony to the power of the Cross"* (368). It is not a matter
of exclusive concentration on the biological process of "conception" *per
se*; it is to be understood as metonymy, a figurative way of expressing the
meaning of her whole life of perfect response to the grace of redemption,
which she proleptically experienced from the very beginning through the
very end of her earthly existence. The two other, much briefer reflections
both focus on the readings of the feast, the first emphasizing the element
of "dramatic dialogue" (373) in the texts, drawing from and echoing as
they do both the imagery of the Song of Songs and the exchange with the
angelic messenger at the Annunciation: "God, the Divine Bridegroom,
speaks to Mary; she in turn speaks to Him and to us, and we, for our part,
speak mostly to her" (373). The other commentary on "some themes
from the office" (375) sets the feast and the doctrine firmly within the
context of Christ's redemptive work, and warns against any sort of mys-
tification that would obscure this connection: "Unless we see the Feast of
the Immaculate Conception as a celebration of the victory of Christ over
sin and death and the devil, we cannot understand it; Mary without Jesus
is nothing; {the} Immaculate Conception without the Cross is less than
nothing, a pure illusion" (376).

For good measure, one final Marian conference (378–80), not
linked to any particular feast, is found in these additional materials,
drawn largely from the writings on Mary and the priesthood of his friend
the French Dominican Paul Philippe.[27] As in the Marian material in Part

---

27. Merton met Fr. Philippe when he visited Gethsemani and corresponded with
him in connection with his work in the Congregation for Religious at the Vatican,
where he eventually become a curial archbishop and secretary of the Congregation of

II, Merton is particularly interested in the figure of Mary at the foot of the cross: "Mary was necessary to Jesus in the Passion—He willed to have her consolation, her compassion, her understanding, her sharing with Him His great act of love for men. She shared His solitude, and she alone could; thus she shared His divine gift of penetrating into the inmost hearts of all" (379). Once again the emphasis is on the paschal character of Mary's vocation, and in this regard, on her special role in guiding and interceding for the priest, whose sacramental ministry is profoundly paschal as well. Like much of the material that, for whatever reason, is not found in the final mimeograph of "Liturgical Feasts and Seasons," this conference supplements and reinforces themes and ideas that do appear there.

~

Thomas Merton certainly was no apologist for the liturgical status quo. He had no sympathy whatsoever for liturgical pomp and grandiosity. He is at his most scathing in his critique of the florid pageantry of the pontifical High Mass celebrated on Easter morning:

> Interminable pontifical maneuverings, with the "Master of Ceremonies" calling every play, and trying to marshal the ministers into formation and keep things moving. Purple zucchetto and cappa magna and of course it had to be our Mexican novice who was appointed to carry the long train (this inwardly made me furious and practically choked any desire I may have had to sing alleluias). The church was stifling with solemn, feudal, and unbreathable fictions. This taste for plush, for ornamentation, for display strikes me as secular, no matter how much it is supposed to be "for the glory of God." The spring outside seemed much more sacred.[28]

Yet Merton's deep appreciation and affection for the liturgy that had played a central role in forming his own monastic life led to a certain ambivalence toward the changes that would take place during the final decade of his life. Even at the very time he was completing the novitiate

the Doctrine of the Faith. Merton was in correspondence with Fr. Philippe in August and September of 1960 concerning his attempts to move to Dom Gregorio Lemercier's monastery in Cuernavaca, Mexico (see Merton, *Witness to Freedom*, 221–26, 229); see also Merton's April 5, 1963, letter congratulating Philippe on his elevation to the archbishopric, which goes on to include an extensive discussion of monastic renewal in the context of the Second Vatican Council (Merton, *School of Charity*, 162–66).

28. Merton, *Conjectures of a Guilty Bystander*, 269–70.

liturgy conferences, he was expressing some discomfort with changes already being made to the liturgical calendar. On January 12, 1958, he wrote in his journal:

> It is sad it is not the Sunday within the Octave of Epiphany. The new changes in the Liturgy seem to me to be in many ways bewildering and senseless—a matter of juggling with words and manipulating the rubrics rather than a real vital adjustment. So the Octave of the Epiphany has, for some reason, been abolished, yet the office remains essentially the same. Tomorrow, the Liturgy of the Octave Day will be what it always has been. But it will be the "Feast of the Commemoration of the Baptism of the Lord"! This is the mouse which our mountain is bringing forth. We are all wrapt up in our liturgical red tape.[29]

Preferring "Octave of the Epiphany" to "Baptism of the Lord" may seem rather captious, but in the context is perhaps an expression of his unease with change that is presented as significant but is mainly a matter of relabeling, more cosmetic than substantial. Almost two years later, on December 7, 1959, he has a similar complaint: "We no longer have Vigil of the Immaculate Conception in the Liturgy. A pity—I miss all the Vigils. Why on earth were they suddenly suppressed?"[30] There may also be a certain defensiveness on his part that he is not perceived by some of his fellow monks as a supporter of liturgical reform because of his own proclivity for solitude and silence. On December 19, 1960, he writes in his journal:

> Certainly the liturgical mysteries are the "highest" and most valuable and most Christian worship. But when it comes to personal tastes and preference, solitary contemplative prayer is to me the source of the greatest joy and hope and strength, and I *like* it. I think I have a right to—and to spend as much time in it as I like outside of choir. But this *preference*, even though it is nobody's business but my own, seems to be something they resent intensely.[31]

Whether "they" do in fact resent his contemplative bent to the degree he suspects or whether this is a bit of projection on his part, it no doubt has some bearing on his mixed feelings about liturgical reforms that will

29. Merton, *Search for Solitude*, 154.

30. Merton, *Search for Solitude*, 354.

31. Merton, *Turning Toward the World*, 77.

of course be one of the principal changes brought about by the Second Vatican Council.

His initial response, however, to *Sacrosanctum Concilium*, the Constitution on the Sacred Liturgy promulgated at the end of the second session of the Council, is very positive, as it will continue to be despite his reservations and hesitations about some of the ways it will be implemented. He writes in his journal on December 15, 1963, "Began reading the Council's constitution on liturgy. . . . It is really remarkable. There is no question that great things have been done by the Bishops, and Pope John was truly inspired. When one reads quotations from some of the statements one is more and more impressed by their fullness of meaning."[32] On the following day, he writes to Dom Aelred Graham with an even more extensive positive evaluation: "The new Constitution on Liturgy from the Council is most exciting and very rich, it seems to me. I am going through it with the novices. There is great work ahead. This is the first real liturgical reform in 1600 years, and if it is properly understood and implemented, it will amount to a revolution in the sense of a metanoia for the whole Church." He is realistic about the inevitable difficulties that translating vision into praxis will involve, yet he is fundamentally hopeful: "I know that there will be some false starts and some blunders, but the Holy Spirit will take care of us." He goes on to disclaim any title to being "an avant-garde liturgist . . . bubbling over with projects" and adds: "I want to make it my business to try to stand up for some monastic values that might get lost in all this: for instance the preservation of *some* 'sacred silence' somewhere in all the singing and reading and acclaiming that we are promised,"[33] and this will indeed by his primary focus in the months and years ahead.

Writing three weeks later, on January 4, 1964, to Fr. Chrysogonus Waddell, Gethsemani's leading liturgist, who was studying in Rome at the time, Merton foresees the transition to an English liturgy, but strikes a note of caution about the disappearance of a sung Latin office that has stood the test of time:

> I think that in the long run there will have to be readings in the vernacular, but I wonder if there are not quite a few complexities to consider. There is first of all the matter of Gregorian chant. Whatever may be my evil reputation among chant people, I am

32. Merton, *Dancing in the Water of Life*, 44–45.
33. Merton, *School of Charity*, 188.

really deeply in love with the chant. I think it is certainly the greatest religious music we have available to us. I also like the Latin office myself, and am so far demented as to love the Vulgate Psalter. I know that I may have to give this up for the good of others, eventually. But at the same time I think we ought to recognize that something valuable and great in itself cannot be discarded thoughtlessly. I certainly think that it will not be easy to replace it by something objectively half as good, though of course for the benefit of those concerned, there will be immense advantages.[34]

He strikes a somewhat different note in a letter to the distinguished Benedictine liturgist Godfrey Diekmann, OSB. He calls *Sacrosanctum Concilium* "a splendid and lively document" and expresses the hope that it may "really herald the true, deep, universal renewal of the spirit of worship, and the practice of real liturgy at last, on a wide scale, not just for the few," then goes on to question whether "the old forms will do," with regard to "the singing" in particular. "Not being too much of a pastoral liturgy man," he comments, he has no grand plan to offer, but questions "if we are yet ready to create new forms that will be 'eternal.' Better perhaps to envisage a long state of transition and experimentation, and hope that plenty of freedom will be granted . . . and properly used!"[35] Far from being opposed to change, he expresses a concern here lest the process be cut off too quickly, before the possibility of reaching a real discernment of what is transient and what is of permanent value in the renewal.

Considering the monastic context in particular, even before the reforms have begun to be implemented, he is already concerned that monasteries may embrace changes that have not been thoroughly considered, with questionable results. "Our great danger," he writes to a Carthusian friend on December 9, 1963, before having had the opportunity to read the liturgy constitution, "is to throw away things that are excellent, which we do not understand, and replace them with mediocre forms which seem to us to be more meaningful and which in fact are only trite."[36] Simply changing forms, or even languages, without a deeper transformation of attitudes will effect no lasting solution, as he notes in a February 14, 1964 letter to Ronald Roloff, OSB:

---

34. Merton, *School of Charity*, 193.
35. Merton, *Seeds of Destruction*, 317 [undated, but evidently early 1964].
36. Merton, *School of Charity* 187.

If the old office did not mean anything to them, where is the guarantee that the new one will mean more? Merely singing the psalms in English is not going to make the office any deeper and any better for people who are just not interested in praying. . . . My own personal feeling about the vernacular office is that it had better be good, because to me it was a relief to get the substance and richness of the Latin office we have here, with Gregorian, etc. This I know is not popular talk, but I speak only for myself. . . . I have never had any trouble with our office as such. I have certainly been bothered to death by some of the policies in choir, and some of the monastic nonsense that has taken place under the guise that nothing is to be preferred to the *Opus Dei* (therefore make it as much of an impossible project as you can). I came here with a good knowledge of Latin and a love for the Psalms, the Bible and the Fathers. I have never had any trouble understanding the office, or "getting something out of it." . . . I do feel though that for a while the vernacular may be an improvement because it will have to be simpler. It will have to be fairly experimental, and non-professional, and hence we will escape perhaps for a few years from our benighted perfectionism and just pray like humans for a while.[37]

When the new rite for Mass is introduced, he is unimpressed by the English translations of the scriptural readings, which he calls "extremely trite and pedestrian" and marked by a "total lack of imagination, of creativity, of a sense of worship!"[38] and while he notes "there are good things about" the new rite, he considers it "obviously transitional,"[39] and finds that it "ends too abruptly."[40] His initial ambivalence about concelebrated Mass seems to be rooted more in his conflicted relationship with Dom James Fox, his abbot, who was of course principal celebrant at these Masses, than in objections in theory or even in practice. On July 12, 1965, the day after the first regular Sunday concelebration, he reflected in his journal: "It makes sense to concelebrate on the Lord's Day and though in many ways I do not 'like' it I see that this is best, and will sign up for it. There is no question that this makes far more sense than the old way (private Mass, then High Mass) for here the community *all* assembles, and most go to communion, and guests are there, etc. My difficulties are

---

37. Merton, *School of Charity* 201–2.

38. Merton, *Dancing in the Water of Life*, 227 [April 13, 1965].

39. Merton, *Dancing in the Water of Life*, 215 [March 9, 1965].

40. Merton, *Dancing in the Water of Life*, 215 [March 10, 1965].

not with the principle or the idea, but still with the way we do it, and our apparent attitude. But this is of no real importance."[41] A week later, after Dom James has authorized his permanent residence at the hermitage, Merton feels much more reconciled to his abbot and much more at ease at Mass: "Concelebration after that was a moving, humbling and consoling experience, and I think I will have no more of my foolish feelings about it. Thank God for enough light to see my childishness."[42] In January 1966, having turned down the invitation to become involved in the translation process for the new missal, he notes in his journal that while he regards much of the conservative opposition to the liturgical changes as "pretty neurotic," he can "objectively . . . see reasons for some of the criticisms."[43] By October of that year, he has reached a kind of liturgical equilibrium that enables him to appreciate the freewheeling Mass he concelebrated with Daniel Berrigan, with its "very moving simple English text" (not officially approved and evidently borrowed from the Anglicans), but still value the "sober, austere, solemn, intense" Mass he had celebrated for Jacques Maritain the previous week, "old style." He concluded, "Somehow I think the new is really better," but added, "I have nothing against the old."[44] This represents his considered position on the matter for the remaining two years of his life.[45]

41. Merton, *Dancing in the Water of Life*, 268; for earlier comments on concelebration see the journal entries for January 27, 1965, and July 5, 1965 (Merton, *Dancing in the Water of Life*, 196, 264), and the March 28, 1965, letter to Dame Marcella Van Bruyn, OSB (Merton, *School of Charity*, 270–71).

42. Merton, *Dancing in the Water of Life*, 273.

43. Merton, *Learning to Love*, 13 [January 29, 1966].

44. Merton, *Learning to Love*, 149.

45. See for example his journal entry of May 30, 1967: "More changes in the Mass—elimination of a lot of signs of the cross, kisses of altar etc. In a way it relaxes tensions—is more honest—more true to the non-hieratic feeling of the modern America—but I had no real objection to the old formal ritual gestures either" (Merton, *Learning to Love*, 241); see also his comments of July 13, 1967: "I still feel there is a great deal of uncertainty about the meaning of the new Liturgy . . . because of the gap between the theological statements *about what it ought to be* and the actuality of what it is. The theologians declare that the Liturgy is the place of God's power and visible presence: but is that what one 'sees'? I admit that when one believes, then the Liturgy *is* a place of holiness and sharing in God's presence and in His peace. But for me this was even more true in the old Liturgy—though also true of concelebration, true of my own Mass—I can't seem to find the differences that are declared to be so important. True, there is a lot of ambivalence in me because I am a non-liturgical type, and because, isolated as I am, I am very little aware of what is really going on" (Merton, *Learning to Love*, 262–63).

As for his own liturgical practice, his move to the hermitage enabled him to retain the form of the office and the version of the Scriptures that had nourished him for the previous quarter-century. On July 19, 1965, he wrote in his journal, "The Latin psalter is for me! It is a deep communion with the Lord and His saints, of my Latin Church. To be in communion with the Saints of *my* tradition is by that fact to be more authentically in communion with those of the Greek, Syriac, etc. traditions, who reach me through my own Fathers."[46] A year later, in August 1966, he wrote to Dame Marcella Van Bruyn, "I still say the old office (the community dropped Prime and rearranged all the psalms). I am going to keep the office in Latin *usque ad mortem.* I read the Vulgate for my *lectio divina.* I am horribly conservative in these respects," then added: "Otherwise I am using some Zen Buddhism, etc."[47]—a perfect illustration of the impossibility of confining Thomas Merton to neat ideological categories.

Among Merton's more amusing observations on liturgical life, one pertinent to the present volume, comes from his sardonic journal entry of January 20, 1961: "In the refectory we are being boomed at by a liturgical tape—that is, by a tape-recorded talk on the liturgy. A harangue, ardent, deafening, blasting everybody's head off. The material itself is fair—the usual, not too bad, present-day emphasis on the theology on the mysteries of Xt in the liturgy. All standard since *Mediator Dei*—and certainly nothing beyond or besides *Mediator Dei.* But the blasting, the emphasis—(*everything* is emphasized)—the impassioned pointing to the 'Ca-ROSS!'" His reaction to this liturgical pontificating was to distance himself personally from it as far as possible: "One thing that went through my mind during this tape: the resolution never to publish my book on the liturgy: I mean the novitiate liturgy conferences."[48] There is no indication that he had actually thought seriously about publishing *Liturgical Feasts and Seasons,* but his spontaneous response to this "haranguing" was to renounce any complicity in a similar enterprise, no matter that his conferences were hardly marked by a similar tone.

46. Merton, *Dancing in the Water of Life,* 273–74.

47. Merton, *School of Charity,* 311.

48. Merton, *Turning toward the World,* 87–88; see also the revised version of this passage (which doesn't mention the novitiate conferences) in Merton, *Conjectures of a Guilty Bystander,* 29–30.

But this resolution did not prevent Merton from gathering together and publishing a collection of liturgical essays a few years later. *Seasons of Celebration* appeared in December 1965[49] but was already conceived in October 1963[50] and assembled by February 1964.[51] It includes fifteen essays, some of them predating the novitiate liturgy conferences; its subtitle, *Meditations on the Cycle of Liturgical Feasts*, found only on the dustcover of the first edition, nowhere in the book itself, is not completely representative of the contents, as less than half the chapters actually focus on particular feasts, but all have at least some connection to liturgy. As "my book on the liturgy" that did in fact get published, it is worth considering in some detail, particularly as it overlaps with the present volume in that its third essay is "Time and the Liturgy," a further reworked version of "The Opening of the Liturgical Year," the original introduction to the novitiate conferences that serves as a kind of prelude to the essays that follow it in *Seasons of Celebration* as well.

There are about two dozen alterations in the text of this essay, most of them fairly minor, but the beginning and the end of the article are completely rewritten and expanded. The first eight sentences are omitted, and replaced by three and a half pages of new material, which immediately begins the discussion of time with an emphasis on the Christian perspective that time is no longer an enemy, no longer a threat to freedom, for a redeemed humanity: "when man recovers, in Christ, the freedom of the Sons of God, he lives in time *without predetermination*, because grace will always protect his freedom against the tyranny of evil."[52] Time is not a threat because human transience and mortality are no longer seen as the final word on human destiny. Without explicitly using the terms *chronos* and *kairos*, Merton points out that the liturgy presents a deeper sense of time that is not simply quantitative and sequential; liturgical time is experienced as "a 'sacred time,' a primordial time which mysteriously recurs and is present in the very heart of secular time."[53] The end of time is now to be recognized not as an extinction but as a fulfillment, already experienced in mystery in the liturgy. At this point the revised text rejoins the original with its reference to living in the messianic kingdom in the

49. Merton, *Dancing in the Water of Life*, 277.

50. Merton, *Dancing in the Water of Life*, 21.

51. Merton, *Dancing in the Water of Life*, 77.

52. Merton, *Seasons of Celebration*, 46.

53. Merton, *Seasons of Celebration*, 47.

present age. After some expansion of the material on cyclic time with references to Hellenistic mystery religions and Platonism, in which time is regarded as a prison of eternal spirits,[54] and a corresponding addition to the following section on contemporary "mass man" deprived even of "the anguish of dualism or the comfort of myth,"[55] the revised text remains close to the original until reaching the quotation from *Mediator Dei*,[56] after which its conclusion is completely original. Where "The Opening of the Liturgical Year" ends with a focus on liturgy as a contemplative exercise, "the fountainhead of all true Christian mysticism" (308), "Time and the Liturgy" asks whether the cycle of liturgical feasts does not in fact "finally reduce the Christian liturgy to a glorified and spiritualized cult of natural fecundity and rebirth."[57] Merton's answer is to stress the eschatological character of the true Christian understanding of history in which the coming of Christ has ushered in "the time of the end";[58] even the cycle of the liturgy is always oriented toward the absolute future of God's reign, and thus is always a sign of contradiction to the spurious security of "merely temporal and social patterns," always a challenge to "the complacent celebration of the *status quo*."[59] In this shift from an emphasis on the liturgy as the entry of eternity into time (see 309) to the more dynamic focus on an "eschatological hope" transcending "visible and familiar" institutional structures,[60] the mature voice of the more prophetic Merton of the mid-1960s is heard, but emerges so naturally from what has preceded that only by comparing earlier and later conclusions is one made aware of the evolution in his understanding not just of time but of the Christian life in the decade that separates the first and the final versions of these reflections.

54. See Merton, *Seasons of Celebration*, 50.

55. Merton, *Seasons of Celebration*, 51.

56. Merton, *Seasons of Celebration*, 59.

57. Merton, *Seasons of Celebration*, 59.

58. Merton, *Seasons of Celebration*, 59; this phrase, which has become familiar from one of Merton's best-known essays, "The Time of the End Is the Time of No Room" (Merton, *Raids on the Unspeakable*, 65–75), itself a "liturgical" reflection on the meaning of Christmas, is credited in a footnote to Gunther Anders, who "has coined this striking expression to describe the change of perspective that followed the dropping of the first Atomic Bomb on Hiroshima"—giving a sense of the precariousness of human achievement and of human history which Merton says was "in a very real sense . . . already that of the first Christians" (Merton, *Seasons of Celebration*, 59–60).

59. Merton, *Seasons of Celebration*, 60.

60. Merton, *Seasons of Celebration*, 60.

The article on time is then followed by a half-dozen essays on specific celebrations of the liturgical calendar, three on Advent/Christmas and three on Lent/Easter, followed by five more thematic pieces, of varying degrees of liturgical relevance. None of these was written specifically for this collection; they were assembled from already written and for the most part previously published essays, so that they constitute a somewhat heterogeneous gathering.

Among the earliest, and longest, pieces in the book is "The Sacrament of Advent in the Spirituality of St. Bernard,"[61] identified by Merton himself in his "Author's Note" as presented "to students of Patristic theology in 1952."[62] Drawing extensively on Bernard's series of Advent sermons, Merton emphasizes especially his teaching on the three Advents (found in briefer form in the novitiate conference on the First Sunday of Advent [see 5–6]), the first coming on Christmas, the final coming at the parousia, and the "*medius Adventus*" which "is in a certain sense the most important for us," the "present Advent that is taking place at every moment of our own earthly life as wayfarers."[63] Christ's coming now, in this time and place, in liturgy, in Scripture and in spiritual experience, both puts us in touch with the foundational events of faith and with their final realization, and is invitation and challenge to ongoing conversion. "Advent: Hope or Delusion?" the more provocative title given to the following piece,[64] signals a more recent treatment of the season, and indeed dates from 1963, but there are strong elements of continuity with the preceding essay, as here too Merton stresses "the coming and indeed the *presence* of Christ in our world . . . even in the midst of all its inscrutable problems and tragedies."[65] But as the last words of this quotation suggest, more attention is paid to the present condition of the world, to the need "to seek and find Christ in our world as it is, and not as it *might be*,"[66] recognizing the just demands of contemporary people "to *see* in us some evidence of the presence and action of Christ, some visible manifestation

61. Merton, *Seasons of Celebration*, 61–87.

62. Merton, *Seasons of Celebration*, vii; published in French translation as "Le Sacrement de l'Avent dans la Spiritualité de Saint Bernard" but previously unpublished in English.

63. Merton, *Seasons of Celebration*, 76–77.

64. Merton, *Seasons of Celebration*, 88–100; originally published in 1963 as "The Advent Mystery."

65. Merton, *Seasons of Celebration*, 89.

66. Merton, *Seasons of Celebration*, 90.

of the *Pneuma*,"[67] which can happen only if Christians share in Christ's own *kenosis*, emptying themselves of arrogance and self-centeredness and along with Christ entering into compassionate identification with "the unfortunate, the sinful, the destitute—those who were 'empty.'"[68] Here the meaning of Advent for a justice-centered spirituality is vividly expressed—it is a call to bring the future into the present, to incarnate the kingdom of God here and now.[69] This first triad of essays concludes with "The Nativity Kerygma,"[70] a homily originally published as a Christmas gift book in 1958.[71] Again the emphasis is on the fact that the salvation brought by the birth of Jesus is a present reality, "not merely an old thing which happened long ago, but a new thing which happens today."[72] Here also the theme of *kenosis*, the revelation of the divine majesty in the humility and hiddenness of the Child in the stable, is highlighted: "In 'emptying Himself' and taking the form of a servant, the Lord laid aside His majesty and His divine power, in order to dwell among us in goodness and mercy."[73] Those "who have seen the light of Christ are obliged, by the greatness of the grace that has been given us, to make known the presence of the Savior to the ends of the earth,"[74] so that the entire creation, which groans in expectation for the revelation of the children of God, will be drawn into the saving events initiated on Christmas Day. This proclamation of the message of salvation, Merton reminds his audience, is to be made not only through what one says but by how one lives, so that Christians themselves become a manifestation, an "Epiphany" of Christ to the world.

The second group begins with "Ash Wednesday,"[75] somewhat paradoxically presented as "a day of happiness, a Christian feast," since it is the initiation of "the great Easter cycle" that celebrates Christ's "definitive

---

67. Merton, *Seasons of Celebration*, 93.

68. Merton, *Seasons of Celebration*, 95.

69. "Yet we believe that He who has come and will come is present here and now: that we are in His Kingdom. Not only that, but we *are* His Kingdom" (Merton, *Seasons of Celebration*, 92).

70. Merton, *Seasons of Celebration*, 101–12.

71. Merton, *Nativity Kerygma*; subsequently published in *Worship* in 1959.

72. Merton, *Seasons of Celebration*, 102.

73. Merton, *Seasons of Celebration*, 108.

74. Merton, *Seasons of Celebration*, 112.

75. Merton, *Seasons of Celebration*, 113–24; originally published in *Worship* in 1959.

victory over sin and death."[76] Even the ashes themselves, signed in the form of a cross, are a reminder not merely of mortality but of Christ's passage through death, through the cross, to risen and glorified life, and of the promise that all who bear the cross, who share Christ's death, will also share his resurrection. The asceticism of fasting and other Lenten practices is not to be understood merely as self-discipline, self-mastery, but as a sign and a means of participating in the Paschal mystery, "the mystery of our burial with Christ in order to rise with Him to a new life."[77]

"Christian Self-Denial"[78] is the earliest of the essays, originally dating from 1950, but the version published here has been considerably augmented and updated. For example, the original version declares:

> There is no better or more complete manual of ascetical theology than the Missal. Quite apart from the teaching in the Epistles and Gospels, which are the actual word of God, the Church offers us in her collects and other prayers a most exhaustive and monumental theology of self-denial and supernatural living. To *live* the Mass that we all offer, by reading and understanding the prayers of the Mass, and incorporating them into our lives, is the best way to acquire the true Christian sense of abnegation.[79]

This has become in *Seasons of Celebration*:

> There is no better or more complete source of ascetical theology than the Liturgy. Quite apart from the teaching in the Psalms and Bible texts, which are the actual word of God, the Church offers us in her collects and other prayers a most exhaustive and monumental theology of self-denial and supernatural living. To *live* the Mass that we all offer by active and intelligent participation is the normal expression of Christian metanoia.[80]

The language of the revised version is both more biblical ("metanoia" for "abnegation") and more attuned to the spirit of liturgical renewal ("active and intelligent participation" for "reading and understanding the prayers of the Mass, and incorporating them into our lives"). Thus the tone of the

---

76. Merton, *Seasons of Celebration*, 113.

77. Merton, *Seasons of Celebration*, 122.

78. Merton, *Seasons of Celebration*, 125–43; originally published as "Self-Denial and the Christian" in *The Commonweal* in 1950, reprinted in Merton, *Early Essays*, 60–72.

79. Merton, *Early Essays*, 65.

80. Merton, *Seasons of Celebration*, 131.

article does not clash with that of the other, more recent articles. The major point remains basically the same: that authentic Christian self-denial must "lead us to a positive increase of spiritual energy and life,"[81] but whereas in the original it "keeps encouraging us with the hope of the happiness that lies ahead" and "puts heaven, so to speak, in our hearts here and now,"[82] in revised form it "keeps encouraging us to understand that our existence in 'the world' and in time becomes fruitful and meaningful in proportion as we are able to assume spiritual and Christian responsibility for our life, our work, and even for the world we live in" and "enables us to enter into the confusion of the world bearing something of the light of Truth in our hearts, and capable of exercising something of the mysterious, transforming power of the Cross, of love and of sacrifice."[83] These alterations provide in miniature an illustration of the same process of re-visioning by which *Seeds of Contemplation* became *New Seeds of Contemplation* more than a decade later. The newer version also concludes, as the earlier did not, with the explicit statement that "Self-denial, however rigorous, lacks all Christian meaning apart from the Cross and Resurrection of Christ,"[84] followed by two final paragraphs on Lent and on the Lenten practices of "fasts, renunciations and alms deeds" as having "an essential part to play as signs of a full participation in the Easter Mystery,"[85] thus situating this article more specifically in the sequence of the liturgical cycle being presented.

This second group of three culminates with "Easter: The New Life,"[86] which once again calls attention to the paschal significance not only of the liturgical cycle as a whole but of every single celebration of the Mass, in which "we die with Christ, rise with Him and receive from Him the Spirit of Promise who transforms us and unites us to the Father in and through the Son."[87] What is particular to Easter, coming after the asceticism of Lent, is the experience of definitive liberation, not only from sin but from the Law, from a spirituality centered on duty, issuing in inevitable failure and thus deserving of judgment. "To die to death and live

---

81. Merton, *Early Essays*, 64; Merton, *Seasons of Celebration*, 130.

82. Merton, *Early Essays*, 65.

83. Merton, *Seasons of Celebration*, 132.

84. Merton, *Seasons of Celebration*, 142.

85. Merton, *Seasons of Celebration*, 143.

86. Merton, *Seasons of Celebration*, 144–57, originally published in *Worship* in 1959.

87. Merton, *Seasons of Celebration*, 145.

a new life in Christ," Merton affirms, "we must die not only to sin *but also to the Law. . . .* not only as one who seeks salvation but as one who *is saved.* One might almost say that this truth is the great 'scandal' of Christianity."[88] Easter proclaims freedom from having to earn salvation, to deserve redemption by striving "to keep the Law of God considered as a formal code imposed on him from without."[89] Faced with the apparent alternatives of either living according to the flesh or living according to the law, the Christian learns from the risen Christ that there is "a third possibility . . . . It is the grace of God in Christ our Lord or, to be more succinct, *it is Christ Himself in us.* It is our new life in Christ. By our life of love and hope in Christ we rise above the dilemma and thus resolve it,"[90] not by becoming completely sinless, but by being drawn into a new relationship with the God of infinite mercy, a relationship in which sin is overcome not by "dutiful observance"[91] but by love, the love of God that empowers a reciprocal love for God because it is the Spirit of God that loves through and with and in the redeemed person. This is Merton's insight into the transformation effected by Christ's invitation to his disciples to share in his resurrected life and his return to the Father.

Each of the five thematic essays that follow has some liturgical resonance without being focused on a particular feast. "A Homily on Light and the Virgin Mary"[92] reflects on the ways in which the liturgy applies a whole series of Old Testament texts on light to Mary, "the perfect rekindling of the pure light which had been extinguished by the sin of Adam. In Mary, the lamp was once more perfectly clean, burning with pure light, standing on the lampstand, illuminating the whole house of God, restoring meaning to all God's creatures, and showing the rest of men the way to return to the light."[93] Perhaps most striking are those passages from the sapiential books in which Wisdom is presented as the "brightness of the eternal light and a mirror without stain,"[94] and the image of the woman "clothed with the sun" in the Apocalypse, identified in the

88. Merton, *Seasons of Celebration,* 146–47.

89. Merton, *Seasons of Celebration,* 156.

90. Merton, *Seasons of Celebration,* 156.

91. Merton, *Seasons of Celebration,* 156.

92. Merton, *Seasons of Celebration,* 158–70, originally published in *Worship* in 1963.

93. Merton, *Seasons of Celebration,* 163–64.

94. Merton, *Seasons of Celebration,* 164.

liturgy with Mary "filled with the light of the transfigured Christ"[95] and therefore a model for the redeemed Christian, who is called to live in the light so that "light will pass through him to pervade and transfigure the whole of creation."[96]

"The Good Samaritan,"[97] a conference given to the entire Gethsemani community on the Feast of the Transfiguration, 1961,[98] situates the parable of Luke 10:29–37 and its question of "Who is my neighbor?" in the context of the Old Testament concept of *chesed* (or *ḥesed*), the "gratuitous mercy that considers no fitness, no worthiness and no return. . . . the way the Lord looks upon the guilty and with His look makes them at once innocent."[99] As God's love transcends all considerations of worthiness, so the *"chasid"*—the one who has become the embodiment of divine mercy because he has experienced that divine mercy in his own life—renounces all attempts to classify others into the worthy and unworthy, neighbor and stranger. "The folly of the *chasid* is manifested in his love and concern for his neighbor, the sinner. . . . The professionally pious man, on the contrary, makes a whole career out of being distinguishable from sinners."[100] In the end, Merton suggests, *chesed* is the power of the Spirit of God that enables one both to see in others and to be for others the presence of the Lord. "It is Christ Himself Who lies wounded by the roadside. It is Christ Who comes by in the person of the Samaritan. And Christ is the bond, the compassion and the understanding between them."[101] Here Merton draws on the resources of recent Scripture scholarship and applies it in creative ways, reminiscent of patristic exegesis, to express to his community his own growing sense of the centrality of compassion for (and from) the marginalized to the Christian and even the monastic vocation.

---

95. Merton, *Seasons of Celebration*, 164–65.

96. Merton, *Seasons of Celebration*, 167.

97. Merton, *Seasons of Celebration*, 171–82, published there for the first time.

98. See Merton's journal entry for August 6, 1961: "I had to give the Conference in chapter—on the Good Samaritan, and the '*chesed*' of God" (Merton, *Turning toward the World*, 147). He evidently intended to have it printed on a hand press in Vermont, but apparently nothing came of this plan—see his journal entry for August 11, 1961: "Will send the Good Samaritan to Claude Fredericks today. What lovely things he prints at Pawlet. What perfection! And no question that it has a special grace and nobility which you can't get with a machine" (Merton, *Turning toward the World*, 150).

99. Merton, *Seasons of Celebration*, 178.

100. Merton, *Seasons of Celebration*, 179.

101. Merton, *Seasons of Celebration*, 181.

> Where there is on the one hand a helpless one, beaten and half
> dead, and on the other an outcast with no moral standing and
> the one leans down in pity to help the other, then there takes
> place a divine epiphany and awakening. . . . This is what we are
> talking about when we speak of "doing the will of God." Not
> only fulfilling precepts, and praying, and being holy, but being
> instruments of mercy, and fastening ourselves and others to
> God in the bonds of *chesed*.[102]

The following article, "The Name of the Lord,"[103] also more scriptural than strictly liturgical in its approach, begins by citing the opening
verses of the Letter to the Hebrews, where the superiority of the Son to
the angels and of His ministry to theirs is related to his inheritance of
"a name superior to theirs,"[104] as in the Hebrew Scriptures the revelation of the divine name transcends God's communications through "the
angel of the Lord." Merton then goes on to examine in some detail the
various passages relating to the name Yahweh, the various suggestions of
Scripture scholars as to its implications in both preserving the mystery
of God's "ineffable Nature" while at the same time "clearly and forcefully
manifesting *His presence and His being as a Person* with a free and salvific
plan emanating from an abyss of incomprehensible and loving mercy."[105]
Only in the very last paragraph of the article does Merton circle back to
the initial focus on the name of the Son, briefly but powerfully pointing
out that the "Name which was given by Joseph to Mary's child, at the
command of the angel" is in fact "Ye-shua, *Yahweh saves* . . . . the same 'I
am' revealed to Moses, present in the midst of the People of God throughout the Salvation history," the name claimed by Jesus when he declares,
"Before Abraham was, *I am*" (John 8:58). Thus, Merton concludes, "The
Christian faith . . . sees in the *Person* of Jesus the living, actual presence
of the ineffable Name."[106]

The liturgical dimension initially seems most peripheral to the following essay, "'In Silentio,'"[107] an abridged version of the Introduction

---

102. Merton, *Seasons of Celebration*, 182.

103. Merton, *Seasons of Celebration*, 183–203, originally published in *Worship* in
1964.

104. Merton, *Seasons of Celebration*, 183.

105. Merton, *Seasons of Celebration*, 191.

106. Merton, *Seasons of Celebration*, 203.

107. Merton, *Seasons of Celebration*, 204–15.

Merton wrote for the monastic photographic volume *Silence in Heaven*.[108] Here the focus is also scriptural, centered on the origin and fall stories of Genesis and on the new creation begun with the Spirit of God once again moving over the waters at the baptism of Jesus, who then departed for the desert to confront the power of evil and to restore the original harmony of paradise. This is the context for an authentic understanding of the monastic vocation both as "a life of consecration, trial, solitary combat, of obedience to the Holy Spirit in an eschatological battle between light and darkness,"[109] and as a call "to spend [one's] entire life in cultivating the spiritual Eden, the 'new creation' of space and light marvellously effected by God through the Incarnation, Passion and Resurrection of His Son."[110] The monk is recognized both as "a man of sorrow, a man discontented with every illusion, aware of his own poverty, impatient of evasion, who seeks the naked realities that only the desert can reveal," and as "a man of joy, a man at peace with the emptiness of the wilderness, glad of his limitations, loving reality as he finds it, and therefore secure in his humility," above all "a man of desires . . . . because he lives by pure hope."[111] The only explicitly monastic essay in the book, "'In Silentio'" may seem to be somewhat out of place, but its inclusion actually is a way for Merton to integrate monasticism into the broader texture of Christian life presented by the volume as a whole, and in its powerful and beautiful conclusion the liturgical dimension is at least metaphorically invoked in the midst of solitude in the image of wisdom's "unending, sunlit, inexpressible song: the private song she sings to the solitary soul. . . . the unique, irreplaceable song that each soul sings for himself with the unknown Spirit, as he sits on the doorstep of his own being, the place where his existence opens out into the abyss of God's nameless, limitless freedom."[112] This solitary, secret song is then recognized as but one expression of "the song that each one of us must sing,"[113] that God Himself sings within each person, a song that "blends also in secret with the unheard notes of every other individual song," forming "a great choir whose music is heard only in

---

108. Merton, *Silence in Heaven*, 17–30; originally published in French as *Silence dans le Ciel* by the Benedictine Abbey of La-Pierre-Qui-Vire. For a discussion of this work see O'Connell, "Thomas Merton's *Silence in Heaven* and *The Silent Life.*"

109. Merton, *Seasons of Celebration*, 206.

110. Merton, *Seasons of Celebration*, 207.

111. Merton, *Seasons of Celebration*, 208.

112. Merton, *Seasons of Celebration*, 214.

113. Merton, *Seasons of Celebration*, 214.

the depths of silence, because it is more silent than the silence itself,"[114] a paradoxical affirmation that incorporates and transcends distinctions between liturgy and contemplation, that brings together monastics and laity, the living and the dead, all of whom join in the one song "welling up like a stream out of the very heart of God's creative and redemptive love."[115]

The last in this series of thematic essays, "Community of Pardon,"[116] written in 1963,[117] focuses not just on the reconciliation of the sinful individual with God, but on the social significance of the Church's presence in the world as a reconciled community, a sign and instrument of the unity that is God's will for the human race. "Christ will not be visible to the world in His Church except in proportion as Christians seek peace and unity with one another and with all men. . . . In so far as the Church is a community of pardon it is an epiphany of the Divine Love, Agape: the Love that underlies the mystery of creation and redemption."[118] This unity is to be understood as the work of the Holy Spirit, "the bond of union between the Father and the Son, . . . also the bond of union between the faithful who have been reconciled to the Father through the Son, and with one another in the Church."[119] It is a communion not of the perfect but of the forgiven, those pardoned by God and by one another, united in a recognition of their own frailty and the mercy that each of them has received. It is in this context that Merton situates the power of what was still being exclusively called the sacrament of penance, but it is also at the heart of every Eucharistic celebration, in which communion is preceded by the exchange of the kiss of peace, by which "we give the Holy Spirit to our brother, as if the flame of one candle were transferred to enlighten another."[120] This is the church that prays in the postcommunion of the Easter Mass for the gift of the Spirit to "lead those who have received the Paschal Sacraments to be of one heart."[121] Once again Merton points to the meaning of participation in Christ's death and resurrection

---

114. Merton, *Seasons of Celebration*, 215.

115. Merton, *Seasons of Celebration*, 214.

116. Merton, *Seasons of Celebration*, 216–30, published there for the first time.

117. See Merton, *Seasons of Celebration*, 230.

118. Merton, *Seasons of Celebration*, 216–17.

119. Merton, *Seasons of Celebration*, 218.

120. Merton, *Seasons of Celebration*, 227.

121. Merton, *Seasons of Celebration*, 228.

as the renunciation of one's separate, alienated self in order to become one with Christ and therefore with all others who are likewise united to him through the paschal mystery. "No one can rest in his own individual virtues and interior life. No man lives for himself alone. . . . We grow and flourish in our own lives in so far as we live for others and through others. . . . Hence we must always remain open to one another so that we can always share with each other,"[122] a receptivity and trust that Merton sees exemplified in Pope John XXIII's symbolic gesture of beginning his papacy by flinging opening a window.[123]

One other thematic article was evidently considered so different from these others that it was not grouped with them but placed immediately before "Time and the Liturgy." With its patristic focus, "Church and Bishop in St. Ignatius of Antioch"[124] might seem somewhat out of place in this collection, even if set apart from the main body of the essays, but Merton's main point in the article is that for Ignatius the church itself is created and sustained by its gathering together as a community in worship around its bishop. Moreover, his seven letters themselves, written as he was on his way to Rome and martyrdom, were a kind of liturgical proclamation, "written to be read in the liturgical assembly,"[125] a "*kerygma* and acclamation."[126] Merton writes that "His theology of the Church . . . is not a collection of dogmatic theses but a liturgy, a hymn of praise, surrounding an act of sacrifice."[127] Likewise the total self-surrender of martyrdom is to be recognized as "the fulfillment of the Eucharistic participation, in which the passion is represented by the union and solidarity of the faithful in love."[128] Ignatius's description of the Eucharist as the "medicine of immortality"[129] refers not only, according to Merton, to the risen life in the new creation, but to the experience of eternal life here and now in the communion of all believers in the one risen Lord received

122. Merton, *Seasons of Celebration*, 229.

123. It should be noted that this focus on openness immediately precedes the final article in the volume, "Liturgical Renewal: The Open Approach" (to be considered below).

124. Merton, *Seasons of Celebration*, 28–44, originally published in *Worship* in 1963.

125. Merton, *Seasons of Celebration*, 33.

126. Merton, *Seasons of Celebration*, 29.

127. Merton, *Seasons of Celebration*, 29.

128. Merton, *Seasons of Celebration*, 39.

129. Merton, *Seasons of Celebration*, 42.

sacramentally. Merton concludes that the key to a full appreciation of
Ignatius's rich ecclesiology is his "faith in the *reality* of the Body and
Spirit of the Incarnate Word, the *reality* of the Passion and Resurrection
of Christ, and the *reality* of our sacramental communion in His Body
and Blood in those sublime liturgical mysteries where the members of
Christ are 'consummated in unity.'"[130] Far from being out of place, this
article roots much of the discussion to follow in the heart of the liturgical
tradition of the early church that the contemporary liturgical movement
had worked to recover and that came to a certain fruition in the reforms
of the Second Vatican Council.

It is the Council and its Constitution on the Liturgy, *Sacrosanctum
Concilium*, that provides the overall framework for *Seasons of Celebration*, as both its first and its last article highlight the significance of the
renewal of the liturgy called for by the Council for the renewal of the
church as a whole. In this context it is particularly noteworthy that the
opening article, "Liturgy and Spiritual Personalism"[131] was actually written, and published, in 1960,[132] two years before the Council opened and
three years before *Sacrosanctum Concilium* was promulgated. But Merton evidently believed the perspective he presented there was so consistent with that of the Constitution that in the revised version as found
in *Seasons of Celebration*, extensive quotation and commentary on the
document are seamlessly integrated into the article in such a way as to
suggest (to the few readers that might take notice) that Merton's perspective on liturgical renewal was already completely consistent with what the
Council would officially teach a few years later. Merton was thus "ahead
of the curve" in this area as well as in issues of social justice and interre-
ligious dialogue, though here as elsewhere he would certainly emphasize
that he was expressing not merely his own insights but the wisdom he
had gleaned from his wide reading and his contemplative receptivity to
the Word of God.

The original version of the article traces the meaning of the term
leitourgia to its roots in the classical Greek notion of a public work
performed by a free citizen, and points out that in the church, where
all are free citizens with "the privilege of free and spontaneous speech

---

130. Merton, *Seasons of Celebration*, 44.

131. Merton, *Seasons of Celebration*, 1–27.

132. The article was completed on May 29, 1960 (see Merton, *Turning toward the
World*, 4) and published later that year in *Worship*.

(*parrhesia*) in the Father's Presence,"¹³³ all are called to be not passive observers but active participants in worship. Liturgy is thus the exercise of each person's mature responsibility for the public, communal worship of God. While the priest has a unique role in the celebration, all are members of the priestly people of God who together offer sacrifice to God. This is an exercise of authentic personalism, the expression of one's own deepest identity, as contrasted both with a subjective individualism that reflects a contemporary elevation of an autonomous self and with a collectivism that is simply a conformity to "convention, fashion, and prejudice"¹³⁴ while catering to an illusion of free self-expression that is no more than "the capricious eccentricities of atoms in a mass-society."¹³⁵ Because authentic relationships are an intrinsic dimension of genuine personalism, the communal experience of liturgical worship is not a diminishment but a fulfillment of each person's innermost identity, which is discovered and developed through "the public act by which the whole Church reenacts the Christian pasch, the passage from death to life in the mystery of the death and resurrection of Christ. . . . which is the guarantee of each Christian's individual spiritual freedom, and at the same time constitutes the People of God."¹³⁶ Ultimately, Merton reminds his audience, "what is manifested, proclaimed, celebrated and consummated in the liturgy is not *my* personality or *your* personality: it is the personality of Christ the Lord who, when two or three of us are gathered together in His name, *is present in the midst of us.* This presence of Christ in the liturgical celebration leads to our discovery and declaration of our own secret and spiritual self."¹³⁷ Thus the "public work" of liturgy, far from being opposed to contemplation or an alternative to it, orients the believer toward this "final perfection of Christian personalism . . . the intimate realization of one's perfect union with Christ 'in one Spirit.' The highest paradox of Christian personalism is for an individual to be 'found in Christ Jesus'

133. Merton, "Liturgy and Spiritual Personalism," 495; Merton, *Seasons of Celebration,* 5.

134. Merton, "Liturgy and Spiritual Personalism," 503; Merton, *Seasons of Celebration,* 20.

135. Merton, "Liturgy and Spiritual Personalism," 503; Merton, *Seasons of Celebration,* 21.

136. Merton, "Liturgy and Spiritual Personalism," 499; Merton, *Seasons of Celebration,* 14.

137. Merton, "Liturgy and Spiritual Personalism," 504; Merton, *Seasons of Celebration,* 22–23.

and thus 'lost' to all that can be regarded, in a mundane way, as his 'self.' This means to be at the same time one's self and Christ."[138]

Into this presentation Merton introduces dozens of changes in the revised version, in which little is omitted but much is added, beginning with two pages on the Council's ratification of the efforts for renewal that the twentieth-century liturgical movement had championed. He finds in the Constitution "the beginning of a broad and general Liturgical reform which, it is hoped, will accomplish the most striking and significant changes in every form of Catholic Worship. This is to be, and in fact already is, the greatest development in liturgy since the Patristic age and the most thorough reform in liturgy the Church has ever known."[139] Its essential characteristic, Merton points out, quoting from *Sacrosanctum Concilium*, is the "full, conscious and active participation of all the faithful,"[140] which is of course precisely the point he was already making in the article about liturgy as the public work of free citizens of the City of God. As such, he continues, it cannot be implemented by an "authoritarian reform" that would be "imposed by means of constraint from above" but must be "the creative joint effort of all Catholics to attain a new understanding of worship itself."[141] Only with such an understanding will the people be able to "affirm and exercise their full spiritual rights as citizens in the Kingdom of God."[142] A proper appreciation of the relationship between liturgy and authentic Christian personalism, Merton suggests, can make an essential contribution to the development of this understanding. Periodically throughout the essay, Merton introduces relevant discussion and quotation from the Liturgy Constitution, noting the stress on the presence of Christ in the midst of the assembly as presented in the introduction and the opening chapter;[143] the emphasis on the participatory role of the laity, particularly in the proclamation of the Word, also found in chapter 1;[144] the council's rejection of what has been termed "validism," in which rubrical correctness rather than active participation

---

138. Merton, "Liturgy and Spiritual Personalism," 506; Merton, *Seasons of Celebration*, 26.

139. Merton, *Seasons of Celebration*, 1–2.

140. Merton, *Seasons of Celebration*, 2.

141. Merton, *Seasons of Celebration*, 2.

142. Merton, *Seasons of Celebration*, 3.

143. Merton, *Seasons of Celebration*, 8–9.

144. Merton, *Seasons of Celebration*, 12–13.

is considered the primary criterion for guaranteeing the proper effects of the Mass;[145] and finally the Council's recognition that

> liturgical reform is essential to the reform of the Church itself, and that the active participation of all the faithful in the Liturgy is essential to liturgical reform. . . . The faithful Christian who participates actively in liturgical reform . . . . is offering his personal contribution to the great work of Christian renewal undertaken by the Council. In one word, to participate intelligently in liturgical worship is now to participate actively in the reform of the whole Church.[146]

Such a perspective, Merton believes, "brings out what we have said about the 'political' character of liturgical participation, with the word 'political' being used in a special sense—the activity of concerned citizens of the city (or *polis*) of the Church"[147]—thus situating his own reflections on the personalist dimension of the public work of Christian worship in the context of the movement for broad ecclesial reform that he sees as the heart of the Council's vision of liturgical renewal.

"Liturgical Renewal: The Open Approach,"[148] the article with which *Seasons of Celebration* concludes, is more in the nature of a progress report "after nearly a year of the 'new Mass,'" affirming that "the changes are pointing in the right direction"[149] but that much still needs to be worked out. Published in the popular Catholic magazine *The Critic*,[150] rather than in *Worship*, the premier American liturgical publication where "Liturgy and Spiritual Personalism" and the majority of the other articles in *Seasons of Celebration* first appeared, it is a more accessible treatment of its topic that adopts a tone intended to conciliate readers across the spectrum of what was already becoming a sharply polarized response to liturgical changes. He gently critiques both "misplaced enthusiasms" and "resentful non-participation" and recommends "a spirit of sober and reasonable experimentation" that is willing to engage in a process of "trial

---

145. Merton, *Seasons of Celebration*, 15–16.

146. Merton, *Seasons of Celebration*, 18–19.

147. Merton, *Seasons of Celebration*, 19.

148. Merton, *Seasons of Celebration*, 231–48.

149. Merton, *Seasons of Celebration*, 231–32.

150. In a September 23, 1964 letter to Leslie Dewart, Merton makes the self-deprecating comment, "I have a rather silly article on liturgy coming out in the *Critic* in December, but that is only a gesture of good will" (Merton, *Witness to Freedom*, 298).

and error" in order to develop a truly participatory form of worship.[151] He endorses the vernacular, still used only in part of the Mass: "The logic of Liturgical renewal certainly requires that the entire Mass be said in the language of the people, and this must eventually come,"[152] but he also hopes that the old Latin liturgies (not just the Roman but the Ambrosian and others) can be preserved in some monastic settings. Echoing some of his private comments in journals and correspondence, he acknowledges the defects of the lectionary translations ("Our Bible readings are now in English. But what English!"[153]) and the shortcomings, compared to Gregorian chant, of some of the congregational singing, but points out that "at least it is something that everyone can do."[154] His principal point is that "It is not the old forms that must go so much as the old spirit,"[155] which he identifies as "a consecrated impersonality and . . . business-like despatch" that creates "a deadly atmosphere of officialism in cult, a pervasive and deadening influence which one is expected to counteract by interior and subjective worship, governed entirely by one's own individual tastes and needs."[156] At the same time he is critical of a kind of superficial, breezy informality that can easily lose a sense of the sacred: "'The Lord be with you' is something else again than 'Hello gang!' So the whole idea of 'renewal' means something else than saying the formulas of prayer in a familiar language and with the intonations of colloquial and rotarian togetherness."[157] Reminiscing about his first encounters with the Mass at Corpus Christi Church in his student days at Columbia, he points out that an "atmosphere of joy, light, and at least relative openness and spontaneity"[158] was quite possible even with the Tridentine form of the Mass, so that "it is not the style that matters but the spirit, the taste, the living sense of rightness and of truth, and basically the respect for God's creation, God's people, God's house."[159] While affirming the need to respect the directives of the church, he emphasizes that from its very

---

151. Merton, *Seasons of Celebration*, 233–34.

152. Merton, *Seasons of Celebration*, 232.

153. Merton, *Seasons of Celebration*, 233.

154. Merton, *Seasons of Celebration*, 233.

155. Merton, *Seasons of Celebration*, 234.

156. Merton, *Seasons of Celebration*, 234–35.

157. Merton, *Seasons of Celebration*, 236.

158. Merton, *Seasons of Celebration*, 237.

159. Merton, *Seasons of Celebration*, 238.

beginnings in the first communities Christian worship was "marked by a general, explicit, uncompromising refusal of constraint,"[160] and he faults both conservatives and progressives for attempts to impose their vision of effective liturgy. "Obviously, it will do no good simply to constrain progressives to be content with old forms that seem to them lifeless. Just as obviously, those who do not feel or understand the need for renewal cannot be brought into open and living participation merely by constraint."[161] If conservatives tend toward narrow legalism, progressives sometimes try to apply psychological pressure, which Merton sees as ultimately counterproductive. Neither "childishly rebellious" conservatives averse to all change nor progressives "pushing forward blindly and recklessly" against inertia and resistance to reform[162] represent the authentic spirit of liturgical worship. Above all, Merton recommends openness, not just to new ideas and forms but openness to other people, even those with a different perspective: "it would be disastrous if the liturgical renewal were to rely on the replacement of one kind of constraint by the other. Renewal means, on the contrary, the replacement of constraint by the openness of simple and joyous participation."[163] He counsels patience, mutual respect, and a willingness to be flexible, and finally recommends approaching liturgy "in a spirit of *play*," exemplified in the unselfconscious spirit of children and the spontaneous sense of celebration found in the "new nations" of Africa and elsewhere, for "it is in play that the human heart is at once open, engaged, joyous, serious and self-forgetful."[164] Here the Merton reader may recognize that his prescriptions for genuine liturgical renewal that conclude this essay and *Seasons of Celebration* as a whole echo his invitation in the final words of *New Seeds of Contemplation* to "forget ourselves on purpose, cast our awful solemnity to the winds and join in the general dance."[165]

Merton wrote one other programmatic essay on liturgical renewal in the context of the Second Vatican Council that was not included in *Seasons of Celebration* and was not in fact published at all during his

160. Merton, *Seasons of Celebration*, 239.
161. Merton, *Seasons of Celebration*, 240.
162. Merton, *Seasons of Celebration*, 243.
163. Merton, *Seasons of Celebration*, 243.
164. Merton, *Seasons of Celebration*, 248.
165. Merton, *New Seeds of Contemplation*, 297.

lifetime.[166] Circulated in mimeographed form, "Christian Worship and Social Reform" was evidently written some time between late October 1962 and early December 1963, since it includes an extensive quotation from the "Message to Humanity" issued by the Council on October 20, 1962,[167] shortly after the opening of the first session, but makes no reference to *Sacrosanctum Concilium*, promulgated on December 4, 1963. It was perhaps omitted from *Seasons of Celebration* because Merton considered it already outdated, since it had been written before the Constitution on the Liturgy had been issued, though he could have updated it as he had "Liturgy and Spiritual Personalism." Certainly its focus on the relationship between liturgy and "the struggle for peace and brotherhood in the great crises of the twentieth century,"[168] its consideration of the issues of racism, materialism, and technology in the context of Eucharistic celebration, provides important insights on Merton's conviction of the integral relationship between ecclesial worship and work for justice. Merton begins by emphasizing that "One cannot understand the liturgy merely by looking at it 'objectively.' One must be personally and religiously involved in it, to grasp its real meaning."[169] This involvement is essentially soteriological, an experience of the redemptive power of Christ's death and resurrection that encompasses not only personal salvation but the transformation of the world, "dimensions that are not only social but even cosmic and eschatological."[170] The sacramental inclusion of bread and wine and other material elements draws creation into the act of worship of God in Christ, but also signifies the spiritual potential of created things. "They are present as signs and tokens, reminding man of his obligation to the world, to his fellow man and to Christ: his divine vocation to live and work in such a way that his ordinary use of material things contributes his share of the building of the Kingdom of God—the new creation."[171] Even more significantly, the communal nature of Christian worship expresses the intimate bond of solidarity that unites all human beings as children of one Father, and summons those who participate to incarnate that solidarity in the concrete circumstances of their daily lives.

---

166. It appeared in the *Merton Seasonal* in 2009.

167. See Abbott, ed., *Documents*, 3–7.

168. Merton, "Christian Worship and Social Reform," 9.

169. Merton, "Christian Worship and Social Reform," 4.

170. Merton, "Christian Worship and Social Reform," 5.

171. Merton, "Christian Worship and Social Reform," 5.

"Man's communion with nature and with his fellow man is not, and can never be, a 'purely spiritual' affair. . . . Liturgy is itself a 'common work', a sharing in worship. Liturgy therefore expresses a communal responsibility and reciprocity which, after taking a religious form in the sacred cult, afterwards incarnates itself in work characterized by a similar responsibility and reciprocity."[172] But because this dimension of liturgy is obscured for contemporary Christians by a lack of familiarity with the worldview in which it originally took form, Merton notes, "we must certainly recognize, with the Fathers of the Second Vatican Council, that the time for 'renewal' of the liturgical forms is long overdue."[173] While continuity with the tradition must be maintained, liturgy must express as well "the most important realities of our modern human and social situation" and be "intimately concerned with the most critical problems of our society,"[174] such as racial injustice or reliance on "the technological instruments of power which we all cooperate in creating and manipulating."[175] The purpose of active participation in the liturgy by the assembly is not merely to "keep the congregation awake and to stir up emotions appropriate to a communal ceremony,"[176] but to connect the experience of liturgy with the experience of life. Issues of social justice and peace are pertinent to liturgy not through some logical deduction from general principles but as an intrinsic dimension of the very meaning of the paschal mystery of redemption that is celebrated in church but lived out in the world. "The social dimension of the liturgy is then manifest in the awareness, in the responsibility that is awakened in each participant who comes to recognize his sacred duty to carry out a redemptive and sanctifying function in the world . . . . Such is our ideal and our vocation. Unfortunately," Merton concludes, "we are still very far from realizing it."[177] The implicit hope expressed in the article is that the Vatican Council, whose "main theme" had already been expressed by the Council Fathers as "the relation of spiritual renewal with man's social development," a connection based on "the Church's faith in the Incarnation, a faith which embraces all that is

172. Merton, "Christian Worship and Social Reform," 6.

173. Merton, "Christian Worship and Social Reform," 7.

174. Merton, "Christian Worship and Social Reform," 9.

175. Merton, "Christian Worship and Social Reform," 10.

176. Merton, "Christian Worship and Social Reform," 9.

177. Merton, "Christian Worship and Social Reform," 10.

best in the idea of Christian humanism which it elevates to the plane of evangelical fulfillment,"[178] might bring such a vision closer to realization.

Merton's *Meditations on the Cycle of Liturgical Feasts*, as the subtitle of *Seasons of Celebration* has it, did not of course simply cease with the publication of that volume. Two reflections on Christmas, written almost simultaneously, appear in subsequent collections of essays: "The Time of the End Is the Time of No Room" in *Raids on the Unspeakable*,[179] and "The Good News of the Nativity" in the posthumous volume *Love and Living*.[180] The two complement each other in approaching the mystery of the incarnation from different perspectives.

The first is presented in an introductory note as "a sober statement about the climate of our time, a time of finality and of fulfillment."[181] Christ's identity with the excluded is recognized as an eschatological sign that signals the end of the old world and the arrival of a radically different vision of justice and love, a time both "of great tribulation" and "certainly and above all the time of The Great Joy" announced by the angelic choir.[182] It is a recognition that the good news is proclaimed not to the powerful, the comfortable, the complacent, but to those living "in silence, loneliness and darkness," the descendants of the desert-dwellers, the faithful but neglected remnant, the *anawim*.[183] And the good news is precisely that the Lord God Himself has come to share their lot, to be born and to live and even to die as an outsider, excluded from the frenetic, aimless, demonic busyness of the faceless crowds. "Into this world, this demented inn, in which there is absolutely no room for Him at all, Christ has come uninvited. But because He cannot be at home in it, because He is out of place in it, and yet He must be in it, His place is with those others for

178. Merton, "Christian Worship and Social Reform," 8–9.

179. Merton, *Raids on the Unspeakable*, 65–75, originally published in *Motive* in 1965. Merton mentions the article as scheduled for publication in an August 31, 1965 letter to Naomi Burton Stone (Merton, *Witness to Freedom*, 147).

180. Merton, *Love and Living*, 220–32, originally published in *The Bible Today* in 1965. In an August 28, 1965 journal entry, Merton writes, "In the afternoon I finished a first draft for the *Bible Today* article (for their December issue) and had less trouble with it than I expected. I had been dreading it because I am no Bible scholar. But if they wanted technical competency they would not have asked me" (Merton, *Dancing in the Water of Life*, 287).

181. Merton, *Raids on the Unspeakable*, 65.

182. Merton, *Raids on the Unspeakable*, 74.

183. Merton, *Raids on the Unspeakable*, 69.

whom there is no room."[184] For Merton the birth of Christ is the inbreaking of a disruptive power that shatters the presumptive order of a world that no longer has room for the divine presence, a terrifying prospect for those invested in the present age and implicated in its duplicities. Only for those willing to take the risk of hope, Merton concludes, is the time of the end "not the last gasp of exhausted possibilities but the first taste of all that is beyond conceiving as actual."[185]

The second essay begins in a more detached, objective mode, acknowledging the question of the historicity of the Nativity gospels, wondering if the only alternatives are to settle for "a low-protein diet of one or two authenticated facts upon which everybody *must* agree"[186] or to "adopt a fundamentalist position"[187] that defends an absolutely literal interpretation of the Christmas stories in a way that is "rigid and artificial"[188] and dismissive of the very real problems these stories raise. Merton's response to this dilemma is to remind his audience that the primary purpose of the Christmas gospels is not to provide factual biographical data but to serve as "kerygmatic recitals embodying the inerrant truth of revelation"[189]—to proclaim the salvific significance of God's total identification with humanity in the incarnation and to invite the hearers of this message to put their faith in this "good news," not merely by intellectual acceptance but with wholehearted commitment. This approach, he maintains, is consistent with a traditional "monastic reading" of the Scriptures,[190] responding to the Word of God not with "scientific" detachment but as a summons to *metanoia*, a transformed consciousness leading to a transformed life. From this perspective the birth narratives are not merely attractive and comforting stories of the sweet Christ Child and his sweet mother but "a solemn proclamation of an event which is the turning point of all history . . . the manifestation of the fullness of time . . . . of a decisive eschatological event, a liberation from all incomplete and fragmentary religious forms," the inbreaking of the kingdom of God.[191] However great or small the fac-

184. Merton, *Raids on the Unspeakable*, 72.

185. Merton, *Raids on the Unspeakable*, 75.

186. Merton, *Love and Living*, 220.

187. Merton, *Love and Living*, 220.

188. Merton, *Love and Living*, 221.

189. Merton, *Love and Living*, 221.

190. Merton, *Love and Living*, 222.

191. Merton, *Love and Living*, 223.

tual accuracy of the details may be, this is the theological and spiritual essence of the good news of the Nativity, conveyed in the angelic message to the shepherds of the birth of a Savior (Luke 2:10–11)—"the message not only of joy but of *the* joy: the great joy which all the people of the world have always expected without fully realizing what it was.... the joy of eschatological fulfillment."[192] Once this central point is recognized the various details of each Nativity story can be properly appreciated as contributing to "this inner revelation, which the Church at once announces (in her kerygma) and celebrates (in her liturgy)"[193]—whether Matthew's reflections on Christ as the realization of the messianic prophecies of the Old Testament or Luke's emphasis on "the infinite motherly compassion of God for men"[194] that is in its own way embodied in Mary's tender care for her Child. This approach is "not a matter of religious psychology but of living theology" as experienced in "the prayer of the Church."[195] It "has grave consequences for our lives," Merton maintains, for by "accepting One for whom there is no room in the 'inn' of an excited and distraught world .... as our God, then we accept our own obligation to grow with Him in a world of arrogant power and travel with Him as He ascends to Jerusalem and to the Cross, which is the denial of power."[196] As it draws to its conclusion, the theme of this essay converges with that of "The Time of the End Is the Time of No Room." The proclamation of the incarnation already has paschal implications: "It is not enough to respond to the joy and charm of Bethlehem. We must recognize that if we belong to Christ, we must die with Him in order to rise with Him," for "from the point of view of the Gospels, without the Cross and without the Resurrection, *there can be no full meaning in the life of man.* If the Cross is God's 'No' to worldly arrogance, then our decision for Christ must be a renunciation of all reliance on worldly power."[197] It is instead a reliance on the power of the Holy Spirit, breathed out upon the church by Christ from the cross and in his resurrection appearances, but "already present in the Church's recital of the Nativity."[198] It is ultimately the Spirit that enables the church and its members "to recognize Christ when the word

192. Merton, *Love and Living*, 224.

193. Merton, *Love and Living*, 227.

194. Merton, *Love and Living*, 227.

195. Merton, *Love and Living*, 229.

196. Merton, *Love and Living*, 230.

197. Merton, *Love and Living*, 230–31.

198. Merton, *Love and Living*, 232.

of his Nativity is proclaimed in the liturgy of the Church," to reply to that word with the "'free' and confident speech of sons (*parrhesia*)," and to respond confidently to the invitation presented by Christ's full embrace of the human condition—to be united to him in his life, death, and resurrection and so to become "co-heirs with Him in the Great Joy which is His victory over death, and in His meekness, which has inherited the earth."[199] The "end" of the gospel, both its conclusion and its purpose, is already present at its beginning for those with eyes to see and ears to hear and a spirit open to the Spirit sent by the risen Christ. From this perspective, questions of the factual historicity of specific details of the Nativity narratives are put in context and recognized as secondary to the central religious message of these narratives.

Despite his extensive series of publications on liturgy in *Worship* and elsewhere, Merton never claimed to be a "professional" liturgist—quite the contrary. In his September 23, 1964, letter to Leslie Dewart he writes:

> this liturgy thing has, at least in monasteries, become so much of a professional specialty that I am not one of those that can afford initiatives and declarations. I go along with it, and enjoy what is offered, but I cannot do the offering (of new texts and ideas) though people have pestered me a little to write hymns and whatnot. I don't intend to touch any of it because I think it is all extremely fluid (as it ought to be) and the flowing is usually a mile ahead of me, as I cannot keep up with the required information, attend conferences, and so on. It would be naive of me to try to contribute anything worthwhile.[200]

Yet despite these disclaimers his interest in liturgical matters and especially in the liturgical dimension of monastic life is evident both in the length and breadth of his conferences for the novices, not only in *Liturgical Feasts and Seasons* but in the detailed discussions of the daily cycle of monastic life, in large part focused on the office[201] and the Mass,[202] in *Monastic Observances*, as well as in the extent of his published writings on liturgy both before and during the process of renewal brought about by the Second Vatican Council. Merton's "last word" on the liturgical

199. Merton, *Love and Living*, 232.

200. Merton, *Witness to Freedom*, 298.

201. Merton, *Monastic Observances*, 38–45, 57–75 (vigils); 92–103 (lauds); 189–98 (prime).

202. Merton, *Monastic Observances*, 104–46.

dimension of Christian and monastic life can be found in the posthumously published volume *The Climate of Monastic Prayer*,[203] which is concerned primarily with the solitary prayer of the contemplative but which repeatedly emphasizes that the public, communal prayer of the liturgy and personal, contemplative prayer can and should complement one another:

> The early Christian tradition and the spiritual writers of the Middle Ages knew no conflict between "public" and "private" prayer, or between the liturgy and contemplation. This is a modern problem. Or perhaps it would be more accurate to say it is a pseudo-problem. Liturgy by its very nature tends to prolong itself in individual contemplative prayer, and mental prayer in its turn disposes us for and seeks fulfillment in liturgical worship.[204]

Liturgy and sacraments must have a contemplative dimension to be meaningful, while contemplative union with God in Christ is the completion, the full personal actualization, of the paschal mystery encountered liturgically and sacramentally. A contemplative appreciation of and participation in the mysterious transforming action of the liturgy will in turn provide the insight and impetus for authentic Christian action in the world. "Without the spirit of contemplation in all our worship—that is to say without the adoration and love of God above all, for his own sake, because he is God—the liturgy will not nourish a really Christian apostolate based on Christ's love and carried out in the power of the *Pneuma*."[205] Despite one-sided claims for the superiority of contemplation to communal prayer and vice versa, Merton maintains that "at the present time it is once again becoming clear that . . . the true vocation of the monks of the Benedictine family is not to fight for contemplation against action, but to restore the ancient, harmonious and organic balance between the two. . . . The answer is not liturgy alone, or meditation alone, but a full and many-sided life of prayer in which all these things can receive their proper emphasis."[206] Although he often describes himself as a "non-liturgical type,"[207] the evidence of the present volume

203. Virtually the same text was subsequently published as *Contemplative Prayer*, with the pagination ten pages behind that of *Climate of Monastic Prayer*.

204. Merton, *Climate of Monastic Prayer*, 65.

205. Merton, *Climate of Monastic Prayer*, 153–54.

206. Merton, *Climate of Monastic Prayer*, 91.

207. Merton, *Learning to Love*, 263.

of conferences reinforces the ample evidence provided throughout his writings of his own commitment to living out this "full and many-sided life of prayer" and to nurturing a similar commitment in the young men entrusted to his pastoral care.

∽

In conclusion I would like to express my gratitude to all those who have made this volume possible:

- to the Trustees of the Merton Legacy Trust, Peggy Fox, Anne McCormick, and Mary Somerville, for permission to publish the *Liturgical Feasts and Seasons* conferences and for their constant support in this and other projects;

- to Brother Paul Quenon, OCSO, monk and longtime cantor at the Abbey of Gethsemani, for his lovely Foreword to this volume that draws on his own experience as novice under Fr. Louis to illuminate the content and context of these conferences;

- to Paul M. Pearson, director and archivist of the Merton Center, and Mark C. Meade, assistant director, for their gracious hospitality and valued assistance during my research visits to the Center;

- to the Gannon University Research Committee, which provided a grant that allowed me to pursue research on this project at the Merton Center and at various libraries;

- to Mary Beth Earll and Betsy Garloch of the interlibrary loan department of the Nash Library, Gannon University, for once again providing invaluable assistance by locating and procuring various obscure volumes;

- to Patrick Lawlor of the Columbia University Rare Book and Manuscript Library for his generous and gracious efforts to locate and make available the *Liturgical Feasts and Seasons* materials in the Columbia archives;

- to library staff of the Hesburgh Library of the University of Notre Dame, and the Institute of Cistercian Studies Collection at the Waldo Library, Western Michigan University, especially Neil Chase, for assistance in locating important materials in their collections;

- to all those at Wipf and Stock who have brought this volume to publication with grace and effciency, particularly K. C. Hanson, editor; George Callihan, editorial administrator; Jeremy Funk, copy editor; and Heather Carraher, typesetter;

- again and always to my wife, Suzanne, and our children for their continual love, support, and encouragement in this and other projects.

LITURGICAL *FEASTS* AND *SEASONS*
Part I

Conferences Given in the Choir Novitiate
Abbey of Gethsemani

TABLE OF CONTENTS
I

FIRST SUNDAY IN ADVENT

The liturgy is the expression of the Church's love for God. Hence it is a school of love. It forms our hearts, minds, wills, sensibilities and taste. But this formation is not merely psychological. We are formed by the objective reality of God's love for us, acting upon us in and through the liturgy. This formation gives us a "mind" and "heart" greater than our own. It takes us above and beyond ourselves. We rise to the level of the liturgy, and this makes us greater than we were before. The liturgy elevates us; it broadens our horizons, makes us capable of greater things. Jesus Himself forms our souls as we pray and sing with the liturgy.

The action of the liturgy on our hearts is meant to be to a great extent felt and sensible, not in the sense that the liturgy should be expected to produce sentimental effects—emotion for its own sake—but it certainly works upon and forms our sensibilities. This is quite evident in the various liturgical seasons—the joy of Easter, for instance, or the compunction and attentive devotion of Lent. Here in Advent, the Church's love for the Redeemer expresses itself mostly in terms of *desire*. The liturgy of Advent forms our minds, hearts and wills with loving, humble desire, a desire which has in past ages burned in the hearts of all the saints. It is a desire which is found in the Heart of God Himself—His love as our Father and Redeemer.

The hymn *Conditor alme siderum*[1] sets the tone for Advent (both words and melody). Its character is *simple, sober* and *sincere*. It is objective—focused upon the power, compassion and love of the Redeemer. It sees Him as Creator and as Judge—as King of all ages—as the Holy One—but always as the One Who has pity on our infirmities and comes from afar to save us from complete destruction—the creatures of His own hands. The *humility*, reverence {and} confidence in the hymn are most striking. Where, in what individual composition, could we find something that would be capable of raising the hearts of all men universally to so high a level with such simplicity?

Darkness and light {is} a prominent theme in the Advent and Christmas liturgy. {In} the Incarnation, the light shines in the darkness and the darkness comprehends it not.[2] In the vesper hymn, Jesus is "*Aeterna lux*

---

1. "Dear Creator of the stars" (vespers hymn: Saturday before the First Sunday of Advent, etc.) (*Breviarium Cisterciense, Pars Hiemalis*, 175).

2. John 1:5.

credentium."[3] In the hymn of vigils, the Word comes to save the world: "*Cursu declivi temporis*"[4] ({note the} suggestion of the world's nightfall); we pray: "*Illumina nunc pectora, Tuoque amore concrema.*"[5] Love burns like a vigil light in the darkness. In the epistle, The night is past, day has arrived—Let us put away the works of darkness,[6] etc.

{In} *the Mass, {we pray in the} introit: Ad te levavi*[7]—lifting up our soul to God. What does this mean?—confidence, expectation, hope, in the face of trial and darkness, and the desire to learn His ways—*Vias tuas Domine demonstra mihi.*[8] With what humility we should learn to utter these words. How reverently and with what a spirit of supplication we should beg to learn His will, and appreciate His ways. This implies gratitude for what He has shown us of His will so far, sorrow for having appreciated His graces less, resolve to make better use of grace in the future. The introit implies a new resolve, a plan to live an entirely new life, with the new Church year. We are able with confidence to put away our tepidity and negligence and renew our vigilant love, because once again we contemplate the mercy and the promises of our long-suffering Redeemer.

Three Dimensions of Prophecy: in Advent we share in a special way in the longing and the hope of the patriarchs and prophets. Just as there are three Advents,[9] so there are three dimensions of prophecy:

1. *The First Advent*—Jesus came fulfilling the prophecies of the Old Testament on one level—the historical level. The promised Redeemer comes in time.

2. *The Second Advent* continues to fulfill the prophecies on another level, moral and spiritual. The Redeemer comes to us as individuals. The same promises made regarding His historical coming apply to His

3. "Eternal light of believers" (l. 2) (*Breviarium Cisterciense, Hiemalis*, 175).

4. "in the course of declining time" ("*Verbum Supernum Prodiens*," l. 4) (*Breviarium Cisterciense, Hiemalis*, 176).

5. "Now illuminate our hearts; set them on fire with your love" (l. 5) (*Breviarium Cisterciense, Hiemalis*, 176).

6. Rom 13:12 (epistle: First Sunday of Advent) (*Missale Romanum*, 2; *Missale Cisterciense*, 2).

7. "To You [O Lord] I have lifted [up my soul]" (Ps 24[25]:1) (*Missale Romanum*, 1; *Missale Cisterciense*, 1).

8. "Show me your ways, Lord" (Ps 24[25]:4) (*Missale Romanum*, 1; *Missale Cisterciense*, 1).

9. Merton draws here particularly on St. Bernard's Advent sermons: see Merton, *Seasons of Celebration*, 75–83, and the Introduction above, page lvi.

spiritual coming to our souls in grace. These are the most important from the point of view of *personal devotion*. What are some of them? (Use them as subjects of meditation and as ejaculatory prayers—to get {the} Advent spirit). "*Ecce ego venio et habitabo in medio tui*"[10] (*Benedictus*—first Tuesday); "*Lux mundi Dominus cum potentia venit*"[11] (*Magnificat*—first Tuesday); "*Veni Domine visitare nos in pace, ut laetemur coram te corde perfecto*"[12] (*Magnificat*—first Saturday); "*Salvabo te et liberabo te, noli timere*"[13] (Saturday—*Benedictus*); "*Noli timere, ecce Deus tuus veniet*"[14] (first responsory—second Sunday); "*Doluit Dominus super te et auferet a te omnem tribulationem*"[15] (fourth responsory—first Sunday).

3. *The Third Advent*—with the grace of the second Advent, we join the prophets, our eyes are illuminated with their faith and their hope, and all together we look forward to the Third Advent, the final coming. This is most important from the point of view of the whole Church—{the} ardent desire for God's Kingdom finally to be established. He must reign! Our desire really helps to bring that day closer! *Alieni non transibunt per Jerusalem amplius*[16] (tenth responsory—first Sunday). The enemies of God will no longer defile His Church, but Christ shall reign in peace and His elect will praise Him in perfect joy.

ADVENT LITURGY—Some Practical Notes (Saturday before the First Sunday of Advent):

1) *Advent* {is} the season of *desire*—for the presence of God, for salvation; of *vocation*—our desire for Him and His desire for us; of

---

10. "Behold, I shall come and dwell in your midst" (Zech 2:14) (*Breviarium Cisterciense, Hiemalis*, 190).

11. "The Lord, the Light of the world, comes with power" (*Breviarium Cisterciense, Hiemalis*, 190).

12. "Come Lord, visit us in peace, that we may rejoice before you with a perfect heart" (actually lauds antiphon: first Saturday of Advent) (*Breviarium Cisterciense, Hiemalis*, 192).

13. "I will save you and set you free; do not fear" (actually part of the first responsory for the first nocturn: second Sunday of Advent) (*Breviarium Cisterciense, Hiemalis*, 193).

14. "Do not fear; behold your God will come" (actually Magnificat antiphon: first Saturday of Advent) (*Breviarium Cisterciense, Hiemalis*, 192).

15. "The Lord grieves for you, and will take away from you all your tribulation" (actually fourth responsory for the first nocturn: second Saturday of Advent) (*Breviarium Cisterciense, Hiemalis*, 194).

16. "Foreigners will not pass through Jerusalem any longer" (*Breviarium Cisterciense, Hiemalis*, 183).

expectation and vigilance—waiting for what? Christmas? for *Jesus*—He comes as a thief in the night.[17] The fruit of His coming in Advent will be known at Christmas; {of} *"penance,"* in the sense of removing obstacles to grace. Put aside everything that can keep us from responding, all that impedes desire. Let Him act in our souls.

2) *Vespers* (note the picture in the breviary[18]): {the} *capitulum* {is} Awake from sleep[19]—our salvation is nearer. Distinguish the liturgy from the mere seasonal cycle: in {the} dead of winter, near {the} solstice, we think of the coming of life and light. {It is even} deeper than that—He is present. {In the} *responsorium*—*"Missus est"*[20]—God comes unexpectedly to Mary (*"Expavescit Virgo de lumine"*[21])—God comes to *reign*—(". . . of His kingdom there shall be no end"[22]—words which always thrilled St. Teresa of Avila[23])—*Love reigns.* {In} *the hymn* {we pray}, Christ, the Creator of the stars and the eternal light of the believers, the Redeemer of all, hear our prayers. You have had pity on the sick world and hast brought us a remedy to save us from death. As the evening of the world descended, You came forth as a bridegroom from the pure womb of Mary. All beings, in heaven and on earth, shall kneel in subjection to Your great power. We pray You, holy One, Thou Who wilt come as Judge of the world, preserve

---

17. 1 Thes 5:2.

18. The full-page drawing opposite the beginning of the text for the Saturday before the First Sunday of Advent (*Breviarium Cisterciense, Hiemalis,* 174) features an enthroned Christ flanked by a crowned Virgin Mary and John the Baptist, with smaller inset drawings above and below; the quarter-page drawing immediately above the text is of Isaiah being cleansed on his lips with a coal by one of the seraphim, with the text *"Et volavit ad me unus de seraphim. Is. 6.6"* below it (*Breviarium Cisterciense, Hiemalis,* 175).

19. *"de somno surgere"* (Rom. 13:11) (*Breviarium Cisterciense, Hiemalis,* 175).

20. "[The Angel Gabriel] was sent" (Luke 1:26) (*Breviarium Cisterciense, Hiemalis,* 175).

21. "the Virgin was terrified by the light" (*Breviarium Cisterciense, Hiemalis,* 175).

22. Luke 1:33.

23. This may refer to the famous passage in the first chapter of the *Life* in which the child Teresa and her brother decide to go off to be martyred by the Moors "to attain as quickly as possible to the fruition of the great blessings which, as I read, were laid up in Heaven. . . . It used to cause us great astonishment when we were told that both pain and glory would last for ever. We would spend long periods talking about this and we liked to repeat again and again, 'For ever—ever—ever!' Through our frequent repetition of these words, it pleased the Lord that in my earliest years I should receive a lasting impression of the way of truth" (Peers, ed. and trans., *Saint Teresa,* 1.11).

us in time from the arrows of the treacherous enemy.[24] {The} *Magnificat antiphon* {is}: "*Ecce* nomen *Domini venit de longinquo.*"[25] This is taken up again in more solemnity in the long first responsory, "*Aspiciens a longe*": I see the power of God coming from afar and mist covers the whole earth. Go out to Him and say: tell us if thou be He who is to reign over the people of Israel?[26]

3) *The Vigils*: the *invitatory* {is}: "*Ecce venit Rex*"[27]—Let us run forth to meet Him. These things mean less in our day when the arrival of a king is nothing. Modern society has lost the power to furnish symbols of the City of God. *Lessons* of {the} first nocturn—Read Isaias 1:[28] Israel has not

---

24. "*Conditor alme siderum, / Aeterna lux credentium, / Christe Redemptor omnium, / Exaudi preces supplicum. // Qui condolens interitu / Mortis perire saeculum, / Salvasti mundum languidum, / Donans reis remedium, // Vergente mundi vespere, / Uti sponsus de thalamo / Egressus honestissima / Virginis Matris clausula. // Cuius forti potentiae / Genu curvantur omnia, / Coelestia, terrestria, / Nutu fatentur subdita. // Te, deprecamur agie, / Venture Judex saeculi, / Conserva nos in tempore / Hostis a telo perfidi*" (*Breviarium Cisterciense, Hiemalis*, 175–76).

25. "Behold the Name of the Lord comes from afar" (*Breviarium Cisterciense, Hiemalis*, 176).

26. "*Aspiciens a longe, ecce video Dei potentiam venientem, et nebulam totam terram tegentem. Ite obviam ei, et dicite; Nuntia nobis, si tu es ipse Qui regnaturus es in populo Israel*" (*Breviarium Cisterciense, Hiemalis*, 177).

27. "Behold the King is coming" (*Breviarium Cisterciense, Hiemalis*, 176).

28. "The vision of Isaias the son of Amos, which he saw concerning Juda and Jerusalem in the days of Ozias, Joathan, Achaz, and Ezechias, kings of Juda. Hear, O ye heavens, and give ear, O earth, for the Lord hath spoken. I have brought up children, and exalted them: but they have despised me. The ox knoweth his owner, and the ass his master's crib: but Israel hath not known me, and my people hath not understood. Woe to the sinful nation, a people laden with iniquity, a wicked seed, ungracious children: they have forsaken the Lord, they have blasphemed the Holy One of Israel, they are gone away backwards. For what shall I strike you any more, you that increase transgression? the whole head is sick, and the whole heart is sad. From the sole of the foot unto the top of the head, there is no soundness therein: wounds and bruises and swelling sores: they are not bound up, nor dressed, nor fomented with oil. Your land is desolate, your cities are burnt with fire: your country strangers devour before your face, and it shall be desolate as when wasted by enemies. And the daughter of Sion shall be left as a covert in a vineyard, and as a lodge in a garden of cucumbers, and as a city that is laid waste. Except the Lord of hosts had left us seed, we had been as Sodom, and we should have been like to Gomorrha. Hear the word of the Lord, ye rulers of Sodom, give ear to the law of our God, ye people of Gomorrha. To what purpose do you offer me the multitude of your victims, saith the Lord? I am full, I desire not holocausts of rams, and fat of fatlings, and blood of calves, and lambs, and buck goats" (Isa 1:1–11) (*Breviarium Cisterciense, Hiemalis*, 177–78; first lesson: vv. 1–3; second lesson: vv. 4–6; third lesson: vv. 7–9; fourth lesson: vv. 10–11).

known. Woe to the sinful people. Where shall I strike you? The daughter of Sion shall be left deserted. The princes of Sion are the princes of Sodom. Sacrifices are of no use. Unless the Lord has left us a seed (Christ, the promised Messias), we had been as cities to be destroyed utterly. Read on to verse 18 of *Isaias* 1:[29] "if your sins be as scarlet they shall be made as white as snow." {Here we find} compunction, love, desire, faith in Christ Who is present, Whose presence is judgement.

Advent—Second and Third Sundays—Saint John the Baptist:

1. The liturgical texts are full of joy and hope:

a) *Second Sunday*: {the} *introit* {is} "*Ecce Dominus veniet ad salvandas gentes . . . auditam faciet gloriam vocis suae.*"[30] {The point is to} awaken attention, {to} *realize.* {Note} the glory of His voice, unlike any other voice; His words are not our words, His thoughts not our thoughts. {He is} the Almighty—His voice arouses at once fear and confidence; {He is} the Holy One: {the} *glory* of His voice suggests that glory is produced in us by hearing Him, {bringing a} likeness to Him, {a} splendor; He speaks in the liturgy. {The} "*Alleluia*" {is}: "I rejoiced in the things that were said to me, we shall go into the house of the Lord."[31] {In the} *offertory* {we pray}: "*Deus tu conversus vivificabis nos et plebs tua laetabitur in te.*"[32] {In the} *communio* {we say}: "Arise O Jerusalem, and stand on high and behold the joy that cometh to thee from God."[33] {The} joy that cometh from

29. "When you came to appear before me, who required these things at your hands, that you should walk in my courts? Offer sacrifice no more in vain: incense is an abomination to me. The new moons, and the sabbaths, and other festivals I will not abide, your assemblies are wicked. My soul hateth your new moons, and your solemnities: they are become troublesome to me, I am weary of bearing them. And when you stretch forth your hands, I will turn away my eyes from you: and when you multiply prayer, I will not hear: for your hands are full of blood. Wash yourselves, be clean, take away the evil of your devices from my eyes: cease to do perversely, Learn to do well: seek judgment, relieve the oppressed, judge for the fatherless, defend the widow. And then come, and accuse me, saith the Lord: if your sins be as scarlet, they shall be made as white as snow: and if they be red as crimson, they shall be white as wool."

30. "Behold, the Lord will come to save the nations, . . . He will make the glory of his voice heard" (Isa 30:30) (*Missale Romanum,* 4; *Missale Cisterciense,* 4).

31. "*Laetatus sum in his, quae dicta sunt mihi: in domum Domini ibimus*" (*Missale Romanum,* 4; *Missale Cisterciense,* 4).

32. "Having turned, God, You will give us life, and Your people will rejoice in You" (Ps 84[85]:7) (*Missale Romanum,* 5; *Missale Cisterciense,* 5).

33. "*Jerusalem surge, et sta in excelso, et vide jucundatem, quae veniet tibi a Deo*

God {is the} same as the glory of His voice—the life-giving effect of God's action—and we rejoice in Him. Stand on high—as St. Bernard would say,[34] recognize your dignity as an intelligent and loving creature made for union with God. {The} *vesper antiphons* {read}: "*Urbs fortitudinis nostrae—aperite portas quia nobiscum Dominus*"[35] ({from the Book of} Judith, {symbolizing} victory over sin—{note the} connection with the Immaculate Conception); *Ecce apparebit,*[36] etc.—*si moram fecerit*[37] (in time of trial, {of} apparent frustration of hopes, {the} fruitfulness of waiting in faith); "The hills and mountains sing praises to God"[38] (sext)—"all the trees clap their hands because the Lord is coming to reign forever."[39]

b) *Third Sunday*: {the} *introit* {is}: "*Gaudete*"[40]—this is not just a joyful interlude in a penitential season, but a more joyous climax in a joyful season; {note the expression of} modesty and trust, {the} expectation of light ({cf. the} collect:[41] how much we need light); cf.

---

tuo" (Bar 5:5; 4:30) (*Missale Romanum*, 5; *Missale Cisterciense*, 5).

34. See *De Diligendo Deo*, II.2: "*Quaerat enim homo eminentiora bona sua in ea parte sui, qua praeeminet sibi, hoc est in anima quae sunt dignitas, scientia, virtus. Dignitatem in homine liberum arbitrium dico: in quo ei nimirum datum est caeteris non solum praeeminere, sed et praesidere animantibus. Scientiam vero, qua eamdem in se dignitatem agnoscat, non a se tamen. Porro virtutem, qua subinde ipsum a quo est, et inquirat non segniter, et teneat fortiter cum invenerit*" ("Let man seek his higher goods, which are dignity, knowledge, virtue, in that part of himself by which he rises above himself, that is, in the soul. I call dignity in man his free will, in which it is certainly given to him not only to be superior to other creatures, but to rule over them; knowledge is that by which he recognizes this same dignity in himself, and that it does not come from himself; virtue, finally, is that by which he continually and untiringly seeks the One from Whom he has being, and when he finds Him holds to Him strongly") (Migne, *PL* 182, col. 976A).

35. "The city of our fortitude . . . open the gates because the Lord is with us" (Jdt 13:13) (*Breviarium Cisterciense, Hiemalis*, 198, which reads: ". . . *nobiscum Deus*").

36. "Behold [the Lord] will appear" (*Breviarium Cisterciense, Hiemalis*, 198).

37. "If he makes a delay, [await Him]" (*Breviarium Cisterciense, Hiemalis*, 198).

38. "*Montes et colles cantabunt coram Deo laudes*" (*Breviarium Cisterciense, Hiemalis*, 198).

39. "*et omnia ligna silvarum plaudent manibus: quoniam veniet Dominus dominator in regnum aeternum*" (*Breviarium Cisterciense, Hiemalis*, 198).

40. "Rejoice [in the Lord always]" (Phil 4:4) (*Missale Romanum*, 5; *Missale Cisterciense*, 5).

41. "*Aurem tuam, quaesumus, Domine, precibus nostris accommoda: et mentis nostrae tenebras, gratia tuae visitationis illustra*" (*Missale Romanum*, 5; *Missale Cisterciense*, 5); (lauds collect) (*Breviarium Cisterciense, Hiemalis*, 208).

{the} last vesper antiphon of {the} Second Sunday;[42] also {the} first antiphon of this Third Sunday of Advent: "*Veniet Dominus et non tardabit,* ET ILLUMINABIT ABSCONDITA TENEBRARUM";[43] cf. {the} vespers of Wednesday after {the} Second Sunday: "*Sion renovaberis, et videbis justum tuum qui venturus est in te*";[44] cf. responsory ten of this Third Sunday: "Docebit nos Dominus vias suas *et ambulabimus in semitis ejus.*"[45] All these thoughts form the profound content (mystical) of the liturgy: God comes to change us from within, to rule us, to guide us, to form us, to teach us His ways. Without all this, we will not be able to recognize Him. We know Him if, when He comes, we are living according to His will. Then His ways are prepared; hence the importance of the Precursor, St. John the Baptist in the Advent liturgy.

2. *St. John the Baptist*: John appears before us as a *living model* of one perfectly prepared to receive the Lord at His coming. Totally empty of self, he receives into his whole being the light of the Lord, disappears in order that the Lord may be made manifest in him. St. John the Baptist is set before us because in Advent the Church takes on his spirit (the spirit and power of Elias[46])—his "interior form"—in order to receive the Messias.

  a) We have already seen something of John's preaching: repent (be changed), and to the Pharisees, "ye brood of vipers."[47] John {is} a sign of contradiction—a challenge—a "judgement," because the Pharisees and Herod reject him, and thus lose their chance.

  b) The Baptism of Jesus: in John 1 we have the following account (gospel of {the} Third Sunday);[48] first of all, John's testimony before the

---

42. "*Ecce Dominus noster cum virtute veniet, et illuminabit oculos servorum suorum, alleluia*" ("Behold Our Lord will come with power, and he will bring light to the eyes of his servants, alleluia") (*Breviarium Cisterciense, Hiemalis,* 198).

43. "The Lord will come, and will not delay, and He will bring light to those hidden in darkness" (*Breviarium Cisterciense, Hiemalis,* 209).

44. "Sion, you will be renewed, and you will see your Just One, Who will have come upon you" (Magnificat antiphon) (*Breviarium Cisterciense, Hiemalis,* 201).

45. "The Lord will teach us His ways, and we shall walk in His paths" (Isa 2:3) (*Breviarium Cisterciense, Hiemalis,* 206).

46. Luke 1:17.

47. Matt 3:7; Luke 3:7.

48. John 1:19–28 (*Missale Romanum,* 5–6; *Missale Cisterciense,* 6).

formal delegation of the Jews: "I am not the Christ" (1:20); "I am not Elias, or the prophet" (1:21) (John as an individual). What has thou to say of thyself? "I am a *voice* crying in the wilderness"[49]—a voice {that} passes away {for in the} wilderness {there is} no one to hear. Here too we get a sense of solemnity, the finality, and in a certain sense the ineffectiveness of his mission—and his own lack of personal importance. He does not claim any importance as an individual. He has a mission; his mission is important until it is fulfilled. After that, he must disappear. Then they question his baptism (25ff.). John replies: "I baptize with water"—again, his baptism has no value of its own; {it is} purely a sign and a figure of the true baptism that is to come. {Note} *the witness and judgement of John*—{and} contrast with the Jews—John exemplifies perfectly the attitude of one who knows that he belongs to the Old Testament and yet knows that the Old Testament must disappear, that it is nothing, only a shadow. The Jews are rooted in the Old Testament as in something permanent. They crucify Jesus to prevent its alteration. *Note*: John could have done as his disciples did, left all and followed Jesus. No, he had to remain "outside the kingdom" in which even the lowest would be higher than he. {This is the} *first tremendous lesson*: if we are to receive the Lord, our whole spiritual universe must, in a sense, be laid waste. We are nothing, our ideals are nothing, when compared to the reality of which they are but the shadow. We must be able to relinquish the shadow in order to receive the reality. Then John formally proclaims (John 1:26): "but there hath stood one in the midst of you whom you know not." The Lord has *already come*: {this has} important implications. He whom we expect is already here; let us not, like the Jews, put off His advent into the distant future. He will baptize with the Holy Spirit and with Fire (Matthew 3:11). He who is to come after me has been set before me because he is above me (John 1:15 and 1:30). John declares the absolute transcendence of the Christ.

3. *The Gospel of the Second Sunday*:[50] the Church does not present this gospel as a problem in the career of John, merely as a testimony to the coming of the Christ, as a proof that He has come. For us, as we consider John, our model for Advent, we can look into the problem which the

---

49. John 1:22–23.

50. Matt 11:2–10 (*Missale Romanum*, 4–5; *Missale Cisterciense*, 4–5).

text offers. At the end of his career, in prison, John apparently begins to question whether he was formerly right in identifying Jesus as the Christ {and} sends disciples to make sure. Some hold that this was only for the benefit of the disciples. The Gospel text seems to suggest that John was asking for his own reassurance: "Now when John had heard in prison the works of Christ, sending two of his disciples he said to Him: art thou He that art to come, or look we for another?" (Matthew 11:2 and 3). Guardini[51] explains this hesitation: John at the time of the Baptism was under a charismatic grace, given not for him but for others, {and so} recognized Jesus as the Christ. Later, in captivity, without the light of prophecy, in his own poverty, struggling in faith, he asks for reassurance from Jesus Himself—not from a sign. Note that John asks Jesus Himself, and rests content. So first of all this is a supreme act of faith in Jesus' word, rather than in a sign from heaven. He asks as if he himself had not been the Precursor and witness. He speaks as though he were only a prisoner, not a Precursor. However, the fact remains that he is reduced to intense interior poverty. Not only is he in prison, not only does Jesus leave him in prison, not only is his work destroyed ({or} rather sublimated in Christ), not only is his whole prophetic career at an end, but now his mystical light has failed. In his poverty, John is content to go to death for Christ, with no other support than faith in the word of Jesus. This is the supreme ideal of the monk. This makes John the Baptist so like Our Lady, who lived in pure faith, whose faith was the gateway by which Jesus came into the world. Then Jesus canonizes John as the perfect monk—not a reed— not clothed in soft garments, *more* than a prophet.

ADVENT—EMBER WEEK

Theology in the Collects: (1) the solemnity of our Redemption will bring both temporal assistance and eternal happiness (Wednesday:

---

51. See Guardini, *The Lord*, 22–25.

oration;[52] Saturday: third oration;[53] Saturday: postcommunion[54]); (2) He comes with special consolations to those who trust Him (Wednesday: second oration[55]); (3) especially through the transforming effect of the Eucharist (Wednesday: postcommunion etc.[56]); (4) Christmas will bring us liberation from the yoke of sin and its effects (Saturday: second collect[57]).

{This is} *Our Lady's Week*: Wednesday—the Annunciation[58] (the offertory;[59] *"Ave Maria"*); Friday—the Visitation.[60]

---

52. *"Praesta, quaesumus, omnipotens Deus: ut redemptionis nostrae ventura so-lemnitas, et praesentis nobis vitae subsidia conferat, et aeternae beatitudinis praemia largiatur"* ("Grant, we beg, Almighty God, that the approaching celebration of our redemption may both bring assistance to us in this present life and bestow the rewards of eternal happiness") (*Missale Romanum*, 6; *Missale Cisterciense*, 6); (lauds collect) (*Breviarium Cisterciense, Hiemalis*, 212).

53. *"Deus, qui conspicis, quia ex nostra pravitate affligimur: concede propitius; ut ex tua visitatione consolemur"* ("God, Who see that we are afflicted by our iniquity, graciously grant that we may be consoled by Your visitation") (*Missale Romanum*, 9; *Missale Cisterciense*, 9); (lauds collect) (*Breviarium Cisterciense, Hiemalis*, 217).

54 *"Quaesumus, Domine Deus noster: ut sacrosancta mysteria, quae pro separationis nostrae munimine contulisti; et praesens nobis remedium esse facias et futurum"* ("Lord our God, we beg that You may make the most holy mysteries, which You have bestowed as protection of our liberation, a remedy for us both now and in the future") (*Missale Romanum*, 12; *Missale Cisterciense*, 12).

55. *"Festina, quaesumus Domine, ne tardaveris, et auxilium nobis supernae virtu-tis impende: ut adventus tui consolationibus subleventur, qui in tua pietate confidunt"* ("Hasten, Lord, we beg; do not delay, and grant to us the assistance of Your heavenly power, so that those who trust in Your goodness may be raised up by the consolations of Your coming") (*Missale Romanum*, 7; *Missale Cisterciense*, 7).

56. *"Salutaris tui, Domine, munere satiati, supplices deprecamur: ut, cujus laetamur gustu, renovemur effectu"* ("Filled with the gift of Your salvation, Lord, we suppliants pray to be renewed by the effect of that which brings joy by its taste") (*Missale Roma-num*, 8; *Missale Cisterciense*, 8).

57. *"Concede, quaesumus, omnipotens Deus: ut, qui sub peccati jugo ex vetusta ser-vitute deprimimur: exspectata unigeniti Filii tui nova nativitate liberemur"* ("Grant, we beg, Almighty God, that we who are oppressed by our old bondage under the yoke of sin may be freed by the new birth of Your Only-begotten Son for which we look") (*Missale Romanum*, 9; *Missale Cisterciense*, 9).

58. Luke 1:26–38 (gospel reading) (*Missale Romanum*, 7; *Missale Cisterciense*, 7).

59. Isa 35:4 (*Missale Romanum*, 7; *Missale Cisterciense*, 8).

60. Luke 1:39–47 (gospel reading) (*Missale Romanum*, 8; *Missale Cisterciense*, 8).

Third Sunday: {the} *epistle*[61] (*Modestia vestra* . .[62]) {teaches} confidence and peace {as} our perfect preparation for Christmas, in spite of trial. *Nihil solliciti sitis*:[63] {this is} only possible with heroic faith and prayer—prayer and supplication {in an} ardent expression of our needs to God, with thanksgiving, {which} adds to confidence {through our} recognition of Him and His goodness. {The} *pax Dei*[64] {is} not just any peace, but the peace of *God, beyond all feeling* and all understanding. (It must come from Him in a way we know not, and not just be produced by us. We must *let Him give* what we need, as He wills and when He wills— He is God.) {We pray} *custodiat* corda[65]—from fluctuations of emotion and doubt, from anxious desires and needs; {*custodiat*} intelligentias[66]— from error, presumption, restless curiosity, etc.

FOURTH SUNDAY {IN} ADVENT—*Epistle*:[67] reaction to ordinations and to Advent—{it is} beautiful to be ordained in December Ember Days, {or} Pentecost week (Ascension Day). *Sic nos existimet homo*[68]—what people think of the priest: Jesus said, You are the salt of the earth . . . . light of the world.[69] All must *see* the light of the world. One of the great trials of a priest is to be constantly held up as a model to others by his very position. Yet he is, like others, a weak man.

1. People should consider not the man but the priest—the representative of Christ—supernatural reverence {should be shown} for {the} holiness of his office and order.

2. The priest should concern himself above all with his own fidelity: "*ut fidelis inveniatur*"[70] (cf. Jesus' parable of {the} master returning at night and surprising his servants[71]). This is a personal matter between the priest and Christ in the sanctuary of his own conscience. One must learn to live in the sight of God and deal directly with

61. Phil 4:4–7 (*Missale Romanum*, 5; *Missale Cisterciense*, 5).

62. "Let your moderation [be made known]" (v. 5).

63. "Do not be anxious" (vs. 6).

64. "peace of God" (vs. 7).

65. "guard your hearts" (v. 7).

66. "guard your minds" (v. 7).

67. 1 Cor 4:1–5 (*Missale Romanum*, 12–13; *Missale Cisterciense*, 12).

68. "Let someone so consider us" (v. 1).

69. Matt 5:13, 14.

70. "that someone be found trustworthy" (1 Cor 4:2).

71. Luke 12:35–38.

Him. *There are some* points on which a priest cannot ask advice from anyone or speak *to anyone* (problems in confession sometimes).

3. *A minimo est ut a viris judicer:*[72] {he} must not be swayed from duty by *fear of displeasing people* {or} *fear of opposition*, or be influenced too greatly by {a} *desire to please everyone.* "How can you believe who seek glory one from another?"[73] {It is a} matter of faith and supernatural spirit.

4. *Neque meipsum judico:*[74] avoid {the} other extreme, being too confident in one's own judgement; {avoid} arrogance, "always {being} right," self-righteousness, aggressive pharisaism, or *contempt* for authority and virtue—{leading to} danger of scandal.

5. {The} right attitude {is} true humility, *faith*, hoping in God's mercy. {Put} total reliance on God—His light will reveal all. Seek Him alone. *Tunc laus erit unicuique a Deo.*[75] "Good and faithful servant"[76]—this is true glory.

FURTHER ADVENT NOTES: *Dominus prope est!*[77] Advent is not so much for us a time in which God comes from "afar," as one in which we are purified to realize that He *is near.* Isaias is the prophet of Advent, first because he sees the coming Messias more clearly than any of the other prophets—he sees Him "closer"; also because he most clearly announces the consolations of Israel and the goodness of God to them, after the coming of the Redeemer; but also because he shows the infidelities and foretells the purification of Israel, to prepare for the coming of the Redeemer. Advent is a time of hope, of joy in coming consolation, but also a time of trial and interior purification—always for individuals, sometimes as now (1956), for the whole Church and the entire world. All through Isaias we find the two-fold theme that is announced in the first and second chapters. It is repeated over and over again: Israel has been faithless, but God Who is faithful, precisely because He is faithful, will punish Israel, will allow Jerusalem to be destroyed, and will afterwards

---

72. "It matters very little to me that I be judged by human beings" (1 Cor 4:3).

73. John 5:44.

74. "I do not judge myself" (1 Cor 4:3).

75. "Then each will have praise from God" (v. 4).

76. Matt 25:21, 23.

77. "The Lord is near" (Phil 4:5) (introit: third Sunday of Advent) (*Missale Romanum*, 5; *Missale Cisterciense*, 5).

reestablish Israel after destroying the gentile invader, and not only that, but also in the end all nations will enter the Church and there will be a reign of universal peace, to be established by the King Messias, the Just One, the Servant of the Lord—by His sufferings, in which He takes upon Himself the sins of the whole world. Such, in a word, is the message of Isaias. But each passage in which this theme is reiterated in one way or another can very well apply to our own souls. READ chapter 29:4–8:[78] the threatened destruction of Jerusalem, to be followed by her rebirth and the destructions of the nations; 25:1–5 and 8–10[79]—prophecies of joy. We must realize that all this applies to us, to Christian nations and to our own souls. There is indeed "judgement" ahead—"*in spiritu ardoris*"[80]—and in Advent we certainly feel the purifying touch of this flame. But there is also rebirth and renewal and life in God. The purpose of all Isaias's teaching in Advent is to teach us all, individuals and nations, that THERE IS NO HOPE AND NO PEACE SAVE IN GOD AND IN HIS CHRIST. We must

78. "Thou shalt be brought down, thou shalt speak out of the earth, and thy speech shall be heard out of the ground: and thy voice shall be from the earth like that of the python, and out of the ground thy speech shall mutter. And the multitude of them that fan thee, shall be like small dust: and as ashes passing away, the multitude of them that have prevailed against thee. And it shall be at an instant suddenly. A visitation shall come from the Lord of hosts in thunder, and with earthquake, and with a great noise of whirlwind and tempest, and with the flame of devouring fire. And the multitude of all nations that have fought against Ariel, shall be as the dream of a vision by night, and all that have fought, and besieged and prevailed against it. And as he that is hungry dreameth, and eateth, but when he is awake, his soul is empty: and as he that is thirsty dreameth, and drinketh, and after he is awake, is yet faint with thirst, and his soul is empty: so shall be the multitude of all the Gentiles, that have fought against mount Sion."

79. "O Lord, thou art my God, I will exalt thee, and give glory to thy name: for thou hast done wonderful things, thy designs of old faithful, amen. For thou hast reduced the city to a heap, the strong city to ruin, the house of strangers, to be no city, and to be no more built up for ever. Therefore shall a strong people praise thee, the city of mighty nations shall fear thee. Because thou hast been a strength to the poor, a strength to the needy in his distress: a refuge from the whirlwind, a shadow from the heat. For the blast of the mighty is like a whirlwind beating against a wall. Thou shalt bring down the tumult of strangers, as heat in thirst: and as with heat under a burning cloud, thou shalt make the branch of the mighty to wither away. . . . He shall cast death down headlong for ever: and the Lord God shall wipe away tears from every face, and the reproach of his people he shall take away from off the whole earth: for the Lord hath spoken it. And they shall say in that day: Lo, this is our God, we have waited for him, and he will save us: this is the Lord, we have patiently waited for him, we shall rejoice and be joyful in his salvation. For the hand of the Lord shall rest in this mountain: and Moab shall be trodden down under him, as straw is broken in pieces with the wain."

80. "in a spirit of burning" (Isa 4:4).

therefore learn to abandon all hope in anything else, especially in human expedients and schemes (whether for our own souls or for the world), and look for help from God, draw our strength from faith in Him and obedience to His will.

Advent shows us again and again how all human strength and human pride is brought low in order that God may have a free hand to do good to men, overwhelming all their resistance to Him. READ 30:15–21[81]—the great lesson. Israel should have learned this one great truth: IN SILENCE AND HOPE SHALL YOUR STRENGTH BE. She would not. She must be destroyed, but after the destruction resulting from her trust in her own schemes, God would have His way, and take away her sorrow and hear her prayers. "Thy eyes shall see thy Teacher"—{receive} intimate guidance by God. For ourselves then: rest in *hope*, true hope; look at God, not at ourselves. The great Advent lesson {is} to LOOK UP, to get away from preoccupation with ourselves and look at God our Savior, Jesus our peace: *ipse est pax nostra.*[82] *Ipsum audite.*[83] Advent brings a light that surrounds us like the bright cloud on Thabor, even in our trials.

THE O ANTIPHONS: {these are} seven great and solemn invocations, the cry of the Church bringing down the Savior from heaven. The Church, the Bride, lifts her voice in the darkness of the world, and her voice, filled with the power of the Holy Spirit and with the longing of all mankind, resounds sweetly and irresistibly in heaven. All the supernatural longing of the inspired prophets and patriarchs is concentrated here. In these great cries of love, adoration and supplication, we are intimately united with Abraham and Isaias, and the saints of the Old Law. We are intimately

---

81. "For thus saith the Lord God the Holy One of Israel: If you return and be quiet, you shall be saved: in silence and in hope shall your strength be. And you would not: But have said: No, but we will flee to horses: therefore shall you flee. And we will mount upon swift ones: therefore shall they be swifter that shall pursue after you. A thousand men shall flee for fear of one: and for fear of five shall you flee, till you be left as the mast of a ship on the top of a mountain, and as an ensign upon a hill. Therefore the Lord waiteth that he may have mercy on you: and therefore shall he be exalted sparing you: because the Lord is the God of judgment: blessed are all they that wait for him. For the people of Sion shall dwell in Jerusalem: weeping thou shalt not weep, he will surely have pity on thee: at the voice of thy cry, as soon as he shall hear, he will answer thee. And the Lord will give you spare bread, and short water: and will not cause thy teacher to flee away from thee any more, and thy eyes shall see thy teacher. And thy ears shall hear the word of one admonishing thee behind thy back: This is the way, walk ye in it: and go not aside neither to the right hand, nor to the left."

82. Eph 2:14.

83. "Listen to Him" (Matt 17:5; Mark 9:6; Luke 10:35).

united with the prayers and longings of Our Lady. We are united with the whole Church, all the blessed and all the saved on earth and in the bosom of Christ, who cry out for the second coming. And we are at the same time united with the inarticulate longings of all the peoples who, though they do not know the name of Jesus our Redeemer, yet seek God in ways that are hard to identify and recognize. Finally, and above all, we are giving voice to the cry of the oppressed, the poor, the downtrodden, the persecuted, all those whom Christ seeks out with preference.

All this is in our hearts when we sing the O antiphons. They contain the very essence of Advent prayer. They resume the longing of the Old Testament for the Messias by repeating the sevenfold call with seven different names of the Holy One. These names succeed one another in order so that they resume the whole history of salvation and the gradual manifestation of the Word Incarnate—from the "Wisdom" that presided over creation to "Emmanuel" or God with us. Note the mystery and meaning of a "Name" for our tradition. (Names have lost significance in {the} modern world—a "Rose by any other name would smell as sweet."[84] Anyone can make up a new "brand" name which means nothing.)

O SAPIENTIA:[85] "In the beginning was the Word, and the Word was with God, and the Word was God. . . . All things were made by Him and without Him was made nothing that was made" (John 1:1–3; cf. Wisdom[86]). In the depths of our hearts we call upon the very Wisdom in Whom our being is rooted, in whom "all things consist,"[87] He Who was from the beginning and is now and ever shall be, He Who alone truly IS, and all the rest exists in Him and by Him. He comes forth eternally from the Father, and all creation is uttered in Him. He embraces all in His power and His mercy—*attingens a fine usque ad finem fortiter.*[88] We who cry out feel ourselves held in the strong power of the Holy One—*Agios ischyros.*[89] *Suaviter disponens omnia*[90]—and we recognize that His Providence wisely and sweetly rules all. Let us yield to the sweetness and

---

84. Shakespeare, *Romeo and Juliet*, II.ii.43–44.

85. "O Wisdom" (*Breviarium Cisterciense, Hiemalis,* 228).

86. See Prov 8:27–31.

87. Col 1:17.

88. "reaching from end to end mightily" (*Breviarium Cisterciense, Hiemalis,* 228).

89. "Holy Mighty One" (from the "Trisagion" of the liturgy of the Eastern Church) (chorus, improperia: Good Friday) (*Missale Romanum,* 184; *Missale Cisterciense,* 159).

90. "sweetly arranging all things" (*Breviarium Cisterciense, Hiemalis,* 228, which reads: "*suaviterque . . .*").

power of His will, open our hearts to His action, abandon ourselves to the great stream of His powerful and merciful plan which we do not understand—but how? *Veni ad docendum nos viam prudentiae*[91]—if we are to unite ourselves consciously and fully with Him, He must awaken our minds and hearts with light and strength to see His ways and to learn the "path of prudence" or of holy wisdom.

O ADONAI:[92] here we call upon Him as the Holy Lawgiver and Leader of His People, the God of Sinai and of the desert. The same idea as in the previous antiphon becomes more particularized and more precise. We remind Him—and ourselves—of His manifestation of Himself to Moses in the burning bush, and we remember with the Greek Fathers that all creation burns always with His invisible fire. READ *Exodus* 3:1–9:[93] "I have heard their cry. . . ." The Holy One is the God of mercy, Who will come to save the poor and the oppressed, but in order to lead them into the desert and give them His Law. So that too must be our resolution. READ *Exodus* 20:1–6 and 18–21.[94] This is the atmosphere of holy fear

---

91. "come to teach us the path of prudence" (*Breviarium Cisterciense, Hiemalis*, 228).

92. "O Lord" (*Breviarium Cisterciense, Hiemalis*, 228).

93. "Now Moses fed the sheep of Jethro his father in law, the priest of Madian: and he drove the flock to the inner parts of the desert, and came to the mountain of God, Horeb. And the Lord appeared to him in a flame of fire out of the midst of a bush: and he saw that the bush was on fire and was not burnt. And Moses said: I will go and see this great sight, why the bush is not burnt. And when the Lord saw that he went forward to see, he called to him out of the midst of the bush, and said: Moses, Moses. And he answered: Here I am. And he said: Come not nigh hither, put off the shoes from thy feet: for the place whereon thou standest is holy ground. And he said: I am the God of thy father, the God of Abraham, the God of Isaac, and the God of Jacob. Moses hid his face: for he durst not look at God. And the Lord said to him: I have seen the affliction of my people in Egypt, and I have heard their cry because of the rigour of them that are over the works: And knowing their sorrow, I am come down to deliver them out of the hands of the Egyptians, and to bring them out of that land into a good and spacious land, into a land that floweth with milk and honey, to the places of the Chanaanite, and Hethite, and Amorrhite, and Pherezite, and Hevite, and Jebusite. For the cry of the children of Israel is come unto me: and I have seen their affliction, wherewith they are oppressed by the Egyptians."

94. "And the Lord spoke all these words: I am the Lord thy God, who brought thee out of the land of Egypt, out of the house of bondage. Thou shalt not have strange gods before me. Thou shalt not make to thyself a graven thing, nor the likeness of any thing that is in heaven above, or in the earth beneath, nor of those things that are in the waters under the earth. Thou shalt not adore them, nor serve them: I am the Lord thy God, mighty, jealous, visiting the iniquity of the fathers upon the children, unto the third and fourth generation of them that hate me: And shewing mercy unto thousands

and adoration and love and desire to obey God; this should inspire us in all our prayer. Then the Lord will come to redeem us "with outstretched arm."[95] READ *Exodus* 14:19–27.[96]

O RADIX JESSE:[97] here we have a different picture—the first view of the Messias—the establishment of the Kingdom of peace, by a descendant of Jesse, upon Whom the Holy Spirit will descend with all His gifts. The Blessed Mother is also in the picture. READ Isaias 11:1–9:[98] here too,

---

to them that love me, and keep my commandments . . . . And all the people saw the voices and the flames, and the sound of the trumpet, and the mount smoking: and being terrified and struck with fear, they stood afar off, Saying to Moses: Speak thou to us, and we will hear: let not the Lord speak to us, lest we die. And Moses said to the people: Fear not: for God is come to prove you, and that the dread of him might be in you, and you should not sin. And the people stood afar off. But Moses went to the dark cloud wherein God was."

95. "*in brachio extento*" (*Breviarium Cisterciense, Hiemalis*, 228).

96. "And the angel of God, who went before the camp of Israel, removing, went behind them: and together with him the pillar of the cloud, leaving the forepart, Stood behind, between the Egyptians' camp and the camp of Israel: and it was a dark cloud, and enlightening the night, so that they could not come at one another all the night. And when Moses had stretched forth his hand over the sea, the Lord took it away by a strong and burning wind blowing all the night, and turned it into dry ground: and the water was divided. And the children of Israel went in through the midst of the sea dried up: for the water was as a wall on their right hand and on their left. And the Egyptians pursuing went in after them, and all Pharao's horses, his chariots and horsemen through the midst of the sea, And now the morning watch was come, and behold the Lord looking upon the Egyptian army through the pillar of fire and of the cloud, slew their host. And overthrew the wheels of the chariots, and they were carried into the deep. And the Egyptians said: Let us flee from Israel: for the Lord fighteth for them against us. And the Lord said to Moses: Stretch forth thy hand over the sea, that the waters may come again upon the Egyptians, upon their chariots and horsemen. And when Moses had stretched forth his hand towards the sea, it returned at the first break of day to the former place: and as the Egyptians were fleeing away, the waters came upon them, and the Lord shut them up in the middle of the waves."

97. "O Root of Jesse" (*Breviarium Cisterciense, Hiemalis*, 228).

98. "And there shall come forth a rod out of the root of Jesse, and a flower shall rise up out of his root. And the spirit of the Lord shall rest upon him: the spirit of wisdom, and of understanding, the spirit of counsel, and of fortitude, the spirit of knowledge, and of godliness. And he shall be filled with the spirit of the fear of the Lord. He shall not judge according to the sight of the eyes, nor reprove according to the hearing of the ears. But he shall judge the poor with justice, and shall reprove with equity for the meek of the earth: and he shall strike the earth with the rod of his mouth, and with the breath of his lips he shall slay the wicked. And justice shall be the girdle of his loins: and faith the girdle of his reins. The wolf shall dwell with the lamb: and the leopard shall lie down with the kid: the calf and the lion, and the sheep shall abide together, and a little child shall lead them. The calf and the bear shall feed: their young ones shall

He is not merely a leader of the Jews but a sign for the gentiles—gathering the gentiles together from the four corners of the world into His one Church: And He shall be the King of Kings.[99] READ Isaias 9:6–7:[100] "A child is born to us . . . ."

O CLAVIS DAVID:[101] {He is} the Judge, the one with final judicial power, the founder of the Church. He alone can release those who are in prison, under the tyranny of death and sin; He alone can make saints of the persecuted ones. In this antiphon we pray not only for liberation from our sins but also for the captives and all those who, by violence and injustice, are prevented from adoring God in freedom. READ Apocalypse 3:7–10:[102] faith and patience are what will enable us to pass through the door He opens for us into the new dimension of eternity; and fortitude is also necessary. For the key is the symbol of His strength, and for us to be liberated by strength we must share in His strength by strong faith and patient abandonment to His will. Our times demand great courage, and so does our vocation. O Key of David, open in the depths of our hearts the treasury of faith and courage; make us Thy witnesses and Thy martyrs. And so lead us out into the light of eternal glory.

---

rest together: and the lion shall eat straw like the ox. And the sucking child shall play on the hole of the asp: and the weaned child shall thrust his hand into the den of the basilisk. They shall not hurt, nor shall they kill in all my holy mountain, for the earth is filled with knowledge of the Lord, as the covering waters of the sea."

99. Rev 17:14, 19:16.

100. "For a child is born to us, and a son is given to us, and the government is upon his shoulder: and his name shall be called, Wonderful, Counsellor, God the Mighty, the Father of the world to come, the Prince of Peace. His empire shall be multiplied, and there shall be no end of peace: he shall sit upon the throne of David, and upon his kingdom; to establish it and strengthen it with judgment and with justice, from henceforth and for ever: the zeal of the Lord of hosts will perform this."

101. "O Key of David" (*Breviarium Cisterciense, Hiemalis,* 228).

102. "And to the angel of the church of Philadelphia, write: These things saith the Holy One and the true one, he that hath the key of David: he that openeth, and no man shutteth; shutteth, and no man openeth: I know thy works. Behold, I have given before thee a door opened, which no man can shut: because thou hast a little strength, and hast kept my word, and hast not denied my name. Behold, I will bring of the synagogue of Satan, who say they are Jews, and are not, but do lie. Behold, I will make them to come and adore before thy feet. And they shall know that I have loved thee. Because thou hast kept the word of my patience, I will also keep thee from the hour of temptation, which shall come upon the whole world to try them that dwell upon the earth."

O ORIENS:[103] the Lord now rises like the dawn, the dawn of His eternal day, the *Pascha Christi*,[104] the Easter, the Day which the Lord has made.[105] In the root of Jesse and the Key of David we see symbols of the Cross: here we see the Resurrection. In the two antiphons above He is the King of Martyrs; here He is the King of Glory, the Splendor of the eternal light, radiating *peace* and calm brilliancy over the face of the earth, the peace of eternal victory and unending life, the peace of God which surpasses all understanding[106] which must guard our hearts from sin. Let the light of Thy peace shine upon us in darkness. Fill our hearts with the *deifying light of faith* which has brought us to the monastery and keeps us here. Let us pray for monks and contemplatives, those who live in the peace of the cloister which is sometimes a paradise and sometimes a valley of the shadow of death to our human feelings. We must live in the light of the eternal day. READ John 20:1-2, 19-23:[107] the Risen Lord brings peace to His disciples. He gives them the Holy Spirit and the power to administer the sacrament of pardon and peace.

O REX GENTIUM:[108] the desired King, the *cornerstone*[109]—here Christ is called upon as the only strong foundation for the unity of mankind. There is no true peace for nations but by unity in the Church of God. Here we contrast the strength of the Rock, Christ, with the weakness of man "formed from the slime of the earth,"[110] and beg Him to bring

---

103. "O Dawn" (*Breviarium Cisterciense, Hiemalis*, 228).

104. "Christ's Passover."

105. Ps 117[118]:24.

106. Phil 4:7.

107. "And on the first day of the week, Mary Magdalen cometh early, when it was yet dark, unto the sepulchre; and she saw the stone taken away from the sepulchre. She ran, therefore, and cometh to Simon Peter, and to the other disciple whom Jesus loved, and saith to them: They have taken away the Lord out of the sepulchre, and we know not where they have laid him. . . . Now when it was late that same day, the first of the week, and the doors were shut, where the disciples were gathered together, for fear of the Jews, Jesus came and stood in the midst, and said to them: Peace be to you. And when he had said this, he shewed them his hands and his side. The disciples therefore were glad, when they saw the Lord. He said therefore to them again: Peace be to you. As the Father hath sent me, I also send you. When he had said this, he breathed on them; and he said to them: Receive ye the Holy Ghost. Whose sins you shall forgive, they are forgiven them; and whose sins you shall retain, they are retained."

108. "O King of the Nations" (*Breviarium Cisterciense, Hiemalis*, 228).

109. "*lapis angularis*" (*Breviarium Cisterciense, Hiemalis*, 228).

110. Gen 2:7.

us back into oneness with one another in Him. READ Aggaeus 2:7–10:[111] the second temple, the Church; Isaias 2:2–5:[112] the reign of peace, the union of all nations who desire to "walk in the law of the Lord."

O EMMANUEL:[113] {this} resumes everything—God with us, our King, our Lawgiver, the *Savior* of the world, come to save us. All is included in the word *salvation*, which embraces everything. Where is the Lord more truly "Emmanuel" than in the Blessed Sacrament!

THE MYSTERY OF THE INCARNATION

1. "*Ecce Sponsus venit.*"[114] First of all, God *manifests* Himself. Unless He revealed Himself we could never have known Him as He is. He manifests Himself not in a doctrine but in a *fact* (a mystery). Christmas is the great revelation of God, giving Himself to us in the Incarnation of His Word, manifesting Himself to us in a way in which we can receive Him and apprehend Him and know Him and love Him, and thus come, through the Incarnate Word, to union with the Father in the Holy Spirit. Admire and adore the divine wisdom of God's plan, giving us Jesus, a way of salvation by love, implanted in the depths of our nature. Cling to the simplicity of God's plan and do not add to it the inventions of human pride. {Show} gratitude for this manifestation, for this renewal of the mystery of Christmas in which we are called to participate. The epistles of the three Christmas Masses[115] are so many exclamations of the Church at the great

---

111. "For thus saith the Lord of hosts: Yet one little while, and I will move the heaven and the earth, and the sea, and the dry land. And I will move all nations: and the desired of all nations shall come: and I will fill this house with glory: saith the Lord of hosts. The silver is mine, and the gold is mine, saith the Lord of hosts. Great shall be the glory of this last house more than of the first, saith the Lord of hosts: and in this place I will give peace, saith the Lord of hosts."

112. "And in the last days the mountain of the house of the Lord shall be prepared on the top of the mountains, and it shall be exalted above the hills, and all nations shall flow unto it. And many people shall go, and say: come and let us go up to the mountain of the Lord, and to the house of the God of Jacob, and he will teach us his ways, and we will walk in his paths: for the law shall come forth from Sion, and the word of the Lord from Jerusalem. And he shall judge the Gentiles, and rebuke many people: and they shall turn their swords into ploughshares, and their spears into sickles: nation shall not lift up sword against nation, neither shall they be exercised any more to war. O house of Jacob, come ye, and let us walk in the light of the Lord."

113. *Breviarium Cisterciense, Hiemalis*, 228.

114. "Behold the Bridegroom is coming" (Matt 25:6).

115. Titus 2:11–15 (*Missale Romanum*, 15; *Missale Cisterciense*, 15), Titus 3:4–7 (*Missale Romanum*, 17; *Missale Cisterciense*, 17), and Heb 1:1–12 (*Missale Romanum*,

mystery of God's coming to dwell among us. "The grace of God our Savior hath appeared . . . ."[116] "The goodness and kindness of God our Savior hath appeared . . . ."[117] "God Who at sundry times and in divers manners spoke in times past to the Fathers by the prophets, last of all in these days hath spoken to us in His Son, Whom He hath appointed heir of all things, by Whom He made the world . . . ."[118] And in the gospel[119] from the Prologue of St. John: "In the beginning was the Word and the Word was with God and the Word was God. . . . And the Word was made flesh and dwelt among us, and we saw His glory, the glory as it were of the only-begotten of the Father, full of grace and truth. . . ."[120] But "He came unto His own and His own received Him not."[121] {It is} useless for Jesus to come if no one receives Him. Christmas celebrates not only the fact of His coming *but the fact of His reception* (accentuated by the non-reception by the citizens of Bethlehem—this is part of the mystery). {There is} no room for Him in our hearts preoccupied with ourselves; {he is} perfectly received by Mary, received by the shepherds and {the} magi—{the} simple and {the} learned. "*Attollite portas, principes, vestras, et elevamini portae aeternales, et introibit Rex Gloriae. Quis est iste Rex Gloriae?*" (Psalm 23).[122] The King of Glory comes forth from eternity, through the gates of great mystery, and having taken flesh in the womb of the Blessed Virgin, enters into the world, and the Church acclaims Him with her faith and her praise, seeing Him emerge from His tabernacle in the Sun and exult like a giant to run His course.[123] But Who is this King of Glory? We must open the eyes of our faith. We must listen and assent to the solemn words in which the Church herself proclaims her faith in the Incarnate Son of God: "*Sed necessarium est ad aeternam salutem ut Incarnationem quoque*

18–19; *Missale Cisterciense*, 18), respectively.

116. Titus 2:11.

117. Titus 3:4.

118. Heb 1:1–2.

119. John 1:1–14 (gospel: third Mass of Christmas) (*Missale Romanum*, 19; *Missale Cisterciense*, 19).

120. John 1:1, 14.

121. John 1:11.

122. "Lift up your gates, princes, and be raised, eternal gates, and the King of Glory will enter. Who is this King of Glory?" (Ps 23[24]:7, 9) (offertory: vigil of Christmas) (*Missale Romanum*, 14; *Missale Cisterciense*, 14).

123. Ps 18[19]:6.

Domini nostri Jesu Christi fideliter credat . . . ." (Athanasian Creed).[124] *Est ergo* fides recta[125] (not just any faith); *Ut* credamus *et* confiteamur[126] (in the Christmas liturgy); *Quia* Dominus Noster Jesus Christus Dei Filius Deus *et* Homo *est*[127] (the unity of two natures in one Person—Christ is God); *Deus est ex substantia Patris ante saecula natus;*[128] *Homo est ex substantia Matris in saeculo natus;*[129] PERFECTUS DEUS[130] (in no sense a real diminution of the divinity), PERFECTUS HOMO[131] (man just as we are, but without sin); *Ex anima rationali et humana carne subsistens, Aequalis Patri secundum divinitatem, Minor Patre secundum humanitatem.*[132] Qui licet Deus sit et homo, non duo tamen sed UNUS EST CHRISTUS. *Unus autem non conversione divinitatis in carnem* SED ASSUMPTIONE HUMANI-TATIS IN DEUM[133] ({*this is*} *the heart of the Mystery*). True contemplation means to penetrate by love into the reality of the mystery which these words contain, to know Jesus not just as an imagined human being at our side with the label of divinity, but Jesus as He is, God and Man. In the liturgy we join the whole Church of God in "believing" and "confessing" this great mystery, and in so doing we receive Christ Himself into our hearts, for He has become incarnate not for Himself, not for the Father only, but for us. Indeed, the Incarnation, which is the fulfillment of all the prophecies and promises of God, demands to be fulfilled in us. Jesus has come not only to be God and Man, not only to be God and Man in one Person, but to unite mankind to God in Himself. Hence the epistles of the three Masses say again: "He has appeared to teach us . . . to live in hope of the [second] advent of the glory of our great God and Savior Jesus Christ

124. "But it is necessary for eternal salvation that one also believe faithfully in the Incarnation of Our Lord Jesus Christ" (prime: Sunday) (*Breviarium Cisterciense, Hiemalis,* 131–32).

125. "For this is the correct faith."

126. "that we believe and confess."

127. "that Our Lord Jesus Christ the Son of God is God and Man."

128. "He is God, born from the substance of the Father before all ages" (". . . *saecula genitus*" in text).

129. "He is man, born from the substance of his mother in time."

130. "perfect God."

131. "perfect man."

132. "subsisting from a rational soul and human flesh, equal to the Father in his divinity, less than the Father in his humanity."

133. "Though he be God and man, Christ is not two but one—one not by the transformation of his humanity into divinity but by the assuming of his humanity into God."

. . . Who gave Himself for us *to cleanse for Himself a people acceptable,* a pursuer of good works . . . ."[134] "The goodness of God has appeared . . . not through the works of our justice, but by His mercy, by the laver of regeneration and renovation of the Holy Spirit Whom He hath poured forth abundantly upon us through Christ Jesus our Savior . . . that we may be heirs of life everlasting in Christ Jesus our Lord."[135] And {see} the Prologue of St. John's Gospel: "He came unto His own . . . and as many as received Him He gave them power to become the sons of God, to them that believe in His Name: Who are born not of blood, nor of the will of the flesh, nor of the will of man, but of God."[136]

2. The fulfillment of the divine mystery is then not merely the revelation of God, Who appears in order to be seen and praised by us, but the sending and coming of *a Savior who is given to us and born for us,* that we may receive Him, and have life in His Name, and live in Him, and be found "in Christ," and so that God may be glorified in all those who have become "one flesh" with His Divine Son. Hence it is that Christ comes down from the hills of eternity to seek humanity as His bride. He is the Bridegroom for Whose coming we have been waiting for centuries, the Savior who will raise up our nature to union with God and open to us again the gates of Paradise. "Behold the Bridegroom cometh; go forth ye to meet Him!"[137] God reveals Himself not in a doctrine but in His own Person, Jesus—and Jesus is God, and God is love. "*Deus caritas est.*"[138] To enter into the mystery of God is to be united, in charity, with Jesus, Who is God, Who is Charity. Just as all through the Old Testament Yahweh regarded Israel as His Spouse and reproached her for her infidelity, yet kept promising that He would return and forgive her and espouse her to Himself, so now Jesus comes as the Spouse, to unite to Himself the true Israel, the faithful people, the redeemed sinners, the Holy Church. "I will espouse thee to Me for ever: and I will espouse thee to me in justice and judgement and in mercy and in commiserations: AND I WILL ESPOUSE THEE TO ME IN FAITH: and thou shalt know that I am the Lord. And it shall come to pass in that day [the *hodie*[139] of Christmas] I will hear, saith

---

134. Titus 2:11–14.

135. Titus 3:4–7.

136. John 1:11–13.

137. Matt 25:6.

138. "God is love" (1 John 4:8).

139. "today."

the Lord: I will hear the heavens and they shall hear the earth . . . . And I will sow her unto Me in the earth, and I will have mercy on her that was without mercy, and I WILL SAY TO THAT WHICH WAS NOT MY PEOPLE: THOU ART MY PEOPLE, AND THEY SHALL SAY THOU ART MY GOD" (Osee 2—at {the} end[140]). *Espousals*: what is the justification of this image of espousals to signify our union with God? {The} *meaning of espousal* {is seen when} Adam says in Genesis 2:23–24: "This now is bone of my bones and flesh of my flesh. . . . Wherefore a man shall leave father and mother and shall cleave to his wife, and they shall be two in one flesh." This contains several important ideas:

a) Man and wife are two beings of a common nature; they belong together. (The Word, coming forth "from God" and taking flesh, espouses humanity, which came forth from God, and which belongs to God. He comes into His own; He takes possession of His own, of what was made to share the divine nature.)

b) Because man and wife belong together, then man leaves his father and mother and completes himself by uniting himself to his wife: the elements of *leaving, going forth, seeking,* and *becoming united to another*—these are all important elements in the idea of espousals. (Behold the Bridegroom cometh—the Word goes forth from eternity and enters into time. "Go ye forth to meet Him"—we in our turn must go out of ourselves, of our human and worldly life, by faith, hope and love, to meet Him.)

c) They shall be two in one flesh. Man and wife live together as a single person, with one heart, one mind, one will, and all things in common. Thus they form the basic cell in human society, in mankind. The individual is not complete in himself: he becomes complete when he gives himself to another and receives from another. (The Word espouses human nature: two natures in "one flesh," if the expression may be permitted—in one person. Then He joins us all to Himself "*in one Spirit*."[141])

d) Marriage is a "sacrament" or symbol of the union of Christ and His Church, says St. Paul (Ephesians 5:31–32, quoting the text from Genesis): "Husbands love your wives as Christ also loved the Church and delivered Himself up for it, that He might sanctify it,

140. Hos 2:21–23, 25.
141. 1 Cor 12:13.

cleansing it by the laver of water in the word of life, that He might present it to Himself a glorious Church, not having spot or wrinkle or any such thing: but that it should be holy and without blemish" (Ephesians 5). In other words, Christ came to espouse the Church to Himself, to dwell in the midst of us as one Person with all of us, He the Head and we His members.

3. "THROUGH ONE OF US THE WORD HAS TAKEN UP HIS ABODE IN ALL OF US" (St. Cyril of Alexandria[142]). The life of Christ in His Church is the fulfillment of His Incarnation. He became Incarnate precisely in order to unite us perfectly to Himself and to live in us. The humanity which God united to Himself, the humanity of Jesus, is filled with the light and life of God. But when we receive Him, He fills us with His own light and life and strength and love. The Humanity which He united to Himself has the power to sanctify and save all mankind, and it saves them by *contact*, by *union*. "*Virtus ex illo exibat et sanabat omnes.*"[143] Let us look at the humanity of Christ in the mystery of the hypostatic union:

1) The human nature of Christ is a human nature belonging to God. It is God's nature, though not the divine nature. Christ the Man is God.

2) The humanity of Christ is therefore transfigured and assimilated to the Word by grace and glory, sharing in everything that belongs to the divine nature, in so far as a human nature can do so.

3) The humanity of Christ is then the conjoined instrument by which the Word effects the sanctification and redemption and unites to God all mankind. Scheeben says: (Christ—anointed): "the anointing of Christ is nothing but the fullness of the divinity of the Logos, which is substantially joined to the humanity and dwells in it incarnate, which so permeates and perfumes it with its fragrance and life-giving force that through the humanity it can extend its influence to others and imbue them also with its power and its fragrance" (*Mysteries of Christianity*, p. 332[144]).

---

142. "*In omnibus itaque Verbum habitavit per unum*" (*In Evangelium Joannis*, I.9 [Migne, *PG* 73, col. 162C]).

143. "Power went forth from him and healed all" (Luke 6:19).

144. Scheeben, *Mysteries of Christianity*, 332, which reads: "nothing less than . . ."

Our Union with Christ:

1) First of all we are united to Him by faith and grace and baptism. He then sends His Spirit into our hearts, and dwells in us by His Spirit. Through the movement and inspiration of grace, our actions become the actions of Christ, our thoughts are His thoughts, etc. Above all, the Holy Spirit produced in us the humility and poverty, and the spirit of love and sacrifice, the simplicity of the God–MAN and all His other characteristics, especially His charity.

2) In the Blessed Eucharist {there is} a most intimate sacramental union with the very flesh of the Incarnate Word, in which He comes to us also in His soul and divinity. The Catechism of the Council of Trent says: the Eucharist, which contains "Christ the Lord Who is true grace and the source of all divine favors"; and communion "unites us to Christ, and makes us partakers of His flesh and of His divinity, and reconciles and unites us to one another in the same Christ."[145]

CONCLUSION: God reveals and gives Himself totally to us in the mystery of the Incarnation. He comes to us as the Bridegroom Who unites human nature and all His elect, personally to God in Himself. His sacred humanity is the conjoined instrument of His divinity in effecting this work, through faith and the sacraments of faith. And we must go forth to Him in faith bringing the gift of ourself, our whole life, denouncing our own human way of seeing and doing things, in order to live on His level and above our own nature. Our monastic life is a prolongation of the Incarnation, a life entirely in Christ. {The} Mystery of Christmas— a *coming* and a *receiving*—that is the monastic life.

THE CHRISTMAS LITURGY—The Three Masses

The great day ("*Dies sanctificatus*") has come. "The sanctified day hath shone upon us" (*alleluia*: third Mass[146]). All through Advent the prophets looked forward and spoke of what would come in "that day" in the future—*in {illo} die*.[147] They were speaking, in their time, of the fullness of time, the fulfillment of God's promises. But now we say Hodie *Christus*

---

145. "*Christum Dominum, qui vera gratia atque omnium charismatum fons est . . . .* [*hoc sacramentum*] *Christo nos copulat, atque eius carnis et deitatis participes effecit, nosque inter nos in eodem Christo conciliat ac coniungit*" (*Catechismus ex Decreto Concilii Tridentini*, 161 [II.iv: "*De Sacramento Eucharistiae*," iii, iv]; Merton's translation here does not correspond to that found in *Catechism of the Council of Trent*, 214, 215).

146. *Missale Romanum*, 19; *Missale Cisterciense*, 19.

147. "on that day" (typescript reads: "*illa*").

natus est.[148] The Church, liturgically, in the great mystery of Christmas, now renews the *coming* of the fullness of time, the promised "day" of God's coming into the world as Redeemer and Savior. Although on every day of the year God comes to us in the liturgy, yet on this day is especially renewed the very mystery of His coming, of His first appearance in the world, Incarnate, coming as Savior to save that which was lost, as King to take possession of what rightfully belongs to Him. In this mystery, at the same time, we enter into participation in the Word's eternal birth and coming forth from the Father, and His birth in our souls, and His second coming, as Judge for the final reckoning. These great realities are all present together in the telescoping of time and eternity which is effected by the liturgy.

The theology of the feast is tremendously rich and varied. The chant brings out, as nowhere else in the liturgical year, the rich meaning of the texts. Our prayer is at its highest intensity in the great introits, graduals, alleluias, offertories and communions of the first and third Masses. The theological and contemplative richness of these texts, and those of the collects and epistles, is overwhelmed by the simplicity of the gospels which *announce*, *proclaim* in the plainest and most direct terms, the birth of the Redeemer—and then finally, in the third Mass, sum up the whole feast in the prologue of St. John.

It is not enough to associate with each Mass some one of three births of Christ—this simple scheme cannot be made to fit. There is something of each birth in each one of the Masses. For example, in the Midnight Mass, the introit and communion open and close the Mass with the eternal generation of the Word,[149] and the gospel declares His temporal birth and manifestation to the shepherds.[150] The third Mass, in the introit and communion,[151] speaks of His birth and manifestation to the world, and the gospel had both His eternal and temporal birth.[152] The second Mass does not fit into any scheme, really. The real distinction between the three Masses is not due to any abstract systematic schema. They are Masses which differ in character, in attitude, in tone. The thing to do is to be

148. "Today Christ is born."

149. Ps 2:7 and Ps 109[110]:3, respectively (*Missale Romanum*, 15, 16; *Missale Cisterciense*, 15, 16).

150. Luke 2:1–14 (*Missale Romanum*, 16; *Missale Cisterciense*, 16).

151. Isa 9:6 and Ps 97[98]:3, respectively (*Missale Romanum*, 18, 19; *Missale Cisterciense*, 18, 19).

152. John 1:1–14 (*Missale Romanum*, 19; *Missale Cisterciense*, 19).

attuned to these differences of mood, differences which simply belong to the *time* at which they are celebrated.

The Midnight Mass {focuses on} light shining in the darkness, {the} secrecy and wonder of the "most sacred night"[153] in which the mystery takes place, the night that comes alive with heavenly light and angels, the night of God's coming into the world, the night which is the threshold of eternity. The cool wind of eternity blows into our faces, and the warm light of Christ shines in our midst, in the crib. The night Mass has its own character of ineffable wonder, of awakening to the tremendous, unspeakable mystery of God in our midst, with His peace. In the night of the *lucis mysterium*[154] (truly a vigil—cf. Holy Saturday) we reflect on the eternal birth of the Word, on the Father as the source from Whom He comes (*In splendoribus sanctorum*[155]). In the luminous darkness of the holy night, our hearts open out into the abyss of God, the "brightness of the holies," dark but bright, and from Him we too are born, in the light of the Son.

The Dawn Mass is really and truly a *morning* Mass. The Incarnation has now another modality, the freshness of morning light, a frosty December dawn (how perfectly the dawn Mass fits the state of those who awaken refreshed after the second sleep in the monastery, following the night Mass)—the awakening when you come back to yourself and realize that it is really Christmas—but really—that Christ has indeed come! It has even a little of the businesslike character of the awakening of the monastery priests, who now have work to do, who will soon ascend the altar for *their* Christmas. The atmosphere is brisk and purposeful. Read {the} gospel.[156] *Pastoresque loquebantur, transeamus usque Bethlehem*[157]

153. *"hanc sacratissimam noctem"* (collect) (*Missale Romanum*, 15; *Missale Cisterciense*, 15).

154. "mystery of light" (collect).

155. "in the brightness of the saints" (communion) (*Missale Romanum*, 16; *Missale Cisterciense*, 16).

156. Luke 2:15–20: "And it came to pass, after the angels departed from them into heaven, the shepherds said one to another: Let us go over to Bethlehem, and let us see this word that is come to pass, which the Lord hath shewed to us. And they came with haste; and they found Mary and Joseph, and the infant lying in the manger. And seeing, they understood of the word that had been spoken to them concerning this child. And all that heard, wondered; and at those things that were told them by the shepherds. But Mary kept all these words, pondering them in her heart. And the shepherds returned, glorifying and praising God, for all the things they had heard and seen, as it was told unto them."

157. "And the shepherds were saying, let us go over to Bethlehem" (Luke 2:15) (*Missale Romanum*, 17; *Missale Cisterciense*, 16).

(coming down from the dormitory in the atmosphere of mutual encouragement prescribed in the *Rule!*[158]); Et venerunt festinantes . . . *Videntes cognoverunt*[159] (we re-live the tremendous experience of the night on another level). {This is the} genius of the liturgy, which here captures perfectly the mood of rediscovery of what we have already found: "It is really true!"—and the universal admiration: with Mary keeping all the words in her heart, the shepherds go again, glorifying God; action fills the gospel. Meanwhile St. Anastasia gets in with a commemoration,[160] adding to the busy and social atmosphere of the dawn Mass. The note of *admiration* and praise dominates in this Mass, too. The enthusiasm is caught up by the collects and here too Christ is seen as King, dressed in glory (*Dominus regnavit, decorem indutus est*[161]). (*Ecce rex tuus venit sanctus et Salvator*[162]—communion).

The Midday Mass is the oldest and most majestic of the three Masses. In it the Church, the community as such, takes cognizance of the great mystery. *Puer natus est nobis*[163] (introit). The epistle, long and meditative, goes over the whole thing theologically, with the solemn and formal declaration that while God spoke to His people formerly through the prophets, now He speaks to it through His Son.[164] Then the Church takes note of the fact that *all the ends of the earth* have seen the salvation of our God (gradual[165]). She calls all the nations to adore Him (alleluia[166]). This Mass is a great solemnity in which we are no longer focusing our attention on the divine Child, but on the Church itself who receives Him, who is herself the continuation and fulfillment of the Incarnation—or rather the

---

158. See the emphasis on mutual support in *Rule*, chapter 72, "Of the Good Zeal Which Monks Ought to Have" (McCann, ed. and trans., *Rule of St. Benedict*, 159, 161).

159. "And they came hurrying . . . seeing they understood" (Luke 2:16, 17).

160. A second collect and second secret (*Missale Romanum*, 17, 18; *Missale Cisterciense*, 17, 18).

161. "The Lord has reigned; He is clothed in beauty" (Ps 92[93]:1) (alleluia) (*Missale Romanum*, 17; *Missale Cisterciense*, 17).

162. "Behold your King comes, the Holy One and Savior" (Zech 9:9) (*Missale Romanum*, 18; *Missale Cisterciense*, 18).

163. "A Child is born for us" (Isa 9:6) (*Missale Romanum*, 18; *Missale Cisterciense*, 18).

164. Heb 1:1–12 (*Missale Romanum*, 18–19; *Missale Cisterciense*, 18).

165. Ps. 97[98]:3–4, 2 (*Missale Romanum*, 19; *Missale Cisterciense*, 18).

166. *Missale Romanum*, 19; *Missale Cisterciense*, 19.

Church is conscious of her unity as she proclaims the great theological revelation of her Head.

Hodie—of the melodies with which the Church sings the coming of the great day, it has been said:

> It is only when the Church intones her Gregorian chant that the soul is fully touched by the mystery of God's coming. In these chants there are unforgettable passages which raise up the heart—melodies of an unearthly sweetness. And yet they remain nevertheless songs of the earth, possible only on earth, only to be expressed by human lips. Once again the liturgy will cause such melodies to be heard, and in a still more moving fashion, with the first alleluia of the Easter Vigil. After centuries of exile and penance, behold how the gates of Paradise are opened again. It is like the rustle in the leaves of Paradise at the approach of God. God returns at last to His garden in the afternoon air. The Spouse lifts up her hands towards the Bridegroom as He comes. *Ad te levavi animam meam.* (Dame Aemiliana Loehr[167])

Main Themes: light—in all the Masses the coming of the Word is the coming of light in darkness, the light of faith. His light must shine in our hearts if we are to receive Him at all. The mystery of Christmas is a mystery of light. It is *the shining forth of the light of eternity.* The "sanctified day" which shines out upon us is the day of eternity, the *hodie* in which the Son comes forth as the splendor of the Father (epistle and gospel, third Mass). The day is the Child Himself. He Himself is the light. Hence we can see Him at midnight, without any other light than His own. He is

---

167. "C'est seulement lorsque se font entendre les chants grégoriens que l'âme est touchée par le mystère de l'avènement. Il y a là, dans l'antienne de l'introït, dans le chant de la communion, mais surtout à la fin du chant d'offertoire, quelques intervalles inoubliables qui élèvent le coeur: mélodies d'une douceur supraterrestre et cependant, en ce qu'elles ont de retenu et d'encore inavoué, véritable chant de la terre, possible seulement sur la terre, uniquement exprimable par des lèvres humaines. Une fois encore, la liturgie en fera entendre de semblables, et d'une manière encore plus émouvante, au premier alleluia de la vigile de Pâques. Après des siècles d'exil et de pénitence, voici que les portes du paradis s'ouvrent de nouveau. C'est le frissonnement qui se produit dans la ramure de l'arbre de vie à l'approche de Dieu: Dieu revient enfin dans son jardin 'a la brise du jour.' Ce sont les mains de l'épouse qui se lèvent à la rencontre de l'époux: 'Seigneur j'ai levé vers vous mon âme'" (Loehr, *L'Année de Seigneur,* 1:91; Merton almost certainly translates from this French version rather than from the German original; he is not using the published English translation: Löhr, *Mass through the Year,* 1.42; the quoted scripture passages are taken from Gen 3:8 and Ps 24[25]:1 ["To you I lift up my soul"]).

the day that dawns *ante luciferum*.[168] All these nuances point to the fact that the feast is one in which we celebrate the spiritual and divine birth of Christ in our hearts as light.

Some Texts: collect, first Mass: "O God who hast made this most holy night to shine forth with brightness of the true light [Christ], grant we beseech Thee that we may enjoy His happiness in heaven, the mystery of Whose light we have known on earth"[169] (indicating that Christmas is indeed a foretaste of paradise, a participation in the same unfailing light and peace which shine forth in paradise). "*Lux fulgebit hodie super nos quia natus est nobis Dominus*"[170] (introit: second Mass). Collect of the second Mass: "Grant we beseech Thee almighty God, that we who are bathed in the new light of Thy Word made flesh, may show forth in our actions that which by faith shineth in our minds."[171] This introduces us to the moral consequences of the illumination. Jesus comes not to shine upon us as passive spectators. He comes to enter into our lives and our actions. Our actions must be filled with His light, that is to say with His Truth. They must correspond to the supernatural reality of our divine sonship. This is clear in the epistle of the first Mass (read[172]). {The} light of Christ shines forth in our sobriety, piety, justice, our rejection of the impiety of the world and of secular desires. The reception of this light brings about a transformation in our lives. Like the shepherds we come, and go away changed, and the change is expressed with happiness, "newness" and praise. {See the} postcommunion {of the} first Mass: "that we who rejoice in celebrating these mysteries of the Nativity of Our Lord, may by

168. "before the morning star" (communion: first Mass) (*Missale Romanum*, 16; *Missale Cisterciense*, 16).

169. "*Deus, qui hanc sacratissimam noctem veri luminis fecisti illustratione clarescere; da, quaesumus; ut, cujus lucis mysteria in terra cognovimus, ejus quoque gaudiis in caelo perfruamur*" (*Missale Romanum*, 15; *Missale Cisterciense*, 15).

170. "Today a light will shine on us because the Lord is born for us" (*Missale Romanum*, 17; *Missale Cisterciense*, 17).

171. "*Da nobis, quaesumus, omnipotens Deus: ut, qui nova incarnati Verbi tui luce perfundimur; hoc in nostro resplendeat opere, quod per fidem fulget in mente*" (*Missale Romanum*, 17; *Missale Cisterciense*, 17).

172. Titus 2:11–15: "For the grace of God our Saviour hath appeared to all men: Instructing us, that, denying ungodliness and worldly desires, we should live soberly, and justly, and godly in this world, Looking for the blessed hope and coming of the glory of the great God and our Saviour Jesus Christ, Who gave himself for us, that he might redeem us from all iniquity, and might cleanse to himself a people acceptable, a pursuer of good works. These things speak, and exhort and rebuke with all authority" (*Missale Romanum*, 15; *Missale Cisterciense*, 15).

a fitting life become worthy to attain to union with Him."[173] *The transformation is sacramental however, even more than it is moral.* {See the} secret {of the} second Mass: "May our gifts . . . be agreeable to the mysteries of this day's nativity and ever pour down upon us peace, that even as He who was born Man shone forth as God, so these earthly fruits may bestow upon us that which is divine."[174] {There is a} deep sacramental theology here. Again, in the postcommunion of the second Mass {we find} the same sacramental theology: "May the new life derived from this sacrament ever revive us O Lord, since it is His sacrament Whose wonderful birth has cast out the oldness of human nature [the ancient corruption of human nature]."[175] In summary, the triumphant alleluia of the third Mass calls all nations to "walk in the light of the Lord" (Isaias[176]). "A sanctified day hath shone upon us. Come ye gentiles and adore the Lord, for this day a *great light hath descended* upon the earth."[177] (Note how the Mass of Christmas Eve is an impassioned prayer for Christ to appear and for the Light to shine forth. The introit is a *promise* that we shall see His glory.[178] The collect prays that we may see Him without fear as our Judge.[179] In the gradual {we find} *"Qui sedes super Cherubim, appare . . ."*[180])

---

173. "*ut, qui Nativitatem Domini nostri Jesu Christi mysteriis nos frequentare gaudemus; dignis conversationibus ad ejus mereamur pervenire consortium*" (*Missale Romanum*, 17; *Missale Cisterciense*, 16).

174. "*Munera nostra . . . Nativitatis hodiernae mysteriis apta proveniant, et pacem nobis semper infundant; ut, sicut homo genitus idem refulsit et Deus, sic nobis haec terrena substantia conferat, quod divinum est*" (*Missale Romanum*, 18; *Missale Cisterciense*, 17).

175. "*Hujus nos, Domine, sacramenti semper novitas natalis instauret: cujus Nativitas singularis humanam repulit vetustatem*" (*Missale Romanum*, 18; *Missale Cisterciense*, 18).

176. Isa 2:5.

177. "*Dies sanctificatus illuxit nobis: venite gentes, et adorate Dominum: quia hodie descendit lux magna super terram*" (*Missale Romanum*, 19; *Missale Cisterciense*, 19).

178. Exod 16:6, 7 (*Missale Romanum*, 13; *Missale Cisterciense*, 13).

179. "*Deus, qui nos redemptionis nostrae annua exspectatione laetificas: praesta; ut Unigenitum tuum, quem Redemptorem laeti suscipimus, venientem quoque judicem securi videamus, Dominum nostrum Jesum Christum Filium tuum*" ("God, Who bring joy by the annual expectation of our redemption, grant that we may confidently see Your only-begotten, whom we joyfully welcome as our Redeemer, come also as judge, Our Lord Jesus Christ Your Son") (*Missale Romanum*, 13; *Missale Cisterciense*, 13).

180. "You who sit upon the Cherubim, come forth" (Ps 79[80]:2) (*Missale Romanum*, 14; *Missale Cisterciense*, 14).

New Life {is} another most important theme. Christ comes as light, but also as Life. The liturgical mystery of Christmas brings refreshment, nourishment (postcommunion: Vigil[181]), liberation (collect of {the} third Mass, and of the office[182]).

Christmas—our contemplation of the mystery: the Christmas cycle is one of the most "contemplative" portions of the Church year. (In Lent, we are busy with the activity of penance and the "illumination" of holy doctrine; in the Easter cycle we are above and beyond even contemplation—we are sharing in the life of the Risen Lord, and anticipating the triumphant life of heaven which is the life of glory rather than the life of contemplation as we know it.) In the Christmas liturgy more plainly than anywhere else, the Church teaches us *her* way of contemplation. It is a way singularly simple and efficacious. It puts us in the most effective possible contact with Jesus Himself, the Way, the Truth and the Life. What is contemplation in this connection? *to enter into the mystery of the divine Light, through love of the Infant Jesus, the Incarnate Word, embraced by faith and charity, and received sacramentally into our hearts that He may there transform us into sons of God by grace.*

Before we consider these points in detail, let us first remark on the fact that the Church thus teaches us to become contemplatives.

1. It is the will of God that the Church form us as contemplative: "that they may see the dispensation of the mystery which hath been hidden from eternity in God Who created all things . . . to be strengthened by His Spirit with might to the inward man that Christ may dwell by faith in your hearts, being rooted and founded in charity . . . that you may be able to comprehend with all the saints . . . to know the charity of Christ which surpasseth all understanding, that you may be filled with all the fullness of God" (Ephesians 3:9 etc.) This, according to Paul, is to be the fruit of his preaching: (a) that we know God as He is; (b) which can only be done if He reveals Himself to us; (c) but He has revealed Himself to us in the great Mystery of Christ—God and Man and the Head of

---

181. "*Da nobis, quaesumus, Domine; unigeniti Filii tui recensita nativitate respirare; cujus caelesti mysterio pascimur et potamur*" ("Grant us, Lord, we beg, to be renewed as we recall the nativity of Your only-begotten Son, through Whose heavenly mystery we are given food and drink") (*Missale Romanum*, 14; *Missale Cisterciense*, 14).

182. "*Concede, quaesumus, omnipotens Deus: ut nos Unigeniti tui nova per carnem Nativitas liberet, quos sub peccati jugo vetusta servitus tenet*" ("Grant, we beg You, Almighty God, that the birth of Your only-begotten Son in the flesh might free us, who are held by the old enslavement under the yoke of sin") (*Missale Romanum*, 18; *Missale Cisterciense*, 18; *Breviarium Cisterciense, Hiemalis*, 236).

the Mystical Body, in Whom and through Whom all are brought to the Father; (d) to know this, we must be united to Christ; we must form part of the Body; (e) this is only possible by love—love for Jesus, for the Father in Him, for one another in Him; (f) Jesus therefore calls us to the crib to admire the wonderful mercy of God, to love Him, to be united with one another and with God, in Him, in perfect peace.

2. This way of contemplation is sure and easy. We do not have to learn some strange technique; *we have only to love and believe.* We have only to *unite ourselves with the Church* as she contemplates the great mystery. She will lead us herself into the depths of the divine light. For this the most necessary dispositions are the readiness to *believe*, to *love* and to *wonder.* For this we must be simple and childlike; we must be able to open our eyes and see what is there. Those who are too preoccupied with their own selfish interests and ambitions, and with worldly things, and the aims of a secular culture, have lost the simplicity and genuineness which are required if we are to "see" what is there to be seen. They are blind. Furthermore, the Sacrament of the Holy Eucharist makes the way all the more sure, for our faith teaches us that here we receive into our hearts the very One Who comes to bring us grace and light from God, indeed the Body and Blood of the Incarnate Word, with His soul and divinity, accompanied by the Father and the Holy Spirit from Whom He is inseparable. The rich liturgical texts which surround the great act by which we participate ritually in the mystery itself, strive in every way to tell us how great is this "Child" Who comes to us, and words exhaust themselves without fully expressing the content of the mystery. But then He Himself comes to us with all the fullness and all the reality which words cannot express, and the Savior is born in our hearts, as we ourselves participate in His Divine Sonship and with Him look to the Father, while we are spiritually begotten by the Father in the Son.

A. *We enter into the mystery of the divine light.* All the "sanctification" and purification of Advent has been ordered to this—to empty and prepare our souls to receive the divine light, born in us in the darkness of Christmas night, a light which is heavenly and not of this world, which has nothing to do with human science, human wisdom, human learning; a light which no one can perceive, by any amount of effort and application, unless God Himself sheds a ray of it into his heart by a pure gift of love. The Person of Jesus is "light": *Tu*

lumen, tu splendor Patris (hymn: vespers[183]). "God Who hast made
this most holy night to shine forth with the brightness of true light
. . ." (collect: Midnight Mass[184]). "Grant that we who have *known the*
mystery of this light on earth, may also rejoice in its delight in heaven
. . ." (*idem*). *What is the light Jesus brings to us?* It is the very light of
the Word which is begotten from the bosom of the Father from the
beginning: "*In splendoribus sanctorum ex utero ante luciferum genui*
te."[185] It is indeed the very glory and brightness of the Father. {There
are} three modes of illumination {found in} the three Masses: (1)
mysterious and sweet; (2) joyful and active; (3) splendid, universal,
triumphant. *How does this light reach us?* through our faith in the
Incarnation and good works which we are inspired to carry out by
the grace of Christ present within us. {See the} collect, dawn Mass:
"That we who are bathed [*perfundimur*] in the new light of the Word
made flesh . . . [we are bathed, suffused, soaked in light—a *new* light,
a special "nativity of light," which takes place only at Christmas] may
shine forth in our *actions* that which *faith* makes to show resplen-
dently in our minds."[186] Actually the light of faith does not strike the
intelligence alone, but here illuminates the intimate depths of the
spirit, the "high point" of the soul, the *scintilla animae*, above both
will and intelligence, if the expression be permitted, and from there
it sheds its radiance over all our faculties. It is Jesus Himself Who is
born and enthroned in the summit of our soul, Who there "rules"
us by the radiance of His light, and really instructs and forms us.
{See the} epistle {for} Midnight Mass: "The grace of God our Savior
hath appeared [yes, in the most intimate center of our own being,
because if it does not appear there it does not "appear" at all] to all
men, instructing us that *denying ungodliness and worldly desires* we
should live soberly and godly and justly in this world looking for
the blessed hope . . ."[187] etc. Especially it is the Holy Sacrament that

183. "You [who are] the Light, the Splendor of the Father" ("*Christe Redemptor*
omnium," l. 5) (*Breviarium Cisterciense, Hiemalis*, 235).

184. "*Deus, qui hanc sacratissimam noctem veri luminis fecisti illustratione clares-*
cere: . . ." (*Missale Romanum*, 15; *Missale Cisterciense*, 15).

185. "In the splendor of holiness I have begotten you before the morning star" (Ps
109[110]:3) (communion: first Mass) (*Missale Romanum*, 16; *Missale Cisterciense*, 16).

186. "*ut, qui nova incarnati Verbi tui luce perfundimur; hoc in nostro resplendeat*
opere, quod per fidem fulget in mente" (*Missale Romanum*, 17; *Missale Cisterciense*, 17).

187. Titus 2:11–13 (*Missale Romanum*, 15; *Missale Cisterciense*, 15).

brings us God: "This earthly substance confers on us what is Divine" (secret: dawn Mass).[188]

What are some other effects of this light? {It brings} *admiration,* wonder—we are seized with divine awe (cf. introit: dawn Mass: "*Lux fulgebit . . . vocabitur* admirabilis"[189] etc. "*O admirabile commercium*"[190]). Admiration (*admiror*) {is} looking in silence, when our thoughts are beyond utterance; our whole being becomes a witness to the goodness of what we see—hence, contemplation gives great glory to God. {It brings} *adoration,* and a sweeping sense of the universality of God's love—an adoration that ascends to the Father and at the same time reaches out to the whole earth, *calling all people to adore with us the God* Who has manifested Himself. (This is in particular the theme of the third Mass.) "*Dies sanctificatus illuxit nobis—*VENITE GENTES ET ADORATE DOMINUM*—quia hodie descendit lux magna super terram.*"[191] When the Church sings this, she is not merely expressing a pious wish. Her voice is the voice of power, inspired by the presence of the Son of God speaking in the midst of her. It is the voice of the great King and Savior calling all men to salvation in the new light. As we sing this it is really the King with a commanding voice who calls solemnly to the whole earth to unite and prostrate itself before the throne of the Father's majesty. This voice goes forth with infallible effect, but secretly, in the realm of grace, and what we sing in our basilica is repeated and heard all over the earth in the secrecy of men's hearts, even behind the iron curtain, for we sing in Him Who is present to all as the King and center of all hearts. {It brings} *joy:* universal joy is the fruit of the great outpouring of love which makes the divine Word present and "sensed" in our hearts: "Let the heavens rejoice, and let the earth be glad before the FACE OF THE LORD, FOR HE HATH COME"

---

188. "*nobis haec terrena substantia conferat, quod divinum est*" (*Missale Romanum,* 18; *Missale Cisterciense,* 17).

189. "The light will shine forth . . . He will be called Wonderful . . ." (Isa 9:2, 6) (*Missale Romanum,* 17; *Missale Cisterciense,* 17).

190. "O wondrous exchange" (vespers antiphon: Feast of the Circumcision) (*Breviarium Cisterciense, Hiemalis,* 304).

191. "A sanctified day has shone on us—come, nations, and adore the Lord, for today a great Light has descended upon the earth" (alleluia: third Mass) (*Missale Romanum,* 19; *Missale Cisterciense,* 19).

(offertory: Midnight Mass[192]). The source of this joy is the realization, the thrill, of being present in the sacred mysteries, at the nativity (postcommunion: Midnight Mass[193]). {It brings} *purification, liberation, newness of life.* The light shed by the divine presence in our hearts *purifies and renovates our entire being,* so that we are born again with the newborn Christ, and "cleansed for Him an acceptable people"[194] (epistle: Midnight Mass). "That the new birth in the flesh of Thy only-begotten Son may *set us free* whom the old bondage doth hold under the yoke of sin" (collect: third Mass[195]). {It brings} *hope of heaven,* {a} *pledge of future glory* in Him Who has come to save us. We are sons of God and heirs of heaven, and our joy in Him is a pledge of our future glory, of which this contemplative light is a foretaste. "*Sicut divinae generationis nobis est auctor, ita et immortalitatis sit ipse largitor*" (postcommunion: third Mass[196]). {It brings} *firm confidence and perfect abandonment* in union with the Child in the crib, and in the arms of Mary. He comes in truth to bring us an increase of divine life, to make us sons of God, and He will complete His work by giving us the gift of immortality. "That being justified by His grace we may be heirs according to hope of life everlasting"[197] (epistle: dawn Mass). In this sense the Child Who is born comes as the FATHER OF THE WORLD TO COME (introit: dawn Mass[198]), with work to do preparing a Kingdom for the Father—not merely to give us temporal consolation. {It brings} *knowledge of the Father in the Son.* We can hear the Father saying to us as He says to the Son: *Filius meus es tu*[199]—*ego hodie genui te*[200]—*ex utero ante luciferum genui te* (introit: third Mass[201]).

---

192. Ps 95[96]:11, 13 (*Missale Romanum*, 16; *Missale Cisterciense*, 16).

193. See n. 173.

194. Titus 2:14 (*Missale Romanum*, 15; *Missale Cisterciense*, 15).

195. "*ut nos Unigeniti tui nova per carnem Nativitas liberet: quos sub peccati jugo vetusta servitus tenet*" (*Missale Romanum*, 18; *Missale Cisterciense*, 18).

196. "As He is for us the Author of divine regeneration, so may He also be the Giver of immortality" (*Missale Romanum*, 19; *Missale Cisterciense*, 19).

197. Titus 3:7 (*Missale Romanum*, 17; *Missale Cisterciense*, 17).

198. Isa 9:6 (*Missale Romanum*, 17; *Missale Cisterciense*, 17).

199. "You are My Son" (Ps 2:7) (introit: Midnight Mass) (*Missale Romanum*, 15; *Missale Cisterciense*, 15).

200. "today I have begotten You" (Ps 109[110]:3) (gradual: Midnight Mass) (*Missale Romanum*, 16; *Missale Cisterciense*, 15).

201. "I have begotten you before the morning star" (Isa 9:6; Ps 97[98]:1) (*Missale*

B. *All this is effected purely and simply by our personal love for Jesus Who is born to us.* There is no other way. No matter how much we may study the theology of the feast, or strive to be contemplatives, or exercise our powers in other ways, if we do not go directly by love to the PERSON OF JESUS, the Infant Who is born, the feast is sterile. Everything depends today on the reception of the PERSON WHO IS BORN—music, ceremonies, and *a fortiori* other celebrations mean nothing whatever except in so far as they are aids and reminders that help our infirmity to conceive the possibility of this union of love, or to express the overflowing joy of our faith. They help bring before us a human, inadequate, idea of what is going on, of Who comes to us—but we have to start somewhere. What is important is not where we start, but where we finish. Our love terminates in the Person of Christ. And He is much closer to us than we think—even in the depths of our own heart.

This love is tested and proved by our love for others around us. Hence, Christmas is supereminently a feast of fraternal union and charity. It is indeed *necessary* that the light of Christ shine not only in the hearts of individuals, but *that it radiate from one individual to another* so that we may contemplate *Jesus mysteriously present in the community.* Here is the true Babe Who is born to us—the "newness," the "new light," the "new joy" which ineffably manifests itself throughout the monastery and in all our brothers, the joy that binds us together on a pure and spiritual plane (and for which perhaps the trials and difficulties of Advent have been a necessary preparation), {bringing} reconciliations, the ability to see wonderful new qualities in our brother, the ability to do things for him more easily, to give in with less difficulty, etc., etc. Read 1 John 4:2ff.–14:[202] By this is

---

Romanum, 18; *Missale Cisterciense*, 18).

202. "By this is the spirit of God known. Every spirit which confesseth that Jesus Christ is come in the flesh, is of God: And every spirit that dissolveth Jesus is not of God: and this is Antichrist, of whom you have heard that he cometh, and he is now already in the world. You are of God, little children, and have overcome him. Because greater is he that is in you, than he that is in the world. They are of the world: therefore of the world they speak, and the world heareth them. We are of God. He that knoweth God, heareth us. He that is not of God, heareth us not. By this we know the spirit of truth, and the spirit of error. Dearly beloved, let us love one another, for charity is of God. And every one that loveth, is born of God, and knoweth God. He that loveth not, knoweth not God: for God is charity. By this hath the charity of God appeared towards us, because God hath sent his only begotten Son into the world, that we may live by him. In this is charity: not as though we had loved God, but because he hath first loved us, and sent his Son to be a propitiation for our sins. My dearest, if God hath so loved

the Spirit of God known—every spirit which CONFESSETH THAT JESUS CHRIST IS COME IN THE FLESH, IS OF GOD ({note the} tremendous importance of this for Christmas!). "WE ARE OF GOD . . . . LET US LOVE ONE ANOTHER. . . . EVERYONE THAT LOVETH IS BORN OF GOD AND KNOWETH GOD. . . . GOD HAS SENT HIS ONLY-BEGOTTEN SON THAT WE MAY LIVE BY HIM. . . . IF GOD HATH SO LOVED US WE OUGHT ALSO TO LOVE ONE ANOTHER. . . . IF WE LOVE ONE ANOTHER GOD ABIDETH IN US AND HIS CHARITY IS PERFECTED IN US. . . . AND WE HAVE SEEN AND DO TESTIFY THAT GOD HATH SENT HIS SON TO BE THE SAVIOR OF THE WORLD."

Conclusion: the only conclusion to all this is that when the light of the Savior fills our hearts and transforms our whole life in charity, there is nothing left but to rest in joy and in peace, because the *Lord has come*, and He has brought with Him His *peace*.

THE PRINCE OF PEACE—Christmas Season:

1. *The Messianic Kingdom is to be the Kingdom of Justice and Peace.* Read *Isaias* 65:17–25;[203] 11:1–9.[204] {Note the} *paradox*: Jesus said He came to

---

us: we also ought to love one another. No man hath seen God at any time. If we love one another, God abideth in us, and his charity is perfected in us. In this we know that we abide in him, and he in us: because he hath given us of his spirit. And we have seen, and do testify, that the Father hath sent his Son to be the Saviour of the world."

203. "For behold I create new heavens, and a new earth: and the former things shall not be in remembrance, and they shall not come upon the heart. But you shall be glad and rejoice for ever in these things, which I create: for behold I create Jerusalem a rejoicing, and the people thereof joy. And I will rejoice in Jerusalem, and joy in my people, and the voice of weeping shall no more be heard in her, nor the voice of crying. There shall no more be an infant of days there, nor an old man that shall not fill up his days: for the child shall die a hundred years old, and the sinner being a hundred years old shall be accursed. And they shall build houses, and inhabit them: and they shall plant vineyards, and eat the fruits of them. They shall not build, and another inhabit; they shall not plant, and another eat: for as the days of a tree, so shall be the days of my people, and the works of their hands shall be of long continuance. My elect shall not labour in vain, nor bring forth in trouble: for they are the seed of the blessed of the Lord, and their posterity with them. And it shall come to pass that, before they call, I will hear: as they are yet speaking, I will hear. The wolf and the lamb shall feed together: the lion and the ox shall eat straw; and dust shall be the serpent's food: they shall not hurt nor kill in all my holy mountain, saith the Lord."

204. "And there shall come forth a rod out of the root of Jesse, and a flower shall rise up out of his root. And the spirit of the Lord shall rest upon him: the spirit of wisdom, and of understanding, the spirit of counsel, and of fortitude, the spirit of knowledge, and of godliness. And he shall be filled with the spirit of the fear of the Lord. He shall not judge according to the sight of the eyes, nor reprove according to the hearing of the ears. But he shall judge the poor with justice, and shall reprove with equity for the meek of the earth: and he shall strike the earth with the rod of his mouth,

bring not peace but the sword;[205] yet, "My peace I give to you, not as the world giveth do I give unto you. Let not your heart be troubled, nor let it be afraid."[206] What is the solution? Christians, and especially priests and monks, are to be *peacemakers*. The peace of Christ must exist in the world *through our efforts*—our efforts to make peace in community and first of all in our own hearts by sacrifice of ourselves. {The} monastery {is to be} a "pattern" for {the} working out of this—this is {the} meaning of monastic sacrifice.

2. *The Example of St. Stephen, the Proto-Martyr*: {note} how this example can be misunderstood. *Hypocritical meekness is a disguised form of aggression* (Uriah Heep[207]). {It} is not based on self-sacrifice but {is a} roundabout way of self-assertion, subtle aggression which makes the other appear to be the aggressor, makes him perform the outwardly guilty act. We are then smugly justified before the bar of our own conscience. But Truth is not mocked, and there remains a residue of anguish under the surface of our self-deception. *Read* Matthew 5:38–44:[208] love your enemies. But we have no enemies in the monastery. If we treat our brothers as "enemies" even by a pious "forgiveness," we may be subtly attacking them. This {serves as} an innocent "outlet" for spite and vindictiveness.

3. The solution {is} *true mercifulness*, {being} big enough to understand our own smallness and {the} smallness of others. {To} *really forgive*:

---

and with the breath of his lips he shall slay the wicked. And justice shall be the girdle of his loins: and faith the girdle of his reins. The wolf shall dwell with the lamb: and the leopard shall lie down with the kid: the calf and the lion, and the sheep shall abide together, and a little child shall lead them. The calf and the bear shall feed: their young ones shall rest together: and the lion shall eat straw like the ox. And the sucking child shall play on the hole of the asp: and the weaned child shall thrust his hand into the den of the basilisk. They shall not hurt, nor shall they kill in all my holy mountain, for the earth is filled with the knowledge of the Lord, as the covering waters of the sea."

205. Matt 10:34.

206. John 14:27.

207. The hypocritical character in Charles Dickens's *David Copperfield* (1850).

208. "You have heard that it hath been said, An eye for an eye, and a tooth for a tooth. But I say to you not to resist evil: but if one strike thee on thy right cheek, turn to him also the other: And if a man will contend with thee in judgment, and take away thy coat, let go thy cloak also unto him. And whosoever will force thee one mile, go with him other two. Give to him that asketh of thee, and from him that would borrow of thee turn not away. You have heard that it hath been said, Thou shalt love thy neighbour, and hate thy enemy. But I say to you, Love your enemies: do good to them that hate you: and pray for them that persecute and calumniate you."

a) means first of all, to understand, *to identify oneself spiritually with {one's} brother.* The interior resistance, the effort to "thrust him aside" mentally, is an act of aggression (hidden). Distinguish {between} explicit and implicit acts of aggression: "treating him as if he didn't exist"; criticizing him, looking for faults, stressing differences and incompatibilities; "excommunicating" him mentally; impatience, anger, rudeness, coldness. No, we must *fully accept him, as he is, with his faults, as our brother*—accept his differences.

b) means to give in reasonably—except when it is more charitable not to (consult {one's} director). It can be necessary to correct, to say "no"; who is to judge? {Do} not decide "I am right" and he must be told. {The} basic principle {is that} we complete one another. No one is the whole cheese. No one knows it all. Sometimes we are very "understanding" in a way that implies we know it all—we are *generally only half-right*—sometimes much less than that.

4. {The major} *obstacle* {is} our interior idol (read from Müller[209]): the greater the idol, the greater our intolerance, because the greater our vulnerability {For} Müller {this is} a "fundamental principle":

> The way to overcome incredulity which destroys our original union with God and progressively enchains us, obstructing our inner communion with other men is not to be found in *proving to man externally* that he should return to God, but rather in making clear, in the concrete life of an individual man or class of men, that they have *placed a creature in the way of the Creator,* a finite being in the place of the infinite. . . . He has deified a creature; he is pursuing his own love of himself which can never lead him to love of the community and of others. An idol is incapable of real solidarity [comment: has to be the center]. It is indeed the enemy of solidarity. If in laying bare man's inner life we discover to him his special idol and disillusion him in that idol, we will surely bring him to the true God. The destruction of the idol is the first step toward God.

{The solution is} finding our true selves in God by giving up our false selves. {What is} *the way*—all monastic asceticism points the way. But asceticism can be perverted, or reduced to words, and outward motions.

---

209. This may be a reference to an unidentified passage by Franz H. Mueller (1900–94), German-American sociologist and, along with his wife Therese (1905–2002), a pioneer of the liturgical movement in America.

{By} obedience, God *uses* {the} *superior* to destroy {the} idol—even when he does not seem to "understand" us. Do not exaggerate blindly passive obedience. But maybe the superior has a point—maybe {he is} not as dumb as he looks. {Practice} fraternal charity (seventy times seven[210]). {Look to} Jesus in the crib, *defenseless*, completely at the mercy of men, the "least" of all, a baby. {Look to} Jesus washing the feet of the disciples. READ Matthew 20:20–28[211] (comment); Mark 9:32–40[212] (comment); John 13:12–17[213] (the washing of the feet): note the last line—not only knowing but doing.

210. Matt 18:22.

211. "Then came to him the mother of the sons of Zebedee with her sons, adoring and asking something of him. Who said to her: What wilt thou? She saith to him: Say that these my two sons may sit, the one on thy right hand, and the other on thy left, in thy kingdom. And Jesus answering, said: You know not what you ask. Can you drink the chalice that I shall drink? They say to him: We can. He saith to them: My chalice indeed you shall drink; but to sit on my right or left hand, is not mine to give to you, but to them for whom it is prepared by my Father. And the ten hearing it, were moved with indignation against the two brethren. But Jesus called them to him, and said: You know that the princes of the Gentiles lord it over them; and they that are the greater, exercise power upon them. It shall not be so among you: but whosoever will be the greater among you, let him be your minister: And he that will be first among you, shall be your servant. Even as the Son of man is not come to be ministered unto, but to minister, and to give his life a redemption for many."

212. "And they came to Capharnaum. And when they were in the house, he asked them: What did you treat of in the way? But they held their peace, for in the way they had disputed among themselves, which of them should be the greatest. And sitting down, he called the twelve, and saith to them: If any man desire to be first, he shall be the last of all, and the minister of all. And taking a child he set him in the midst of them. Whom when he had embraced, he saith to them: Whosoever shall receive one such child as this in my name, receiveth me. And whosoever shall receive me, receiveth not me, but him that sent me. John answered him, saying: Master, we saw one casting out devils in thy name, who followeth not us, and we forbade him. But Jesus said: Do not forbid him. For there is no man that doth a miracle in my name, and can soon speak ill of me. For he that is not against you, is for you. For whosoever shall give you to drink a cup of water in my name, because you belong to Christ: amen I say to you, he shall not lose his reward."

213. "Then after he had washed their feet, and taken his garments, being set down again, he said to them: Know you what I have done to you? You call me Master, and Lord; and you say well, for so I am. If then I being your Lord and Master, have washed your feet: you also ought to wash one another's feet. For I have given you an example, that as I have done to you, so you do also. Amen, amen I say to you: The servant is not greater than his lord; neither is the apostle greater than he that sent him. If you know these things, you shall be blessed if you do them."

Sᴜɴᴅᴀʏ ᴡɪᴛʜɪɴ {ᴛʜᴇ} Oᴄᴛᴀᴠᴇ ᴏғ Cʜʀɪsᴛᴍᴀs: much of the proper of the Mass is from the *Christmas dawn Mass*. *The epistle*[214] stresses the idea of our sonship and adoption. The *Spirit* of Sonship is the Holy Spirit, crying in our hearts "Abba, Father."[215] The ability to look to God our Father in perfect trust and confidence is proof that the Holy Spirit is working in us. Our prayer should lead to an ever-growing peaceful dependence on God our Father. *The gospel*[216] {teaches that} we are brothers of Jesus—we have the same Mother. Mary brought forth Jesus in joy, us in sorrow. "Thine own soul a sword shall pierce"[217]—especially the sword of sorrow at the opposition of men to the Savior. Simeon definitely predicts the Passion, center of a great struggle around the Person of the Redeemer. No neutrality is possible. He comes to ask us to leave all and die to ourselves, and this is hard. Contact with Him makes known what we are in ourselves. Mary's sorrows {involve the result} "that out of many hearts thoughts may be revealed"[218]—a mysterious saying. St. Jerome's interpretation (eleventh lesson)[219] {is} that Mary's heart will be pierced by the word of God, searching the inmost depths of her being to reveal *who she is*. {The} same will happen to all the faithful. Hence all who will follow Jesus will share in His suffering and in those of the Blessed Mother; {they will experience} conflict {and} rejection. We have no settled place in this world, and must not expect to find one. Exile, doubt, confusion, anguish {are our lot} until we come to the perfect vision of Truth in heaven.

Cɪʀᴄᴜᴍᴄɪsɪᴏɴ (January 1): {The} *Benedictus* antiphon {is} *Mirabile mysterium declaratur hodie*.[220] {This refers} *not* {to a} "Mystery of the Circumcision" but still {to} the Incarnation (finally *one day* with Christmas). *Note* how far in {the} background is the Circumcision, only mentioned in passing in the gospel. {There is} nothing about "bloodshedding" *anywhere* in the liturgy; in {the} first nocturn we are fortified by *faith* and ɴᴏᴛ by

---

214. Gal 4:1–7 (*Missale Romanum*, 26; *Missale Cisterciense*, 28).

215. Gal 4:6; see also Rom 8:15.

216. Luke 2:33–40 (*Missale Romanum*, 26; *Missale Cisterciense*, 29).

217. Luke 2:35.

218. Luke 2:35.

219. *Breviarium Cisterciense, Hiemalis*, 294 (the reading is from St. Ambrose [*In Lucam*, 2.2] rather than St. Jerome).

220. "Today a marvelous mystery is declared" (*Breviarium Cisterciense, Hiemalis*, 320).

circumcision.²²¹ *Innovantur naturae. Deus homo factus est*²²²—not merely human—*a man. "Id quod fuit permansit et quod non fuit assumpsit."*²²³ *"Non commixtionem passus neque divisionem."*²²⁴ {He is} ᴏɴᴇ being, *one Person*—two natures completely distinct but united in one Person—*not mixed* like water and wine, or two created substances; *not* transubstantiation ({this} would be docetism²²⁵). The *Holy Name* of Jesus involves and somehow contains this unity.

Tʜᴇ Oғғɪᴄᴇ ᴏғ ᴛʜᴇ Eᴘɪᴘʜᴀɴʏ ᴏғ Oᴜʀ Lᴏʀᴅ: {the} keynote of the whole office {is} majesty and solemnity, {a} sense of the sacredness, the transcendence of God Who appears to us, {a sense of} dynamic action. The Child in the crib is seen in great majesty against the cosmic background (Psalms) of the great storm in which we see the *Rex Terribilis*²²⁶—the Lord of Hosts, leading His people through the desert, and the *King coming at the Last Judgement*. This office has *a cosmic scope*. The Lord not only appears to all men but He manifests Himself *in all creation*.

1. {At} *vespers*, the tone is solemn, but simple and quiet. *Ante luciferum genitus, et ante saecula.*²²⁷ The star of the Magi suggests the text from the psalms: "born before the Day Star."²²⁸ Every word of this antiphon has great importance. *Dominus—Salvator—noster—hodie—mundo—apparuit.*²²⁹ The Church in adoration and in the vigilance of perfect faith sees the tremendous content of the mystery. *Venit*

221. The readings of the first nocturn (Rom 3:1–4; 3:5–6, 29–31; 4:1–4; 4:5–7) focus on justification by faith (*Breviarium Cisterciense, Hiemalis*, 311).

222. "Nature is renewed; God is made man" (Benedictus antiphon) (*Breviarium Cisterciense, Hiemalis*, 320).

223. "that which He was He continued to be, and that which He was not He took upon Himself" (*Breviarium Cisterciense, Hiemalis*, 320, which reads: "… *non erat assumpsit*").

224. "suffering neither mixing nor division" (*Breviarium Cisterciense, Hiemalis*, 320).

225. I.e. appearing to be human but actually only divine—as the Eucharistic elements appear to be bread and wine but are now the body and blood of Christ.

226. "the awesome King" (Ps 46[47]:3) (first nocturn, psalm) (*Breviarium Cisterciense, Hiemalis*, 351).

227. "Begotten before the morning star, and before the ages" (first antiphon, vespers) (*Breviarium Cisterciense, Hiemalis*, 349).

228. Ps 109[110]:3.

229. The Lord our Savior has appeared in the world this day" (*Breviarium Cisterciense, Hiemalis*, 349).

lumen tuum:[230] Christ has come as the light of His Church. This thought dominates vespers, especially in the magnificent responsory *Illuminare, illuminare Jerusalem*.[231] *The Magi* have a role in vespers (third and fourth antiphons[232]) but they do not dominate the scene entirely; they are simply secondary. *The hymn*[233] {includes} Herod's anger and vain fear; *the Magi*—their faith and their gifts; the Baptism of Christ; the Marriage of Cana.

2. *The Psalms of Vigils*: the invitatory is simple,[234] a repetition of Christmas. Then come the *psalms*. If you are not attuned to the psalms of this night, you miss the real Epiphany. {This is} one of the greatest offices of the year. It is the Last Judgement. The Magi are in the picture still (responsories; lessons), but we look up into the sky where they have seen their Star. And whereas they *saw then* the star we *see now* (in the same mystery) the coming of the Light of the World and fulfillment {of} all the prophecies of the Old Testament! {In} *Psalm 28*[235] {we pray} *Afferte Domino filii Dei*:[236] we are sons of God; we bring to the Lord sacrifice and glory. {The psalm tells of} *the thunder of the God of majesty*: His voice is heard in power, in *magnificence* (Sing great things with tremendous power and lavishness[237]), awaking the cedars of Libanus. See the storm on the mountains, splitting up the trees. His voice {is} coming through the fire, His voice

230. "Your light has come" (second antiphon, vespers) (*Breviarium Cisterciense, Hiemalis*, 349).

231. "Shine, shine, Jerusalem" (responsory: capitulum) (*Breviarium Cisterciense, Hiemalis*, 349).

232. "*Apertis thesauris suis, obtulerunt Magi Domini aurum, thus, et myrrham, alleluia*" ("Having opened their treasures, the Magi brought the Lord gold, frankincense and myrrh, alleluia"); "*Stella ista sicut flamma coruscat et Regem regum Deum demonstrat; Magi eum viderunt, et Christo Regi munera obtulerunt*" ("That star flashes like a flame and shows God, the King of kings; the Magi saw Him, and brought gifts to Christ the King") (*Breviarium Cisterciense, Hiemalis*, 349).

233. "*Hostis Herodes impie*" ("Herod, impious foe") (*Breviarium Cisterciense, Hiemalis*, 349–50).

234. "*Christus apparuit nobis: Venite adoremus*" ("Christ has appeared to us: Come let us adore") (*Breviarium Cisterciense, Hiemalis*, 350).

235. *Breviarium Cisterciense, Hiemalis*, 350–51.

236. "Bring to the Lord, sons of God" (v. 1) (*Breviarium Cisterciense, Hiemalis*, 350).

237. "*Vox Domini in virtute: vox Domini in magnificentia*" ("The voice of the Lord in power; the voice of the Lord in lavishness") (v. 4) (*Breviarium Cisterciense, Hiemalis*, 350).

shaking the desert, God sitting like a king over the great downpour of rain; and He brings His people in peace. {The} Jews, protected in the Temple, sing His glory. {The} antiphon (meditative and solemn) {is} "Bring to the Lord, sons of God [your sacrifice]; adore the Lord in His holy house."[238] {This is followed by} *Psalm 45:*[239] God is our refuge; mountains fall into the sea; the rivers {are} flowing into the city of God, {with} God in the middle of His city, which stands firm, but at the voice of God the nations are moved; the God of peace will end wars and burn the weapons of war. {Then comes} *Psalm 46:*[240] All nations praise Him: "*Jubilate Domino.*"[241] *Dominus excelsus terribilis . . .*[242] He goes up into heaven with the sound of trumpets. He is our God, Who has chosen us and loved us and put the nations under our feet. Here we see how the Magi are only a token. All the kings of the earth shall cast down their crowns[243] before the great king and adore Him. {The} antiphon {is} *Psallite Deo nostro, psallite: psallite Regi nostro, psallite sapienter.*[244] Know what you are singing and to Whom you are singing. He is the King of the whole earth, the Lord of Lords. *Psalm 65* {follows}: "*Quam terribilia sunt opera tua Domine, in multitudine virtutis tuae mentientur tibi inimici tui.*"[245] Here we have the exodus of the chosen people. He has made the sea like dry land. "Come and see the works of the Lord,"[246] *His Epiphany in our own tribulations (a new theme).* He has tried us in fire. He has placed men over us and delivered us from their power. He has brought us into a trap and then delivered us. We have gone through fire and water and we come out to sacrifice to Him and praise Him in His holy temple. {In} *Psalm 71,*[247] even more clearly, the Judgement

---

238. "*Afferte Domino, filii Dei, adorate Dominum in aula sancta ejus*" (*Breviarium Cisterciense, Hiemalis,* 351).

239. *Breviarium Cisterciense, Hiemalis,* 351.

240. *Breviarium Cisterciense, Hiemalis,* 351–52.

241. "Rejoice in the Lord" (v. 2) (*Breviarium Cisterciense, Hiemalis,* 351).

242. "the most high, awesome Lord" (v. 3) (*Breviarium Cisterciense, Hiemalis,* 351).

243. See Rev 4:10.

244. "Sing praise to our God, sing praise; sing praise to our King, sing wisely" (*Breviarium Cisterciense, Hiemalis,* 352).

245. "How awesome are your works, Lord; Your enemies honor you grudgingly for the mightiness of Your power" (v. 3) (*Breviarium Cisterciense, Hiemalis,* 352).

246. Ps 65[66]:5.

247. *Breviarium Cisterciense, Hiemalis,* 353–54.

{is evident}: *Deus judicium tuum regi da.*[248] He comes to do justice
to His people and to the poor, {to bring} the peace of His reign. *He
descends like dew on the fleece.*[249] {In} *Psalm 85*[250] finally {comes} the
prayer of the poor man {to} trust in God's mercy, trust to go by His
ways, for in these He manifests Himself to us. Note {the} last antiphon of the first nocturn: Omnes *gentes*[251]—all will adore the Lord;
{see also} the versicle: "Omnis *terra adoret te, et psallat tibi*";[252] {and}
the beginning of the first lesson: *Omnes sitientes venite ad aquas.*[253]
{The} beautiful lesson from Isaias[254] shows in what sense the feast is
universal. *All* will inevitably bow down and adore the King—those
who love Him and those who do not. But the Epiphany *of Love* is
only for those who realize that *they need a Savior*, the *sitientes*, the
poor, those who have no money, those who are willing to be saved
gratis, those who ardently thirst. The rich, like Herod, who are attached to what they have, will not listen, but they insist on throwing
away their money and their energy on what has no substance, and
can never satisfy them (read Isaias 55—{the} first half[255]).

248. "God, give to the king Your judgement" (vs. 1) (*Breviarium Cisterciense, Hiemalis*, 353).

249. "*Descendet sicut pluvia in vellus*" (v. 6).

250. *Breviarium Cisterciense, Hiemalis*, 354–55.

251. "All the nations" (v. 9) (*Breviarium Cisterciense, Hiemalis*, 354).

252. "Let all the earth adore You, and sing praise to You" (*Breviarium Cisterciense,
Hiemalis*, 355).

253. "All who thirst, come to the waters" (Is 55:1) (*Breviarium Cisterciense, Hiemalis*, 355).

254. Isa 55:1–4; 60:1–3; 60:4–6; 61:10–62:1 (*Breviarium Cisterciense, Hiemalis*,
355–56).

255. "All you that thirst, come to the waters: and you that have no money make
haste, buy, and eat: come ye, buy wine and milk without money, and without any price.
Why do you spend money for that which is not bread, and your labour for that which
doth not satisfy you? Hearken diligently to me, and eat that which is good, and your
soul shall be delighted in fatness. Incline your ear and come to me: hear and your soul
shall live, and I will make an everlasting covenant with you, the faithful mercies of
David. Behold I have given him for a witness to the people, for a leader and a master to
the Gentiles. Behold thou shalt call a nation, which thou knewest not: and the nations
that knew not thee shall run to thee, because of the Lord thy God, and for the Holy
One of Israel, for he hath glorified thee" (Isa 55: 1–5).

EPIPHANY {and} *Missions*: praying for those who sit in darkness—
VOCATION AND RESPONSE (based on St. Leo's *Sixth Epiphany Sermon*[256]).
"No one comes to me unless the Father draws him."[257] *Epiphany* {is the}
manifestation of {the} Glory of God in Christ the Incarnate Word. {The}
vocation of the Gentiles {is} to see the glory of God in Christ; and to
adore Him in His Church—Jerusalem. "*Dies quo primum gentibus Salvator mundi Christus apparuit*"[258] (St. Leo).

{The} *Grace of Epiphany* {relates to the} basic structure of {the} spiritual life: call it {a} response {which is} "personal": "Thou and I." God calls
us to Him by *words* in many places. Here in the Epiphany, the Word, the
glory of the Father, is Himself the manifestation of the Father, Who calls
us to come to the Father in Him. St. Leo {says}: *Illa hodie cordibus nostris
concipienda sunt gaudia, quae in trium {Magorum} fuere pectoribus quando Regem coeli et terrae . . . adoravere conspicuum.*[259] Think of the joy that
was in the hearts of the Magi when they found Him whom they sought.
This joy {should be} in our own hearts when the light of God arises upon
us, when we hear the Spirit like living water saying "come to the Father"
(St. Ignatius of Antioch[260]). {It is} the joy of a faith that not only *seeks*
but *finds God*—in obscurity, yes; but this obscurity is itself our light. The
light that illumines us is the understanding that darkness is our light,
and that we do not have to see; rather that to see is not to see, and not to
see is to see. The grace of conversion to the faith in so many souls daily
is a renewal of the grace of the Epiphany (St. Leo[261]). The cradle Catholic
must have this same illumination somewhere along the line also. {It is}
no special prerogative of converts! All must "find" the Savior. N.B. {the
role of} Herod: the devil today plays Herod's part, trying to frustrate the
work of conversions—to lead them astray, or to frighten them—to kill
the Child newly born in them (St. Leo[262]). So too with our vocation: *surge*

---

256. *Sermo 36* (*In Epiphaniae Solemnitate 6*) (Migne, *PL* 54, cols. 253C–256C).

257. John 6:44.

258. "The day on which the Savior of the world first appeared to the Gentiles"
(*Sermo* 36.1 [Migne, *PL* 54, col. 253C, which reads: "*Dies, dilectissimi, quo . . .*"]).

259. "On that day, our hearts must recognize the joys which were in the breasts of
the three Magi when they saw and adored the King of heaven and earth" (Migne, *PL*
54, col. 253C) (text reads: "*Majorum*").

260. Ignatius of Antioch, Romans, 7 (*Epistles of Clement and Ignatius*, 83).

261. Migne, *PL* 54, col. 254AC.

262. Migne, *PL* 54, cols. 254C–255B.

illuminare![263] Graces {are} in line with our vocation—certainty; doubts and difficulties {are} caused by "Herod"; {the} old man doesn't want to relinquish his kingship.

OUR RESPONSE: ADORATION—GIFTS. {We are called} to adore, to cast oneself down before Christ, to acknowledge He is *all* and we are but creatures of His. Practically, for us, {the} fundamental form of adoration is *obedience*, by which we "cast down" before Him our "crown" (cf. {the} 24 elders—*Apocalypse*[264]). *The Gifts of the Magi* (St. Leo) {are}: GOLD, "from the treasury of our own soul,"[265] is the acknowledgement of Christ as King of the Universe (here, *obedience*); MYRRH {is} faith in the Incarnation (God became Man); our flesh has become the temple of God by baptism; our bodies are united to the Incarnate Word, sacramentally, in Holy Communion; this faith should bear fruit in great respect for our flesh which is pure and consecrated to God (but we must struggle to keep it pure by chastity and mortification—basic bodily mortification here {is} connected with weather and work, colds, etc., chapping, sweating, rashes—minimum care); INCENSE {is} faith in the Divinity of Christ: He is equal in all things to the Father (*read Colossians*: "All the riches of the Father in Him" [*Colossians* 2:9]), but He became poor, that by His poverty we might be enriched ({2 Cor. 8:9}[266]); our vow of poverty {means} renouncing all to share {the} poverty of Christ; to possess the riches of the Father in Him. {We must} struggle to keep the vows. St. Leo says the homage the devil once received through sacrifices to idols, he now receives through sin.[267] How? {see} St. Leo, *Sermo 7*:[268] the Magi did not see the Savior cast out devils or work miracles. The only prodigy they saw in Him was His humility, His holy childhood. This was His preaching to them. This was the beginning of His victory over the devil, a victory also consummated by humility. "*Omnipotens Deus causam nostram nimis malam humilitatis privilegio bonam fecit.*"[269] "*Christianae sapientiae disciplina non in abundantia verbi, non in astutia disputandi, neque in*

263. "Arise, shine" (Isa 60:1) (second lesson, first nocturn) (*Breviarium Cisterciense, Hiemalis*, 355).

264. Rev 4:10.

265. "*de thesauri animi sui*" (Migne, *PL* 54, col. 254C).

266. Reference left blank in text.

267. Migne, *PL* 54, cols. 255A–256C.

268. Migne, *PL* 54, col. 257C.

269. "Almighty God made our very bad situation good by the privilege of humility" (Migne, *PL* 54, col. 258A).

appetitu laudis et gloriae, sed in vera et voluntaria humilitate consistit quam Dominus noster Jesus Christus elegit et docuit.[270]

Conclusion: fidelity to God's call {is essential}: not starting out for Him and then living for ourselves—to really *follow* the star until we find Him, each day going deeper into our vocation, {progressing} *from faith to vision.*

HOLY BAPTISM—Octave of the Epiphany

St. Paul says, "By baptism we are buried together with Christ in death."[271] The Octave of the Epiphany celebrates the fact that Christ's baptism in the Jordan is an "appearance," {an} "epiphany" or manifestation of God, in Christ. The gospel of the Mass makes this clear. St. John says: "I knew Him not, but in order *that He might be manifested* in Israel, therefore came I baptizing in water."[272] John did not just happen to point out Christ. The baptism was an *essential part* of the "epiphany." The lesson of the gospel is that St. John, acting as prophet and precursor, formally identifies the Christ, the anointed, the One on Whom the Holy Spirit descends, the One Who in turn will baptize with the Holy Spirit and with fire. God Himself had to make known His Son. No one else could discover Him Who came forth from God to sanctify men by the Spirit of God and bring them back to Him. In Christ's baptism we see revealed not only Jesus Himself, but also the great truth that baptism is itself the sacrament of our illumination and incorporation in Him. If it is so, it is only because Christ's baptism is already a type of His death on the Cross, His victorious struggle with sin and with the evil one. And our baptism, in turn, is a death and resurrection with Christ, in a liturgical rite, which unites us to Him in the mystery of His "*Pascha*" and makes us new men, conformed to Him, clad with His sacred Being as with a white garment—other Christs, anointed with the Holy Spirit.

The Liturgy of the Octave:

---

270. "The discipline of Christian wisdom consists not in an abundance of words, nor in skill in argument, nor in a desire for praise and glory, but in genuine and willing humility which Our Lord Jesus Christ chose and taught" (Migne, *PL* 54, col. 258BC, which reads: "... *Dominus Jesus Christus ... elegit ...*").

271. Rom 6:4.

272. John 1:31.

1. The Mass is as of the Epiphany, except for special collects and gospel (of the baptism[273]). The collects emphasize the fact of our sanctification and transformation in Christ: "grant that we may be inwardly reformed by Him whom we recognize to have been outwardly like unto ourselves" (collect).[274] To be inwardly reformed means to be baptized in the Holy Spirit. The postcommunion (like that of the day itself) asks for light to penetrate the Eucharistic mystery of which we have been partakers and which is our true Epiphany, the true appearance of Christ in mystery, the manifestation of God in Him, with Whom we are united sacramentally in the Eucharist: "that we may discern with a clear mind the mystery of which Thou hast willed that we should be partakers."[275]

2. Lessons of the second and third nocturns are special—dealing with baptism. They show the difference between Eastern and Western approaches to the mystery of {the} Epiphany. St. Augustine (third nocturn)[276] emphasizes the fact of the *one baptism*, that in every minister who baptizes, Christ Himself baptizes. The mysticism of the West is centered on the Church and her outward acts, which manifest Christ. The Orient (St. Gregory Nazianzen: second nocturn[277]) is more exalted, speaking of the Illumination of all by Christ, of His sanctification of the waters by His own baptism, of His sanctification of John, of the mystical purification of the whole world by the baptism of Christ. The main points of St. Gregory's lessons are:

(1) In being "illuminated" (baptized), Christ rather illuminates us with the radiance of His glory. "Christ is baptized; let us therefore go down together with Him, in order that we may also come up again with Him."[278] (Go down: descent, death, passion; Ascent: resurrection. The Greeks were very much aware of the mystery of the *pascha Christi*.)

273. John 1:29–34 (*Missale Romanum*, 45; *Missale Cisterciense*, 38–39).

274. "*praesta . . . ut per eum, quem similem nobis foris agnovimus, intus reformari mereamur*" (*Missale Romanum*, 45; *Missale Cisterciense*, 38); (collect, lauds) (*Breviarium Cisterciense, Hiemalis*, 384).

275. "*ut mysterium, cujus nos participes esse voluisti, et puro cernamus intuitu*" (*Missale Romanum*, 45; *Missale Cisterciense*, 39).

276. *Tractatus 6 in Joannem* (*Breviarium Cisterciense, Hiemalis*, 382–83).

277. *Oratio in Sancta Lumina* (*Breviarium Cisterciense, Hiemalis*, 380–81).

278. "*Christus baptizatur, simul et nos descendamus, ut cum ipso pariter ascendamus*" (fifth lesson) (*Breviarium Cisterciense, Hiemalis*, 380).

(2) Jesus sanctifies John who baptizes Him. He "buries the old Adam in the waters," and above all He "sanctifies the waters of the Jordan."[279] Contact of the waters with Christ, the source of all holiness, sanctifies them. Note {that} it is necessary for this contact to take place in a ritual action which manifested God's will in the matter.

(3) "Jesus ascended from the waters, as it were, bringing out with Himself the whole world which He had submerged and drawn up. And the heavens were then opened [not divided] to show that the gates of paradise were again open to men in Christ."[280]

(4) And the Holy Spirit gives testimony that Christ came down from heaven and will take us back to heaven.[281] (Note: the Greeks were acutely aware of the intimate connection between the *Baptism* of Jesus and the *Transfiguration*.)

Antiphons: the unusual antiphons of the day hours in our breviary all come from the Orient. They have a Greek character about them, and are often more or less paraphrases of texts in the Oriental liturgy. *Tierce*:[282] the antiphon is taken from the *Idiomeles* of tierce of the Great Hours in the Byzantine liturgy, which reads:

> The hand of the Precursor, of the Baptist, of the prophet most honored among the Prophets, was seized with trembling when he saw Thee, O Lamb of God, that takest away the sins of the world. Shaken with anguish he cried out: "I dare not touch Thy head, O Word of God, Thou O compassionate One, do Thou thyself sanctify and illuminate me, for Thou art the Light and the Peace of the world."[283]

279. *"et veterem Adam sepeliat in aquis . . . sanctificentur aquae Jordanis"* (sixth lesson) (*Breviarium Cisterciense, Hiemalis*, 381).

280. *"Ascendit Jesus de aqua, secum quodammodo demersum educens et elevans mundum: et vidit non dividi coelum, sed aperiri"* (seventh lesson) (*Breviarium Cisterciense, Hiemalis*, 381).

281. Eighth lesson (*Breviarium Cisterciense, Hiemalis*, 381).

282. *"Baptista contremit, et non audet tangere sanctum Dei verticem, sed clamat cum tremore: Sanctifica me, Salvator"* ("The Baptist trembles, and does not dare to touch the holy head of God, but cries out trembling: sanctify me, Savior") (*Breviarium Cisterciense, Hiemalis*, 384).

283. "La main droite de Précurseur, du Baptiste, du Prophète plus honoré que tous les prophètes, fut prise de tremblement lorsqu'il Vous vit, Agneau de Dieu qui effacez les péchés du monde; et, pris d'angoisse, il Vous cria: 'Je n'ose toucher votre tête, ô Verbe; Vous même ô compatissant sanctifiez-moi et illuminez-moi, car Vous êtes la

"(Cf. another *Idiomeles*, of the night vigils: "Thou Who in the Spirit and in fire dost purify the sins of the world, when St. John saw Thee coming to Him he cried out, 'I dare not touch Thy most pure head, but Thou, Master, sole friend of men, sanctify me by Thy Epiphany.'"[284]) *Sext*: our antiphon[285] emphasizes the fact of the great struggle that is contained in the sacrament of baptism. Christ's death and resurrection were a great victory over sin and death, the final and complete victory over the great enemies of man, especially the devil. The dragon dwelt in the waters—i.e. used material creation, which was completely under his sway, to exercise his tyranny over men, also his slaves. Descending into the waters, Christ sanctifies material creation by wresting it from the power of the devil and making it the instrument of His sanctifying power, by virtue of His death on the Cross. Jesus says to the Baptist (in the *Idiomeles* of the Great Hours—*sext*: Byzantine Liturgy): "Prophet, come and baptize me, I thy Creator, Who enlighten all things and purify them by grace. . . . Prophet, make haste, for I have work to do. . . . I go to deal the death-blow to the enemy hidden in the waters, the prince of darkness, to deliver the world from his snares and bring eternal life, for I am the friend of men."[286] Note the antiphons of lauds and of the Magnificat: corrupt nature is re-captured, regained, brought back into the power of Christ, through the waters which He has sanctified (*lauds*);[287] *Magnificat*: "The fountains of waters were sanctified when Christ appeared in glory. All the world,

---

vie, la lumière et la paix du monde'" (Mercenier, *Prière des Églises de Rite Byzantin*, 2.1:250).

284. "Vous qui, dans l'Esprit et le feu, purifiez le péché du monde, Jean-Baptiste Vous vit venir à lui et, dans la crainte et le tremblement, il s'écria; 'Je n'ose touché votre tête immaculée! Mais Vous, Maître, seul ami des hommes, sanctifiez-moi par votre Épiphane'" (Mercenier, *Prière des Églises de Rite Byzantin* 2.1:286).

285. "*Caput draconis Salvator contrivit in Jordane flumine, et ab ejus potestate omnes eripuit*" ("The Savior crushed the head of the dragon in the River Jordan, and snatched all from his power") (*Breviarium Cisterciense, Hiemalis*, 384).

286. "Prophète, viens me baptiser, moi ton créateur, qui illumine par la grâce et qui purifie tous les hommes. . . . Prophète, laisse faire à présent, car je suis venu ac-complir toute justice. . . . j'ai hâte de faire périr l'ennemi caché dans les eaux, le prince des ténèbres, pour délivrer le monde de ses filets en lui accordant la vie eternelle, car je suis ami des hommes'" (Mercenier, *Prière des Églises de Rite Byzantin*, 2.1:255–56).

287. "*Veterem hominem renovans Salvator venit ad baptismum, ut naturam quae corrupta est, per aquam recuperaret: incorruptibili veste circumamictans nos*" ("Renew-ing the old man, the Savior comes to baptism so that he might heal through the water our nature which was corrupted, clothing us with an incorruptible robe") (*Breviarium Cisterciense, Hiemalis*, 384).

come and drink waters from the Savior's fountains, for at that time Christ our God sanctified all creatures."[288] Once again {we find} the complete Christian view of the created world, flowing from the Church's contemplation of the mystery of the Incarnation. But we have to pass through the struggle of Christ with sin and death, die with Him on the Cross. The fact that the sacraments bring us the light and strength of Christ does not exempt us from the necessity to fight, ascetically, against the evil one in ourselves. Jesus dwells in our hearts, and gives us strength most secretly and surely from within, but He also wishes to die and rise *again in our actions*. Each day the Eucharist will be our food and our strength. Each day we will die sacramentally with Christ our God and rise with Him, and in the strength of His resurrection will find the power to combat the evil tendencies which still remain in our flesh.

Conclusion: the Octave of the Epiphany then closes the circle of the mystery of the Incarnation as it is presented to us in the Christmas liturgy. We see clearly that the God Who has become Incarnate has come with work to do, with a battle to fight. He has come to die on the Cross and destroy our enemies, in order to raise us up with Him. We now see the full meaning of the message of the angels to the shepherds: Christ is born to us a *Savior*.[289] In the Baptism of Christ we have a foreshadowing of Easter and Pentecost, with Jesus emerging from the tomb and the Holy Spirit descending upon Him (the Church).

SEPTUAGESIMA: The Mystery of Sin (cf. Vonier, *Victory of Christ*;[290] Scheeben, *Mysteries of Christianity*,[291] etc.) "Through one man sin entered into the world, and by sin death, and thus to all men death passed on, since all sinned in him" (Romans 5:12).

What does our faith teach us about original sin? The following truths, defined by the Council of Trent, are to be believed with firm faith by every Catholic:

---

288. *"Fontes aquarum sanctificati sunt, Christo apparente in gloria. Orbis terrarum, haurite aquas de fonte Salvatoris: sanctificavit enim tunc omnem creaturam Christus Deus noster"* (*Breviarium Cisterciense, Hiemalis*, 384–85).

289. Luke 2:11.

290. Vonier, *The Victory of Christ* (1934), in Vonier, *Collected Works*, 1:258–62.

291. Scheeben, *Mysteries of Christianity*, Part 3: "The Mystery of Sin," 243–310.

1. Adam sinned by disobeying God's command. His primal sin was one of *disobedience*, and pride. (Session V, canon 1 [DB 788[292]])

2. As effects of this sin:

    I. (a) He lost the sanctity and justice in which he had been constituted; (b) he incurred the anger and indignation of God; (c) hence he incurred the penalty of death; (d) and as a consequence of this he became a captive under the power of the prince of death, the devil; (e) the whole Adam, body and soul, was by this sin reduced to a corrupt state (*in deterius commutatum*) (all canon 1[293]).

    II. But Adam did not only harm himself by his sin. It passed over to us (canon 2): (a) the state of sanctity and justice was lost not only for him, but for us; (b) the punishment of death in the body passed over to all of us; (c) and with it passed over also that much worse punishment, *death of the soul.*[294]

    III. This sin and its effects can in no way be taken away by any natural means, by any effort of man. It inheres in each unregenerate human soul and is *his* sin. The only remedy for sin is the merit of Our Savior Jesus Christ, imparted to the soul in the sacrament of baptism.[295]

---

292. Denzinger and Bannwart, eds., *Enchiridion Symbolorum*, 263–64.

293. "... *statim sanctitatem et iustitiam, in qua constitutus fuerat, amississe, incurrisseque per offensam praevaricationis huiusmodi iram et indignationem Dei atque ideo mortem, quam antea illi comminatus fuerat Deus, et cum morte captivitatem sub eius potestate, qui mortis deinde habuit imperium, hoc est diaboli, totumque Adam per illam praevaricationis offensam secundum corpus et animam in deterius commutatum fuisse ...*"

294. "*Si quis Adae praevaricationem sibi soli, et non eius propagini asserit nocuisse, et acceptam a Deo sanctitatem et iustitiam, quam perdidit, sibi soli, et non nobis etiam eum perdidisse; aut inquinatum illum per inoboedientiae peccatum mortem et poenas corporis tantum in omne genus humanum transfudisse, non autem et peccatum, quod mors est animae: A*[*nathema*] *S*[*it*]" (Denzinger and Bannwart, eds., *Enchiridion Symbolorum*, 264 [#789]).

295. "*Si quis hoc Adae peccatum, quod origine unum est, et propagatione, non imitatione, transfusum omnibus inest unicuique proprium, vel per humanae naturae vires, vel per aliud remedium asserit tolli, quam per meritum unius mediatoris Domini nostri Iesu Christi, qui nos Deo reconciliavit in sanguine suo*, factus nobis iustitia, sanctificatio et redemptio [1 Cor. 1, 30], *aut negat ipsum Christi Iesu meritum per baptismi sacramentum in forma Ecclesiae rite collatum tam adultis quam parvulis applicari: A*[*nathema*] *S*[*it*]" (Denzinger and Bannwart, eds., *Enchiridion Symbolorum*, 264 [#790]).

The Liturgy of Septuagesima, the beginning of the great Easter Cycle, starts the Church's meditation of the Easter Mystery, by considering sin. But in the distance, we must see the Victory of Christ, His death on the Cross, His Resurrection from the dead, and the imparting to our souls His grace and salvation by baptism (Easter night).

Let us consider some deeper aspects of sin:

1. *The Reign of Evil in the World*, established by the sin of Adam. "The realm of evil was definitely established on the day of the Fall, through the triple tyranny of Satan, sin and death" (Vonier[296]). Adam's sin, says Vonier, was the greatest sin ever committed.[297] All other sins are but a participation in this diabolical revolt of man against his Father and Creator. The source of Adam's sin was a lie of the devil, that disobedience would not mean death. Satan promised illumination of the mind as a result of disobedience. Death was the "main object of his machinations" (Vonier[298]). Vonier proves this by the statement of Christ that Satan was a murderer from the beginning—and adds that he was envious of man's immortality.[299] "God created man incorruptible, and to the image of His own likeness He made him. But by the envy of the devil, death came into the world" (Wis. 2:23).[300] Death was the most important result of this sin, to Satan, "because it meant the destruction of a divine plan of immense greatness and beauty."[301] What was this plan? the unity of man in charity, in the divine likeness, in a paradisiacal life of contemplation and peace, a perfect spiritual life, in preparation for a pure vision of God in heaven, a life in which God's wisdom and greatness would be manifested in the unity of man on earth, in which the whole world would offer to God praise through man, its high priest, the son of God. The whole universe would thus be an image of the divine wisdom (SOPHIA). Instead of this unity, the perfect trust of man in God, friendship of man with his Father ("walking in the garden in the afternoon time"[302]), union of man with man in peace—instead of all this, the vast sea of human wills, from the

296. Vonier, *Collected Works*, 1:255.

297. "For the rebellion of Adam and Eve was the gravest sin ever committed by man" (Vonier, *Complete Works*, 1:255).

298. Vonier, *Collected Works*, 1:255, which reads: ". . . machination."

299. Vonier, *Collected Works*, 1:256.

300. Quoted in Vonier, *Collected Works*, 1:256.

301. Vonier, *Collected Works*, 1:256, which reads: "for it meant . . ."

302. Gen 3:8.

beginning of time until its end, is shot through with evil, with pride, with selfishness, with sin, with death. One after another, new wills come into being and deny God, turn away from Him, fly from Him, eaten up with selfishness, with mendacity, with fear, with evil; and yet the good is there too, but mixed up, wounded, defiled, frustrated. And over this chaotic sea of human wills moves the evil spirit, filling everything with darkness and poison. This "sin" of Adam is a unity, *peccatum*, says Vonier.[303] All sins are one in his sin, and yet they are unnumerable. God sees humanity as a unit. Satan, sin and death then form "an active, organized and purposeful empire."[304] In this empire, evil is more than a negation, more than an absence of good. It is evil inherent in what ought to be good. Sin is not just the abstract deordination, but the will itself infected with rebellion and evil.

2. *Sin is a mystery*, a spiritual reality in its own right, but one that does not come from God. "It is a mystery of nothingness, of darkness, of evil; a mystery of iniquity. And this mystery does not come from God. It comes from the creature which, wrested from nothingness and darkness by a divine act, rises up in rebellion against its Creator and extinguishes in itself the mystery of His grace" (Scheeben, p. 243[305]). What is it? disorder, annihilation of good, darkness opposed to the light of reason, active enmity to reason and to truth. Sin is an act by which a child of God dishonors and defiles the divine likeness in himself, ruins the splendor and the reality of his spiritual sonship by an act of formal rebellion against the truth and order of God, which even runs counter to his own interior hunger for God and his own innate instinct for justice and goodness (go on: Scheeben's analysis of the soul's defection from God [p. 261 ff.][306]).

SEPTUAGESIMA {is} the beginning of the Easter Season (two and a half weeks of pre-Lenten preparation). Christmas has brought the

---

303. Vonier, *Collected Works*, 1:257.

304. Vonier, *Collected Works*, 1:257.

305. Text reads: ". . . a mystery of nothingness, . . . God, it . . ."

306. Scheeben emphasizes that alienation from God presupposes initial union with God, and points out that one's total dependence on God is a motive for gratitude and self-surrender, but can also become a source of resentment "at the thought that what he is and has is not of himself; when he longs to use and enjoy the good he has received according to his own arbitrary pleasure, as if he had not received it; when, finally, he demands more than God with loving liberality has assigned to him; in a word, when he wishes to be like God" (Scheeben, *Mysteries of Christianity*, 262).

Redeemer—the Light has come into the world, but the darkness comprehended it not[307] (read Parsch[308]). Lent {is the} time in which the Church prepares to renew her baptismal consecration in union with the catechumens whom she prepares for baptism. {The} Lenten liturgy {is} a catechesis (for those to be prepared), a mystery (for the mature Christians). {It} realizes again the struggle between light and darkness: darkness in us {is} sin. There is in us a principle opposed to the Light of God. Our self-will crucified Him. There must be struggle: He dies and rises in us (a) sacramentally (baptism and Eucharist); (b) ascetically (prayer and penance prolong the sacramental action of baptism and the Eucharist). Lent prepares for the great fifty-day Feast of Easter. Lent is not the chief reality. Easter is. Lent is the preparation. Don't put the cart before the horse. Light is more important than darkness.

The Alleluia {is a} song of joy—on all Sundays, especially. {The} joy of Christians springs from the Risen Christ. Note: in St. Benedict the *Alleluia* is said *usque ad* caput Quadragesimae[309] (first Sunday {of} Lent). Ash Wednesday {was} not introduced until {the} eighth century, 300 years after St. Benedict. Septuagesima, etc., {was} introduced in {the} eighth century, under the influence of {the} Oriental liturgy. Dom Trethowan says the liturgy reflects disturbed political conditions of the time.[310] For the Greeks, Septuagesima begins the Liturgical Year, and that is why we begin Genesis in the first nocturn of Septuagesima.[311] Dom Guéranger makes a great fuss over the solemn cessation of the *Alleluia* at vespers before Septuagesima, reproaching Catholics of his time for taking no notice.[312] However, the cessation of the *Alleluia* is only an accidental,

---

307. John 1:5.

308. "Christmas is a 'light' feast, a fact that determined its position in the calendar. December twenty-fifth is not the historical anniversary of Christ's nativity (that date is unknown). The winter solstice was chosen for the feast in order to supplant and christianize the pagan festivities associated with the birth of the sun-god (Sol Invictus). Christ is the true Sun-god who overcomes and vanquishes the darkness of hell. Hence the feast of His birth is most appropriately placed at that point of time when the sun again begins its ascent" (Parsch, *Church's Year of Grace*, 1:205–6).

309. "up to the beginning of Lent" (c. 15) (McCann, ed. and trans., *Rule of St. Benedict*, 58).

310. "The fact seems to be that the Masses of Septuagesima and Sexagesima, in practice, reflect the very threatening political conditions of the 6th century" (Trethowan, *Christ in the Liturgy*, 83).

311. Gen 1:1–5, 6–8, 9–11, 12–13 (*Breviarium Cisterciense, Hiemalis*, 431–32).

312 Guéranger, *Liturgical Year*, 4:106–15.

not the very essence of Septuagesima. A "complete office" of farewell is quoted by Guéranger[313]—from fifth-century Spain, with elements of the "*Itinerarium.*"[314]

Septuagesima {is a} *preamble,* {the} beginning of the Easter cycle, {a} season of penance to prepare us for celebration of the mystery of our Redemption. *We have to know we need a Redeemer,* and at the same time (a) the need to do something about it; (b) the fact that no matter how much we do, we cannot by ourselves do enough; (c) {a} realization that God's grace and mercy are our only salvation—Jesus Who said "Ask and you shall receive, knock and it shall be opened unto you"[315] here stirs up our faith and compunction in order that we may press forward with hope; (d) {that} salvation {is} a gift which we must receive on God's own terms, in His Church.

1. The *Introit* (note {the} combination of urgency and hope): *Circumdederunt me*[316]—it is in our greatest sorrow that the Lord prepares us to cry out in such a way that He will hear us. Tribulation is a grace. We must accept it, not refuse it. The Church never stresses the dark side, never {is} gloomy or pessimistic. Right away she adds, *In tribulatione invocavi Dominum et exaudivit. . . . Diligam te Domine fortitudo mea.*[317] When we are brought low, it is that we may remember that the Lord is our strength. {The} *collect* {shows the} same balance: *Qui juste pro peccatis affligimur pro tui nominis gloria misericorditer liberemur*[318] (cf. *gradual*[319]).

2. *Epistle:*[320] {this shows} (a) {the} *uncertainty of salvation;* (b) {the} *necessity of good works, especially works of penance,* {by which we} deny ourselves what holds us back, what constitutes our attachment, what

313. Guéranger, *Liturgical Year,* 4:110–13.

314. I.e. prayers for someone going on a journey: see *Breviarium Cisterciense,* 227–29*.

315. Matt 7:7; Luke 11:9.

316. "[The waters of death] have surrounded me" (Ps 17[18]:5) (*Missale Romanum,* 57; *Missale Cisterciense,* 47).

317. "In my distress I called upon the Lord and He heard me . . . . I will love the Lord my strength" (Ps 17[18]:7, 2) (*Missale Romanum,* 57; *Missale Cisterciense,* 47).

318. "that we who are justly afflicted for our sins may be mercifully freed for the glory of Your name" (*Missale Romanum,* 57; *Missale Cisterciense,* 47) (collect, lauds) (*Breviarium Cisterciense, Hiemalis,* 437).

319. Ps 9:9–10, 19–20 (*Missale Romanum,* 57; *Missale Cisterciense,* 47).

320. 1 Cor 9:24–10:5 (*Missale Romanum,* 57; *Missale Cisterciense,* 47).

blocks grace, what is in God's way—especially attachment to self; (c) {as an} *illustration*, {see} the children of Israel in the desert—God {is} not well pleased—why? {see} *Numbers* 14:26–30 (punishment for murmuring); cf. c. 13:28–14:1–11: How long will this people detract me . . . *how long will they not believe?*

3. *Gospel:*[321] see the same lesson—salvation and sanctity are God's gifts. He gives as He pleases. Those attached to their own works murmur at God's generosity to those who *do less*. Many {are} called, few chosen? (vide CBL[322]).

SEXAGESIMA: "That on the good ground are they who in a *good and perfect heart, hearing the word, keep it and bring forth fruit in patience.*"[323]

   A. {There are} *three things necessary for perfection:* (1) good dispositions, in the very center of our being—*good will*, complete *sincerity*, {a} combination of gifts of nature and grace, above all grace; (2) to hear the Word and keep it {in a} spirit of faith—to "hear" is to believe; {in a} spirit of understanding—{to} see to some extent; {and in a} spirit of obedience; (3) {to} bring forth fruit in patience—it takes time.

   B. St. Paul, {in} the epistle,[324] gives us an admirable picture of these dispositions: (1) Paul does not rely upon or presume on his natural gifts; (2) {nor on} his sufferings—yet he does not advance these as proofs of strength—he glories in his infirmity; (3) {nor on} his visions—he does not glory in these, but again, in his infirmity; (4) {he is aware of} *his real self:* he remembers his weaknesses and limitations, the sting of the flesh, humiliation, the unanswered prayer—God prefers him to be humbled. *His conclusion* {is that} grace is sufficient; power is made perfect in infirmities. Paul *accepts* his infirmities, abandons himself to Christ, goes ahead into situations where his weakness alone would fail, but where he is sustained by the power of Christ.

---

321. Matt 20:1–16 (*Missale Romanum*, 57–58; *Missale Cisterciense*, 48).

322. "The ominous: Many are called but few are chosen, is perhaps not authentic here—Mark omits—but drawn from 22:14" (Jones, "Matthew," *Catholic Commentary*, 887).

323. Luke 8:15 (gospel) (*Missale Romanum*, 60; *Missale Cisterciense*, 50).

324. 2 Cor 11:19—12:9 (*Missale Romanum*, 59; *Missale Cisterciense*, 49).

This is what we also must learn to do, to go forward with our weaknesses, by *means of them*, and not be too impatient to get rid of them.

QUINQUAGESIMA—THE FORTY HOURS: "*Deus qui nobis sub sacramento mirabili passionis tuae memoriam reliquisti . . .*"[325] {It is} this "marvelous sacrament," inexhaustible wonder of the greatest of the sacraments by which Jesus Himself, Body, Blood, Soul, Divinity, remains with us, and not only that, but actually renews His sacred passion each day in the midst of His faithful: "that we may so reverence the sacred mysteries of Thy Body and Blood, that we may forever perceive within us the fruit of Thy Redemption."[326] The fruit of the Redemption is manifested above all by charity. {We encounter} Jesus in the Blessed Sacrament, our Redeemer, our strength, our life, our hope, our joy. All good flows to us from Him, by reason of His love for us. The veneration He seeks from us is a return of love. In proportion as we love Him, we unite ourselves with Him in His sacrifice. Love alone can give us the strength to do this. Each time this sacrifice is renewed, the *work of our Redemption is accomplished*. {There is a} union with priests in adoration throughout the world, holy priests {and a} holy people. "O sacred banquet in which Christ is received; the memory of His passion is renewed; the mind is filled with grace; and a pledge of future glory is given to us."[327]

Preparation for Lent: we may say more about this {for} Ash Wednesday. At the moment, we can thank God for the grace to prepare remotely for Lent in these forty hours, hours of love, in which our hearts will be purified of blindness and self-love, and will be made ready for sacrifice. Emptying our hearts before Easter, *Ecce ascendimus Jerosolymam*;[328] {it is a} time of *purification* and *enlightenment* to prepare for Easter and *union*. Both purification and enlightenment flow into our souls from the blessed

---

325. "O God, who have left us a memorial of your passion in this marvelous sacrament . . ." (collect, vespers, lauds: Corpus Christi) (*Breviarium Cisterciense, Pars Aestivalis*, 194, 211).

326. "*ita nos Corporis et Sanguinis tua sacra mysteria venerari; ut redemptionis tuae fructum in nobis jugiter sentiamus*" (*Breviarium Cisterciense, Aestivalis*, 194, 211).

327. "*O sacrum convivium, in quo Christus sumitur: recolitur memoria passionis eius; mens impletur gratia et futurae gloriae nobis pignus datur*" (prayer written according to tradition by St. Thomas Aquinas) (*Raccolta*, 117–18 [#180]).

328. "Behold we are going up to Jerusalem" (Luke 18:31) (gospel for Quinquagesima) (*Missale Romanum*, 61; *Missale Cisterciense*, 51).

Cross of our Savior. Purification {is a} cleansing by fire, the fire of Jesus' love, which creates in us zeal and fervor. {It is a} medicinal penance, a time of healing, {a} restoration of health and grace. But the spiritual life and its methods {are} like a pharmacy—we cannot just go in and help ourselves; we might get poisoned. The tragedy of souls that do this, pick their own medicine, {is evident}. Yet at the same time, they should know their disease. They should be able to come and point to the complaint that needs to be cured. Then {a} suitable remedy will be given them. In other words, we should have self-knowledge—pray for it, and in Lent apply a proper remedy that will really purify. {It is} useless, when you have a cancer, to concentrate on dandruff or trench mouth to the exclusion of everything else. Choose penances that will help us *to grow in charity and Christlikeness*, especially *attention to obedience* (we often assume we are obedient and it turns out we really neglect obedience), and also to *charity*. {Pay} attention to the main rules of our life—silence, prayer, mortification. Look over {the} Sermon on Mount,[329] or {the} Instruments of Good Works,[330] or chapter 13 of 1 Corinthians. {Follow} daily practices, {such as} meditation on {*The*} *Imitation* {*of Christ*} or on {the} *Rule*—get {such} practices approved.

FORTY HOURS—{*The*} *Mystery of the Eucharist*: we *adore* the Blessed Sacrament. But a sacrament is in a certain sense a created thing, yet the Blessed Sacrament "is God." {This is the} great mystery of the sacraments—midway between God and His creation (cf. Vonier[331]).

1. *Real Presence*: the Blessed Sacrament contains not only grace, but the Author of grace, the Risen Christ. Jesus is really, truly and substantially present—as a Person. Pius IX {said}: "He himself willed to be present and sustain us by His divinity—the most perfect safeguard of our spiritual life." The Blessed Sacrament is the source of our strength, "giving us the full certitude that He has loved us to the end."[332] {According to} Leo XIII, {the} Blessed Sacrament {is} the *source of our hope and confidence*: "In the

---

329. Matt 5–7.

330. *Rule*, c. 4 (McCann, ed. and trans., *Rule of St. Benedict*, 26–32).

331. "that intermediate world which lies between the creature and the uncreated God, the sacramental world, which is neither nature nor divinity, yet which partakes of both" (*A Key to the Doctrine of the Eucharist*, c. 5 [Vonier, *Collected Works*, 2.248]).

332. Pius IX, *Amantissimi* (May 3, 1858), translated by Merton from *Liturgie: Enseignements Pontificaux*, 123 (#149): "Lui-même notre soutien et notre force par la présence de sa divinité, sauvegarde la plus assurée de la vie spirituelle. . . . Il a voulu nous donner la pleine certitude que ceux qu'Il a aimés, Il les a aimés jusqu'à la fin."

Blessed Sacrament is the only true hope and peace for the world, and the only real solution for all the problems of our times";[333] but pride blinds men to this. The Blessed Sacrament is the Bread of Life: "*caro mea pro mundi vita.*"[334]

2. *Sacramental Participation in the Mystery of Christ*:

a) {is} to realize always in ourselves the *Redemptionis Fructum.*[335] Each time this Holy Sacrifice is offered, the work of our redemption is accomplished (liturgy). Jesus renews His redemptive sacrifice in the Mass. It is His great act of Love. We participate in this great act most perfectly by our Eucharistic communion, offering ourselves with Him, abandoning all care in the jubilation of trust and thanksgiving, to live always in a spirit of fraternal union and thanksgiving—this is the Eucharistic life.

b) *Sacramental communion* {is} a feast of Love. Pius XII {in} *Mediator Dei* {writes}: "The Church of Jesus Christ has only this Bread to *satisfy the aspirations and desires of your souls.*" Liturgy, says Pius XII, aims above all at manifesting the unity of the Mystical Body (*Mediator Dei* {#587}): "to unite them most closely to Christ Jesus"; "to form them into one Body, and unite them with one another as brothers who sit down at the same table to partake of the same *remedy of immortality.*"[336] In this unity we sit down to eat with Jesus and the disciples. We satisfy His desire, Who said: "With desire have I

---

333. Leo XIII, *Mirae Caritatis* (May 28, 1902); *Liturgie: Enseignements Pontificaux*, 152 (#183): ". . . ce sacrement adorable, qui est à Nos yeux le gage principal de nos espérances et de la réalisation du salut et de la paix, objets des voeux inquiets de tous."

334. "my flesh for the life of the world" (John 6:51).

335. "the fruit of redemption" (postcommunion: Mass of the Seven Holy Founders of the Servites [Feb. 12]) (*Missale Romanum*, 512; not in *Missale Cisterciense*).

336. Pius XII, *Mediator Dei* (#120); *Liturgie: Enseignements Pontificaux*, 377: "L'Église de Jésus-Christ n'a que ce seul pain pour satisfaire les aspirations et les désirs de nos âmes, pour les unir très étroitement au Christ Jésus, pour faire finalement 'un seul corps' et les unir entre eux, comme des frères qui s'assoient à la même table pour prendre le remède de l'immortalité en partageant un même pain." Copy text reads "#588" (which refers, like the rest of the numbers in this volume, to its own enumeration of excerpts, not to the documents' original paragraph numbers). The italicized words at the conclusion of Merton's translation are from Ignatius of Antioch, *Letter to the Ephesians*, 20; the quoted words in the French are from 1 Cor 10:17.

desired to eat this Pasch with you."[337] *We sit down in the banquet of heaven* with all the elect—they want our company. *We participate in the Agape of the Divine Persons: omni benedictione coelesti et gratia repleamur.*[338]

Conclusion (Pius XII): "In the Sacrament of the Altar is the center of all Christianity—there God Himself lives in the midst of us and remains with us, Jesus Christ, our Lord, until the end of time. . . . Jesus Christ reigning today triumphantly in heaven as King, hides Himself in our tabernacles . . . waits for us, unites us, calls us to Him in a divine banquet in which He gives Himself as our food, as a prelude to paradise where the veil of faith having been torn asunder, He will give Himself to us face to face in a vision of eternal joy."[339] Meditate on the *Adoro Te,*[340] *Pange Lingua,*[341] *Lauda Sion,*[342] etc. "*Tibi se cor meum totum subjicit / Quia te contemplans totum deficit.*"[343]

ASH WEDNESDAY

"When you fast . . . be not sad" (gospel[344]—looking forward to {the} nuptial feast of Easter). {Note} the paradox of joy on this day of penance. The whole keynote of Lent is not the severity and justice of God, but rather His mercy and goodness to those who are sorry for their sins and

---

337. Luke 22:15.

338. "that we may be filled with every heavenly blessing and grace" ("*Supplices te rogamus*" prayer: canon of the Mass) (*Missale Romanum,* 328; *Missale Cisterciense,* 224).

339. Pius XII, homily at Pontifical Mass, March 3, 1940; *Liturgie: Enseignements Pontificaux,* 273 (#420): "Dans le sacrement de l'autel se trouve le centre de tout le christianisme: là vit et se tient au milieu de nous et avec nous, jusqu'à la consommation des siècles, Dieu Lui-même, Notre-Seigneur Jésus-Christ . . . aujourd'hui roi triomphant dans le ciel, qui mille fois chaque jour se cache dans nos tabernacles sous les espèces du pain transformé par les paroles et les mains des prêtres, et nous attend, nous invite, nous appelle près de Lui à un repas divin, dans lequel Il se donne Lui-même en nourriture, comme un prélude du paradis où, le voile de la foi s'étant déchiré, Il se donnera face à face dans une vision d'éternelle joie."

340. "I adore You [devoutly]" (*Breviarium Cisterciense,* 255*).

341. "Sing, my tongue, [the Savior's glory]" (*Breviarium Cisterciense, Pars Vernalis,* 239–40; *Aestivalis,* 193–94; *Pars Autumnalis,* 314–15).

342. "Sion, sing praise" (sequence: Corpus Christi) (*Missale Romanum,* 398).

343. "My entire heart submits itself to you / since contemplating you it gives way completely" ("*Adoro te,*" ll. 3–4).

344. Matt 6:16–21 (*Missale Romanum,* 65; *Missale Cisterciense,* 55).

who have confidence in Him. *The purpose of Lent* {is} to purify our hearts and open them wide to grace, to draw us nearer to God, that we may be united with Him in the Risen Christ at Easter. But we cannot be drawn to someone of whom we are terrified. This "hiding" of the severity of God is not a kind of trick, or a subterfuge of God. The reality is in fact that in Himself He is *not severe*. He is of Himself loving and merciful. He becomes severe only when we resist Him, and the change is not in Him but *in our relation to Him*. The great law is that we must adapt ourselves to His will (which is all mercy and love), not that He must adapt Himself to our will. If we bend ourselves to His Will, then we are in a position to know Him and be united to Him as He is, as a God of mercy and a loving Father. Only if we refuse this adaptation does He become (in our case) severe. The severity flows not from His nature but from our opposition to Him. {The} atmosphere of peace in Lent is a guarantee of grace. We are not like Atlas carrying the world on his shoulders, but united with the whole Church.

How many expressions of confidence in the divine mercy {there are} in the *Ash* Wednesday liturgy: *Misereris omnium et nihil odisti omnium quae fecisti* (introit[345]); *Exaudi nos Domine quoniam benigna est misericordia tua* (antiphon of {the} blessing of ashes[346]) ({these are} two keynote texts—the openers of the Mass and the blessing, respectively); "The multitude of Thy tender mercies . . ." (antiphon—blessing[347]); "*Serenissima pietas* . . ." (first prayer—blessing[348]); "O God, Who desirest not the death but the repentance of sinners . . ." (second prayer[349]). He is a God Who "looks down most graciously upon the frailty of human nature."[350] He is "moved by humiliation and appeased by satisfaction."[351] He had mercy

---

345. "You have mercy on all and hate nothing of all You have made" (Wis 11:24) (*Missale Romanum*, 63; *Missale Cisterciense*, 54, which read: ". . . *eorum quae* . . .").

346. "Hear us, Lord, for your mercy is gracious" (Ps 68[69]:17) (*Missale Romanum*, 62; *Missale Cisterciense*, 53).

347. "*multitudinem miserationum tuarum*" (*Missale Romanum*, 62; *Missale Cisterciense*, 53).

348. "most serene graciousness" (*Missale Romanum*, 62; *Missale Cisterciense*, 52, which read: "*serenissimam pietatem*").

349. "*Deus, qui non mortem, sed poenitentiam desideras peccatorum*" (*Missale Romanum*, 62; *Missale Cisterciense*, 53).

350. "*fragilitatem conditionis humanae benignissime respice*" (second prayer, which is imperative rather than indicative: "look down . . .") (*Missale Romanum*, 62; *Missale Cisterciense*, 53).

351. "*qui humiliatione flecteris, et satisfactione placaris*" (third prayer) (*Missale*

upon the pagan Ninivites, in spite of the threats of Jonas (the prophet was disappointed!). This mixture of joy and sorrow, confidence and humility, trust in God and distrust of self, is *characteristic of holy compunction*, a grace among others granted to us by worthy participation in the day's liturgy.

Other effects (the ashes are a sacramental!) {include} redemption from sin; health of body and soul; pardon of all sin; grace to earn the reward promised to penitents; and {grace} to gain firm possession of the good spiritual things we need; grace, self-denial and strength to resist our spiritual enemies; the grace to please God by our Lent, etc. (see the prayers of the blessing[352]). Jesus therefore commands us to be joyful. (So does St. Benedict—we expect Easter with "holy joy."[353]) The whole lesson of the gospel[354] is that what most matters is a supernatural intention, a desire to please God. It is not *what* we offer God in itself, that counts; it is the will to please God. But at the same time this intention must be something besides *blind and unenlightened* "good will," or well-meaning stupidity. We must understand Who God is, that He desires of us what we can offer, not some impossible task, but real, sincere generosity within the limits of our capacity. The widow's mite[355] was pleasing to God not because of the quantity—others gave a larger sum—but because it represented the devotion of her *whole heart*. This is a subject on which we have so many wrong ideas. The important thing is the ability to be glad that our Father sees and appreciates what we offer Him. This is to "have our treasure in heaven," and our heart also, {in} simplicity and faith. "Lay up treasures in heaven."[356] Jesus wants us to have true peace that no creature can take away.

Ash Wednesday (II): the blessing of the ashes. It would be a mistake to regard the liturgy of the day as one of unrelieved darkness. {There is} poignancy and compunction—a good school of compunction. Note the themes—and the melodies. THEMES {include}:

Romanum, 63; *Missale Cisterciense*, 53).

352. *Missale Romanum*, 62–63; *Missale Cisterciense*, 52–53.

353. *Rule*, c. 49 (McCann, ed. and trans., *Rule of St. Benedict*, 114, which reads: "*cum spiritalis desiderii gaudio sanctum Pascha exspectet*" ["with the joy of spiritual desire await the holy paschal feast"]).

354. Matt 6:16–21 (*Missale Romanum*, 65; *Missale Cisterciense*, 55).

355. Luke 21:1–4.

356. Matt 5:20.

1. *Mercy of God*: the mercy of God is always uppermost. {See the} *introit* of the Mass: *Misereris omnium et nihil odisti eorum quae fecisti.*[357] God is a loving Creator, looking with love and pity upon His creatures. *Dissimulans peccata*;[358] but He will not look at the sins of those who love Him, if they are repentant. He sees only the repentance and makes as if the sins were not there (in fact, He blots them out in the Blood of Christ—this is the full meaning of *dissimulans*). *Benigna est misericordia tua*[359] (antiphon—note the poignant melody), and the "multitude of His mercies,"[360] {the} infinite treasure of mercy. *Respice nos*:[361] to be looked at by God! (Compunction is the foundation of monastic spirituality—absorb the meaning of these chants.) "*God who desireth not the death of the sinner but his repentance*, look down graciously upon the frailty of human nature . . ."[362] "O God *Who art moved by humiliation* and appeased by satisfaction . . ."[363] (God has pity on those who are reduced to nothing.) Note the expression, His *serenissima pietas*[364] (blessing of ashes); hence the resulting *confidence*. Without this confidence the whole rite is a mockery.

2. *Sense of Sin*:

a) *Intraverunt aquae usque ad animam meam*:[365] {we} feel like drowning men, like a sinking ship, {with} the waters of death seeping into the most inmost part of our being.

b) We who know that we are dust and for the demerits of our wickedness are to return to dust (blessing), {have a} sense that sin has made us revert to nothingness, {a} sense of emptiness of our being without God. Note how deep, how existential, this sense of sin {is}—not an emotional or theatrical display of shame {but a} deep and sincere

---

357. See n. 345 above.

358. "overlooking the sins" (introit) (Wis 11:23) (*Missale Romanum*, 63; *Missale Cisterciense*, 54).

359. See n. 346 above.

360. See n. 347 above.

361. "Look upon us" (Ps 68[69]:17) (*Missale Romanum*, 62; *Missale Cisterciense*, 53).

362. Second prayer (*Missale Romanum*, 62; *Missale Cisterciense*, 53).

363. Third prayer (*Missale Romanum*, 63; *Missale Cisterciense*, 53).

364. See n. 348 above.

365. "The waters have come even up to my soul" (Ps 68[69]:2) (blessing antiphon) (*Missale Romanum*, 62; *Missale Cisterciense*, 53).

penetration into the mystery of culpability before God, {which} can only be expressed by discretion and reserve. {There is a} sense that sin has entered into our inmost being.

3. *Effects of the Blessing* (graces imparted by the sacramental of ashes):

a) They are a *remedium salubre*[366] to all who call upon His Name.

b) They impart *corporis sanitatem et animae tutelam.*[367]

c) They impart pardon of all sins and the rewards promised to penitents (i.e. if they indicate the beginning of a time of penance!—not *ex opere operato*[368]).

d) They bring a special blessing from God, to fill us with compunction, and also to make our prayers and fasts powerful to obtain every grace from Him.

e) Thus we shall have done penance and not be overtaken by death unprepared.

f) In general, we obtain all the graces necessary for the holy war which is Lent, strength to meet temptation and overcome the wiles of evil spirits.

FIRST SUNDAY OF LENT: {this is} a great monastic day in the liturgy, in so far as monks, above all, participate in the mystery of Jesus' fast and temptation in the desert. *The Lenten Curtain:*[369] (a) reminds us that Paradise was closed to fallen man (but it is to be reopened to us by the Risen Savior); (b) {reminds us of} the darkness that stands between us and God (this dark cloud is penetrated by faith and humble prayer) {and} reminds us that God is more truly seen here below in darkness than in light—{and thus} inspires compunction and humility, which bring us closer to God. The Psalm *"Qui Habitat"*[370] (tract): this is the great Lenten Psalm. St. Ber-

---

366. "a wholesome remedy" (first prayer) (*Missale Romanum*, 62; *Missale Cisterciense*, 52).

367. "health of the body and safety of the soul" (first prayer) (*Missale Romanum*, 62; *Missale Cisterciense*, 53).

368. "by the power of the work itself."

369. For the use of the purple curtain, hung in front of the presbytery on the First Sunday of Lent, see *Regulations*, 112 (#234).

370. "He who dwells" (Ps 90[91]) (*Missale Romanum*, 71–72; *Missale Cisterciense*, 61).

nard, preaching on it in Lent, produced a real spiritual directory.[371] {Its} theme {is that} God is the protector of those who hope in Him alone. The psalm is a list of all the dangers from which we can escape by prayer. *Penance* detaches us from human consolations, and makes us rely more purely on God alone. *Prayer* is the big thing. A verse of Psalm 90 is also taken for the introit (*Invocabit me et ego exaudiam eum*[372]). *The epistle*[373] again {provides} a list of sufferings and good works which are the sign of the *acceptable time in which God hears and answers our prayers.* Lent is such a time. {In} *the gospel,*[374] the mystery of Christ's debate with the evil spirit is beyond our level of understanding. Is there, can there be a really satisfactory explanation of these things? (a) Christ was truly tempted; (b) the identity of the "tempter" or "*diabolus*"—we are crazy if we really think we know exactly what a devil is; (c) the meaning of the triple temptation. By meditation on the text, we see that the devil uses the mysteries of Scripture in a subtle but relatively shallow way (relative to Christ, but not to us), and Jesus replies in a much more mysterious way. The devil's phrases can mean many things. Jesus' replies contain, in some way, *everything*. From a certain point of view the three temptations are different; from another, they are all one. They all tend to pride and self-assertion, deviation from God's order; and all these, explicitly or implicitly, invoke adoration of the devil. Note {that} Jesus' second answer can be taken as a direct, simple reply to Satan: "In tempting me you are tempting the Lord Your God." The real mystery of this gospel *lies in the innumerable different depths and possibilities of meaning in each answer given by the Lord.*

SECOND SUNDAY OF LENT

Why the Gospel of the Transfiguration?[375] Jesus, Moses, Elias all fasted for forty days. (N.B. Moses and Elias in the lessons of ember week[376]).

---

371. Migne, *PL* 183, cols. 185B–254C.

372. "He will call me and I shall answer Him" (v. 15) (*Missale Romanum*, 71; *Missale Cisterciense*, 60).

373. 2 Cor 6:1–10 (*Missale Romanum*, 71; *Missale Cisterciense*, 60–61).

374. Matt 4:1–11 (*Missale Romanum*, 72; *Missale Cisterciense*, 61).

375. Matt 17:1–9 (*Missale Romanum*, 85; *Missale Cisterciense*, 74).

376. The lessons for Wednesday of Ember Week in Lent are Exod 24:12–18, which concludes with mention of Moses's forty days and forty nights on Mount Sinai (*Missale Romanum*, 76; *Missale Cisterciense*, 65–66); and 3 Kgs [1 Kgs] 19:3–8, which is the story of Elijah's journey of forty days and forty nights to Mount Horeb on the strength of the food given him by the angel (*Missale Romanum*, 76; *Missale Cisterciense*, 66).

The light of the Risen Christ will shine in us and "transfigure" our souls at Easter if we are generous in Lent. *Points on this gospel* {include}:

1. Peter does not sufficiently distinguish between Jesus, Moses, Elias. He seems to put all on an equal plane; hence the bright cloud and the voice from heaven, "This is my beloved Son, hear ye *Him*"[377]— no longer the law and the prophets. Then {comes a} great fear, and they see Jesus alone.

2. Degrees of the Spiritual Life: (a) consolations and joys, the "lights" of contemplation; (b) the "darkness" of contemplation—humiliation and trial; (c) the revelation of *Jesus alone*; (d) in the highest maturity of the spiritual life, all is again ordinary, but now truly one sees Jesus alone in all things. "*Jesus Alone*": we must truly learn to see Jesus alone, in events—all events have their purpose, especially those we find crucifying; in companions and superiors—all are instruments of God—we need one another; *in the community itself*: learn to consider the good of the whole as far more important than our own private good, {with} charity, {in} unity—the good of all and our own too at the same time. To see Jesus alone is to forget ourselves and give up our own private good for the unity and the common aims of the community, to give up one's own projects and aims in order to fall in with plans of superiors, to see Jesus in a unified community where the first superior works through his officers and associates, all with one common purpose. {Beware} the *sin of sowing division*, creating distrust, {playing} "politics" in community. "Is the Church divided?" "Is Christ divided?"[378] See each member in the whole body, not taking a "disintegrated" and separatist view, pitting individuals against one another (especially superiors). Hence the importance of the statute on detraction (read today in chapter[379]). Everything depends on *how we think* about others, and especially about superiors.

---

377. Matt 17:5.

378. 1 Cor 1:13.

379. Originally read by the cantor on the First Sunday of Advent (*Regulations*, 103, 282 [##215, 594]), subsequently switched to the Second Sunday of Lent (handwritten note to *Regulations*, #232 [111] in copy at the Abbey of Gethsemani).

Wednesday of the Fourth Week in Lent: the "Great Scrutiny"

Even to one who knows nothing of the history of the liturgy, it is clear from the Mass texts that this day's liturgy has much to do with the holy sacrament of baptism. {We hear} in the introit:[380] "I will pour upon you clean water and you shall be cleansed from all your filthiness and I will give you a new spirit." The first lesson from Ezechiel[381] repeats these words, of which it is the source. It gives further details about the "new spirit"—the Holy Ghost will be given to the faithful. In the gradual[382] that follows this lesson—*accedite ad eum et illuminamini*[383]—baptism is the sacrament of illumination. In the lesson from Isaias,[384] full remission of sins is promised: "if your sins be as scarlet, they shall be made white as snow, and if they be red as crimson they shall be made white as wool." Above all, the gospel,[385] in which the man born blind is sent to wash in the pool of Siloe, and in which he recognizes Jesus as the Son of God and adores Him, obviously is a preparation for baptism. At the same time, however, the "illumination" spoken of in the first gradual refers to the Scriptures. The gradual after the epistle[386] more explicitly points to the word of God and to the Spirit: "By the word of the Lord the heavens were established and all the power of them by the spirit of His mouth." (Word and spirit here literally refer to the command and the creative power of God; by application they mean the Second and Third Persons of the Holy Trinity.) Finally, the "recognition" of Christ by the man born blind refers also to the grace by which the new catechumens will know Jesus in the Scriptures.

This rich liturgy is then full of special graces and meanings. To understand it we must go back to the "great scrutiny." On this day the candidates for baptism at Easter were assembled, recognized and adopted by the Church officially as catechumens, and began their proximate preparation for baptism. What happened? (1) Special prayers were recited over the assembled candidates, and blessings were given, and they became catechumens officially; (2) Some of the rites of baptism were performed

380. Ezek 36:23–26 (*Missale Romanum*, 114; *Missale Cisterciense*, 104).

381. Ezek 36:23–28 (*Missale Romanum*, 115; *Missale Cisterciense*, 104–105).

382. Ps 33[34]:12, 6 (*Missale Romanum*, 115; *Missale Cisterciense*, 105).

383. "Draw near to him and be enlightened."

384. Isa 1:16–19 (*Missale Romanum*, 115; *Missale Cisterciense*, 105).

385. John 9:1–38 (*Missale Romanum*, 116–17; *Missale Cisterciense*, 105–106).

386. Ps 32[33]:12, 6 (*Missale Romanum*, 115; *Missale Cisterciense*, 105).

at this time, notably the tasting of the salt and the "opening of the ears" (*ephpheta*),[387] both of which have reference to the Scriptures. The four Gospels were then introduced to the catechumens by readings and a brief explanation of what the "Gospel" is. Finally the creed was recited, and they were taught the *Pater* with a brief commentary.

The Wednesday of the fourth week of Lent is for us the beginning of the last stage of Lent, the final preparation for Holy Week and Easter. It reminds us above all that *the Easter mystery is the mystery of our death and resurrection in Christ by baptism*, that we relive this mystery each time we participate in the Holy Eucharist, and also each time we do so we receive the Holy Spirit and advance in sanctification, while the whole Body of Christ progresses toward the final consummation, the glorious Easter of eternity. Let us meditate on the profound mystery of *renewal* and new birth, the transforming action of the Spirit of God in the Easter mystery in which we are divinized in the death and resurrection of the Savior and become one spirit with Him and the Father.

Passiontide

We now come to the heart of the liturgical year. The liturgy cannot be understood by one who has not lived with the Church the Easter mystery. This understanding cannot be gained from books and conferences, even though they may be "about" the liturgy. These may indeed open to us the way to a more fruitful participation, but *participation itself is the only key to the mystery*. Note: Holy Week is not the *end* but the beginning. Lent and Holy Week are the *preparation for Easter which lasts 50 days!*

First of all, note that each day we celebrate and share in the Easter mystery in Holy Mass. But it is also necessary that at this culminating point in the liturgical year the whole mystery itself be explicitly set out before us and that we celebrate it in all its fullness and in all its aspects. And so now, after a period of purification and instruction, we turn our whole attention *to the celebration of the Passion of Christ by the People of God*. {We need to understand} the word "celebration": to celebrate is to solemnize publicly, with sacred rites, which *proclaim the glory* of the act celebrated, and in the fullest sense *communicate* to those who share in the celebration *a share in that glory*. What we celebrate in the Passion is not the sufferings of Christ but *His victory*. More precisely, we who celebrate His victory declare the glory He has won by His victory over

---

387. "be opened" (Mark 7:34).

death, and in which He reigns enthroned at the right hand of the Father. We celebrate this glory by living through His struggle and victory over death. But this is done in mystery, and in the fullest imaginable sense by the fact that He Who reigns in glory, *during this celebration, actually dies and rises again in us.* How? spiritually, mystically—by grace; through the sacramental action of the liturgy. {We must} distinguish—it is not a physical participation in the Passion (feelings of suffering do not add to the celebration), nor is it a moral or psychological participation. *The participation is mystical and sacramental,* through the action of the liturgy. The liturgy does not work by magic. The rites and prayers are not incantations. Our *participation* is what counts. This means:

a) Receiving the word of God in the great liturgical texts, with a heart wide open to grace; hence the *invitatorium* of vigils {for} Passion Sunday: "Today if you should hear His voice, harden not your hearts."[388] See also the gospel: "if any man shall keep my word he shall not taste death forever."[389]

b) Devotion in the celebration of the *Paschale sacramentum* (St. Leo, fifth lesson: Passion Sunday[390])—entering into the liturgical sacrifice of Christ.

c) By *commune consortium Crucis Christi*[391]—fasting, penance, suffering, trial, as St. Leo points out (second nocturn). The grace of the Cross gives us strength to bear our own cross throughout life, as we travel to join the risen Savior in eternity. {These are} the last renunciations that will purify our hearts before Easter; let us not refuse them.

388. "*Hodie si vocem Domini audieritis, Nolite obdurare corda vestra*" (*Breviarium Cisterciense, Vernalis,* 239).

389. John 8:51 (*Missale Romanum,* 124; *Missale Cisterciense,* 114).

390. "paschal sacrament" (*Sermo 9 de Quadragesima*) (*Breviarium Cisterciense, Vernalis,* 242).

391. "a common participation in the cross of Christ" (*Breviarium Cisterciense, Vernalis,* 242).

Some Big Themes of the Liturgy:

1. *Judica me*[392]—Why is the psalm *judica* suppressed in the prayers at the foot of the altar?[393] not because it has become unimportant; on the contrary, here is where this psalm has its rightful place in the Mass itself—{the} *introit* of Passion Sunday,[394] {the} *gradual* {for} Tuesday.[395] {It} strikes the keynote of the Passion: the Just One is stricken for our sins. But He speaks the psalm *in us*. Because of His presence in us, we who are sinners become just. We can dare challenge the Father to judge us, for we are loved and redeemed by the Son (*discerne causam meam de gente non sancta*[396]); we *pass over* in Christ from the ungodly to the godly. We are like Jacob in the garments of Esau. God sends forth the light of Truth that drew Christ Himself to the mount of Calvary and thence to the Holy Mountain of the heavenly Sion and into the tabernacle of heaven. This light will shine on us in the great liturgical mystery. The cry of the Just One unjustly delivered into the hands of sinners rings out through the whole of Passion time. From this we realize that the Church contemplates the interior sufferings of Christ even more than His physical sufferings. These are the sufferings of God, the God of Truth, delivered into the hands of liars; of Light, become a prey to darkness; of Love delivered over to hatred. In a word, through the interior sufferings of Christ we can begin to glimpse dimly something of the awful mystery of the opposition of sin to God, and of God "becoming sin"[397] and allowing Himself to die in order that we might live, in order that our death may be changed into life, our lies into truth, our darkness into light. Notice especially the anguish of Truth delivered over to the injustice and lies!

Insurrexerunt in me testes iniqui, et mentita est iniquitas sibi.[398] One of the most profound and terrible revelations of the mystery of sin {is} the corrupt witness of sinners against the Truth itself, {which} ends only in the defeat of sin and untruth by its own iniquity. One sees here at

392. Ps 42[43].

393. *Missale Romanum*, 226; *Missale Cisterciense*, 178 (omitted from Passion Sunday through Holy Thursday, inclusive).

394. Ps 42[43]:1–3 (*Missale Romanum*, 123; *Missale Cisterciense*, 113).

395. Ps 42[43]:1, 3 (*Missale Romanum*, 128; *Missale Cisterciense*, 117).

396. "distinguish my cause from that of an unholy people" (Ps 42[43]:1).

397. 2 Cor 5:21.

398. "False witnesses have risen up against me, and wickedness has lied to itself" (Ps 26[27]:12) (versicle, second nocturn: Passion Sunday) (*Breviarium Cisterciense, Vernalis*, 242).

once the tragedy of Christ delivered into the hands of the unjust, and the inevitable victory of Christ over their injustice—because since there is and can be nothing in common between light and darkness, in defeating the light the darkness only defeats itself, for darkness is nothing but the absence of light. Yet we sense the dreadful mystery of darkness that sought to abolish itself by abolishing the Light without which it could not even be darkness.

Tota die contristatus ingrediebar quoniam anima mea repleta est illusionibus.[399] {Here we find} the Truth of God suffering in us, the anguish of the Spirit within us, as we are ground between the millstones of suffering, the opposition of light and darkness in our own souls, our share in the agony of Christ. This theme of struggle against iniquity and falsity comes out most poignantly in the gospel of the day[400] (John 8): "If I say the truth to you, why do you not believe me?"[401] He promises eternal life, and in it the fulfillment of all the promises, all that the Jews have awaited for centuries. He points to Abraham and shows He is the fulfillment, and the Jews say He has a devil. He shows not only His own innocence but the very nature of innocence and justice, and He is essentially both: "I honor My Father—you have dishonored Me."[402] (Have we lost the sense of words like dishonor, treachery?) "If I glorify Myself My glory is nothing: it is My Father that glorifieth Me of Whom *you say* He is your God . . . . I know Him, and if I say I know Him not I shall be like to you a liar."[403] Jesus is truth, because He does not seek His own glory, does not live for Himself. The Pharisees are falsity and darkness because they seek only themselves; and they think they are just in doing so, not realizing that they abide in death because they refuse the only hope of salvation from the darkness with which they are satisfied. All through this, we see the great theme that GOD ALONE is the help of the Just One, and in this consists the justice of Jesus as well as our own: the repeated cries to God to defend Him, to vindicate Him, to save Him. These cries must be ours, but we address them to the Savior Himself Who, in us, as we cry to Him, cries out to the Father in us. The summary of this whole theme of truth

399. "The whole day I go about saddened, for my soul is filed with illusions" (Ps 37[38]:7–8) (responsory, eighth lesson: Passion Sunday) (*Breviarium Cisterciense, Vernalis,* 243, which reads: ". . . *ingrediebar Domine quoniam . . .*").

400. John 8:46–59 (*Missale Romanum,* 124; *Missale Cisterciense,* 114).

401. John 8:46.

402. John 8:49.

403. John 8:54, 55.

rejected and outraged justice {is found in} the antiphons of *sext* and *none* during Passion Week: *Popule meus, quid feci tibi? Aut quid molestus fui? Responde mihi*[404] (cf. the *Improperia* of Good Friday[405]). *Numquid redditur pro bono malum? Quia foderunt foveam animae meae.*[406] In neither of these do we get any indication of a God that hates His sinful creature and seeks only revenge; rather it is the voice of a God of love Who seeks only to do good to His creatures. They judge themselves in rejecting Him. The antiphon of none is as it were the cry of God's truth in the very law of our nature which He created; for it is even against man's nature to render evil for good. Yet God protests {that} we not only violate the natural law flagrantly among ourselves, but man has even seized the opportunity to render infinite evil to God Who has given him every good. The suffering Redeemer is everywhere in the liturgy of Passiontide, which thereby becomes a true spiritual commentary on many texts of the Old Testament, especially of the psalms. We find Jesus in Daniel in the lions' den (Tuesday, Passion Week[407]); Jeremias (lessons of {the} night office;[408] epistle: Friday in Passion Week;[409] Saturday *ibid.*;[410] epistle, Tuesday of Holy Week,[411] and especially the Lamentations[412]); the Servant of Yahweh, Isaias 53 (Wednesday of Holy Week[413]); *Psalms* 118[414] (all the little hours, last three

---

404. "My people, what have I done to you? How have I offended you? Answer me" (*Breviarium Cisterciense, Vernalis*, 251).

405. *Missale Romanum*, 184–85; *Missale Cisterciense*, 157–59.

406. "Is evil returned for good? For they have dug a pit for my soul" (Jer 18:20) (*Breviarium Cisterciense, Vernalis*, 251).

407. Dan 14:27, 28–42 (*Missale Romanum*, 127–28; *Missale Cisterciense*, 117).

408. Jer 1:1–16 (first nocturn: Passion Sunday); Jer 2:12–32 (first nocturn: Palm Sunday) (*Breviarium Cisterciense, Vernalis*, 240–41, 261–62).

409. Jer 17:13–18 (*Missale Romanum*, 134; *Missale Cisterciense*, 122).

410. Jer 18:18–23 (*Missale Romanum*, 136; *Missale Cisterciense*, 123).

411. Jer 11:18–20 (*Missale Romanum*, 154; *Missale Cisterciense*, 136).

412. Tract: Feast of the Seven Dolors (Friday in Passion Week) (1:12) (*Missale Romanum*, 538–39; *Missale Cisterciense*, 394); antiphon, terce: Passion Sunday (3:58); first nocturn: Holy Thursday (c. 1); first nocturn: Good Friday (cc. 2, 3); first nocturn: Holy Saturday (cc. 3, 4, 5) (*Breviarium Cisterciense, Vernalis*, 247, 277–79, 287–89, 296–97).

413. vv. 1–12 (*Missale Romanum*, 160; *Missale Cisterciense*, 140–41).

414. Offertory: Passion Sunday (vv. 17, 107); introit: Thursday, Passion Week (v. 1); communion: Thursday, Passion Week (vv. 49–50); offertory: Friday, Saturday, Passion Week (vv. 12, 121, 42) (*Missale Romanum*, 124, 131, 133, 135, 137; *Missale Cisterciense*, 114, 120, 121, 123, 124).

days of Holy Week[415]), 54,[416] 53,[417] 102,[418] 6,[419] 26,[420] 13,[421] 9,[422] 24,[423] 17,[424] 29,[425] 25,[426] 30,[427] especially *Psalm* 21 (the tract for Palm Sunday, etc.[428]).

2. *The Triumph of the Cross*: although we have so far seen the sufferings of the Redeemer, especially in so far as in Him Truth and Love are destroyed by falsity and hatred, yet always and essentially the Passion is the TRIUMPH OF TRUTH AND OF LOVE. Hence even in the darkest hours of Passiontide, the note of triumph and victory sounds out clear

415. *Breviarium Cisterciense, Vernalis*, 284–85.

416. Introit: Thursday after Ash Wednesday (vv. 17, 19, 20, 23); gradual (vv. 23, 17–19); gradual: Tuesday, second week (vv. 23, 17–19); offertory: Monday, third week (vv. 2–3); introit: Tuesday, fourth week (vv. 2–4) (*Missale Romanum*, 66, 67, 87, 99, 113; *Missale Cisterciense*, 56, 77, 89, 103).

417. Gradual: Monday, Passion Week (vv. 4, 3) (*Missale Romanum*, 126; *Missale Cisterciense*, 116); prime: Holy Thursday; second nocturn: Good Friday; third nocturn: Holy Saturday (*Breviarium Cisterciense, Vernalis*, 284, 289, 300).

418. Tract, Ash Wednesday, Monday of second week (v. 10) (*Missale Romanum*, 65–66; *Missale Cisterciense*, 54–55).

419. Offertory: Monday, Passion Week (v. 5) (*Missale Romanum*, 126; *Missale Cisterciense*, 116).

420. Introit: Tuesday, Passion Week (vv. 14, 1) (*Missale Romanum*, 127; *Missale Cisterciense*, 117); first nocturn: Good Friday; second nocturn: Holy Saturday (*Breviarium Cisterciense, Vernalis*, 287, 298).

421. Communion: Monday of third week (v. 7) (*Missale Romanum*, 99; *Missale Cisterciense*, 89).

422. Offertory: Tuesday, Passion Week (vv. 11–13) (*Missale Romanum*, 128; *Missale Cisterciense*, 118).

423. Communion: Tuesday, Passion Week (v. 22) (*Missale Romanum*, 129; *Missale Cisterciense*, 118).

424. Gradual: Passion Sunday (vv. 48–49); introit: Wednesday, Passion Week (vv. 48–49, 2–3) (*Missale Romanum*, 124, 129; *Missale Cisterciense*, 114, 118).

425. Gradual: Wednesday, Passion Week (vv. 2–4) (*Missale Romanum*, 130; *Missale Cisterciense*, 119); second nocturn: Holy Saturday (*Breviarium Cisterciense, Vernalis*, 298).

426. Communion: Wednesday, Passion Week (vv. 6–7) (*Missale Romanum*, 131; *Missale Cisterciense*, 120).

427. Introit: Friday, Saturday, Passion Week (vv. 10, 16, 18, 2) (*Missale Romanum*, 134, 136; *Missale Cisterciense*, 122, 123); compline: Holy Thursday (*Breviarium Cisterciense, Vernalis*, 285).

428. Introit: Palm Sunday (vv. 20, 22); tract: Palm Sunday (vv. 2–9, 18–19, 22, 24, 32); stripping of the altars: Holy Thursday (*Missale Romanum*, 146, 170; *Missale Cisterciense*, 128, 129); responsory, versicle, vespers: Passion Sunday (v. 22); versicle, responsory, first nocturn: Monday, Passion Week (v. 19); first nocturn: Good Friday (*Breviarium Cisterciense, Vernalis*, 248, 249, 287).

and unmistakable above every other. We should realize that this note of victory is the forerunner of Easter, and ties in the Passion with Easter. Some people act as if there were a break, a division, between the Passion and the Resurrection in the liturgy, as if the main thing were to commemorate the Passion and then stop, and rest up—during Paschal time—as though Easter were only a negative of Holy Week, a time when we "no longer think about suffering and the Cross so much," but go back to our everyday concerns. How truly un-Christian such an attitude would be! And equally un-Christian would be one which insisted that "though Holy Week is over we must continue to think above all of the sufferings of Jesus and His shameful death." A most important distinction must be made. Surely we must at all times honor and love the Cross above all else, but precisely because it is the *sign of victory*. We must not forget the Passion of Christ, indeed, but we must remember it as part of His triumph. Otherwise the whole thing is meaningless. If Christ be not risen from the dead, vain is our faith.[429] In the early days of the Church the "crown of life" was given to the baptized at Easter and also placed upon the Cross, as a token of the Easter victory. The *Vexilla Regis*[430] is one of the most stately hymns of triumph in the liturgy. It belongs to the days when the crucifixes in our churches were splendid with gems and represented Christ as a King. (Only in the Middle Ages did the piety of the faithful turn rather to the more realistic representation of the suffering Redeemer.) *Fulget Crucis Mysterium*:[431] in this great mystery we see the radiance of the divine light, of pure Truth, of supreme wisdom, the wisdom of God, which is only revealed in mystery, and in one mystery, the mystery of Christ. The note of suffering is by no means absent, but always subservient to the great mystery. *Carne carnis Conditor suspensus est patibulo—Manavit unda et sanguine ut nos lavaret crimine.*[432] However, Christ triumphs on the Cross: *Regnavit a ligno Deus;*[433] the cross is *Arbor decora et fulgida or-*

429. 1 Cor 15:14.

430. "Standard of the King" (vespers: Passion Sunday) (*Breviarium Cisterciense, Vernalis*, 248–49).

431. "the mystery of the Cross shines forth" (l. 2).

432. "The Creator of the flesh was suspended in the flesh from the cross; . . . He poured forth water and blood to cleanse us from sin" (ll. 3–4, 8, 7).

433. "God reigned from the tree" (l. 12).

nata Regis purpura.[434] In conclusion we pray: *Quos per crucis mysterium salvas rege per saecula.*[435]

3. *The Pascha Christi*—the true Passover (see the epistle for Passion Sunday: *Hebrews* 9[436]): *Christus assistens Pontifex futurorum bonorum.*[437] Christ *stands*; He now stands representing us, in the sanctuary of heaven, the true priest, the High Priest, not of this world, not of the things of time, not of a merely outward purification, a merely transient rite, but of the "good things to come," the life of heaven and *eternal redemption.* "He has entered into the Holy of Holies, with the sacrifice of His own blood."[438] This sacrifice is offered for us now. Where? on our own altars, by Christ Himself. What is done visibly by the priest at the altar is done invisibly by Christ at the altar, and in heaven. It is the sacrifice of perfect love, the pure love of the Incarnate Word for His Father and for us. He sheds His own Blood in order that we, entering into His sacrifice with Him, may be able to offer our love and reparation to the Father, and above all may be able to offer the sacrifice of our own hearts and our own wills, with His, to the Father. It is thus that we are "cleansed from dead works to serve the living God."[439] All works done without Christ are dead, for without His love and His sacrifice, everything that is done is done without love for God, and indeed all remains outside the sphere of His love and in the sphere of corruption and hatred. "Therefore He is the Mediator of the New Testament . . . that they that are called may receive the promise of eternal inheritance in Christ Jesus Our Lord."[440] If Christ our pasch is slain,[441] we too must enter with Him into the Holy of Holies. But the liturgy does not make clear what this involves until we reach the culminating point of the mystery in the Paschal Vigil. What we look forward to, then, in these two weeks, is a specific liturgical action, for which all the rest is a preparation; it is the sacred rite of the Easter Vigil, the Holy Eucharist, celebrated in the night illuminated by the *new fire* of the Resurrection. Our "*pascha*"— our passage in mystery from death to life—is *our participation in this*

434. "a beautiful and shining tree, adorned with the King's purple" (ll. 13–14).

435. "Rule forever those whom You save through the mystery of the Cross" (ll. 31–32).

436. Heb 9:11–15 (*Missale Romanum*, 123–24; *Missale Cisterciense*, 114).

437. "Christ present as the High Priest of future goods" (vs. 11).

438. Heb 9:11, 12.

439. Heb 9:14.

440. Heb 9:15.

441. See 1 Cor 5:7.

sacred mystery. The Easter Vigil will reawaken our minds to the great truth that each day, in our Mass, we share in the *pascha Christi*, the Easter mystery, and death is vanquished by life, darkness by light, hatred by love. One thing however is emphasized in the Passiontide liturgy: the *pascha Christi*, by which Christ Himself leads us through death to eternal life, is accomplished as a *sacrifice*. More than that, not only is the slaying of Christ our *pasch a* sacrifice, but it is *the* only true sacrifice, the only one that avails in God's sight to atone for sin, to bring souls to union with Him, and to give Him true glory. The value of Christ's sacrifice is *infinite*. Our communion in His sacrifice, and our union with God through this sacred mystery, is *perfect*. Finally, His sacrifice unites us perfectly with one another, in Christ Who is slain, and Who rises from the dead to live, by His Holy Spirit, in all His members. We believe that Jesus offered Himself on the Cross as a perfect sacrifice for the sins of the world, to liberate man from sin and unite him to God redeemed and sanctified. This sacrifice was consummated once for all on the Cross, but Jesus in the Mass gave His Church a divine mystery in which the one, perfect sacrifice could be renewed over and over again in an unbloody manner. Having first offered this sacrifice Himself at the Last Supper, He placed it in the hands of His priests, instructing them to offer it with Him and in Him to the end of time. Our Mass is the same sacrifice, the same offering of the same victim, by the same priest, but in a different manner. This is the Paschal Mystery. There are many other evidences of this triumphant paschal spirit all through Passiontide, for instance, the preface of Passiontide. The *preface* is always a great hymn of thanksgiving, solemnly opening the canon of the Eucharistic sacrifice, the supreme sacrifice of thanksgiving and praise. This is true also of Passion time: It is truly meet and just, right and availing to salvation, that we should *at all times and in all places give thanks* to Thee, O Holy God.[442] This is at once the pure paschal spirit, and the connecting bond that unifies the whole liturgy in all its seasons; it is *always* and *above all* a sacrifice of praise, thanksgiving, jubilation. What is the motive of thanksgiving in Passiontide? "Who didst set the salvation of mankind upon the tree of the Cross"—or better, "Who didst make the salvation of mankind depend on the Cross—*so that whence came death thence also life might rise again*, and that he that overcame by the tree

---

442. "*Vere dignum et justum est, aequum et salutare, nos tibi semper, et ubique gratias agere: Domine sancte*" (preface of the Holy Cross: the wording is identical to the standard preface) (*Missale Romanum*, 312; *Missale Cisterciense*, 211).

on the tree also might be overcome."[443] This is the characteristic Easter perspective. Death has been conquered by the death of Christ, and man's vocation is to be saved and to jubilantly praise God's plan for eternity, in this wonderful mystery. For the Cross is the great revelation of the unconquerable love and mercy of God.

Palm Sunday opens Holy Week with a day of triumph. Palm Sunday gives us a very good opportunity to see the difference between what the Fathers called *literal* and *spiritual* interpretation of the Scriptures. {According to} the letter, the Jews who were about to crucify Christ received Him with shouts of acclamation when He entered Jerusalem. Some pious writers labor the idea that the "very same" Jews who acclaimed Him on Sunday, cried *Crucifige*[444] on Good Friday. That may have been true; and in any case, the Jewish people certainly acclaimed Him on Sunday and crucified Him on Friday. But Palm Sunday is *something more* than a manifestation of fickle enthusiasm on the part of the Jews, and this is what we must try to understand. The inner reality of the Palm Sunday celebration, particularly the procession and what goes with it, is a *representation in mystery of Christ's triumph* which was to come through the Passion and Resurrection, and it is equally a representation in mystery of the triumph of the Whole Christ, the entrance of the Mystical Body into the glory of the Father. In one way there is a contrast between Palm Sunday and Easter Sunday, but in another sense they are different aspects of the same mystery. The "human" triumph of Palm Sunday already contains in figure and in mystery the triumph of Easter and the crowning victory of the Last Day. Jesus consented, indeed willed, to enter Jerusalem in triumph, because He was indeed a King, and this triumph was, in figure, a true triumph. When the Pharisees told Him to rebuke the children who cried Hosanna, He rebuked the Pharisees in turn for not realizing that a fulfillment of scriptural prophecy was taking place before their very eyes, not only in the acclamations of the children, but in *everything* that went on at that time.[445] We must realize the same thing: here is fulfillment, and further prophecy. Here we enter with Jesus in the greatest of sacred

443. "*Qui salutem humani generis in ligno Crucis constituisti: ut unde mors oriebatur, inde vita resurgeret; et qui in ligno vincebat, in ligno quoque vinceretur*" (preface of the Holy Cross) (*Missale Romanum*, 312; *Missale Cisterciense*, 211).

444. "Crucify [him]" (Matt 27:23; Mark 15:13, 14; Luke 23:21; John 19:15).

445. Luke 19:39–40.

realities, which includes our own salvation. The Church prays before the Blessing of the Palms: "O God, Whom to love above all is righteousness [*quem diligere et amare justitia est*], multiply in us the gifts of Thy ineffable grace, and since Thou hast given us in the death of Thy Son to hope for those things which we believe, grant us by the Resurrection of the same to attain to the end to which we aspire."[446] {This is a} rich collect, full of theology. From the Cross, we receive faith, to realize what God has promised, {and} hope, which will merit possession of the promises. But we remain at present in the darkness of faith and hope in which the promises are veiled under figures and attained only in mystery. However, this real grasp of the substance of what is promised is gained for us by the Cross, *now*. Through the Resurrection, we will actually enter into the full and clear possession of the good things of God promised and won for us by Christ; cf. St. Thomas, III, q. 49, a. 5:[447] since sin is the obstacle that prevents us from entering heaven, the Passion of Christ, by destroying sin, has opened to us the gate of heaven. {See} III, q. 56, a. 1 and 2:[448] the Resurrection of Christ is the efficient cause of the resurrection of our bodies and of our souls. See a. 1, ad 1: "The resurrection of Christ is the cause of our resurrection by the power of the Word united to His flesh. And this works according to His will. Hence the effect ought not necessarily to follow right away, but rather according to the way the Word of God has disposed that it should take effect, namely, that we should first be conformed to Christ suffering and dying, in this suffering and mortal life, and then that we may attain to participation in the likeness of His

---

446. "*Deus, quem diligere et amare justitia est, ineffabilis gratiae tuae in nobis dona multiplica: et qui fecisti nos in morte Filii tui sperare quae credimus; fac nos eodem resurgente pervenire quo tendimus*" (*Missale Romanum*, 139).

447. St. Thomas Aquinas, *Summa Theologiae, Pars Tertia*, q. 49, a. 5: "*Utrum Christus sua passione aperuerit nobis januam caeli*" ("Whether by His Passion Christ opened the gate of heaven to us") (Aquinas, *Opera Omnia*, 4.219–20).

448. "*De Resurrectionis Christi Causalitate: 1. Utrum resurrectio Christi sit causa resurrectionis corporum*" ("On the Causality of the Resurrection of Christ: 1. Whether the resurrection of Christ is the cause of the resurrection of bodies") (St. Thomas Aquinas, *Opera Omnia*, 4:246–47); "*2. Utrum resurrectio Christi sit causa resurrectionis animarum*" ("2. Whether the resurrection of Christ is the cause of the resurrection of souls") (St. Thomas Aquinas, *Opera Omnia*, 4:247–48).

Resurrection."[449] {See} {ad} 4:[450] both His Passion and His Resurrection cause (by efficient causality), by divine power, our justification in two respects—by the destruction of sin, and the conferring of a new life. But from the point of view of exemplar causality, the Passion causes the destruction of sin and the resurrection causes the bestowal of new life.

In the Palm Sunday procession we take the part of the *Pueri Hebraeorum*,[451] and hail Christ as our King. The procession symbolizes our life's course through the world, a course in which we are faced with the decision of choosing between Christ and the leaders of the people, moved by purely expedient and pragmatic motives: how to defend the immediate interests of those in power. (The responsory—*collegerunt*:[452] note the solemn and ominous tone of this responsory; it is a *council*, a deliberation, of the "world." On the basis of pure expediency, with an apparent good in view, it is decided to sacrifice Christ and save the people. {Note} the irony of Caiphas' prophecy—PROPHETAVIT *dicens!*[453]—the awful mystery that Christ is indeed delivered to death by His people, and the People is nevertheless saved by Him.) The mystery of Palm Sunday opens our eyes to this, and makes us resolve to be among the poor and the unworldly who are united to Christ and perhaps have to suffer persecution at the hands of the powerful, for we will inevitably stand in the way of their "wise plan." Hence we decide, we choose Christ, we prostrate in adoration, and with our hearts full of faith we choose Christ, not the world. (*Ave Rex Noster*[454]—see Holy Week outline[455].) Then the angels

449. "*resurrectio Christi est causa nostrae resurrectionis per virtutem Verbi uniti; quod quidem operatur secundum voluntatem. Et ideo non oportet quod statim sequatur effectus, sed secundum dispositionem Verbi Dei, ut scilicet primo conformemur Christo patienti et morienti in hac vita passibili et mortali; deinde perveniamus ad participandum similitudinem resurrectionis ipsius*" (St. Thomas Aquinas, *Opera Omnia*, 4:247).

450. St. Thomas Aquinas, *Opera Omnia*, 4.247 (text reads: "a. 4").

451. "the children of the Hebrews" (procession, first antiphon) (*Missale Romanum*, 144; *Missale Cisterciense*, 127).

452. "[the princes of the nations] have gathered together" (John 11:47) (*Missale Romanum*, 140).

453. "speaking, he prophesied" (John 11:51) (*Missale Romanum*, 140).

454. "Hail, Our King" (procession hymn) (*Missale Cisterciense*, 127; not in *Missale Romanum*).

455. See below, 94–97.

in heaven (*gloria laus*[456]—inside the Church door), and the Church triumphant, intone the prophetic chant prefiguring the triumph of the last day, and we, the Church, in mystery, enter into heaven with the Savior (symbolized by our entrance into the basilica). At the same time we enter with Christ into the sanctuary where He is offered in sacrifice.

WEDNESDAY OF HOLY WEEK

Isaias 53: The Passion of the Servant of Yahweh (cf. {the} Four Songs of the Servant: 42:1–4 [Advent Liturgy[457]]; 49:1–6 [Feast {of} St. John {the} Baptist[458]]; 50:4–9 [Monday, Holy Week[459]]; 52:13–53{:12} [Wednesday, Holy Week[460]]). The prophet announces that the Servant of Yahweh will not only fail but will be put to death by His People, who do not know how to recognize in Him the Messias. But the conversion of the Gentiles will be the fruit of His death. {This is} one of the Old Testament texts in which the *agape* of God's love for me is most mysteriously and deeply revealed. God's love comes *to us in a form which we can easily despise*. It appears to us as weakness. It is a scandal—it even can be seen and condemned under the guise of evil.

Line 1: no one has believed the prophet. No one has accepted the revelation of the power of God in the weakness of the servant of Yahweh. {*Line*} 2: the promised rod rising out of the root of Jesse shall rise up in barren and arid soil, in a time, in circumstances that the people do not expect and do not prize. {There is} no form or majesty to attract their human ideas of power and fulfillment (*eros*), nothing to make them take delight in Him. {*Line*} 3: despised, poor, a man of sorrows, ACQUAINTED WITH INFIRMITY, hidden, despised, we esteemed Him not. {*Line*} 4: the Jews thought Him a sinner, that is to say, one punished by God for sins with leprosy and poverty, etc. But in reality, He was bearing upon Himself *their* sins. They could not understand the divine Love which appeared to them in Christ, a love which took upon itself all their evils and infirmities

456. "Glory, praise" (procession hymn) (*Missale Romanum*, 145; *Missale Cisterciense*, 128).

457. First lesson, first nocturn: Tuesday, Fourth Week of Advent (*Breviarium Cisterciense, Hiemalis*, 225).

458. Introit: Nativity of St. John the Baptist (vv. 1–2) (*Missale Romanum*, 619; *Missale Cisterciense*, 444); capitulum, vespers (v. 1); capitulum, terce (v. 1); capitulum, sext (vv. 5, 6); capitulum, none (v. 7) (*Breviarium Cisterciense, Aestivalis*, 355, 364).

459. *Missale Romanum*, 152; *Missale Cisterciense*, 134–35.

460. 53:1–12 (*Missale Romanum*, 160; *Missale Cisterciense*, 141).

in order to share with them all His goodness. {*Line*} 5: He was wounded for our iniquities; by His bruises we are healed. He was *pierced through* for our *rebellions*. The idea of self-will here appears again. {*Line*} 6: like sheep going astray, *everyone has turned aside into his own way*, but instead of here stressing the punishment of the people, as the prophets so often do, Isaias now reveals the tremendous fact that this punishment, so terrible and unthinkable, *has been laid upon the shoulders of the Messias*; and this {was done} by the Lord—the iniquity *of us all*, not of this or that group, but of all, Jews and Gentiles, holy and unholy, etc. Let us realize that Jesus takes on our weakness, our helplessness. He is never closer to us in this Valley of Tears than when we are weak and helpless and realize our helplessness before our enemies and abandon our own stratagems and plans, simply in order to do His will. Then truly He resists temptation and conquers in our own hearts. {*Line*} 7: {He} offered {Himself} of His own free will, led like a sheep to the slaughter, without complaint, or opening His mouth. Line 8: after arrest and sentence He was taken off, and on His fate who reflected? He was cut off from the land of the living, and for the rebellion of His people He was stricken to death. They made his grave with the wicked and with the rich man His sepulchre. Lines 10–12: "Truly He gave Himself as a guilt offering. He shall see seed that prolongs days [a great progeny is the fruit of His sacrifice—the Mystical Body]. After His travail of soul He shall see light . . . . THEREFORE I WILL ASSIGN THE MANY FOR HIS PORTION AND NUMBERLESS SHALL BE HIS SPOIL, AND WITH THE REBELLIOUS HE WAS NUMBERED BUT HE BORE THE SIN OF MANY AND FOR THE REBELLIOUS HE INTERCEDES."

THE EASTER MYSTERY

Proem: *Holy Week and Easter* {are the} center of {the} liturgical year, because {they are the} center of our whole Christian life—the *Easter Mystery*. {It is} wrong to separate Holy Week from Easter, as if it were all over on Good Friday. {The} Church sets aside every other celebration to concentrate on this central mystery which includes all others. We should also keep our hearts free from everything else, and enter into the celebration with full attention. Every day of the year the Easter Mystery is renewed in the Mass—{the} sacrifice of Christ. This {is} only possible because He died and is risen. Otherwise it would be a mere commemoration. In Holy Week everything else is put aside so that we may renew and deepen our consciousness of the fact that the Mass is the great "memorial" of the death and resurrection of the Lord. The nature of that memorial {is} a mystery which makes His salvific action actually present, and unites us with Him in it.

What is Holy Week? {Is it} a week set aside for commemoration of an historical event? No, {it is} not a celebration like a civic holiday. {Is it} a week set aside for study of a truth? No, {it is} not like a Catholic Bible week, etc. Christianity is more than a doctrine, more than a speculative truth, more than a moral system. In Holy Week we do not merely meditate on the Passion, contemplate the sufferings of Jesus, rouse our hearts to affection for Him, and resolve to intensify our ascetic efforts. This is not even the beginning of Holy Week. We can, and do, do that all the year round. {Is it} a week set aside, like a retreat, for meditation on sacred realities, and stirring up good resolutions? No, Holy Week is something much more than all this. IT IS THE CELEBRATION OF THE EASTER MYS-TERY, THE REPRESENTATION OF A SACRED ACTION, A SACRED FACT, IN WHICH GOD GAVE US THE MOST PERFECT MANIFESTATION OF HIS LOVE FOR US, OF HIS NATURE WHICH IS CHARITY (*agape*). BY PARTICIPATION IN THIS MYSTERY WE (1) do the most effective thing possible to unite ourselves to Him; (2) we give Him supreme glory; (3) we do what is most pleasing to Him—we carry out the action decreed by His all-wise and all-loving plan for the salvation of mankind; (4) in doing this we come to know more of Him, though in mystery; we are more closely united to the Word and enlightened by Him; (5) in doing this we grow in charity and are transformed in God—we are "new creatures" in the mystical renewal of our baptismal life. The Easter Mystery is the *mystery of regeneration,* the Christian spring festival and new life in Christ, in which not only the individual, but the Church herself, and, indirectly, the whole world, feels the force of the vivifying action of the Divine Spirit poured out into our souls by the Risen Savior. Hence our celebration of the Easter mystery has a tremendous effect on the whole world, though this effect remains hidden.

The Mystery: {it is} important to understand the sense of the traditional term "mystery." Without this understanding our liturgical life becomes largely a matter of rubrics or spiritual nosegays. The liturgical life is not a life of meditations based on the liturgy. It is a life in Christ, an awareness of "the mystery" that can only be gained by full participation in it. Why Mystery? (a) as opposed to *mysteries* (this contains them all); (b) {it is} not only a hidden truth, but a *fact*; (c) a *fact which is evident*, but which has a hidden and divine effect; (d) and which is renewed in a divine manner, reproducing the same effect. To speak of the *Easter Mystery* {is} not merely a liturgical fashion, or an esoteric way of thinking made up by some theological innovators. {It is} in the full tradition of the Fathers, and the New Testament. For instance, St. Ambrose has left us two treatises, *De Sacramentis*[461] and *De Mysteriis*;[462] they contain his "Easter catechesis," {the} final touches given to the instruction of the catechumens when they are "illuminated" by baptism. Previously they had received instruction in the Scriptures and in the Creed, but now they are initiated *into the mysteries*; that is to say, they receive baptism and the Eucharist, and at the same time the hidden meaning of the sacraments is explained to them. Rather, the sacramental (system and) mystery is laid open to them in an explanation of (a) the rites of baptism and the Eucharist; (b) the mysterious typological texts of the Old Testament used in the Easter rites. So St. Ambrose's catechesis on the mysteries is an explanation of the Easter rites which *shows the meaning of the rites by hidden types contained in the Scriptures that the liturgy uses.* These hidden types show forth not moral truths (which the catechumens have learned in previous instructions on Scripture), but *sacred facts or realities*—the reality of Christ's redeeming action and His gift of His Spirit, and His Body and Blood, to us, in the sacraments. The *catechesis de mysteriis* is therefore an opening up of the salvific action of Christ veiled in the symbolism of rites and scriptures. The purpose of this is to bring the newly baptized into full contact with the sacred action itself, *to bring him into immediate union with Christ Who carries out this action in mystery.* St. Ambrose says (*De Mysteriis*):

> We gave you each day moral instructions while they were reading to you now the history of the Patriarchs, now the maxims of Proverbs . . . . The purpose of this was to make you walk in the way of your ancestors [Abraham, etc.], follow their footsteps and obey the oracles of God, and that thus after you had been regenerated by baptism, you should lead a life worthy of those who had been purified. *But now we have come to speak to you of the mysteries* [the spiritual sense of the Scriptures], and to explain to you the sacraments [the sacred rites]. [He says he did not want to explain these before baptism because it would have been a violation of the *arcana*, and besides, he adds, the light of the mysteries penetrates more deeply into those who are not expecting such graces, than if some explanation had preceded them.] *Open then your ears, and breathe in the good odor of eternal life, which has been poured out upon you by the gift of*

461. Migne, *PL* 16, cols. 417A–462A.
462. Migne, *PL* 16, cols. 389A–410A.

the sacraments. [These should be our dispositions also when we enter Holy Week. He adds later:] you see the Levites and Bishop present. But do not look at the mere outward surface; God, Who acts through them is present in them: BELIEVE THEN IN THE PRESENCE OF GOD HERE. CAN YOU BELIEVE THAT HE IS ACTING HERE IF HE IS NOT HERE PRESENT? WHENCE WOULD COME HIS ACTION IF HIS PRESENCE WERE NOT THERE FIRST? (*De Mysteriis* I.8)[463]

2. From this first quotation we reach another conclusion: the sacred mystery is an action performed by whom? BY GOD HIMSELF; BY JESUS CHRIST THE HIGH PRIEST, IN UNION WITH HIS CHURCH. Some texts from the Encyclical *Mediator Dei*, on the liturgy in general, prove this in particular of the Easter Mystery. "The Divine Redeemer willed that His priestly life begun with the supplication and sacrifice of His mortal Body should continue down the ages in His Mystical Body which is the Church."[464] "ALONG WITH THE CHURCH THE DIVINE FOUNDER IS PRESENT AT EVERY LITURGICAL FUNCTION. . . . THE SACRED LITURGY IS CONSEQUENTLY THE PUBLIC WORSHIP WHICH OUR REDEEMER AS HEAD OF THE CHURCH RENDERS TO THE FATHER, AS WELL AS THE WORSHIP WHICH THE COMMUNITY OF THE FAITHFUL RENDERS TO ITS FOUNDER, AND THROUGH HIM TO THE HEAVENLY FATHER."[465] In Holy Week the Church not only renews the Holy Sacrifice, but also renews it in {a} *ritual celebration that elaborates the very details of its first offering and of the institution of the Sacrament by which it is perpetuated.* For example, {in} the *Mass of Holy Thursday*: (1) the texts of the Mass itself describe the Last Supper (gospel[466]), and the early Christian *Agape* (St. Paul[467]); (2) there is only one Mass—the abbot gives communion to all the other priests and people. Both these facts, together with the *mandatum* intimately connected with the Holy Thursday Mass, and the Scripture reading from St. John in chapter ({the} discourse at {the} Last Supper[468]), bring vividly

463. Cc. 1.1–3, 2.8 (Migne, *PL* 16, cols. 389A–390A, 391BC).

464. Pius XII, *Mediator Dei*, 4 (#2), which reads: ". . . Redeemer has so willed it . . . that the priestly . . . continue without intermission down . . ."

465. Pius XII, *Mediator Dei*, 10 (#20), which reads: ". . . Church, therefore, her divine . . ."

466. John 13:1–15 (*Missale Romanum*, 167; *Missale Cisterciense*, 148).

467. 1 Cor 11:20–32 (*Missale Romanum*, 166–67; *Missale Cisterciense*, 147–48).

468. The reading of the Farewell Discourse (John 13:1—18:1) took place in the chapter room immediately before the Mass for Holy Thursday (Br. Paul Quenon, OCSO: personal communication).

before us the Last Supper itself. So on Holy Thursday, this aspect of the "Mystery" is re-lived in a very special way. Although every Mass renews the sacrifice consummated on Calvary and first offered in the Cenacle, yet this Mass brings us back "in mystery" to the Last Supper in particular. Hence {comes} the grace of Holy Thursday—recapturing the simplicity and reality of Jesus' intimacy with His disciples, and what this intimacy constitutes. Read John 13:1 (gospel of Holy Thursday): "Knowing that *His hour* was come [Holy Thursday brings to us *that hour* in which we were present to Him and He *is* present to us] ... that He should *pass out of this world* to the Father [the *Pascha—transitus*: all the Exodus allusions {are} to be seen in light of this text—Christ our true Pasch; our Holy Week {must be} a *passage*, a *transitus*]. Having loved His own [Love, in all the depth and simplicity of the word—a human heart full of the divine *Agape*], He loved them *unto the end* [{there are} no limits to God's love or of His power to make that love effective in our lives]." And the liturgy thus makes us more conscious of Jesus present as High Priest, the divine Victim who instituted the Mass.

3. But the Easter Mystery is more than the liturgical representation of the Last Supper, and of Calvary, and of the Resurrection. It is a ritual presentation of the whole recapitulation in Christ which Paul simply calls "THE MYSTERY." Paul speaks of "THE MYSTERY WHICH WAS KEPT SECRET FROM ETERNITY WHICH NOW IS MADE MANIFEST BY THE SCRIPTURES OF THE PROPHETS ACCORDING TO THE PRECEPT OF THE ETERNAL GOD FOR THE OBEDIENCE OF FAITH" (*Romans* 16:26; read also *Ephesians* 3:8–11[469]). But what is the full meaning of the mystery? Mersch says it is the doctrine of man's *incorporation in Christ and of his divinization in Christ.* "INCORPORATION IN CHRIST IS THE 'MYSTERY,' AND THE MYSTERY IS THE ACT WHEREBY GOD IN HIS MERCY UNITES ALL MEN TO HIMSELF AND DEIFIES THEM IN HIS WELL-BELOVED SON" (Mersch[470]). But how is this done? by sharing in the death and resurrection of Christ, BY PARTICIPATION IN THE

---

469. "To me, the least of all the saints, is given this grace, to preach among the Gentiles, the unsearchable riches of Christ, And to enlighten all men, that they may see what is the dispensation of the mystery which hath been hidden from eternity in God, who created all things: That the manifold wisdom of God may be made known to the principalities and powers in heavenly places through the church, According to the eternal purpose, which he made, in Christ Jesus our Lord."

470. Mersch, *Whole Christ*, which reads: "We must remember, too, that according to Paul incorporation in Christ is the 'mystery,' and that this mystery is the act whereby God in His mercy unites all men to Himself and deifies them all in His well-beloved Son."

ACTION BY WHICH CHRIST REDEEMED MANKIND—and this is the Easter Mystery. By actively participating, with intelligent faith and enlightened love, in the ritual mystery of Easter, we are entering deeper into the FACT of our incorporation and divinization in Christ. How {can we} make this more understandable? by realizing {the} meaning of {the} texts and rites.

HOLY WEEK (A Brief Outline)

Preamble: Note the collect for Saturday in Passion week—{the} Church looks forward to Holy Week and prays for special grace to profit by it: "That Thy People instructed by the Sacred Rites [*sacris actionibus erudita*], they may become more pleasing to Thy majesty and thus be granted richer blessings."[471] It is therefore a sacred action which instructs us in the mystery of Christ, unites us more closely to God, makes us capable of greater graces. In the secret we ask to be preserved from dangers by virtue of our "participation in so great a mystery."[472] In the postcommunion, we ask that we ever live in this participation in the mystery of the *Pascha Christi*.[473]

Outline of the "Sacred Actions" (we will go more into their meaning later):

1. Palm Sunday {is} the triumphal opening of Holy Week, the "Advent" of the Savior as King and Conqueror—but not in the way human aspirations would expect. "*Ecce Rex tuus venit tibi mansuetus, sedens super asinam.*"[474] He comes in meekness and poverty, {and} in so doing fulfills all the prophecies (One given to stand for all). Everything in the Palm Sunday procession centers on this Advent of the King and Savior. After the blessing, we become the children of the chosen people, hailing the Messias (chant: *Pueri Hebraeorum*[475]): "*Potenti triumphatori*

---

471. "*plebs tibi dicata piae devotionis affectu: ut sacris actionibus erudita, quanto majestati tuae fit gratior, tanto donis potioribus augeatur*" (*Missale Romanum*, 136; *Missale Cisterciense*, 123).

472. "*tanti mysterii . . . consortes*" (*Missale Romanum*, 138; *Missale Cisterciense*, 124–25).

473. "*Divini muneris largitate satiati, quaesumus, Domine Deus noster: ut hujus semper participatione vivamus*" ("Filled with the abundance of the divine gift, Lord Our God, we ask that we may always live by participation in this") (*Missale Romanum*, 138; *Missale Cisterciense*, 125).

474. Behold your gentle King comes to you seated upon an ass" (Matt 21:5, citing Zech 9:9) (*Missale Romanum*, 140; *Missale Cisterciense*, 128).

475. "*Pueri Hebraeorum, portantes ramos olivarum, obviaverunt Domino,*

digna dant obsequia."[476] {The} procession ({which is} different from {the} Roman {rite}) {includes the} (1) responsory: *Collegerunt*[477]—the plot of the High Priests against Jesus; (2) in reply, we the faithful people bow down to the Cross, and sing AVE REX NOSTER (very moving, not in {the} Roman liturgy): "HAIL OUR KING, SON OF DAVID, REDEEMER OF THE WORLD, WHOM THE PROPHETS DECLARED WOULDST COME AS SAVIOR TO THE HOUSE OF ISRAEL, THEE THE FATHER HAS SENT AS A SAVING VICTIM INTO THE WORLD, THEE ALL THE SAINTS HAVE AWAITED SINCE THE BEGINNING OF THE WORLD, AND NOW, HOSANNA TO THE SON OF DAVID, BLESSED IS HE THAT COMES IN THE NAME OF THE LORD! HOSANNA IN THE HIGHEST."[478] As a reply to the last invitation of the Church, the "angels" reply "in the highest" (behind the closed doors of the sanctuary[479]) from heaven which is closed to us: GLORIA LAUS[480] which becomes an antiphonal chorus of praise with men and angels alternately hailing the King and Savior. One beautiful strophe in the Roman {liturgy} is missing in ours: "HI TIBI PASSURO SOLVEBANT MUNIA LAUDIS / NOS TIBI REGNANTI PANGIMUS ECCE MELOS."[481] Finally the church doors open and the procession enters the church (reminding us of how the Church will enter glorious into heaven with the Risen Savior when He has come again

---

clamantes, et dicentes: Hosanna in excelsis" ("The children of the Hebrews, carrying olive branches, went out to meet the Lord, crying out and saying: Hosanna in the highest") (*Missale Romanum*, 144; *Missale Cisterciense*, 127).

476. "They give obedience proper to a powerful conqueror" (procession, antiphon) (*Missale Romanum*, 145).

477. "*Collegerunt pontifices et pharisei concilium et dicebant quid facimus quia hic homo multa signa facit si dimittimus eum sic omnes credent in eum ne forte veniant Romani et tollant nostrum locum et gentem*" ("The chief priests, therefore, and the Pharisees gathered a council and said: What do we, for this man doth many miracles? If we let him alone so, all will believe in him; and the Romans will come, and take away our place and nation") (John 11:47–48).

478. "*Ave, Rex noster, Fili David, Redemptor mundi, quem prophetae praedixerunt Salvatorem domui Israel esse venturum. Te enim ad salutarem victimam Pater misit in mundum, quem exspectabant omnes sancti ab origine mundi, et nunc: Hosanna Filio David, Benedictus qui venit in nomine Domini. Hosanna in excelsis*" (prayer at the conclusion of the Palm Sunday procession, mentioned, but not quoted, in *Missale Cisterciense*, 127, and *Regulations*, 114–15).

479. See *Regulations*, 114–15 (#240).

480. "*Gloria, laus et honor tibi sit, Rex Christe Redemptor: Cui puerile decus promp-sit Hosanna pium*" ("Glory, praise and honor to you, Christ Redeemer King, to whom the reverent honor of the children gave rise to Hosanna") (*Missale Romanum*, 145).

481. "These paid a tribute of praise to You as You were about to suffer; behold, we make a song to You as You reign" (*Missale Romanum*, 145).

to take us to Himself); this is implied in the opening words: *Ingrediente Domino sanctam civitatem.*[482]

The Mass of Palm Sunday introduces us to the Passion of the Savior. Psalm 21 gives the keynote (introit and tract)[483]—contemplation of the "mystery" of the Passion in the Old Testament prophecy of David. {The} *epistle* (Philippians,[484] again) {provides} the keynote of Holy Week, the true "action" that is demanded of us: "HOC ENIM SENTITE IN VOBIS QUOD ET IN CHRISTO JESU . . . HUMILIAVIT SEMETIPSUM, FACTUS OBEDIENS USQUE AD MORTEM. PROPTER QUOD DEUS EXALTAVIT ILLUM."[485] {The} *gradual* {follows}: "*Tenuisti manum dexteram meam et in voluntate tua deduxisti me.*"[486] {Then comes} the St. Matthew Passion.[487] {Note the} poignancy of the communion antiphon, after the Passion has been seen in preview, in its entirety: "*Pater, si non potest transire hic calix . . . fiat voluntas tua.*"[488]

{On} *Monday*, {there is} no Passion, but {the} epistle {from} Isaias[489] {presents the} servant of Yahweh (c. 50): "The Lord hath opened my ear and I do not resist . . ." {In the} *gospel*,[490] Mary Magdalen anoints the feet of Jesus with precious ointment for His burial.

{On} *Tuesday* {we hear} the St. Mark Passion.[491]

{On} *Wednesday*, {the} *first lesson* {is} triumphant: "*Quis est iste qui venit de Edom tinctis vestibus de Bosra*"[492] ({this} will be one of the Easter

---

482. "to the Lord entering the holy city" (responsory following "*Gloria laus*") (*Missale Romanum*, 145).

483. vv. 20, 22, 2 and 2–9, 18–19, 22, 24, 32, respectively (*Missale Romanum*, 146; *Missale Cisterciense*, 128, 129).

484. Phil 2:5–11 (*Missale Romanum*, 146; *Missale Cisterciense*, 129).

485. "Have this mind in yourselves which you have in Christ Jesus . . . He humbled Himself, obedient even to the point of death. Because of this God exalted Him" (vv. 5, 8–9).

486. "You have held my right hand and You have led me in Your will" (Ps 72[73]:24) (*Missale Romanum*, 146; *Missale Cisterciense*, 129).

487. Matt 26:36–27:60 (*Missale Romanum*, 147–51; *Missale Cisterciense*, 129–34).

488. "Father, if this cup cannot pass away . . . may Your will be done" (Matt 26:42) (*Missale Romanum*, 148; *Missale Cisterciense*, 130).

489. Isa 50:5–10 (*Missale Romanum*, 152; *Missale Cisterciense*, 134–35).

490. John 12:1–9 (*Missale Romanum*, 153; *Missale Cisterciense*, 135).

491. Mark 14:32–15:46 (*Missale Romanum*, 154–58; *Missale Cisterciense*, 137–40).

492. "Who is that who comes from Edom, with clothes dyed from Bosra" (Isa 63:1) (*Missale Romanum*, 159; *Missale Cisterciense*, 140).

canticles[493]) (Isaias 62). {The} epistle {is again} the Suffering Servant of Yahweh (Isaias 53[494]) {and the gospel} the St. Luke Passion.[495]

THE LAST THREE DAYS OF HOLY WEEK

In general, {there is}: (1) no Lenten curtain;[496] (2) no *Gloria Patri*[497] (come prepared, especially at *vespers* and *compline*), no blessings[498] and *tu autem*[499] or *Rule* in chapter;[500] (3) {a} special tone for the psalms of the little hours[501] (all *Psalm* 118 each day[502]—{the} will of God); (4) *Tenebrae*: darkness at {the} end of *lauds*,[503] Lamentations,[504] etc.; (5) *see Usages* #251[505] for grace in refectory, etc. (mimeographed papers).

MAUNDY THURSDAY (*Maundy* {from} *mandatum*[506]):

1. *Mandatum of {the} Poor*—novices should stay {and} may join in if an extra {person is there}. "*Suscepimus Deus misericordiam tuam in medio templi tui.*"[507] "Blessed are the merciful for they shall receive mercy"[508]—{the} mystery of charity and love in Christ. "Love one another as I have loved you."[509] The action of charity and the Eucharist {are closely

---

493. Isa 63:1–5 (canticle, third nocturn) (*Breviarium Cisterciense, Vernalis*, 309).

494. *Missale Romanum*, 160; *Missale Cisterciense*, 141.

495. Luke 22:39–23:53 (*Missale Romanum*, 161–64; *Missale Cisterciense*, 143–45).

496. For the removal of the purple curtain, hung in front of the presbytery on the First Sunday of Lent, see *Regulations*, 115–16 (#240).

497. *Breviarium Cisterciense, Vernalis*, 277–303.

498. *Regulations*, 116 (#243).

499. *Regulations*, 122–23 (#251).

500. According to *Regulations* #245 (118): "The Holy Rule is sung without the blessing being asked."

501. *Regulations*, 116 (#242).

502. *Breviarium Cisterciense, Vernalis*, 284.

503. *Regulations*, 117 (#244).

504. *Regulations*, 116 (#243); *Breviarium Cisterciense, Vernalis*, 277–79 (Thursday); 281–89 (Friday); 296–97 (Saturday).

505. *Regulations*, 122–23.

506. "command" (i.e. the "new commandment" of John 13:34).

507. "We have received Your mercy, God, in the midst of Your temple" (Ps 47[48]:10).

508. Matt 5:7.

509. John 13:34.

related}: {the} Mystical Body and {the} Sacramental Body of Christ. (The abbot waits on them at table in the guest house.)

2. {The} GREAT MANDATUM: we sing the usual *Mandatum* antiphons, etc., but one is peculiar to Holy Thursday, about Jesus washing the feet of His disciples and solemnly commanding them to follow His example. He was not instituting a rite by this, so much as urging us to charity and mutual service. (St. Bernard[510] regards it as a "sacrament," i.e., {a} sacramental.) The rite is valuable in so far as it instructs us in the meaning of our common life, but it also increases charity for those who enter into it. "Quanto magis *vos debetis alter alterius lavare pedes.*"[511] Fraternal charity and unity in Christ {is} the "*res sacramenti* of the Eucharist" (St. Thomas[512]). The whole purpose of the "sacred actions" of Holy Week {is} to deepen and purify our union in Christ by humility and obedience, which come from sharing in the love which He showed in His sacred Passion. *Maundy: mandatum novum do vobis, ut diligatis invicem sicut dilexi vos.*"[513] Charity, says St. Paul, is the fulfillment of the Law.[514] "In this shall all men know that you are My disciples, if you love one another"[515] (*antiphon: In hoc cognoscent omnes . . .*[516]). Meditate on these antiphons! (The tone of Holy Thursday {is found} in these and {in} the Mass.)

{3.} {The} Mass of the day {is} evening Mass (preceded by mental prayer) at the very hour when the Blessed Sacrament was instituted! About 4:00 the Mass begins; the two bells are rung at the *Gloria in excelsis,*[517] but thereafter, nothing but the clapper {is used} until Holy Saturday. (Watch out for {the} end of work and bells for office, etc.; do not prostrate on desks; {go} out of {the} stalls at {the} collect). *The Mass*

---

510. "*Nam ut de remissione quotidianorum minime dubitorum, habemus ejus sacramentum, pedum ablutionem*" ("For with respect to the remission of slight daily faults we have His sacrament, the washing of feet" ("*Sermo in Coena Domini*" [Migne, *PL* 183, col. 272D]).

511. "How much more ought you to wash one another's feet" (John 13:14).

512. St. Thomas Aquinas, *Summa Theologiae*, III, q. 73, a. 3: "*res hujus sacramenti est unitas corporis mystici*" ("the matter of this sacrament is the unity of the mystical body") (St. Thomas Aquinas, *Opera Omnia*, 4.334).

513. "I give you a new commandment, that you love one another as I have loved you" (John 13:34).

514. Rom 13:10.

515. John 13:35.

516. Sixth antiphon for the footwashing (*Missale Romanum*, 170–71).

517. "Glory [to God] in the highest" (*Missale Romanum*, 166; *Missale Cisterciense*, 147).

{in relation to} the Last Supper {is} evident here—Reverend Father {as} Christ, the priests {as} His apostles, the rest {as} disciples. {The} *epistle*[518] {focuses on} the Agape of the first Christians; {the} *gospel*[519] {is that of} the washing of the feet.

GOOD FRIDAY

({The} night office {is} as usual in these days. After {taking the} discipline,[520] leave shoes and socks in {the} cell. {There is both} frustulum and interval.) Prime and PSALTER lasts about four hours (*re* {the} Psalter, {see} *Consuetudines* #22[521]—{the} entire Psalter {is} recited in chapter after prime;[522] *Expleto Psalterio*, all the day {is} for reading, said the *Consuetudines*). After Psalter {there is an} interval of about half an hour, then tierce, then sext, examen, *angelus*. Dinner {is} at 11:00 because of communion (bread and water), and {then there is a} long interval (about two hours, followed by Lenten reading). Lenten reading {continues}, and about 2:30 {comes} none and {the} office of the day.

Office of Good Friday (afternoon)—Lessons and Passion:

Part 1: Reverend Father and {the} ministers enter barefoot without lights, prostrate before the bare altar while the acolytes spread a cloth on the altar, and the prior comes out to sing the lesson from *Osee:*[523] "Come, let us return to the Lord. He strikes and heals us."[524] HE WILL REVIVE US AFTER TWO DAYS AND ON THE THIRD DAY HE WILL RAISE US UP AND WE SHALL LIVE IN HIS SIGHT AND WE SHALL KNOW AND WE SHALL FOLLOW ON THAT WE MAY KNOW THE LORD . . .[525] {Note the} dynamic character of this office; {it is} not a static contemplation of the Passion without any issue: (a) we are identified with the Crucified here; (b) we shall rise with Him and know Him; (c) all this {is} done by the hand of the Lord Who

518. 1 Cor 11:20-32 (*Missale Romanum*, 166-67; *Missale Cisterciense*, 147-48).

519. John 13:1-15 (*Missale Romanum*, 167; *Missale Cisterciense*, 148).

520. On this penitential practice, see *Regulations*, 173 (##362-63) and Merton, *Monastic Observances*, 249-50.

521. "*Dicta autem prima . . . Psalterium ex integro persolvant. Expleto Psalterio per totam diem vacent fratres lectioni*" ("After prime has been said, . . . let them recite the psalter in full. Once the psalter has been completed the brothers may devote the entire day to *lectio*") (*Nomasticon*, 102).

522. See also *Regulations*, 127 (#256).

523. Hos 6:1-6 (*Missale Romanum*, 172; *Missale Cisterciense*, 150-51).

524. Hos 6:1.

525. Hos 6:2-3.

has struck us; (d) and thereafter we shall follow Him Whom we have come to know. MISERICORDIAM VOLUI ET NON SACRIFICIUM ET SCIENTIAM DEI PLUS QUAM HOLOCAUSTA . . .[526] {These are} remarkable words on Good Friday, when there is in fact no sacrifice, and when we are preparing to enter into the full mercy and knowledge of God in the Easter Sacrifice. Then {comes the} tract, from Habacuc, on the wonder of the wisdom of God manifested in the Passion.[527] (Note: this text is also used at Christmas.[528]) {This is followed by the} lesson from Exodus[529] on the Paschal Lamb and the Paschal supper, {and the} tract from Psalm 139:[530] "Eripe me Domine ab homine malo."[531] Then the PASSION according to St. John[532] immediately begins.

Part 2: the prayers:[533] (1) for the peace of the Church in the whole world ({for the} Church to persevere in faith, even unto martyrdom); through Christ in Whom God has revealed His glory to the whole world; this peace {is} to rest on faith (stabili fide in confessione tui nominis perseveret[534])—{this is} important in our time! We are praying for martyrs; (2) for the pope; (3) for all bishops, priests, etc., down to doorkeepers; then confessors, virgins and widows—that they may all faithfully serve God; (4) for the catechumens, to grow in faith and understanding; (5) that the whole Church may be purged of all errors, that sicknesses may be dispelled, that famine cease, that prisons be opened, that pilgrims and travelers may return safely home, for all in tribulation; (6) for heretics and schismatics, deceived by the devil; (7) for the Jews (no flectamus genua[535]), that they may no more be blind, but may open their eyes to the Light of Christ; (8) for pagans and idolators. The Adoration of the Cross

---

526. "I have desired mercy and not sacrifice, and the knowledge of God more than holocausts" (Hos 6:6).

527. Hab 3:1–3 (Missale Romanum, 172; Missale Cisterciense, 151).

528. Responsory, fifth lesson, second nocturn (v. 1) (Breviarium Cisterciense, Hiemalis, 248).

529. Exod 12:1–11 (Missale Romanum, 173; Missale Cisterciense, 151).

530. Ps 139[140]:2–10, 14 (Missale Romanum, 173; Missale Cisterciense, 151–52).

531. "Deliver me, Lord, from the evil man" (Ps 139[140]:1).

532. John 18:1—19:42 (Missale Romanum, 173–76; Missale Cisterciense, 152–55).

533. Missale Romanum, 177–83; Missale Cisterciense, 155–57.

534. "May [the Church] persevere in steadfast faith in the confession of Your name" (Missale Romanum, 177; Missale Cisterciense, 155).

535. "Let us bend our knees" (Missale Romanum, 182; Missale Cisterciense, 157).

begins with the *improperia*, or the "Reproaches."[536] Two priests solemnly bring forth the veiled crucifix from behind the altar where it is hidden. In the Roman rite it is first unveiled, but here only after the singing of the *improperia*: *Popule meus*—{a} dialogue between the two priests in the sanctuary and the two monks at the sanctuary step, with the choir joining in, {emphasizing} sorrow for sin, penance. "*Popule meus, quid feci tibi?*"[537] God is speaking to Israel, but we too are Israel. We have all sinned against Him. We have crucified Jesus by *our* sins too. We too are ungrateful to One Who has nothing but love and mercy toward us. "In what have I grieved thee, answer me!"[538] "I led thee out of Egypt and thou hast prepared a cross for thy Savior."[539] *Agios O Theos*:[540] Holy God, holy strong One, holy immortal One, have mercy on us. God's reproaches continue, each verse ending with the refrain: "Thou hast prepared a cross for thy Savior; thou hast with a lance opened the side of thy Savior." Then they uncover the cross, singing, "*Ecce lignum crucis*,"[541] summoning us to adore (on knuckles when they intone this; kneel upright for "*Beati immaculati*";[542] continue singing; repeat "*Ecce lignum . . .*" while the two priests adore; then we begin our adoration). Note: on adoration of {the} cross—keep together, two and two, {in} order, peace, quiet; return through {the} upper opening (?). *The Pange Lingua*[543] again {shows the} *triumph of the cross*. Finally, {the} *super omnia*:[544] the cross stands out above all other "trees."

Part III. *The Mass of the Presanctified*: religious go first to {the} repository. Candles are lighted. {There is a} slow and solemn procession

536. *Missale Romanum*, 184–85; *Missale Cisterciense*, 157–59.

537. "My people, what have I done to you?" (*Missale Romanum*, 184; *Missale Cisterciense*, 157).

538. "*in quo contristavi te? responde mihi*" (*Missale Romanum*, 184; *Missale Cisterciense*, 157).

539. "*eduxi te de terra Aegypti: parasti Crucem Salvatori tuo*" (*Missale Romanum*, 184; *Missale Cisterciense*, 157).

540. "O holy God" (Greek choric response to the Improperia) (*Missale Romanum*, 184; *Missale Cisterciense*, 158).

541. "Behold the wood of the Cross" (*Missale Romanum*, 183; *Missale Cisterciense*, 159).

542. "Blessed [are they who walk] spotless" (Ps 118[119]:1) (*Missale Cisterciense*, 159).

543. "Sing my tongue" (*Missale Romanum*, 185; *Missale Cisterciense*, 159).

544. "Above all [trees]" (final antiphon for the "*Pange Lingua*") (*Missale Cisterciense*, 160).

around {the} high altar, bringing the Eucharistic Christ to the altar for communion (*note: junior novices lead*). Incense {is used, then the} *Orate Fratres*[545] and *Pater*[546] {are said, the} "*libera nos*"[547] is sung, {and} then {there is} communion.

HOLY SATURDAY ("*Mater omnium sanctarum vigiliarium*"
—St. Augustine[548])

In order that we may participate more fruitfully in the mystery, the prayer of the Church obtains a special grace for the *new fire* which will become, mystically, the Light of Christ (*Lumen Christi*[549]): "O God, Who through Thy Son Who is the cornerstone, hast enkindled in the faithful *the fire of Thy brightness*, deign *to sanctify unto our profit this fire struck from flint*, and grant us by this paschal festival to be so inflamed with heavenly desire, that we may finally come purified in mind to the feast of the never-ending light."[550] Again, {there is} the mystery of our entrance, in and with Christ, into the light of heaven. Later {we pray}: "Do thou, O unseen Redeemer of life, enkindle the brightness of this night, so that not only the sacrifice offered tonight *may glow with a mysterious mingling of Thy Light*, but also that *wherever any part of this holy sacramental is brought, the treachery of Satan may give place to Thy presence in power and majesty*"[551] (cf. {the} ancient custom of the Greeks—carrying holy fire to their homes; {thus we} bring {the} new fire to {the} novitiate for Masses).

Jesus' work is finished on Good Friday. His victory is won, but the fruits of the victory remain to be gathered. Meanwhile, Holy Saturday is the Last Sabbath, and Sunday the eighth day will be the dawn of the new creation. "If Christ be not risen, vain is our preaching, vain is your faith."[552] The RESURRECTION is necessary:

---

545. "Pray, brothers" (*Missale Romanum*, 187; *Missale Cisterciense*, 161).

546. "[Our] Father" (*Missale Romanum*, 187; *Missale Cisterciense*, 161–62).

547. "Deliver us" (*Missale Romanum*, 188; *Missale Cisterciense*, 162).

548. "The Mother of all holy vigils" (*Sermo 219: In Vigiliis Paschae*, 1 [Migne, *PL* 38, col. 1088, which reads: "*Matre...*"]).

549. *Missale Romanum*, 190; *Missale Cisterciense*, 164.

550. Prayer for the blessing of the new fire (*Missale Romanum*, 189; *Missale Cisterciense*, 163).

551. Prayer for the blessing of the paschal candle (*Missale Romanum*, 190; *Missale Cisterciense*, 163–64).

552. 1 Cor 15:14.

a) {It is} the acceptance and ratification of the Son's sacrifice by His Father.

b) In His humanity He enters fully into the glory of the Word, reaping the reward of His obedience.

c) His humanity becomes the instrument for the sanctification and transformation of the whole world. By the *agape* of His risen life He can reach out into all hearts and lead them to the glory of the Father. His humanity becomes the point from which the Holy Spirit goes forth into all souls. He lives in heaven and in us!

d) Now that He is victorious and risen, He can communicate the Holy Spirit to souls in the mystery of baptism, but more—{he can} give His humanity itself to us in the Eucharist.

e) *gratia capitis jugiter influit.*[553]

Bouyer says:

> We see how closely bound are the resurrection of Christ and the founding of the Church; how the very existence of the Church depends on the Resurrection; *how, by its very existence, the Church bears witness to the Resurrection.* We understand then that the feast of Easter, the feast of the Risen Christ, *is, in the Church, the feast of her incorporation in Christ;* for the neophytes it is the feast of their new birth in baptism, and for the already "perfect" Christian, the *feast of the renewal of their life by the eucharistic banquet....* The whole liturgy of the great paschal night must be interpreted in this light: it celebrates the Resurrection of Christ in celebrating our reconciliation with the Father as an accomplished fact. That is, it celebrates our new life in the

---

553. "The grace of the Head flows perpetually into" the members: this is the theological theme of "capital grace"—that the grace of the Incarnate Christ is the source of all grace in the church, the Body of Christ. The idea, though not the precise phrasing, is found, for example, in St. Thomas Aquinas, *Summa Theologiae, Pars Tertia,* q. 8: "*De Gratia Christi Secundum Quod Est Caput Ecclesiae*" ("On the Grace of Christ, according to His Being the Head of the Church") (St. Thomas Aquinas, *Opera Omnia,* 4:47–53) and in chapter 16 of the decree "*De Justificatione*" of the Council of Trent: "*ille ipse Christus Jesus tamquam caput in membra et tamquam vitis in palmites in ipsos justificatos jugiter virtutem influat*" ("Christ Jesus himself, as the head into the members and the vine into the branches, continually infuses strength into those justified") (Schroeder, *Canons and Decrees of Trent,* 319, 41).

Eucharist and more precisely the indefinite expansion of that life by baptism. (*Paschal Mystery*,[554] p. 263)

The Vigil Has Three Parts:[555]

1. *Lucernarium*—{the} feast of lights: {the} new fire and *lumen Christi*.

2. The Vigil proper: final instruction of the catechumens, in readings from the Old Testament.

3. The "feast of water": blessing of the font, baptism, Eucharistic banquet.

Part I. The New Fire and the Paschal Candle: *Lumen Christi*—the light shines in darkness {as a sign of the} Resurrection. {In} the *Exultet*,[556] with great solemnity the Church hails the Risen Lord and *proclaims the Easter Mystery* with all its consequences and fruits. The deacon, as minister of the Church, prepares for this most solemn declaration of the mystery:

1) He is blessed, as for the singing of the gospel.

2) He is blessed by the Lord to announce His Paschal *praeconium* (*praeco*: herald). It is simply another aspect of the *Evangelium*—it is the "good news" that comes to us from God in this night.

3) He incenses the book, and all the monks stand in ceremony as for the gospel. He sings on the same tone as the (ancient) preface, hence the *Exultet* is a great "eucharistic prayer"—of thanksgiving, involving all the orders of creation.

Outline of the Exultet: the deacon officially, in the name of the Lord, summons the angels in heaven and the whole earth to acclaim the Resurrection. The trumpet of salvation must sound forth, for the victory of the great King. In all the earth, the radiance of the eternal King has driven away darkness. But above all the Church, resplendent with the blazing glory of His Light, rejoices, and therefore let this church resound with the triumphant songs of a huge assembly. (Then the deacon asks them all to pray that he may be worthy to go on and praise the Easter Mystery symbolized by the Paschal candle, rather, by the action surrounding the

---

554. Bouyer, *Paschal Mystery*, which reads: ". . . depends upon the . . . incorporation with Christ . . . of the new birth . . . of the general renewal . . ." (emphasis added).

555. See Bouyer, *Paschal Mystery*, 263–64.

556. *Missale Romanum*, 190–99; *Missale Cisterciense*, 164–70.

Paschal candle. Note: the mere fact that the Paschal candle "is lit" is not a symbol of the Resurrection. But the fact that the Church gathers together and lights the candle and proclaims the mystery—*this* is the liturgical resurrection.) We praise the eternal Father with our whole heart because Jesus has paid the debt of Adam, fulfilled the type of the paschal lamb and the exodus from Egypt. This indeed is the night (*Haec nox* est[557]—{note the relation of} liturgy and time!—the past {and} present {are one} in mystery) in which *we* pass through the Red Sea, in which Christ rises in triumph from hell. (Again note {the} importance of this fulfillment of "mysteries" in Scripture.) We are redeemed! Our life has a purpose and a goal! There follow a series of exclamations on the great mercy of God, including "*O felix culpa.*"[558] To really understand this we must have passed over entirely to God—remember *Septuagesima* and the *massa damnata*[559]—quite a contrast! Then lights are taken from the candle and lamps are lit throughout the church. (Note {the} custom in Russia {of} peasants taking home the holy fire.) The deacon concludes by asking that the light of the candle may be an acceptable evening sacrifice to God, and that we may be filled with grace and brought to everlasting peace and our eternal victory in the Lord.

The Prophecies: their function is to show how the Easter Mystery was already present in the types of the Old Testament, and how these are fulfilled in us. {The} collect following {each} prophecy gives {a} clue to {the} mystery contained in it:

1. The *Creation*[560]—{the} collect shows it refers also to the second creation, the new world made by the victory of Christ, {and to} baptism.

2. *Exodus*[561] (fourth in *St. Andrew's Missal*[562])—this too is an "ancient miracle which we feel to blaze forth in our own time"[563] (collect).

557. "This is the night" (*Missale Romanum*, 195; *Missale Cisterciense*, 167).

558. "O happy fault" (*Missale Romanum*, 195; *Missale Cisterciense*, 167).

559. Second nocturn, lesson seven: "*de malis in mala praecipitabatur totius humani generis massa damnata*" ("the condemned mass of the entire human race was thrown from evil into evil") (St. Augustine, *Enchiridion*, c. 27 [Migne, *PL* 40, col. 245]) (*Breviarium Cisterciense, Hiemalis*, 434); Merton mentions this text in *Sign of Jonas*, 158 [February 13, 1949].

560. Gen 1:1–2:2 (*Missale Romanum*, 199–201; *Missale Cisterciense*, 170–71).

561. Exod 14:24–15:1 (*Missale Romanum*, 203–204; *Missale Cisterciense*, 171–72).

562. Lefebvre, *Saint Andrew Daily Missal*, 3:68 (the order is that of the Roman Rite).

563. *Missale Romanum*, 204; *Missale Cisterciense*, 172.

3. *Isaias*[564] (eighth in *St. Andrew's Missal*[565])—the idea of the *remnant* of Israel {is} introduced here, followed by the canticle of the vine.[566]

4. *Isaias*[567] (fifth in *St. Andrew's Missal*[568])—heavenly life {is} offered us in Christ {through} baptism and {the} Eucharist; "*Omnes sitientes venite ad aquas*"[569] (read it[570]).

The tract, "*Sicut cervus*,"[571] {is} followed by this collect, which is self-explanatory: "Grant we beseech thee, Almighty God, that we who celebrate the Paschal feast, may be enkindled with heavenly desires and may thirst for the fount of life."[572] After that begins the Mass (in our rite {there is} nothing of {the} baptismal font, etc.)

Holy Saturday {is} the "Sabbath" rest of Jesus in the tomb, after finishing the work of the new creation, into which we all enter on Easter

---

564. Isa 4:2–6 (*Missale Romanum*, 206–207; *Missale Cisterciense*, 172).

565. Lefebvre, *Saint Andrew Daily Missal*, 3:74.

566. Isa 5:1, 2, 7 (*Missale Romanum*, 207; *Missale Cisterciense*, 172).

567. Isa 54:17–55:11 (*Missale Romanum*, 204; *Missale Cisterciense*, 172–73).

568. Lefebvre, *Saint Andrew Daily Missal*, 3:69–70.

569. "All you who thirst, come to the waters" (v. 1).

570. "This is the inheritance of the servants of the Lord, and their justice with me, saith the Lord. All you that thirst, come to the waters: and you that have no money make haste, buy, and eat: come ye, buy wine and milk without money, and without any price. Why do you spend money for that which is not bread, and your labour for that which doth not satisfy you? Hearken diligently to me, and eat that which is good, and your soul shall be delighted in fatness. Incline your ear and come to me: hear and your soul shall live, and I will make an everlasting covenant with you, the faithful mercies of David. Behold I have given him for a witness to the people, for a leader and a master to the Gentiles. Behold thou shalt call a nation, which thou knewest not: and the nations that knew not thee shall run to thee, because of the Lord thy God, and for the Holy One of Israel, for he hath glorified thee. Seek ye the Lord, while he may be found: call upon him, while he is near. Let the wicked forsake his way, and the unjust man his thoughts, and let him return to the Lord, and he will have mercy on him, and to our God: for he is bountiful to forgive. For my thoughts are not your thoughts: nor your ways my ways, saith the Lord. For as the heavens are exalted above the earth, so are my ways exalted above your ways, and my thoughts above your thoughts. And as the rain and the snow come down from heaven, and return no more thither, but soak the earth, and water it, and make it to spring, and give seed to the sower, and bread to the eater: So shall my word be, which shall go forth from my mouth: it shall not return to me void, but it shall do whatsoever I please, and shall prosper in the things for which I sent it."

571. "As the deer" (Ps 41[42]:1–3) (*Missale Romanum*, 210; *Missale Cisterciense*, 173).

572. *Missale Cisterciense*, 173 (the *Missale Romanum* has a different prayer).

night, in the triumph of His Resurrection. {On} *the burial of Jesus,* some points from St. Thomas:

1. The death of Christ is to us a cause of life. It causes the death of our death. "Whatever happened to the body of Christ, even separated from the soul, was to us a cause of salvation by virtue of the power of the divinity united to that body" (III, q. 50, a. 6).[573] "The effects of the death of Christ are seen in the destruction of those things which stand in the way of our salvation—death of the soul, death of the body" (*ibid.*).[574]

2. The burial of Christ not only proves the reality of His death and resurrection (III, q. 51, a. l),[575] but also has a spiritual and salutary efficacy in those who are "buried together with Him by baptism."[576] The fact that He is buried in a tomb belonging to another is the ultimate in poverty shown in His Passion (III, q. 51, a. 2, ad 4[577]). However, it was a *new* tomb, for as Origen says, "*omnia quae sunt circa corpus Jesu munda sunt et nova et valde magna*" (quoted in III, q. 51, a. 2, ad 4[578]). During the burial of Christ, He was *all* in the tomb, for the whole *Person* was there, united to the body, and He was *all* in Limbo, for the whole Person of the Word was united to the soul (III, q. 52, a. 3[579]) (read 1 *Peter* 3:18–22[580]).

---

573. "*ideo quidquid contigit circa carnem Christi, etiam anima separata, fuit nobis salutiferum virtute divinitatis unitae*" (St. Thomas Aquinas, *Opera Omnia*, 4:225).

574. "*effectus mortis Christi attenditur circa remotionem eorum quae contrariantur nostrae saluti; quae quidem sunt mors animae, et mors corporis*" (St. Thomas Aquinas, *Opera Omnia*, 4:225).

575. St. Thomas Aquinas, *Opera Omnia*, 4.225.

576. Col 2:12.

577. St. Thomas Aquinas, *Opera Omnia*, 4.226.

578. "All things which are around the body of Jesus are pure and new and very great" (St. Thomas Aquinas, *Opera Omnia*, 4:226, quoting Origen, *Tractatus 35 in Matthaeum*).

579. St. Thomas Aquinas, *Opera Omnia*, 4:230.

580. "Because Christ also died once for our sins, the just for the unjust: that he might offer us to God, being put to death indeed in the flesh, but enlivened in the spirit, In which also coming he preached to those spirits that were in prison: Which had been some time incredulous, when they waited for the patience of God in the days of Noe, when the ark was a building: wherein a few, that is, eight souls, were saved by water. Whereunto baptism being of the like form, now saveth you also: not the putting away of the filth of the flesh, but the examination of a good conscience towards God by the resurrection of Jesus Christ. Who is on the right hand of God, swallowing down

The Descent of Jesus into Hell {is understood}:

1. as part of our punishment which He took upon Himself (though He did not suffer in hell); by his descent into hell He saves His elect from descending there (III, q. 52, a. 1[581]).

2. as part of His victory over the devil—He delivers the souls in Limbo.

3. to show His power in hell, *"visitando et illuminando,"*[582] i.e. manifesting His divinity *clearly*: "As the power of the passion of Christ is applied to the living, conforming us to His passion, so that same power is applied to the dead by His descent into hell."[583] *See the hymn of Easter Vigils*: "Christ the unconquered lion arises and the dragon is laid low, and crying out with His loud living voice, He raises the dead from their sleep. Greedy hell gives back the prey it had devoured, and delivered from captivity, the army of the dead follows Jesus."[584]

4. However, He did not descend into the hell of the damned, except by the *effect* of His resurrection, confounding them for their malice and infidelity (q. 52, a. 2[585]). He went into purgatory by the "effect" of His Resurrection, bringing them hope. *Sanctis autem patribus qui pro solo originali peccato detinebantur in inferno lumen aeternae gloriae infudit (idem).*[586] To Adam, Abraham, Moses, David, Isaias, etc., to the saints of the Old Law and to the saints of the natural law—like Lao Tse and Confucius and Buddha, no doubt—He brought the light of glory. In a word, He appeared in Limbo in His

death, that we might be made heirs of life everlasting: being gone into heaven, the angels and powers and virtues being made subject to him."

581. St. Thomas Aquinas, *Opera Omnia*, 4:228–29.

582. "by His visitation and illumination" (St. Thomas Aquinas, *Opera Omnia*, 4:228).

583. *"Unde sicut virtus passionis Christi applicatur viventibus per sacramenta configurantia nos passioni Christi; ita etiam applicata est mortuis per decensum Christi ad inferos"* (St. Thomas Aquinas, q. 52, a. 1, ad 2) (St. Thomas Aquinas, *Opera Omnia*, 4:229).

584. *"Christus invictus Leo / Dracone surgens obruto, / Dum voce viva personat, / A morte functos excitat. / Quam devorarat improbus / Praedam refudit tartarus: / Captivitate libera / Jesum sequuntur agmina"* (ll. 5-12) (*Breviarium Cisterciense, Vernalis*, 305).

585. St. Thomas Aquinas, *Opera Omnia*, 4:229–30.

586. "The light of eternal glory shone upon the holy fathers who were kept in hell because of original sin" (St. Thomas Aquinas, *Opera Omnia*, 4:230, which reads: ". . . peccato originali . . .").

glory—{His} glorious soul—the effect of His divinity reached into the lowest depths of hell; those who were ready to receive Him, who had somehow believed in Him, then came to Him by the attraction of His glory and followed Him away. The others were confounded. He also liberated from purgatory those who were "ready," says St. Thomas.[587] But it does not seem fitting that *any* should be left to suffer, on a day of victory.

EASTER SEASON

{We must strive} for a Paschal outlook on life. A predominantly *negative* attitude towards life is to be regarded as a dangerous temptation against Christian hope and a menace to the development of our risen life in Christ. We must not make a virtue out of wallowing in our miseries, as if our helplessness were utterly hopeless and the only way we could glorify God is by constant falls followed by prolonged lamentation of our nothingness. {We must} not regard God as One who takes delight in crushing our nothingness, and leaving us in a state of utter degradation. We are risen with Christ. We seek the things that are above. We live in a new creation. How shall we return to the *vetustas*[588] of the flesh? The devil is the accuser who never ceases to point out our faults. We are delivered from his power by the Resurrection; let us not return to it by our passivity. Let us not ruin our spiritual life with a program of continual self-condemnation and self-frustration. Let us stop calling ourselves evil and dare to *be good*. Let us face the fact that if we are risen with Christ we are good, we are holy, we are *saints*. All you who have risen with Christ have put on Christ.[589] The ferment of malice and falsity has been purged out of our lives. We have washed our feet; how should we defile them? Precisely by going back to wallowing in our misery, we tend to make void the work of Christ. If we keep saying, "O, I am nothing, I am useless, I can do nothing but evil," we will be able to silence our conscience and make a virtue out of defeat and cling to the *vetustas* and slavery and negativism of our old lives. No, we have risen with Christ and we are saints. That does not mean *we are faultless*—faultlessness is not the point. It means that though we may slip and make mistakes, our lives are now good and

---

587. "*qui jam sufficienter purgati erant*" (q. 52, a. 8, ad 1) (St. Thomas Aquinas, *Opera Omnia*, 4:233).

588. "old way."

589. See Col 3:1; Gal 3:27.

totally pleasing to God and full of greater potentialities for pleasing Him. Our bad will is done away with. We love God and seek Him alone, in spite of our weakness. *We are redeemed*—we do not have to keep redeeming ourselves over and over again day and night, as if it did not "take" the first time. If we really sin, yes, we need to do penance and rise again from our sins. *But the fact that we are not faultless and impeccable* is of little consequence if we sincerely try to love and glorify God and *make our lives fruitful.* Our lives must become positive, creative; the greatness that lies within us now must be allowed to come forth. We must respond to the call of Christ. We must rise up and come to Him ourselves. Read *Canticles of Canticles* 1:4–7,[590] 2:10–17.[591]

EASTER THEMES: Proem: {note} the progression of the gospel narratives in the Mass: Holy Saturday:[592] earthquake; Easter Sunday:[593] more calm; Easter Monday:[594] disciples of Emmaus; later: *Pax vobis*;[595] Low Sunday:[596] Thomas—"My Lord and my God."[597]

590. "I am black but beautiful, O ye daughters of Jerusalem, as the tents of Cedar, as the curtains of Solomon. Do not consider me that I am brown, because the sun hath altered my colour: the sons of my mother have fought against me, they have made me the keeper in the vineyards: my vineyard I have not kept. Shew me, O thou whom my soul loveth, where thou feedest, where thou liest in the midday, lest I begin to wander after the flocks of thy companions. If thou know not thyself, O fairest among women, go forth, and follow after the steps of the flocks, and feed thy kids beside the tents of the shepherds."

591. "Behold my beloved speaketh to me: Arise, make haste, my love, my dove, my beautiful one, and come. For winter is now past, the rain is over and gone. The flowers have appeared in our land, the time of pruning is come: the voice of the turtle is heard in our land: The fig tree hath put forth her green figs: the vines in flower yield their sweet smell. Arise, my love, my beautiful one, and come: My dove in the clefts of the rock, in the hollow places of the wall, shew me thy face, let thy voice sound in my ears: for thy voice is sweet, and thy face comely. Catch us the little foxes that destroy the vines: for our vineyard hath flourished. My beloved to me, and I to him who feedeth among the lilies, Till the day break, and the shadows retire. Return: be like, my beloved, to a roe, or to a young hart upon the mountains of Bether."

592. Matt 28:1–7 (*Missale Romanum*, 223; *Missale Cisterciense*, 176).

593. Mark 16:1–7 (*Missale Romanum*, 344; *Missale Cisterciense*, 236).

594. Luke 24:13–35 (*Missale Romanum*, 345–46; *Missale Cisterciense*, 237).

595. "Peace to you" (Luke 24:36) (gospel of Easter Tuesday) (*Missale Romanum*, 347; *Missale Cisterciense*, 238).

596. John 20:19–31 (*Missale Romanum*, 357–58; *Missale Cisterciense*, 246).

597. John 20:28.

1. *Surrexit Dominus vere.*[598]

2. *Haec dies quam fecit Dominus:*[599]

    a) *Beata Quinquagesima*[600] (*Pentecostes*); {it is the} day of eternity, {the} new creation in which Christ the Sun has risen; {it is the} *Prima Sabbati*[601] (*gospel*[602])—an entirely new order of being (cf. secret: Easter Day;[603] collect: Easter Wednesday[604]) .

    b) {It is the day} in which Christ walks with us, in preparation for the face–to–face vision (but {the} Holy Spirit replaces the corporeal presence of the glorified Redeemer) {and} instructs us: cf. {the} gospel of Easter Tuesday:[605] "*aperuit illis sensum ut intelligerent Scripturas*";[606] "*Mane nobiscum Domine.*"[607] (i) our hearts {were} burning within us (ii) at the breaking of {the} bread.[608]

    c) Moral implications (St. Paul's Epistles): "*Si consurrexistis cum Christo quae sursum sunt sapite*";[609] "*Mortui estis et vita vestra*

---

598. "The Lord has truly risen" (second nocturn, versicle: Easter) (*Breviarium Cisterciense, Vernalis,* 307).

599. "This is the day the Lord has made" (Ps 117[118]:24) (gradual: Easter) (*Missale Romanum,* 343; *Missale Cisterciense,* 235); (versicle, lauds: Easter) (*Breviarium Cisterciense, Vernalis,* 313).

600. "Blessed fifty days."

601. "the first day of the Sabbath."

602. "on the first day of the week" (Mark 16:2) (*Missale Romanum,* 344; *Missale Cisterciense,* 236).

603. "*Suscipe, quaesumus, Domine, preces populi tui cum oblationibus hostiarum: ut paschalis initiata mysteriis, ad aeternitatis nobis medelam, te operante, proficient*" ("Accept, Lord, we beg, the prayers of Your people with the sacrificial offerings, so that what has been begun by the paschal mysteries may through Your work profit us for an everlasting reward") (*Missale Romanum,* 344; *Missale Cisterciense,* 236).

604. "*Deus, qui nos Resurrectionis Dominicae annua solemnitate laetificas: concede propitius; ut per temporalia festa quae agimus, pervenire ad gaudia aeterna mereamur*" ("God, Who bring us joy through the annual celebration of the Lord's Resurrection, mercifully grant that through the temporal feasts we commemorate, we may become worthy to arrive at eternal joys") (*Missale Romanum,* 348; *Missale Cisterciense,* 239).

605. Luke 24:36–47 (*Missale Romanum,* 347–48; *Missale Cisterciense,* 238–39).

606. "He opened their minds for them so that they might understand the scriptures" (Luke 24:45).

607. "Stay with us Lord" (Luke 24:29).

608. Luke 24:32.

609. "If you have risen with Christ, . . . taste the things that are above" (Col 3:1, 2) (epistle: Easter Vigil) (*Missale Romanum,* 222; *Missale Cisterciense,* 175).

abscondita est cum Christo in Deo";[610] "*Cum Christus apparu-
erit, tunc et vos apparebitis*"[611] (eschatology); "*Expurgate vetus
fermentum*"[612] (cf. lessons, first nocturn: Easter Sunday[613]);
"*Itaque epulemur in azymis sinceritatis et veritatis.*"[614] {It brings
about} *unity* (Easter Day postcommunion;[615] *Soli polique pa-
triam unam facit rempublicam*[616]) {and} *peace*: "*Pax vobis.*"[617]

3. Why? "*Pascha nostrum immolatus est Christus.*"[618]

4. "*Itaque epulemur.* ALLELUIA!"[619]

EASTER SUNDAY: {the} *Paschal Season* {represents the} mystical life
{and reveals the} most sublime mysteries, {which are} hardest to understand, yet easy to participate in. *Resurrection* {means} (1) we are dead to
sin; (2) we are baptized in the death of Christ; (3) more precisely, we are
buried with Him by baptism into death so that we may rise in newness
of life; (4) if we are buried with Him in death, we shall rise with Him;
(5) our old man is crucified with Him that we may serve sin no longer,
for he that is dead is justified from sin; (6) if we be dead with Christ we
shall live together with Christ; (7) you are dead to sin but alive to God in
Christ Jesus Our Lord.[620] What do these statements mean? *How do we die*

---

610. "You have died, and your life is hidden with Christ in God" (Col 3:3).

611. "When Christ appears, then you too will appear [with Him]" (Col 3:4).

612. "Throw out the old yeast" (1 Cor 5:7) (epistle: Easter) (*Missale Romanum*,
343; *Missale Cisterciense*, 235).

613. Rom 6:2–10 (*Breviarium Cisterciense, Vernalis*, 306–7).

614. "Therefore let us feast on the unleavened bread of sincerity and truth" (1 Cor
5:8) (epistle, communion: Easter) (*Missale Romanum*, 343; *Missale Cisterciense*, 235,
236).

615. "*Spiritum nobis, Domine, tuae caritatis infunde: ut, quos sacramentis paschali-
bus satiasti, tum facias pietate concordes*" ("Lord, pour forth on us the Spirit of Your
love, so that You may by Your goodness make of one mind those whom You have filled
with the paschal sacraments") (*Missale Romanum*, 344; *Missale Cisterciense*, 236).

616. "He makes one country, a fatherland for earth and sun" (vigil hymn: Easter, ll.
15–16) (*Breviarium Cisterciense, Vernalis*, 307).

617. "Peace to you" (Luke 24:36) (gospel: Easter Tuesday) (*Missale Romanum*, 347;
Missale Cisterciense, 238).

618. "Christ our Pasch has been sacrificed" (1 Cor 5:7) (epistle, versicle, communion: Easter) (*Missale Romanum*, 343, 344; *Missale Cisterciense*, 235, 236).

619. "Therefore let us feast" (1 Cor 5:8) (epistle, communion: Easter) (*Missale Romanum*, 343, 344; *Missale Cisterciense*, 235, 236).

620. See Rom 6:1–13 (lessons, first nocturn: Easter) (*Breviarium Cisterciense, Vernalis*, 306–307).

to sin and live in Christ? Since this is the heart of the Easter Mystery, our understanding of it is all-important—all-important too, for our whole contemplative life (e.g. taking {the} monastic habit). {It is} most important not to repeat these formulas automatically; we must live our faith and really know it. *Remember:*

1. By original sin man *is dead to God*, and a *captive under a law he cannot keep.* (He cannot avoid all sin without grace.)

2. Man is incapable by himself of repairing his condition. He *must die;* he must *die in sin,* unless God intervenes.

3. St. Ambrose explains (*De Sacramentis*[621]): sin and death are the punishment; the punishment *must be undergone* to satisfy God's justice. When we die, *we pay the debt for sin,* and *we cease to sin,* but, unfortunately, we are dead. Christ's answer {to this dilemma is that} He takes upon Himself sin and death. He dies, paying our debt. (He is a man like us.) But He *then rises from the dead* and leaves us a means whereby we can make His death our own: (a) before we die (so as to be free from sin); (b) when we die. How? As God He can and does *institute* a means, an action which we can perform in Him and with Him. If we can die and rise with Him we shall (1) pay our debt; (2) stop sinning; (3) go on living with a restored nature (cf. {the} escape of Edmond Dantès in *Count of Monte Cristo*[622]).

4. How do we do this? (1) by faith; (2) the sacraments; (3) our new Life—especially the life of our vows: *conversion of manners* makes our life a paschal life in the Risen Christ.

The Easter Liturgy: the whole spirit of the Easter season is a spirit of joy and victory. Why? because the joy and fullness of God's love have come down to fill the world of man. We are no longer of "this world" (no longer under the "elements" of this world according to St. Paul[623]), no longer slaves of death and time; but into His creation God has come Himself to dwell with man whom He has lifted up to union with Himself

---

621. *De Sacramentis,* 2.6 (Migne, *PL* 16, cols. 428B–429B).

622. After the death of his mentor, the Abbé Faria, the unjustly imprisoned Dantès switches places with the corpse, and concealed inside the abbé's shroud, is tossed from the parapet of the Château d'If into the sea—the customary "burial" given to dead prisoners—and so makes his escape: see chapter 20, "The Cemetery of the Château d'If," in Dumas, *Count of Monte Cristo,* 232–37.

623. Col 2:20.

in His Risen Son, our Divine Savior. The liturgy repeatedly brings before us the *"conversatio"*[624] of the Risen Christ with His disciples during the time between His Resurrection and His Ascension, in order to remind us of the fact that He still dwells with us, and deals with us even more intimately, not in His Risen Humanity in a visible and experiential way, but through His Spirit and in the Blessed Eucharist, where His humanity and divinity alike are hidden. Christ lives in His Church, and throughout all the members of His Mystical Body He radiates the glory of His risen life; He communicates His light and love in the Holy Spirit. This mystery of Christ is the great manifestation of the Divine Wisdom; and in Paschaltide all is flooded with the radiance of this Wisdom.

The fifty days of Paschal time are the symbol of plenitude and fullness. It was the time of growing and harvest in Palestine, a time of thanksgiving not only for the good things of the earth but for the riches of divine life given us in the charity of Christ. Paschal time has an eschatological aspect, however. The Last Judgement is brought before us in the canticles of the third nocturn.[625] Easter gives us a growing awareness of the fact that Christ, though risen, must also ascend to the glory of His Father in order to prepare a place for us. His first message to His apostles is this: "I ascend to My Father and your Father."[626] Even the life of joy in God which is given us as members of the Mystical Christ on this earth is not definitive; it is only a step to something else more perfect and more complete: our life in glory, the glorious Church, the clearly manifested life of the Risen Christ in all His members, in heaven. Hence the Paschal season is a *growing progression* of fullness and joy from Easter to Pentecost, so that the giving of the Holy Spirit at Pentecost is in fact the culmination of the Easter triumph.

---

624. See Monday, Easter Week: Luke 24:13–35 (*Missale Romanum*, 345–46; *Missale Cisterciense*, 237); Tuesday, Easter Week: Luke 24:36–47 (*Missale Romanum*, 347–48; *Missale Cisterciense*, 238–39); Wednesday, Easter Week: John 21:1–14 (*Missale Romanum*, 349–50; *Missale Cisterciense*, 240); Thursday, Easter Week: John 20:11–19 (*Missale Romanum*, 352; *Missale Cisterciense*, 242); Friday, Easter Week: Matt 28:16–20 (*Missale Romanum*, 354; *Missale Cisterciense*, 243); Saturday, Easter Week: John 20:1–9 (*Missale Romanum*, 356; *Missale Cisterciense*, 244); Low Sunday: John 20:19–31 (*Missale Romanum*, 357–58; *Missale Cisterciense*, 245); Ascension: Acts 1:1–11; Mark 16:14–20 (*Missale Romanum*, 368–69; *Missale Cisterciense*, 256–57).

625. Isa 63:1–6; Hos 6:1–6; Zeph 3:8–13 (*Breviarium Cisterciense, Vernalis*, 309–10).

626. John 20:17.

The whole Easter cycle is not something which ascends to Easter as to its high point and then descends again to Pentecost, tapering off. It is a constant ascent to Pentecost, and the tapering off does not begin until after Pentecost. St. Augustine says, "Easter is the beginning of grace; Pentecost is its crown" (quoted in Flicoteaux, *Triomphe de Pâques*, 17[627]). Guéranger says: "Eternity in heaven is the true Pasch: hence, our pasch here on earth is the feast of feasts, the solemnity of solemnities [cf. Gregory Nazianzen in the night office[628]]. . . . The Church would have us consider ourselves as having risen with Jesus, and having already taken possession of eternal life."[629] Not only that, but this Paschal spirit of joy and victory goes throughout the year, for *every Sunday* is a renewal of the Easter solemnity. Every Sunday should be celebrated in the spirit of Easter and of eternity. It is the "eighth day," the day of eternity, outside our "weeks," beyond and above time.

Abundant graces of charity and joy and light will be given to us during this season, and it is our part to cooperate with them, to open our hearts to the light of Christ, especially in the liturgy and the Scriptures, and to nourish in our hearts and our community life the fervor of charity which is the fount of true joy, and the infallible sign of our new life in Christ, for we know that we have "passed from death to life if we love the brethren."[630] Like all other graces, the joy of Paschaltide is not something which comes to us automatically and passively, without our having to do anything. The joy is all there in the liturgy, and it is easy to get. Yet we must wish to *deepen* it in ourselves by digging deeper roots of faith into the mystery of the Resurrection. Paschaltide is a Eucharistic season par excellence, that is, a season of praise and thanksgiving to God

---

627. Pseudo-Augustine, *Sermo* 43.2 (*In Die Pentecostes I*): "*Solemnitas enim Paschae pervenit usque ad finem, non perdens jucunditatem, sed praeparans dignitatem: ut enim fuit initium gratiae, sic hodie finita est laus canticorum*" (Hamman, *Patrologiae Latinae, Supplementum*, 2.996) ("The solemnity of Easter extends all the way to the end, not losing its joyfulness, but enhancing its dignity; as it was the beginning of grace, so today the praise of the canticles is brought to completion"), paraphrased in Flicoteaux, *Triomphe de Pâques* ("Pâques a été le commencement de la grace, la Pentecôte en est le couronnement").

628. "*Haec nobis festivitatum festivitas, et celebritatum celebritas*" ("This is for us the festivity of festivities, and the celebration of celebrations") (*Sermo 1 de Paschate*) (*Breviarium Cisterciense, Vernalis*, 307).

629. Guéranger, *Liturgical Year*, 7:15, which reads: ". . . Church would, therefore, have us . . . having already risen with our Jesus, and as having . . ."

630. 1 John 3:14.

because He is good—not just because He is good *to us*, but because He is infinitely good in Himself. *Confitemini Domino quoniam bonus.*[631] How do we come to appreciate this better? by a deeper realization that the Paschal mystery is the great revelation of His love and His mercy: *quoniam in aeternum misericordia ejus.*[632] This atmosphere of victory especially surrounds our altars at Holy Mass during the Paschal season. The Lamb, slain for the sins of the world, is radiant in victory. *Dux vitae mortuus regnat vivus.*[633] Here above all we are overwhelmed with the realization that Jesus *lives*, and He is love. Our response {is} love and exultant thanksgiving to the Father, in the glorious Christ. Easter joy {is} the full expression of superabundant spiritual *life*.

Further points for Easter: the *Vidi aquam*[634] {is to be} contrasted with the *Asperges*.[635] {It has a note of} triumph rather than the suppliant and penitential view taken at other seasons. Note, it is the *same grace* that we receive, but now with a paschal aspect, an emphasis on the abundance of life that is poured out by God. All who are reached by the saving water are sanctified and sing the glorious song of triumph, *Alleluia*, {the} song of power and gratitude, proclaiming the victory of God. {Let us look at} some passages from Isaias on the Messianic Kingdom. But this is the Kingdom of God, the Kingdom in which the banquet of Jesus with His

---

631. "Proclaim the Lord, for He is good" (Ps 117[118]:1) (versicle: Easter Vigil) (*Missale Romanum*, 222; *Missale Cisterciense*, 175); (gradual: Easter) (*Missale Romanum*, 343; *Missale Cisterciense*, 235).

632. "because His mercy [endures] forever" (Ps 117[118]:1).

633. "The Leader of life Who was dead now reigns alive" (sequence: Easter, l. 7) (*Missale Romanum*, 344).

634. "I saw the water" (antiphon for the sprinkling of holy water before Mass used from Easter through Pentecost).

635. "Sprinkle [me with hyssop]" (antiphon for the sprinkling of holy water before Mass used for the rest of the liturgical year).

disciples is "fulfilled." READ: Isaias 44:1–8;[636] Isaias 49:8–23:[637] God's love for men revealed in the outpouring of His grace and the great multitude of the faithful ({the} theme of the Shepherd: cf. Good Shepherd Sunday);

636. "And now hear, O Jacob, my servant, and Israel whom I have chosen. Thus saith the Lord that made and formed thee, thy helper from the womb: Fear not, O my servant Jacob, and thou most righteous whom I have chosen. For I will pour out waters upon the thirsty ground, and streams upon the dry land: I will pour out my spirit upon thy seed, and my blessing upon thy stock. And they shall spring up among the herbs, as willows beside the running waters. One shall say: I am the Lord's, and another shall call himself by the name of Jacob, and another shall subscribe with his hand, To the Lord, and surname himself by the name of Israel. Thus saith the Lord the king of Israel, and his redeemer the Lord of hosts: I am the first, and I am the last, and besides me there is no God. Who is like to me? let him call and declare: and let him set before me the order, since I appointed the ancient people: and the things to come, and that shall be hereafter, let them shew unto them. Fear ye not, neither be ye troubled, from that time I have made thee to hear, and have declared: you are my witnesses. Is there a God besides me, a maker, whom I have not known?"

637. "Thus saith the Lord: In an acceptable time I have heard thee, and in the day of salvation I have helped thee: and I have preserved thee, and given thee to be a covenant of the people, that thou mightest raise up the earth, and possess the inheritances that were destroyed: That thou mightest say to them that are bound: Come forth: and to them that are in darkness: Shew yourselves. They shall feed in the ways, and their pastures shall be in every plain. They shall not hunger, nor thirst, neither shall the heat nor the sun strike them: for he that is merciful to them, shall be their shepherd, and at the fountains of waters he shall give them drink. And I will make all my mountains a way, and my paths shall be exalted. Behold these shall come from afar, and behold these from the north and from the sea, and these from the south country. Give praise, O ye heavens, and rejoice, O earth, ye mountains, give praise with jubilation: because the Lord hath comforted his people, and will have mercy on his poor ones. And Sion said: The Lord hath forsaken me, and the Lord hath forgotten me. Can a woman forget her infant, so as not to have pity on the son of her womb? and if she should forget, yet will not I forget thee. Behold, I have graven thee in my hands: thy walls are always before my eyes. Thy builders are come: they that destroy thee and make thee waste shall go out of thee. Lift up thy eyes round about, and see all these are gathered together, they are come to thee: I live, saith the Lord, thou shalt be clothed with all these as with an ornament, and as a bride thou shalt put them about thee. For thy deserts, and thy desolate places, and the land of thy destruction shall now be too narrow by reason of the inhabitants, and they that swallowed thee up shall be chased far away. The children of thy barrenness shall still say in thy ears: The place is too strait for me, make me room to dwell in. And thou shalt say in thy heart: Who hath begotten these? I was barren and brought not forth, led away, and captive: and who hath brought up these? I was destitute and alone: and these, where were they? Thus saith the Lord God: Behold I will lift up my hand to the Gentiles, and will set up my standard to the people. And they shall bring thy sons in their arms, and carry thy daughters upon their shoulders. And kings shall be thy nursing fathers, and queens thy nurses: they shall worship thee with their face toward the earth, and they shall lick up the dust of thy feet. And thou shalt know that I am the Lord, for they shall not be confounded that wait for him."

Isaias 55:1–5:[638] the gratuity of God's love for us, and of the gift of fruitfulness, by which He draws to the Church those He has called from the ends of the earth; Isaias 65:17–25:[639] the new Creation, the new Jerusalem, the peace and joy of the people of God who "shall not labor in vain"; the mercy of the Messianic Kingdom; Isaias 66:9–13:[640] "Shall not I that make others to bring forth children, Myself bring forth, saith the Lord?" The divine Wisdom is our Mother. All these texts show us the fruitfulness of the new life of the Church, the fruitfulness of the font and of the life-giving Spirit Who will come to us in all fullness at Pentecost.

638. "All you that thirst, come to the waters: and you that have no money make haste, buy, and eat: come ye, buy wine and milk without money, and without any price. Why do you spend money for that which is not bread, and your labour for that which doth not satisfy you? Hearken diligently to me, and eat that which is good, and your soul shall be delighted in fatness. Incline your ear and come to me: hear and your soul shall live, and I will make an everlasting covenant with you, the faithful mercies of David. Behold I have given him for a witness to the people, for a leader and a master to the Gentiles. Behold thou shalt call a nation, which thou knewest not: and the nations that knew not thee shall run to thee, because of the Lord thy God, and for the Holy One of Israel, for he hath glorified thee."

639. "For behold I create new heavens, and a new earth: and the former things shall not be in remembrance, and they shall not come upon the heart. But you shall be glad and rejoice for ever in these things, which I create: for behold I create Jerusalem a rejoicing, and the people thereof joy. And I will rejoice in Jerusalem, and joy in my people, and the voice of weeping shall no more be heard in her, nor the voice of crying. There shall no more be an infant of days there, nor an old man that shall not fill up his days: for the child shall die a hundred years old, and the sinner being a hundred years old shall be accursed. And they shall build houses, and inhabit them; and they shall plant vineyards, and eat the fruits of them. They shall not build, and another inhabit; they shall not plant, and another eat: for as the days of a tree, so shall be the days of my people, and the works of their hands shall be of long continuance. My elect shall not labour in vain, nor bring forth in trouble; for they are the seed of the blessed of the Lord, and their posterity with them. And it shall come to pass that, before they call, I will hear; as they are yet speaking, I will hear. The wolf and the lamb shall feed together; the lion and the ox shall eat straw; and dust shall be the serpent's food: they shall not hurt nor kill in all my holy mountain, saith the Lord."

640. "Shall not I that make others to bring forth children, myself bring forth, saith the Lord? shall I, that give generation to others, be barren, saith the Lord thy God? Rejoice with Jerusalem, and be glad with her, all you that love her: rejoice for joy with her, all you that mourn for her. That you may suck, and be filled with the breasts of her consolations: that you may milk out, and flow with delights, from the abundance of her glory. For thus saith the Lord: Behold I will bring upon her as it were a river of peace, and as an overflowing torrent the glory of the Gentiles, which you shall suck; you shall be carried at the breasts, and upon the knees they shall caress you. As one whom the mother caresseth, so will I comfort you, and you shall be comforted in Jerusalem."

GOOD SHEPHERD SUNDAY (Second Sunday after Easter)

Deus qui in Filii tui humilitate jacentem mundum erexisti (collect[641]). The entire cosmos is "lifted up" and spiritualized by the love of Christ for us and for all His creatures. He is truly the Good Shepherd Who has taken great care of all that belonged to Him, and has "loved everything that He had made,"[642] and has not suffered anything to be lost. Hence, *Misericordia Domini plena est terra*:[643] the earth is no longer an arid desert where we seek God in vain, but it is the temple of God, and He dwells in His temple, which is also the image and figure of the sanctuary where He dwells in heaven. All creatures are signs of God and speak of His mercy. {In the} *epistle*,[644] St. Peter shows how Christ is indeed the Servant of Yahweh prophesied in Isaias 53. This Mass is interesting for its *paschal view* of the Passion (cf. also the Feast of the Invention of the Holy Cross[645]). The Passion is everywhere, but "transfigured" by the Paschal victory. {The} *gospel* (John 10), {presents Christ as the} fulfillment of all Old Testament prophecies—cf. Yahweh as the shepherd of Israel (cf. Ezechiel 34:11–23; Psalms 22, 77, 78, etc.). Zacharias had said the Shepherd would be struck and the sheep scattered (Zach. 13:7), and yet, *by the Resurrection, Jesus gathered His scattered flock into unity.* This Mass looks forward to Pentecost as well as to {the} Ascension (first nocturn[646]). The theme of *a promised eschatological unity* (*unum ovile et unus pastor*[647]) rings out at the end of the gospel as a *very important paschal theme.* And we must hasten the day of this unity by forgetting ourselves and following in the footsteps of the Good Shepherd (epistle; gospel) to lay down our lives for "our sheep"—the souls entrusted to us by Divine Providence, especially Christians in Russia, separated Christians, etc. *The Sacrament of*

641. "God, Who have raised up a fallen world through the humility of Your Son" (*Missale Romanum*, 359; *Missale Cisterciense*, 248); (collect, lauds) (*Breviarium Cisterciense, Vernalis*, 335).

642. "*Omnia diligit Deus quae fecit*" (St. Augustine, *Tractatus 110 in Joannem* [Migne, *PL* 35, col. 1924], quoted in Aquinas, I, q. 20, a. 3 [*Opera Omnia*, 1.94]).

643. "The earth is filled with the mercy of the Lord" (Ps 32[33]:5) (introit: second Sunday after Easter) (*Missale Romanum*, 359; *Missale Cisterciense*, 247).

644. 1 Pet 2:21–25 (*Missale Romanum*, 359; *Missale Cisterciense*, 248).

645. May 3 (epistle: Phil 2:5–11; gospel: John 3:1–15) (*Missale Romanum*, 565–67; *Missale Cisterciense*, 412–14; *Breviarium Cisterciense, Vernalis*, 529–42).

646. Lessons 1–4: Acts 1:1–12 (*Breviarium Cisterciense, Vernalis*, 329–30); the lessons for the first nocturn of the Ascension are Acts 1:1–14 (*Breviarium Cisterciense, Vernalis*, 363–64).

647. "one flock and one shepherd" (John 10:16).

Unity—the Eucharist—is the means by which the Good Shepherd brings His flock into unity, giving Himself to them as their food so that they *recognize* Him; they are enlightened with divine light, in the "breaking of the bread"[648] (*Alleluia* verse: *Roman Missal*[649]). In this we see a definite relation of this day's Mass to *Holy Thursday*. Paschal time is the promised fulfillment when Jesus eats and drinks with His disciples *in the Kingdom of Heaven*—{the} "new wine."[650] *The idea of recognition, awakening, re-alization* is stressed in the *alleluia* verses—and our response is love and fidelity to our Risen Lord Who is "with us all days even to the end of the world,"[651] as our Good Shepherd, leading us by His ways so that we never need to fear. We need only remember, more and more, the implications of the tremendous fact that we *belong to Him*. It is through *His Church* and in His Church that Jesus acts as the Good Shepherd in our lives.

Fourth Sunday after Easter

Note the beautiful introits of all the Sundays after Easter; they are among the most magnificent and comprehensive of the whole year, *praising God and embracing the whole work of salvation*. They throw a "paschal" light on the whole Old Testament. Today {presents} a new view of the words of Psalm {97}: "He hath revealed His justice in the sight of the Gentiles."[652] How? by raising Christ from the dead, after destroying death and sin on the Cross. The text looks forward to Pentecost in which again He will even more clearly reveal the whole plan of His "justice" in the Church. Justice here embraces all the sanctity of God Who is Charity. {The} *collect*[653] {focuses on the} unity of the faithful, {having} one will, one charity. This union in love of the will of God, in desiring what He

---

648. Luke 24:35.

649. *Missale Romanum*, 359; the alleluia verse in the *Missale Cisterciense* is taken from Matt 28:2.

650. Matt 26:29; Mark 14:25.

651. Matt 28:20.

652. Ps 97[98]:2 (introit) (*Missale Romanum*, 361; *Missale Cisterciense*, 250) ("17" in copy text).

653. "*Deus, qui fidelium mentes unius efficis voluntatis: da populis tuis id amare quod praecipis, id desiderare quod promittis; ut inter mundanas varietates ibi nostra fixa sint corda, ubi vera sunt gaudia*" ("God, Who make the minds of the faithful to be of one will, grant Your people to love what You command, to desire what You promise, so that amidst worldly changes our hearts may be fixed where there are true joys") (*Missale Romanum*, 362; *Missale Cisterciense*, 250); (collect, lauds) (*Breviarium Cisterciense, Vernalis*, 349).

commands, is the guarantee of peace, true peace. This is the way of peace. We have to *work at this*. It is not done for us without effort on our part. Our efforts and generosity make us better able to live a risen life with Christ above the turmoil and dissension of the "old man." {With regard to the} *epistle*,[654] {note the} close connection between {the} epistle and {the} collect: (1) {the} idea of stability (in God) and change ({in} all that is outside of God); (2) {the} idea that by our virtue we participate in the stability of God; (3) the life of peace and unity is a *gift of God*; (4) given in the "engrafted word"[655] that saves our souls; (5) silence, meekness, chastity {are fundamental}. *The anger of man does not work the justice of God.* We have to work to overcome our nature. Do not try to correct everybody else, or teach everybody else, or punish others. Keep still, keep quiet. It is the *duty* of a Christian to bear meekly with injuries, and *not to take offense*. {Considering the} *gospel*, {this} beautiful gospel[656] tells us {for} the first time now of the coming of the Paraclete.

1. *Expedit vobis ut ego vadam.*[657] If Jesus does not go, the Holy Spirit will not be sent. When the Holy Spirit comes He will work both *exteriorly and interiorly*.

2. *Exteriorly*, {by} the open vindication and glorification of Jesus: *Ille me clarificabit.*[658] The clear condemnation of the world {is shown}: the world, not Jesus, has sinned; the world, not Jesus, is unjust; the world, not Jesus, is judged. This will be made clear by the Holy Spirit *in the Church*—{through} the sanctity and the charismata of the Church.

3. *Interiorly*, the Holy Spirit will also glorify Jesus in the souls of the apostles, teaching them all truth—not His own truth, but that of Jesus. {The} Holy Spirit brings *an abiding presence of God*, of Jesus, a constant teaching, guidance and sanctification in our souls.

654. James 1:17–21 (*Missale Romanum*, 362; *Missale Cisterciense*, 250).

655. James 1:21.

656. John 16:5–14 (*Missale Romanum*, 362; *Missale Cisterciense*, 250–51).

657. "It is beneficial for you that I depart" (John 16:7).

658. "He will illuminate Me" (John 16:14).

FIFTH SUNDAY AFTER EASTER

1. *Resurrexit in eo mundus, resurrexit in eo coelum, resurrexit in eo terra* (St. Ambrose: second nocturn[659]). As we near the end of Paschal Time and are ready for the consummation of Christ's triumph in the giving of the Holy Spirit, our attention is drawn by the liturgy to the *restoration of all things* in Christ which is precisely the work of the Spirit. Berdyaev says: "The world has been imprisoned by evil, and it can only be delivered by love."[660] It is as a result of man's sin that the world, with man himself, is subject to *inertia* and *necessity*, to laws that lead inevitably and inexorably to dissolution and death. Since the fall, all nature tends downwards to nothingness. But with the coming of Christ, the second Adam, love and liberty are once again in the world, and once again creation is ordered not towards inertia, necessity and death, but liberty, creativity and life. Why? because in Christ, God and man become one, and man is elevated above the determinism of nature, above merely natural laws of life and death. The whole world is his kingdom and helps him to serve God; the whole world is elevated with him and ordered with him to a spiritual end. This will be fully apparent only at the last day.

2. *Petite et accipietis*[661] (St. Augustine: third nocturn[662]). Do we really believe this? (1) Everything we ask in Jesus' Name will be granted. (2) But what is asked *"contra rationem salutis"*[663] is not asked in His Name. (3) We must ask, knowing Who Jesus is, and what salvation means, and our prayer must accord with this Christian view. (4) We will not necessarily be heard for others (*they* may put obstacles in the way), but will always be heard for ourselves. (5) Above all, the

---

659. "In Him the world is raised, in Him the heaven is raised, in Him the earth is raised" (*De Fide Resurrectionis*, 102 [Migne, *PL* 16, col. 1354]) (eighth lesson) (*Breviarium Cisterciense, Vernalis*, 353–54).

660. "Le monde a été enchaîné par le mal et ne peut être délivré que par l'amour" (Berdyaev, *Sens de la Création*, 199). Merton was reading this work in April and May 1957 (see Merton, *Search for Solitude*, 85–89, 92–94).

661. "Ask and you shall receive" (John 16:24) (third nocturn: fifth Sunday after Easter) (*Breviarium Cisterciense, Vernalis*, 356); (gospel: fifth Sunday after Easter) (*Missale Romanum*, 363; *Missale Cisterciense*, 252).

662. *Tractatus 102 in Joannem* (lessons 9–12) (*Breviarium Cisterciense, Vernalis*, 354–55).

663. "contrary to the way of salvation" (ninth lesson) (*Breviarium Cisterciense, Vernalis*, 354).

supreme gift will be given us "that your joy may be full."[664] To ask for anything else but eternal life or the means thereto is nothing. Courage, hope and magnanimity in the life of prayer {are essential}.

3. *Processions*: yet in the rogation processions we simply and humbly ask for good crops. {Here there is} the idea of a *lustral* procession (rogations; Sundays): {they} always should terminate in a Mass (n.b. {they are of} pagan origin). What about the procession on Ascension Day? {It is} commemorative of the mystery. And Corpus Christi?

LITANIAE MAJORES[665] AND ROGATION DAYS

The "St. Mark's Procession" has really nothing to do with St. Mark. {The} litany was fixed for this day before St. Mark's feast existed. It existed before St. Gregory the Great, who fixed it on this day. {It} goes back to {the} pagan *Robigalia*.[666] {With regard to the} litany, remember {that} St. Benedict in the *Rule* calls the "*Kyrie*" "*Litaniae*."[667] Properly, a litany is a penitential prayer of supplication chanted while proceeding from place to place. The major litanies and rogation-day processions are traditionally supposed to start out from a parish or other church and proceed through town or countryside, to call down a blessing from God. In the monastery, we would better keep the spirit of the procession if we went *outside*, and paused to call down special blessing on our fields and crops. Actually, usually one priest and a companion go all over the farm during the afternoon work.

The litanies remind us of the great truth that God is the Master of the crops, the giver of rain and good weather, the Father from Whom all blessings come, and not a mere spectator Who stands by and approves while we go ahead with our marvelous technical methods for increasing production. Again, litanies are *penitential*; {they} remind us that by our sins we have merited to have all blessings withdrawn from us; {they are} a protestation of submission to the divine will and obedience for the future.

---

664. John 15:11, 16:24.

665. "Greater litanies" (*Missale Romanum*, 364–66; *Missale Cisterciense*, 252–54), the term used to refer to the "rogation day" kept on April 25, the Feast of St. Mark, as distinguished from the "lesser litanies" of the three days preceding the Feast of the Ascension.

666. A festival held on April 25 to propitiate an archaic deity who was considered responsible for various agricultural diseases.

667. *Rule*, c. 9 (McCann, ed. and trans., *Rule of St. Benedict*, 50).

For many years April 25 was a day of abstinence—so too the rogation days. The rogation days, instituted by St. Mamertus, Bishop of Vienne, in time of earthquakes, {are} a kind of supplement to the ember days (processions {are made} barefoot, with ashes on heads). The rogation processions {are} a sacramental by which the Church strives to sanctify our daily life. Pray for your special intentions; sanctify your manual labor. {See} *Guardini* on processions—to walk with full human dignity is to add beauty and meaning to prayer. "Walking expresses the nobility of man. He is upright, the master of his movements, advances with assurance. This is his privilege. To walk upright signifies to be a man. But we are not only men, we are also sons of God. . . . Christ lives and walks about the world in us. . . . remember God's counsel to Abraham, '*Ambula coram me et esto perfectus* . . . .'"[668] ({We} should have some sense of this, and not just walk like animals on their hind legs.)

ASCENSION DAY

1. Remember that Ascension and Pentecost are really parts of the Easter solemnity—the *sacra quinquagesima*.[669] The Ascension is the logical consequence of Jesus' Resurrection from the dead. The sending of the Holy Spirit is also a necessary consequence of the Resurrection and Ascension. Since Jesus is in heaven and yet also in us, it is necessary that the Spirit be sent, for it is by the Holy Spirit that Jesus lives in us and we in Him.

2. As monks, our whole life is an imitation of Jesus. Jesus sums up His whole life: "I came forth from the Father and came into the world: again I leave the world and go to the Father" (John 16: gospel of {the} fifth Sunday after Easter[670]). Dom Anselme Stolz, OSB says that the monk's imitation of Christ reproduces all these movements in our lives.[671] As Jesus came forth from the Father, we leave our own families and what is

---

668. "La marche n'exprime-t-il pas la noblesse de l'homme? Car ce corps droit, maître de ses mouvements, qui va d'un pas assuré, est son privilège. Marcher le corps droit signifie être homme. Mais nous ne sommes pas seulement des hommes. 'Vous êtes de race divine' nous dit l'Écriture. . . . Le Christ vit en nous de façon spéciale. . . . Ce cerait, transfiguré, l'accomplissement de conseil: Ambula coram me et esto perfectus" (Guardini, *Signes Sacrés*, 41–42; the quotation is from Gen 17:1: "Walk in My presence and be perfect").

669. "holy fifty days."

670. *Missale Romanum*, 363; *Missale Cisterciense*, 252.

671. Stolz, *L'Ascèse Chrétienne*, 85–86.

our own, like Abraham: *exi de terra tua et cognatione tua.*[672] By mortification we "go out" of our own human nature and our own will. Then we leave the world and go to the Father, by prayer. It is above all then by our life of prayer that we return with Jesus to the Father. {The} Ascension {is a} feast of the contemplative life.

3. {See the relevant} texts: {at} *the vigil, Pater venit hora, clarifica Filium tuum.*[673] The "hour" literally referred to is that of the Passion and Resurrection. The Ascension is here pointed out therefore as the final glorification involved in Christ's victory over death. Actually, the "glorification" is inseparably involved in the Passion, Resurrection and Ascension. But we are focusing on the Ascension now as pure and unmixed glory. {In the} *epistle* of the vigil[674] (Ephesians 4), the Ascension {is seen as the} fruit of the victory of Christ, compared to a triumph of a conquering general, in which we are led with Him, and share in His spoils. He portions out to us graces according to His own largesse, because "*He ascended above the heavens that He might fill all things.*"[675] His gifts {are} vocations, which give us an active share in the great mystery of His kingdom. {The} Ascension {is} part of our vocation. The end {is} in view: "Until we all meet into the unity of faith and of the knowledge of the Son of God, unto a perfect man, unto the measure of the age of the fullness of Christ."[676] {In} the gospel of the vigil[677] (John 17), {we hear}: "Father, the hour has come"[678] (theme of the vigil); "You have given Him power over all flesh, that to all He may give life eternal";[679] "Eternal life {is} to know Thee and Jesus Christ";[680] "I have finished the work . . . now glorify Thou Me";[681] "Now they have known that all that Thou hast given Me are from Thee"[682] (the Church knows the Father in the Son; no longer {is there}

672. "Leave your land and your relatives" (Gen 12:1) (quoted in Stolz, *L'Ascèse Chrétienne*).

673. "Father, the hour has come; glorify Your Son" (John 17:1) (Benedictus antiphon) (*Breviarium Cisterciense, Vernalis,* 358).

674. Eph 4:7–13 (*Missale Romanum,* 366; *Missale Cisterciense,* 254).

675. Eph 4:10.

676. Eph 4:13.

677. John 17:1–11 (*Missale Romanum,* 367; *Missale Cisterciense,* 255).

678. John 17:1.

679. John 17:2.

680. John 17:3.

681. John 17:4, 5.

682. John 17:7.

any need for the Son to occupy the center of the stage in His historical Person, for the Mystical Christ is the One Son of God, knowing, loving, serving and praising the Father, in the Spirit); "I pray for them—they are in the world, and I come to Thee"[683] (we remain in the world as members in whom Christ still works, struggles and suffers, while He reigns gloriously in heaven, all power being in His divine hands).

4. *The Office of Ascension Day*: vespers {has the} usual clear sequence of antiphons[684] (replacing the *Alleluia*). *Vado parare vobis locum*:[685] faith in the life of glory destined for us, as we share in the triumph of Jesus, as a reward for our participation in His sufferings. *Iterum veniam ad vos*:[686] this reward will not be without the presence of Jesus Himself; indeed, He is our reward, and He comes to lead us into the reward, the Kingdom. *Non vos relinquam*:[687] the same idea {is} repeated, with a tender emphasis on the fact that we shall not be left orphans, and we shall rejoice when He comes again—not only at the Parousia, but also He comes in the Spirit, for the Holy Spirit makes Jesus dwell intimately in our own inmost being, or rather, the Holy Spirit opens up the depths of our being, showing us that heaven is there and Jesus reigns within, and we did not realize it. *Pacem meam do vobis*:[688] {the} Ascension {is} a feast of peace, peace in faith and perfect hope. The paradox of the Christian life {is that} we do not seek full peace and hope in the world; we place all our hope in heaven; and yet in doing so we realize that we possess everything, that we lack nothing, that nothing is wanting to us to know. The same heaven which we shall possess in clear vision we already possess in hope. *Sic veniet*:[689] He shall certainly return to judge the world and glorify the elect. {The} *hymn*[690] {is} apparently of late composition; {in} admiration of the mercy of God triumphant in Jesus, {it} looks back over the Incarnation of the Word and Creator of the world, the Passion, the descent into hell and the liberation of the captives, the triumph of the King rising to take His place at the right hand of the Father, and the future glory, the clear

---

683. John 17:9, 11.

684. *Breviarium Cisterciense, Vernalis*, 361.

685. "I go to prepare a place for you" (John 14:3) (first antiphon).

686. "I shall come to you again" (John 14:3) (first antiphon).

687. "I will not leave you [orphans]" (John 14:18) (second antiphon).

688. My peace I give to you" (John 14:27) (third antiphon).

689. "Thus He will come" (Acts 1:11) (fourth antiphon).

690. "*Jesu nostra Redemptio*" ("Jesus our Redemption") (*Breviarium Cisterciense, Vernalis*, 361–62).

vision of God promised to us. {The} *collect* (*Ipsi quoque mente in coeles-tibus habitemus*[691]) {focuses on} the grace of the feast: to dwell in heaven by prayer and faith and purity of heart. But this means, after all, realizing that Jesus dwells within us on earth, and His prayer and His Spirit have separated us from the world, which cannot harm us, and opened to us the mystery of His infinite reality present and resplendent within all things. {The} *first nocturn*, {from the} Acts of the Apostles,[692] {is the} narrative of the Ascension. {The} responsories of all the nocturns {are} from the Acts, Psalms, St. John, mostly. {In the} *second nocturn*, {the} lessons of St. Leo[693] give the theology of the feast, particularly seven and eight. *Human nature* is seen ascending above all the other orders of creation, even above the angels and archangels, to be seated together with the eternal Father in glory, because united hypostatically to the Son in the Incarnation. Hence, *Christi ascensio nostra provectio est. Quo praecessit gloria capitis, eo spes vocatur et corporis.* {. . .} *Coelorum in Christo superna penetravimus.*[694] "Today we have become not only possessors of Paradise, *but we have even entered the highest heavens in Christ,* having gained far more by the ineffable grace of Christ than we had lost by the envy of the devil."[695] {The} amazing consequences of this doctrine, which makes possible the Christian life by contemplation, {are that} *we are already living in heaven by hope.*

5. *The Mass*: the narrative of the Ascension {is} in the epistle:[696]

a) How Jesus told the apostles to wait in Jerusalem for the coming of the Holy Ghost. This coming is the "promise of the Father which you have heard from my lips."[697] John baptized with water; you will

---

691. "May we ourselves also dwell in spirit in the heavenly places" (*Missale Romanum*, 368; *Missale Cisterciense*, 256; *Breviarium Cisterciense, Vernalis*, 362, 369).

692. Acts 1:1–14 (*Breviarium Cisterciense, Vernalis*, 363–64).

693. *Sermo 1 de Ascensione* (*Breviarium Cisterciense, Vernalis*, 365–66).

694. "The ascension of Christ is our arising. Where the glory of the Head has led the way, there also the hope of the Body is called. . . . In Christ we have entered the highest heavens" (eighth lesson) (*Breviarium Cisterciense, Vernalis*, 366, which reads: ". . . *est, et quo* . . .").

695. "*Hodie enim non solum paradisi possessores firmati sumus, sed etiam coelorum in Christo superna penetravimus, ampliora adepti per ineffabilem Christi gratiam, quam per diaboli amiseramus invidiam*" (*Breviarium Cisterciense, Vernalis*, 366).

696. Acts 1:1–11 (*Missale Romanum*, 368–69; *Missale Cisterciense*, 256–57).

697. Acts 1:4.

be baptized with the Holy Ghost.[698] (What a tremendous reality—to be baptized not with a created thing but with God, anointed with the Spirit Who made Jesus the Christ, the Lord's Anointed.)

b) The question of the disciples: still seeing things from a purely human point of view, not understanding the things of God, they ask if the Kingdom they have been expecting will now be established. (We too are always clinging to some foolish hope concretized in a silly question which we repeatedly ask Him.)

c) The answer of Jesus: He says neither "yes" nor "no": "It is not for you to know the times which the Father has placed in His own power."[699] But there is something much greater than this knowledge, which is not proper to us: "You shall receive the power of the Holy Ghost coming upon you."[700] "You shall be my witnesses . . . in Jerusalem, Samaria, and in the uttermost parts of the earth."[701]

d) He is taken up into heaven, and the angels appear to chide them for standing dumbfounded: He will return again as they have seen Him going.

{In} the gospel,[702] again {we see} the reproach of the incredulity of the apostles (a theme running through this feast—St. Gregory emphasizes this in the third nocturn[703]), {then} the mission of the apostles to the whole world (cf. {the} epistle of the vigil,[704] {presenting the} Ascension {as a} triumph, {the} sharing of spoils: the spoils of the Christ's victory are to be distributed over the whole world). Conditions for receiving them {are} belief {and} baptism: "Qui crediderit et baptizatus fuerit . . ."[705] Evidences of belief {are} charismatic graces. The result {is that} the apostles preach "Domino cooperante."[706] Mark telescopes the narrative, not speaking of Pentecost. But it is in and through the Holy Spirit that the Lord Jesus works with His apostles.

698. Acts 1:5.

699. Acts 1:7.

700. Acts 1:8.

701. Acts 1:8.

702. Mark 16:14–20 (Missale Romanum, 369; Missale Cisterciense, 257).

703. Homilia 29 in Evangelia (Breviarium Cisterciense, Vernalis, 367–68).

704. Eph 4:7–13 (Missale Romanum, 366; Missale Cisterciense, 254).

705. "the one who believes and is baptized" (Mark 16:16).

706. "with the Lord working [with them]" (Mark 16:20).

6. *The Ascension Psalm* (Psalm 46):[707] it is a hymn to God as King of the world. Some commentators think it refers to a procession with the Ark ascending to the Temple and Gentile allies being invited to praise God with Israel. However, the Church looks at it as a messianic and eschatological psalm. In the messianic age, the Gentiles will praise God with the Jews, and God will be King over the whole earth. The ascension of Christ is the ascension of the victorious King to His throne, and all the world joins in praising Him; the great ones of the earth belong to God. At present this is still hidden by the veils of faith, but it will be manifest when He comes again, "as we have seen Him ascending into heaven."[708]

ASCENSION AND PENTECOST

Originally the two feasts were celebrated in one, on the day of Pentecost (up until the fourth century). At Jerusalem, the coming of the Holy Ghost was celebrated in the evening at the Cenacle, and the Ascension was commemorated on the Mount of Olives in the afternoon. The two feasts are indeed closely connected, and form part of the whole Easter Mystery of which they are the *consummation*.

1. {They are} *feasts of wonder* {and} admiration. The *admirabilis Ascensio* {reveals the} importance of wonder, joy, jubilation in the spiritual life, {as} essential to our contacts with God in the Church (cf. Isaias 60: {the} epistle for the Epiphany,[709] which has much the same object and spirit as these feasts: "Then shalt thou see and abound and *thy heart shall wonder and be enlarged*"[710]). The Ascension {and} the giving of the Holy Spirit culminate in the *conversion of the Gentiles* ({see the} gospel of {the} Ascension[711] {and the} epistle of Pentecost). Read {the} *epistle* {for} Pentecost:[712] "They were all amazed and wondered . . . we have heard

707. Introit (v. 2); alleluia (v. 6); offertory (v. 6) (*Missale Romanum*, 368, 369; *Missale Cisterciense*, 256, 257).

708. Acts 1:11 (introit; epistle) (*Missale Romanum*, 368; *Missale Cisterciense*, 256, 257).

709. Isa 60:1–6 (*Missale Romanum*, 39; *Missale Cisterciense*, 35–36).

710. Isa 60:5.

711. Mark 16:14–20 (*Missale Romanum*, 369; *Missale Cisterciense*, 257).

712. Acts 2:1–11 (*Missale Romanum*, 378; *Missale Cisterciense*, 264–65): "And when the days of the Pentecost were accomplished, they were all together in one place: And suddenly there came a sound from heaven, as of a mighty wind coming, and it filled the whole house where they were sitting. And there appeared to them parted tongues as it were of fire, and it sat upon every one of them: And they were all filled with the Holy Ghost, and they began to speak with divers tongues, according

them speak in our own tongues the wonderful works of God." {Among the} great wonders of the Ascension {is the question}: *where* does Jesus go? into an entirely new realm, a spiritual "place."

2. *Feasts of Fullness: Spiritus Domini* replevit *orbem terrarum.*[713] *Cum* complerentur *dies.*[714] Reple *tuorum corda fidelium.*[715] *Reple cordis intima.*[716] *Repleti sunt omnes Spiritu Sancto.*[717] God Himself comes to dwell within us—the Father, Son and Holy Spirit "remain" in us (gospel: Pentecost[718]). We are not only filled but *purified* (*Spiritus Sancti illustratione emunda*[719]) and fecundated (*tui roris intima aspersione fecundet*[720]). All this begins with the Ascension: *Ascendit* UT IMPLERET OMNIA[721] (epistle: vigil of {the} Ascension). *Read* {the} epistle of {the} vigil:[722]

---

as the Holy Ghost gave them to speak. Now there were dwelling at Jerusalem, Jews, devout men, out of every nation under heaven. And when this was noised abroad, the multitude came together, and were confounded in mind, because that every man heard them speak in his own tongue. And they were all amazed, and wondered, saying: Behold, are not all these, that speak, Galileans? And how have we heard, every man our own tongue wherein we were born? Parthians, and Medes, and Elamites, and inhabitants of Mesopotamia, Judea, and Cappadocia, Pontus and Asia, Phrygia, and Pamphylia, Egypt, and the parts of Libya about Cyrene, and strangers of Rome, Jews also and proselytes, Cretes, and Arabians: we have heard them speak in our own tongues the wonderful works of God."

713. "The Spirit of the Lord has filled the whole earth" (Wis 1:7) (introit: Pentecost) (*Missale Romanum*, 378; *Missale Cisterciense*, 264).

714. "When the days were fulfilled" (Acts 2:1) (epistle: Pentecost) (*Missale Romanum*, 378; *Missale Cisterciense*, 264).

715. "Fill the hearts of Your faithful" (alleluia versicle: Pentecost) (*Missale Romanum*, 379; *Missale Cisterciense*, 265).

716. "Fill the inmost heart" (sequence: Pentecost, l. 14) (*Missale Romanum*, 379).

717. "All were filled with the Holy Spirit" (Acts 2:4) (epistle: Pentecost) (*Missale Romanum*, 378; *Missale Cisterciense*, 264).

718. John 14:23–31 (*Missale Romanum*, 379; *Missale Cisterciense*, 265).

719. "purify [our hearts] by the light of the Holy Spirit" (secret: Pentecost) (*Missale Romanum*, 379; *Missale Cisterciense*, 265).

720. "May it make fertile by the inward sprinkling of Your dew" (postcommunion: Pentecost) (*Missale Romanum*, 379; *Missale Cisterciense*, 265).

721. "He ascended . . . that He might fill all things" (Eph 4:10).

722. Eph 4:7–13 (*Missale Romanum*, 366; *Missale Cisterciense*, 254): "But to every one of us is given grace, according to the measure of the giving of Christ. Wherefore he saith: Ascending on high, he led captivity captive; he gave gifts to men. Now that he ascended, what is it, but because he also descended first into the lower parts of the earth? He that descended is the same also that ascended above all the heavens, that he might fill all things. And he gave some apostles, and some prophets, and other some evangelists, and other some pastors and doctors, For the perfecting of the saints, for

Captivam duxit captivitatem.[723] {This is} His triumph: *He takes us with Him* (see St. Leo, second nocturn[724]): hence our great joy! Unitam sibi fragilitatis nostrae substantiam *in gloriae tuae dextera collocavit*[725] (communicantes: Ascension); ut nos divinitatis suae tribueret esse participes[726] (preface: Ascension). Here indeed we have the overwhelming fullness of the Mystery of Christ!! Our nature *in its weakness* is seated in heaven. In our trials, temptations and sufferings our own humanity is enthroned with Jesus, *as long as* we are sharers in His divinity. How? by the Holy Spirit. {This is} a sublime and consoling truth. Not just our souls and our "interior life" {are} sanctified, but *all* is elevated and transformed in Christ; all is heavenly; all is divine. Understand why we sing the *Alleluia,* and long for the Holy Spirit: our offices, jobs and functions—all are sanctified by the Holy Spirit as we come together to form *one body.* "*Ut in omnibus glorificetur Deus.*"[727] Read {the} epistle for {the} Sunday within {the} Octave {of the Ascension}.[728]

Vigil of Pentecost

What do we mean—the Holy Ghost *comes?*

1. *The Collects after the Prophecies:*[729] note how these collects explain the scriptures, particularly *Exodus.* The light of the New Testament "unlocks" the hidden mystery of the great events in Exodus (collect two[730]):

---

the work of the ministry, for the edifying of the body of Christ: Until we all meet into the unity of faith, and of the knowledge of the Son of God, unto a perfect man, unto the measure of the age of the fulness of Christ."

723. "He led captivity captive" (Eph 4:8, citing Ps 67[68]:19).

724. See above, nn. 693–695.

725. "He placed at the right hand of Your glory the substance of our weak nature, united to Himself" (*Missale Romanum,* 324; *Missale Cisterciense,* 219).

726. "so that he might allow us to be sharers of His divinity" (*Missale Romanum,* 314; *Missale Cisterciense,* 203).

727. "so that God might be glorified in all things" (1 Pet 4:11).

728. 1 Pet 4:7–11 (*Missale Romanum,* 370; *Missale Cisterciense,* 258): "Be prudent therefore, and watch in prayers. But before all things have a constant mutual charity among yourselves: for charity covereth a multitude of sins. Using hospitality one towards another, without murmuring, As every man hath received grace, ministering the same one to another: as good stewards of the manifold grace of God. If any man speak, let him speak, as the words of God. If any man minister, let him do it, as of the power, which God administereth: that in all things God may be honoured through Jesus Christ."

729. *Missale Romanum,* 372–75; *Missale Cisterciense,* 260–62.

730. *Missale Romanum,* 372; *Missale Cisterciense,* 260–61.

{the} typology of {the} Red Sea (baptism); deliverance of the Chosen People (all the sacraments). Regeneration {comes} by *partaking of the Holy Spirit*. What does it mean to partake of the Holy Spirit? {See} collect three:[731] God Himself is the glory of the faithful and the life of the just. {In the} *liturgy*, "by singing sacred canticles"[732] we are taught by God. {In} collect five, the prophets in general teach us to "*Temporalia relinquere atque ad aeterna festinare!*"[733] Our hearts must be empty to receive the Holy Ghost. But the Holy Ghost Himself must empty them. Our part {is} to remove obstacles and "let go" of what we are holding onto. We need His grace to know the commandments and to put them into practice. Without Him we can do nothing. {Therefore we must form a} resolution to refuse Him nothing, in order that He may have perfect freedom of action in our souls. "*O lux beatissima / Reple cordis intima / Tuorum fidelium.*"[734]

2. *The Mass: Claritatis tuae super nos splendor effulgeat*[735] (collect). His light will be strength and confirmation in grace. *Fortitude* {is} a great grace of Pentecost, a most important gift—{the} divine energy to overcome the inertia of our nature and confess God before the world. In what way does the Holy Spirit become a fountain of living waters in our hearts?

3. *Vespers*: see especially the mystery of the Church and God's clear manifestation of Himself in the Church as a result of the sending of the Holy Spirit. "*Erant omnes pariter in eodem loco.*"[736] Common life attracts the Holy Spirit, especially; {along with} liturgical prayer {it is} the "place" where the Holy Spirit is most active.

Pentecost

The Liturgy of the Vigil and of the Feast: in the early times, Pentecost was celebrated, like Easter, with a night vigil. Baptism was administered

---

731. *Missale Romanum*, 372; *Missale Cisterciense*, 261.

732. "*modulatione sacri carminis*" (*Missale Romanum*, 373; *Missale Cisterciense*, 260; this is actually collect three in the Roman Rite).

733. "to let go of temporal things and hasten toward the eternal" (*Missale Romanum*, 375; *Missale Cisterciense*, 261; the enumeration is according to the Roman Rite; collect four in the Cistercian Rite).

734. "O blessed Light / Fill the inmost heart / Of your faithful" (sequence: Pentecost, ll. 13–15) (*Missale Romanum*, 379).

735. "May the splendor of Your brightness shine upon us" (*Missale Romanum*, 376; *Missale Cisterciense*, 262).

736. "They were all together in the same place" (Acts. 2:1) (capitulum) (*Breviarium Cisterciense, Vernalis*, 389).

to catechumens who were not able to be baptized at Easter. {Note} the prophecies and orations of the vigil (*Cistercian Missal*: in our missal we have on {the} vigil of Pentecost the lessons that were omitted in {the} Easter Vigil[737]).

1. *Abraham* (842):[738] the obedience of Abraham, the readiness to sacrifice Isaac, looks back to the Passion of Christ, but the important theme, for the liturgy of this vigil, is the promise of God to multiply Abraham's seed as the sands of the sea. In this lesson we see: (a) the Heavenly Father offering Jesus His Son, "providing" another victim than Isaac, the child of the Promise; {here we find the} mystery of Providence—and Abraham's faith and obedience; (b) the Sacrifice of the Son; (c) and its fruitfulness. {In the} *collect*, the Church herself meditates on this lesson, asking God, Who gave Abraham as an example of obedience to the human race, to give us the grace to "break the perversity of our own will" and to "fulfill in all things the integrity of Thy precepts."[739]

2. *Moses* (855)[740] teaches his canticle to the Chosen People, gives the Levites the book of the Law to keep in the Ark, reproves them for their obstinacy and prophesies that after his death they will continue to disobey God, and says that the words of the Law will remain as a witness against them. {The} *tract* {is} the Canticle of Moses (part of Deuteronomy 32),[741] {including} texts about the word of God "descending like dew"[742] (again {the} implication of fertility and mercy), {revealing} the fidelity and perfection of God's promises. {In the} *collect*, God is invoked as the glory of the faithful and the life of the just, "Who through Moses didst will that Thy people should be taught [Thy ways] in the singing of the canticle."[743] (This points out the singular importance of the canticle of

737. Gen 22:1–19; Deut 31:22–30; Isa 4:1–6 (this reading had not been omitted at the Easter Vigil; see n. 564 above and n. 748 below); Bar 3:9–39 (*Missale Cisterciense*, 259–62); the Roman Rite includes in addition Exod 14:24—15:1 and Ezek 37:1–14 as the second and sixth readings, respectively (*Missale Romanum*, 371–75).

738. *Missale Romanum*, 371–72; *Missale Cisterciense*, 259–60 (the parenthetical numbers have not been identified).

739. "*nostrae voluntatis pravitatem frangere; tuorum praeceptorum rectitudinem in omnibus adimplere*" ("break the evil of our will; fill the righteousness of Your commandments in all") (*Missale Romanum*, 372; *Missale Cisterciense*, 260).

740. *Missale Romanum*, 372; *Missale Cisterciense*, 260.

741. Deut 32:1–4 (*Missale Romanum*, 373; *Missale Cisterciense*, 260; in the Roman Rite the lesson and its tract and collect are third in order).

742. "*descendant sicut ros*" (Deut 32:2).

743. "*Qui per Moysen famulum tuum nos quoque modulatione sacri carminis*

Deuteronomy, and what our attitude towards it should be; note: in our missal much of the longer collect in {the} Roman {rite}[744] is omitted.) "Bestow the gift of Thy mercy on all peoples, giving blessedness and taking away terror, that what was uttered as a condemnation may be changed into an eternal remedy."[745] *Note* {the} deep theology of this: it is Paul's theology of the law of grace superabounding where sin had once abounded.[746] This should be our attitude to the canticle of *Deuteronomy*. Sing it aware of our miseries and infidelities, but trusting in the grace and mercy of God, and conscious of the fact that the Church by the power of the Blood of the Savior is able to see the wrath and justice of God in an entirely new light.

3. *Isaias* (851)[747] {speaks of} the Remnant (this was also used on Holy Saturday[748]) {and of the} poverty of the people ({there are} no men, so that polygamy is practiced), but the "bud of the Lord"[749] shall germinate them and "all who are left in Jerusalem shall be saved."[750] God shall purify His people and shall overshadow His Church with a protecting cloud. {The} *tract*[751] {speaks of} the vineyard of the Lord {and of} God's loving care for His vineyard. {In the} *collect*,[752] the Church here looks to the prophets for God's teaching that we must leave temporal things. (Note {that} this tells us one of the lessons we must expect to find in the prophets. {It is} a clue to help our understanding of them. In fact it is one of the great themes of the prophets—renunciation of hope in temporal strength and human alliances, in order to trust entirely in the will and the

---

erudisti" ("Who through Moses Your servant have instructed us also by the music of the sacred song") (*Missale Romanum*, 373; *Missale Cisterciense*, 260).

744. Actually the identical collect is found in the Roman Rite. Merton is apparently confused by the fact that a completely different sequence of tract (Exod 15:1-2) and collect followed the second lesson (Exod 14:24-15:1) in the Roman Rite (*Missale Romanum*, 373), which is not included in the Cistercian Rite.

745. "*universis Gentibus misericordiae tuae munus operare, tribuendo beatitudinem, auferendo terrorem: ut, quod pronuntiatum est ad supplicium in remedium transferatur aeternum*" (*Missale Romanum*, 373; *Missale Cisterciense*, 260-61).

746. Rom 5:20.

747. *Missale Romanum*, 373; *Missale Cisterciense*, 261.

748. *Missale Romanum*, 206-207; *Missale Cisterciense*, 172.

749. Isa 4:2.

750. Isa 4:3.

751. Isa 5:1-2, 7 (*Missale Romanum*, 373; *Missale Cisterciense*, 261).

752. *Missale Romanum*, 374; *Missale Cisterciense*, 261.

promises of God.) *Temporalia relinquere et ad aeterna festinare.*[753] Grant
that what we have known to be commanded by Thee, we may carry out by
heavenly inspirations.[754] (It is the Holy Spirit Who both reveals to us what
God has commanded and gives us the grace and strength to carry it out.)

4. *Baruch* (847):[755] {this is} a magnificent prophecy:

(1) Israel is exiled in the land of the dead;

(2) for having forsaken the fountain of wisdom.

(3) Learn where is wisdom (a classic passage—compare Job—in
the sapiential tradition: where is wisdom hidden? She is not to
be found by the philosophy of the pagans).

(4) Wisdom is from God alone. He is infinitely above all the science of man and the philosophy of the gentiles. "How great is
the House of God . . . it is high and immense."[756]

(5) Man's strength and human gifts do not entitle him to wisdom.
The wise man is the little one to whom God chooses to reveal
Himself. To find wisdom one must be called by a special gift
of God. "He chose not the giants."[757] "And because they had
no wisdom they perished in their folly."[758] So wisdom is also
essential for salvation.

(6) Who is our God that gives wisdom? {There are} beautiful verses
on God the Creator, obeyed and served by His creation.

(7) The conclusion: "This is our God, and there shall be no other. . . . He gave the way of knowledge to Jacob, His servant
. . . . Afterwards He was seen upon earth and conversed with
men."[759]

---

753. "to let go of temporal things and hasten toward the eternal" (*Missale Romanum*, 375; *Missale Cisterciense*, 261).

754. "*ut, quae a te jussa cognovimus, implore coelisti inspiratione valeamus*" (*Missale Romanum*, 375; *Missale Cisterciense*, 261).

755. *Missale Romanum*, 374; *Missale Cisterciense*, 261–62.

756. Bar 3:24–25.

757. Bar 3:26–27.

758. Bar 3:28.

759. Bar 3:36–38.

{The} collect {is}: "*Domine Deus virtutum, qui collapsa reparas, et reparata conservas: auge populos in tui nominis sanctificatione renovandos; ut omnes qui sacro baptismate diluuntur, tua semper inspiratione dirigantur.*"[760] ({This} gives a good idea of the relation of baptism and confirmation: baptism {is} necessary to purify; the Holy Spirit must be with us all our life long, inspiring us with actual graces to enable us to live our baptismal consecration.) {The} tract {is}: "*Sicut cervus desiderat ad fontes aquarum . . .* "[761] {The} final collect, summing up all this part of the vigil, {is} Concede . . . ut qui solemnitatem doni Sancti Spiritus colimus, coelestibus desideriis accensi, fontem vitae sitiamus.[762]

Corpus Christi

The extraordinary richness of the *office of Corpus Christi* reminds us of the fact that in giving Himself to us to be our spiritual food, Jesus has given us *everything*. {In the} solemn responsory of vespers,[763] this is the divine banquet to which we are admitted, the banquet typified by the feast Assuerus made for Esther, but in fact much greater than any earthly banquet: we sit down with the angels and saints, and the divine Persons Themselves in heaven, for charity is the banquet of the Blessed Trinity. Everything here is summed up in the one word *Love*. Jesus loved us unto the end,[764] in giving us this Blessed Sacrament. He laid down His life for us in order to share with us His love for the Father and His love for mankind, in order to unite Himself to our hearts in Holy Communion. "With desire have I desired to eat this Pasch with you."[765] We

---

760. "Lord God, Who repair what has fallen and preserve what has been repaired, bless the peoples to be renewed in the sanctification of Your name, so that all who are washed by holy baptism may always be directed by Your inspiration" (*Missale Romanum*, 375; *Missale Cisterciense*, 262).

761. "As the deer longs for springs of water" (Ps 41[42]:2) (*Missale Romanum*, 375; *Missale Cisterciense*, 262).

762. "Grant . . . that we who celebrate the solemn feast of the gift of the Holy Spirit, enflamed by heavenly desires, may thirst for the fountain of life" (*Missale Romanum*, 376; *Missale Cisterciense*, 262).

763. "*Fecit Assuerus grande convivium cunctis principibus, et pueris suis, ut ostenderet divitias gloriae regni sui*" ("Assuerus made a great feast for all his nobles and his children in order to display the riches of the glory of his kingdom") (Esth 1:3) (*Breviarium Cisterciense, Aestivalis*, 193).

764. John 13:1.

765. Luke 22:15 (responsory, vespers: Corpus Christi) (*Breviarium Cisterciense, Aestivalis*, 193).

must above all believe in the love with which Jesus gives Himself to us. Communion is not a mere automatic operation: it is a personal act of love of Jesus for us, and of the Father for us in Jesus. We can only come to communion because Jesus draws us, the Father draws us to Him. Jesus wants this union with our souls, in order that He may give us life, in order that He may *do us good*. God, our Creator, wills to perfect the work of His creation by giving us His own life. Everything He does for us and in us tends to fulfill His desire to make us grow, to share with us His own life. In order to do this He must transform us, elevating us beyond the level of our nature, a thing inconceivable to us. But this is the great work of His love, which demands the cooperation of our freedom. Jesus comes to give us the strength to cooperate with Him, light to know how, love and courage to persevere, because the work is not *done for us*—we must do it, and thus Jesus Himself will do the work in us.

{Note the} *effects of communion as shown in the office*: {in the} *first antiphon* {of} *vespers*,[766] Jesus is our viaticum; through Him we come to the day of everlasting light (cf. fourth responsory:[767] Elias). {In the} *fourth antiphon* {of} *vespers*, the Bread of Life incorporates us with Himself.[768] (As the Living Father has sent Me, and I live by the Father, so he who eats Me lives by Me.[769]) The rest of the antiphon tells how: by perfect charity.[770] {In the} *Magnificat antiphon*,[771] He comes to give us consolation in our journey. {He gives us} strength against our enemies (fifth antiphon {for the} *first nocturn*[772]). {The} Blessed Eucharist overcomes temptation and {the} effects of sin, wipes out venial sin, helps {us} to resist and {to} advance. Joy and exultation {predominate}—cf. {the} third antiphon {for

---

766. *"nostrum viaticum"* (*Breviarium Cisterciense, Aestivalis*, 191).

767. 3 Kgs [1 Kgs] 19:6, 8 (*Breviarium Cisterciense, Aestivalis*, 200).

768. *"Sibi nos incorporat panis vitae"* (*Breviarium Cisterciense, Aestivalis*, 193).

769. John 6:58.

770. *"charitate perfecta"* (*Breviarium Cisterciense, Aestivalis*, 193).

771. *"in peregrinatione . . . consolationem"* (*Breviarium Cisterciense, Aestivalis*, 194).

772. *"adversus omnes qui tribulant nos"* ("against all who trouble us") (*Breviarium Cisterciense, Aestivalis*, 197).

the} second nocturn[773]—also {the} fifth[774] and sixth antiphons.[775] He divinizes us: *"ut homines deos faceret, factus homo"*[776] (fifth lesson, {from} St. *Thomas*[777]). Union with Jesus (and {the} exultation that belongs to this) {is the} main effect (fifth responsory[778]). He is our hope and our strength (sixth responsory[779]). This sacrament {is the} great manifestation of divine wisdom (third nocturn: canticles[780] and antiphon[781]). {The} lessons[782] and responsory[783] of {the} third nocturn emphasize the great mystery of our union in Christ, {the} other great effect of {the} Eucharist. {The} *res sacramenti*[784]—{the} *Corpus Christi* eschatology—looks forward to {the} last judgement.

FEAST OF THE SACRED HEART OF JESUS

All the mysteries of our faith are united and concentrated in the Sacred Heart, the vital center from which flows all the life of the Church. *In the Cistercian Missal and Breviary* {we find}:

A. *The Mass*: {the} introit[785] ("Mercy shall be His work"[786]) {puts the} emphasis *on the merciful love of Jesus*: "It is not in His Heart to afflict

---

773. *"in quem cor et caro nostra exultant"* ("in Whom our heart and flesh rejoice") (*Breviarium Cisterciense, Aestivalis*, 202).

774. *"Miserator et misericors Dominus replet in bonis desiderium tuum"* ("May the compassionate and merciful Lord fulfill your desire in good things") (*Breviarium Cisterciense, Aestivalis*, 204).

775. *"Educas panem de terra, et vinum laetificet cor hominis"* ("May you bring forth bread from the earth, and may wine bring joy to the heart of man") (*Breviarium Cisterciense, Aestivalis*, 205).

776. "He became human in order to make humans divine" (*Breviarium Cisterciense, Aestivalis*, 205-206).

777. *In Opusculum 57* (*Breviarium Cisterciense, Aestivalis*, 205–206).

778. John 6:55–56 (*Breviarium Cisterciense, Aestivalis*, 206).

779. John 6:58 (*Breviarium Cisterciense, Aestivalis*, 206).

780. Prov 9:1–12; Jer 31:10–14; Wis 16:20–17:1 (*Breviarium Cisterciense, Aestivalis*, 207–8).

781. Prov 9:1–2; Ps 103[104]:14–15 (*Breviarium Cisterciense, Aestivalis*, 207–208).

782. St. Augustine, *Tractatus 26 in Joannem* (*Breviarium Cisterciense, Aestivalis*, 208-10).

783. 1 Cor 10:17 (first responsory) (*Breviarium Cisterciense, Aestivalis*, 209).

784. "the matter of the sacrament" (see n. 512 above).

785. *Missale Cisterciense*, 428; the introit of the Roman Rite is Ps 32[33]:11, 19, 1 (*Missale Romanum*, 402).

786. *"Miseribitur secundum multitudinem miserationum suarum"* ("He will have mercy according to the multitude of His mercies") (Lam 3:32).

mankind."[787] {This is the} true idea of the Sacred Heart. He is *not* aggressive and vengeful, and His complaints to St. Margaret Mary are to be understood not as those of a person easily offended, but as the complaint of *infinite mercy* which is not understood or accepted by men. The hardness of heart is all on the side of men. It is indeed the attitude of many that God is a hard taskmaster, and that He asks too much, is exorbitant. It is of this that the Sacred Heart complains; the coldness of men refuses love as "hard" and unbearable. This is not true of sinners only, but of a certain type of pious person (cf. the Christmas sermons of Bl. Guerric[788]), always stressing the "demands" made by God and weighing out their own fulfillment of these demands. "*No, the Lord is good to those who trust Him.*"[789] Here is the true attitude. {It is} not a question of constant irate demands which must be met slavishly by our unwilling efforts, but of *a trust that implies total self-surrender to the mercy of God*, never hardening our hearts and holding back in fear, never cringing in distrust, seeing Jesus' love in everything, hard or easy, and embracing it with perfect trust. {The} *collect* reinforces these dispositions by recalling "*praecipua in nos charitatis ejus beneficia,*"[790] in order to rejoice in them and their fruits (cf. *offertory*[791]). {The} *epistle*[792] {declares}: "Ah, it is God who is here to save

---

787. "*non enim humiliavit ex corde suo et abiecit filios hominis*" (Lam 3:33).

788. The reference is evidently not directly to the five Nativity sermons of Guerric [Migne, *PL* 185, cols. 29B–46D] but to Merton's essay with this title that accompanies Sr. Rose of Lima's translations of the sermons in *Christmas Sermons of Bl. Guerric of Igny*, 1–25, in which he develops this idea in more detail: "Sadness, fully consented to, is a denial of God's mercy—it leads to infidelity and despair. . . . The ungrateful man hardens his heart and refuses to see the goodness and mercy of God. He does not want to see them! . . . If the gift of God is to be seen as it really is, we must realize that He has made salvation easy for us. But the sad ones, whom Bl. Guerric rebukes so roundly, are always precisely complaining of the hardness of their lot, of the sufferings and crosses and labors which they have to undergo, as if God had not done everything to make life sweet and easy for them. They refuse to turn their eyes to the merciful love which lightens all our burdens" (12–13); "Guerric brings out all that we have been saying about the spirit of sadness and ingratitude, of contention, hard-heartedness, and resistance to love. . . . The spirit of ingratitude and coldness is also a spirit of envy. Unable to see the goodness and mercy of God in His gift to us, it not only refuses the gift but tries to prevent others from receiving it" (16).

789. "*Bonus est Dominus sperantibus in eum*" (Lam 3:25).

790. "the blessings of His love for us are overwhelming" (*Missale Cisterciense*, 428).

791. Ps 102[103]:2, 5 (*Missale Cisterciense*, 429).

792. Isa 12:1–6 (*Missale Cisterciense*, 428–29; the epistle in the Roman Rite is Eph 3:8–19 [*Missale Romanum*, 402]).

me. . . . *I will go forward confidently and never be afraid*,"[793] not trusting in my own works, yet generously doing what I can. "But from the Lord comes my strength."[794] To embrace His will, even when it seems impossible, merits special grace and strength from Him. "You shall rejoice as you draw water from the Savior's fountains."[795] The *gospel*[796] {focuses on} the Cross, the greatest and most complete expression of His love for us and hence the greatest motive of our trust.

B. *The Office*: {the} second nocturn (not really by St. Bernard[797]) {focuses on} transformation in Jesus:

a) *to dwell in His Heart* (read *John* 15:1–11:[798] "*Manete in me . . .* "[799]); to renounce all other loves; to be sustained by His love alone. This implies sacrifice, but above all trust: "casting all my care on the Heart of the Lord Jesus."[800]

b) *His Heart is a temple in which God is perfectly adored*; hence we ask to be drawn entirely into this mystical sanctuary, so as to praise God perfectly.[801]

---

793. Isa 12:2.

794. Isa 12:2.

795. Isa 12:3.

796. John 19:31–37 (*Missale Romanum*, 403; *Missale Cisterciense*, 429).

797. *De Vite Mystica* (*The Mystical Vine*), c. 3 (*Breviarium Cisterciense, Aestivalis*, 323–25).

798. "I am the true vine; and my Father is the husbandman. Every branch in me, that beareth not fruit, he will take away: and every one that beareth fruit, he will purge it, that it may bring forth more fruit. Now you are clean by reason of the word, which I have spoken to you. Abide in me, and I in you. As the branch cannot bear fruit of itself, unless it abide in the vine, so neither can you, unless you abide in me. I am the vine; you the branches: he that abideth in me, and I in him, the same beareth much fruit: for without me you can do nothing. If any one abide not in me, he shall be cast forth as a branch, and shall wither, and they shall gather him up, and cast him into the fire, and he burneth. If you abide in me, and my words abide in you, you shall ask whatever you will, and it shall be done unto you. In this is my Father glorified; that you bring forth very much fruit, and become my disciples. As the Father hath loved me, I also have loved you. Abide in my love. If you keep my commandments, you shall abide in my love; as I also have kept my Father's commandments, and do abide in his love. These things I have spoken to you, that my joy may be in you, and your joy may be filled."

799. "Remain in me" (John 15:4).

800. "*jactans omne cogitatum meum in Cor Domini Jesu*" (fifth lesson) (*Breviarium Cisterciense, Aestivalis*, 324).

801. Sixth lesson (*Breviarium Cisterciense, Aestivalis*, 324).

c) *To "find" the Heart of Jesus* is at once to "find" our own heart and His[802] (cf. Oriental spirituality: "seeking" and "finding" the heart[803]). The Sacred Heart, King and Center of all hearts,[804] *is the inmost center of our own heart* (because of our Eucharistic communions especially, and the action of the Holy Spirit conforming our heart to His).

d) {He is} the *Way*: there is only one sure way and His Heart teaches us this way to conformity—to experience in ourselves the humility of Jesus. "Learn of Me that I am meek and humble of heart" (antiphon: lauds).[805]

THE MEANING OF SUNDAY (cf. *Dictionnaire de Spiritualité*: "Dimanche"[806])

We are not fully Christians if we do not appreciate Sunday.

1. Wrong Approach: {from a} secular {perspective, it is} merely a day off; {from a} puritanical {perspective, a} day of bluenose gloom; {from a} pharisaical {perspective, a} day on which one is bound by many prescriptions, especially negative {ones}. All these approaches are negative. Sunday is "not one of the other days" of the week. These approaches are human and imperfect, not Christian.

2. The Problem in the World Today: {At} La Salette, Our Lady laments the neglect of Sunday.[807] {Under} communism, {there is} no Sunday on the calendar; no one day of rest. {With the rise of} secularism, {there is} spiritual inertia, even of Catholics—going to Mass under protest and then spending the day as children of the world. In the monastery? {Is there a} proper use of Sunday? {Do we merely} accumulate devotions

---

802. Sixth lesson (*Breviarium Cisterciense, Aestivalis*, 324).

803. For a thorough overview of this key dimension of Eastern Christian spirituality, see Ware, "How Do We Enter the Heart."

804. A phrase taken from the Litany of the Sacred Heart of Jesus (*Raccolta*, 160 [#245]).

805. Matt 11:29 (*Breviarium Cisterciense, Aestivalis*, 328).

806. Gaillard, "Dimanche."

807. Part of the message reported by the two young visionaries from the apparition of the Blessed Virgin at La Salette on September 19, 1846, were the words, "I have appointed you six days for working. The seventh I have reserved for myself. And no one will give it to me. This it is which causes the weight of my son's arm to be so crushing" (Kennedy, *Light on the Mountain*, 31).

and activities to keep things moving? {This is to} bury the true sense of Sunday.

3. Since {the} fifth century, each Sunday has begun to acquire its own character and liturgy: v.g. Septuagesima, Sundays of Lent, etc.[808] {This is} good, but we must remember the essence of Sunday, underneath these accidental modifications. Otherwise we see Sundays as recurring "feasts"—{a} cyclic return of days with special characteristics. {We need to} see the *unity of Sunday: Sunday is always Easter.* It is a day which brings us to the very heart and essence of our life in Christ, a "sacramental" day in which God is closer to man.

4. Sunday and Sabbath: Sunday is not a mere substitute for or transposition of the Jewish Sabbath.[809] In the beginning the apostles observed both the Sabbath and the *Lord's Day.* They are not the same. St. Paul (Col. 2:16–17), {recognizing that the} *Sabbath {was} made for man, not man for the Sabbath,*[810] providentially saved Christianity from these complications (cf. Council of Jerusalem: Acts 15). {The} Sabbath {was} abandoned; Sunday {is the} witness of Christian liberty. {But} *Sunday {is} the fulfillment of the Sabbath*: Jesus came not to destroy but to fulfill. His conflicts with {the} Pharisees over the Sabbath {centered on the fact that} for them man was the servant of the Sabbath (light vs. darkness; life against death). If the Sabbath were held on to, we would have forgotten that Jesus had given it its true spiritual fulfillment. How? by showing us *God is our life*—life is not in what we do only, but {what we do} in Him. {According to} Hebrews 4:3–11, we are called to participate in God's divine rest of eternity by ceasing from slavery to human works, attitudes, "elements of this world,"[811] etc., {by} living in Christ. Sunday perpetually reminds us of this; {it is} the day on which we live purely and perfectly "in Christ"—Sunday and Paschal time. {There is a} difference between {this and} observing a Sabbath rest, as if one day were better than another, one food pure and another impure, etc.—not because of the day, but because of God. "Keep {the} Sabbath day holy"[812]—not in the sense that we have to make it holy—but it is a day on which we remember that Christ has made us holy and free. {It is} not a day in which to strive to produce

808. See Gaillard, "Dimanche," col. 962.

809. See Gaillard, "Dimanche," cols. 950–51.

810. Mark 2:27.

811. Gal 4:3.

812. Exod 20:8.

some special effect, but to rejoice in the effect which God has produced in us. This effect {is} charity, union of wills, peace. {It is a} *Eucharistic day*, {a day for} remembering God and thanking Him (Psalm 117). {There are} three elements in Sunday: (1) rest: natural man needs rest, change, leisure; this is good; (2) faith: this day of "rest" becomes a sacrament of our rest in God by abandoning concern with self; (3) God Himself makes Himself known to us above all created things. {It is the} Lord's Day. READ John 20:19–23[813] etc.: {the} Paschal appearances give {the proper Sunday} tone.

5. Sunday and the Fathers: {according to} St. Ignatius, to abandon the old law and to live in hope in Christ is "*to live according to the Lord's Day*"[814]—that is to say, to live according to the hope of Christ Who rose from the dead, and raised us with Himself to new life. "If Christ be not risen, vain is our preaching, vain is your faith."[815] {The} *true Sabbath* is freedom from sin, from self-love, from self-will, freedom from slavery to "things"—in Christ. This Sabbath is perpetual: every day is a feast (feria); every day is Easter Sunday. We have passed from death to life in Christ, {by} charity. But Sunday comes each week to remind us of this and to preserve our "Paschal life" in Christ. Our "*conversatio in coelis*,"[816] our Eucharistic life, {is} thanking God because we *know* He is good. According to St. Thomas,[817] Sunday is the reminder of the *new creation*, a reminder which is necessary because the annual feast of Easter would not be enough.

6. The Character of Sunday (cf. St. John 20):

a) As we have seen, it sets the tone for the whole Christian life. Hence, to fail to observe Sunday is to lose {the} Christian sense, outlook, character, bit by bit.

---

813. "Now when it was late that same day, the first of the week, and the doors were shut, where the disciples were gathered together, for fear of the Jews, Jesus came and stood in the midst, and said to them: Peace be to you. And when he had said this, he shewed them his hands and his side. The disciples therefore were glad, when they saw the Lord. He said therefore to them again: Peace be to you. As the Father hath sent me, I also send you. When he had said this, he breathed on them: and he said to them: Receive ye the Holy Ghost. Whose sins you shall forgive, they are forgiven them; and whose sins you shall retain, they are retained."

814. Magnesians, 9.1, quoted in Gaillard, "Dimanche," col. 952.

815. 1 Cor 15:14.

816. "Our citizenship in heaven" (Phil 3:20).

817. *De Duobus Preceptis*, quoted in Gaillard, "Dimanche," col. 968.

b) Sunday {is} a *day of light*, {the} "first day" on which light was made, {the} day when Christ, {the} true Light, rose from the tomb (*lumen Christi*[818]) to shine forever. {The} light of grace {shines} in our hearts {on this} day of grace, {this} day on which Jesus comes, the doors being shut, and says, "Peace be to you."[819] {See the} hymns of our Breviary, "*Aeterne Rerum Conditor*"[820] {and} "*Splendor Paternae Gloriae*."[821] *Aeterne Rerum* {speaks of} God disposing and ruling time: {at} cockcrow, the rising sun dispels {the} darkness of sin and error, brings courage {and} repentance, revives our energy {with the} awakening of faith and good resolve, {of} hope, {from the} memory of Jesus looking on Peter. (This hymn is more a vigil hymn than a Sunday one, however.) *Splendor Paternae Gloriae* {is} a lauds hymn, especially appropriate for Sunday: "*Lux lucis et fons luminis*,"[822] the true sun, pouring the light of the Holy Spirit into our hearts etc.

c) *Sunday* {is} the day which the Lord hath made (*Haec dies quam fecit dominus; exultemus et laetemur in ea*[823]). This applies to creation and to the new creation, Easter, the day on which we approach something of what we ought to be, {and} rest in Him. Let *Him* make the day—we rejoice in it.

d) Hence {it is} a day of joy—not mere secular rest, but the day that corresponds most truly to God's will. On the other six days we labor in the sweat of our brow, as the result of Adam's sin. {On} Sunday we return to the life of rest in God for which we were created (as opposed to the communist idea!).

e) But above all {it is} a day of *triumph and victory*. Our joy springs from the Resurrection of Christ, {His} victory over sin, death, {the} devil, {bringing} freedom, strength, confidence. Hence we proclaim Him LORD. {It is the} victory of life over death,

---

818. "the light of Christ."

819. Luke 24:36; John 20:19, 21, 26.

820. "Eternal Creator of all things" (*Breviarium Cisterciense, Hiemalis*, 20–21 etc.).

821. "Splendor of the Father's glory" (*Breviarium Cisterciense, Hiemalis*, 41 etc.).

822. "Light of light and fount of light" (*Breviarium Cisterciense, Hiemalis*, 41 etc.).

823. "This is the day the Lord has made; let us be glad and rejoice in it" (Ps 117[118]:24) (responsory, versicle: Sunday) (*Breviarium Cisterciense, Hiemalis*, 41 etc.).

{the} victory of life through death, {the} mystery of the Cross. Sunday truly hails {the} triumph of {the} Cross.

f) How? because it is *a day of unity*, the calling together of the faithful (*ecclesia*)—the Christian community manifests its unity in Christ (a) assembling to hear the word of God, to make contact with the Lord, and to acclaim Him; thus light shines forth in the Church; (b) assembling to be united with Him in the Eucharist, and thus manifest their unity in Him— the Sacred Banquet—{the} expression of joy in unity {and the} ascent through unity and Eucharist to the Holy Trinity: *"Cognitio Trinitatis in unitate est finis totius vitae nostrae"*[824] (St. Thomas).

g) But for this, Sunday must be a day of purification, purging out the old leaven of hypocrisy, worldliness, jealousy, competitive spirit, self-love, greed, laziness, etc., etc., {a} day of virtue, charity, prayer, almsgiving.

h) But not a day of fasting. The Fathers regarded sadness on Sunday as a sin, and fasting was forbidden. They did not even allow kneeling in prayer (because we are risen in Christ). The early Christians also took care not to observe the complete idleness of the Jews, but {they} avoided secular business and gave themselves to prayer and union in Christ—with time allowed for innocent recreations. {The} Christian spirit {is} not puritanical. Early monastic rules even prescribed light reading rather than study of psalms on Sunday.

The whole spirit of Sunday is therefore strictly a Gospel spirit, in which everything is centered upon faith in the Cross, faith in the power of Christ's redemptive death and His Resurrection, putting aside trust in our own concerns and anxieties, and seeking salvation (finding it) in the Eucharistic assembly of the faithful, in charity, simplicity, union, joy, with rest and recreation included—not because these are demanded by sense, but because Christ has liberated us from vain concerns with a million binding practices that blind and fetter the spirit, {leading to a} trust that implies we can give a little rest and joy to our humanity, in its entirety,

824. "Knowledge of the Trinity in unity is the goal of our entire life" (*In Quatuor Libros Sententiarum*, I, d. 2, *expositio textus* [St Thomas Aquinas, *Opera Omnia*, 6:27, which reads: "*Cognitio enim . . . est fructus et finis . . .*"]), quoted in Gaillard, "Dimanche," col. 970.

body and soul, without incurring {the} displeasure of a manichean deity! Note Cassian's banquet on Sunday, in Egypt (the five olives, etc.).[825]

7. *Sunday in the Monastery* {shows the} application of these principles. {As it is the} Lord's Day, let Him make the day what it ought to be.

a) Resist anxieties and compulsions to be busy with many things. This resistance is required as the virtue God seeks of us, as the expression of faith; {it is a} day to rise above compulsive living, anxieties, scruples, fretting about ourselves and our activities.

b) Do not be afraid to follow legitimate attractions. God wants you to follow these, unless of course His will blocks them.

c) Different reading from other days {is} recommended; light reading {is} all right. Avoid studies (when scholastics) unless necessary. {It is a} good time for a long spiritual reading period outside, {and for} time in church, preferably a silent time when others are not milling around. Follow the inner voice that leads you to peace and joy in God wherever He indicates.

d) {Note the} beauty of peace and silence in {the} monastic family on Sunday, reading together in the garden or scriptorium—{an} image of heaven; {a} monastic paradise. But do not become attached to the paradise aspect of {the} monastery—remember it is only to be purchased by the Cross.

e) Sunday {is} a day of sacrifice ("almsgiving") for those who have to devote themselves to some useful task; {there is} merit {and} no loss of peace involved if one is truly united to Jesus.

f) {It is} a day for the word of God—in chapter, in conferences; for {the} brothers, {a day for} confessions and visits to Father Masters or Reverend Father.

g) {It is} a day for Jesus in the Blessed Sacrament—a Eucharistic day.

h) {The} rosary {should be said} this day at least.

{According to} Ida of Léau,[826] the true essence of Sunday {is} peace in Jesus, ineffable love and joy, {with} not too much reading, etc., {a foretaste of} eternity.

825. *Conf.* 8.1 (Migne, *PL* 49, col. 720), quoted in Gaillard, "Dimanche," col. 955.

826. For Merton's biographical sketch of Ida of Léau, Cistercian nun of Brabant (c. 1211–1290), see Merton, *Valley of Wormwood*, 380–87, based on the contemporary

8. *The Mystery of Sunday*: "the first day" ({the day of the} creation of light, {of the} Resurrection, {of the} descent of the Holy Spirit) {and} "the eighth day" (figure and promise of eternity: St. Basil[827]). St. Augustine teaches that we now live in the "seventh day" of the world's history whose ending will be not in night but in the light of the eighth day, eternity, prefigured by Sunday. "This seventh age is our Sabbath, whose ending will not be night but Sunday, which like an eternal eighth day, made sacred by the Resurrection of Christ, prefiguring the repose not only of spirit but of body. There we shall be free, and we shall see. We shall see and love and we shall praise. For what other end have we but to arrive at the kingdom which has no end" (last words of *The City of God*[828]). In conclusion, Sunday is a weekly feast of the Risen Lord, a memorial of the whole economy of Redemption, a prefiguring of its final consummation, a making present of the mystery of Christ in His Church by the full assembly of the Christian family in the Eucharistic banquet.

SEVENTH SUNDAY AFTER PENTECOST

"*Deus cujus Providentia in sui dispositione non fallitur*" (collect).[829] The mystery of Providence is the very essence of the New Testament. To love and serve Jesus without abandonment to the loving care of the Father just does not make sense—this is the main theme of the Sermon

---

Vita as found in the *Acta Sanctorum, Octobris* XIII, 107–24 (October 29). Merton points out that "especially after her Communions, and on Sundays, she would often remain the whole day completely absorbed in God, even though she was not altogether robbed of the use of her senses" (382), though the *Vita* indicates that typically Sundays were actually quite busy for Ida: "*Vacans ergo dulcis Yda soli Deo, ducens in consuetudinem omni die dominica Christi corpus recipere, de virtute in virtutem progrediens, in scripturis occupans sensus exterius corporales, studiose libros ecclesiae scribens, corrigens quemdam librum ferialem non minimum, in quo leguntur in Matutinis lectiones, et plures alios conscripsit diligentius*" ("Therefore sweet Ida, focusing on God alone, became accustomed to receiving the body of Christ every Lord's Day, advancing from virtue to virtue; she engaged her bodily senses with the scriptures, studiously copying books of the Church, not least correcting a certain ferial book, in which were read the readings for the morning, and also copied much else quite diligently") (*Acta Sanctorum, Octobris* XIII, 113).

827. *De Spiritu Sancto*, 27 (Migne, *PG* 32, col. 192), quoted in Gaillard, "Dimanche," col. 959.

828. St. Augustine, *De Civitate Dei*, 22.30.5 (Migne, *PL* 41, col. 804), quoted in Gaillard, "Dimanche," col. 960.

829. "God, Whose Providence does not fail in its working out" (*Missale Romanum*, 410; *Missale Cisterciense*, 288).

on the Mount. "You cannot serve God and Mammon."[830] To serve God is to abandon solicitude, seeking first the kingdom of heaven and letting Him take care of all the rest. God's Providence is *never deceived*. This is the central truth which we must believe. *Nothing that happens is purely accidental*, nothing mere "fate" or "chance" or "bad luck." *Everything that happens in our lives is foreseen, taken into account, willed or at least permitted*; all is part of a very definite plan of *an infinitely wise and conscious love* for us personally. All is *equally* foreseen; all is equally part of the plan; all is equally for our good—not only the "good things," our successes, joys, etc., but the "bad things" also, defeats, mistakes, setbacks, accidents; *even our sins* fall into a plan of God's love, in a certain sense. He *never wills sin*, but He *wills the results of sin for our good* and for the universal good at the same time. Providence, says Guardini (*Living God*, p. 22), implies an order which does not constrain me, does not use me, *but is governed by my needs*. "Everything that happens would have me in mind."[831] "*There is a seeing Mind behind everything that happens and {. . .} I am the object of its seeing.*"[832] This does not do away with harsh realities, but sees them in the light of "God's loving purpose for His dear ones."[833] This requires a heroic living faith in our souls. This makes us true Christians—and it is something which we then *experience*. Providence {is} not a machine but a "mystery of the Living God—you will experience it to the extent that you surrender yourself to it, not letting it merely pass over you, but co-operating with it. . . . *As a living person you must stand within the living activity of God*" (p. 27). But if we fail to abandon ourselves to the Providence of God, it is because we prefer our own providence. What a contrast! God *sees* everything, and is never deceived by anything. He knows all because all is in His wisdom—all things only reflect the thoughts of His mind. We see little or nothing, and in the little we see we are so easily deceived. The more we think we understand, the more we deceive ourselves. God *controls* everything; there is nothing in the world that can move or act without His will, even our own will. We control so little; we cannot even control our own thoughts and passions. Yet we

830. Matt 6:24; Luke 16:13.

831. Guardini, *Living God*, 22–23.

832. Guardini, *Living God*, 22 (italics added).

833. "Providence means that every thing in the world retains its own nature and reality but serves a supreme purpose which transcends the world: the loving purpose of God. But this love of God for His creatures whom He has made is alive like that of a human being for his dear ones" (Guardini, *Living God*, 24).

struggle to control others, by manipulation; and then how often we fail. The hidden recesses of the mind and will of others totally escape us. God *loves* everything and everyone, wills the true good of all and can bring it about. We tend to seek our own good before all else, at the expense of others, and then in the struggle to assert ourselves we fail. If we really love God, let us not be "false prophets" of our own providence, seeking by devious ways to assert our own will ("within they are ravening wolves"[834]). Let us bring forth the *fruits of God's will*, not just *say* we want to abandon ourselves, but really do so—*really want God's will to be carried out in all things.* {Note} the danger of being glib about abandonment. Those who "know all about" God's will usually just do their own. {The} secret of true abandonment {is} precisely to respect the *mystery* of God's inscrutable designs, and yield to a plan we cannot see. The gentleness and interior peace produced by abandonment {is} essential for {a} contemplative life.

Ninth Sunday after Pentecost

1. In the night office {is a text from} *Ecclesiastes*.[835] {The} true spirit of *Ecclesiastes* {is} not just sophisticated worldly disgust but detachment and "disillusionment" in the good sense of the word, freedom from the bewitching lure of creatures and from vain and pointless pursuit of goods that have no substance. {It involves the} principle of *risk* (see Orientation Notes: "Ecclesiastes"[836]).

2. {In the} gospel[837] {we read}: "If thou hadst known, and that in this day, the things that are to thy peace."[838] Jesus weeps over the blindness of Jerusalem. He is not afflicted by sins of weakness, but by obstinate

---

834. Matt 7:15.

835. Eccl 1:1–17 (*Breviarium Cisterciense, Aestivalis*, 259–61; this is actually the first nocturn for the second Sunday in August rather than for the ninth Sunday after Pentecost).

836. Merton, "The Scandal, Perspectives and Lessons of *Ecclesiastes*," part V: "The Scriptures as Medicine," 54: "6. 'Cast thy bread upon the waters.' *The principle of risk.* Two practical conclusions follow from the 'alternation of contraries'—The first is that we must be willing to take risks, to face uncertainties. We must do things anyway, even if we do not know what the result will be. In other words, we must leave the results of our works to God. *We must abandon ourselves in matters that are beyond our control and have confidence in life itself which God has made*—our undertakings will not all succeed, but even our failures will probably serve us in good stead if we live right (cf. St. Paul—'All things work together for the good of those that love God'—completes and elevates this principle)."

837. Luke 19:41–47 (*Missale Romanum*, 413; *Missale Cisterciense*, 290–91).

838. Luke 19:42.

attachment to vanity and blindness. What did Jerusalem fail to see? that it was necessary to *risk* the newness of the Kingdom of God and drop attachment to familiar dreams of national and worldly glory, worldly ends. {The} destruction of Jerusalem {is prophesied} "because thou hast not known the time of thy visitation."[839] Jesus comes to us under despised and apparently unworthy appearances—*not what we expect*. We must always be ready for the time of visitation. Grace often comes in very humiliating trials, hardships and temptations, or through a person we do not respect, or through the *same* message we have heard many times before. But today it may have a new meaning.

3. {The} *epistle*[840] throws light on {the} spiritual meaning of *Exodus*.

Tenth Sunday after Pentecost

1. *Deus qui omnipotentiam parcendo maxime, et miserando manifestas* (collect).[841] This should make us reflect that we do no honor to God in thinking of Him as One Who thirsts for revenge and Who likes to punish. Over and over again in the life of Jesus we see His superabundant mercy for sinners. Above all, it was the omnipotent God Who died on the Cross for us, showing His *infinite love*—His *final answer* to sin! {Thus we see} the paradoxical character of the divine attributes.

2. *The Pharisee and the Publican*[842] {reveals} what this teaches us about prayer:

a) Note the connection between *compunction* and *recollection*. The publican is pierced to the heart. God is truly present to him. He does not need to bother about others. The pharisee is pleased with himself. He is looking at himself rather than God. (He is also paying a lot of attention to other people.) He is just asking God to approve His own self-worship. To confirm himself in his complacency he looks down on others. He is living in total unreality—reflected in the mirror of his own mind and the mind of others. Truth is in the mind of God. {It must be sought on the} horizontal and vertical plane—the pharisee has not discovered the right dimension.

---

839. Luke 19:44.

840. 1 Cor 10:6–13 (*Missale Romanum*, 412–13; *Missale Cisterciense*, 290).

841. "God, who show Your omnipotence to the utmost by sparing and being merciful" (*Missale Romanum*, 413; *Missale Cisterciense*, 291, which read: ". . . omnipotentiam tuam parcendo . . .").

842. Luke 18:9–14 (*Missale Romanum*, 414; *Missale Cisterciense*, 292).

b) Conclusions: to be heard by God, one does not have to be propor-
tionally virtuous, but sincere and poor in spirit, and to know one's
own nothingness. We must *be humble.* How many do not know
what it means to "humble oneself," {and the} vital importance of
true humility. Be humbled "under the hand of God."[843] Interior
suffering {is} one of His greatest gifts. He has mercy on us by sending us suffering.

September Ember Days

{We must see} the beauty of penance. {These} Mass texts {are} all
the more beautiful by their interrelationship. {The} spirit of feasting and
{that of} fasting {are} mingled. {There is a} close relation of the September ember days to the Feast of the Exaltation of the Holy Cross, a *feast*
centered on the Cross; and the ember days—*fasts*—{are} centered on the
idea of thanksgiving for the harvest. It is not so much that we fast because of the harvest. The ember-day fast here, as in the other seasons, is
connected rather with the forthcoming ordinations. But it is a season of
harvest; hence the atmosphere is above all one of joy, especially Ember
Wednesday. The ember days of September recall the ancient Jewish Feast
of Tabernacles. See {the} second lesson of Ember Saturday (Leviticus 23):
"You shall dwell in bowers seven days; everyone that is of the race of
Israel shall dwell in tabernacles that your posterity may know that I made
the children of Israel to dwell in tabernacles when I brought them out
of Egypt."[844] The lesson of Michaeas[845] on Ember Saturday also recalls
this. The time when Israel was in the desert, supported directly by God,
was the ideal time of the history of the Chosen People. God was their
Shepherd. They were "the flock of thy inheritance, they that dwell alone
in the forest according to the days of old."[846] The lesson from Zacharias[847]
again emphasizes the mercy of God, and links the idea of this fast with
the divine mercy. In the epistle[848] of Ember Saturday, St. Paul brings out
the mystical meaning of the Mosaic tabernacle. Christ has entered into
the holy of holies, and that is why we rejoice, not because we have reached

---

843. 1 Pet 5:6.

844. Lev 23:42–43 (*Missale Romanum,* 429; *Missale Cisterciense,* 306).

845. Mic 7:14, 16, 18–20 (*Missale Romanum,* 429; *Missale Cisterciense,* 306).

846. Mic 7:14.

847. Zech 8:14–19 (*Missale Romanum,* 429–30; *Missale Cisterciense,* 306).

848. Heb 9:2–12 (*Missale Romanum,* 431; *Missale Cisterciense,* 307–308).

an earthly promised land but because the true promised land of heaven is opened to us by an "eternal redemption."[849] Above all, {consider} the beautiful lesson from Osee,[850] {the} Ember Friday epistle, {in which} the mercy of God makes Israel like a fruitful tree {and} Israel promises to turn away from idols. The lesson from Esdras[851] {on} Ember Wednesday {presents} the rediscovery of the law after the return from Babylon.

All these beautiful texts on penance are capped by the three gospels of these days. {On} Saturday,[852] the triumphant mercy of Christ supersedes the legalism of the Old Testament. The barren fig tree will be cultivated again for a year, in order that it may have another chance to bear fruit. And we, no doubt, when bringing in the fruits of the earth, may realize that our hearts have been fruitless and sterile. His mercy will give us another chance. And He will come and "untie" us in our captivity, like the little woman in the gospel, bent over for eighteen years. {The} idea {is} that after a *long wait* and long suffering, the Savior will not leave us without mercy and assistance. {On} Ember Friday[853] {we hear} the most beautiful of gospels on penance, the washing and anointing of Christ's feet by Mary Magdalen. Love is everything—love for Jesus the Savior. This is true penance: not just tears because we have sinned, but tears for having hurt Him, Who loves us so much. Finally {in} the gospel of Ember Wednesday[854] {there are} two great points:

1. The basic, fundamental importance of *faith*. Jesus reproaches the people rather hotly: "O generation without faith, how long will I have to stand you!"[855] "If thou canst believe all things are possible . . ."[856] {This is a} reproach to the weak faith of the man who doubts whether Jesus "can do anything."[857] Most beautiful of all {is} the touching simplicity and sincerity of the man of weak faith who, suddenly touched, cries out with tears: "I do believe, Lord, help Thou my unbelief,"[858] throwing the burden back upon the Savior!

849. Heb 9:12.

850. Hos 14:2–10 (*Missale Romanum*, 426–27; *Missale Cisterciense*, 304).

851. 2 Esd [Neh] 8:1–10 (*Missale Romanum*, 424–25; *Missale Cisterciense*, 302).

852. Luke 13:6–17 (*Missale Romanum*, 431–32; *Missale Cisterciense*, 308).

853. Luke 7:36–50 (*Missale Romanum*, 427; *Missale Cisterciense*, 304).

854. Mark 9:16–28 (*Missale Romanum*, 425; *Missale Cisterciense*, 302–3).

855. Mark 9:18.

856. Mark 9:22.

857. Mark 9:21.

858. Mark 9:23.

2. Prayer and fasting {are the foundation of} the apostolic power of the contemplative life.[859]

EIGHTEENTH SUNDAY AFTER PENTECOST

Da pacem:[860] praying for peace, not just any peace but the peace that has been promised by God from the beginning and which will infallibly be given, because the prophets *are* faithful (i.e. truthful). What peace? not just a compromise, an absence of hostilities, a temporal truce, {but} eternal peace in the house of the Lord. *Laetatus sum in his quae dicta sunt mihi*[861] (Psalm 121, quoted both in the introit and {in the} gradual[862]). *Fiat pax in virtute tua*:[863] peace in the power of God's merciful love. What is this *"virtus"*? It is the *miserationis operatio*,[864] {the} action of His mercy within us (in the collect). "We cannot please Thee without Thee."[865] Peace {is found} in pleasing God, by virtue of His love in us. {At the} end of the year, we look to the end of all—eternal rest, eternal light, in Christ (secret[866]). *"Ipse est pax nostra,"*[867] for He can give confidence by taking away the burden of our sins (gospel[868]).

---

859. See Mark 9:28.

860. "Give peace" (Eccli [Sir] 36:18) (introit) (*Missale Romanum*, 432; *Missale Cisterciense*, 309).

861. "I rejoiced in those things that were said to me" (v. 1) (*Missale Romanum*, 432; *Missale Cisterciense*, 309).

862. Vv. 1, 7 (*Missale Romanum*, 433; *Missale Cisterciense*, 309).

863. "May peace be done in your power" (Ps 121[122]:7).

864. "the working of mercy" (collect) (*Missale Romanum*, 433; *Missale Cisterciense*, 309).

865. *"tibi sine te placere non possumus"* (collect) (*Missale Romanum*, 433; *Missale Cisterciense*, 309).

866. *"Deus, qui nos per hujus sacrificii veneranda commercia, unius summae divinitatis participes effecis: praesta, quaesumus; ut, sicut tuam cognoscimus veritatem, sic eam dignis moribus assequamur"* ("God, Who through the adorable interchange of this sacrifice make us sharers in the one supreme divinity, grant we pray that as we recognize Your truth, so we may reach it by worthy behavior") (*Missale Romanum*, 433; *Missale Cisterciense*, 310).

867. "He Himself is our Peace" (Eph 2:14).

868. Matt 9:1-8 (*Missale Romanum*, 433; *Missale Cisterciense*, 309).

Nineteenth Sunday after Pentecost

Note that many {of the} texts that are sung are the same as in the Mass for mid-Lent. A prominent theme of the Mass {is} *vocation.* {The} *epistle*[869] {focuses on} the New Man. {The} *gospel* {is the parable of} the Wedding Feast,[870] {which tells of} the lavish generosity of the king {and} the indifference of "those who were called." "They neglected and went their own way"[871] (*inobedientiae desidia*[872]). The king sends his servants out "into the highways" (in another gospel[873] it says: *compel them to enter*). But one must come with a wedding garment—not so much an abstract "state of grace" or an official, juridical sanctity, but LOVE. The beautiful *collect* (*universa nobis adversantia exclude*[874]) {teaches that} God alone can remove all the obstacles to love. *Mente et corpore pariter expediti:*[875] {one must be} ready to travel, {as the} Jews {were} ready to cross {the} Red Sea—{with} no useless baggage, whether of mind or body—just what we *need.* But we are not all able to get along with "nothing." Each one should take the little that he really needs. You can't swim the Atlantic. *Quae tua sunt liberis mentibus exsequamur:*[876] understand well that the "things of God" for us are the occupations of our everyday life in the monastery. But they must be His business, not just our own. And we must carry out everything with *freedom of heart.* How to find freedom of heart? What is it?

Twenty-First Sunday after Pentecost

1. {In the} introit, note the adoration of God's holy will, a frequent theme in these Sunday Masses. "*In voluntate tua Domine* universa sunt posita."[877] Nothing whatever escapes the domination of His will.[878]

---

869. Eph 4:23–28 (*Missale Romanum*, 434; *Missale Cisterciense*, 310).

870. Matt 22:1–14 (*Missale Romanum*, 434–35; *Missale Cisterciense*, 310–11).

871. Matt 22:5.

872. "the sloth of disobedience" (*Rule*, Prologue) (McCann, ed. and trans., *Rule of St. Benedict*, 6).

873. Luke 14:23.

874. "remove everything that is opposed to us" (*Missale Romanum*, 434; *Missale Cisterciense*, 310).

875. "equally prepared in mind and body."

876. "that we may with free minds carry out that which is Yours."

877. "Lord, in Your will all things have been placed" (Esth 13:9) (*Missale Romanum*, 436; *Missale Cisterciense*, 312).

878. "*non est qui posit resistere voluntati tuae*" (Esth 13:36) (*Missale Romanum*, 436; *Missale Cisterciense*, 312).

2. The theme of struggle {is central}, not against flesh and blood, but against spiritual enemies—how we tend to underestimate the subtlety and power of spiritual beings. They can make their voice sound like the voice of our own conscience and of our own freedom itself, even though they cannot move our will directly. How can we resist? only with the *armor of God*—spiritual weapons:[879] *truth* {means} seeking at all times to be strictly in accordance with our conscience and with God's will; *justice* here means especially devoted and careful fulfillment of the will of God[880] (and not just "giving to every man his due,"[881] a pagan ethical conception, which is all right as far as it goes); {the} *gospel of peace* should guide our steps in the ways of peace, meekness, etc. (cf. the Sermon on the Mount); *faith* {is} the essential shield; {the} *helmet of salvation* {is} hope in God; *the sword of the Spirit which is the word of God*: how do we use it as a sword? by "killing" the thoughts that arise from temptation (cf. St. Benedict:[882] dashing the newborn thoughts of evil against the rock—Christ). This theme also runs through the rest of the Mass: {the} *offertory* shows us Job, delivered over to Satan to be tried;[883] {in the} *communion*,[884] our hope is in the word of the Lord.

3. *The gospel*[885] {is} one of the clearest, simplest and most beautiful of the whole year: the servant who received remittance of a debt of 1000 talents,[886] and would not forgive the fellow servant who owed him 100 pence. How clear and unmistakable is Jesus' meaning. This is what the *Kingdom of Heaven* is like (i.e. the Church). The life of a Christian is *essentially a life of mercy*; {it} consists in forgiving and being forgiven. St. Benedict stresses this: "forgive us our trespasses."[887] {It must come} *"from*

879. Eph 6:10–17 (epistle) (*Missale Romanum*, 436–37; *Missale Cisterciense*, 312–13).

880. For an extensive discussion of the Christian conception of justice, see Merton, *Life of the Vows*, 52–65.

881. See Cicero, *De Natura Deorum*, 3.15.38 (p. 320): "*Iustitia suum cuique distribuit*" ("Justice . . . assigns to each his own").

882. *Rule*, c. 4 (McCann, ed. and trans., *Rule of St. Benedict*, 28).

883. Job 1:1—2:7 (condensed) (*Missale Romanum*, 437; *Missale Cisterciense*, 313).

884. Ps 118[119]:81, 84, 86 (*Missale Romanum*, 437; *Missale Cisterciense*, 313).

885. Matt 18:23–35 (*Missale Romanum*, 437; *Missale Cisterciense*, 313).

886. actually ten thousand talents (Matt 18:24).

887. *Rule*, c. 13 (McCann, ed. and trans., *Rule of St. Benedict*, 56).

the heart"[888]—St. Gregory (third nocturn[889]) makes this also clear and inescapable. It is not just a matter of saying, "I have forgiven him; let him do what he likes, I don't care!" {It is} not just a question of "wiping out" both the offense and the offender in our own hearts. {There is an} obligation to return to a union of love with him, as if nothing had happened. *"Juxta nostram mentem sententia Dei flectitur atque mutatur"*[890] (St. Gregory).

THE LAST SUNDAY AFTER PENTECOST

Holy Church ends the liturgical year by contemplating the end of the world. We who have stood and listened to the singing of this gospel,[891] and have seen the Lord descend again upon the altar in the Sacred Mysteries today, have been present in mystery at the Last Judgement.

1. The foremost thing mentioned by Jesus in His own description of what is to come {is} *the apparent triumph of falsity, corruption and sin*:

    a) *The abomination of desolation (read Daniel 9:26–27*[892]) *literally* {is} the destruction of Jerusalem and the profanation of the Temple; *typically* {it is the} desolation and desecration of all that is holy at the end of the world.

    b) *The presence of false Christs and false prophets everywhere* {brings} great danger that the elect themselves will be deceived.

    c) {Note the} *utter desperateness of the situation.* All must fly— woe to those burdened with a child to slow them down ({there is} necessity of complete freedom).

---

888. Matt 18:35.

889. The lessons are actually from St. Jerome's *Commentary on Matthew 18* (*Breviarium Cisterciense, Autumnalis*, 263–64) (Gregory's *Homily 28 on the Gospels* was the source of the lessons for the previous Sunday [*Breviarium Cisterciense, Autumnalis*, 262]).

890. "the judgement of God is adjusted and changed to correspond to our attitude" (twelfth lesson) (*Breviarium Cisterciense, Autumnalis*, 264).

891. Matt 24:15–35 (*Missale Romanum*, 445–46; *Missale Cisterciense*, 317).

892. "And after sixty-two weeks Christ shall be slain: and the people that shall deny him shall not be his. And a people with their leader that shall come, shall destroy the city and the sanctuary: and the end thereof shall be waste, and after the end of the war the appointed desolation. And he shall confirm the covenant with many, in one week: and in the half of the week the victim and the sacrifice shall fall: and there shall be in the temple the abomination of desolation: and the desolation shall continue even to the consummation, and to the end."

2. The destruction of the world (cf. Luke 21: gospel {for the} first Sunday {of} Advent[893]):

    a) {There are} signs in the heavens: *"virtutes coelorum commovebuntur"*[894]—{the} *disruption of {the} order of the universe.*

    b) Men {will be} withering away for fear; all the tribes of the earth shall mourn.

    c) The angels and the trumpets {announce} the appearance of the Son of Man on the clouds of heaven.

Theology teaches (de Fide[895]) {that} the world will be destroyed by fire, and suddenly. There will be a new creation after all have risen from the dead and been judged by the Lord.

---

893. Luke 21:25–33 (*Missale Romanum*, 2; *Missale Cisterciense*, 2–3).

894. "the powers of heaven will be shaken" (Matt 24:29).

895. "as a matter of faith."

LITURGICAL *FEASTS* AND *SEASONS*
Part II

TABLE OF CONTENTS

THE MYSTERY OF MARY AND THE CHURCH

We must reduce our spiritual life to simplicity, and in order to do this we must see that the many different ideas, concepts, mysteries, devotions and so forth which seem to make up our religion, are really aspects of one great reality in which they all converge and in which they have their true life and meaning. This one great reality is the Mystery of Christ in His Church. As long as we do not reach this simple view of things, which is what St. Paul wanted his disciples to have and which is in fact the true essence of the Christian outlook, we will be perplexed, imagining that one idea stands in the way of another, one devotion rules out another, etc. For instance, so many are still uneasy about devotion to Our Lady, as if that took away something from our faith in Jesus, as if Jesus and Mary could possibly be rivals for our love and devotion. In fact, we see Jesus in and through Mary, and Mary in Him. We are united to Him and to her at the same time because the grace which He sends us comes to us through her intercession. Her love acts upon us as the instrument of His love, making our love His instrument also. Can we not see that it is really all one LOVE, poured forth in our hearts, and in hers, by the Holy Spirit Who is given us? To really understand the place of Mary in our life, and the impossibility of her interfering with the mediatorship of Christ Our Lord, we must see how closely the mystery of Our Lady is connected with the mystery of the Church. They are two great aspects of the mystery of Christ. Steps to an understanding of the mystery {include}:

1. The Incarnation: Jesus comes to save us, to share with us the light, the love, the mercy of God, to make us Sons of God, to bring us back, in and with Himself, to the Father. {This is} the purpose of the divine plan: *instaurare omnia in Christo.*[1]

2. Mary is the Mother of the Lord, who by her *fiat*[2] cooperates in the great work of the Incarnation, who by her compassion on Calvary cooperates in the objective Redemption of man. Through Mary, whom Christ willed to have as His collaborator in His great work, all grace is given to the mystical members of Christ, who therefore have her for their mother in a much more intimate sense than the natural man is united to his own mother. The natural man received life from his mother, but goes on living without her. In the supernatural order it is not so. We not only receive life from Mary, but we continue to receive it at every moment, remaining

---

1. "to restore all things in Christ" (Eph 1:10).
2. "let it be done" (Luke 1:38).

always in complete dependence on her for the life of grace. {We are} like infants in the womb, therefore, in the supernatural order.

3. All who are called to membership and life in Christ are called, like Mary (but in a less strict sense), to collaborate with Jesus in the work of the Redemption—we "redeem" one another. Each one of us is his brother's keeper. We obtain grace for one another. We help and educate one another in the faith; we grow together in the knowledge of Christ; we share His gifts with one another, until we all become "one Christ loving Himself" (St. Augustine[3]).

4. Hence, though Jesus is our only Savior, He wills that we should all cooperate in our own salvation and in that of others. In this we are all His instruments, Mary principally, but each one of us also in a more remote and partial fashion. THE WHOLE MYSTERY OF MAN'S COLLABORATION WITH CHRIST IN THE WORK OF SALVATION IS THE MYSTERY OF THE CHURCH. MARY IS THE PERFECT TYPE OF THE CHURCH. IN HER PERSONALLY WAS REALIZED ALL THAT THE CHURCH, COLLECTIVELY, MUST BE. BOTH MARY AND THE CHURCH ARE THE BRIDE OF CHRIST. MARY IS AS IT WERE THE MODEL AND CENTER AROUND WHICH THE CHURCH'S LIFE IS BUILT. TO LIVE IN THE CHURCH IS TO LIVE IN HER.

5. From the very first, Mary understood all that was to be realized in and by the Church:

a) She is holy and without spot, immaculate. The Church too is without spot, holy, but made up of members *who progressively become holy*. In doing so, they become more and more like Mary. They feel more and more the maternal influence of Mary. Mary {is} the model and type of holiness. By the action of the Holy Spirit, each member of the Church gradually achieves the likeness to this model, and Christ is formed perfectly in him. Mary {is} as it were the mould—as long as we qualify this image, and remember that we are all supposed to be different.

b) Mary {is} perfectly united to Jesus, one body and one spirit with Him in the Incarnation, suffering with Him on Calvary, united with Him in His Resurrection, reigning with Him in glory. The Church is His body. Each member becomes gradually "one body and one spirit"[4] with Christ (mainly through {the} Eucharist).

3. "*unus Christus amans seipsum*" (*In Epistola Joannis ad Parthos*, 10.3) (Migne, PL 35, col. 2055).

4. Eph 4:4.

The Church shares in His sufferings. Each one fills out his little share in the sufferings of Jesus,[5] so that together we form one "Bride" of Christ, perfectly conformed to Mary the Co-redeemer. The Church shares in His risen life, and looks forward to the day when, in the resurrection of the flesh, all the members will be enthroned in the glory where Mary has preceded us.

c) In Mary, the perfect and complete member, the Church begins her life. In Mary, the Church realizes, to begin with, her most intimate and inalienable essence: union with Christ.

6. Father Laurentin points out (*Initiation Theologique*,[6] iv, p. 300) that in the beginning, theologians made practically no distinction between the Church and Mary. Texts from Scripture were taken to represent Mary and the Church indiscriminately, so that it is often impossible to tell which one is being talked about. The "first golden age" of the Church is that in which, in fact, Mary herself alone *was* the whole Church. Gradually the Church began to realize itself apart from her; at Pentecost, for example, the Church is Mary *and* the disciples. Pentecost is the feast at which the Church takes cognizance of its identity apart from Mary, but united with her in her communion of the Word, in the Holy Spirit. The Church also takes cognizance of her vocation as mother—the fruitful womb of baptism, the seed of the Word. The "last golden age" of the Church is that in which, united with Mary in the glory of the Lord, all will surround the throne of God. Mary has already entered into that glory. In between these two terms, the Church grows in knowledge of herself and of Mary, her perfection and her model. The Church realizes at once her limits and the perfection of Mary, especially the power and importance of Mary's intercession.

7. *Conclusions*: "There is between the *Virgo Maria* and the *Virgo Ecclesia* an interpenetration and reciprocal inclusion in which Scheeben liked to see an image of the Trinitarian Circumincession."[7] In so far as the Church is a hierarchical body, visibly representing Christ and preaching

5. See Col 1:24.

6. Laurentin, "La Vièrge Marie," *Initiation Théologique*, Tome 4: *L'Économie du Salut*: Livre 2: "Marie et l'Église" (c. 5).

7. "Il y a entre la *Virgo Maria* et la *Virgo Ecclesia* une inclusion réciproque et une interpénétration où Scheeben se plaisait à voir une image de la circumincession trinitaire" (Laurentin, *Initiation Théologique*, 301); see Scheeben, *Mariology*, 1:216–17; 2:66–67; 2:250–51.

to all nations, Mary is hidden in the Church. In so far as the Church is an interior and mystical reality, united to Christ, invisibly communing with Him, then Mary in whom this union is perfectly realized, as it were, contains the Church within herself. Union with Mary is therefore perfection of the interior life of the Church, {a} life of communion with the Word.

Saint Bernard's Sermons for the Feast of Saint Andrew

On the Love of the Cross: in the *Imitation* we read (Bk. II, ch. 12): "In the Cross is infusion of heavenly sweetness, in the Cross is strength of mind; in the Cross is joy of spirit."[8] This thought is an important one in St. Bernard. For him, the monk must strive not merely to suffer for Christ, but to suffer willingly and joyously, just as he must practice virtue not exteriorly but with ardent interior love. If we accept suffering unwillingly, or bear the Cross grudgingly and with complaints, then that which is given us for our salvation helps us little or not at all. At the same time, however, it is useless to try in one jump to pass from the lowest degree of the spiritual life to the highest, and to embrace the Cross with ardent desire and love when our love is still weak and untried. We must accept the sufferings and difficulties proportionate to our state and our strength and God will give us grace to take what He will send us later on.

The first Sermon of St. Bernard on the Feast of St. Andrew[9] teaches us what he means by the love of the Cross:

n. 1: The joy of St. Andrew as he receives the Cross {is great}: there is no sorrow in this feast; all is rejoicing and gladness: *Nemo ex nobis compassus est sic patienti.*[10]

n. 2: Yet the question arises: what is this rejoicing? How can one take delight in suffering? because the Cross is not the sign of death but of life, not {of} destruction but fructification. It is not loved for suffering's sake, but for the sake of the grace and union with God which we can reach by loving the Cross. *Semper lignum crucis vitam germinat* (505).[11] The cross is the tree of life; otherwise it would not be planted in the midst of the paradise of the Church. There is no place for a tree of death and destruction in the garden of Christ. But the manna that is given to us in this paradise, the fruit of this tree of life, *is hidden* from us. It is a secret which

---

8. Thomas à Kempis, *Imitation of Christ*, 142.

9. Migne, *PL* 183, cols. 503D–509A.

10. "None of us has suffered with such patience" (Migne, *PL* 183, col. 503D).

11. "The wood of the Cross always produces life" (Migne, *PL* 183, col. 505B).

we must discover in order to rejoice in the Cross; and it is necessary to discover this secret if we would *win a complete victory over the powers of evil.* This is one of the fundamental doctrines of St. Bernard: *sapientia vincit malitiam.*[12] But *sapientia* is *sapor boni,*[13] and the Cross is our greatest good on earth. Hence if we do not have a *sapor,* a taste, for the Cross, there is still something lacking in us. There is something missing in our spontaneity and fervor of love.

n. 3: The devil tries to cast us down by impatience or the love of pleasure. But if one really loves the Cross he will not be distressed by either of these movements and he will have a perfect defense against the tempter. Now, since St. Andrew was a fisherman, St. Bernard begins to talk about the followers of Christ under the symbol of three kinds of fish, which he finds in Leviticus 11:9 (the pure fish which it is lawful to eat): "All that hath fins and scales, as well in the sea as in the rivers and in the pools, you shall eat."[14] The apostles are fishers of men, catching souls like fish for the heavenly banquet. There are three kinds of fish: those in the sea are those who live holy lives in the world; those who are in the rivers are those who become saints by preaching the Gospel in the world; those in the pools are those who become saints in the cloister, protected from the outside world and patiently waiting to be caught by the Lord, saying, "*Quando veniet qui me deferat?*"[15]

n. 4: Again there are three degrees in the spiritual life: the beginners, guided by fear (the beginning of wisdom), must be content to bear the Cross patiently; {the} progressives, whose lives are dominated by hope for a reward, which they begin to see in the future, bear the Cross willingly; the perfect, who are totally governed by charity, embrace the Cross with ardent love and prefer it. St. Bernard, with his usual prudence and knowledge of human nature, spends much time explaining the first degree. No one should be downcast because he feels repugnance for the Cross at first! Jesus Himself mercifully willed to suffer agony in

12. "Wisdom overcomes malice" (Wis 7:30) (*De Diversis,* 14 [Migne, *PL* 183, col. 574D]; *In Cantica,* 82 [Migne, *PL* 183, col. 1180D]; *In Cantica,* 85 [Migne, *PL* 183, col. 1192A]).

13. "a taste of the good" (*In Cantica,* 85 [Migne, *PL* 183, cols. 1191A, 1192A, 1192B]).

14. "*Hujusmodi siquidem pisces mundos esse legalis sanctio judicabat, qui et pinnis levantur, et proteguntur squamis: sive illi in mari sint, sive in flumine, sive in stagno*" (Migne, *PL* 183, cols. 505D–506A).

15. "When will He come Who will take me away?" (Migne, *PL* 183, col. 506B).

the garden, when it would have been perfectly easy for Him to accept the Cross with even greater joy and indifference than St. Andrew; indeed He could have suffered without the slightest shadow or sorrow or inconvenience. But instead, for our sake, He willed to take upon Himself all our weakness and moral torment. *Quid enim? Agnosco vocem meam in Salvatore, et de salute desperem?*[16] His example and the graces He has gained for us enable us to practice patience. His fear has made us courageous; His sorrow has brought us joy; His anguish has brought us peace; His desolation leaves us consoled ({507}[17]). However, we must not make a virtue out of weakness and simply rest in it without seeking to love generously. This is quietism. We must make our weakness an occasion of greater strength and confidence. For the perfect it is not enough to suffer bravely, with hope, dominating our passions by reason and courage. One thing more is needed—to suffer with joy, with abandon and delight. This joy is not possible without a special gift of the Holy Ghost, and is indeed a sign that He has taken complete possession of our soul.

n. 10: Only love (not fear or hope) is strong as death. Whereas *fear* accepts the Cross saying, "It is fitting that I suffer (I have deserved it)," and *hope* accepts the Cross saying, "It is good for me to suffer—I will gain by it," LOVE says, "*Sic volo, sic cupio, sic desidero vehementer.*"[18] He adds that there were many at Clairvaux who had reached this degree, and so the others should not hesitate to try to imitate them. But how? *Nemo repente fit summus.*[19] You cannot rise all at once from the bottom of the ladder to the top; you have to climb all the various rungs. We climb these rungs with two feet, *meditation* and *prayer*. Meditation teaches us what we lack, and shows us the danger we are in. Prayer obtains for us what we lack and delivers us from danger by the grace of Our Lord.

Second Sermon for {the} Feast of St. Andrew: On Obedience:

1. {This is} a magnificent sermon[20] on religious obedience, based on the consideration of the promptitude with which St. Andrew followed Jesus when he was called. All Christians are bound to obey, but most

---

16. "What then? I recognize my voice in the Savior, and should I despair of salvation?" (Migne, *PL* 183, col. 507D).

17. Copy text reads: "807."

18. "So I want, so I wish, so I vehemently desire" (Migne, *PL* 183, col. 508D).

19. "No one reaches the summit immediately" (Migne, *PL* 183, col. 509A).

20. Migne, *PL* 183, cols. 509B–514A.

especially the monk, who by his very profession is a *debitor obedientiae*.[21] We owe obedience in justice. That is to say that if we do not obey, our monastic life is unreal. For justice is that virtue by which we conform to what we should be by giving what is due from us. Obedience is like a coin we have received from Wisdom Itself and which we must pay back. *If we criticize and analyze*, pick and choose what commands to obey, and obey only those we like, we give back a broken coin—not the proper weight. *If we obey exteriorly while murmuring interiorly*, the coin is false; it is lead and not silver.

2. The obedience of Peter and Andrew when called by the Lord {was genuine}: *Nihil dijudicantes aut haesitantes, non solliciti unde viverent, non considerantes quomodo . . . praedicatores fieri possent: Nihil interrogantes, sine mora.*[22] This is the example the Church wants monks to see each year, and put into effect. How? by *charity*. It is love that makes obedience worthwhile. *Sola enim est charitas quae obedientiam gratam facit et acceptabilem Deo.*[23] We must be "joyful givers"[24] (here we rejoin the theme of the First Sermon).

3. St. Andrew's joy and exultation on going to the Cross was not merely human. It could only be a special gift from God, a heroic charity stronger than death, poured forth in his soul by the Holy Spirit. We in our turn, aware of our weakness, knowing its cause ({and the} need of special grace) should ardently desire the strength from God. *The very fact of desiring this grace is a sign that its first fruits have already been granted us.* All that is necessary is to ask, but to ask with faith and fervor, and really ardent desire. Beg at all times, without hesitation, *for the gift of the Holy Spirit*, for if we desire Christ, we must despise self, and if we seek His will we must renounce our own. But, says St. Bernard, instead of this fervent desire, we too often entertain only feelings of false security. Though surrounded by enemies, we sleep in a fatal security; we are lazy and silly, indulging in foolish jokes, and we are negligent of our spiritual exercises as if they really had little importance (see col. 512AB). Negligence would

---

21. "one who owes obedience" (Migne, *PL* 183, col. 509B, which reads: "*debitores*").

22. "Not pondering or hesitating; not concerned about where they would live; not considering how they could become preachers; asking nothing; without delay" (Migne, *PL* 183, col. 509D, which reads: ". . . *considerantes quoniam . . . Nihil denique . . . sine omni mora*").

23. "It is love alone which makes obedience pleasing and acceptable to God" (Migne, *PL* 183, col. 509D).

24. 2 Cor 9:7 (Migne, *PL* 183, col. 509D).

be a sign either that we have secretly sold out to the enemy, or that if we are still friends of God we are ungrateful for His protection.

4. The Cross is our salvation, but only if we bear it with manly courage. The four corners of the Cross {symbolize how} the Cross protects us against four great temptations[25] (cf. *Psalm* 90).

A demonio meridiano[26]

Pride and self-complacency

A sagitta volante in die[27]   *A negotio perambulante in tenebris*[28]

Insults—fear of being despised   Flattery—harmful love

A timore nocturno[29]

Fear of mortification

THE PRIEST IN THE MONASTERY—Feast of St. Thomas the Apostle[30]

1. In the Common of the Apostles, the Church reminds us of the fact that the apostles and their successors are the special friends of Jesus. *Nimis honorati sunt amici tui Deus. . . .*[31] *Isti sunt triumphatores et amici Dei. . . .*[32] *Vos estis qui permansistis mecum in tentationibus meis. . . .*[33] And in the Mass of Ordination, at the end, the responsory is sung: "*Iam non dicam vos servos sed amicos*"[34] ({which is} also {the} gospel of the vigil of an Apostle[35]). The calling to the priesthood is the loftiest of all vocations and dignities. The priest is another Christ, deputed to consecrate the Sacred Victim, the Lamb of God Who takes away the sins of the world. *The power of the priest* {includes the power} to destroy sin, to turn back the enemies of God; to give infinite glory to God (in the Mass); to purify

---

25. Migne, *PL* 183, cols. 512A–513A.

26. "from the noonday demon" (Ps 90[91]:6).

27. "from the arrow that flies by day" (Ps 90[91]:5).

28. "from the business walking in the darkness" (Ps 90[91]:6).

29. "from the fear at night" (Ps 90[91]:5).

30. December 21.

31. "God, Your friends are very highly honored" (Ps 138[139]:17) (introit, alleluia) (*Missale Romanum*, 474; *Missale Cisterciense*, 337); (hymn versicle, vespers; versicle, seventh lesson) (*Breviarium Cisterciense*, 2*, 14*).

32. "They are victors and friends of God" (responsory, sixth lesson, second nocturn) (*Breviarium Cisterciense*, 14*).

33. "You are they who have remained with me in my trials" (Luke 22:28).

34. "I shall not call you servants but friends" (John 15:15) (*Pontificale Romanum*, 30).

35. John 15:12–16 (*Missale Romanum*, (2); *Missale Cisterciense*, 2*).

souls {and} reconcile them to God; to satisfy their hunger for truth—{he is} the only one who has the final answer: the priest speaks for the Teaching Church, as an aid to the bishop; to satisfy their desire for security and salvation; to lead souls on the sure path to God. Yet he himself is a frail creature, and is constantly confronted by human frailty in himself and in others at all times, so that he is constantly caught in between God and sin. When we see this, we no longer desire the priesthood as a dignity, but rather tremble at the burden. The only way in which the burden can be borne {is that} the priest must indeed be what he is called, above all, a friend of Christ, another Christ. He must always be filled with that charity than which there is no greater: to desire to lay down his life for his God, his Master and his Friend. Yet alas! how often we are more aware than ever of our own weakness, for the priest is often kept conscious of a *special* weakness in himself in order that like St. Paul[36] he may learn to glory in his infirmities, that the power of Christ may triumph in and through him. It brings him very close to Jesus, and close to souls at the same time, but it creates difficulty and even conflict.

2. To be a friend of Jesus in this special way means sharing:

a) His *humility*: *Tollite jugum meum super vos et discite a me quia mitis sum et humilis corde.*[37] {This must be} a meekness that does not get angry at unavoidable evils and obstacles, that does not lose patience with the frailties of human nature, that does not fight back and condemn. The priest must be more charitable, more discreet, more patient, more understanding than anyone else. {He must have} humility *of heart*, a deep, peaceful humility that comes from the full acceptance of reality, and union with Jesus in truth. As a religious, the priest must be especially *obedient*; in this he must see a means of finding Jesus, his Friend, and pleasing Him.

b) His *trials*: Jesus was rejected and misunderstood by those He came to save. The priest must above all be patient with misunderstanding, with the defense that fallen nature instinctively puts up against him. Jesus felt the full force of *desolation* which consumes the heart of the sinner. The priest must always, in the depths of his soul, be aware of the awful solitude of the

36. See 2 Cor 12:7–9.

37. "Take My yoke upon you and learn from Me for I am meek and humble of heart" (Matt 11:29).

sinner far from God; he must share something of that isolation in order to be able to understand and seek out the lost sheep. Jesus had to die for us as a victim on the Cross, and the priest too must lay down his whole life for the truth, for souls—that is to say, he must forget his own interests entirely for the interests of Jesus. He must be like Jesus a Good Shepherd who lays down his life for his sheep.[38] This is impossible unless he is himself a docile sheep of the Good Shepherd. In the monastery the priests *often have far more trials*, crosses and burdens than anyone else, especially if they share in the care of souls or have other jobs. At the same time, the priest is *often more gravely tempted* than the other religious or the laybrothers. His exalted position may put him in the way of serious occasions of sin; his superior may have an exaggerated, misplaced confidence in him, and the priest himself may have too great a trust in his own powers, and the mistake may not be discovered until it is too late. We seldom realize how often priests, particularly in religion, are burdened beyond their talents and their strength. This is true in the active life, as well as in the diocesan priesthood. It can also be true in a contemplative monastery. It often happens that a person of mediocre qualities and talents, who would perhaps be very good and edifying in a lesser position, becomes a priest in the monastery and has to take on heavy burdens, too heavy for him to carry. He is crushed under them.

c) *His charity*: hence if we are to bear the burden of the priesthood we can only do so with a completely self-sacrificing charity like that of Jesus. We must be consumed with love for the Father, with desire for the coming of the Kingdom of God, for the salvation of souls, for the glory of God, for the triumph of the Gospel. If a priest merely loves himself and seeks to advance his own interests, his own petty ambitions, the result is lamentable, and everybody sees it. For the priest is a light placed on a high lampstand and his faults often come out very clearly and have a very bad effect on others. Here too he has no recourse but to fly to Jesus with love and trust. Hence, though the priest ought to take care to lead an edifying life, others ought also

38. See John 10:11.

to remember the difficulty of his position, and overlook his faults, and pray for him, and excuse him, and never treat him with disrespect. Remember that in spite of his limitations he is another Christ, and is venerated with a special respect by the angels and by Our Lady and by God Himself.

d) His manifestation of divine Truth: the priest is ordained to of-fer sacrifice, first of all, but also to see that the Gospel reaches all men. Our preaching in the monastery is limited; however, it is none the less important. *The Word of God* nourishes souls. We should take our preaching in chapter seriously; it should be simple, solid, Catholic. We are not permitted merely to air our own opinions and put ourselves on display; we have a seri-ous obligation to preach Christ Crucified, to realize that "He must increase and I must decrease."[39] We must really try to give souls the spiritual food they need, for there are souls starving for truth even in the monastery. {Note the importance of} *ex-ample*: it cannot be too often repeated that the priest preaches more by his example than by his words, especially in our silent monasteries. He who sees the priest, must see Christ in him.

e) His contemplation: the priest in a contemplative monastery is called above all to enter into the great Mystery of Christ and live it to the full. He above all should be a man well-versed in the Scriptures and in theology, indeed, but above all, a man of prayer, a man who lives the Mystery of the Eucharist, and not merely one who "says Mass." His Mass must be not just an incident in the day; it must be the heart of a life of prayer centered on the sacrifice of the Word Incarnate. He must be a man of faith more than the others.

3. How the Church prepares us for the priesthood: besides our courses in philosophy and theology, besides the spiritual instruction and direction that must be received by the candidates for orders, the Church prepares us for ordination by the liturgy itself leading us gradually to the priesthood by successive steps: the four minor orders, the subdiaconate and the diaconate. Ideally speaking, with each order the candidate gets a chance to exercise himself in some of those functions which pertain to the priestly office. Also the rite of ordination is in each case a simple and

39. John 3:30.

profound instruction which throws light on the nature of the priesthood; not only that, but each order is a sacrament, or, in the case of the minor orders, at least a sacramental, and special graces are imparted which form the soul of the future priest.

4. {See} some of the instructions contained in the rite for the ordination of subdeacons. The first instruction bears especially on the obligation of perpetual chastity which the subdeacon assumes. The candidates are warned that if they do not feel themselves capable of assuming this burden, it is better to turn back before it is too late.[40] The second instruction {focuses on}:

a) the simple, exterior duties of the subdeacon. They may strike us at first as prosaic, but the Church takes them seriously. Actually she is very wise, and it is a pity that we no longer today carry out all the functions proper to each order—for instance here, the washing of altar linens.[41] The Church expects that by conscientiously carrying out these simple jobs, we will be formed for higher things.

b) In fact, the altar, altar linens, etc. have a symbolic meaning: the subdeacon must be aware of the mystery of the Mystical Body and of the higher obligation of "cleansing" the souls of the faithful by preaching the word of truth.[42]

40. "*Filii dilectissimi, ad sacrum Subdiaconatus Ordinem promovendi, iterum atque iterum considerare debetis attente, quod onus hodie ultro appetitis. Hactenus enim liberi estis, licetque vobis pro arbitrio ad saecularia vota transire; quod si hunc Ordinem susceperitis, amplius non licebit a proposito resilire, sed Deo, cui servire regnare est, perpetuo famulari, et castitatem, illo adjuvante, servare oportebit, atque in Ecclesiae ministerio semper esse mancipatos. Proinde, dum tempus est, cogitate, et, si in sancto proposito perseverare placet, in nomine Domini huc accedite*" ("Most beloved sons, who are about to be advanced to the sacred order of the subdiaconate, again and again you should carefully consider the burden that you voluntarily seek today. For thus far you are free, and are permitted according to your own decision to pass over to a secular way of life; but if you have taken on this order, you will no longer be allowed to step back from your commitment, but will have become a permanent servant of God, to serve Whom is to reign, and with His assistance you will be required to observe celibacy, and will always be engaged in the ministry of the Church. Therefore, while there is time, think, and if it pleases you to persevere in this sacred commitment, come forward in the name of the Lord") (*Pontificale Romanum*, 15).

41. "*pallas altaris, et corporalia abluere*" (*Pontificale Romanum*, 16).

42. "*Si itaque humana fragilitate contingat in aliquo fideles maculari, praebenda est a vobis aqua coelestis doctrinae, qua purificati, ad ornamentum altaris, et cultum divini sacrificii redeant*" ("So if through human weakness it happens that the faithful are soiled in some way, they should be provided by you with the water of heavenly

c) They must themselves live in a spirit of deep faith, and also be zealous for their duties, and live virtuously. They must be "valiant and
watchful sentinels of the heavenly army."[43] If they earnestly try to
fulfill this assignment, they will receive an abundant outpouring of
the Gifts of the Holy Ghost.

The vestments {have symbolic significance}. {Does} the amice
{signify} moderation in speech? modesty? restraint? {It is} hard to say
exactly what is meant by "*castigatio vocis*";[44] {it is related to the} "helmet
of salvation."[45] The alb of course signifies purity of heart. The maniple
{represents} "fruits of good works" (*Pontificale*[46]); the prayer we say when
putting it on emphasizes rather that we may be "worthy to bear the maniple of mourning and of tears, that with rejoicing we may receive the
reward of our labors."[47] The tunicle {is the} "*tunica jucunditatis*."[48] (He
also receives the Book of the Epistles, to sing the epistles "for the living
and the dead."[49])

CANDLEMAS (February 2)

The blessing of the candles:[50] {this is a} case where an important
sacramental is intimately connected with the Holy Sacrifice of the Mass
itself, and with the liturgy of the day—but only more or less by accident;
there is no essential link between them. This gives us occasion to admire
the simplicity and depth with which the Church teaches and sanctifies us
by her symbolic rites and her sacramental actions. {The} *purpose of the
blessing* {is in a} *primary* {sense} to make us love and appreciate the symbolism and sacramental value of blessed candles, and of light in general
as used in {the} liturgy, and of course above all to provide the Church

---

teaching, through which they may return purified to the adornment of the altar and
the worship of the divine sacrifice") (*Pontificale Romanum*, 16).

43. "*strenuos sollicitosque coelestis militia . . . excubitores*" (*Pontificale Romanum*,
17).

44. "correction of the voice" (*Pontificale Romanum*, 17).

45. Eph 6:17.

46. "*fructus bonorum operum*" (*Pontificale Romanum*, 17).

47. "*Merear, Domine, portare manipulum fletus et doloris; ut cum exsultatione re-
cipiam mercedem laboris*" (*Missale Romanum*, xlviii; *Missale Cisterciense*, xxviii).

48. "the tunic of joy" (*Pontificale Romanum*, 17).

49. "*tam pro vivis, quam pro defunctis*" (*Pontificale Romanum*, 17).

50. *Missale Romanum*, 499–501; *Missale Cisterciense*, 366–68.

and the faithful with candles for their use: the *use* of the candles by the Church at Holy Mass and in other liturgical rites {and} by the faithful to obtain special graces and protection, especially at the hour of death. *Note*: on February 3 {the} candles {are} immediately used for the blessing of the throats. {A} *secondary*, and accidental, {purpose is} to enhance the liturgy of the feast with a procession, and to "absorb" the ancient pagan feast of the Lupercalia (the procession with torches in honor of Ceres looking for Proserpine[51]), or other authors say the Amburbalia.[52]

The prayers said by the Church tell us the power of the holy candles:

a. *Ad sanitatem corporum et animarum, sive in terra sive in aquis.*[53] But how is this efficacy realized? by the invocation of the Name of Jesus, and by the intercession of the Blessed Mother (first prayer).

b. *sancto igne dulcissimae charitatis tuae succensi in templo sancto gloriae tuae repraesentari mereamur*[54] (second collect). Here we see how much the Church packs into a short space of a few lines, {providing} a real insight into her contemplation, which we share by the liturgy:

(1) {It} begins with reference to the Presentation of Jesus in the Temple, received into the arms of old Simeon.

(2) Then {comes a} reference to the fact that the candles are blessed and given us to carry in procession, and they are enkindled not only with earthly fire, but with a heavenly blessing, which is the spiritual light of Christ. We bear the light of Christ mystically for the glory of the Father.

(3) While we are actually doing this, the spiritual efficacy of the sacred rite merits for us grace to be enkindled interiorly ourselves with charity, which is the grace of Christ in our hearts, and we experience a foretaste, in holy hope, of our own entrance to the Kingdom of glory, the splendor of the heavenly Jerusalem, in

51. In the myth of Proserpine (Persephone), she is carried away by Pluto (Hades) into the underworld and sought by her mother Ceres (Demeter), goddess of agriculture; eventually her daughter is allowed to return to earth for part of the year, which results in the alternation of the seasons.

52. See Lambing, *Sacramentals*, 235–36; the Amburbalia was a feast of purification of the city celebrated by torchlight processions at Rome in February every five years.

53. "for the health of bodies and souls, whether on land or seas" (*Missale Romanum*, 499; *Missale Cisterciense*, 366).

54. "inflamed by the holy fire of Your most sweet love, we may be found worthy to be made present in the holy temple of Your glory" (*Missale Romanum*, 499; *Missale Cisterciense*, 367).

which we will exchange the dim light of faith for the glory of the beatific vision, which will be enkindled in us as the flame itself on the candle.

c. {There is} a special prayer to Christ the true light that enlightens every man coming into the world:[55] "Pour forth Thy blessing on these candles, and sanctify them by the visible light; dispel the darkness of the night, so our hearts burning with invisible fire *and enlightened by the grace of the Holy Ghost* [{the} Latin itself is more forceful and direct—it says "enkindled with invisible fire,"[56] *that is,* with the Holy Spirit] may be delivered from all the blindness of sin."[57] Hence the grace of this sacramental is *interior illumination and purgation so that we are delivered by true compunction from our hidden sins,* "that we may discern those things which are pleasing to Thee and beneficial to our souls." And again {there is} a reference to our passage from the darkness of this world to the light of heaven. Read the last two prayers,[58] which sum up the same teaching

---

55. John 1:9.

56. "*accensa . . . invisibili igne.*"

57. "*effunde benedictionem tuam super hos cereos, et sanctifica eos lumine gratiae tuae, et concede propitius; ut, sicut haec luminaria igne visibili accensa nocturnas depellunt tenebras; ita corda nostra invisibili igne, id est, Sancti Spiritus splendore illustrata, omnium vitiorum caecitate careant*" (*Missale Romanum,* 500; *Missale Cisterciense,* 367).

58. "*Omnipotens sempiterne Deus, qui per Moysen famulum tuum, purissimum olei liquorem ad luminaria ante conspectum tuum jugiter concinnanda praeparari jussisti: benedictionis tuae gratiam super hos cereos benignus infunde: quatenus sic administrant lumen exterius, ut, te donante, lumen Spiritus tui nostris non desit mentibus interius*" ("Almighty, eternal God, who commanded through Your servant Moses that the purest liquid of oil be prepared for lamps to be burned perpetually in Your sight, kindly pour forth the grace of Your blessing upon these candles, that as they provide light exteriorly, so through Your gift the light of Your Spirit may not be lacking interiorly for our minds"); "*Domine Jesu Christi, qui hodierna die in nostrae carnis substantia inter homines apparens, a parentibus in templo es praesentatus: quem Simeon venerabilis senex, lumine Spiritus tui irradiatus, agnovit, suscepit, et benedixit: praesta propitius; ut ejusdem Spiritus sancti gratia illuminati atque edocti, te veraciter agnoscamus, et fideliter diligemus*" ("Lord Jesus Christ, Who on this day, appearing among men in the substance of our flesh, were presented by Your parents in the temple; Whom the venerable old man Simeon, illumined by the light of Your Spirit, recognized, took up and blessed, mercifully grant that enlightened and taught by the grace of the same Holy Spirit, we may truly recognize You and faithfully love You" (*Missale Romanum,* 500; *Missale Cisterciense,* 367).

once again. The *Nunc Dimittis*[59] and {the} antiphon *"Lumen"*[60] {are} (a) a confession of faith, like that of Simeon; receiving the lighted candle we mystically receive Jesus and we acknowledge Him; (b) a manifestation of Christ to the world; (c) a prayer that His Kingdom may come to the whole world: the mystery of the missionary apostolate {is thereby} symbolized.

The Procession[61] (*Hypapante*[62]): the theme of the feast, as the Greek title indicates, is the meeting of the people of God with the Divine Bride-groom, the Word made Flesh, in which He comes forth and manifests Himself to the people in public (though few see Him) by an act of obedience and worship (cf. the invitatory of vigils: "Go forth to meet thy God"[63]). The theme of the meeting is uppermost in the first antiphon of the procession, *Adorna* (read the text—it is beautiful!): "Adorn thy bride-chamber, O Sion, and receive Christ, thy King; salute Mary, the Gate of Heaven, for she beareth the King of Glory Who is the new light. The Virgin stands, bringing in her hands the Son [the Greek Text[64] {is} Mary comes as a bright cloud bearing in her flesh, her Son begotten before the Day Star] begotten before the day star; Whom Simeon receiving into his arms declared Him to His people as the Lord of life and death, the Savior of the world."[65] {This is} one of the most magnificent texts in the Roman Liturgy; it is from the Orient. The others, simpler and less mystical, simply narrate the Presentation of Jesus in the Temple. From

---

59. "Now dismiss [Your servant]" (Luke 2:29–32) (*Missale Romanum*, 500; *Missale Cisterciense*, 368).

60. "light [of revelation to the Gentiles]" (Luke 2:32) (*Missale Romanum*, 500; *Missale Cisterciense*, 368).

61. *Missale Romanum*, 500–501; *Missale Cisterciense*, 368.

62. "encounter" (see Mercenier, *Prière des Églises de Rite Byzantin*, 2.1:310).

63. *"occurrens Deo tuo"* (*Breviarium Cisterciense, Pars Hiemalis*, 599).

64. "Ornez votre chambre nuptiale, Sion, et recevez le Christ Roi; embrassez Marie, la porte du ciel, car elle est semblable au trône des chérubins: elle porte le Roi de gloire. La Vierge est une nuée de lumière, portant dans sa chair son Fils né avant l'étoile du matin. Le recevant dans ses bras, Siméon annonça aux peuples qu'Il était le Maître de la vie et de la mort, et le Sauveur du monde" (Mercenier, *Prière des Églises de Rite Byzantin*, 2.1:321–22).

65. "*Adorna thalamum tuum, Sion, et suscipe Regem Christum: amplectere Mariam, quae est caelestis porta: ipsa enim portat Regem gloriae novi luminis: subsistit Virgo, adducens manibus Filium ante luciferum genitum: quem accipiens Simeon in ulnas suas, praedicavit populis, Dominum eum esse vitae et mortis, et Salvatorem mundi*" (*Missale Romanum*, 501).

the Oriental liturgy we see the following: "Tell us, O Simeon, what you carry in your arms that makes you so joyful in the Temple; to Whom do you address this cry, 'Let me depart in peace'?" "It is this Child born of a Virgin. He is the Word of God, Incarnate for us, the Savior of mankind. Let us adore Him, let us adore Him."[66] "Receive, O Simeon, Him Whom Moses saw in the cloud, giving the Law, and Who is now a Child, submitting to the Law. It is He Who spoke by the Law. It is He Who made Himself heard through the prophets, Who is incarnate for us and Who saves mankind. Let us adore Him"[67] (three times). "Let us also go, to the sound of sacred and inspired chants, and meet the Christ, meet Him in Whom Simeon has seen salvation. He it is that David foretold. He it is that spoke in the prophets, Who is incarnate for us, and speaks to us in the Law. Let us adore Him"[68] (three times). "He Whom, in the liturgy of heaven, the spirits supplicate with trembling fear, is received here below into the bodily arms of Simeon, and the old man proclaims the union of God with men."[69] "The Mother who knew not man carries in her arms the One Who from all eternity shines forth from the Father and has come down in these last days in her virginal womb. . . . The Virgin Mother of God carries in her arms the One Who goes forth riding on the cars of the cherubim and is hymned by the seraphim."[70] "O you heavens, spread out by the wisdom of God, rejoice, and thou, o earth, tremble, for your

66. "Dites-nous, Siméon, qui portez-vous dans vos bras pour être si joyeux dans le temple? À qui addressez-vous ces mots: Maintenant je vais être délivré car j'ai vu mon Saveur?—C'est cet enfant né d'une Vierge. Il est Dieu, le Verbe de Dieu qui s'est incarné pour nous et qui sauve l'humanité. Adorons-Le" (Mercenier, *Prière des Églises de Rite Byzantin*, 2.1:315).

67. "Accueillez, Siméon, celui que Moïse vit jadis dans la nuée donnant la loi au Sinaï et qui a parlé par la loi; c'est Lui qui c'est fait entendre dans les prophètes, qui s'est incarné pour nous et qui sauve l'humanité. Adorons-Le" (Mercenier, *Prière des Églises de Rite Byzantin*, 2.1:316).

68. "Allons nous aussi, au son des chants inspirés, à la rencontre du Christ et accueillons celui dont Siméon a vu le salut. Il est celui qui David a annoncé. Il est celui qui a parlé dans les prophètes, celui qui c'est incarné pour nous et qui nous parle dans le loi. Adorons-Le" (Mercenier, *Prière des Églises de Rite Byzantin*, 2.1:316).

69. "Celui que, dans la liturgie d'en haut, les esprits supplient avec tremblement, est reçu ici-bas dans les bras corporels de Siméon, et celui-ci proclame l'union de la divinité avec les hommes" (Mercenier, *Prière des Églises de Rite Byzantin*, 2.1:320).

70. "Celui qui resplendit du Père avant les siècles et, dans ces derniers temps sortit d'un sien virginal, sa Mère qui ne connut point de marriage Le porte dans le temple. . . . La Mère de Dieu, Marie, portait dans ses bras celui qui s'avance porté sur les chars des chérubins et qui est célébré par les hymnes des séraphins" (Mercenier, *Prière des Églises de Rite Byzantin*, 2.1:322).

Maker, coming forth from the abyss of the Godhead, Christ, is offered to God by His Virgin Mother as a Child, He Who exists before all things: for He has covered Himself with glory."[71]

Other passages {include this} from a sequence by Notker of St. Gall: "Rejoice, O Mary, on whom the Little One Whose look gives joy and being to the world, looked and smiled. . . . Since we cannot, because we are weak, follow the wondrous humility of a God, let us take Mary as our model. Praise to the Father of glory, Who hath united us all into one, by revealing His Son to both the Gentiles and the people of Israel. Praise to the Son, Who hath given us fellowship with the citizens of heaven, by reconciling us by His Blood to the Father. Praise, too, be forever to the Holy Ghost. Amen."[72]

SAINT AILRED—*Cistercian Life in His Time*
(Feast of St. Ailred: February 3)

To know our Fathers and the way they lived—their attitude, their outlook—{is the way} to become a monk, by contact with real monks.

Ailred's Life and Character: {he was} born at Hexham {in} 1110 {and} educated at {the} court of Scotland, etc; {he was} the Bernard of England. {For} character sketches:

1. Read from Jocelyn of Furness (Powicke, p. xxxiii[73]): (a) how he made good use of his gifts, though they were not extraordinary; (b) {he

---

71. "Cieux étendus par l'Intelligence réjouissez-vous, et toi, terre, tressaille: votre artisan, sortant du sien de la Divinité, le Christ, est offert comme enfant à Dieu son Père par la Vierge, sa mère, Lui qui existe avant toutes choses: Il s'est couvert d'une gloire éclatante" (Mercenier, *Prière des Églises de Rite Byzantin*, 2.1:327–28).

72. "*Exsulta, cui parvulus arrisit tunc, Maria, qui laetari omnibus et consistere suo nutu tribuit. . . . Si non Dei possumus tantam exsequi tardi humilitatem, forma sit nobis ejus Genitrix. Laus Patri gloriae, qui suum Filium Gentibus et populo revelans, Israel nos sociat. Laus ejus Filio, qui suo sanguine nos Patri reconcilians, supernis sociavit civibus. Laus quoque Spiritui Sancto sit per aevum*" (from the sequence "*Concentu parili hic te, Maria*" as quoted and translated in Guéranger, *Liturgical Year*, 3:498, which reads: ". . . his people of Israel. . . .").

73. "He was a man of fine old English stock (*ex ueterem Anglorum illustri stipe procreatu*). He left school early and was brought up from boyhood in the court of King David with Henry the king's son and Waldef. In course of time he became first a monk, afterwards abbot of Rievaulx. His school learning was slight, but as a result of careful self-discipline in the exercise of his acute natural powers, he was cultured above many who have been thoroughly trained in secular learning. He drilled himself in the study of Holy Scripture, and left a lasting memorial behind him in writings distinguished by their lucid style, and wealth of edifying instruction, for he was wholly inspired by a spirit of wisdom and understanding. Moreover, he was a man of the

was} a student of Scripture and a contemplative; (c) {and} a man of the highest integrity {and} practical wisdom (cf. St. Benedict's cellarer[74]); (d) {he was} witty and eloquent, a pleasant companion, generous and discreet; (e) above all, {he was full of} patience and tenderness, {and} sympathy for the infirmities, both physical and moral, of others. ({cf.} St. Benedict: instruments of good works[75]).

2. Gilbert of Hoyland: commenting on the Canticle of Canticles, in Sermon 41[76] Gilbert introduces a passage in praise of Ailred, recently dead:

a) {he} praises the purity of his life and the prudence of his doctrine;

b) {he} speaks especially of his great sufferings, accompanied by clarity of mind and peace of heart, due to his great charity; he was consumed by his love for God, even in the midst of his sickness, {and} he praised God always, with great fervor;

c) his bearing was always tranquil; he was slow to speak, modest and patient in his talk (some of the monks around him were impetuous); Gilbert speaks of him as *opportune loquens et opportune silens*;[77]

d) he does not call him even "slow to anger,"[78] because there was no anger in him at all;

e) speaking of the great sweetness of his spirit, Gilbert says[79] it came entirely from the fact that he was a completely spiritual man, living entirely in hope of heaven;

---

highest integrity, of great practical wisdom, witty and eloquent, a pleasant companion, generous and discreet. And, with all these qualities, he exceeded all his fellow prelates of the Church in his patience and tenderness. He was full of sympathy for the infirmities, both physical and moral, of others" (Jocelyn of Furness, *Life of St. Waldef*, in Daniel, *Life of Ailred*).

74. *Rule*, c. 31 (McCann, ed. and trans., *Rule of St. Benedict*, 80, 82).

75. *Rule*, c. 4 (McCann, ed. and trans., *Rule of St. Benedict*, 26–32).

76. Migne, *PL* 184, cols. 214A–219D.

77. "speaking when appropriate and keeping silent when appropriate" (Migne, *PL* 184, col. 217A).

78. Migne, *PL* 184, col. 217A.

79. Migne, *PL* 184, col. 217C.

f) he kept the sweetness of his spirit by avoiding controversies and sterile disputes; he was *prudens eloquii mystici*;[80] he excelled in consoling the little ones and aiding them to rise up to heavenly things; his sermons were easy to understand but full of fervor.

3. Some facts about his life from Walter Daniel: he never expelled anyone from the monastery, even the man who threw him in the fire. {For a} description of Cistercian life and spirit, {see} Walter Daniel, p. 11; {for a} description of Rievaulx, {see} p. 12 (read[81]). Ailred's entrance into the novitiate (p. 16) {describes} how, in the novitiate, he submitted his own will to the other novices, which was a "martyrdom,"[82] or a laying down of one's own life for others. {Walter describes} Ailred as a young monk at work (p. 21) {and} Ailred as novice master:[83] the cold spring;[84] the *Speculum*.[85] {He was} sent on foundation to Revesby (p. 27). Ailred as Abbot of Rievaulx was criticized and maligned by enemies. Rievaulx under St. Ailred (p. 36ff.) {was}:

a) {a} stronghold for sustaining the weak (problem cases came from everywhere);

80. "skilled in spiritual speech" (Migne, *PL* 184, col. 217D).

81. "The spot was by a powerful stream called the Rie in a broad valley stretching on either side. The name of their little settlement and the valley, Rievaulx. High hills surrounded the valley, encircling it like a crown. These are clothed by trees of various sorts and maintain in pleasant retreats the privacy of the vale, providing for the monks a kind of second paradise of wooded delight. From the loftiest rocks the waters wind and tumble down to the valley below, and as they make their hasty way through the lesser passages and narrower beds and spread themselves in wider rills, they give out a gentle murmur of soft sound and join together in the sweet notes of a delicious melody. And when the branches of lovely trees rustle and sing together and the leaves flutter gently to the earth, the happy listener is filled increasingly with a glad jubilee of harmonious sound, as so many various things conspire together in such a sweet consent, in music whose every diverse note is equal to the rest. His ears drink in the feast prepared for them, and are satisfied" (Daniel, *Life of Ailred*, 12–13).

82. Daniel, *Life of Ailred*, 17.

83. Daniel, *Life of Ailred*, 25.

84. "I should not omit to tell how he had built a small chamber of brick under the floor of the novice-house, like a little tank, into which water flowed from hidden rills. Its opening was shut by a very broad stone in such a way that nobody would notice it. Ailred would enter this contrivance, when he was alone and undisturbed, and immerse his whole body in the icy cold water, and so quench the heat in himself of every vice" (Daniel, *Life of Ailred*, 25).

85. I.e. the *Speculum Caritatis* (*Mirror of Charity*) (Migne, *PL* 195, cols. 621–58), Aelred's first book (see Daniel, *Life of Ailred*, 25–26).

b) {an} abode of perfect charity;

c) {the} supreme glory of Rievaulx {is} that it teaches tolerance of the infirm and compassion with others: "The house which withholds tolerance from the weak is not to be regarded as a house of religion."[86]

{Walter also provides a} description of the big community (p. 38) {and of} the brethren gathering in his sick room (p. 40).

The Feast of Saint Joseph (March 19)

St. Joseph is the last of the Patriarchs. St. Joseph has a very special place in our life of prayer and devotion. He is one of the greatest saints in the Church triumphant, and one of the closest to all of us. He plays a special and intimate part in the lives of us all.

a) Just as he was chosen as the instrument of divine Providence to be in a most special way the Protector and Provider for the Holy Family, Mary and the divine Child, so too he enters intimately into God's providential plans for the whole Church, and for every individual member of the Church.

b) Note, we speak of him usually as Provider and Protector of the persons of Mary and of Jesus. In point of fact this means that he was providentially appointed to *watch over the accomplishment of the great Mystery of the Incarnation*, at least in its development and fulfillment. This explains his greatness. Joseph is the Protector of the Blessed Virgin, and it is due to his special devoted care that Our Lady came safely to the time appointed for bringing forth her Son. St. Joseph is the Protector of the Mother and Child at the Nativity and immediately after it, when he takes them into Egypt and brings them back. He is also the Protector of them for many years of the hidden life at Nazareth—the head of the Holy Family.

c) But in St. Joseph we see the characteristics of all the patriarchs merge together and reach a higher fulfillment. The patriarchs are, above all, "Fathers," preparing the way for the Redeemer. To St. Joseph it is given to resume in himself all the fatherhood of Abraham, Isaac, Jacob and all the rest. It is as though in him the patriarchs stood by their great descendant the Messias. Joseph is then the one mentioned in

---

86. Daniel, *Life of Ailred,* 38, which reads: ". . . toleration . . ."

the genealogies. Moreover, *like the patriarchs, St. Joseph is under the direct guidance of God*—indeed, even more than they. Like them, he is commanded to undertake strange and dangerous tasks, without knowing exactly what will come to them. Like them he has to leave {his} country and go into an unknown land at the command of God. The spirituality of St. Joseph resumes in itself all that we know about the inner life of Abraham, Isaac, Jacob (except that his character differs greatly from that of the shrewd and aggressive Jacob!).

d) But all fatherhood is from above, from the Father of lights.[87] St. Joseph, like the patriarchs, *is a kind of figure of the Heavenly Father*—all the more so because he stands in the place of the Heavenly Father, in time, in history, in the economy of the Incarnation.

The Joys and Sufferings of St. Joseph: these are told us with great simplicity in the Gospel, and they give us a real insight into Joseph's character and into the quality of his sanctity, his "spirit." In this sense Joseph is a well-known saint, one who is close to all of us, one about whose inner life we really have some knowledge. Yet at the same time, his simplicity is a tremendous mystery, and it is not wise to say too much about him. He escapes analysis and definition, like Our Lady. He is so simple that he is beyond us. He is "unknown." However, let us read the passages in question. READ Matthew 1:18–25:[88] the great trial of his faith and of his justice which is greater than that of the scribes and Pharisees (v. 19), because he does not do what they would have done to solve the problem! He does the opposite. READ Matthew 2:13–15 and 19–23:[89] the flight into Egypt.

---

87. See Jas 1:17.

88. "Now the generation of Christ was in this wise. When as his mother Mary was espoused to Joseph, before they came together, she was found with child, of the Holy Ghost. Whereupon Joseph her husband, being a just man, and not willing publicly to expose her, was minded to put her away privately. But while he thought on these things, behold the angel of the Lord appeared to him in his sleep, saying: Joseph, son of David, fear not to take unto thee Mary thy wife, for that which is conceived in her, is of the Holy Ghost. And she shall bring forth a son: and thou shalt call his name Jesus. For he shall save his people from their sins. Now all this was done that it might be fulfilled which the Lord spoke by the prophet, saying: Behold a virgin shall be with child, and bring forth a son, and they shall call his name Emmanuel, which being interpreted is, God with us. And Joseph rising up from sleep, did as the angel of the Lord had commanded him, and took unto him his wife. And he knew her not till she brought forth her firstborn son: and he called his name Jesus."

89. "And after they were departed, behold an angel of the Lord appeared in sleep to Joseph, saying: Arise, and take the child and his mother, and fly into Egypt: and be

READ Luke 2:40–52:[90] Jesus lost in Jerusalem. {Reflect on} the faith it must have taken to be obeyed by the Son of God—and the unthinkable trial of losing Him! The greatness of St. Joseph's sanctity has two foundations: (a) his closeness to the Incarnation, to the Incarnate Word, the source of all sanctity; (b) his perfect union with God's will, his perfection as an instrument of Divine Providence, his plasticity and simplicity in a vocation utterly extraordinary, for which there were and could be neither rules nor precedents.

St. Joseph the Worker: for this very special vocation God chose a *poor man*, a true representative of the Anawim for whom God alone was their hope and their support (the singers of the Psalms). How often we hear St. Joseph speaking in the Psalms. We know him well! Like Mary, he resumes in himself all the spirit of trust and faith that we find in every line of the Psalms. If St. Joseph looks back to the patriarchs, he looks forward also to the innumerable multitude of the poor and the faithful in whom Christ truly lives and suffers and continues His work of the

---

there until I shall tell thee. For it will come to pass that Herod will seek the child to destroy him. Who arose, and took the child and his mother by night, and retired into Egypt: and he was there until the death of Herod: That it might be fulfilled which the Lord spoke by the prophet, saying: Out of Egypt have I called my son. . . . But when Herod was dead, behold an angel of the Lord appeared in sleep to Joseph in Egypt, Saying: Arise, and take the child and his mother, and go into the land of Israel. For they are dead that sought the life of the child. Who arose, and took the child and his mother, and came into the land of Israel. But hearing that Archelaus reigned in Judea in the room of Herod his father, he was afraid to go thither: and being warned in sleep retired into the quarters of Galilee. And coming he dwelt in a city called Nazareth: that it might be fulfilled which was said by prophets: That he shall be called a Nazarene."

90. "And the child grew, and waxed strong, full of wisdom; and the grace of God was in him. And his parents went every year to Jerusalem, at the solemn day of the pasch, And when he was twelve years old, they going up into Jerusalem, according to the custom of the feast, And having fulfilled the days, when they returned, the child Jesus remained in Jerusalem; and his parents knew it not. And thinking that he was in the company, they came a day's journey, and sought him among their kinsfolks and acquaintance. And not finding him, they returned into Jerusalem, seeking him. And it came to pass, that, after three days, they found him in the temple, sitting in the midst of the doctors, hearing them, and asking them questions. And all that heard him were astonished at his wisdom and his answers. And seeing him they wondered. And his mother said to him: Son, why hast thou done so to us? behold thy father and I have sought thee sorrowing. And he said to them: How is it that you sought me? did you not know, that I must be about my father's business? And they understood not the word that he spoke unto them. And he went down with them, and came to Nazareth, and was subject to them. And his mother kept all these words in her heart. And Jesus advanced in wisdom, and age, and grace with God and men."

Redemption of the world. Note that St. Joseph had little evident place
in the Church's life of devotion and prayer when society was Catholic,
when the visible Church tended to be rich and powerful, and when her
hierarchy were also temporal lords. St. Joseph came back into view in a
time of trouble and dissention, that looked forward to the revolutions of
the modern world. Today he has come into his own! For St. Joseph is the
patron of all the millions of poor and oppressed, the displaced persons,
the proletariat, the slave-laborers, the prisoners in concentration camps,
for it is among these that the true future of the world is being worked
out. Do we realize sufficiently that these poor are, in the most real sense,
"the Church," the "Body of Christ"? They come to him and cry out to him
from the four corners of the earth like the starving multitudes who came
to the Patriarch Joseph in Egypt.[91] St. Joseph alone knows the answer to
their plight, because no one else seems to be able to do anything effective.
(Note the horrible irony of Stalin's first name!) The future of humanity
depends on our imitating the humble, hidden, laborious virtues of St.
Joseph, and above all his trust and his plasticity in the hands of God.

But this is and has long been quite evident for us monks. As Cistercians we have deliberately embraced a life which is *in every respect like
the life of the Holy Family*. It is a poor, simple, laborious family life that
is also a life of prayer centered on Christ dwelling in the midst of us. We
have sought Him in the poverty which He Himself embraced on earth.
We have sought Him in the labor, the ordinariness, the obscurity, which
were His chosen portion for the greater part of His life. We have sought a
life with Mary, in intimacy and hiddenness. In living this life, we should
ask St. Joseph to teach us to live, as did Charles de Foucauld, in a *constant
awareness* of the life of the Holy Family, lived through the mystery of eternity in which we are present to them and they to us. Charles de Foucauld
used to think like this: "It is now 8 p.m. Blessed Mother, St. Joseph, what
are you doing now? In a few moments you will kneel in your evening
prayer together" etc. It does not matter if all that he imagines may not
be absolutely accurate; the point is the *reality* of the presence of the Holy
Family to those who share their life. And Charles de Foucauld wanted
to *share that life perfectly, especially in its poverty, hiddenness, labor, simplicity*. Our sincerity in this matter depends entirely on the resoluteness
with which we ask ourselves: "Is this compatible with the life of the Holy
Family? Is this the way Jesus acted? Is this comparable to their poverty,

91. See Gen 41:57.

their labor," etc. Charles de Foucauld wanted to arrive at an *absolutely literal* reproduction. What matters is a *relative* conformity—meaning conformity to the standards of the poor in our own time. That alone is a tremendous challenge. Can we say we have met it? We must ask ourselves to what extent our lives are poor in terms of (a) dependence—not being self-sufficient and able to get what we want when we want it; (b) deprivation—being content to "do without"; (c) labor—being able and ready to embrace whatever work we can get, in order to earn our living. N.B. in our monastic vocation we are supposed to be delivered, to some extent, from the insecurity of the poor, but our relative security is justified only if it is based on one *common effort* and the work of the community. We must *not* allow work to become the most important thing in our lives, however.

FEAST OF OUR HOLY FATHER SAINT BENEDICT (March 21)

What does the office of our Father, St. Benedict, teach us about his spirit? Indeed, it is for this "spirit" that we pray in the collect, and where will we better find out about it than in the other texts, the *proper* texts which make up the office. The Spirit "Whom St. Benedict served"[92] was, of course, the Holy Spirit. But when we speak of the "spirit of St. Benedict" we are speaking of something special and characteristic in his own way of life, willed especially for his monastic family by the Holy Spirit. Let us look particularly at those texts which were written about St. Benedict himself and are not simply applied to him from the Common of Confessors.

1. *Responsory of Vespers:* "St. Benedict sought rather to suffer hard things from the world than to accept its praise, and preferred to be worn out by labors for God than to be lifted up by the good things of the present life. For, being inspired by divine grace, he longed more and more for the things of heaven."[93] This strikes the keynote of Benedictine sacrifice:

a) We come here to be humble and obscure. A humble man is not merely one who enjoys the *advantages* of humility. But in order truly to have this peace, we must pay the price for it; we must be ready for humiliation, ready to give up our self-esteem, our reputation, and to do without the praise and respect of others. We must really be

---

92. "*cui beatus Benedictus . . . servivit*" (vespers prayer) (*Breviarium Cisterciense, Pars Vernalis,* 448).

93. "*Sanctus Benedictus plus appetiit mala mundi perpeti, quam laudes, Malens pro Deo laboribus fatigari, quam vitae hujus favoribus extolli*" (*Breviarium Cisterciense, Vernalis,* 447).

detached in this matter. It is one of the signs of a Benedictine vocation: *si sollicitus sit ad opprobria*.[94] If the novice is too sensitive and fussy about his own feelings and his own self-respect, he cannot last in the monastery. But above all, a little honest sensitivity is better than the simulated humility which keeps quiet but seeks in devious ways to get its own back, and wages a silent, undercover war with the superior, resenting commands and indeed authority as such!

b) We must expect sometimes to get tired as a result of our generous efforts. The monastic life is not a life of ease and comfort, in which everything is ordered to our own satisfaction. We have to sacrifice ourselves, give up our time and our freedom, embrace difficult and boring tasks as our share in the burden of supporting the community. The true monk, with a genuine spirit of sacrifice, *prefers* the humble way of thankless and unspectacular tasks, and does not seek privileges and exemptions on every side; especially {he} does not seek to be called *rabbi*, and to have a privileged place in the community (cf. {the} gospel[95] {for the} second Wednesday of Lent, which falls this year [1957] on the eve of St. Benedict's feast; cf. {also} the gospel of Lazarus and Dives[96] which falls on the feast itself: "Son, remember that thou hast received good things in thy life, and Lazarus has received evil"[97]).

c) We do not merely sacrifice ourselves doggedly, blindly, in a purely negative way. We have our eyes open, in supernatural hope, to the joys of heaven, and to the supreme reward of pleasing God. It is this grace which gives us strength to bear our trials. We *cannot* bear them without this supernatural view of the hundredfold reward and life everlasting, and the realization that the sufferings of this life are as nothing compared with the joys of the life to come, or even indeed, with the consolations of prayer which God gives even in this life to those who are faithful to their vocation. *Magis ac magis ad superna animo suspirabat.*[98] Progress in the spiritual life is progress

---

94. "if he is eager for humiliations" (*Rule*, c. 58) (McCann, ed. and trans., *Rule of St. Benedict*, 130, which reads: "*si sollicitus est . . . ad opprobria*").

95. Matt 20:17–28 (*Missale Romanum*, 89; *Missale Cisterciense*, 79).

96. Luke 16:19–31 (*Missale Romanum*, 90–91; *Missale Cisterciense*, 80).

97. Luke 16:25.

98. "more and more he aspired in his spirit for the highest things" (vespers versicle) (*Breviarium Cisterciense, Vernalis*, 447).

in the purity and intensity of our desire for heavenly things, which in turn grows in proportion as we are detached from earthly things.

The Hymns: {at} vespers,[99] {it is} a survey of his life: how in his childhood he fled into solitude; how he chastised his flesh, wrote his *Rule*, drove out the last traces of paganism from his country; how finally from heaven he sends consolations to his devoted sons. The hymn of vigils[100] develops the theme that in St. Benedict there dwelt the "spirit of all the just"[101]—he was at the same time an Abraham, {an} Isaac, {a} Moses. The hymn of lauds[102] returns to his monastic vocation.

The antiphons and responsories of vigils[103] sketch out the broad outlines of his life. They are drawn from the early biography by St. Gregory the Great.[104] In them, besides St. Benedict's power as a miracle worker, we see *other special characteristics of his spirit*:

1. His contempt for the world, due to the *special discretion*, the prudent sense of values which marked him even from childhood: he saw at once that the world and its values was a deception, and withdrew before he had been corrupted by them. He also showed a special contempt for worldly knowledge, and knew that the way to God was rather a way of "unknowing": *recessit igitur scienter nescius et sapienter indoctus.*[105] Note that this in no way conflicts with the wise Benedictine emphasis on true learning.

2. His spirit of prayer and contemplation: having risen above earthly things, he saw the whole world in God "as though in one ray of the sun."[106] So great was his love of prayer that he died standing in prayer, upheld by his sons, in the monastic oratory, after having received the Blessed Eucharist.[107] This shows in particular his love of communal prayer.

---

99. *"Laudibus cives"* (*Breviarium Cisterciense, Vernalis*, 447).

100. *"Quidquid antiqui"* (*Breviarium Cisterciense, Vernalis*, 448).

101. Preface (*Missale Cisterciense, Prefationes* 2*) (St. Gregory the Great, *Dialogues*, 2.8.8).

102. *"Inter aeternas"* (*Breviarium Cisterciense, Vernalis*, 455–56).

103. *Breviarium Cisterciense, Vernalis*, 449–54 (also lessons 5–8).

104. Migne, *PL* 66, cols. 125A–294C.

105. "Therefore he withdrew, knowingly ignorant and wisely untaught" (first nocturn, sixth antiphon) (*Breviarium Cisterciense, Vernalis*, 449).

106. *"velut sub uno solis radio"* (responsory, seventh lesson) (*Breviarium Cisterciense, Vernalis*, 452).

107. Tenth responsory, third nocturn (*Breviarium Cisterciense, Vernalis*, 454).

3. His patience and charity are only hinted at, in the story of the monks of Vicovaro who tried to poison him.[108] He forgave them and retired to solitude without anger. He was thus with all his persecutors and enemies. The miracle worked by St. Scholastica[109] seems again to be a divine approval of the spirit of discretion and charity (this time Benedict's own severity is over-ridden.)

In order to complete this picture we should return more and more frequently to the *Holy Rule*, which is the true source of our knowledge of his heart and of his life. Here by meditating on the precepts he has left us and by incorporating them perfectly in our own lives, we will grow in humility, obedience, the spirit of prayer and praise, and self-forgetfulness, learning above all to do that which in few words gives the full picture of St. Benedict: "To prefer absolutely nothing to the love of Christ."[110]

The Feast of the Annunciation

The Mystery (read the gospel of the Feast:[111] the Angel of the Lord is sent to Our Lady, and by her *fiat*[112] she becomes the Mother of God. By our faith and our obedience, we enter with her into the mystery of the Incarnation. The angel tells her how she will become the Mother of God:

108. Third responsory, second nocturn (*Breviarium Cisterciense, Vernalis*, 450).

109. I.e. the storm that arises after Scholastica's prayer that she and Benedict might not have to part at the end of their day together, their last encounter before her death (*Vita Benedicti*, c. 33; Migne, *PL* 66, col. 194).

110. "*Nihil amori Christi praeponere*" (*Rule*, c. 4) (McCann, ed. and trans., *Rule of St. Benedict*, 26).

111. "And in the sixth month, the angel Gabriel was sent from God into a city of Galilee, called Nazareth, To a virgin espoused to a man whose name was Joseph, of the house of David; and the virgin's name was Mary. And the angel being come in, said unto her: Hail, full of grace, the Lord is with thee: blessed art thou among women. Who having heard, was troubled at his saying, and thought with herself what manner of salutation this should be. And the angel said to her: Fear not, Mary, for thou hast found grace with God. Behold thou shalt conceive in thy womb, and shalt bring forth a son; and thou shalt call his name Jesus. He shall be great, and shall be called the Son of the most High; and the Lord God shall give unto him the throne of David his father; and he shall reign in the house of Jacob for ever. And of his kingdom there shall be no end. And Mary said to the angel: How shall this be done, because I know not man? And the angel answering, said to her: The Holy Ghost shall come upon thee, and the power of the most High shall overshadow thee. And therefore also the Holy which shall be born of thee shall be called the Son of God. And behold thy cousin Elizabeth, she also hath conceived a son in her old age; and this is the sixth month with her that is called barren: Because no word shall be impossible with God. And Mary said: Behold the handmaid of the Lord; be it done to me according to thy word. And the angel departed from her" (Luke 1:26–38) (*Missale Romanum*, 534; *Missale Cisterciense*, 393).

112. "Let it be done."

"The Holy Ghost shall descend upon thee and the power of the Most High shall overshadow thee. Through the power of her *fiat*, the Holy Ghost descends also upon us and fills us with the dark faith which liberates us from the illusions and shortcomings of a purely human and natural view of things. But it takes courage to accept the liberation that is offered to us. To renew our strength we must constantly appeal to Mary our Mother and deepen our faith in her Divine Motherhood: *ut qui vere eam Dei genetricem credimus ejus apud te intercessionibus adjuvemur* (collect).[113] The more we focus our faith on this mystery, the more we are aided by her prayers. Without this faith, our devotion to her is mere sentiment. Mary, Mother of God, is Mother of Mercy. Through her the divine mercy has come into the world. Without her *fiat*, there would be nothing but the darkness of sin, and the unending misery of captivity under the forces of evil. Without her there would be *no hope*. How true it is to call her, as we do in the *Salve Regina*, Mother of Mercy, our Life, our Sweetness and our Hope. But hope comes to us in the darkness of struggle, in which we share in her "overshadowing."

Liberation: without Mary, there would be nothing but captivity to Satan. For some, there might be an "easy" and "happy" life on earth—with pleasures and power, but no satisfaction, only unrest and horror, but this life itself would be based on cruelty and injustice, and for others, hell on earth, slaves of the powerful, victims of injustice; and for both—no escape from eternal damnation. Think how unutterably evil the world would now be if there had never been any grace, any sanctity, any supernatural love. But even though we are freed, yet we live in a world of sin and there are in ourselves the remains of the tyranny of sin. The liberty that goes with our divine sonship is still only enjoyed in the darkness of faith, and we cannot escape in our lives the "servitude of corruption."[114] Though the Church is supremely free in Christ, yet in the world we live in she is humiliated and suppressed by the injustice of her enemies, and more than this, she suffers from within from the failings and shortcomings, the sins of her own members. Hence the Church herself, though free, is in darkness, and sighs for the full and final liberation. And we, her sons, must *struggle* for this liberation. It will not come automatically, and the victory will not be given to those who have not conquered by

---

113. "That we who believe her to be truly the Mother of God may be assisted by her intercessions with You" (*Missale Romanum*, 533; *Missale Cisterciense*, 392).

114. Rom 8:21.

their faith, their obedience, their charity, their humility and all the other virtues which unite us to Our Lady in her *fiat*.

Freedom and Captivity in the Contemplative Life: as contemplatives we have embraced a life of faith that liberates us from the snares and illusions of life in the world. Yet we are at times painfully aware of our darkness and captivity, more so than we would be perhaps in the active life. The truth is that there are two laws struggling together within us, and that what is freedom for the one is captivity for the other. We have our fallen nature, which longs for its own kind of liberty, the license to do and think as it pleases, and this in reality is captivity to the devil (but we do not always feel it to be so). On the other hand we have the Spirit of God, and grace aspires to liberty by total subjection to the love and will of God: for this liberty, attachment to our own will and to creatures is a real misery and an enslavement. The contemplative life is often indeed a life of light and peace and joy, but much more often it is a life of darkness and struggle. At times we taste the liberty of the sons of God in a way we had never before dreamed possible, liberty in God, in the silence of interior prayer, in the freedom bought by sacrifice. We must love and seek these joys, not for our own satisfaction but because they do bring us closer to God. But at the same time we feel our limitations. We remain bound by faults and attachments, which we are sometimes helpless to shake off. We are weighed down by the burden of our own character and temperament, the bitter slavery of our selfhood, our practical inability to be perfect, our helplessness to follow out the good that we want to do. We realize fully, with St. Paul, that we are "carnal, sold under sin"[115] and we cry with him, "who will deliver me from the body of this death?"[116] More than this, we keenly feel the limitations of others, of society as a whole, of the Church's hierarchy (READ *Romans* 7:14 to the end[117]). Grace alone can deliver us from this captivity.

115. Rom 7:14.

116. Rom 7:24.

117. "For we know that the law is spiritual; but I am carnal, sold under sin. For that which I work, I understand not. For I do not that good which I will; but the evil which I hate, that I do. If then I do that which I will not, I consent to the law, that it is good. Now then it is no more I that do it, but sin that dwelleth in me. For I know that there dwelleth not in me, that is to say, in my flesh, that which is good. For to will, is present with me; but to accomplish that which is good, I find not. For the good which I will, I do not; but the evil which I will not, that I do. Now if I do that which I will not, it is no more I that do it, but sin that dwelleth in me. I find then a law, that when I have a will to do good, evil is present with me. For I am delighted with the law of God, according

Fr. Thomas Philippe, OP[118] writes of the inner crucifixion of the contemplative who embraces a high ideal of prayer, silence and interior liberty, and suffers from his own limitations and the limitations of the community around him. The contemplative life, by its nature, aims at the highest liberty, complete inner freedom, the beginning of eternal life in which there is no law, and nothing but the reign of eternal love. To have a contemplative vocation is to have at least an obscure appreciation of this fact which is central to the contemplative ideal. Indeed, our ideal is nothing but this: to love for the sake of loving, with no obstruction and no obstacle, to be able to escape totally from selfhood and self-preoccupation

---

to the inward man: But I see another law in my members, fighting against the law of my mind, and captivating me in the law of sin, that is in my members. Unhappy man that I am, who shall deliver me from the body of this death? The grace of God, by Jesus Christ our Lord. Therefore, I myself, with the mind serve the law of God; but with the flesh, the law of sin."

118. Thomas Philippe (1905–1993) was a French Dominican who became the spiritual director of Jean Vanier and was the original inspiration behind the L'Arche movement founded by Vanier. In 1953 Robert Lax wrote to Merton: "I send you a letter from Jean Vanier (who is the son of the Canadian Ambassador to France & who runs a house for lay contemplatives & students, where I live a lot of the time.) He wonders if you would read a book by his spiritual director Pere Thomas Phillipe [sic], O.P. (who was co-founder with Jacques Maritain of this house.) The essays are all on the Blessed Virgin Mary & the Contemplative Life, and those Ive read Ive certainly found good" (Merton/Lax, *When Prophecy* 119). In a second letter he writes: "Here it is five months later. . . . Here too is the letter from Vanier. I have met and talked a couple of times with Pere Thomas Philippe and he is wonderful (a living flame) and marvel of sweetness (his qualities are totally communicable). Think hell be writing and translating for Rices magazine. . . . Cant for the moment find Vaniers letter describing Eau Vive & Pere Thomas but will send it soon" (Merton/Lax, *When Prophecy* 120-21). There is no Vanier letter in the Merton archives at Bellarmine University, and no further information on the book that is mentioned in the first letter; various mimeographed sets of his conferences in French had been produced, some of which Merton was familiar with. In his December 1967 retreat for contemplative prioresses at Gethsemani, he refers to material by Thomas Philippe as "marvelous stuff" circulating in "mimeographed conferences" (Merton, *Solitude and Togetherness*); in the published transcription of the retreat this material is erroneously attributed to "Paul Philippe, formerly secretary of the congregation for religious" (Merton, *Springs* 49-50), whereas what Merton actually said was that Thomas Philippe was "no relation to Paul Philippe, who used to be the secretary of the congregation." It is likely that the material cited here, otherwise unidentified and no longer extant at the Abbey of Gethsemani, was drawn from this mimeographed material referred to by Merton. Philippe is now known to have been a serial sexual abuser of adult women under his direction, a fact largely concealed during his lifetime; shortly after the death of Jean Vanier it became known that he too had abusive relationships with women, evidently under the influence of Philippe's bizarre esoteric sexual theories.

(not to mention every form of sin) in order to fly to God in perfect freedom, and rise above the miseries of this life. We have all tasted something of this in the very fact of our vocation. Yet, Fr. T. Philippe says, there is this paradox that on earth the contemplatives are the ones who are in fact *most captive* and groan under the burden of their captivity. At such times, he says, we must remember Our Lady of Mercy—Our Blessed Mother is *the one who ransoms captives*. We are in prison, and she is paying our ransom. Today, in this feast, we are reminded of this fact. We are like the souls of the Fathers in Limbo described by St. Bernard.[119]

The sense of captivity: so often we feel bound in *utter helplessness* and frustration. We feel we will never make any progress, that our life will never have any real meaning again. All is finished; we are up a blind alley for good and all! We feel acutely in ourselves *everything that is opposed to our ideal*, everything that blocks charity, everything that is opposed to God Himself. Fr. Thomas Philippe says that this *sense of captivity* is in reality a grace reserved for those who are called to a higher life by God. Those who are content with activity and the routine of life in the world never feel this—they are satisfied, more or less, and higher aspirations

---

119. See *De Laudibus Virginis Matris* (Homilies on the *Missus Est*) Sermo 4.8 (Migne, *PL* 182, col. 83CD): "*Exspectat angelus responsum: tempus est enim ut revertatur ad Deum qui misit illum. Exspectamus et nos, o Domina, verbum miserationis, quos miserabiliter premit sententia damnationis. Et ecce offertur tibi pretium salutis nostrae: statim liberabimur si consentis. In sempiterno Dei Verbo facti sumus omnes, et ecce morimur: in tuo brevi responso sumus reficiendi, ut ad vitam revocemur. Hoc supplicat a te, o pia Virgo, flebilis Adam cum misera sobole sua exsul de paradiso, hoc Abraham, hoc David. Hoc caeteri flagitant sancti Patres, patres scilicet tui, qui et ipsi habitant in regione umbrae mortis. Hoc totus mundus tuis genibus provolutus exspectat. Nec immerito quando ex ore tuo pendet consolatio miserorum, redemptio captivorum, liberatio damnatorum: salus denique universorum filiorum Adam, totius generis tui. Da, Virgo, responsum festinanter. O Domina, responde verbum, quod terra, quod inferi, quod exspectant et superi*" ("The angel awaits an answer, for it is time for him to return to the God Who sent him. We also, O Lady, are waiting for a word of mercy, on whom the sentence of condemnation wretchedly weighs. Behold, the price of our salvation is offered to you: if you consent, we shall be freed at once. We were all made by the Eternal Word of God, and behold, we die: in your short response we are to be remade, so that we may be recalled to life. O holy Virgin, weeping Adam, exiled from paradise with his wretched offspring, begs this from you, likewise Abraham, likewise David. The other holy fathers, your own fathers, who are themselves still dwelling in the region of the shadow of death, ask for this. The entire world, prostrate at your feet, awaits this. Not without reason, when the consolation of the wretched, the redemption of captives, the freedom of the condemned, depends on your word: indeed the salvation of all the children of Adam, of your entire race. Give your answer quickly, Virgin; O Lady, reply with the word that the earth, the world below and the world above are waiting for.")

seem to them to be nonsense. Are we then crazy? No. God has given us a secret taste of the joy to which we are called and we can never again be contented with lower things. We *must* go forward into the midst of contradictions. We must advance in darkness, without knowing where we are going, without seeing any evident hope of arriving, yet trusting in God and abandoned to Him. To turn back will never give us peace; it will only help us momentarily to forget, and then when we die we will face again the problem and the paradox we have tried to escape. For this paradox must be faced by *everyone* who wishes to enter heaven. The active man finds it often in the defeat of his work or opposition he meets in the world. The contemplative finds it in himself and in his community. But we must evaluate this darkness at its real worth. It is an "overshadowing" that makes our life extremely fruitful and rich in faith; it forces us to love by the Holy Spirit and not by our own will.

The Way to Liberty: we must be convinced that our liberation depends entirely on Our Lady. If she does not ransom us, if she does not give us the means to escape, we cannot escape this captivity. If we try to escape by our own efforts, if we try to work out the solution with our own reason, we will inevitably fall further into the darkness and hopelessness of our captivity, because then the devil will be able to delude us and bring us under his own sway. Our reason and the devil—when we are faced by this paradox and frustration—have the following method: they tell us to *reason*, to analyze, to find out what is wrong, to show up the wrong, to right it by our own efforts. We then begin to criticize and complain. We blame those around us for the chains that hold us back. If we have not made progress, it is then the fault of the Order, the house. The spiritual life is not properly understood here. The monastic life is not lived as it should be. There is a special "problem" in this house—the superiors do not give the proper formation; our directors do not understand us, etc. etc. Criticism gives us a sense of pseudo-superiority. As Thomas Philippe remarks: "Those who revolt are in fact those who do not have the courage to break their own interior chains. For when these are broken, the others do not matter." If we listen to our conscience, we sense that this is indeed the root of the trouble. We criticize because we hate ourselves for not breaking our chains.

Our Lady gives us two ways to liberty which are in reality one and the same: *the way of humility and the way of love*. This is Mary's own way—it was her *fiat*. To judge and criticize is the attitude of one who thinks he knows. Humility does not claim to know. How can we know the inscrutable plan of God? Humility simply accepts everything in the light of God's mercy and our own weakness. It does not seek to explain anything. It simply verifies the fact that this is the will of God, and it recognizes its own limitations and expects nothing else than the sense of helplessness and captivity. It does not try to analyze what does not need to be analyzed. But in this, humility becomes our greatest strength—it leaves God free to break our chains for us.

This attitude can alone solve all our difficulties. It does not refuse to look at the truth. It accepts our faults, and recognizes them and fully accepts the responsibility of overcoming them by the grace of God—but with patience. It accepts the suffering of a long and arduous struggle. Above all it is an attitude of love. *It is the recognition that love itself is the only true liberty.* When we are content to love as best we can, in spite of the exterior limitations and obstacles, then we are interiorly free and fly beyond and above all obstacles. Until then, obstacles stop us completely. After that, they no longer exist.

Mary asks that we make good use of these means. The contemplative, who is called to share her faith and her love, must not be content to sit down in the darkness and give up, or run to other expedients, or rebel and try to solve everything himself. He must seek liberty by Mary's way—the way of humility and love. This is not just a matter of preference, something one can choose or not; it is for the contemplative an *imperious necessity.* He must go forward—there is no turning back at all. It is either liberty or stagnation—and liberty is bought at the price of great trust and great suffering. It is not an ideal we can ever abandon. All that we can give up is our own plan for realizing the ideal. We must put ourselves then entirely in Mary's hands—say *fiat* to her as she herself said *fiat* to the angel. Conclude: READ {the} first lesson, from Isaias 7[120] (Achaz, the human spirit, refusing to do things God's way, not giving up to God).

FEAST OF THE SEVEN DOLORS (Friday in Passion Week)—
The Mystery of Mary's Compassion

---

120. "And the Lord spoke again to Achaz, saying: Ask thee a sign of the Lord thy God either unto the depth of hell, or unto the height above. And Achaz said: I will not ask, and I will not tempt the Lord. And he said: Hear ye therefore, O house of David: Is it a small thing for you to be grievous to men, that you are grievous to my God also? Therefore the Lord himself shall give you a sign. Behold a virgin shall conceive, and bear a son, and his name shall be called Emmanuel. He shall eat butter and honey, that he may know to refuse the evil, and to choose the good" (Isa 7:10–15) (*Missale Romanum*, 533; *Missale Cisterciense*, 392–93).

1. Preamble—a theological note: in the sacrifice of the Cross, mankind is objectively redeemed. *Subjective redemption* {is the process} in which by our satisfactions and merits we cooperate in the distribution of graces to one another. Mary is the only human being who cooperated in the *objective redemption* of mankind. She did so in the strict sense, by her *fiat* to the Incarnation. It is also certain that Mary, morally united with Jesus on Calvary, satisfied and merited for all men. Thus her participation in Calvary comes at least under subjective redemption. Some theologians also argue that her *fiat* on Calvary was a strict, direct and immediate cooperation with Jesus on the Cross in effecting man's objective redemption. {The} argument {is that} since her *fiat* at the Incarnation was a direct and immediate cooperation, and since her *fiat* at the Cross is a completion of the *fiat* at the Annunciation, *ergo* . . . Scheeben says: "By reason of this intimate participation of Mary in the redeeming sacrifice, one can say that with Christ she offered to God satisfaction for sin, that she merited grace and redeemed the world . . . all this in and by the sacrifice of the Cross, in so far as she was co-offerer."[121]

2. *Mary's Share in Calvary*: in the office, the selection of antiphons at vespers from the Canticle of Canticles tells of the supremely intimate mystical union between the souls of Jesus and Mary in the great act of sacrificial love, of *Agape*, by which man was redeemed. *Vadam ad montem myrrhae*:[122] she goes up to the mountain of myrrh and of incense, ascending to a mystical sacrifice of herself in union with her Son. *Fulcite me floribus stipate me malis quia amore langueo*:[123] she dies of love with her Son. But the death of Mary on Calvary seems to have consisted formally in the *separation from Jesus, with Whom, nevertheless, she was at that*

---

121. See Scheeben, *Mariology*, 2:225–26: "Because of its intimacy, Mary's participation forms one whole with Christ's activity, so that, according to the divine plan, Christ acts as little apart from and without her as she can act apart from and without Him. But for that very reason all effects of His sacrifice must be regarded as effected and obtained conjointly by her in and through this sacrifice. Therefore, we can say that Mary with Christ, that is, by her cooperation with Him, gave satisfaction to God for sin, merited grace, and thus redeemed the world . . . in and through Christ's sacrifice, in so far as she shared in offering this sacrifice with Him." The differences in this version may be due to Merton making his own translation from a French version of the work, or finding this quotation in a secondary source.

122. "I shall go to the mountain of myrrh" (Song 4:6) (first antiphon, vespers) (*Breviarium Cisterciense, Vernalis*, 470).

123. "Support me with flowers, surround me with apples, for I languish with love" (Song 2:5) (fourth antiphon) (*Breviarium Cisterciense, Vernalis*, 472).

moment most perfectly united (Quo abiit dilectus tuus . . .[124])—just as Jesus, at the moment supremely united with the will of the Father, seems to
be separated from the Father. Note the elements in the death on Calvary:
death is separation of soul from body, of that which lives from the source
of its life. But Jesus' soul {is} apparently separated from the Father and
from His own divinity (at least mystically—as the result of taking upon
Himself the "death" of sin). Jesus' soul {is} separated from {His} body.
Mary {is} "separated" mystically from Jesus (she too then feels something
of what it is to be in "sin," yet in this separation she is most intimately
united to Him, AND TO US). Jesus, Who by His Incarnation entered into
union with us in all our human affections and feelings and sufferings,
besides sin, in His Passion enters *most intimately into the loneliness of
each sinner separated from God and from other men*, as though at the moment of His death, Jesus, mystically separated from the Father and from
Himself, having in His Father's bosom and in His own divinity "nowhere
to rest His Head,"[125] becomes divided into a million exiled souls, seeking
His refuge in the souls of numberless sinful men, all men, exiled from
God. It is as if at the moment Jesus had no being except my being, my
loneliness, my weakness, my misery—our loneliness rather—as if, exiled
from God, He lived momentarily only in sinful men, who died in Him
while He lived in them. At that moment, as it were in the flash of a great
mystical cataclysm, He reached out and took possession of all our souls
by seeking there the only refuge that was left for Him to find. At one great
bound He had leaped finally over the gulf that separated God and man,
as if to say, "See, now, I am not in heaven, not above you; I am only in
the souls of sinners, nowhere else, in this moment of my death." Will we
fear Him, then? At this moment, too, Mary, sharing the same separation,
enters into intimate union with us also—the exchange of John for Jesus.
So she too, in her compassion, says to us: "See, I have no longer any Son; I
am no longer the Mother of God, but the mother, as it were, of a criminal;
and He has died, leaving me to be cared for by the other criminals whom
He had made His friends. Will you fear now to take me for your Mother?"
The exchange of John for Jesus—of us for Jesus—was, says St. Bernard,
a sword piercing Mary's heart. "Was not that word more to thee than a

---

124. "Where has your Beloved gone?" (Song 6:1) (third antiphon) (*Breviarium
Cisterciense, Vernalis*, 471).

125. Matt 8:20; Luke 9:58.

sword, passing right through thy soul and reaching unto the division of the soul and the spirit? Woman, behold thy son?"[126] (lesson 6).

3. *Elements in the Martyrdom of Mary*:

a) First, her human affection for her Son is crucified; St. Bernard stresses that insensibility was one of the great sins of the Gentiles, and that Mary by no means was affected with such a fault (lesson 8[127]). Therefore she suffered in her soul, by love, most intensely all the wounds inflicted on Jesus' body.

b) She willed to accept this sacrifice of "separation from Jesus" in order to receive us in exchange.

c) Although she firmly believed and hoped in the Resurrection, yet her sacrifice was made in the darkness of perfect faith and hope. *She did not know for certain*, with clear human evidence. Her clinging to this truth by divine evidence alone was a martyrdom of spirit in the darkness of faith, for everything indicated, humanly speaking, that Jesus had failed and was not God.

d) At the same time, with Jesus, and like Him, she contemplated in Him not so much His own wounds as the salvation of the world. "O Virgin, thou lookest upon Him with loving eyes, contemplating in Him not so much the tearing of the wounds as the salvation of the world."[128]

e) In making this sacrifice of herself she offered Jesus to the Father on our behalf, and herself with Him, and also made the supreme sacrifice of love *for us*. In offering Jesus to the Father, she was mystically giving Him up for us. Even though Jesus would rise again, she would never possess Him in the same way that she had done before, when He was only her Child. Now, she would be united with Him and His members together, and always see Him in them and them in Him. *Mary can no longer look at Jesus without seeing me in Him.*

---

126. "*An non tibi plusquam gladius fuit sermo ille, revera pertransiens animam, et pertingens usque ad divisionem animae et spiritus: Mulier, ecce filius tuus?*" (*Sermo de Duodecim Stellis*) (*Breviarium Cisterciense, Vernalis*, 483).

127. *Breviarium Cisterciense, Vernalis*, 484.

128. "*Piis, o Virgo, spectas eum oculis, contemplans in eo non tam vulnerum livorem, quam mundi salutem*" (second lesson, versicle) (*Breviarium Cisterciense, Vernalis*, 477).

SAINT ROBERT AND THE FOUNDATION OF CÎTEAUX
(Notes for the Feast of our Father, St. Robert) (April 29)

St. Robert:[129] his predominant part {was} as the *inspiration* of the {Cistercian} movement. He is not the "founder of the Order," but he is the founder of Cîteaux, and the moving spirit of the whole Cistercian reform. He was influential above all as a saintly person, as a father and guide of souls, as an abbot. In the monastic tradition, the "charismatic" vocation of certain persons who embody in themselves a whole ideal is of supreme importance (cf. St. Anthony,[130] the Russian "staretz,"[131] etc.). St. Robert was of this type. In order to understand his importance, we must not look for writings or for teaching left by him, nor for a monastic code drawn up by him; we have to try to see him as his contemporaries saw him. He was above all a wonderful saintly *person* who drew others to God by the fact that God brought them under his influence. (*N.B.* the thirteenth-century "Life" of St. Robert[132] is not to be trusted.)

1. St. Robert *attracted into solitude* not only numerous souls, but great souls; not only men like our Fathers, Sts. Alberic, Stephen, etc., but also St. Bruno, {who} prepared for his foundation of Grande Chartreuse by a stay at a dependency of Molesme—Seche Fontaine.

2. St. Robert was like many other saints typical of his age of monastic reform: St. John Gualbert, St. Bernard of Tiron, St. Vital, founder of Savigny,[133] etc.—men who longed for the pure simplicity of monastic life. They wanted solitude, simplicity, poverty, labor, a true life of prayer given to God alone, away from the world.

3. The life of St. Robert was a constant succession of attempts to break with the conventional monasticism of his time, to return to primitive simplicity, probably a semi-eremitical sort of life such as was led at Colan. As the *Exordium Parvum* succinctly says, they sought

---

129. For Merton's early biographical sketch of Robert, see Merton, *Valley of Wormwood*, 143–52.

130. On St. Anthony, see Merton, *Cassian and the Fathers*, 31–39; and Merton, *Pre-Benedictine Monasticism*, 17–24.

131. On this figure of the charismatic Russian monastic spiritual father, see Merton's essay "Russian Mystics," in Merton, *Mystics and Zen Masters*, 178–87.

132. Migne, *PL* 157, cols. 278–88; on this work see Merton, *Medieval Cistercian History*, 49.

133. On these figures, see Merton, *Medieval Cistercian History*, 33–36.

QUIES MONASTICA[134]—monastic peace—peace to give themselves to God without being trammeled by useless and futile occupations not proper to the life of a monk.

4. {He was} Robert a *Champenois*—from the province of Champagne, a land of plains, a natural passageway for armies and migrations {and} scene of many great battles (v.g. in the last two World Wars: Verdun, Château-Thierry). The people of the region are quiet; they see the world go by their cottage door and say nothing; {they are} simple and prosaic, but deep.

The Life of Robert: {he was} born about 1028, {and} entered Saint Pierre de Celle at fifteen, {where he has a} long monastic preparation, in silence {and} spends about twenty-five years in the Benedictine cenobitic life; nothing is known of him there. At around forty-two he is elected abbot of Saint Michel de Tonnerre. Soon after, the hermits of Colan invite him to become their Father. He was not able to leave (the monks prevented it), but later he became abbot of another Benedictine monastery (St. Ayoul); but in 1074 the group at Colan gets permission from Rome to have Robert with them. He goes to Colan, which soon becomes Molesme. Here too, with the growth of the community and the reception of many gifts, the original spirit declined, and Robert saw that his ideal was again frustrated. With Stephen and Alberic and others, {he proposed a} project of return to simplicity {which} was placed before the chapter of the community, without success. Secession to Cîteaux took place. Later Robert, then very old, was recalled by the Holy See to Molesme.[135] One fact stands out: *everybody wanted him* as superior, as spiritual father. He was a holy man, venerated by all, who exercised an extraordinary influence over all, who brought peace wherever he went (he was recalled to Molesme because he alone could restore peace there). In a word, he was a man who sought peace—peace in the will of God, peace in monastic simplicity, peace in abandonment beyond and above a monastic ideal. In one word, he was through and through a *man of God*. It was not what he did that counted, but what he *was*. He died in 1111, {on} April 17.

---

134. The phrase is found in the letter from Pope Paschal, the so-called Roman Privilege (c. 14): "*Locum igitur illum quem inhabitandum pro quiete monastica elegistis*" ("that place in which you have chosen to dwell for monastic quiet") (*Nomasticon*, 61).

135. On the controversy surrounding this return, see Merton, *Medieval Cistercian History*, 52–58.

The Ideal of the Founders of Cîteaux: our Fathers sought primarily and above all to be *true monks*. They did not leave Molesme in order to be better than everyone else, nor did they even emphasize the idea of "keeping the *Rule* better" than the Black Benedictines (later, in the controversies that arose, this attitude was taken by some Cistercians). Content to leave the Benedictines with their own approved observance, the founders of Cîteaux wished to keep the *Rule* according to the norms really laid down in black and white by St. Benedict.[136] They did not want just an approximation; they wanted the genuine thing. It was, then, an attempt at *renovation*, but also at *adaptation* of the Benedictine life. For they did allow some small variations in the life, in order to adapt it to the time and place. The life led at Cîteaux and in the monasteries of the new Order was *not exactly* in every precise detail the life that was led at Subiaco or Monte Cassino by St. Benedict, but it was essentially the same, the same *in all that really mattered*. (Differences for instance {included} conventual Mass, laybrothers, no oblate children in the monastery.)

The complaints of the Cistercians against Cluny can be summed up as follows: *Cluny had destroyed the true balance of the Benedictine life*. The office was overlaid with excessively long public vocal prayers—litanies, little offices, etc. Manual labor had dwindled down to nothing, or was a mere formality. *Lectio divina* tended to become study of pagan literature. There was much bureaucratic clerical work. *Cluny had lost true monastic simplicity*. It was certain, of course, that many saintly monks lived in the Black Benedictine monasteries, and that there was much humility and self-effacement and silence in the common life of these great houses, but nevertheless simplicity was not perfect, for the monastery was too much involved in the affairs of the world. It was too close to the heart of feudal society. The monks participated in the exploitation of the poor—benevolently, no doubt. There was not real poverty; perhaps in many cases the monks could indeed find *personal* poverty, but the monastery itself was rich, and the community was rich—and its riches came from the labor of serfs and the contributions of the poor. The pressure of extra prayer and business made an *easier regime* seem permissible and even necessary. Consequently, the monastic life was *complicated and turbulent*. A monk cannot really have peace in his heart if he is merely living in the monastery much the same life as he led in the world.

Our Fathers sought a simple, quiet, monastic life. They did not seek severity for its own sake, but austerity as a way of *purchasing true inner*

---

136. On the foundation of Cîteaux, see Merton, *Medieval Cistercian History*, 38–45, 49–52.

peace and leisure for prayer by purifying the heart and liberating it from attachments, giving it over entirely to God. The ways of the world are not the ways of God. Worldly prudence is opposed to the prudence of God (Read Romans 8[137]). The monk must live by the spirit, not by the flesh. St. Robert understood this well. It is an illusion to seek the protection and the benefits of monastic life without paying the price that is necessary. Simplicity and solitude are not just a beautiful spiritual luxury; they must be *earned*. They do not drop into the lap of those who have an honest desire for them. The struggle begins in our own hearts. We must practice constant detachment from things, from persons, from self, and really free ourselves so that we can give our hearts entirely to God, that we may be led by His Spirit. Let us bless and thank God for the example and zeal of our founders, and let us be faithful to the tradition they have handed down to us. Particularly let us study and love that tradition, and realize that we have been chosen to make it live on.

May—Consecration to Our Lady

Our Lady as co-redeemer and mediatrix of all grace takes an active and central part in all God's work for the salvation and sanctification of souls. May is the time to remember this above all. May, the most beautiful month of the year, is *her* month (October, the next most beautiful, {is} also hers), because the world was made for her and for Jesus, for the Mystical Christ, the Church, of which she is the type. And she is the most perfect of all God's creatures, the summit of His creation, and so to her are given special gifts which *are for* the rest of creation, and which will reach it through her love. We receive these gifts by participating in her *fiat*, and indeed the grace to do this contains in itself all her gifts to us. Her *fiat* led to the salvation of us all, and we are all saved in so far as we are united to this *fiat* which she pronounced in our name. For us, particularly, as contemplatives, she has very special gifts and special care. Our contemplative life by its very nature is a life of "consecration" to Mary, of more intimate dependence on her, and more perfect participation in her most special virtues of *faith, obedience, purity of heart, love, humility*.

137. Rom 8:6–10: "For the wisdom of the flesh is death; but the wisdom of the spirit is life and peace. Because the wisdom of the flesh is an enemy to God; for it is not subject to the law of God, neither can it be. And they who are in the flesh, cannot please God. But you are not in the flesh, but in the spirit, if so be that the Spirit of God dwell in you. Now if any man have not the Spirit of Christ, he is none of his. And if Christ be in you, the body indeed is dead, because of sin; but the spirit liveth because of justification."

However, in order to appreciate this, we should explicitly consecrate ourselves to Mary in the novitiate as a sign of our willingness to persevere. (This consecration should take the place of those private vows which are not to be advised in the novitiate.) Mary will then *take over* and do for us what we cannot do ourselves. Mary wants to obtain for us a share above all in *her humility*, so important for all Christians, vitally important above all for contemplatives.

1. We need *light*, faith; otherwise we are in error and confusion, and remain helpless because we don't know what we are doing. But *pride and false humility* are the great sources of darkness and delusion in our lives, {of} so much unconscious self-deception, springing from our *demands* and *expectations*, our hidden *resentments*, flowing from illusions about ourselves.

2. {A} negative attitude in {the} spiritual life can flow from resentment, from pride and frustrated aggression. Mary's *meekness* will help us to grow *strong*. Realize the paradox of meekness and strength: it takes great strength to really say *fiat*, and abandon ourselves truly to the will of God.

3. *Humility* and *magnanimity*, perfectly united in Mary, will also be united in the soul consecrated to her. But we do not understand humility like hers, or humility like that of Jesus. We do not really know what humility is—even holy people often make serious mistakes in misjudging what they consider to be {the} pride of others, which may not be pride at all. After all, the Pharisees thought Jesus was a proud and contumacious rebel.

4. To love Mary and to give ourselves to her is to *enter into mystery*, but we must then remain very loyal to what we know to be God's will: charity, our *Rule*, our monastic way of life.

MARY IN THE PASSION (Day of Recollection: May)

"*Mulier cum parit, tristitiam habet, quia venit hora ejus.*"[138] "*Mulier, ecce filius tuus*"[139] (read *John* 19:25–27[140]). There is a beautiful

138. "When a woman is giving birth she is sad, because her hour has come" (John 16:21).

139. "Woman, behold your son" (John 19:26).

140. "Now there stood by the cross of Jesus, his mother, and his mother's sister, Mary of Cleophas, and Mary Magdalen. When Jesus therefore had seen his mother

correspondence between the gospel of {the} third Sunday after Easter[141] and the gospel of the Votive Mass of Our Lady in paschal time.[142] Mary became our mother on Calvary, in sorrow, and we are united to her in joy. In three poignant and simple lines, the Gospel of the Beloved Disciple points to the very essence of Mary's participation in the Passion of Jesus. Jesus, seeing His mother and the Beloved Disciple, the two persons He most loved, gave Mary to John to be his mother; John to Mary to be her son. Before the Passion, Mary had not been John's mother. John had not been her son. This special relationship is the fruit of the Passion. It is the last supreme gift of Jesus' love. *It is the beginning of the Church.* This special relationship continues the life of Christ on earth ({as} if {a} forest fire). John represents all who follow Christ, all the members of the Mystical Christ. To be a member of Christ means to be a child of Mary. The love that unites us to Mary, as sons to a mother, is the love of Jesus Himself, living in us. By this love Jesus lives on mystically in the world, prolongs His Incarnation. Mary's part in the Passion was, then, to become mother of us all, mother of the whole Church, and thus Mother of Christ over and over again each time a new member is born to life in Christ.

In a word, Mary's principal part in the Passion was to receive *us* from the hands of Jesus in exchange for Jesus dying on the Cross, and thus to *find and keep Jesus* in us. We are the supreme gift of Jesus to His mother; we are the reward for her *fiat,* for the faith with which she accepted the Incarnation and the sacrifice of her Son. We are the reward for her love of Jesus, her fidelity to Jesus. Her love and fidelity merit to become so fruitful in us that Jesus lives in us all. No one ever makes a sacrifice for Jesus without being repaid for it a hundredfold. It is in us all that Jesus gives Himself back to Mary not a hundred times over, but millions and millions of times over, in reward for the faith with which she consented to be parted from Him by His death on the Cross. So Jesus gives Himself to Mary, in us. But this depends on our own freedom, our own love. *We are at once the Crown of Our Lady and her Cross.* Jesus in giving us to her was making the supreme gift of His love, but in receiving us in exchange for Him on Calvary, with all our sins, infidelities, weaknesses, rebellions, Mary was indeed receiving a "Cross." Whatever she suffered on Calvary

and the disciple standing whom he loved, he saith to his mother: Woman, behold thy son. After that, he saith to the disciple: Behold thy mother. And from that hour, the disciple took her to his own."

141. John 16:16–22 (*Missale Romanum*, 361; *Missale Cisterciense*, 249).

142. John 19:25–27 (*Missale Romanum*, (50); *Missale Cisterciense*, 50*).

came from the sins of the ones entrusted to her by Jesus (and the whole world was entrusted to her). In this way she shared Jesus' own sufferings on account of our sins. Jesus is in us. But *we* are in ourselves, too. Mary receives the new man in us, but something of the old man is still there.

We need not dwell here on the totality, the universality, the completeness, the intensity of the sufferings of Jesus. Everything that could be suffered by a human body and soul was suffered by Jesus on the Cross. All that was suffered by Him physically was suffered by Mary mystically. His sufferings were, moreover, something more than ours—not only sufferings of a human nature but of a *divine Person*. Only Mary was capable of appreciating what that meant, and of sharing His sufferings. Mary's participation in the Passion {was} not just *quantitative*, but *qualitative*—not just the sufferings themselves but the added pain that comes from knowing the *full inner significance* of each indignity visited upon the Son of God. The Passion {was} an all-out offensive of evil against good, of hatred against love, lies against truth. It is the great battle between the *non serviam*[143] of Satan and the *fiat*[144] of Jesus and Mary ({note} the frightful "logic" of the crimes committed against Christ in the Passion). Every incident in the Passion was an argument, intended to prove that Satan was right and Jesus was wrong; that falsehood is able to overcome truth; that truth doesn't matter; that love is powerless against hate; that good must be overcome by evil. Each new insult, torment, defection, injustice, was Satan's way of saying triumphantly, "See, You are wrong; You can't win." Here as always, Satan is in his role as the *Accuser*, the critic, the one who pulls down what God has built up, tears apart what love has brought together. Now the main thing that Satan wanted to tear apart was the human race; he wanted to prevent Jesus from uniting men in one Spirit, one love, one truth, one Church. In order to do this, {he} turned the chosen people against Jesus, used all the instruments prepared by God as weapons *against* the work of God—for instance, the holiness and knowledge of the Pharisees became weapons against Jesus.

This shows us {the} special significance of the rejection of Jesus and the choice of Barabbas. The priests, the "holy men," the doctors of law, "custodians of God's truth and justice," prefer a rebel, {a} murderer, and reject the Son of God and Savior. {The} devil says: "See, after all You have done to draw them to You, after all Your mercy to them, all Your patience

---

143. "I shall not serve" (Jer 2:20).

144. "Let it be done" (Matt 26:42; Luke 22:42; Luke 1:38).

with them, they prefer me; they prefer hatred to love; I can get them with a snap of my fingers; they don't want You." Jesus' reply to this was silence and obedience. Mary shared in His silence and His obedience. So did John. So must we. If we share the silence and obedience of Jesus on the Cross, then we will effectively be His gift to His Mother. But the devil wants to "tear us apart" also, tear us away from Mary, make us follow Barabbas, so he can say to Jesus: "See, You gave everything for them, and I give them nothing, but I can still get them to follow me." If we are to be Mary's joy and consolation, and form part of her crown instead of adding to her sorrows, we must enter with her into the mystery of the silence and obedience of the dying Son of God. Obedience may be simple when we realize {the} superior is right; {we} may not feel like obeying, but our conscience is on his side. Trouble comes when we have *formed a moral judgement* which is contradicted by {the} superior. This means in fact, not that we go against conscience, but that *we must be willing to admit that our judgement was wrong, and to reform our judgement according to that of the superior.* (Conscience itself dictates this revision of our judgement.) This is very difficult. We get around it by appeal to the principle that we don't have to give up our speculative judgement. Quite true—but under pretext of keeping our speculative judgement, we refuse to change our practical judgement. {For} example, {the} superior commands {a} job which I think {is} against {the} spirit and rule of {our} Order. {This} example supposes he is fully within his rights, but it is something *less good*, speculatively, than what I would do myself. It is really a lesser good, but not an evil. Speculatively, true, this *is* a lesser good. I continue to hold that. But I am not permitted to infer that because this is a lesser good, therefore God prefers the greater good and does not will what is willed by the superior. This is an act of disobedience, or will lead to disobedience. I am not permitted to make this judgement. It is a *practical* judgement—what is to be done—and I do the will of the superior, telling myself that God does not really want this. This is where we fail. This is where we fail in faith too—cutting down God to our level: since it appears better *to me*, then it *must be* willed by God. God cannot will a lesser good in a particular instance, etc. Satan, the accuser, gets in here, and shows us how the "superior is not following the will of God." The way is prepared for a flat *non serviam*. If we are to share in the Passion of Christ and be sons of Mary, we must be ready to give up the idea that we are always right. As long as we cling to this, we will choose Barabbas. Another common illusion {is seen in} those who think that because they can accept the orders of the superior without anger they are obedient. They just tolerate orders but don't carry them out. They are good sports about taking orders, but they don't bother to do the will of another. {We} must not only *hear* but *do*, not just interiorly agree with {the} superior {and} approve of his order. {It is a} question of duty: to be aware of duty is to see God confusedly; to do it is to possess Him.

Let us return to our original theme. As a reward for Mary's fidelity to Him, Jesus gives Himself to her in us. But He does so in so far as we give ourselves. Hence it follows {that} if we desire to love Our Lady and console her as a Mother, we must seek to live in such a way that it is *easy and spontaneous* for us to give ourselves to her at all times. For this, avoid too *negative and subjective* {a} spirituality; a spirituality of *fault-finding*, thinking always of ourselves and of our faults, and then thinking of faults of others. This leaves us no time to think of God. {*The*} *great reality in our life is not the fact that we are evil, but that God is good.* Some spiritual men believe in evil more than they believe in good. {The} Cross means the goodness and kindness of God to us. Mary {is} a loving Mother who wants us to approach her with confidence. {We need a} *right understanding of confidence*, not merely concentrating on *what we don't have*, and expecting to get it. This {is} negative. *We may not, in fact, get this particular thing.* Then what? Confidence is part of love, is immersed in love—love which sees we already *are receiving and do receive* all we need, for we have Jesus, we have Mary, we need nothing else (read *John* 16:21[145]).

The Nativity of St. John the Baptist (June 24)

Note, this is not simply the feast of St. John the Baptist, but the feast of his *nativity*—not so much the celebration of all his virtues and sanctity, as the commemoration of a great and significant event, the birth of the Precursor. Why is this nativity important? because it raises the curtain upon the great mystery of the Incarnation. It reminds us of the great fundamental truths of our faith: (1) we need a Redeemer; (2) we cannot find Him by ourselves—He must be pointed out to us as sent by God; (3) we have to know how to prepare ourselves to meet Him. St. John is sent to point out the Redeemer, and to prepare the way for Him, so that people will recognize Him and come to Him and listen to Him. The mission of John is clearly shown forth by God in the nativity of the great

---

145. "A woman, when she is in labour, hath sorrow, because her hour is come; but when she hath brought forth the child, she remembereth no more the anguish, for joy that a man is born into the world."

Precursor, full of signs and wonders that proclaim he will be the last and greatest of all the prophets. Remember {that} St. John {the} Baptist is the great saint of Advent, and so this feast has something of the character of Advent—{a} mixture of joy and penance, hope and austerity; {it is} a feast of renunciation, of "going forth into the desert." But there is color and fire which we do not find in the Advent liturgy, the flaming "spirit and power of Elias."[146] John is a burning and shining light. Furthermore, the great difference between this feast and the Advent liturgy is that it is not so much marked by expectation as by fulfillment already begun: "God hath visited and wrought redemption of His People."[147] In the birth of the Precursor, as we celebrate it in this feast, redemption is regarded as an accomplished fact, which we celebrate with joy.

Some points from the liturgy:

Joy: the collect of the feast emphasizes "the grace of spiritual joys" as characteristic of this feast. "*Da populis tuis spiritualium gratiam gaudiorum.*"[148] In the gospel,[149] Zachary, after receiving back the power of speech, is filled with the Holy Spirit and prophesies—a joyous thing. In the postcommunion, again the theme of joy {predominates}: "*Sumat Ecclesia tua Deus beati Joannis Baptistae generatione laetitiam.*"[150] Why? Through him we recognize the *regenerationis Auctor.*[151]

The joy of the feast is the joy of our new life in God, the joy that is given us in Christ and in His Spirit of joy. For joy is the overflow of superabundance of life and love. "He shall be filled with the Holy Spirit from his mother's womb, and many shall rejoice in his birth"[152] (introit: vigil). {According to} St. Ambrose (third nocturn): "The birth of the saints brings joy because it is a 'common good.'"[153]

---

146. Luke 1:17 (vespers antiphon) (*Breviarium Cisterciense, Pars Aestivalis,* 355).

147. Luke 1:68 (*Breviarium Cisterciense, Aestivalis,* 363).

148. "Give Your people the grace of spiritual joys" (*Missale Romanum,* 618; *Missale Cisterciense,* 444).

149. Luke 1:57–68 (*Missale Romanum,* 619; *Missale Cisterciense,* 445).

150. "God, may Your Church take joy in the birth of blessed John the Baptist" (*Missale Romanum,* 619; *Missale Cisterciense,* 445).

151. "Author of regeneration" (*Missale Romanum,* 619; *Missale Cisterciense,* 445, which read: "*auctorem*").

152. Luke 1:15, 14 (*Missale Romanum,* 615; *Missale Cisterciense,* 442).

153. "*Habet sanctorum editio laetitiam plurimorum, quia commune est bonum*" (*In Lucam,* 2.1) (ninth lesson) (*Breviarium Cisterciense, Aestivalis,* 361).

Abundant power: everywhere in the liturgy of this feast we find expressions of overflowing richness and abundance of the power of God, of His hand stretched forth to save and regenerate—especially from the great prophets, from Isaias, in the Messianic songs of the Servant of Yahweh, and from Jeremias, {a} type of Christ—so that the words that reveal God's action in Christ Himself are here applied to the Precursor. The birth of St. John represents an overflowing of God's charismatic gifts. He is filled with the Holy Spirit from his mother's womb (cf. the Visitation). The other Prophets were called in later life. St. John was called in the womb of Elizabeth. Read the *epistle of the vigil*:[154] "Before I formed thee in the bowels of thy mother, I knew thee."[155] This of course can be said of everyone, in a general way. But in the particular sense in which it is used here, in the Old Testament sense, it has particular meaning: God had already "thought" of the Precursor, was already "fixing His attention" upon this vessel of election in a creative and dynamic way, making him a prophet and an instrument of power. Contrast the weakness of the infant: Jeremias in mature years was struck dumb like an infant, but St. John actually was an infant when he felt the hand of the Lord upon him. The helplessness of the human instrument contrasts with the might of God's power. God chooses the weak and helpless and reserves for Himself the privilege of secretly giving them unexpected grace to strengthen them, while even leaving them manifestly poor and weak. "Do not fear, I am with thee."[156] "His hand touched my mouth."[157] And then the might and universality of John's mission {is declared}: "Behold, I have given My words in thy mouth, I have set thee this day over nations and kingdoms

---

154. Jer 1:4–10: "And the word of the Lord came to me, saying: Before I formed thee in the bowels of thy mother, I knew thee: and before thou camest forth out of the womb, I sanctified thee, and made thee a prophet unto the nations. And I said: Ah, ah, ah, Lord God: behold, I cannot speak, for I am a child. And the Lord said to me: Say not: I am a child: for thou shalt go to all that I shall send thee: and whatsoever I shall command thee, thou shalt speak. Be not afraid at their presence: for I am with thee to deliver thee, saith the Lord. And the Lord put forth his hand, and touched my mouth: and the Lord said to me: Behold I have given my words in thy mouth: Lo, I have set thee this day over the nations, and over kingdoms, to root up, and to pull down, and to waste, and to destroy, and to build, and to plant" (*Missale Romanum*, 616; *Missale Cisterciense*, 443).

155. Jer 1:5.

156. Jer 1:8.

157. Jer 1:9.

to root up and to pull down and to waste and destroy, to build and to plant, saith the Lord Almighty."[158]

{In the} *epistle of the feast*[159] {is found} the richness of this great proclamation of the Messias to all the ends of the earth—the herald of a Mighty King speaks out! "Give ear, ye islands, and hearken ye people from afar"[160] etc. Again {we find} the same theme—the prophet's credentials: "*Dominus ab utero vocavit me . . .* "[161] Again {there is} the idea of God "remembering" his name in his mother's womb.[162] How can God remember something which had not existed before? Why is He said to do so? It suggests the reality and the individual vocation of the prophet being drawn forth slowly and deliberately from the infinite abyss of God's wisdom and providence. {Other themes include} God's power and "accuracy": the mouth of the prophet is as {a} sharp sword;[163] God's protection: in the shadow of His hand the Precursor is protected;[164] God's wisdom: the Baptist is specially chosen as a *sagitta electa*[165] and hidden in the quiver of divine Providence—a marvelous symbol; the lavishness and magnificence of God in the vocation of the Precursor: "And now saith the Lord that formed me from the womb to be His servant: behold I have given thee to be the *light of the Gentiles,* that thou mayest be My salvation even unto the ends of the earth [note St. John {the} Baptist is himself "God's salvation"]. Kings shall see and princes shall rise up and adore for the Lord's sake and for the Holy One of Israel who hath chosen thee."[166]

Hence, the prodigality of God's grace in the vocation of St. John makes him, as the office frequently reminds us, one of the greatest of saints, "*inter natos mulierum non surrexit major Joanne Baptista*"[167] (twelfth responsory, {which} sums everything up). The liberality of God descends even to the smallest details, so that God Himself gives the

---

158. Jer 1:9–10.

159. Isa 49:1–3, 5, 6, 7 (*Missale Romanum,* 618; *Missale Cisterciense,* 444–45).

160. Isa 49:1.

161. "The Lord has called me from the womb" (Isa 49:1).

162. Isa 49:1.

163. Isa 49:2.

164. Isa 49:2.

165. "a chosen arrow" (Isa 49:2).

166. Isa 49:5, 6, 7.

167. "Among those born of woman none has arisen greater than John the Baptist" (Matt 11:11; Luke 7:28) (*Breviarium Cisterciense, Aestivalis,* 362).

Baptist his name (hence the emphasis on the fact that God remembered his *name* even in the womb of his mother).

The hymn for lauds[168] celebrates the great outpouring of grace and sanctity in St. John. In the first verse, he is of exceeding great merit, a virgin, a powerful martyr, a hermit, and the greatest of the prophets. Others have earned a thirtyfold or twentyfold income on their talent; he has increased his talent three-hundredfold, etc. Hence, because of all this evidence of the action of God, it is a feast of *wonder and admiration*. Note the tremendous importance of wonder in the liturgy. It is essential for our adoration of the All-Holy God to cultivate a sense of the great wonder of all His works. It is because we lack this sense of wonder and sacred awe (really the "fear of the Lord") that we lack the sense of liturgical prayer, and our worship lacks strength and dignity. We are pious enough, no doubt, but we do not have the great, burning spirit of adoration that makes for really religious men. Let us make no mistake; this is a very serious lack, due not to our own fault, but to the fact that we are members of a materialistic and pragmatist civilization, in which there is no sense of wonder at God, and all our wonder and admiration is poured out on the achievements of men; yet these, instead of being fruitful and redemptive, are destructive, and lead to damnation and sterility. The grace of this feast should awaken in us joy and wonder at the magnificence of the divine action in the spirit of man redeemed by Him.

Preparing the Way of the Lord: this is an Advent theme, which we have seen already to some extent: "*Parare Domino plebem perfectam.*"[169] This reminds us of St. John's great vocation as patron of monks. In the literal sense of the gospel text, it refers to those who are to hear the Christ and believe—the first members of the Church. St. John prepared many of the apostles (for instance, James and John) to be disciples of Jesus. In an applied sense, the Precursor is the great patron of all those who have left everything to follow Jesus in darkness and to be "light in the Lord" (*lux in Domino*[170]). Each one of us can apply to himself: the words "*Et tu puer propheta altissimi vocaberis,*"[171] chanted at the time of our vestition.[172] To be a monk is to be a prophet in the sense of one who *knows* and recognizes

---

168. "O nimis felix" (*Breviarium Cisterciense, Aestivalis*, 363).

169. "to prepare for the Lord a perfect people" (Luke 1:17) (vigil: gospel) (*Missale Romanum*, 616–17; *Missale Cisterciense*, 443).

170. Eph 5:8.

171. "And you, child, shall be called prophet of the Most High" (Luke 1:76).

172. *Rituale*, 155; the entire *Benedictus* (Luke 1:68–79) is chanted.

Jesus in a world that sees Him not. ("There hath stood One in the midst of you Whom you know not," said John—all this in {the} Advent liturgy.) How do we do this?

1) by the completeness of our renunciation: we must leave *all* {and embrace a} love of poverty, silence, solitude, humility, abandonment, renunciation of our own will and judgement;

2) by the totality of our consecration: "He must increase and I must decrease,"[173] that is to say, by a self-dedication that accepts total effacement to live no longer in ourselves but in Christ;

3) by our love for souls, by the ardent missionary spirit with which we thirst for the salvation of the millions who do not know the Savior.

SAINTS PETER AND PAUL (June 29)

Some points from St. Bernard's Sermons (cf. sculptured figures on romanesque basilicas):

1) They are masters and mediators who show us the way of life and to Whom we entrust ourselves with security (*Sermo* I,[174] n. 1 [405]—taught directly by God the Master of all [I, n. 3]).

2) Yet they were sinners who learned from their own sins to have mercy on others; cf. {the} whole Sermon 3:[175] Paul sinned in the world; Peter sinned "in religion" ({this is} of central importance in Cistercian doctrine—compassion for our brethren and understanding of imperfections). Hence, they are kind, in the mercy with which they receive sinners; powerful, in their protection of sinners; wise, in leading us by the straight way to heaven (I.2) (cf. {the} sermon for the vigil:[176] they are more powerful in heaven, know our needs better, are quick to intercede for us, are more merciful because they stand before God the Fount of Mercy[177]).

3) *What do they teach us?* *not* vain speculative knowledge (Plato and Aristotle): "*non semper discere et nunquam ad cognitionem veritatis*

---

173. John 3:30.
174. Migne, *PL* 183, cols. 405C–408C.
175. Migne, *PL* 183, cols. 412B–416A.
176. Migne, *PL* 183, cols. 403C–406B.
177. Migne, *PL* 183, col. 404CD.

pervenire"[178] (*curiositas*)—still less fishing and tent-making. But
"*Docuerunt me vivere*"[179]—to know how to *live*, {the} science of life,
{which is} all-important. Note {the} practicality of St. Bernard and
of Cistercian thought. (Apply {this} to novitiate formation: {you are}
not here to learn merely rules and exterior practices, or how to sing
psalms, etc., or how to get along without responsibility, but truly to
live in Christ.)

4) *What is it to love well?* "*Mala pati—Bona facere.*"[180] "*Bona facere:
vivere—ordinabiliter tibi* (self-custody); *sociabiliter proximo—amari
et amare; humiliter Dei;*[181]

*Mala pati: austeritas poenitentiae; vexatio malitiae; flagellum
correctionis.*"[182] N.B. St. Bernard's thought revolves around these
three relationships—to ourselves, to others, and to God. *Perfection*
{is} to reach peace and interior solitude, in which are no longer
heard the voices of the world, flesh and devil. This is the highest
wisdom taught by the apostles.

THE FEAST OF THE VISITATION (July 2)

"*Ex abundantia caritatis*"[183] (collect). {This is} one of the most
beautiful of Our Lady's feasts. The infinite, overflowing charity of God
manifests itself *with exuberant fullness* in Mary, in her fraternal charity
to Elizabeth. This simple act, that anyone might perform, is in Mary a
kind of "theophany," a manifestation of God. In the *capitulum* {we hear}:
"*Ecce iste venit saliens in montibus.*"[184] Words that belong to Christ the
Bridegroom are used here because *He* comes to John in Mary.

---

178. "not always to be learning and never to arrive at a knowledge of the truth"
(Migne, *PL* 183, col. 407B, which reads: ". . . *ad veritatis scientiam* . . ."*).

179. "they have taught me to live" (Migne, *PL* 183, col. 407B).

180. "To endure evil—to do good" (Migne, *PL* 183, col. 407B).

181. "to live in an orderly way for yourself, in a sociable way for the neighbor—to
be loved and to love; in a humble way for God" (Migne, *PL* 183, col. 407BC).

182. "the austerity of penance; the tribulation of evildoing; the goad of correction"
(Migne, *PL* 183, col. 407CD).

183. "from the abundance of love" (collect: vespers, lauds) (*Breviarium Cisterciense, Aestivalis,* 419, 426).

184. "Behold He comes leaping the mountains" (Song 2:8) (*Breviarium Cisterciense, Aestivalis,* 419).

{Note} the special interest of one theme in this feast: "*Sonet vox tua in auribus meis*"[185] (read {the} lessons[186] and responsories[187] of {the} first

185. "May [Your] voice sound in my ears" (Song 2:14) (fourth lesson) (*Breviarium Cisterciense, Aestivalis*, 421–22).

186. "*Lectio i: Ego flos campi, et lilium convallium. Sicut lilium inter spinas, sic amica mea inter filias. Sicut malus inter ligna silvarum, sic dilectus meus inter filios. Sub umbra illius, quem desideraveram sedi: et fructus ejus dulcis gutturi meo. Introduxit me in cellam vinariam, ordinavit in me charitatem. Fulcite me floribus, stipate me malis, quia amore langueo. Lectio ii: Laeva ejus sub capite meo, et dextera illius amplexabitur me. Adjuro vos filiae Jerusalem per capreas, cervosque camporum, ne suscitetis, neque evigilare faciatis dilectam, quoadusque ipsa velit. Vox dilecti mei, ecce iste venit saliens in montibus, transiliens colles: similis est dilectus meus capreae, hinnuloque cervorum. En ipse stat post parietem nostrum respiciens per fenestras, prospiciens per cancellos. Lectio iii: En dilectus meus loquitur mihi: Surge, propera amica mea, columba mea, formosa mea, et veni. Jam enim hiems transiit, imber abiit, et recessit. Flores apparuerunt in terra nostra, tempus putationis advenit: vox turturis audita est in terra nostra: ficus protulit grossos suos: vineae florentes dederunt odorem suum. Lectio iv: Surge, amica mea, speciosa mea, et veni: columba mea in foraminibus petrae, in caverna maceriae, ostende mihi faciem tuam, sonet vox tua in auribus meis: vox enim tua dulcis, et facies tua decora. Capite nobis vulpes parvulas, quae demoliuntur vineas: nam vinea nostra floruit. Dilectus meus mihi, et ego illi, qui pascitur inter lilia donec aspiret dies, et inclinentur umbrae. Revertere: similis esto, dilecte mi, capreae, hinnuloque cervorum super montes Bether*" ("First lesson: I am the flower of the field, and the lily of the valleys. As the lily among thorns, so is my love among the daughters. As the apple tree among the trees of the woods, so is my beloved among the sons. I sat down under his shadow, whom I desired: and his fruit was sweet to my palate. He brought me into the cellar of wine, he set in order charity in me. Stay me up with flowers, compass me about with apples: because I languish with love. Second lesson: His left hand is under my head, and his right hand shall embrace me. I adjure you, O ye daughters of Jerusalem, by the roes, and the harts of the fields, that you stir not up, nor make the beloved to awake, till she please. The voice of my beloved, behold he cometh leaping upon the mountains, skipping over the hills. My beloved is like a roe, or a young hart. Behold he standeth behind our wall, looking through the windows, looking through the lattices. Third lesson: Behold my beloved speaketh to me: Arise, make haste, my love, my dove, my beautiful one, and come. For winter is now past, the rain is over and gone. The flowers have appeared in our land, the time of pruning is come: the voice of the turtle is heard in our land: The fig tree hath put forth her green figs: the vines in flower yield their sweet smell. Fourth lesson: Arise, my love, my beautiful one, and come: My dove in the clefts of the rock, in the hollow places of the wall, shew me thy face, let thy voice sound in my ears: for thy voice is sweet, and thy face comely. Catch us the little foxes that destroy the vines: for our vineyard hath flourished. My beloved to me, and I to him who feedeth among the lilies, Till the day break, and the shadows retire. Return: be like, my beloved, to a roe, or to a young hart upon the mountains of Bether" [Song 2:1–11]) (*Breviarium Cisterciense, Aestivalis*, 421–22).

187. "*R: Surge, propera, amica mea, formosa mea, Et veni: jam enim hiems transiit, imber abiit, et recessit. V: Audi, filia, et vide, et inclina aurem tuam*" ("R: Arise, make haste, my love, my dove, my beautiful one, and come. For winter is now past, the rain

nocturn). {The} wonderfully sweet harmony of *voices* {make the} Visitation the feast of the *voice*. The human voice, in Mary, becomes the instrument by {which} God Himself speaks:

a) first of all in the sanctification of John (read the gospel:[188] *Ecce enim ut facta est vox salutationis tuae in auribus meis exultavit in gaudio infans in utero meo*[189]);

b) *then in Mary's Magnificat*,[190] to which we should have a special devotion: this great song of praise, spoken by the Holy Spirit through the Immaculate Heart of Our Lady, offers us a simple and perfect means of uniting ourselves in the Holy Spirit with God, through Mary {in} purity of heart, purity of joy!

c) *then in the divine office*: union with God {is brought about}, as was Mary's, by union of our *thoughts* and *voices* with His. First, we must

---

is over and gone. V: Listen, daughter, and see, and incline your ear"). "R: *En dilectus meus loquitur mihi: Intra praecordia mea dat vocem suam. V: Quam dulcia faucibus meis eloquia tua, Domine, super mel ori meo!*" ("R: Behold my Beloved speaketh to me: into my inmost being He sends His voice. V: How sweet Your words to my throat, Lord, beyond honey to my mouth"). "R: *Ibo ad montem myrrhae festinanter, et videbo verbum hoc, Quod factum est in auribus meis ab Angelo salutante. V: Viam mandatorum tuorum cucurri, juxta verbum tuum*" ("I will go quickly to the mountain of myrrh, and I will see this word, because it was put in my ears by the angel's greeting. V: I have run in the way of Your commands, according to Your word"). "R: *Vox turturis audita est, surge, propera, amica mea, et veni, columba mea in foraminibus petrae, in caverna maceriae: Ostende mihi faciem tuam, sonet vox tua in auribus meis. V: Vox enim tua dulcis, et facies tua decora*" ("The voice of the turtle is heard, arise, make haste, my love, and come, my dove in the cleft of the rock, in the hollow places of the wall; show me your face, let your voice sound in my ears. V: For your voice is sweet, and your face is beautiful") (*Breviarium Cisterciense, Aestivalis*, 421–22).

188. Luke 1:39–47: "And Mary rising up in those days, went into the hill country with haste into a city of Juda. And she entered into the house of Zachary, and saluted Elizabeth. And it came to pass, that when Elizabeth heard the salutation of Mary, the infant leaped in her womb. And Elizabeth was filled with the Holy Ghost: And she cried out with a loud voice, and said: Blessed art thou among women, and blessed is the fruit of thy womb. And whence is this to me, that the mother of my Lord should come to me? For behold as soon as the voice of thy salutation sounded in my ears, the infant in my womb leaped for joy. And blessed art thou that hast believed, because those things shall be accomplished that were spoken to thee by the Lord. And Mary said: My soul doth magnify the Lord. And my spirit hath rejoiced in God my Saviour" (*Missale Romanum*, 619; *Missale Cisterciense*, 457).

189. "For behold as soon as the voice of thy salutation sounded in my ears, the infant in my womb leaped for joy" (Luke 1:44).

190. Luke 1:46–55.

sing; our hearts must go out in chant; our innermost being must be caught up in praise. Above all we must know and mean what we sing. The office is *"vox dilecti,"*[191] the voice of God. In it God also asks to hear *our* voice. He is behind the lattices of the literal sense and visible appearances. If we sing, then we give delight to Him; at the same time He speaks to us in the depths of our own heart: *"Intra praecordia mea dat vocem suam."*[192] "How sweet to my lips are Thy words, O Lord; they are sweeter than honey in my mouth."[193]

> The divine office is such an heavenly thing that in it we find whatsoever we can desire; for sometimes in it we address ourselves to Thee for help and pardon for our sins; and sometimes Thou speakest to us, so that it pierceth and woundeth with desire of Thee the very bottom of our souls; and sometimes Thou teachest a soul to understand more in it of the knowledge of Thee and of herself than ever could have been by all the teaching in the world showed to a soul in five hundred years; for Thy words are works (Dame Gertrude More,[194] quoted in Butler, *Benedictine Monachism*, p. 74).

St. Stephen Harding (I) (Common of Confessors—what is a confessor?) (July 16)

{Here is a} simple outline of the office of vigils for beginners, {beginning with the} preparation (Psalm 3) asking for help.[195] {Then come}:

1. the invitatorium (Ps. 94),[196] {an} invitation to praise God our Creator {and} our Savior; all things are His; He speaks to us as He spoke to the children of Israel; they did not listen, but we must. {In} the invitatory itself, praising St. Stephen, {we pray}: *"In domo Domini plantatus";*[197] *"Gaudemus in ejus* sancta solemnitate."[198]

191. "the voice of the Beloved" (Song 2:8).

192. "into my inmost being He sends His voice" (second responsory) (*Breviarium Cisterciense, Aestivalis*, 421).

193. *"Quam dulcia faucibus meis eloquia tua, Domine, super mel ori meo"* (second versicle) (*Breviarium Cisterciense, Aestivalis*, 421).

194. *Confessions*, 7 (*Writings*, 2.27).

195. *Breviarium Cisterciense, Aestivalis*, 19.

196. *Breviarium Cisterciense, Aestivalis*, 451.

197. "planted in the home of the Lord."

198. "let us rejoice in his holy celebration" (*"gaudeamus . . . in ejus . . . "* in text).

2. the *hymn*[199] {focuses on the} power of the saint: he is in heaven; his virtues {are recalled} on earth, {as well as} his miracles; {we} praise him {and} pray to him.

3. *psalms and canticles* {of} *nocturns* {are} from {the} common of martyrs[200] {but are} good for any saint; {they include the following} themes: (1) *"In lege Domini voluntas ejus"*[201] (Ps. 1; cf. Ps. 14: *"Domine quis habitabit"*;[202] 23); (2) *"Non sic impii, non sic"*[203] (Pss. 2, 5, 10, 20, 63); (3) *"Sperate in Domino"*[204] (Pss. 4, 10); (4) *"Oculi ejus in pauperem respiciunt"*[205] {and} *"Quid est homo quod memor es ejus"*[206] (Pss. 8 and 10); *"Exaltare Domine in virtute tua"*[207] (Pss. 20, 8, 23, 91: *Bonum est confiteri Domino*[208]); (5) *"Replebimini ei bonis domus tuae"*[209] (Ps. 64).

4. *first nocturn lessons*[210] (Ecclesiasticus 44): praise of famous men {and recognition of the} wisdom manifest in their lives; {the} *responsories* celebrate {the} glory and virtues of the saint: he is with God because he trusted in God (cf. resp. 4[211]).

---

199. *"Iste confessor Domini"* (*Breviarium Cisterciense*, 88*).

200. *Breviarium Cisterciense*, 29–33* (Pss 1, 2, 4, 5, 8, 10); 34–38* (Pss 14, 20, 23, 63, 64, 91); 40–41* (Eccli [Sir] 14:20, 15:3–5, Jer 17:78, Eccli [Sir] 31:8–11).

201. "his will is in the law of the Lord" (Ps 1:2) (*Breviarium Cisterciense*, 29*).

202. "Lord, who shall dwell" (Ps 14:1) (*Breviarium Cisterciense*, 34*).

203. "Not so the impious, not so" (Ps 1:4) (*Breviarium Cisterciense*, 29*).

204. "Hope in the Lord" (Ps 4:6) (*Breviarium Cisterciense*, 31*).

205. "His eyes look upon the poor one" (Ps 10[11]:5) (*Breviarium Cisterciense*, 32*).

206. "What is man that you are mindful of him?" (Ps 8:5) (*Breviarium Cisterciense*, 32*).

207. "Be exalted, Lord, in Your power" (Ps 20[21]:14) (*Breviarium Cisterciense*, 35*).

208. "It is good to give praise to the Lord" (Ps 91[92]:2).

209. "You shall fill him with the goods of Your house" (Ps 64[65]:5) (*Breviarium Cisterciense*, 37*).

210. *Breviarium Cisterciense*, 101–102* (lessons for abbots).

211. *"Hic est vir, qui non est derelictus a Deo in die certaminis sui, et ipse conculcavit caput serpentis antiqui: Modo coronatus est, quia fideliter vixit in mandatis Domini"* ("This is the man who has not been abandoned by God on the day of his struggle, and he himself has crushed the head of the ancient serpent: he has now been crowned because he lived faithfully according to the commandments of the Lord") (*Breviarium Cisterciense*, 102*).

5. *second nocturn lessons:*[212] {the} life of the saint.

6. *third nocturn homilies:* {the} gospel[213] and St. Jerome's *explanation:*[214] (1) "We have left all";[215] (2) {it is} not enough to leave all—{we} must *follow Christ* (Crates left all[216]). (3) They shall sit and judge the twelve tribes, because of faith. (4) What does it mean to leave all? St. Jerome mentions two "lists," and concludes: "*Omnes affectus contemnere, atque divitias atque voluptates.*"[217]

7. *Te Deum:* "*Te decet laus—te decet hymnus . . .*"[218] (for private use).

8. Then {the} *gospel*[219] and *lauds*[220] (*note the ascent!!*).

St. Stephen Harding (II) (July 16)

His Life and Spirit:[221] the collect of his feast {reads}: "*Excita Domine in Ecclesia tua spiritum cui beatus Stephanus abbas servivit.*"[222] Go back to him for the true Cistercian spirit. That is the importance of his feast: "*amare quod amavit*"[223]—to share his ideal, his desires; to have in our minds the same goal, the same aim; "*opere exercere quod docuit*"[224]—to carry out what he taught, to use the same means. N.B. {it would be in the} wrong spirit to celebrate the feast merely of an achievement for its

212. *Breviarium Cisterciense, Aestivalis*, 451–53.

213. Matt 19:27–29 (*Breviarium Cisterciense*, 102*).

214. *Liber 3 in Matthaeum*, c. 19 (*Breviarium Cisterciense*, 103–104*).

215. Matt 19:27.

216. "*hoc enim et Crates fecit philosophus*" ("Crates the philosopher also did this") (tenth lesson) (*Breviarium Cisterciense*, 103*). (Crates of Thebes was a Cynic philosopher of the fourth century BCE, a disciple of Diogenes.)

217. "to scorn all attachments and riches and pleasures" (*Breviarium Cisterciense*, 104* which reads: "*contempserint . . . et saeculi voluptates*").

218. "[We praise] You, God . . . Praise belongs to You, the hymn belongs to You" (*Breviarium Cisterciense, Aestivalis*, 33).

219. Matt 19:27–29 (*Breviarium Cisterciense*, 104*).

220. *Breviarium Cisterciense, Aestivalis*, 453.

221. On Stephen, see Merton, *Valley of Wormwood*, 262–77 and Merton, *Medieval Cistercian History*, 37–38, 43–46, 63–68, 121–25.

222. "Arouse, Lord, in Your Church the Spirit Whom the blessed Abbot Stephen served" (collect: vespers, lauds) (*Breviarium Cisterciense, Aestivalis*, 450, 453).

223. "to love what he loved" (collect: vespers, lauds) (*Breviarium Cisterciense, Aestivalis*, 451, 453).

224. "to put into practice what he taught" (collect: vespers, lauds) (*Breviarium Cisterciense, Aestivalis*, 451, 453).

own sake. We celebrate his spirit rather than his achievement, for what is important is the spirit by which he worked. Hence it is futile to laud St. Stephen as the originator of the whole Cistercian idea. That is not correct. Robert was the founder of the *novum monasterium*,[225] and the whole plan was guided and dominated by his personal ideal and influence. Stephen, during the early years at Cîteaux, went through a period of formation in silence, and his contribution came later: (a) the foundation of the Order as such: *Carta Caritatis*[226]—*unity* {and} *peace*; (b) the definitive character given to Cistercian observance: {the} *Consuetudines*[227] {are} dominated by his spirit and genius, but of course fully in line with monastic tradition. The observance of Stephen {is} marked by (1) discipline: it is firm but not *rigid*; (2) simplicity: it casts aside all non-essentials; (3) austerity: it is not weak {and} does not make injurious concessions; (4) authenticity: {it embodies the} true monastic tradition, true to the *needs of living monks*, not merely abstract.

1. {The} spirit of St. Stephen as given in {the} *Exordium Parvum*:[228] Stephen, the author of the *Exordium Parvum*, naturally does not go into great details about himself. He describes himself simply as *"Amator regulae et loci."*[229] *Love for the Rule* means in fact love for St. Benedict and the spirit of St. Benedict, {a} desire to find out and practice the true meaning of St. Benedict, *to live the kind of life St. Benedict would approve of and*

---

225. "the new monastery" (i.e. Cîteaux).

226. *"Charter of Charity"* (*Nomasticon*, 68–81); for a thorough treatment of the complex textual development of the *Carta Caritatis* and critical texts and translations of the *Carta Caritatis Prior*, attributed largely to St. Stephen, and the later, better-known *Carta Caritatis Posterior*, see Waddell, ed. and trans., *Narrative and Legislative Texts*, 261–82, 371–88, 441–50, 498–505. For Merton's discussions of this document, see Merton, *Charter, Customs, Constitutions*, 1–14 and Merton, *Medieval Cistercian History*, 65–68, 70–75.

227. *Nomasticon*, 84–241; the *Consuetudines* consists of three parts, the *Ecclesiastica Officia* (84–211), the *Instituta Capituli Generalis* (212–33) and the *Usus Conversorum* (234–41); for Merton's discussion of the *Ecclesiastica Officia*, the usages of the first generation of Cistercians, see Merton, *Charter, Customs, Constitutions*, 15–56; for his discussion of the *Instituta*, a summary of the early decisions of the Cistercian General Chapter, and of the *Usus Conversorum*, the regulations for the laybrothers, see Merton, *Medieval Cistercian History*, 82–88.

228. *Exordium Cisterciensis Coenobii* (*Nomasticon*, 53–65); for a thorough discussion of the composition of the *Exordium Parvum*, attributing the core of the work to St. Stephen, and a critical text and translation, see Waddell, ed. and trans., *Narrative and Legislative Texts*, 199–260, 416–40.

229. "a lover of the *Rule* and of the place" (*Nomasticon*, 64 [c. 17]).

delight in. If we do not have this desire, can we call ourselves monks or Cistercians? Note the difference between this and a mere juridical love for the *Rule.* That comes in too, of course. Stephen had a sense of law, but he transcended {a} mere juridical spirit. *Love of the place* {includes} its solitude, remoteness, poverty. He did everything to protect these, including his firmness in refusing hospitality to {the} Duke of Burgundy and his court. But it implies also love of the community living in the place, and this he had to a marked degree. "*Ne quid in domo Dei remaneret . . . quod superbiam aut superfluitatem, redoleret, aut paupertatem corrumperet.*"[230] The monastery {is} the house and sanctuary of God. "My house shall be called *a house of prayer.*"[231] If we have the spirit of St. Stephen, we will detest everything that offends against the sanctity and peace of the house of God, everything that distracts from the worship of God alone. {We will have a} *sense of the reality and {the} presence of God*—the holiness of God. {Note} Stephen's own custom of "leaving his distractions at the door"[232] as he entered for compline.

{The spirit of St. Stephen is} against *pride*, {against} everything that *tends to glorify man instead of God*, the deviation that seeks honor and reputation for ourselves, our own virtues, our own achievements. {This is the} plague of monastic life. {A} monk is not a monk if he is not humble; {avoid the} scandal of monastic pride and self-sufficiency. {It is} against *useless ornaments and trappings*, vain display, or just {the} accumulation of what is not needed. The real meaning of Cistercian simplicity {is} streamlining, cutting out what is useless and only in the way, what is excessive and hinders real growth. The Cistercian should have a real hatred for the accumulation of junk which hampers his spiritual freedom. Stephen was therefore against {the} use of precious metals when not absolutely necessary; {he} cast out copes, dalmatics and tunics as vain

---

230. "There must not remain in the house of God anything that smacks of pride or excess, or that undermines poverty" (*Nomasticon*, 64 [c. 17], which reads: ". . . *Dei . . . remaneret paupertatem . . . corrumperet*").

231. Matt 21:13, Mark 11:17, Luke 19:46, citing Isa 56:7.

232. "*Cum ecclesiam intraret, ostium ecclesiae manu teneret et digitis firmius quasi pro signo premeret, sicut solent homines signum aut nodum facere, quatenus per hoc admoniti memoriae artius imprimant, quod oblivisci nolunt*" ("When he entered the church, he would hold the door of the church with his hand and press it firmly with his fingers as though for a sign, just as people are accustomed to make a sign or a knot, through which they are reminded and effectively impress on their memory what they do not want to forget") (Konrad of Eberbach, *Exordium Magnum*, 83–84 [c. 26]).

ornaments.[233] {He had a} *love of poverty.* Just like the Franciscan, though in a different way, the Cistercian is married to Lady Poverty—poverty here in the sense of simplicity and labor; {he is the} protector of poverty and hater of everything that corrupts the beauty of poverty. *His charity* appears in two ways in the *Exordium Parvum*:

(1) *the ardor of his prayer*: when the foundation did not get novices, he prayed with great fervor, even though almost on the point of despair. {This was} one of the great trials of his life. "*Die ac nocte longa profundaque trahens suspiria.*"[234] It was the Holy Ghost who thus prayed in him with "unutterable groanings."[235]

(2) *in the formation he gave to the new monks*:

a) He teaches them to fight manfully against their own vices, and the temptations of the devil. *Fortitude* {is a} prominent Cistercian trait. One must resist nature and the evil spirits, without weakness and pusillanimity. Yet at the same time one must recognize that God alone is our strength. {The} peculiar Christian combination of littleness and greatness in Christ {is evident here}.

b) He teaches them that what they imagine to be impossible is in reality possible. This too is a Benedictine trait, not to be too easily deterred by difficulties, but to forge ahead even when the work seems impossible.

c) He teaches them to "bow their proud necks to the sweet yoke of Christ"[236] {and thus to find} peace in humility and obedience.

d) {He teaches them} to ardently love the hard and rugged (*dura et aspera*[237]) prescriptions of the *Rule*;

e) and to fill the house with the joy of fervent charity.

233. *Nomasticon*, 64 (c. 17).

234. "drawing out long and deep sighs day and night" (*Exordium Parvum*, c. 17 [*Nomasticon*, 64], which reads: "*trahentes*" [i.e., referring not to Stephen alone but to the entire community]).

235. Rom 8:26.

236. "*superba colla iugo christi suaui subdere*" (*Exordium Magnum*, c. 21 [Konrad of Eberbach, *Exordium Magnum*, 77]).

237. "hard and austere things" (*Rule*, c. 58) (McCann, ed. and trans., *Rule of St. Benedict*,130), quoted in *Exordium Parvum*, c. 17 (*Nomasticon*, 64).

2. *Other indications of his spirit* {include} his love of authenticity: (a) in the *Rule*, as we have seen; (b) in chant: sending his monks to Metz and Milan to get the authentic texts; (c) in Scripture: he makes his own revision of the Vulgate so that the monks may be chanting the right words in the office.

3. The *Exordium Magnum* calls him "a man of conspicuous sanctity, embellished by the grace of every virtue, a lover of solitude, and a most fervent defender of most holy poverty."[238] His love of prayer {is} proved by the daily Psalter he recited with Peter on the pilgrimage and in the monastery.

Saint Mary Magdalen (July 22)

1. The *gloriosa merita*[239] of a sinner (secret); "*Per peccatricis meritum peccati solve debitum*"[240] (hymn: lauds); "*Multae filiae congregaverunt divitias, tu supergressa es universas*"[241] (capitulum of none). Read the gospel of the feast here.[242] {All these readings focus on} the great merit of Magda-

---

238. "*virum conspicuae sanctitatis omniumque virtutum gratia decoratum, heremi amatorem et ferventissimum sanctae paupertatis aemulatorem*" (Konrad of Eberbach, *Exordium Magnum*, 77 [c. 21]).

239. "glorious merits" (*Missale Romanum*, 664; *Missale Cisterciense*, 468).

240. "Through the merit of a sinner remit the debt of sin" (*Breviarium Cisterciense, Aestivalis*, 474).

241. "Many daughters have accumulated riches, but you have surpassed them all" (Prov 31:29) (*Breviarium Cisterciense, Aestivalis*, 475).

242. Luke 7:36–50: "And one of the Pharisees desired him to eat with him. And he went into the house of the Pharisee, and sat down to meat. And behold a woman that was in the city, a sinner, when she knew that he sat at meat in the Pharisee's house, brought an alabaster box of ointment; And standing behind at his feet, she began to wash his feet, with tears, and wiped them with the hairs of her head, and kissed his feet, and anointed them with the ointment. And the Pharisee, who had invited him, seeing it, spoke within himself, saying: This man, if he were a prophet, would know surely who and what manner of woman this is that toucheth him, that she is a sinner. And Jesus answering, said to him: Simon, I have somewhat to say to thee. But he said: Master, say it. A certain creditor had two debtors, the one owed five hundred pence, and the other fifty. And whereas they had not wherewith to pay, he forgave them both. Which therefore of the two loveth him most? Simon answering, said: I suppose that he to whom he forgave most. And he said to him: Thou hast judged rightly. And turning to the woman, he said unto Simon: Dost thou see this woman? I entered into thy house, thou gavest me no water for my feet; but she with tears hath washed my feet, and with her hairs hath wiped them. Thou gavest me no kiss; but she, since she came in, hath not ceased to kiss my feet. My head with oil thou didst not anoint; but she with ointment hath anointed my feet. Wherefore I say to thee: Many sins are forgiven her, because she hath loved much. But to whom less is forgiven, he loveth less. And he said to her: Thy

len, a sinner:[243] "Many sins are forgiven her because she hath loved much: but to whom less is forgiven, he loveth less"[244] (gospel). Exegetes argue about the precise meaning of this. If we go into the grammar and syntax, we will get inextricably involved.[245] If we look at the context, it is simple. Mary Magdalen has *loved Jesus*; she has honored His Person; she has cast herself entirely at His feet with a love that implies sorrow, gratitude, trust, submission, self-abandonment, everything. In a word, she has loved HIM; and her charity has wiped out a multitude of sins. Simon the Pharisee, on the contrary, unaware that he needs to be forgiven anything, unaware of any special need to love Jesus, considers the Rabbi with cold curiosity, as an equal, perhaps as an inferior. He takes a thoroughly critical attitude towards the reputed holiness of the Master from Galilee, and instead of loving or respecting Him, he is content to have found what he believes to be a deficiency in His holiness. He thinks he has seen through Jesus, and is satisfied. In other words, Simon is characterized by his self-sufficiency, his complacent pride, his hostility, his narrowness. He is selfish. Mary Magdalen is just the opposite—empty of self, totally committed to the need of a Savior, humble, abandoned to His mercy, *seeking only to love and please Him*. Why? She has responded to His goodness. She loves Him because He is good, because of what He is; and *because of Him* she weeps at the evil in herself, since it does not correspond with Him—not because of her ideal of herself. Hence Magdalen, the sinner, wins great merit for her charity, and merits forgiveness for us, while Simon, with his many "good works," is without merit because he has despised Jesus. Like the Publican in the parable[246] she goes down to her house justified. This is one of the most important and central lessons of the Gospel. What matters is LOVE, love for the person of Jesus, love for our brethren in Him, a love impossible without heroic humility and faith and the desire to please Him in everything by doing His Holy Will. "*May the glorious merits of*

---

sins are forgiven thee. And they that sat at meat with him began to say within themselves: Who is this that forgiveth sins also? And he said to the woman: Thy faith hath made thee safe, go in peace" (*Missale Romanum*, 663–64; *Missale Cisterciense*, 468).

243. N.B. Merton presupposes here the traditional identification of Magdalen with the sinful woman of Luke 7:36–50, which is now generally rejected by Scripture scholars.

244. Luke 7:47.

245. See the discussion of this passage in Merton, *Monastic Introduction to Sacred Scripture*, 137–38.

246. Luke 18:9–14.

Blessed Mary Magdalen, we beseech thee, O Lord, make these our offerings to find favor in Thy sight; for Thine only-begotten Son vouchsafed graciously to accept the service she rendered to Him"[247] (secret). Because of her love, Mary Magdalen has power over the Sacred Heart. "It was in answer to her prayers that Thou didst call her brother Lazarus, four days dead, back from the grave"[248] (collect). Hence she has power in our own lives: {see the} beautiful verse from {the} hymn of lauds: "*Pia mater et humilis / Naturae memor fragilis / In hujus vitae fluctibus / Nos rege tuis precibus.*"[249]

2. Some thoughts from the hymns: the hymn of vigils,[250] only one verse and a doxology, laconically tells of Mary Magdalen washing the feet of Jesus with her tears and anointing them with a precious ointment. The hymns of vespers[251] and lauds[252] both bring *the heavenly Father* into the foreground. Through her love for Jesus, Magdalen is reconciled with the heavenly Father, and the hymns portray the love of the Father for her. Instead of punishing and rejecting her, He bends down to her with a tender love and calls her to the throne of glory. There is pathos in the love of Jesus for sinners, but even greater pathos in this love of the Father for weak and errant souls—but we must be able to go to the Father, through Jesus, by Mary. {In the} *hymn for vespers*, it is by looking down tenderly on St. Mary Magdalen that the heavenly Father has filled her with love and melted her cold heart, so that she runs to anoint the feet of Jesus, wounded as she is with love.[253] So great is her charity that it drives out all fear; she stands at the foot of the Cross when others flee; she runs to the tomb before the others, and does not fear the soldiers. Nothing can daunt her love. Hence, we call upon Thee, O Christ, true Charity, to purify us of our sins, and fill our hearts with grace and grant us eternal life

---

247. "*Munera nostra, quaesumus Domine, beatae Mariae Magdalenae gloriosa merita tibi reddant accepta: cujus oblationis obsequium unigenitus Filius tuus clementer suscepit impensum*" (*Missale Romanum*, 664; *Missale Cisterciense*, 468).

248. "*cujus precibus exoratus; quatriduanum fratrem Lazarum vivum ad inferis resuscitasti*" (*Missale Romanum*, 663; *Missale Cisterciense*, 467); N.B. here Magdalen is identified as well with Mary of Bethany.

249. "Humble and pious mother / mindful of our weak nature / In the upheavals of this life / guide us with your prayers" (ll. 13–16) (*Breviarium Cisterciense, Aestivalis*, 474).

250. "*Pater superni luminis*" (*Breviarium Cisterciense, Aestivalis*, 467).

251. "*Nardo Maria pistico*" (*Breviarium Cisterciense, Aestivalis*, 467).

252. "*Aeterni Patris Unice*" (*Breviarium Cisterciense, Aestivalis*, 474).

253. See Song 2:5.

in heaven.[254] {In the} *hymn for lauds*, again we look up to the heavenly Father and ask Him to look upon us with pity, on this day when He calls Magdalen to the throne of glory. Like the lost drachma,[255] she is now re-placed safely in the King's treasury. Like a jewel that has fallen in the mire she regains her original nobility, filled with the light of God.[256] (Note the strength of this verse, stressing the nobility of Magdalen's nature and her preciousness in the sight of God. He values her and seeks her to be part of His treasure, for she belongs to Him. The goodness that she has pros-tituted to men, and which they have perversely desired in her, is nothing else than a gift of God and a reflection of the divine goodness, intended not for temporal squandering, but to lead men to eternal life.)

3. The antiphons of vespers[257] {focus on} the scene at the tomb {and} Mary Magdalen's ardent desire to do honor to Jesus Whom she loves. Note, she does not believe explicitly in the Resurrection; on the contrary, she believed Jesus to be dead. But nevertheless she loves Him. She seeks Him "in the night" (first lesson: "*In lectulo meo per noctes quaesivi quem diligit anima mea*"[258]). For this she is rewarded not merely with the gift of faith, but Jesus appears first to her, before the apostles, and sends her to them to strengthen their faith. "*He appears first to Mary from whom He had cast out seven devils*"[259] (*Benedictus* antiphon). {This symbolizes} the vocation of the contemplative to persevere in love, in darkness, when all seems to be lost. Without this love, we are worthless. It is all we have.

4. The source of all this strength was not her own ardent nature. Her strength and her love came from God. He had endowed her with gifts that made her able to respond wonderfully, but the fact remains that what matters is *trust in the mercy of God*. The office tells us to look at Him and not at ourselves. Do we really believe in the Gospel? Do we really believe that we have a Savior? Are we really convinced that we need a Savior?

---

254. "*O vera, Christe, Charitas, / Tu nostra purga crimina, / Tu corda reple gratia, / Tu redde coeli praemia*" (*Breviarium Cisterciense, Aestivalis*, 467).

255. See Luke 15:8–10.

256. "*Aeterni Patris Unice, / Nos pio vultu respice, / Qui Magdalenam hodie / Vocas ad thronum gloriae. / In thesauro reposita / Regis est drachma perdita: / Gemmaque luce inclyta / De luto luci reddita*" (1.1–8) (*Breviarium Cisterciense, Aestivalis*, 474).

257. *Breviarium Cisterciense, Aestivalis*, 466.

258. "On my bed through the night I sought Him Whom my heart loves" (Song 3:1) (*Breviarium Cisterciense, Aestivalis*, 468).

259. "*apparuit primo Mariae Magdalenae, de qua ejecerat septem daemonia*" (*Breviarium Cisterciense, Aestivalis*, 474).

If not, what are we doing in the monastery? *"Pone me ut signaculum"*[260] (read the end of the epistle[261]). Jesus says to us and to her (epistle and fourth lesson[262]): "Put Me as a seal upon thy heart." The grace of ardent desires comes to melt our hearts and make them receptive. But the important thing is not this "liquifaction" of our being. We are not made merely to be "melted" with love. Those who seek consolation only, seek only to "melt." But we are melted in order that, like wax, we may take on a new form and then resume our solidity and *remain transformed.* Through the work of grace, Mary Magdalen had indeed "melted" with love, but it was in order to receive a seal, to receive Christ stamped upon the depths of her being. What is this seal? It is His own love as manifested in the Passion. When our hearts melt with consolation and with fervor, it is not just to make us feel good and to give us satisfaction with ourselves; it is to make us ready and receptive to take fully the seal of the Cross in our hearts. Without knowing it, in anointing the feet of Jesus, Mary had already received the seal of the Passion in her heart: *ad sepeliendum me fecit.*[263] The love which worked in her was something she had received by contact with Jesus. It was His love, the love that led Him to lay down His life for us. The love we must have in our hearts is not just any "love," but the love of Jesus crucified—that is to say, the love with which He loves us, the love which He gives to us, the love with which we love Him in return as He has loved us. This is a love as strong as death, which cannot be extinguished by many waters. If we give all that we have for this love, the sacrifice is still as nothing, compared to what we receive.

Feast of Saint Anne (July 26)

It would be a sign of lack of faith to be deficient in devotion to those saints about whom little is historically known, especially the great saints intimately connected with the mystery of the Incarnation, like Sts. Joachim and Anne, and St. Joseph. The *Spiritual Directory* says rightly that the faith and devotion of our Order draws us in a special way to these

---

260. "Place me as a seal" (Song 8:6).

261. Song 8:6–7: "Put me as a seal upon thy heart, as a seal upon thy arm, for love is strong as death, jealousy as hard as hell, the lamps thereof are fire and flames. Many waters cannot quench charity, neither can the floods drown it: if a man should give all the substance of his house for love, he shall despise it as nothing" (the first part of the epistle is Song. 3:2–5) (*Missale Romanum*, 663; *Missale Cisterciense*, 467–68).

262. Song 8:6–7 (*Breviarium Cisterciense, Aestivalis*, 469).

263. "She has done this for my burial" (Matt 26:12).

saints.[264] Why? We are hidden in the mystery of the Church and with the Church whose "sense" we should share in a remarkable degree; we find out the truth about these saints, not by the medium of historical knowledge, but by the more intimate and direct intuitions of the Church's own tradition. It is noteworthy that one of the points in which Luther proved his lack of Catholic sense was in his rejection of saints like St. Anne, in particular. It is altogether true that in the late Middle Ages there were a lot of gullible people who went in for exaggerated claims about pictures of Sts. Joachim, Anne and the Blessed Mother, "painted by St. Anne herself." But the Church does not let herself be shaken by follies like these. {We should have} devotion to St. Anne—why? because she prepared, in Mary, a tabernacle for the Lord. The medieval guild of joiners and cabinet-makers had special devotion to St. Anne for this reason (they made tabernacles). They were devoted to the statue of St. Anne instructing the Blessed Mother, with the inscription, "*Sic fingit tabernaculum Deo.*"[265]

At any rate our devotion to St. Anne is our devotion to her mother's love for Mary. As we love everything to do with Our Lady, so our Catholic sense cannot fail by a sure instinct to seek out this particular object, the tender spiritual love and care of the mother for the daughter, and the devotion of Mary to her mother. Love is the most beautiful and most precious reality in the world, because it reflects God Who Himself is love. The love of St. Anne for Mary and of Mary for St. Anne was a most pure and perfect natural love, supernaturalized and transfigured by the Holy Spirit. In this love God lived more perfectly on earth than He had ever done before the Incarnation itself. This love which overshadowed Our Lady was the *shekinah*,[266] or bright cloud that betokened the presence of the divinity Who was to come Himself and take flesh in the tabernacle of her blessed womb. In the love of St. Anne for Mary, God gave the world a presentiment of His wonderful coming in the Incarnation.

{The} cult of St. Anne[267] began in the Orient: a church {was} dedicated to her in the sixth century in Constantinople. {The} Orient commemorated St. Anne and St. Joachim not only {on} September 9 ({the} day after {the} Nativity of {the} Blessed Virgin Mary), but also on December 9 (drawing our attention to the fact that the Immaculate Conception took

264. Lehodey, *Spiritual Directory*, 253–54.

265. "Thus she formed a tabernacle for God" (see Guéranger, *Liturgical Year*, 13:192).

266. On the *shekinah*, see Merton, *Notes on Genesis and Exodus*, 169–74.

267. See Guéranger, *Liturgical Year*, 13:192–94.

place in St. Anne) (she must have been to some extent aware of the great mystery) and {on} July 25: {the} *Dormitio*[268] of St. Anne. Leo III introduced devotion to St. Anne to the West. Carmel helped its propagation. In 1584, Gregory XIII ordered {the} feast to be celebrated by the whole Church. Gregory XV, after a miraculous cure, made it a holy day with the obligation of resting from servile work. {There was a} pilgrimage of St. Anne d'Auray in Brittany: hence {a} special reason for {the} tradition of devotion to St. Anne in {the} Breton-founded monastery of Gethsemani. In our office note the beautiful *Magnificat* antiphons,[269] {the} *Benedictus* antiphon,[270] and the melody of the hymn for matins. This melody beautifully expresses the theme of the second stanza,[271] where the human race raises its head for the first time in darkness to catch the first glimmer of the light of hope "burning in the breast of St. Anne."

Feast of the Transfiguration (August 6)

1. "Today the divine light shines on the earth, the true light has illumined the darkness of mortal men, the glory of God has revealed itself visibly and even bodily to man's world. Today the eternal sun, having moved inside the curtain of fleshly weakness, has blazed forth miraculously on the earth" (Peter the Venerable).[272] *The Transfiguration* {is} the mystery not of a light that is *in* Christ but the mystery of Christ Himself, the light of the world: *Ego sum lux mundi;*[273] *Erat lux vera quae illuminat*

---

268. lit. "falling asleep."

269. "*Gaude, mater magnae prolis, ex te enim processit rutilans stella summi solis*" ("Rejoice, mother of a great offspring, for from you has gone forth the glowing star of the highest Sun"); "*Jucundare genetrix Mariae, quae Virgo Deum peperit, et Mater est Messiae*" ("Be happy, mother of Mary, who gave birth as a virgin to God, and is the mother of the Messiah") (*Breviarium Cisterciense, Aestivalis*, 485, 488).

270. "*Coeleste beneficium introivit in Annam, de qua nata est nobis pia Virgo Maria*" ("A heavenly gift has come in Anne, by whom was born for us the holy Virgin Mary") (*Breviarium Cisterciense, Aestivalis*, 487).

271. "*Jam sperat humanum genus / Caput tenebris excitans, / Lucemque primam conspicit / Annae coruscantem sinu*" ("Now the human race hopes, / Raising its head out of the darkness / And sees the first light / Burning in the breast of Anne") (*Breviarium Cisterciense, Aestivalis*, 485).

272. "*Hodie, . . . quando coeleste lumen in terris emicuit, quando vera lux mortalium tenebras illustravit, quando divinus fulgor humanis saeculis se visibilem etiam corporaliter demonstravit. Hodie aeternus Sol, carneae infirmitatis paululum remota caligine, . . . novo et stupendo miraculo mirabiliter radiando effulsit*" (*Sermo* 1, *De Transfiguratione Domini* [Migne, *PL* 189, col. 953B]).

273. "I am the Light of the world" (John 8:12).

omnem hominem venientem in hunc mundum;[274] *Deum de Deo, lumen de lumine;*[275] *Lumen ad revelationem gentium.*[276] The light of the Transfiguration is the light of a glorified body (St. Thomas, III, q. 45, a. 2[277]).

2. *Why the Transfiguration?*

a) {It is} a revelation of the *glory of the Resurrection* not only of Christ Himself, but of all His members. *Domini transfiguratio sanctorum est futura resurrectio*[278] (Peter the Venerable). The liturgy teaches us this clearly {{see the} capitulum of vespers,[279] etc.). We await a Savior, Our Lord Jesus Christ, *Who will reform the body of our lowliness according to the pattern of the Body of His glory* (Phil. 3). {The} collect {says} *ejusdem gloriae tribuas esse consortes;*[280] cf. {the} third responsory: "We know that when he shall appear *we shall be like unto Him because we shall see Him as He is.*"[281] (Note {the} relation of *likeness* to *contemplation.*) Transformation in the light of Christ {includes} not only our souls, but our bodies: cf. {the} *capitulum* of sext: "We shall be transformed into the same likeness from glory to glory as by the Spirit of the Lord."[282] Indeed, the whole world shall shine with the glory of the Risen Christ.

b) But this was a *preparation for the Passion: per crucem ad lucem*[283] (cf. {the} fourth responsory[284]). We could not persevere to the

274. "He was the true Light enlightening every person coming into this world" (John 1:9).

275. "God from God, Light from Light" (Nicene Creed).

276. "a Light of revelation to the Gentiles" (Luke 2:32).

277. St. Thomas Aquinas, *Summa Theologiae, Pars Tertia, q. 45, a. 2* (St. Thomas Aquinas, *Opera Omnia*, 4:195–96).

278. "The transfiguration of the Lord is the future resurrection of the saints" (Migne, *PL* 189, col. 956A).

279. Phil 3:20–21 (*Breviarium Cisterciense, Aestivalis*, 522).

280. "may You grant us to be sharers of the same glory" (*Missale Romanum*, 687; *Missale Cisterciense*, 486); (collect: vespers, lauds) (*Breviarium Cisterciense, Aestivalis*, 522, 539).

281. 1 John 3:2 (*Breviarium Cisterciense, Aestivalis*, 528).

282. 2 Cor 3:18 (*Breviarium Cisterciense, Aestivalis*, 539–40).

283. "through the cross to the light."

284. "*Ne videntes ejus passionem turbarentur, sed fortiori soliditate firmarentur*" ("so that seeing His passion they might not be made desolate, but might be strengthened in greater firmness") (*Breviarium Cisterciense, Aestivalis*, 528).

end unless we *knew* what glory was promised to us! Keep our eyes on the goal!

3. *The nubes lucida*[285]{symbolizes}:

a) contemplation—the Holy Spirit, purifying by the darkness of contemplation.

b) *claritas mundi innovati, quae erit sanctorum tabernaculum* (St. Thomas, III, q. 45, a. 2, ad 3[286]).

Summary: {the Transfiguration is} the "*adoptio filiorum* perfecta"[287] (collect), the completion of what is begun in baptism.

Saint Lawrence (August 10)

{St. Lawrence is} one of the greatest martyrs, {the} patron of deacons, because of his fortitude and love of the poor. The final total conversion of Rome seems to have been due to him. {The} great basilica of St. Lawrence outside the walls {is a} place of pilgrimage. Many great saints were themselves devoted to St. Lawrence. Most of the office is drawn from a tradition about his martyrdom, supported by St. Ambrose[288] and Prudentius.[289] Undoubtedly some of the details are embellishments—or might be embellishments. Modern scholars who call everything into question have also questioned the authenticity of the *Acta* of St. Lawrence's martyrdom. But we need not fear to accept the *substance* of the story on so strong and well-established a tradition as that which has always existed concerning him at Rome.

Martyrdom was regarded by the Fathers of the Church as the summit of the spiritual life. It held for them the place which modern spiritual writers give to "transforming union." One must admit that in theory the Fathers are much more solid and practical. In practice (as in the martyrdom of St. Agnes), it is seen that the two are in fact equivalent. One cannot

---

285. "bright cloud" (Matt 17:5).

286. "The clarity of the world renewed, which will be the tabernacle of the saints" (St. Thomas Aquinas, *Opera Omnia*, 4:196).

287. "the perfect adoption of sons" (*Missale Romanum*, 687; *Missale Cisterciense*, 486; *Breviarium Cisterciense, Aestivalis*, 522, 539, which read: "*adoptionem filiorum perfectam*").

288. St. Ambrose, *Hymnus LXXIII* (Migne, *PL* 17, cols. 1216–17).

289. Prudentius, *Peristephanon, Hymnus II: Passio S. Laurentii* (Migne, *PL* 60, cols. 294–340).

attain transforming union without an interior martyrdom, a complete death of the old man, and the great martyrs in their "agony" were given graces of prayer which corresponded to their total death to self and their new life in Christ. Martyrdom was regarded by St. Ignatius of Antioch as the consummation of the *Eucharistic life.* The martyr himself becomes the *frumentum Christi,*[290] ground into pure bread by the teeth of lions and tigers. We must never forget the perspectives of heroic love which the Church opens up before us. Too often preachers are content to "reassure" their hearers and to give them an easy and comfortable doctrine that does not involve any disturbance in their more or less worldly lives. It is true, an unwise zeal might merely awaken immature daydreams and fantasies. But the fact remains that we are called to heroism in the Christian life. Our love of Christ our life must be "unto death"—the gospel of the vigil reminds us of this. We are *obliged* to lay down our lives rather than deny Christ. (READ {the} gospel of {the} vigil:[291] He that would save his life must lose it.) See especially the *epistle*[292] *and gospel*[293] *of the Mass of the feast. "Qui parce seminat parce et metet."*[294] {Note here the} relation of {the} Mass of {the} vigil and {the} Mass of {the} feast: Lawrence "sowed abundantly" in giving to the poor. Because he was full of self-forgetful charity, he earned the grace of martyrdom. His fortitude and generosity under torture were based on his generosity in giving to others. Charity to others is {the} basis of our generosity in love of God, because it means true self-forgetfulness. *Hilarem datorem diligit Deus.*[295] *Read* the gospel of the feast.[296]

---

290. "the wheat of Christ" (Ignatius of Antioch, Rom. c. 4, which reads: "God's wheat . . . Christ's pure bread" [Kleist, trans., *Epistles of St. Clement and St. Ignatius,* 82]; see also Merton, *Introduction to Christian Mysticism,* 43–44).

291. Matt 16:24–27: "Then Jesus said to his disciples: If any man will come after me, let him deny himself, and take up his cross, and follow me. For he that will save his life, shall lose it: and he that shall lose his life for my sake, shall find it. For what doth it profit a man, if he gain the whole world, and suffer the loss of his own soul? Or what exchange shall a man give for his soul? For the Son of man shall come in the glory of his Father with his angels: and then will he render to every man according to his works" (*Missale Romanum,* 695; *Missale Cisterciense,* 491).

292. 2 Cor 9:6–10 (*Missale Romanum,* 697; *Missale Cisterciense,* 492).

293. John 12:24–26 (*Missale Romanum,* 697; *Missale Cisterciense,* 492).

294. "He who sows sparingly will also reap sparingly" (2 Cor 9:6).

295. "God loves a cheerful giver" (2 Cor 9:7).

296. "Amen, amen I say to you, unless the grain of wheat falling into the ground die, Itself remaineth alone. But if it die it bringeth forth much fruit. He that loveth his

THE RECEPTION OF THE HOLY CROWN OF THORNS (August 11)

{This is} a feast peculiar to our Order. The second nocturn[297] explains its institution. The Holy Crown of Thorns was sent to St. Louis by Emperor Baldwin of Constantinople. It was brought from Venice by a special escort, and not without miracles. The king came out to meet them as they neared Paris, opened the reliquary with great devotion on the Feast of St. Lawrence; then he and his brother, Prince Robert, themselves carried the reliquary into Paris, barefoot. It was later deposited in the Sainte Chapelle. The king, on very intimate terms with the Cistercian Order, asked the General Chapter to institute a feast to commemorate this occasion.

{It is} a typical medieval liturgical feast, {with} much spiritual application of various texts referring to a crown or a diadem. Emphasis {is placed} on the Passion, and the glory of Jesus, the glory of the Risen Christ reigning in heaven, seen through the Passion as foreground. His Crown of Thorns is seen mystically as His crown of glory. This gives the liturgy of the feast a particular poignancy: for instance, in the third antiphon of vespers, where we see Him "as a Spouse wearing a crown,"[298] the traditional crown of an oriental wedding is changed to the crown of thorns, in which Jesus espouses to Himself, on the Cross, redeemed humanity. {The} *capitulum* of vespers, lauds and tierce again brings in this nuptial theme in a text which may be perplexing: "Go forth, daughters of Sion, and see King Solomon in the diadem with which he was crowned by his mother"[299]—the "mother" in this application is the synagogue. The idea is taken up again in the hymn: "*Christi coronam cernite / Quam Mater ipsa texuit*."[300] In the collect, again the idea of passion and glory {appears}: "That we who venerate the Crown of Thorns on earth, in memory of His Passion, may deserve to be crowned with glory and honor by Him in heaven."[301] Note the twofold significance of our own monastic crown:

---

life shall lose it: and he that hateth his life in this world, keepeth it unto life eternal. If any man minister to me, let him follow me: and where I am, there also shall my minister be. If any man minister to me, him will my Father honour."

297. *Breviarium Cisterciense, Aestivalis*, 560–61.

298. "*quasi sponsum decoratum corona*" (*Breviarium Cisterciense, Aestivalis*, 553).

299. Song 3:11 (*Breviarium Cisterciense, Aestivalis*, 553, 564).

300. "Notice the crown of Christ / Which His mother herself wove" ("*Exite Sion Filiae*," ll. 3–4) (*Breviarium Cisterciense, Aestivalis*, 553).

301. "*ut, qui in memoriam Passionis Domini nostri Jesu Christi Coronam ejus spineam veneramur in terris, ab ipso gloria et honore coronari mereamur in coelis*"

suffering and glory; renunciation and inheritance (cf. {the} ritual for tonsure[302]). {In the} responsories {there are} vague allusions, often mere suggestions, of {an} application to {the} Crown of Thorns: {in responsory} 1, since Adam ate of the forbidden tree, the earth brought forth thorns and thistles for Christ;[303] {in} 2 and 3,[304] {on} the Burning Bush, the allusion is not made very clear, but God speaking to Moses from the midst of the "thorns" of the burning bush suggests the mystery of Christ crowned with thorns; 5[305] {refers to} the sacrifice of Abraham and the ram miraculously found in the thorns; 6[306] and 7[307] {mention} the gold crown on the ark of the covenant and on the altar of incense. These allusions are explained in the hymn of lauds.[308] The twelfth responsory sums up the whole feast: "Christ, knowing suffering and weakness and crowned with thorns, He is the same Who crowns us with mercy and forgiveness."[309]

(*Breviarium Cisterciense, Aestivalis*, 554, 563).

302. "*Omnipotens sempiterne Deus, propitiare peccatis nostris, et ab omni servitute saecularis habitus hunc famulum tuum N. dum capitis comam deponit segrega; ut tua semper perfruatur gratia, et sicut eum similitudinem coronae ornatus tui gestare facimus in capite, sic tua virtute et haereditatem consequi mereatur in corde*" ("Almighty and eternal God, be appeased for our sins, and separate this Your servant [name] from all enslavement to secular behavior as he gives up the hair of his head: so that he may always fully experience Your grace, and as we make him wear on his head the likeness of the crown Your adornment, so by Your power may he merit to attain the inheritance in his heart") (Smets, *Rituale Parvum Cisterciense*, 19).

303. *Breviarium Cisterciense, Aestivalis*, 555.

304. *Breviarium Cisterciense, Aestivalis*, 556.

305. *Breviarium Cisterciense, Aestivalis*, 560.

306. *Breviarium Cisterciense, Aestivalis*, 560.

307. *Breviarium Cisterciense, Aestivalis*, 561.

308. "*Legis figuris pingitur / Christi Corona nobilis: / Implexa spinis victima, / Ardensque testator Rubus. / Arcam corona cinxerat, / Mensaeque sacrum circulum / Aramque thure fumidam / Corona nectit ambiens. / Christi dolorum conscia / Salve Corona gloriae, / Gemmis et auro pulchrior, / Vincens coronas siderum*" ("The noble Crown of Christ / Is embellished with signs of the Law: / A victim entwined with thorns / And a bramble bush, an ardent witness. / The Crown surrounds the ark; / The Crown encircles and encloses / The sacred circle of the table / And the altar smoking with incense. / Hail, Crown of glory, / Aware of the sufferings of Christ, / More beautiful than jewels and gold, / Conquering the crowns of the stars") (*Breviarium Cisterciense, Aestivalis*, 563).

309. "*Christus sciens dolorem et infirmitatem, spinis coronatus, Ipse est qui coronat nos in misericordia, et miserationibus*" (*Breviarium Cisterciense, Aestivalis*, 562).

THE ASSUMPTION OF THE BLESSED VIRGIN MARY (August 15)

1. In this mystery we contemplate above all the supreme bounty of God Who poured out upon Mary all His most perfect gifts and privileges, (a) manifesting in her the perfection of the plan of His Providence, so that all His love for the world is complete in her as in a model for the rest—a great artist who puts all the best of himself into one masterpiece; (b) doing all that can be done to invest a creature with His own life and privileges, so that Mary becomes, as it were, a kind of Incarnation of God's wisdom in His plan for the world. So we look to her as to one in whom God's plan for us all is already completed. "It is our hope that belief in Mary's bodily Assumption into heaven will make our belief in our own resurrection stronger, and render it more effective" (Pius XII: *Munificentissimus Deus*[310]). {It brings an} increase of faith and hope for {the} life to come. {We} rejoice that Mary is in heaven, *gloriosa et felix*.[311]

2. *First vespers:*

a) Mary being assumed into heaven, the angels praise and bless God (first antiphon[312]), adoring the magnificence of His bounty.

b) We rejoice because Mary, assumed into heaven, *reigns* with Christ forever (second antiphon[313]); that is to say, she has not only queenly dignity, but queenly *power*.

c) Hence the gates of Paradise are opened for us by her (fourth antiphon[314]).

d) Why? In all *hearts* she has sought rest (*capitulum*:[315] see {the} context in *Eccli.* 24:11[316]). Mary does not just seek rest in all

---

310. Pius XII, *Munificentissimus Deus*, 18 [#42].

311. "glorious and happy" (vespers: Magnificat antiphon) (*Breviarium Cisterciense, Aestivalis*, 570).

312. *Breviarium Cisterciense, Aestivalis*, 569.

313. *Breviarium Cisterciense, Aestivalis*, 569.

314. *Breviarium Cisterciense, Aestivalis*, 569.

315. "*In omnibus requiem quaesivi, et in haereditate Domini morabor. Tunc praecepit, et dixit mihi Creator omnium: et qui creavit me, requievit in tabernaculo meo*" ("In all I have sought rest, and I will linger in the inheritance of the Lord. Then the Creator of all commanded me, and said to me: and He who created me has rested in my tabernacle") (Sir 24:11–12 [Vulg.]) (*Breviarium Cisterciense, Aestivalis*, 569).

316. "And by my power I have trodden under my feet the hearts of all the high and low: and in all these I sought rest, and I shall abide in the inheritance of the Lord."

things or events, but in hearts. All hearts must be subject to her wise love, just as the Creator of all things rested in her Tabernacle. Mary {is} the *patron of contemplatives*, not only because of her rest in heaven, but because of her action upon souls, in whom she seeks rest for herself and for God. We will never rest until we allow God to rest in us. For God to rest in us we must be content with our own nothingness, and seek only to please Him, not seeking our own pleasure. This was Mary's wisdom.

e) Above all we must believe. *Beata es Maria quae credidisti.*[317] She believed what God told her, and all He said has now been brought to perfection. What has God promised us? See John 5:24–25; 6:39–40, 47–59 (life in Christ, particularly by the Eucharist in which we receive His glorious Body); John 14:1–3 (that we may be with Him), 12–14 (we shall do great works), 23–26 (indwelling gift of the Holy Ghost). To really honor Mary we must always be conscious of these great promises and believe in them as she did.

{*The*} *Assumption of Our Lady in the Byzantine Rite*:

1. {It is} prepared for by a fast beginning August 1, {with a} special vigil on the fourteenth, and the feast goes on until the twenty-third.[318]

2. {There are} some beautiful odes from {the} great matins of the Assumption:

> The mysterious words of the prophets showed, O Christ, that Thy Incarnation of a Virgin would be the splendor of Thy glory and the light of nations; and the abyss shuddered and cried out to Thee: "Glory to Thy power, O Friend of man!" Come, all people, and behold: the Mountain of God, holy and visible to all, rises above the hills of heaven. [Here is an earthly heaven, established upon a heavenly and incorruptible soil.] Thy death, O most Pure One, was a passage to an eternal and better life. From a mortal condition death transports thee to a life truly divine and everlasting, O Immaculate One, and there thou dost contemplate in joy thy Son and Lord. . . . In thy Assumption,

---

317. "Blessed are you, Mary, who have believed" (responsory, vespers capitulum, which reads "*Beata es, Virgo Maria Dei Genetrix, quae credidisti Domino*") (*Breviarium Cisterciense, Aestivalis*, 569).

318. See Mercenier, *Prière des Églises de Rite Byzantin*, 2.1:412.

O Mother of God, the angelic armies trembling and with joy, covered with their most holy wings the body that was so great as to be the dwelling place of God.[319]

The inspired tongues of the theologians, taught by the Holy Spirit, sing a sonorous ode at the departure of the Mother of God and in her honor. "Hail, inexhaustible source of the Incarnation of God, life and salvation of the universe." All things exult in thy divine glory, for thou, O Virgin without stain, thou hast been lifted up to the eternal dwellings and to life without end, and there thou gainest salvation for those who sing to thee. Let the trumpets of the theologians ring out on this day, let all the innumerable tongues of mankind, with all their voices, sing now: let the sky resound, shining with infinite light. Let the angels sing the Dormition of the Virgin. O Virgin, O Mother worthy of all praise, whosoever has been carried away by admiration, whosoever has left his country and consecrated himself to God, whosoever has been inspired by God, all have honored the vessel of election with hymns in thy honor.[320]

In truth, O Virgin of Virgins, thy Child has placed thee in the holy of holies like a clear torch of immaterial flame, like a golden

319. "Les paroles énigmatiques des prophètes ô Christ, montraient d'avance que votre Incarnation d'une Vierge, serait l'éclat de votre gloire pour la lumière des nations; et l'abîme Vous dit en un transport de joie: 'Gloire à votre puissance, ô ami des hommes.' Voyez, peuples, et admirez: la montagne de Dieu, sainte et visible à tous, s'élève au-dessus des collines célestes, ciel terrestre établi sur un sol céleste et incorruptible. Votre mort fut le passage vers une vie éternelle et meilleure, ô Pure; d'une condition mortelle elle vous transporte à une vie vraiment divine et permanente, ô Immaculée, pour contempler dans la joie votre Fils et Seigneur. . . . Dans votre Assomption, Mère de Dieu, les armées angéliques couvraient de leurs ailes très saintes avec tremblement et avec joie, votre corps, assez vaste pour être l'habitacle de la divinité" (fourth ode) (Mercenier, *Prière des Églises de Rite Byzantin*, 2.1:429–30).

320. "Les langues inspirées des théologiens, instruits par l'Esprit, chantent une ode de départ plus sonore que la trompette en l'honneur de la Mère de Dieu: 'Salut, source inépuisable de l'Incarnation de Dieu, vie et salut de l'univers.' Tout est en transports à cause de votre divine gloire, ô Vierge inépousée car vous avez été enlevée de terre vers les demeures éternelles et la vie sans fin, où vous couronnez de salut tous ceux qui vous chantent. Que retentissent en ce jour les trompettes des théologiens, que les langues des humains chantent à present en des parlers divers; que tout alentour l'air retentisse, brillant d'une lumière infinie; que les anges chantent la Dormition de la Vierge. Le vase d'élection se distinguait par ses hymnes en votre honneur, ô Vierge, tout hors de lui, et hors du monde, tout voué à Dieu, étant vraiment et se montrant divinement inspiré, ô Mère de Dieu digne de tout louange" (fifth ode) (Mercenier, *Prière des Églises de Rite Byzantin*, 2.1:430–31).

censer filled with divine fire, like a cup and a scepter, like the tables of the Law written by the finger of God, like the Holy Ark, the table {of} the bread of life.[321]

Young men and virgins, venerating the memory of the Virgin and Mother of God, old men and princes, kings and rulers, sing together, "Thou Who art most worthy of our songs, Lord and God of our Fathers, Thou art blessed."[322]

OFFICE OF THE FEAST OF SAINT BERNARD (August 20)

1. *Vespers*: {there is a} keynote of joy and optimism: St. Bernard in his childhood {is seen as} a chosen soul with divine gifts showing his pre-destination. When we contemplate God's gifts in His saints, we rejoice in the greatness and goodness of God Himself {with} wonder and joy. (The actual words of some of these antiphons[323] are from St. Bernard's *Life of Malachy*[324]). He had the good spirit, was docile—*amabilis valde* (first antiphon[325]). He learned quickly and soon outshone his masters, {being} taught by the Holy Ghost (second antiphon). He grew in wisdom and grace before God and men (third antiphon). And now, to crown it all, he has laid aside his body and entered into glory—an ascent, easy and rapid, due to the loving mercy of God. {This is} encouraging! The responsory[326] {has} a note of lavishness and splendor: a vessel of solid gold, adorned with every precious stone, pours forth the waters of peace upon the earth {and} is like a burning fire and sweet-smelling incense in the days of summer.

321. "En verité, ô Vierge, votre Enfant vous a établie dans le Saint des Saints comme le chandelier brûlant d'une flamme immatérielle, comme l'encensoir d'or rempli de la braise divine, comme la coupe, la verge, la table écrite par Dieu, l'arche sainte, la table du pain de vie" (sixth ode) (Mercenier, *Prière des Églises de Rite Byzantin*, 2.1:431) (copy text reads: ". . . table and the bread . . .").

322. "Jeunes gens et vierges, vénérant la memoire de la Vierge Mère de Dieu, vieil-lards et princes, rois avec les juges, chantez harmonieusement: 'Seigneur et Dieu de nos pères, Vous êtes béni'" (seventh ode) (Mercenier, *Prière des Églises de Rite Byzantin*, 2.1:433); the phrase "Thou who art most worthy of our songs" apparently is adapted by Merton from another matins ode referred to immediately before this passage, the chorus of which reads: "À Vous nos chants, Seigneur et Dieu de nos Pères Vous êtes béni" (Mercenier, *Prière des Églises de Rite Byzantin*, 2.1:364).

323. *Breviarium Cisterciense, Aestivalis*, 583.

324. Migne, *PL* 182, cols. 1073A–1118A.

325. "very lovable" (*Breviarium Cisterciense, Aestivalis*, 583).

326. *Breviarium Cisterciense, Aestivalis*, 583.

2. {The} *hymns*, very simple and rather artless, give {a} summary of his life (typical medieval lyrics of the type discarded later as very bad verse). {Stories include} the presage of his fame as doctor in the barking dog; his vision of the Infant Jesus at Christmas (vespers[327] and vigils[328]); his generosity in resisting temptation; his obedience to the doctor; his miracles (hymn, lauds[329]).

3. {The} *antiphons*[330] {are} full of color and symbols. He has laid hold of the tree of life (first); his prayer {is} compared to the flowering of a lily in the early morning (fourth); he grew up saintly like a cypress or an olive tree (seventh) ({the} cypress grows straight up; {the} olive spreads out); as a priest, his sacrifice at the altar was most pleasing to God (eighth); he greatly increased the Order (tenth[331]), and brought peace to the whole Church because of the joy of his heart filled with charity (twelfth).

4. *Conclusion*: {in the} antiphon of lauds,[332] the whole Church of Cîteaux is filled with the odor of sanctity by Bernard.

Feast of Saint Bernard (second conference):

THE LESSONS OF THE THIRD NOCTURN, texts taken from *Sermo 85 in Cantica*, are used to comment on the gospel[333] of the feast: "You are the salt of the earth"[334] (salt—*sapor*—*sapientia*[335]). If the salt shall lose its savor (*sapor*—*sapientia*), etc. Hence, though these texts were not written on this precise gospel, they are at once a beautiful commentary and a summary of all the teaching of Saint Bernard. Let us summarize these lessons. {In} *lesson nine (sapientia—sapor boni*[336]):

327. "*Bernardus Doctor inclytus*" (*Breviarium Cisterciense, Aestivalis*, 583–84).

328. "*Bernardus inclytis ortus*" (*Breviarium Cisterciense, Aestivalis*, 584–85).

329. "*Intrat Cistercium*" (*Breviarium Cisterciense, Aestivalis*, 591).

330. I.e. of the first and second nocturns (*Breviarium Cisterciense, Aestivalis*, 585, 586–87).

331. Actually the ninth antiphon: "*Ampliavit gentem suam vir justus*" ("The just man increased his group").

332. *Breviarium Cisterciense, Aestivalis*, 591.

333. Matt 5:13–19 (*Breviarium Cisterciense, Aestivalis*, 590–91; *Missale Romanum*, 709; *Missale Cisterciense*, 501).

334. Matt 5:13.

335. "taste—wisdom."

336. "*Nec duxerim reprehendendum, si quis sapientiam saporem boni definiat*" ("I would not consider it misleading if one were to define wisdom as a taste for the good") (*Breviarium Cisterciense, Aestivalis*, 589).

a) Virtue alone is not enough. Virtue without *taste*, without *savor*, is insipid, and eventually will be fruitless. (Note, as Gilson has pointed out,[337] here we have a central truth in St. Bernard drawn directly from the *Rule* [c. 7: end], in which St. Benedict proposes to the monk that he must ascend the degrees of humility in order to reach the *perfect love which casts out fear.*[338]) St. Bernard would add (cf. *Sermones 23–24 in Cantica*[339]) that where there is fear, there is not perfect wisdom, perfect love, perfect peace in God— we still cling to ourselves, and fear prevents us from letting go.

b) Original sin was in fact loss of the *sapor boni*. The *sensus carnis* (taste for lower things, not evil in themselves, but not the proper objects of our desire and complacency for their own sakes) took away the *sapor boni*.

Lesson ten (SAPIENTIA VINCIT MALITIAM[340]) {contains} in three words the whole theology of St. Bernard. The Word, Love, Glory, Truth of the Father, the Wisdom of the Father enters into the world in an infinitely wise plan of God to destroy evil. By the perfection of His loving mercy, a love that goes beyond all bounds, He dies on the Cross for sinners. Then He communicates His love to us in His own Spirit. Entering into our hearts with His love, Jesus, the Incarnate Wisdom of God, enters into our hearts and drives out by His Presence the taste for sin. "*Sensum carnis infatuat / purificat intellectum / cordis palatum sanat et reparat.*"[341] These effects of Jesus {are} present in us how? by *faith*, by *grace*, by *memory* (awareness); doing things for love of Him, we are filled with His love, permitting Him to act in our hearts.

{In} *lesson eleven*,[342] St. Bernard laments that so many do good things without *sapor boni*, just out of habit or routine, or mechanically, or out of necessity; then again, many do evil without any real love of

---

337. Gilson, *Mystical Theology of St. Bernard*, 30–31.

338. 1 John 4:18.

339. Migne, *PL* 183, cols. 884A–894A, 894B–899A.

340. "Wisdom overcomes malice" (Wis 7:30) (St. Bernard, *De Laudibus Virginis Mariae*, 2 [Migne, *PL* 183, col. 62D]; *Breviarium Cisterciense, Aestivalis*, 589).

341. "[Wisdom] beguiles the senses of the flesh, purifies the intellect, heals and restores the palate of the heart."

342. *Breviarium Cisterciense, Aestivalis*, 589–90.

evil—their sin is less. But some have *gone over completely to the love of good*, others to the love of evil.

Lesson twelve {says}: BEATA MENS QUAM SIBI TOTAM VINDICAVIT SAPOR BONI ET ODIUM MALI.[343] Here we have manifest evidence that wisdom has overcome malice, for in our hearts there is no place left for any connaturality with evil. This is the purity of heart, the contemplative peace, which the Cistercian Fathers (like Cassian,[344] etc.) knew to be the end and aim of the monk on earth. It is the foretaste of eternal bliss in heaven.

Sermon outline—Feast of St. Bernard (1958): "In his days the wells of water flowed out, and they were filled as the sea above measure" (*Eccli.* 50:3). Because Jesus thirsted for our souls, we thirst for Him. Living waters {flowed} in {the} golden age of Clairvaux. {Of} the Galapagos Islands, only one has water; on the others {there were only} lava and clinkers. Pirates killed seals and drank their blood. So {it is with the} spiritual life: we land on barren islands; only one has water; we can last for some time on the others, on the blood of seals (explain: spiritualities which accord more or less with our Order {are} the other islands; the one island with water for us {is} St. Benedict—he is the one to whom Jesus has given living water.) St. Bernard helps us find the springs:

1. by his life: {the} overflowing power of God's love and fruitfulness {is found} in {the} life of St. Bernard. Great activity {coexisted with} self-forgetfulness {and} humility; {he} lived only for the Church, lived only for others. Because of his zeal, thousands were able to live {a} contemplative life. (READ *Eccli:* 50:2–11,[345] and apply to St. Bernard.)

---

343. "Blessed the mind which a taste for good and a hatred of evil takes hold of completely for itself" (*Breviarium Cisterciense, Aestivalis*, 590).

344. "*Destinatio vero nostra, id est, scopos, puritas est cordis, sine qua ad illum finem impossibile est quempiam pervenire*" ("Indeed our aim, that is, the target, is purity of heart, without which it is impossible for anyone to reach the ultimate goal") (*Conf.* 1, c. 4) (Migne, *PL* 49, col. 486); see also Merton, *Cassian and the Fathers*, xxxv–xxxix, 204–11.

345. "By him also the height of the temple was founded, the double building and the high walls of the temple. In his days the wells of water flowed out, and they were filled as the sea above measure. He took care of his nation, and delivered it from destruction. He prevailed to enlarge the city, and obtained glory in his conversation with the people: and enlarged the entrance of the house and the court. He shone in his days as the morning star in the midst of a cloud, and as the moon at the full. And as the sun when it shineth, so did he shine in the temple of God. And as the rainbow giving light in the bright clouds, and as the flower of roses in the days of the spring, and as the lilies that are on the brink of the water, and as the sweet smelling frankincense in

2. {by} his character: Bernard {was} a "burning fire"[346] {of} zeal and wisdom. His joy {was} that God should be loved; his sorrow, that God should be offended by sin ({the} Dark Night in St. Bernard—*quid?*). His formula for the spiritual life {is} to know God's ways and follow them, whatever they may be. {We should} not be scandalized by his activity. He is still our model. We don't have to preach crusades, but we must be totally plastic in God's hands and do all as St. Bernard did, out of perfect love.

3. {by} his doctrine: the monastic life—for what?

    a) Man's nature {is} "*celsa creatura in capacitate majestatis*,"[347] {the} image of God. Man's nature is to *love*. {He} has to love. Original sin has turned this love in {the} wrong direction and man has descended below the beasts.

    b) {The} first step {is a} recognition of the interior *contradiction and conflict* between our sublime vocation and our miserable condition: (1) *timor* (*Cant.* 54:8 ff.:[348] "*Aqua timor est*"[349] [54.12]); (2) *zelus* (*Sermo* 20 {in} *Cantica*, n. 4[350]); (3) *sapientia*: "*perfecta charitas*"[351] turns {the} water of fear into wine (*Cant.* 54.12;[352] *Cant.* 85.8[353]); {it is} lost through Eve {and} regained through Mary: "*Sapientia vincit malitiam!*"[354]

    c) {The} second step {is} recognition of the love and mercy of God towards us.

---

the time of summer. As a bright fire, and frankincense burning in the fire. As a massy vessel of gold, adorned with every precious stone. As an olive tree budding forth, and a cypress tree rearing itself on high, when he put on the robe of glory, and was clothed with the perfection of power."

346. Eccli [Sir] 50:9.

347. "a high creature with the capacity for majesty" (*In Cantica*, 80) (Migne, *PL* 183, col. 1163A, which reads: ". . . *capacitate quidem majestatis*").

348. Migne, *PL* 183, col. 1041C.

349. "The water is fear" (Migne, *PL* 183, col. 1043D).

350. Migne, *PL* 183, col. 868D.

351. "perfect charity" (Migne, *PL* 183, col. 1043D).

352. Migne, *PL* 183, cols.1043D–1044B.

353. Migne, *PL* 183, cols. 1191C–1192A.

354. "Wisdom overcomes malice" (Wis 7:30) (St. Bernard, *De Laudibus Virginis Mariae*, 2 [Migne, *PL* 183, col. 62D]).

d) {The} third step {is to} embrace monastic life, to reform {our} nature by penance, obedience, common life, turning our love back in the right direction by making us love others as ourselves.

e) {The} fourth step {is} recognizing the action of God in our souls which has done this, recognizing Jesus in our brother and in ourselves {with} joy, *pietas*, praise ({through the} liturgical life {which is the} life of the Church: nothing so well represents the joy of heaven as a choir in which the brethren praise God with zeal). {There is a} need here for zeal, *industria*, courage, generosity.

f) {The} fifth step {is} loving Jesus with {the} whole *heart*, {the} whole *mind*, {with} all our *strength*.

g) *Amo quia amo.*[355]

4. Bernard {was} all fire.[356] What pleasing sacrifice was offered by Clairvaux in the time of Bernard (READ *Eccli:* 50:12–19[357]).

Conclusions (from *Doctor Mellifluus*[358]): all Christian sanctity must have in it something of the ardent love that was Bernard's, but especially *our* sanctity. But a caution {is in order}: this is not attained by adolescent fantasy and ambition but by humility and self-sacrifice, {by} true

355. "I love because I love" (*In Cantica*, 83.4) (*PL* 183, col. 1183B).

356. See Merton, *Wisdom of the Desert*, 50: "Abbot Lot came to Abbot Joseph and said: Father, according as I am able, I keep my little rule, and my little fast, my prayer, meditation and contemplative silence; and, according as I am able I strive to cleanse my heart of thoughts; now what more should I do? The elder rose up in reply and stretched out his hands to heaven, and his fingers became like ten lamps of fire. He said: Why not be totally changed into fire?" (n. 72).

357. "When he went up to the holy altar, he honoured the vesture of holiness. And when he took the portions out of the hands of the priests, he himself stood by the altar. And about him was the ring of his brethren: and as the cedar planted in mount Libanus, And as branches of palm trees, they stood round about him, and all the sons of Aaron in their glory. And the oblation of the Lord was in their hands, before all the congregation of Israel: and finishing his service, on the altar, to honour the offering of the most high King, He stretched forth his hand to make a libation, and offered of the blood of the grape. He poured out at the foot of the altar a divine odour to the most high Prince. Then the sons of Aaron shouted, they sounded with beaten trumpets, and made a great noise to be heard for a remembrance before God. Then all the people together made haste, and fell down to the earth upon their faces, to adore the Lord their God, and to pray to the Almighty God the most High."

358. See Merton, *Last of the Fathers*, 102–103, and 82–84 (Merton's commentary).

renunciation of self. (The sermon was given in a much simpler form, with other ideas.)

Feast of the Immaculate Heart of Mary (August 21)

1. St. Bernardine of Siena, in the lessons of the second nocturn,[359] touches on the great *mystery* of Our Lady. Though she lived among men as a most ordinary and outwardly unremarkable person, yet her very person and her vocation are a mystery beyond the utterance of any human tongue. St. Bernardine, like St. Bernard, feels his total incapacity to speak of her whom the Father chose before all ages to be the Immaculate Mother of the Son, whom the Son chose as His mother, and whom the Holy Spirit chose to be the dwelling place of all grace. Her Immaculate Heart {is} the dwelling place of God, the dwelling place of perfect love. Jesus says in the Gospel: "A good man from the treasure of his heart brings forth good things."[360] St. Bernardine examines the few words spoken by Mary, and finds they were flames of love that came forth from the fire of pure love that burned in her: "As from a furnace fired to the greatest heat there can come forth nothing but burning fire, so from the heart of the Mother of Christ there could not go forth any word except a word of the highest and most divine love and fervor"[361] (lesson 6).

2. St. Bede[362] (third nocturn) connects the purity of Our Lady's heart with the fact that Jesus not only dwelt in her before He was born (as St. Bernardine emphasizes), but that after He was born she treasured all His actions and words in her heart[363] whether she understood them or not, and in order to keep Him in her heart she remained mostly silent. Instead of preaching, like the apostles, she who would have been the greatest of preachers remained silent.

---

359. *Sermo 9 De Visitatione* (*Breviarium Cisterciense, Aestivalis*, 604–605).

360. Matt 12:35; Luke 7:45 (cited by St. Bernardine in the fifth lesson [*Breviarium Cisterciense, Aestivalis*, 604]).

361. *"sicut a fornace summi ardoris non egreditur nisi incendium fervens: sic de Corde Matris Christi exire non potuit verbum, nisi summi, summeque divini amoris atque ardoris"* (*Breviarium Cisterciense, Aestivalis*, 604–605).

362. *Homilia Hyemalis de Tempore Dominica 1 post Epiphania* (*Breviarium Cisterciense, Aestivalis*, 606–607).

363. See Luke 2:51 (cited by St. Bede in the ninth lesson [*Breviarium Cisterciense, Aestivalis*, 606]).

3. St. Bernard ({in his} *Sermo de Aquaeductu*[364]) {provides} one of the great sermons on Our Lady's mediation. If the universal mediation of Mary is defined as dogma, this sermon will figure prominently in the texts. Jesus is the fountain of Life. Divine life {is} poured forth from Jesus into Mary as into a reservoir, from which an aqueduct brings the waters of life into our souls. St. Bernard adds that through the aqueduct we all receive something of grace, some more, some less: but she receives *all*. She was *full* of the grace of Christ. What was it that made Mary Mediatrix? (1) God chose her before the creation of the world; (2) St. Bernard emphasizes, however, the fact that once chosen, she cooperated perfectly with grace and took a very *active* part in bringing about the Incarnation: it was partly the result of her *prayers*, her *desire*, her *humility*. In other words, St. Bernard stresses the fact that the *purity of Mary's love* and of her humble prayer induced God to come into the world. He poured out into her heart the fullness of His grace, and this did not remain as a kind of static, passive purity; it elicited the perfect response of burning love, pure and total love, total abandonment of herself to God. To say that all God's love comes to us through the Immaculate Heart of Mary is to say that it comes through her love, active, dynamic, spiritual, intelligent, free. Mary is not a kind of magic talisman, but a loving person, and it is her active and burning love that is the point of mediation between Christ and ourselves.

FEAST OF THE NATIVITY OF OUR LADY (September 8)
(Byzantine Rite and Our Rite)

{This feast} lasts in reality from the seventh to the twelfth of September in {the} Greek Church. It is originally the dedication of the Church of the Probatica Pool, which is thought to have been next to the house of St. Anne—hence the date, September 8. {It was} celebrated in the sixth century at Byzantium and Rome, {and} originated in Jerusalem. The story of Mary's parentage and birth is drawn from the apocryphal Proto-gospel of James. The legend follows: Joachim and Anne were without children. They were insulted and reproached for this, and in fact one day Joachim was offering a gift in the Temple and was chased out with insults by the high priest because he was childless. He sadly retired to the country and dwelt with his shepherds. He prayed in the hills while Anne prayed in her garden, and an angel appeared simultaneously to both, announcing the

364. Migne, *PL* 183, cols. 437D–448B.

conception of a child. Joachim hastened back to the city, met Anne in the golden gate, where they embraced one another, and Mary was conceived in the house next to the pool of Probatica. It is fitting that we think especially of Sts. Joachim and Anne on this day. This is the first feast of the liturgical year in the Greek Church. The year begins September 1.[365] Both the Byzantine and Roman liturgies emphasize the fact that this feast is the beginning of a new era, the dawn of the era of salvation, Mary rising like the morning star before the sun of salvation. (St. Anne {is} also compared to a star rising before the sun—Mary—in St. Anne's hymn.[366]) "*Cujus vita inclyta cunctas illustrat ecclesias*"[367] (Mary our light); "*Maria exorta refulget*";[368] "*quibus beatae Virginis partus exstitit salutis exordium*"[369] (collect); "*Ex te ortus est sol justitiae Christus Deus noster.*"[370] Our liturgy emphasizes this note {of} "*salutis exordium,*" and the epistle of the Mass in the Roman Missal,[371] from the book of Wisdom,[372] shows Mary (Wisdom) "set up from eternity and of old before the earth was made. . . . The depths were not yet and I was already conceived. . . . Before the hills I was brought forth. . . . When He prepared the heavens I was there . . . I was

365. See Mercenier, *Prière des Églises de Rite Byzantin*, 2.1:75–77.

366. This seems to be a somewhat inaccurate recollection combining the Magnificat antiphon for the feast of St. Anne—"*Gaude, mater magnae prolis, ex te enim processit rutilans stella summi solis*" ("Rejoice, mother of a great offspring, for from you has gone forth the glowing star of the highest Sun")—with the second stanza of the vigils hymn: "*Jam sperat humanum genus / Caput tenebris excitans, / Lucemque primam conspicit / Annae coruscantem sinu*" ("Now the human race hopes, / Raising its head out of the darkness / And sees the first light / Burning in the breast of Anne") and/or the conclusion of the hymn for lauds: "*Castoque format pectore / Perenne sidus virginum*" ("She formed in her chaste breast / The everlasting star of virgins") (*Breviarium Cisterciense, Aestivalis*, 485, 487). In these passages Mary is the star, Christ the Sun.

367. "whose glorious life illuminates all the Churches" (first antiphon, vespers) (*Breviarium Cisterciense, Pars Autumnalis*, 293).

368. "Mary has arisen and shines forth" (third antiphon) (*Breviarium Cisterciense, Autumnalis*, 293).

369. "for whom the beginning of salvation springs from the birth of the Blessed Virgin" (*Missale Romanum*, 725; *Missale Cisterciense*, 513); (collect, vespers, lauds) (*Breviarium Cisterciense, Autumnalis*, 294, 300).

370. "From you has risen the Sun of justice, Jesus Christ our God" (Magnificat antiphon) (*Breviarium Cisterciense, Autumnalis*, 293, which reads: "*Ex te enim ortus . .*").

371. Prov 8:22–35 (the epistle in the Cistercian Rite is Eccli [Sir] 24:23–31 [*Missale Cisterciense*, 513–14]).

372. The passage (one of Merton's favorites) refers to the figure of Wisdom, but is of course not from the book of Wisdom but from Proverbs 8 (*Missale Romanum*, 725).

with Him forming all things and was delighted every day playing before Him at all times, playing in the world." {Here is seen} the Father's special love for Mary whom He has chosen with a very special choice, and blessed with every grace and privilege because she is to be the Mother of the Incarnate Word, and thus initiate the greatest work of God's love and the unfathomable mystery of His mercy. It is through her that He will accomplish all that is closest to His Heart. The tone of the office and Mass in our rite is strictly *Roman*—solemn, sober, simple, magniloquent, strong, restrained.

The same themes are intoned by the Greek Church with more lyricism and splendor. "This day, from Anne, there has grown out a branch, a divine shoot, which is the Mother of God and the salvation of men. From her, in an unheard-of manner, is born the Creator of all things, and He, being good, has purified by His goodness all the defilement of Adam."[373] "Come, all you lovers of virginity, lovers of purity, come and receive with love the glory of virginity; from the hard rock she makes to spring forth the waters of life, and from a sterile woman, she brings the bush burning with spiritual fire which purifies and illumines our souls."[374] "Having broken the chains of Anne's sterility, the most pure Virgin advances towards men to decide their fate and bring about their pardon."[375] "This day, God, Who sitteth upon the spiritual thrones, hath prepared for Himself on earth a holy throne; He who in His wisdom hath solidly established the heavens hath built, for love of men, a living heaven. . . . God of wonders and hope of the despairing, Lord, glory be to Thee! It is the day of the Lord! Nations, tremble with joy! Behold the nuptial chamber of the Light, the Book of the Word of Life is born from the womb. The Eastern gate is opened, and awaits the entrance of the High Priest: she alone is the door that brings into the world the Christ, and Him alone, for the salvation

---

373. "D'Anne, en ce jour, a poussé un rameau, rejet divin; c'est la Mère de Dieu, le salut des hommes. C'est d'elle qu'est né—qui comprendra?—l'artisan de toutes choses, Lui qui, étant bon, purifie par sa bonté toute la souillure d'Adam" (little vespers) (Mercenier, *Prière des Églises de Rite Byzantine*, 2.1:78–79).

374. "Venez, tous les amis de la virginité et les amants de la pureté; venez, accueillez avec amour la gloire de la virginité; la source de la vie jaillissant d'une pierre dure, le buisson germé sur une terre sterile, buisson au feu immatériel qui purifie et illumine nos âmes" (Mercenier, *Prière des Églises de Rite Byzantine*, 2.1:79).

375. "Après avoir rompu les chaînes de la stérilité d'Anne, la Vierge toute pure s'avança vers les hommes pour leur accorder le pardon" (Mercenier, *Prière des Églises de Rite Byzantin*, 2.1:79); there is nothing corresponding to the phrase "to decide their fate" in the original.

of our souls."[376] "Today is born to us she who is the bridge of life; by her, mortal men have found salvation after their fall into hell and by their hymns they praise Christ, the Giver of life."[377] {The} Greek liturgy {is} characterized by awe and holy exultation, jubilation before God (*Jubilate Deo*) with adoration and compunction {that} touches {the} deepest springs of the human soul {and} transforms us—yet the Roman liturgy is probably better for every day.

Nativity of Our Lady (II): {the} *simplicity and splendor* of the feast {is seen in the office}. The antiphons of vespers sing of the royal glory of Mary, her Queenship, and our total dependence on her in our prayer. Our prayers depend on her prayer. Our prayer-life is a ramification of her prayer-life—a share in her prayer-life: *cujus precibus nos adjuvari mente et spiritu devotissime poscimus.*[378] {The} office {emphasizes} communion in the Word: *nos*—meaning who? {Is it} abstract or concrete? *We* continue the Incarnation in so far as we are one in Christ. {This is} not just a juxtaposition of baptized Christians, "placed end to end," {but an} integration in common life, the Body of Christ. {The} liturgy {is} communion—communication—in the mystery of Christ by celebration of *divine praise* and of the *Eucharistic mysteries*, and by other sacramental actions which "open our eyes" and confer grace. {Note the} *teaching about prayer* contained in these lines:

a) dependence on Mary (we expect nothing from ourselves, all from our Mother); we look to her prayers and not to our own for results.

b) We pray *mente*—with our minds—intelligent prayer (not necessarily *discursive*—intelligence is more perfect in simple intuition)— the prayer that *sees* and *grasps* the truth that Mary holds all in her hands. How {do we} see this? by faith. {Mary is the} "*Mater*

---

376. "En ce jour, le Dieu qui repose sur les trônes spirituels s'est préparé sur terre un trône saint; Celui qui, dans sa sagesse, a solidement établi les cieux, a disposé dans son amour des hommes, un ciel vivant. . . . Dieu de merveilles et espoir des désespérés, Seigneur, gloire à Vous! C'est le jour du Seigneur! Peuples, tresaillez d'allégresse. Voici que la chambre nuptiale de la lumière, le livre du Verbe de vie est sorti d'entrailles humaines. La Porte de l'Orient qui vient de surgir attend l'entrée du grand prêtre; elle est seule à introduire dans l'univers le Christ, et Lui seul, pour le salut de nos âmes" (grand vespers) (Mercenier, *Prière des Églises de Rite Byzantin*, 2.1:80–81).

377. "Aujourd'hui naît celle qui est pont de la vie; par elle, les mortels ont trouvé le salut après leur chute dans l'enfer et ils glorifient par leurs hymnes le Christ qui donne la vie" (first ode, matins) (Mercenier, *Prière des Églises de Rite Byzantin*, 2.1:89).

378. "by whose prayers we ask most devotedly to be aided in mind and spirit" (third antiphon) (*Breviarium Cisterciense, Autumnalis*, 293).

agnitionis"[379]—Mother of knowledge, of recognition. Mary produces in our life the awakening of prayer, conversion to new levels of spirituality, {to a} new humility.

c) We pray *spiritu*—{out of} the very depths of our being—{or} summit of our being—the orientation of our entire life by deep desire and interior submission to Mary. "Spiritual" life {is} not {a} life of imagination, {of} feeling, but of {the} deepest spiritual self. {We must} *empty* ourselves of self to find the "spirit" and center, united to {our} brethren in spirit.

d) {We pray} *devotissime*, {which} implies consecration, {an} eagerness to serve, eagerness to give, eagerness to please; this *devotio* is made up of "fair love" and "holy hope"—*pulchra dilectio*[380]—{it is} fair because {it is} pure, because {it is} reflecting {the} purity of Mary, giving back to her a love like hers for us, with detachment and virginity of spirit. It is TRUE love—faithful, constant and deep.

Blessed Guerric (*Sermo* II, *Nativitas BV*[381]) {calls} Mary Mother of fair love: "My beloved is fair love in Himself, and my Beloved is fair love, and fear and hope and knowledge, in him who believes in Him. He is not only the One we love, fear and know, and the One in Whom we hope; but He also produces all these in us, and by these virtues, as though by certain members and parts, He is formed in us."[382] {Here we find} Guerric's favorite doctrine of the formation of Christ in us through the action of Mary. His likeness is perfect in us when we are perfect in love, not just in that love which *we* as men like to give, but the love by which He acts in us. "Beautifully and properly is Love called 'fair,' since God is love, and by that fact He is supreme beauty, and that virtue of love is all the beauty of the Church."[383] Guerric concludes with a prayer to "Jesus, the beauty

---

379. Eccli [Sir] 24:24 (capitulum) (*Breviarium Cisterciense, Autumnalis*, 293).

380. "fair love" (Eccli [Sir] 24:24) (capitulum) (*Breviarium Cisterciense, Autumnalis*, 293, which reads: "*pulchrae dilectionis*").

381. Migne, *PL* 185, cols. 203C–206C.

382. "*Dilectus meus est pulchra dilectio in se ipso: dilectus meus est pulchra dilectio, timor, et spes, et agnitio in illo qui natus est ex ipso. Ipse enim est non solum quem diligimus, timemus, agnoscimus, et in quem speramus; sed haec etiam omnia in nobis operatur, atque his virtutibus, veluti quibusdam membris et partibus, in nobis perficitur atque formatur*" (Migne, *PL* 185, col. 205B).

383. "*Pulchre autem et proprie dicta est pulchra dilectio, cum charitas Deus sit, ac per hoc summa pulchritudo; sitque virtus ista fere tota pulchritudo Ecclesiae*" (Migne, *PL* 185, col. 206A).

of the saints,"[384] begging Him to reign in the beauty of His love "that the world may love Thee with the same fair and true love with which Thou hast loved the world."[385]

Sancta spes[386] {is} holy because {it is} sanctified by God, and based on His most holy promises of eternal life. Our hope *is all the more holy when it is purified of human motives and supports.* {There is} great boldness in hoping when the world thinks our hope is madness.

FEAST OF THE HOLY NAME OF MARY (September 12[387])

Lessons of the second nocturn[388] (from St. Bernard's Second Homily on the *Missus Est*[389]):

1. Mary, according to St. Bernard, means Star of the Sea.[390] The mystery of the *name* {is that it is} not just an arbitrary tag but somehow indicates the secret inner being of the one named. If there were an adequate Name of God that one could know, one would possess the inner secret of God's own being and power, according to the ancient Jews. In fact, God is beyond all names. The closest we can come to knowing His true Name is to know the Name of Jesus—and this Name is indeed the power of God and the glory of God, {which} fills our hearts with grace when we utter it (cf. {the} Sermon of St. Bernard on the Holy Name[391]).

2. Why is it appropriate to call Mary Star of the Sea? Like the star giving forth its ray without losing anything, Mary brought forth Jesus without detriment to her virginity.

---

384. "*Jesu, pulchritudo Sanctorum*" (Migne, *PL* 185, col. 206C).

385. "*ut illa pulchra et vera dilectione te diligat mundus, qua dilexisti mundum*" (Migne, *PL* 185, col. 206C).

386. "holy hope" (Eccli [Sir] 24:24) (capitulum) (*Breviarium Cisterciense, Autumnalis*, 293, which reads: "*sanctae spei*").

387. This feast was celebrated on the Sunday within the octave of the Nativity of Mary, rather than on a particular date (N.B. TMa reads "Sept. 15"—altered to "Sept. 12" in TMb).

388. *Breviarium Cisterciense, Autumnalis*, 306–308.

389. Migne, *PL* 183, cols. 61B–71A.

390. "*maris stella*" (*Breviarium Cisterciense, Autumnalis*, 306); for a discussion of this image see Merton, *Cistercian Fathers and Their Monastic Theology*, 61–66.

391. St. Bernard, *Sermo 15 in Cantica* (Migne, *PL* 183, cols. 843D–848C).

3. She is the "star risen out of Jacob";[392] her rays "illumine the whole earth."[393] She shines in heaven; she shines on earth; her light even penetrates the nether regions.

4. The effect of her light (which presumably shines in our hearts more fully when with love we utter her name) {is}: *calefaciens magis mentes quam corpora / fovet virtutes / excoquit vitia.*[394] She is a star: *micans meritis, illustrans exemplis.*[395]

5. If we find ourselves in trials, difficulties, dangers, it is in order that we may look up to the star, and call upon Mary. Temptations, tribulations, the assault of our vices, or pride, lust, anger, the remembrance of our sins, the terror of God's judgement: all these are simply signals that we must turn to Mary. If we call upon her, she will surely hear us. And if she hears us, she will give us the grace we need. Hence, the lesson {is} to continually have her name on our lips and in our heart. *Ipsam sequens non devias, ipsam rogans non desperas, ipsam cogitans non erras, ipsa tenente non corruis, ipsa protegente non metuis, ipsa duce non fatigaris, ipsa propitia pervenis.*[396] The whole of our monastic life can be summed up as a trusting love for Our Lady, a love that seeks her face always, that always calls upon her merciful and motherly love.

EXALTATION OF THE HOLY CROSS (September 14)

1. {This} feast {is} "cardinal" ({a} hinge): {it} begins {the} season of penance, {signaling the} Cross in our life; sacrifice {and} transformation; {the need to} renounce self {and to} hate all clinging to self, self-love,

---

392. "*stella ex Jacob orta*" (sixth lesson) (*Breviarium Cisterciense, Autumnalis,* 307).

393. "*universum orbem illuminat*" (sixth lesson) (*Breviarium Cisterciense, Autumnalis,* 307).

394. "warming minds more than bodies, she fosters virtues, burns away vices" (sixth lesson) (*Breviarium Cisterciense, Autumnalis,* 307).

395. "sparkling by her merits, enlightening by her example" (sixth lesson) (*Breviarium Cisterciense, Autumnalis,* 307).

396. "Following her you do not lose your way; asking her you do not despair; thinking of her you do not err; held fast by her you do not fall; protected by her you do not fear; led by her you do not tire; favored by her you reach your goal" (eighth lesson) (*Breviarium Cisterciense, Autumnalis,* 308).

self-justification, self-pity. {See the} *first and second antiphons* {for} vespers (translate[397] and explain).

2. {Note the} story of the feast:[398] the bishop in splendid robes, etc. (second nocturn).

3. *The Glory of the Cross* {is seen in the} invitatory ("*Crux Gemmata*"[399]); the Victory of the Cross {is found in the} fourth antiphon {of the} first nocturn: "*O crucis victoria*"[400] {and also from the} first nocturn: "*Hoc signum crucis.*"[401] We will be judged by the Sign of the Cross. How? cf. in Egypt, the blood of the Paschal Lamb. {The} Cross in this life {is a} sign of mercy.

4. {The} gospel,[402] etc.: how were the devil and death conquered by the Cross?

The Rosary and Its Mysteries (October)

Not only is the rosary in itself one of the most beautiful and truly Catholic forms of prayer, but it is a prayer which the Church insistently recommends to her faithful in our time. Cistercians have sometimes {been} inclined to set aside the rosary in their prayer life, asserting that there is "already too much vocal prayer." There may certainly be cases in which vocal prayer should be kept at an absolute minimum. But we do

---

397. "*Nos autem gloriari oportet in Cruce Domini nostri Jesu Christi*" ("It is right that we should glory in the Cross of Our Lord Jesus Christ"); "*Salva nos, Christe Salvator, per virtutem sanctae Crucis: qui salvasti Petrum in mari, miserere nobis*" ("Save us, Christ Our Savior, through the power of the Holy Cross; You who saved Peter in the sea, have mercy on us") (*Breviarium Cisterciense, Autumnalis*, 313).

398. The Cross had been seized by the Persians and held for fourteen years, until Emperor Heraclius defeated them and demanded the return of the Cross as a condition of peace. Heraclius himself, dressed in gold and jewels, was carrying the Cross back to Calvary, but found it impossible to proceed until he stripped off his ornate garments and walked the rest of the way barefoot and in a common tunic (n.b. it is the emperor, not a bishop, about whom the story is told) (*Breviarium Cisterciense, Autumnalis*, 320–21).

399. "jeweled Cross": the phrase, used to describe medieval decorated crosses, is not actually used in the invitatory: "*Christum Regem pro nobis in Cruce exaltatum, Venite adoremus*" ("Come, let us adore Christ the King raised up for us on the Cross") (*Breviarium Cisterciense, Autumnalis*, 314).

400. "O victory of the Cross" (*Breviarium Cisterciense, Autumnalis*, 315).

401. "This sign of the Cross [will be in the heavens]" (versicle) (*Breviarium Cisterciense, Autumnalis*, 315).

402. John 12:31–36 (*Breviarium Cisterciense, Autumnalis*, 325; *Missale Romanum*, 730; *Missale Cisterciense*, 518).

not need to think that the average religious will find the rosary too great
a burden or too much of a complication in our life, first of all, since we
have now abandoned the Little Office, and secondly, because it is always
perfectly easy to recite the rosary, at least in part, while we walk out to
work, or as we go from place to place in community. The *Spiritual Directory*[403] tells us that it is a time-honored custom of the Order for the
monks to walk out to work saying their beads, as they go in line to the
fields. Indeed, one of the best times to say the rosary, in our life, is when
we are walking outdoors, either on the way to work, or during our *lectio*.
Unless a monk or novice has a special reason for not saying the rosary,
he should not be afraid to keep up the practice which he undoubtedly
had in the world, but with a great freedom of spirit. No one should feel
himself *obliged* to say the rosary each day, or bind himself strictly to say
it at any time. If one were to have made a vow to say the rosary daily,
before entering the monastery, the vow would be suspended from the
moment of temporary profession, and such vows can and should be dis-
pensed during the time of postulancy and novitiate. It is not usually right
that one should undertake to learn and carry out the obligations of the
monastic life with other obligations still binding one. However, each case
should be judged in the light of its own peculiar circumstances. All this
being noted, it is still to be recommended that one say the rosary when
it is possible, with a spirit of freedom and out of love, but one should not
scruple to set it aside when the duties of our monastic life make it difficult
to say the beads with devotion. It is better that a monk or novice should
not find himself hurriedly rattling off his private prayers in bed at night
in order to fulfill a self-imposed obligation. If you have not finished the
beads by bed-time, Our Lady will be more pleased if you simply make
an act of love and trust, and offer to God all the merit of her love in the
fifteen mysteries, then go to bed, for this is the will of God. In doing this
you are in fact uniting yourself more perfectly with Our Lady's obedience, humility and abandonment to the Father's will.

The Special Value of the Rosary: there is no need to take a defen-
sive and apologetic attitude toward the rosary. Most of the "difficulties"
and "objections" to it are simply imaginary, and they vanish when one
says the rosary properly—the matter of repeating prayers more or less

---

403. See Lehodey, *Spiritual Directory*, 378: "We can also begin at this time [distri-
bution of work] to recite ejaculations or pious aspirations which we may count on our
Rosary beads as we go to work or while returning therefrom. This is a very ancient
custom in our Order and we should not allow it to fall into desuetude."

mechanically, for instance. *No one is expected to think of each word of each Hail Mary.* That would, in fact, spoil the whole thing. Each vocal prayer we say as we tell the beads is like the refrain of a song. When we hum a tune, or sing it, returning over and over to the same refrain, we are not fixing our minds with intense concentration on the words; we are just singing. No great amount of thought is required. A song is not something you think about with intent concentration, but something that you *sing*. In order to understand this simple and obvious truth, which is so evident to common sense, it should be enough to think of the singing we did with our friends and family outside, just for the enjoyment of it. We never had any problem of distraction then, and we did not have to try to "fix our minds" on what we were singing. The song "thinks" and "sings" itself. The repetition of the prayers in the rosary is calming, peaceful; it lulls our minds; it creates an atmosphere of prayer; it attunes us to Our Lady's presence; it surrounds us with an aura of love in which our hearts spontaneously open themselves to the grace which she obtains for us by her motherly intercession. While we are reciting the words, we gaze very simply, and lovingly, at the various mysteries. We do not have to meditate on them in a complicated fashion. We know them well, and we simply return to their familiarity with love, and become absorbed in them again. This is possible because the mysteries are at once mysterious and familiar. Their depth is inexhaustible, yet they attract and hold us. What is the power of the mysteries? *This power lies in the fact that they bring us into contact with loved Persons Who love us*; and the Person of Jesus is *divine. The rosary then means the presence of Mary to our minds and hearts, and the presence of Jesus through and with her.* This in itself is the greatest mystery of all, and we should not trouble ourselves trying to analyze and explain to our minds how this takes place. The simplicity of Catholic faith grasps without doubt the reality which our words find such trouble in expressing. Jesus is present to us in Mary and she is present to us in Him, and *as we reflect on the mysteries of the rosary, and devoutly recite the prayers, the grace of God is flowing into our hearts and the mysteries produce their effect in our lives.* Hence the rosary has a very special value because of its *simplicity*, its *efficacy*, its *dogmatic character*, and in a word, because of the fact that it takes us directly to Jesus, the Word Incarnate. The reason why Our Lady wants us to recite the rosary is that it is one of the most effective means of uniting ourselves to Jesus, and because above all, it is one of the most *universal ways* of doing this. After Holy Mass and the sacraments, there is no more effective way for the average Christian to unite himself to Jesus than by the devout use of the rosary.

The Rosary and Contemplation: Fr. Garrigou-Lagrange points out[404] rightly that to say the rosary well is to dispose oneself to contemplative prayer, and to learn how to approach God in simple contemplation. This is true if our recitation of the rosary becomes more and more simple, and at the same time, more deeply affective. That is the clue to most difficulties about the rosary; it is above all, in actual fact, an *affective form of prayer. This means that intellectual considerations and formal thoughts are secondary.* Once one has learned to say the rosary well they remain in the background, giving place to affections. These in turn are very simple and "global"; the rosary does not demand of us that we invent and formulate verbal acts of love, or any other such acts; the vocal prayers prescribed, themselves suffice, and we "experience" each Hail Mary, so to speak, as the breathing of our love, as the rhythmic beating of the heart of love; indeed, in our affection of love, as we say the rosary, the vocal prayers tend to become the united heartbeat of our hearts, the Immaculate Heart of Mary, and the Sacred Heart of Jesus, living and beating in unison. This is the true purpose of the rhythmic character of this prayer. The quasi-physical character of the rhythm set up by repetition therefore has a special importance and value. Nevertheless, as we proceed with our affections and our simple contemplation of the various mysteries, *our intellects are indeed nourished, but in a much higher way, with the truths of faith. The atmosphere of affectivity and love with which we penetrate the mysteries actually perfects our intelligence in a higher and more supernatural way than would be possible by mere intellectual consideration,* because, as St. Thomas points out, in the things of God *our love reaches to the intimate reality which remains obscure to our intelligence.* Hence, he says, "*Melior est amor Dei quam cognitio*"[405] (in the present life) (*Summa*, I, q. 82, a. 3). Why is this? because, St. Thomas says, "*Finis vitae contemplativae habet*

---

404. Garrigou-Lagrange, *Mother of the Saviour and Our Interior Life*, 251–55: "The Rosary: A School of Contemplation."

405. "Love of God is better than intellectual knowledge" (St. Thomas Aquinas, *Opera Omnia*, 1:323); in Merton, *Ascent to Truth*, Merton quotes this statement as one that "is reechoed everywhere in the teachings of the mystics" and "delivers us forever from the delusion that mystical contemplation is learned from books and that the contemplative life reaches its highest fulfillment in the stacks of a university library," while warning his audience "to beware of contemplatives whose mysticism does not have a positive basis in theology," and pointing to Aquinas himself as evidence that God can "pour out His purest graces of mystical prayer even upon a professor" (285).

esse in affectu. . . . Haec est ultima perfectio contemplativae vitae, ut non solum divina veritas videatur sed etiam ut ametur"[406] (II–II, q. 180, a. 7, ad 1). If we can properly grasp this, we can see indeed what a wonderful form of prayer the rosary is. Many souls who find themselves no longer able to "think about" the mysteries, and start straining their heads to do so or to say the words with meticulous care, run the risk of creating a complete disgust for the rosary in their hearts, and abandoning it altogether. If one has loyally meditated on the mysteries for a certain time, and then finds he can no longer do so effectively, in an intellectual way, this may well be because the time has come to taste the real fruits of the rosary devotion. If one has not been careless about the prayer, if one had a growing love of Our Lady and Jesus, a growing need for their presence, united with a kind of dissatisfaction with too much thinking and talking, but a kind of need to be saying the prayers quietly and rhythmically in a solitary and peaceful atmosphere, then one is ready to taste the fruits of the rosary. *These fruits are communicated to us in obscurity and love.* We must not expect to see clearly what we are getting; we must rather desire simply to give our hearts in a simple and uncomplicated way to the contemplation of the mysteries. We are *content with the bare simplicity of the rosary*, content with the quiet sequence of *Aves*, content *with the bare presence of the mysteries*, aware too of a secret and hidden spring of love welling up in our hearts. At such a time, *we are truly and perfectly united to Mary in these mysteries, and we receive obscurely, in the mystery of faith, the fruit of her merits and love.* We receive in our hearts an increase of virtue and charity, and we are more closely united to Jesus in a way we cannot understand. Of course we also gain abundant graces for souls and for the whole Church of God, as well as for ourselves.

Meditation on the Mysteries: before we reach this stage of simplicity, or when we withdraw from it for some reason or other, we need to be aware of the *character of our meditation on the mysteries*. We should never feel it beneath us to return to simple and formal meditation when we have to. This too will always be quite simple. It will consist first of all in *seeing* in a very simple and general way the mystery that takes place, with the *eyes of the imagination*. It will consist in seeing, with the *eyes of the heart*, the virtues and dispositions of Mary and of Jesus in the mystery before us. It will consist above all in a *firm faith* in the dogma

---

406. "The end of the contemplative life has to be in the affections. . . . The ultimate perfection of the contemplative life is this, that the divine truth be not only seen but loved" (St. Thomas Aquinas, *Opera Omnia*, 3:605).

revealed there: in general, the joyful mysteries deal with the dogma of the Incarnation; the sorrowful ones with the mystery of the Redemption; the glorious mysteries with the dogma of eternal life, the application of the fruits of the Cross, our life and vocation to glory in Jesus Christ. When we *see*, in this simple fashion, the content of the mysteries, then we will *go out to Mary and Jesus* with the desire of love and reverence, seeking spiritual communion with them in this mystery. In the mysteries of the rosary Mary "comes to us" mystically and affectively, calling us to come forth and be united to the Incarnate Word in the darkness of faith and the sweetness of obscure love. *Ecce Sponsus venit, exite obviam ei.*[407] How do we "go forth" to meet the grace of God that is offered to us with the "coming" of Our Lady in the mysteries of the rosary? In general, we can say it is above all a matter of uniting ourselves to her experience of joy, sorrow and glory, in each one of the mysteries. Each one of the joyful mysteries represents to us, in a simple and general way, an aspect of joy, a "kind of joy" that Mary experienced in the mystery of the Incarnation. Our meditation of each mystery should not be a mere dry consideration of the fact. We should "go out"—leave our own present disposition, whatever it may be, our occupation with natural things, our preoccupation with things and persons around us, and "enter in" to the *particular mode of joy* which Mary brings us in each mystery. For instance, in the Annunciation, there is a special kind of joy from the fact that Mary is chosen from among all women to be the Mother of God. She is the one who is full of grace, by the ineffable election of the Triune God, and {is} prepared to clothe the humanity of the Word with her pure flesh. She it is too who replies, with infinitely pure joy, "Be it done unto me according to Thy word."[408] In the Visitation, there is another kind of joy, another aspect of the joy of the Incarnation—the fact that human hearts can be united in a specially pure charity in the Mystery of Christ. When Mary greeted Elizabeth, they were able to share, in advance, the joy of communicating and receiving the news of salvation, the Gospel of Jesus Christ. In meditating on this mystery we taste the joy of Mary at the fact that the presence of the Savior is made known to another through her for the first time, and as a result unites her in a special and indissoluble union of charity with Elizabeth and John. In the Nativity, we share the joy of Christmas, the joy of Mary that the Divine Child is brought into the world and manifested to the

---

407. "Behold the Bridegroom comes; go out to meet Him" (Matt 25:6).
408. Luke 1:38.

shepherds, the special joy that the Light of God shines forth in the hearts of all who love this Divine Infant, for this mystery is a mystery of light in darkness. Again, {there is} another modality of joy (mixed with sorrow), when Simeon takes the Child into his arms, and praises God for the fulfillment of all His promises to Israel, and the coming of a Savior to the Gentiles. Mary rejoiced then in the salvation of the whole world by the Cross, and united herself with all the prophets and patriarchs, all the saints of the Old Law rejoicing in Simeon—rejoicing too that the Old Law is now fulfilled and transfigured in Christ. Finally, {there is} the special joy (after sorrow) of finding Jesus with the doctors in the temple, a special sorrowful joy of Mary, in her anticipated sacrifice of the pleasure of an intimate life alone with Jesus, in order that the world may receive His word and His presence. Throughout the sorrowful mysteries too, we see special aspects of Mary's sorrow and suffering of soul as co-redeemer of the human race. In the Agony of the Garden, we share her understanding of the great weight of sorrow that descended upon Jesus as He laid aside His divine power to take on Himself all the weakness and misery and sin of the whole human race, with all the mental and moral suffering which these bring with them. In the scourging we feel with her the wanton brutality of sensual men, as it poured itself out against the Son of God. In the crowning with thorns, it is the refined barbarity of human pride; in the carrying of the Cross, the relentless, implacable hatred of good which is the essence of sin, and the infinite meekness and patience of God's love, bearing this for those who persecute and reject Him. As Jesus dies on the Cross we unite ourselves with the utter fullness of sorrow and sacrifice, the total consummation of Mary's sacrifice with that of Jesus, and we remember that this is the moment when she receives us as her sons. Finally, as Jesus is taken down from the Cross and laid in the arms of His Virgin Mother, we enter into perhaps what is the most inexplicable of all the mysteries, the silence, the "sabbath" that followed the crucifixion; the silence and darkness of Mary's heart when the Word of God is silent in death and the Light of the world has been extinguished. The glorious mysteries then bring us different modes of glory—something much more than joy: Mary's experience of the new life, the new creation initiated by the Resurrection; her rejoicing with Jesus in His Ascension; her immense joy with the coming of the Holy Ghost, and finally her own Assumption and Coronation in heaven.

Holy Rosary (II): *"Fecit mihi magna qui potens est."*[409]

The Rosary and the Magnificat: in both we see the résumé of the entire spiritual life of Mary—that great mystery of God's mercy. In her God showed how much He willed to pour forth His mercies upon His creatures. Also He shows the *way* in which He wills to have mercy. He desires *to transform* and elevate our nothingness. {This is} the great work of our vocation.

a) *Respexit humilitatem:*[410] He takes notice of our nothingness. We have no claim on His attention. (Contrast the Jews—*Isaias: "quare jejunavimus et non aspexisti?"*[411])

b) *Fecit mihi magna qui potens est:* the power and the glory are His, never the creature's. Yet all generations bless *Mary* for God's work in her—not just bless God but the creature whom He has blessed.

c) *Dispersit potentes . . . exaltavit humiles:*[412] He confounds every form of pride, and mercifully lifts up and consoles the humble; He feeds the hungry.

In all the mysteries of the rosary we see God's mercy and Mary's cooperation. Mary {is} present to us in these mysteries with *her* dispositions, bringing Jesus to our hearts to help us carry out the *great work* of our vocation. We come here *to be changed.* In all these mysteries we see the special heroism that is required for perfect docility to grace, and perfect submission to God's will. Works of our own choice (sometimes willed by God) {are} easy—our hearts are spontaneously in them. But when we must put aside our own lights and travel in complete dependence on another, it is very difficult. We are not changed by works of our own choice. God asks us to surrender to Him the running of our lives. Apply {this} to our own life: giving up our own way in prayer to follow {the} liturgy; giving up our own way in reading to read Scripture; giving up our own way in work to do humble tasks; giving up our own way in {the} spiritual life to follow {the} common spirituality. Yet in doing all this we must retain spontaneity and sincerity and *grow* in the liberty and joy that come from God. "In order to go to that which thou knowest not, thou must

---

409. "He Who is mighty has done great things for me" (Luke 1:49).

410. "He has looked upon my lowliness" (Luke 1:48).

411. "Why have we fasted and You have not taken notice?" (Isa 58:3).

412. "He has scattered the proud . . . lifted up the lowly" (Luke 1:51, 52).

travel by a way that thou knowest not" (St. John of the Cross[413]). This was Mary's way—in *joys* ({the} joyful mysteries {as} Mary's novitiate), *sorrows, glories.*

THE ANGELS (Notes for {the} Feast of St. Michael[414] and for {the} Feast of the Guardian Angels[415])

1. *Theology*: the universe is a united whole, integrated, ordered. From lowest material being to highest spiritual being, all creation is united in a hierarchical order, the highest spirits being closest to God, and the higher beings being used by Him as instruments through which He acts upon the lower. This is the order of *nature*. In the realm of *grace*— that is, of charity—angels are united to men by warm fraternal charity, and they act towards us with the perfect charity that springs from their face-to-face vision of God. They love us, in some degree, with God's own love for us. They help us with all their power to attain to blessedness with them, in the Father's house. They love us *in God*, and desire ardently that His will be done in us and that we attain blessedness in Him. The angels are therefore closely concerned in the mystery of divine Providence; they are the instruments of His Providence in our lives. They not only make His will manifest to us, they bring us grace to see it and carry it out; they remove obstacles; they protect us against error; they anticipate difficulties which we cannot see; they produce favorable situations for us to act out of charity. Good inspirations come through our angel. He is the instrument of the Holy Spirit in our regard. These truths are reflected in the collects of the two feasts: (1) O God, Who *in a wonderful order hast established the ministry of angels and of men*, mercifully grant that even as Thy holy angels ever stand before Thee to serve Thee in heaven, so at all times our lives may be protected by them on earth (Feast of St. Michael).[416] In this prayer {the} emphasis {is} on the integrated unity of spirits and rational beings, cooperating in doing God's will. (2) O God, Who in Thine ineffable Providence hast deigned to send Thy holy angels to watch over us,

---

413. *The Ascent of Mount Carmel*, I.xiv.11 (Peers, ed. and trans., *Complete Works of Saint John of the Cross*, 1:63, which reads: "In order to arrive at that . . . thou must go by . . .").

414. September 29.

415. October 2.

416. "*Deus, qui miro ordine Angelorum ministeria, hominumque dispensas: concede propitius; ut, a quibus tibi ministrantibus in coelo semper assistitur, ab his in terra vita nostra muniatur*" (*Missale Romanum*, 745; *Missale Cisterciense*, 528; *Breviarium Cisterciense, Autumnalis*, 346, 361–62).

grant that we who pray to Thee may always *be defended by their protecting power and may share in their company forever.*[417] The existence of angels is *de Fide*, for the Vatican Council teaches that they were created out of nothing together with the material world.[418] It is also *de Fide* that there are evil angels who fell through their own fault. It is also *de Fide* that some good angels are deputed for the protection of men. Every theologian holds that every individual of the elect has a guardian angel; it is also certain that every one of the faithful has a guardian angel. It is commonly held that every human being has one. Other matters about angels are not *de Fide*, but rather common doctrine: for instance, the hierarchies, the "illuminations," etc.

The Guardian Angels: "Man being an essential part of the world, willed and loved for himself, each one of us is the object of a particular providence; it is therefore understandable that God should use, in our case, special and more efficacious means, all the more so since we have been weakened by original sin" (*Initiation Théologique*).[419] Baptism gives each Christian soul a special right to this protection. But all men are potentially members of Christ, and it is fitting that all should be protected by their angels. Angels can act directly on matter, indirectly on our souls, through imagination, etc. They produce good thoughts secretly, without our guessing. They also produce favorable dispositions in our souls so that the will can work better. They act on persons and things

---

417. "*Deus, qui ineffabili providentia sanctos Angelos tuos ad nostram custodiam mittere dignaris: largire supplicibus tuis, et eorum semper protectione defendi, et aeterna societate gaudere*" (*Missale Romanum*, 747; *Missale Cisterciense*, 532; *Breviarium Cisterciense, Autumnalis*, 380, 390).

418. "*Hic solus verus Deus . . . 'simul ab initio temporis utramque de nihilo condidit creaturam, spiritualem et corporalem, angelicam videlicet et mundanam ac deinde humanam . . .*'" (Vatican Council I, *Constitutio Dogmatica de Fide Catholica*, c. 1: *De Deo Rerum Omnium Creatore*) (Denzinger and Bannwart, eds., *Enchiridion Symbolorum*, 473–74 [#1783]); the quoted words are originally from the opening chapter ("*De Fide Catholica*") of the decree *De Trinitate, Sacramentis, Missione Canonica etc.* of the Fourth Lateran Council (1215) (see Denzinger and Bannwart, eds., *Enchiridion Symbolorum*, 189 [#428]).

419. "*Partie essentielle du monde, voulu et aimé pour lui-même, chacun de nous se trouve l'objet d'une 'providence' particulière; on comprend alors que Dieu emploie en notre faveur des moyens spéciaux d'autant plus nécessaires et efficaces que nous sommes plus affaiblis par le péché originel*" (Paul Benoist d'Azy, OSB, "Les Anges dans le Gouvernement Divin," in Laurentin, *Initiation Théologique*, 2:462).

around us (e.g. Père Lamy and the motorcycle[420]). ({See the} *Raccolta*:[421] n.b. {a} novena to {one's} guardian angel {can be made at} any time {and receives} five years {indulgence}—one a day {and a} plenary {indulgence} on completion).

Why is the Eucharist called *Bread of Angels*? (a) Do they receive sacramentally? no; (b) but the light of the Word, the Splendor of the Father, is their "food" and their sustenance; they are fed spiritually by their contemplation of Him; their actions proceed from their close union with Him; (c) we should spiritually eat the flesh of the Incarnate Word, fed not by contemplation of our own operations, but going out entirely to Him, focusing our minds on Him, not on ourselves.

St. Bernard on the Guardian Angels (second nocturn, Feast of the Guardian Angels:[422] from *Sermo 12 on Ps. 90*[423]) St. Bernard is filled with admiration at the immense condescension and love of God towards us, to appoint such magnificent beings as His angels to watch over our lowliness, sublime and blessed beings, closer to Him than any other. And we? nothingness and misery. The fact that these great spirits are our loving friends should make us confident, reverent, devout: *Reverentiam pro praesentia / devotionem pro benevolentia / fiduciam pro custodia.*[424] The *presence of our angels* should keep us from all unseemly thought and action (cf. St. Benedict, first degree of humility[425]—{the} presence of God and presence of the angels are linked up together in devotion). We should have a tender and confident love for those who are to be our companions in glory, especially since their kindness and devotion to us will help us get there. We should have unbounded confidence in these "big brothers"

---

420. The reference is to Père Jean Edouard Lamy (1853–1931), founder of the Congregation of the Servants of Jesus and Mary, who reportedly conversed with his guardian angel and was saved by the Archangel Gabriel from being run over (see Biver, *Père Lamy*, 153–54, which refers to a bicycle rather than to a motorcycle).

421. *Raccolta*, 343–44 (#453).

422. *Breviarium Cisterciense, Autumnalis*, 385–87.

423. Migne, *PL* 183, cols. 231B–235D.

424. "reverence for their presence, devotion for their benevolence, confidence for their guardianship" (sixth lesson) (*Breviarium Cisterciense, Autumnalis*, 386).

425. "*aestimet se homo de caelis a Deo respici omni hora, et facta sua omni loco ab aspectu Divinitatis videri, et ab angelis omni hora renuntiari*" ("one should think of himself as observed by God from heaven at every hour, and his actions seen by the gaze of the Divinity in every place, and reported by the angels at every hour") (*Rule*, c. 7) (McCann, ed. and trans., *Rule of St. Benedict*, 38).

who are so full of truth and power, and we should call upon them without hesitation, incessantly.

Points from the liturgy:

a) First vespers, St. Michael: Michael, *"quis ut Deus"*[426]—the antiphons of vespers[427] present us with the apocalyptic battle between the angels of God and the powers of evil. The strength of the angels lies in their vision and praise of God, their total dedication to His truth and holiness. Michael and the evil one fight together while thousand upon thousand of the heavenly host cry, "Glory to God."[428] (Note the progression in the antiphons—{the} gradual change of focus so as to bring our attention more and more on to the praising multitudes of spirits.) {In} *the hymn,*[429] we join exultantly in the chorus of the angels before the throne of the Incarnate Word, the *Splendor Patris,* and we beg Him, by their help, to bring us back to paradise (note the beauty of the melody). One of the themes of the feast is the union of the liturgy of earth with the liturgy of heaven: *"In conspectu angelorum psallam tibi"*;[430] *"Votis, voce psallimus"*:[431] sing with joy in our hearts.

b) First vespers, Guardian Angels {has} very simple antiphons,[432] two on the angels themselves—that they are appointed to be our guardians, and that they always see the face of the Father in heaven; and two others, exclamations of praise and joy: *"Laudate Deum omnes angeli ejus!"*[433] The capitulum (from Exodus[434]) applies {the} text to {the} guardian angels who will lead us into the place prepared for us by God if we listen to them.

---

426. "Who is like God?" (the meaning of the name Michael).

427. *Breviarium Cisterciense, Autumnalis,* 345.

428. *"Dignus es Domine, accipere gloriam"* ("You are worthy, Lord, to receive glory") (third antiphon) (*Breviarium Cisterciense, Autumnalis,* 345).

429. *"Tibi, Christe, splendor Patris"* ("To You, Christ, Splendor of the Father") (*Breviarium Cisterciense, Autumnalis,* 345).

430. "In the sight of the angels I will sing to You" (vespers hymn, versicle; responsory, third lesson) (*Breviarium Cisterciense, Autumnalis,* 345, 351).

431. "In prayer we raise our voices in song" (vespers hymn, l. 4) (*Breviarium Cisterciense, Autumnalis,* 345).

432. *Breviarium Cisterciense, Autumnalis,* 379.

433. "Praise God, all His angels" (fourth antiphon, vespers) (*Breviarium Cisterciense, Autumnalis,* 379).

434. Exod 23:20–21 (*Breviarium Cisterciense, Autumnalis,* 379).

c) Vigils of the two feasts: {for} *St. Michael*,[435] the antiphons and responsories are apocalyptic, dramatic, jubilant—the battle of Michael with Satan, the joy of the angels in heaven, the splendor of their worship of God, the power and holiness of their prayer, in which we are called to join; they offer our prayers to the Father. Clouds of incense {are} rising up before the golden altar, amid the jubilant chants of the heavenly spirits! {In the} second nocturn,[436] St. Gregory the Great explains the names and functions of the great archangels. {For the} *Guardian Angels*,[437] {the} antiphons and responsories {are} from {the} prophets, {the} Psalms, {and} especially *Tobias*, {which is} most appropriate. The tone of the first feast is more grandiose and dramatic, that of the second, more intimate and gentle.

More about the Angels:

1. *The angel appearing to Daniel*: sometimes the angels appeared in human form in the Old Testament, and were not recognized, as {with} Raphael in Tobias. At other times they appear in a magnificent vision, as in Daniel 7 and 10 (first nocturn: Feast of St. Michael;[438] read Daniel 7:9–18[439]). Daniel 7:9 {presents} the vision of the Ancient of Days {ac-

---

435. *Breviarium Cisterciense, Autumnalis*, 347–60.

436. *Homilia 34 in Evangelium* (*Breviarium Cisterciense, Autumnalis*, 357–58).

437. *Breviarium Cisterciense, Autumnalis*, 381–89.

438. Dan 7:9–10, 10:4–6, 9–14 (*Breviarium Cisterciense, Autumnalis*, 350–51).

439. "I beheld till thrones were placed, and the Ancient of days sat: his garment was white as snow, and the hair of his head like clean wool: his throne like flames of fire: the wheels of it like a burning fire. A swift stream of fire issued forth from before him: thousands of thousands ministered to him, and ten thousand times a hundred thousand stood before him: the judgment sat, and the books were opened. I beheld because of the voice of the great words which that horn spoke: and I saw that the beast was slain, and the body thereof was destroyed, and given to the fire to be burnt: And that the power of the other beasts was taken away: and that times of life were appointed them for a time, and a time. I beheld therefore in the vision of the night, and lo, one like the son of man came with the clouds of heaven, and he came even to the Ancient of days: and they presented him before him. And he gave him power, and glory, and a kingdom: and all peoples, tribes and tongues shall serve him: his power is an everlasting power that shall not be taken away: and his kingdom that shall not be destroyed. My spirit trembled, I Daniel was affrighted at these things, and the visions of my head troubled me. I went near to one of them that stood by, and asked the truth of him concerning all these things, and he told me the interpretation of the words, and instructed me: These four great beasts are four kingdoms, which shall arise out of the earth. But the saints of the most high God shall take the kingdom: and they shall possess the kingdom for ever and ever."

companied by} the thousands of angels {and} the Son of Man. Daniel {is} crushed by the vision {and} asks its explanation, and one of the angels tells him what it means. It is most appropriate that the angel should do this: they contemplate the end of God's plan, for it is for this that they work; they see clearly what they are doing, and what they are working for—we do not. However, our spirituality will be more angelic in proportion as it is more eschatological, and we will understand the last things in proportion as we are pure and detached from the present life. Read Zachary 1:8–17:[440] again, an angel has an all-important function in the vision of the prophet. It is he who speaks within the prophet; again he interprets an eschatological vision—the Lord's mercy upon Jerusalem. Note {the} close connection of angels with the *Church*: each church and altar has an angel guardian; churches are the place of man's meeting with angels. Read Daniel 8:15–19:[441] Gabriel explains an eschatological vision to Daniel. Read Daniel 9:21–27:[442] Daniel in prayer is visited by Gabriel—

440. "I saw by night, and behold a man riding upon a red horse, and he stood among the myrtle trees, that were in the bottom: and behind him were horses, red, speckled, and white. And I said: What are these, my Lord? and the angel that spoke in me, said to me: I will shew thee what these are: And the man that stood among the myrtle trees answered, and said: These are they, whom the Lord hath sent to walk through the earth. And they answered the angel of the Lord, that stood among the myrtle trees, and said: We have walked through the earth, and behold all the earth is inhabited, and is at rest. And the angel of the Lord answered, and said: O Lord of hosts, how long wilt thou not have mercy on Jerusalem, and on the cities of Juda, with which thou hast been angry? this is now the seventieth year. And the Lord answered the angel, that spoke in me, good words, comfortable words. And the angel that spoke in me, said to me: Cry thou, saying: Thus saith the Lord of hosts: I am zealous for Jerusalem, and Sion with a great zeal. And I am angry with a great anger with the wealthy nations: for I was angry a little, but they helped forward the evil. Therefore thus saith the Lord: I will return to Jerusalem in mercies: my house shall be built in it, saith the Lord of hosts: and the building line shall be stretched forth upon Jerusalem. Cry yet, saying: Thus saith the Lord of hosts: My cities shall yet flow with good things: and the Lord will yet comfort Sion, and he will yet choose Jerusalem."

441. "And it came to pass when I Daniel saw the vision, and sought the meaning, that behold there stood before me as it were the appearance of a man. And I heard the voice of a man between Ulai: and he called, and said: Gabriel, make this man to understand the vision. And he came and stood near where I stood: and when he was come, I fell on my face trembling, and he said to me: Understand, O son of man, for in the time of the end the vision shall be fulfilled. And when he spoke to me I fell flat on the ground: and he touched me, and set me upright, And he said to me: I will shew thee what things are to come to pass in the end of the malediction: for the time hath its end."

442. "As I was yet speaking in prayer, behold the man Gabriel, whom I had seen in the vision at the beginning, flying swiftly touched me at the time of the evening

a tremendously important eschatological and messianic prophecy. The angels are centered entirely on the mystery of the Incarnate Word, in which they see the great revelation and manifestation of God, to them as well as to ourselves (cf. Ephesians[443]). Read Daniel 10:9–21:[444] again

sacrifice. And he instructed me, and spoke to me, and said: O Daniel, I am now come forth to teach thee, and that thou mightest understand. From the beginning of thy prayers the word came forth: and I am come to shew it to thee, because thou art a man of desires: therefore do thou mark the word, and understand the vision. Seventy weeks are shortened upon thy people, and upon thy holy city, that transgression may be finished, and sin may have an end, and iniquity may be abolished: and everlasting justice may be brought: and vision and prophecy may be fulfilled; and the saint of saints may be anointed. Know thou therefore, and take notice: that from the going forth of the word, to build up Jerusalem again, unto Christ the prince, there shall be seven weeks, and sixty-two weeks: and the street shall be built again, and the walls in straitness of times. And after sixty-two weeks Christ shall be slain: and the people that shall deny him shall not be his. And a people with their leader that shall come, shall destroy the city and the sanctuary: and the end thereof shall be waste, and after the end of the war the appointed desolation. And he shall confirm the covenant with many, in one week: and in the half of the week the victim and the sacrifice shall fall: and there shall be in the temple the abomination of desolation: and the desolation shall continue even to the consummation, and to the end."

443. See Eph 1:9–10, 21: "the mystery of his will . . . In the dispensation of the fullness of times, to re-establish all things in Christ, that are in heaven and on earth, in him . . . Above all principality, and power, and virtue, and dominion, and every name that is named, not only in this world, but also in that which is to come."

444. "And we have not hearkened to the voice of the Lord our God, to walk in his law, which he set before us by his servants the prophets. And all Israel have transgressed thy law, and have turned away from hearing thy voice, and the malediction, and the curse, which is written in the book of Moses the servant of God, is fallen upon us, because we have sinned against him. And he hath confirmed his words which he spoke against us, and against our princes that judged us, that he would bring in upon us a great evil, such as never was under all the heaven, according to that which hath been done in Jerusalem. As it is written in the law of Moses, all this evil is come upon us: and we entreated not thy face, O Lord our God, that we might turn from our iniquities, and think on thy truth. And the Lord hath watched upon the evil, and hath brought it upon us: the Lord our God is just in all his works which he hath done: for we have not hearkened to his voice. And now, O Lord our God, who hast brought forth thy people out of the land of Egypt with a strong hand, and hast made thee a name as at this day: we have sinned, we have committed iniquity, O Lord, against all thy justice: let thy wrath and thy indignation be turned away, I beseech thee, from thy city Jerusalem, and from thy holy mountain. For by reason of our sins, and the iniquities of our fathers, Jerusalem, and thy people are a reproach to all that are round about us. Now therefore, O our God, hear the supplication of thy servant, and his prayers: and shew thy face upon thy sanctuary which is desolate, for thy own sake. Incline, O my God, thy ear, and hear: open thy eyes, and see our desolation, and the city upon which thy name is called: for it is not for our justifications that we present our prayers

the same thing. Note the importance of (1) Daniel's prayer; (2) Daniel {as a} man of *desires*—this brings him close to the angels ({a} *desire* to know the *will of God* for His people); (3) compunction and humility, self-abasement; (4) {he} receives comfort from the angel in proportion to his weakness and abasement.

2. *The Angel in Tobias*: read *Tobias* 3:[445] Raphael {is} sent to heal the affliction of two holy people distant from each other (read especially

---

before thy face, but for the multitude of thy tender mercies. O Lord, hear: O Lord, be appeased: hearken and do: delay not for thy own sake, O my God: because thy name is invoked upon thy city, and upon thy people. Now while I was yet speaking, and praying, and confessing my sins, and the sins of my people of Israel, and presenting my supplications in the sight of my God, for the holy mountain of my God: As I was yet speaking in prayer, behold the man Gabriel, whom I had seen in the vision at the beginning, flying swiftly touched me at the time of the evening sacrifice."

445. "Then Tobias sighed, and began to pray with tears, Saying: Thou art just, O Lord, and all thy judgments are just, and all thy ways mercy, and truth, and judgment: And now, O Lord, think of me, and take not revenge of my sins, neither remember my offenses, nor those of my parents. For we have not obeyed thy commandments, therefore are we delivered to spoil and to captivity, and death, and are made a fable, and a reproach to all nations, amongst which thou hast scattered us. And now, O Lord, great are thy judgments, because we have not done according to thy precepts, and have not walked sincerely before thee: And now, O Lord, do with me according to thy will, and command my spirit to be received in peace: for it is better for me to die, than to live. Now it happened on the same day, that Sara daughter of Raguel, in Rages a city of the Medes, received a reproach from one of her father's servant maids, Because she had been given to seven husbands, and a devil named Asmodeus had killed them, at their first going in unto her. So when she reproved the maid for her fault, she answered her, saying: May we never see son, or daughter of thee upon the earth, thou murderer of thy husbands. Wilt thou kill me also, as thou hast already killed seven husbands? At these words she went into an upper chamber of her house: and for three days and three nights did neither eat nor drink: But continuing in prayer with tears besought God, that he would deliver her from this reproach. And it came to pass on the third day, when she was making an end of her prayer, blessing the Lord, She said: Blessed is thy name, O God of our fathers: who when thou hast been angry, wilt shew mercy, and in the time of tribulation forgivest the sins of them that call upon thee. To thee, O Lord, I turn my face, to thee I direct my eyes. I beg, O Lord, that thou loose me from the bond of this reproach, or else take me away from the earth. Thou knowest, O Lord, that I never coveted a husband, and have kept my soul clean from all lust. Never have I joined myself with them that play: neither have I made myself partaker with them that walk in lightness. But a husband I consented to take, with thy fear, not with my lust. And neither I was unworthy of them, or they perhaps were not worthy of me: because perhaps thou hast kept me for another man. For thy counsel is not in man's power. But this every one is sure of that worshippeth thee, that his life, if it be under trial, shall be crowned: and if it be under tribulation, it shall be delivered: and if it be under correction, it shall be allowed to come to thy mercy. For thou art not delighted in our being lost: because after a storm thou makest a calm, and after tears and weeping thou

3:21–25). *Note*: old Tobias prayed to die and thought that his prayer was answered, whereas Raphael was sent to heal him. ({Add a} brief comment on {the} rest of Tobias.)

Monastic Peace—Pax Huic Domui[446] (October 18):
Feast of St. Luke (1956)

1. From the gospel of the feast[447] (common of evangelists): it is St. Luke himself who records how, in the sending of the 72 disciples, the Lord said, "Whenever you enter a dwelling, say first of all, Peace to this house, and if there are in the house sons of peace, your peace will remain with them, otherwise it will return to you" (*Luke* 10:5 etc.).

When Jesus was born, He came into the world as the Prince of Peace. Then the angel sang, "Peace on earth to men of good will."[448] St. Paul says that Jesus Himself is our peace: *ipse est pax nostra.*[449] Whenever Jesus appeared to the apostles after His resurrection, He calmed their spirits by saying first of all, "Peace be to you."[450] All this teaches us that Jesus, the Prince of Peace, comes to set our hearts at rest, and in order to prepare His coming He sends peace ahead of Him, for the work He wills to do must be done in peace. However, He also said that He came not to bring peace but the sword,[451] and the meaning of this is that He also allows our souls to be troubled and upset precisely in order that we may learn to desire and seek peace. For God has commanded us to "seek after peace and pursue it" (*Psalm* 33:15). Thus we are faced with a paradox: God wills us to have peace, yet He allows our peace to be disturbed. This is in order to lead us to a higher and more spiritual peace, which we cannot get if we avoid struggle.

2. *Pax*: the Benedictine motto. St. Benedict knows that the Lord wishes to come and dwell in the soul of the monk. The monk must

---

pourest in joyfulness. Be thy name, O God of Israel, blessed for ever. At that time the prayers of them both were heard in the sight of the glory of the most high God: And the holy angel of the Lord, Raphael was sent to heal them both, whose prayers at one time were rehearsed in the sight of the Lord."

446. "Peace to this house" (Luke 10:5).

447. Luke 10:1–9 (*Missale Romanum*, 764; *Missale Cisterciense*, 542).

448. Luke 2:14.

449. "He Himself is our Peace" (Eph 2:14).

450. Luke 24:36; John 20:19, 21, 26.

451. Matt 10:34.

therefore be a *"filius pacis"*[452] in order that the peace brought by the apostle (the spiritual father) may rest upon him. All our life consists in striving to be sons of peace. This is *our share*, our principal part in the work of sanctification which is effected by our free will under the guidance of grace. If we do with our will the works of peace, if we dispose ourselves to live in peace and detachment, then God will do the rest. What are the works of peace? especially doing God's will when it goes against the grain; especially giving in to a brother when it costs {a} sacrifice. However, St. Benedict does all he can to see that the monk lives in peace and not in agitation. The monastery above all is a house of peace. St. Benedict has disposed everything in it to preserve peace. The *Rule* is a rule of peace: for instance, everything must be done at the proper times, *ut nemo perturbetur neque contristetur in domo Dei.*[453] (This is the principal purpose of regularity, according to St. Benedict.) The degrees of humility are in fact also degrees of interior peace that lead to perfect tranquillity and order in the monk's soul. A monk from another monastery may only be received if he is quiet and detached and does not "disturb the monastery by his excessive demands"[454] (c. {61}). Note that the great disturbers of our peace are precisely our own unformulated *demands*. Benedict urges his monks always to seek peace (Prologue[455]), and to be sincere in making peace with one another, indeed, never to let the sun set on conflict between them[456] (c. 4). It is for the sake of peace and charity that all is in the hands of the abbot alone, and the prior is not a second abbot[457] (c. 65). In the matter of exceptions (which are inevitable), those who need less must thank God for it; those who need more must be humble about it, *"et ita omnia membra erunt in pace."*[458] In fact, the great sins of the monk, in the eyes of St. Benedict, are those which disturb this monastic peace, and destroy the conditions so important for the sanctification of souls—sins

452. "son of peace" (Luke 10:6).

453. "so that no one might be disturbed or saddened in the house of God" (c. 31) (McCann, ed. and trans., *Rule of St. Benedict*, 82).

454. "*non . . . superfluitate sua perturbat monasterium*" (McCann, ed. and trans., *Rule of St. Benedict*, 138) (copy text reads: "62").

455. "*Inquire pacem*" (Ps 33[34]:15) (McCann, ed. and trans., *Rule of St. Benedict*, 8).

456. McCann, ed. and trans., *Rule of St. Benedict*, 30.

457. McCann, ed. and trans., *Rule of St. Benedict*, 148.

458. "and thus all members will be in peace" (c. 34) (McCann, ed. and trans., *Rule of St. Benedict*, 86).

of pride and disobedience, which cause factions and unrest; sins of murmuring and criticism, harsh treatment of brothers, impatience, unruly zeal, the refusal to humble ourselves and submit to our brothers and superiors (cf. chapters 72, 71, 70, 69, 64, 65, etc.). Note especially the danger of *suspiciousness* and sensitivity.

3. Read some beautiful texts from the opening pages of Van Houtryve's *Benedictine Peace*: (a) the monastic life {is} preeminently a life of peace (p. ix); (b) the monk must radiate peace (*idem*); (c) St. Benedict {is a} man of *peace*. We must live in the same atmosphere as our founder; (d) quotes from the Fathers (p. x);[459] (e) {an} interesting quote from Louis de Blois[460] (p. xi) is almost a paraphrase from the classic passage in Cassian's first conference on purity of heart;[461] in fact, where Cassian says "*puritas cordis*," St. Benedict might very well put "*pax*," for it comes to the same thing. If we are attached to the *means* of perfection, and make of them ends in themselves, we cannot attain our end, charity, peace in union with God and our brethren.

4. The true secret of peace {is} *contentment with whatever the Lord has given us*, and this implies meekness, poverty of spirit, hunger and thirst for the Lord's will to be done (justice). Peace also implies a certain spirit of mourning; it is not always placid and serene; it is sometimes tinged with sorrow and suffering, because it *has to be paid for by effort and sacrifice*. But we must not confuse effort and agitation. Often when we say "effort," we think of restless and disturbed effort, efforts to do what

---

459. "The monastic institute, remarks the biographer of St. Maurus, demands *summa quies*, the most perfect peace. Life in a monastery, says, St. Anselm, is 'an existence full of peace and tranquility; it is the repose offered by the Lord to those who are engaged in His special service.' Newman tells us, 'There have been great Religious Orders since, whose atmosphere has been conflict, and who have thriven in smiting or in being smitten. It has been their high calling; it has been their particular meritorious service; but, as for the Benedictine, the very air he breathes is peace.'"

460. "You ought chiefly to endeavor to attain to this, that in the liberty and purity of heart—rejecting all self-love—you may always persevere, peaceable and without trouble before God. For this is acceptable to our Lord above all other exercises, be they ever so laborious and hard. Whatsoever, therefore shall hinder this liberty in you, although it be spiritual and seem very profitable, occasion so requiring, leave it, as much as obedience permits. Endeavor, I say, to repel all restlessness of heart, which chokes true peace, perfect trust in God and spiritual progress" (*A Mirror for Monks*, c. 3; Louis de Blois, or Blosius [1506–1566], abbot of the Benedictine monastery of Liessies in what is now Belgium, was a monastic reformer and prolific author on the spiritual life; his *Speculum Monachorum* was written in 1538).

461. Migne, *PL* 49, cols. 481C–524A, esp. cc. 5–10 (cols. 486B–496A).

is not willed by God, efforts to attain the impossible. Note the difference between seeking the *Absolute* and seeking the *impossible*. The truly supernatural person seeks the Absolute, God Himself, He Who IS, and he attains to Him through the medium of what is present and real here and now. To seek the Absolute is to rest content with the actual. The soul whose love of sanctity is based on human motives seeks not the actual, but an impossible ideal based on fantasy and illusions of the imagination.

5. Some Points from John de Bonilla:[462]

a) In order to have true peace, we must remember that our heart was created for love, and that *if we act out of love we can do anything*, but if we act without love we can do nothing, and all our effort ends in frustration.[463] This principle is very Cistercian. It is the foundation of our spirit; secondly, it is very practical.

b) Hence in order to seek peace we must not fix our eyes on a pleasant state which we hope to enjoy, but {decide} *to set our hearts to love* with the grace God has actually given us, and the rest will follow. Love means doing His Will because it pleases Him.[464]

c) In order to act in all things out of love, we have to place a guard upon our senses to make sure that passion and mere blind impulse do not sway us rather than the will of God. We must "have a care that our hearts never become sad or solicitous about anything."[465]

d) We must not be too anxious to plan and direct our own lives. We should rather keep impulse and initiative toned down: "Do not presume to sow; keep the field of your soul free and well-weeded and God will sow in good season."[466] This means abandoning all solicitude, even an inordinate care about our own

---

462. *Pax Animae* (attributed to St. Peter Alcantara, actually by John de Bonilla, OFM); Merton discusses this work in his unpublished conference "Pax Animae—The Treatise of John de Bonilla on *Interior Peace*."

463. *Pax Animae*, 11 (c. 1).

464. *Pax Animae*, 18 (c. 4).

465. *Pax Animae*, 15 (c. 3), which reads: "Have a care never to permit your heart to become sad, concerned, or solicitous for whatsoever happens."

466. *Pax Animae*, 23 (c. 6), which reads: "Do not you presume to till or sow, but keep the field of your soul free and well weeded, and let God sow it in His good season."

spiritual life. Faith and trust are more important than anxious striving.

e) Finally, most important of all, we must *accept trial*; we must embrace it cheerfully and with high motives of faith. Here alone is true peace.[467]

Feast of Saint Luke (II): "*Crucis mortificatio jugiter in corpore suo, pro tui nominis honore portavit.*"[468] {This is} a good description of {the} monastic vocation. But what precisely is the "*crucis mortificatio*"? Some eccentric saints have carried an actual, life-sized wooden cross around in their spare time. Does it mean physical suffering? {According to} monastic tradition (Cassian): "*omnes suas mortificare et crucifigere voluntates.*"[469] {It is the} death of our self-will. {We} die to {the} old man {and} live the new life in Christ. But {this is} not {the} death of all willing, {but} rather {the} liberation of our power to love by loving in union with Jesus. "Ask for nothing; refuse nothing."[470] Let Him decide. The cross is the staff by which the way is made easier, says St. John of the Cross.[471] *Pro tui nominis honore*: His name {is} Who He really is. Our sacrifice {is} a witness to Who God really is. He is *Mercy*; hence we renounce ourselves in order to let ourselves be saved. That is, we do not try to save ourselves. He is *Love*: we cannot give Him any love we have not received from Him; {we} open our hearts in loving faith to receive, and then to give back.

Saints Simon and Jude (October 28)

All through the liturgy of this feast runs the theme of the conflict between the Christian and the world, and the idea that even the religious spirit can be, in some cases, only a worldly spirit in disguise. What is the

467. *Pax Animae*, 25 ff. (c. 7).

468. "for the honor of Your name he carried on his body perpetually the mortification of the Cross" (collect) (*Missale Romanum*, 763; *Missale Cisterciense*, 541; *Breviarium Cisterciense, Autumnalis*, 408, which read: ". . . *mortificationem . . . in suo corpore, . . .*").

469. "To mortify and crucify all one's own desires" (*Conf.* 19.8) (Migne, *PL* 49, col. 1138B).

470. The motto of St. Francis de Sales; in a journal entry on March 14, 1949, Merton quotes these words, which he calls "St. Francis de Sales' principle," during his retreat in preparation for diaconate ordination (Merton, *Entering the Silence*, 289).

471. See *Ascent*, II.vii.7: "the Cross . . . is the staff whereby one may reach him, and whereby the road is greatly lightened and made easy" (Peers, ed. and trans., *Complete Works of Saint John of the Cross*, 1:90–91).

one sure test? love of Our Lord Jesus Christ, and sincere, total abandonment to His will and to His plan for our salvation.

1. Read John 14:16–24,[472] the pericope in which St. Jude asks why
the Lord will give His Spirit to some, but not to the world. "He that hath
My commandments and keepeth them, he it is that loveth Me."[473]

2. The gospel of the Mass (John 15:17–25):[474] instead of choosing
the above pericope, the Church has picked this one, which is much more
somber, and stresses the irreconcilable enmity between the world and
Christ. Those who love Christ must suffer persecution and be hated, like
Him, by the world. To hate Him is to hate the Father also. Our love *must
be tested*. We love when, in spite of all repugnance and sacrifice, we *really
accept* God's will in darkness and faith.

3. The Epistle of St. Jude (first nocturn[475]): Read 1–4:[476] heretics deny
"the *only Sovereign Ruler*, our Lord Jesus Christ" (cf. in the *Rule*: *Christo
vero Regi*[477]). We must, in the words of Jude, "contend earnestly for the

---

472. "And I will ask the Father, and he shall give you another Paraclete, that he may
abide with you for ever. The spirit of truth, whom the world cannot receive, because it
seeth him not, nor knoweth him: but you shall know him; because he shall abide with
you, and shall be in you. I will not leave you orphans, I will come to you. Yet a little
while: and the world seeth me no more. But you see me: because I live, and you shall
live. In that day you shall know, that I am in my Father, and you in me, and I in you. He
that hath my commandments, and keepeth them; he it is that loveth me. And he that
loveth me, shall be loved of my Father: and I will love him, and will manifest myself to
him. Judas saith to him, not the Iscariot: Lord, how is it, that thou wilt manifest thyself
to us, and not to the world? Jesus answered, and said to him: If any one love me, he will
keep my word, and my Father will love him, and we will come to him, and will make
our abode with him. He that loveth me not, keepeth not my words. And the word
which you have heard, is not mine; but the Father's who sent me."

473. John 14:21.

474. *Missale Romanum*, 775; *Missale Cisterciense*, 548.

475. Jude, vv. 1–13 (*Breviarium Cisterciense, Autumnalis*, 417–18).

476. "Jude, the servant of Jesus Christ, and brother of James: to them that are beloved in God the Father, and preserved in Jesus Christ, and called. Mercy unto you,
and peace, and charity be fulfilled. Dearly beloved, taking all care to write unto you
concerning your common salvation, I was under a necessity to write unto you: to
beseech you to contend earnestly for the faith once delivered to the saints. For certain men are secretly entered in, (who were written of long ago unto this judgment,)
ungodly men, turning the grace of our Lord God into riotousness, and denying the
only sovereign Ruler, and our Lord Jesus Christ" (first lesson) (*Breviarium Cisterciense,
Autumnalis*, 417).

477. "to Christ the true King" (*Rule*, Prologue) (McCann, ed. and trans., *Rule of
St. Benedict*, 6).

faith once delivered to the saints."[478] Our Christian faith is a sacred heritage, more precious than any others, given us to be preserved and handed on to others. Heretics in St. Jude's time, and since, corrupted Christianity with elements of pagan and natural mysticism, which savored of sensuality and independence (cf. {the} Sarabaites and Gyrovagues in St. Benedict[479]). {We must preserve} the *purity of our faith* {and} the *purity of our monastic tradition* {by} fidelity to our *Rule* and its spirit, especially fidelity to our sources. Read 12–16, 20–25,[480] for the vehemence and earnestness, and the special vividness, of St. Jude's language.

4. In the collect, *"proficiendo celebrare et celebrando proficere"*:[481] {note the} intimate connection between spiritual growth and participation in the liturgy; *"proficiendo celebrare"*: we come to each feast with deeper, more mature dispositions, having grown in love; *"celebrando proficere"*: celebrating the feast we gain graces which help us grow yet further.

---

478. Jude 3.

479. *Rule*, c. 1 (McCann, ed. and trans., *Rule of St. Benedict*, 14, 16).

480. "These are spots in their banquets, feasting together without fear, feeding themselves, clouds without water, which are carried about by winds, trees of the autumn, unfruitful, twice dead, plucked up by the roots, Raging waves of the sea, foaming out their own confusion; wandering stars, to whom the storm of darkness is reserved for ever. Now of these Enoch also, the seventh from Adam, prophesied, saying: Behold, the Lord cometh with thousands of his saints, To execute judgment upon all, and to reprove all the ungodly for all the works of their ungodliness, whereby they have done ungodly, and of all the hard things which ungodly sinners have spoken against God. These are murmurers, full of complaints, walking according to their own desires, and their mouth speaketh proud things, admiring persons for gain's sake . . . . But you, my beloved, building yourselves upon your most holy faith, praying in the Holy Ghost, Keep yourselves in the love of God, waiting for the mercy of our Lord Jesus Christ, unto life everlasting. And some indeed reprove, being judged: But others save, pulling them out of the fire. And on others have mercy, in fear, hating also the spotted garment which is carnal. Now to him who is able to preserve you without sin, and to present you spotless before the presence of his glory with exceeding joy, in the coming of our Lord Jesus Christ, To the only God our Saviour through Jesus Christ our Lord, be glory and magnificence, empire and power, before all ages, and now, and for all ages of ages. Amen."

481. "to celebrate by progressing and to progress by celebrating" (*Missale Romanum*, 774; *Missale Cisterciense*, 547; *Breviarium Cisterciense, Autumnalis*, 422).

VIGIL OF ALL SAINTS (October 31)

1. *Judicant sancti nationes:*[482] one of the main themes of the Feast of All Saints is brought out especially in the Vigil—the theme that God reigns in His saints. The Kingship of Christ was celebrated for centuries in this Vigil. A special feast had to be instituted only when clergy and faithful were no longer aware of this fact. *Regnabit Dominus Deus illorum in perpetuum.*[483] How do the saints judge the nations? Consider the theme of judgement in St. John. Before the Passion, Jesus says, "Now is the judgement of the world."[484] Jesus judged the world already by coming into it as light into darkness. He came into His own; His own received Him not.[485] By the very fact that they did not receive Him, they judged themselves. So the saints, who have come to Him Who is light, will judge the darkness by the fact that they are in the light.

2. *The Epistle:*[486] (1) *the Lamb enthroned*, the seven spirits, the power of His Love, going forth from His sacrifice to the whole earth; (2) *the opening of the book*—the final meaning of history is now revealed; the worship of Christ as He opens the book {is} worship of the wisdom and love of God: "Thou art worthy to take the Book and open the seals"[487]— the Word Incarnate alone can do this; "Thou hast redeemed us to God in Thy Blood . . . and hast made unto God a Kingdom and priests."[488] (3) So God reigns in His saints, and they in turn praise His wisdom and power, and offer adoration for ever and ever, singing the *new song*—no longer the liturgy of earth, but the liturgy of heaven (which nevertheless already has its echoes in our liturgy).

3. *Scuto bonae voluntatis tuae coronasti nos*[489] (offertory: *Cistercian Missal*): to do God's will is to be protected against every evil and to be in the hands of God (*Justorum animae in manu Dei sunt . . .* etc.[490]); and

---

482. "The saints judge the nations" (Wis 3:8) (introit: vigil) (*Missale Romanum*, 776; *Missale Cisterciense*, 548).

483. "The Lord their God will reign forever" (Wis 3:8).

484. John 12:31.

485. John 1:11.

486. Apoc [Rev] 5:6–12 (*Missale Romanum*, 776; *Missale Cisterciense*, 549).

487. Apoc [Rev] 5:9.

488. Apoc [Rev] 5:9, 10.

489. "You have crowned us with the shield of Your good will" (*Missale Cisterciense*, 549; the offertory in the Roman Rite is Ps 149:5–6 [*Missale Romanum*, 777]).

490. "The souls of the just are in the hands of God" (Wis 3:1) (offertory: feast) (*Missale Romanum*, 779; the offertory in the Cistercian Rite is Ps 67[68]:35–36 [*Missale Cisterciense*, 551]).

to belong to Him perfectly, to let Him reign in us, is our crown and our peace and our joy.

FEAST OF ALL SAINTS (November 1)

"*Mirabilis Deus in sanctis suis*":[491] as usual, {this is} a feast of *wonder*. One of the greatest joys of heaven will be to realize that God is wonderful *in us*, not only individually, but collectively. On this feast, the saints are more interested in us even than we are in them. They are anxious for us to join them that God may be all in all. They are anxious for us to take advantage of our opportunities on earth. {We reach} our collective sanctification as members of a Body. We are not isolated; we all form part of one merciful plan. The mercy of God for one is not unrelated to His mercy for all the others; our salvation goes along with the salvation of countless others. We are helping one another to get to heaven—or hindering one another from getting there.

The Beatitudes (gospel of the feast[492]) {are} a blueprint of true sanctity, {and} just the opposite of the images of sanctity we form for ourselves with the aid of human vanity. One of the greatest obstacles to true holiness is our deficient and too human idea of holiness, which is often quite inhuman. Plaster saints {present an image of} impossible perfection {and of} inertia, {of} death not life!! *Poverty* of spirit excludes these false and vain ideals, {and} prefers the ordinary, the unspectacular, the hidden; {it} does not want to be admired or remarked on {and} does not seek attention. *Meekness* {and} *mercy* {are} centered on the suffering of injury and injustice, the inevitable hurts and injuries that come in social living; {they show} the willingness to give in to others, and *really to forgive*. True forgiveness of true injuries implies real heroism. *Mourning* {and} *hunger and thirst for justice* {reveal that} the way to sanctity is not a way of pleasure and self-satisfaction. We are in exile. God's will (justice) is *not* done, even by us. {We experience} the sorrow of not being saints. The adequation of justice and mercy must be discovered—*bitter zeal*[493] is *not* hunger for justice, because it is unjust (cf. St. Bernard[494]). *Purity of Heart* {and}

---

491. "God, wondrous in His saints" (Ps 67[68]:36).

492. Matt 5:1–12 (*Missale Romanum*, 779; *Missale Cisterciense*, 551).

493. See *Rule*, c. 72: "*zelus amaritudinis malus*" (McCann, ed. and trans., *Rule of St. Benedict*, 158/159).

494. See *Sententiae* 16: "*Nihil enim commune habent murmur et pax, gratiarum actio et detractio, zelus amaritudinis et vox laudis*" ("Complaining and peace,

peace-making {entail} freedom from self and from images of self, radiating love and peace with all; {there is} no peace without sacrifice, without struggle. *God is constantly at work to make us saints.* The sorrow of those who *implicitly give up* trying {must be countered by} the solution: yes, we must give up our own false ideal, but submit to God's ways, which we cannot understand. A deficient ideal of sanctity can be the last refuge of self, and can do great harm in a community. {We should} stick to our objective Benedictine ideal, and to the Gospel.

ALL SAINTS: *the canticle of the third nocturn*[495] (common of martyrs)—everything in the office of All Saints can be summed up under two headings: a) the glory of the saints overflows in the perfect praise which they offer to God, seeing Him as He is, seeing His infinite holiness, and the infinite wisdom of His ways; and in praising Him they also pray that His work may be completed in us; (b) the light which the saints behold and praise is poured out upon us who remain *in agone certaminis*,[496] and by their prayers and example we come to realize how similar was their lot to ours on earth, and that their sanctity consisted in abandoning themselves to the hidden will of God, and passing through darkness and tribulation in order to come to Him. In doing this they fully allowed Him

---

thanksgiving and detraction, zeal of bitterness and the voice of praise have nothing in common") (Migne, *PL* 183, col. 752A). See also *Sermones in Cantica* 49.5, where Bernard emphasizes that genuine zeal must be guided by knowledge and tempered by discretion: "*Importabilis siquidem absque scientia est zelus. Ubi ergo vehemens aemulatio, ibi maxime discretio est necessaria, quae est ordinatio charitatis. Semper quidem zelus absque scientia minus efficax, minusque utilis invenitur; plerumque autem et perniciosus valde sentitur. Quo igitur zelus fervidior, ac vehementior spiritus, profusiorque charitas; eo vigilantiori opus scientia est, quae zelum supprimat, spiritum temperet, ordinet charitatem.... Discretio quippe omni virtuti ordinem ponit; ordo modum tribuit et decorem, etiam et perpetuitatem.... Tolle hanc, et virtus vitium erit, ipsaque affectio naturalis in perturbationem magis convertetur, exterminiumque naturae*" ("And so zeal without knowledge is insupportable. So where there is strong enthusiasm, discretion, which is the ordering of love, is especially necessary. For zeal without knowledge is found to be less effective, less useful; it is even felt to be very harmful. The more eager the zeal, the more intense the spirit, the more abundant the love, so a need for more vigilant knowledge, to control the zeal, to moderate the spirit, to order the love.... Discretion puts order in every virtue, and order brings proportion and beauty, and even permanence.... Take this away, and virtue will become vice, and natural affection itself will be transformed into disorder and destruction of nature") (Migne, *PL* 183, col. 1018BD). For a discussion of this passage see Merton, *Cistercian Fathers and Their Monastic Theology*, 340–46.

495. Wis 3:1–9, 10:17–21 (*Breviarium Cisterciense*, 58*).

496. "in the struggle of combat" (antiphon: canticle) (*Breviarium Cisterciense, Autumnalis*, 438).

to manifest His wisdom in their lives. Sanctity consists then above all in obedience to the will of God which is beyond our understanding, and by obedience to this will we show that we are the meek, poor, merciful, pure ones, etc., who possess the Kingdom of Heaven (cf. gospel[497]). In a word, if we would come to the glory of the saints, we must let God work in our lives, and draw us into that glory, and we must not trust in human wisdom, but live by faith and obedience to God. For God is our sanctity, and we cannot become saints merely by human wisdom and techniques, since His holiness and His wisdom absolutely transcend all our understanding and all our capacity for virtue. And what is human wisdom? wisdom cut down to man's dimensions, cut according to our pattern and our limitations. Such wisdom can never comprehend the infinite God. This is what comes clear in the canticle of the third nocturn, which is one of the most beautiful parts of the office, but which we neglect perhaps, since it is familiar (common of martyrs).

1) Wisdom 3: *Justorum animae in manu Dei sunt.*[498] In order to understand this properly, we must first look at the previous chapters. This is part of a general introduction to the whole Book of Wisdom, in which *the wisdom of the pagans is rejected.* The basic theme is {that} the only true wisdom is that which comes from God. It is a participation in the divine wisdom itself. It can only be had by those who receive it from God. In order to receive wisdom from God they have to be united with Him, and the way to be united to Him is to fear Him and do His will, even though it may be incomprehensible to us at the time. The meaning of His plan will come clear later. First *believe*; then you will understand. *Credo ut intelligam*[499] (read Wisdom 1:5ff.[500]). More precisely, wisdom comes from

497. Matt 5:1–12 (*Missale Romanum*, 779; *Missale Cisterciense*, 551).

498. "The souls of the just are in the hand of God" (Wis 3:1).

499. "I believe that I might understand" (Anselm, *Proslogion*, c. 1 [*PL* 158, col. 227C]; see Merton, *Run to the Mountain*, 292 for Merton's initial encounter with this text [1/16/41]; see also Merton, *Cistercian Fathers and Forefathers*, 55–56, 107–108 for later reflections).

500. "For the Holy Spirit of discipline will flee from the deceitful, and will withdraw himself from thoughts that are without understanding, and he shall not abide when iniquity cometh in. For the spirit of wisdom is benevolent, and will not acquit the evil speaker from his lips: for God is witness of his reins, and he is a true searcher of his heart, and a hearer of his tongue. For the spirit of the Lord hath filled the whole world: and that, which containeth all things, hath knowledge of the voice. Therefore he that speaketh unjust things cannot be hid, neither shall the chastising judgment pass him by. For inquisition shall be made into the thoughts of the ungodly: and the hearing of his words shall come to God, to the chastising of his iniquities. For the ear of

the *Spirit of the Lord*, living and acting in those who do good, and He withdraws Himself from those whose lives are a lie, and who do evil (cf. ch. 1:5ff.). Special emphasis is placed on the fact that the Spirit of Truth cannot and will not live in those who are given to lies, deceitfulness, and other sins against truth, especially *rebellion against God's will*. Now God is the God of life, but the impious really love death more than life and their wisdom is a pact with death (i.e. with unreality). READ chapter 1:12 to {the} end:[501] "Seek not death in the error of your life . . ."[502] Chapter 2 gives a good résumé of the wisdom of the pagans (Greeks), based entirely on the appearances of things. Its basis is *despair*. This leads to a cult of temporal pleasure, getting everything possible out of life while it lasts. But this in turn leads to injustice and oppression as to a logical consequence FOR THAT WHICH IS FEEBLE IS FOUND TO BE NOTHING WORTH (this was the philosophy of Nazism in our own day!). (Read 2:12 to {the} end.[503]) More than this, however, they resent the fact that the poor and

---

jealousy heareth all things, and the tumult of murmuring shall not be hid. Keep yourselves therefore from murmuring, which profiteth nothing, and refrain your tongue from detraction, for an obscure speech shall not go for nought: and the mouth that belieth, killeth the soul" (vv. 5–11).

501. "Seek not death in the error of your life, neither procure ye destruction by the works of your hands. For God made not death, neither hath he pleasure in the destruction of the living. For he created all things that they might be: and he made the nations of the earth for health: and there is no poison of destruction in them, nor kingdom of hell upon the earth. For justice is perpetual and immortal. But the wicked with works and words have called it to them: and esteeming it a friend have fallen away, and have made a covenant with it: because they are worthy to be of the part thereof" (vv. 12–16).

502. Wis 1:12.

503. "Let us therefore lie in wait for the just, because he is not for our turn, and he is contrary to our doings, and upbraideth us with transgressions of the law, and divulgeth against us the sins of our way of life. He boasteth that he hath the knowledge of God, and calleth himself the son of God. He is become a censurer of our thoughts. He is grievous unto us, even to behold: for his life is not like other men's, and his ways are very different. We are esteemed by him as triflers, and he abstaineth from our ways as from filthiness, and he preferreth the latter end of the just, and glorieth that he hath God for his father. Let us see then if his words be true, and let us prove what shall happen to him, and we shall know what his end shall be. For if he be the true son of God, he will defend him, and will deliver him from the hands of his enemies. Let us examine him by outrages and tortures, that we may know his meekness and try his patience. Let us condemn him to a most shameful death: for there shall be respect had unto him by his words. These things they thought, and were deceived: for their own malice blinded them. And they knew not the secrets of God, nor hoped for the wages of justice, nor esteemed the honour of holy souls. For God created man incorruptible, and to the image of his own likeness he made him. But by the envy of the devil, death

the oppressed *reproach them implicitly or openly* by their life which is in the hands of God, and manifests the wisdom of God (ch. 2:12 to the end). The end of chapter 2 then points out that there is an irreconcilable opposition between the wisdom of the world and the wisdom of God, and that God means to use the oppressed just ones to reveal the falsity of the wisdom of the world (cf. 1 *Cor.* 1 and 2), and that *this struggle must come out.* The presence of God's wisdom in the poor who are abandoned to His Providence must be challenged and tested by the wise of this world, whose philosophy is threatened by this mystery. They will put God to the test in persecuting those He loves, and in the persecution His wisdom will vindicate itself and save those that are His.

Now we come to our canticle (ch. 3:1–6), the vindication of God's wisdom in the just: as God is hidden, so the lot of the just is hidden in God. They are in the hand of God precisely in so far as they remain hidden. To be hidden is to be in the power of God, if we are hidden in Him by faith. Desire this hiddenness, not to be too keen to see where we are going, as long as we are doing the will of God. Why is this? because, as 2:23 explains, there is in man an incorruptible image of God. To identify oneself totally with this image and to live in one's true self, the center of one's soul, is to live united with God above all tribulation, above all death and corruption. The man who lives entirely in his outer self will indeed be destroyed by death. But the man who lives with Christ in the Spirit will be above death. Our faith shows us the way to do this, but it requires courage and heroic trust in God, because it means traveling by a way that is invisible and seems foolish to the world. "In the sight of the unwise they seemed to die. . . . Their departure was taken as misery. . . ."[504] "*Et quod a nobis est iter, exterminium . . .*"[505] Their going away from us seemed to be complete destruction,[506] but in reality it was a journey into peace. In the sight of men they suffered torments[507] (this is what was visible and evident to nature), but their hope was full of immortality ("*spes quae videtur non est spes*"[508]). Afflicted in a few things, in many they shall be

---

came into the world: And they follow him that are of his side" (vv. 12–25).

504. Wis 3:2.

505. "And what is the path away from us, destruction" (Wis 3:3).

506. Wis 3:3.

507. Wis 3:4.

508. "hope that is seen is not hope" (Rom 8:24).

rewarded:[509] "eye hath not seen. . ."[510] *Non sunt condignae passiones hujus temporis.*[511] God hath tried them and found them worthy of Himself,[512] by their faith and their hope clinging to the invisible in obedience to His will. As gold in a furnace, then the souls of the saints were perfectly purified by suffering. All that was temporal and imperfect was burnt out by the fire of tribulation which made their desire of God alone ever more and more pure. "As a holocaust He hath received them";[513] their obedience was more pleasing to Him than the greatest of sacrifices, for by it they offered to Him that which was most precious in themselves, and indeed their whole self and their whole life. (Here the second canticle begins.) "*Fulgebunt justi*":[514] the triumph of the just is compared to a fire burning up the stubble in a field, with amazing rapidity and violence and completeness. This will happen in the day when the Lord comes (*BJ* adds this[515]), and because His wisdom has triumphed in them, the Lord will judge the nations through them and in them, for their triumph shall be the vindication of His wisdom and the condemnation of their folly. Indeed the "fire" that breaks forth in the just is the wisdom and power of God. "*Qui confidunt in illo intelligent veritatem . . . donum et pax est electis illius.*"[516] {The} third canticle (from c. 10:17 to {the} end) pictures the passage of the just from death to life under the image of the passage of the Israelites through the Red Sea; the same work of wisdom will be done in the same way in all the saints.

The Poor Souls: there is only one way to the infinitely transcendent God: through fire and darkness. The saints completed the journey in this present life. Those who did not correspond perfectly to the wisdom of God in their lives, through frailty or through some other impediment, must complete the journey after their death. In purgatory the poor souls are tried "as gold in the furnace,"[517] and what is tried is *their love*. What

---

509. Wis 3:5.

510. 1 Cor 2:9.

511. "the sufferings of the present time are not worthy [to be compared to the glory to come]" (Rom 8:18).

512. Wis 3:5.

513. Wis 3:6.

514. "the just will shine" (Wis 3:7).

515. "Au jour de sa visite" (*Sainte Bible*, 872).

516. "those who trust in Him will understand the truth, . . . grace and peace are for His chosen ones" (Wis 3:9).

517. Wis 3:6.

is purgatory? We cannot be too definite about it. It is a "place" (but in what sense?) in which souls are *purified*, and purified *by fire* (but what is this fire?) and in which, by the most terrible punishment, they *expiate* their sins. The Church teaches us definitely that the punishments of purgatory are terrible, that they are necessary to expiate sin, and purify the soul that would see God, and that in our suffrages we can shorten the punishments of the poor souls and speed the work of their purification. In our thoughts about purgatory, while remembering that it is a place of punishment, we should emphasize rather the idea of the purification of love, for the souls in purgatory accept their punishment with pure love: their punishment is not a pure penalty, purely negative, like the *poena damni*,[518] and the whole difference lies in the fact that they are united to God, and closely united to Him. They are, as we have seen in the canticle, "*in manu Dei*";[519] they are only apparently destroyed, but in reality they are in a place of peace (notwithstanding the fact that they are suffering); they are *perfectly united to the will of God*, and their *hope is full of immortality*; they are being purified as gold in the furnace, and the time of their glory and vindication will come (apply the third nocturn canticle[520] to the poor souls). The fire and darkness through which they pass, the mystics tell us, *is the love of God Himself in so far as it is inexorably opposed to all moral imperfection and impurity in their own souls*; and the presence of imperfection is what impedes the final union of their souls with God. Hence they are most eager to be purified so that His will may be perfectly accomplished in them (and this is their chief motive, not merely that they may enjoy for themselves the vision of God—the souls in purgatory have a totally different perspective from ours!).

St. Catherine of Genoa passed through her purgatory in the present life; it was the purgatory of mystical purification. She believes that this is substantially the same purification the souls in purgatory go through.[521]

518. "punishment of the damned."

519. "in the hand of God" (Wis 3:1).

520. Wis. 10:17–21 (*Breviarium Cisterciense*, 58*).

521. Catherine of Genoa, *Treatise on Purgatory*, 17 (c. 1): "This holy Soul found herself, while still in the flesh, placed by the fiery love of God in Purgatory, which burnt her, cleansing whatever in her needed cleansing, to the end that when she passed from this life she might be presented to the sight of God, her dear Love. By means of this loving fire, she understood in her soul the state of the souls of the faithful who are placed in Purgatory to purge them of all the rust and stains of sin of which they have not rid themselves in this life. And since this Soul, placed by the divine fire in this loving Purgatory, was united to that divine love and content with all that was wrought

The same is clear when we study St. John of the Cross. "The dark night is an inflowing of God into the soul, which purifies it from its ignorances and imperfections, . . . the same loving light which purges the blessed spirits and enlightens them is that which here purges the soul and illumines it. . . . this divine light is affliction and torment for the soul . . . etc."[522] Read p. 406, vol. I: "When the divine light assails the soul it causes darkness in it, in so far as the soul is opposed to God . . . it overwhelms and darkens the act of the natural intelligence . . . as two contraries cannot coexist in the one subject, the soul must of necessity have pain and suffering, since it is the subject wherein these two contraries war against each other."[523] (Read especially *The Dark Night*, II.v.5 [p. 407],[524] *ad ibid.*

---

in her, she understood the state of the souls who are in Purgatory."

522. St. John of the Cross, *Dark Night*, II.v.1, 2, which reads: "This dark night . . . which purges it . . . loving wisdom that purges . . . . this Divine wisdom is not only night and darkness for the soul, but is likewise affliction and torment" (Peers, ed. and trans., *Complete Works of Saint John of the Cross*, 1:405–406).

523. *Dark Night*, II.v.3, 4: "In the same way, when this Divine light of contemplation assails the soul which is not yet wholly enlightened, it causes spiritual darkness in it; for not only does it overcome it, but likewise it overwhelms it and darkens the act of its natural intelligence. For this reason S. Dionysius and other mystical theologians call this infused contemplation a ray of darkness—that is to say, for the soul that is not enlightened and purged—for the natural strength of the intellect is transcended and overwhelmed by its great supernatural light. Wherefore David likewise said: That near to God and round about Him are darkness and cloud; not that this is so in fact, but that it is so to our weak understanding, which is blinded and darkened by so vast a light, to which it cannot attain. For this cause the same David then explained himself, saying: Through the great splendor of His presence passed clouds—namely, between God and our understanding. And it is for this cause that, when God sends it out from Himself to the soul that is not yet transformed, this illumining ray of His secret wisdom causes thick darkness in the understanding. And it is clear that this dark contemplation is in these its beginnings painful likewise to the soul; for, as this Divine infused contemplation has many excellences that are extremely good, and the soul that receives them, not being purged, has many miseries that are likewise extremely bad, hence it follows that, as two contraries cannot coexist in one subject—the soul—it must of necessity have pain and suffering, since it is the subject wherein these two contraries war against each other, working the one against the other, by reason of the purgation of the imperfections of the soul which comes to pass through this contemplation. This we shall prove inductively in the manner following" (Peers, ed. and trans., *Complete Works of Saint John of the Cross*, 1:406–407).

524. "In the first place, because the light and wisdom of this contemplation is most bright and pure, and the soul which it assails is dark and impure, it follows that the soul suffers great pain when it receives it in itself, just as, when the eyes are dimmed by humours, and become impure and weak, they suffer pain through the assault of the bright light. And when the soul is indeed assailed by this Divine light, its pain, which

{vi}.6 [p. 412];[525] also 436.[526]) St. Catherine tells us (1) of the extreme

results from its impurity, is immense; because, when this pure light assails the soul, in order to expel its impurity, the soul feels itself to be so impure and miserable that it believes God to be against it, and thinks that it has set itself up against God. This causes it so much grief and pain (because it now believes that God has cast it away) that one of the greatest trials which Job felt when God sent him this experience, was as follows, when he said: Why hast Thou set me against Thee, so that I am grievous and burdensome to myself? For, by means of this pure light, the soul now sees its impurity clearly (although darkly), and knows clearly that it is unworthy of God or of any creature. And what gives it most pain is that it thinks that it will never be worthy and that its good things are all over for it. This is caused by the profound immersion of its spirit in the knowledge and realization of its evils and miseries; for this Divine and dark light now reveals them all to the eye, that it may see clearly how in its own strength it can never have aught else. In this sense we may understand that passage from David, which says: For iniquity Thou hast corrected man and hast undone his soul: he consumes away as the spider" (Peers, ed. and trans., *Complete Works of Saint John of the Cross*, 1.407–408). The remainder of chapter v (Peers, ed. and trans., *Complete Works of Saint John of the Cross*, 1:408) discusses the second source of the soul's pain, its natural, moral and spiritual weakness, which is unable to endure the divine presence in contemplation even though this is in actuality light and gentle.

525.   Chapter vi discusses the third and fourth kinds of pain the soul suffers in the dark night: the encounter of the divine and the human in the purgative contemplation that strips the soul of its habitual attachments, and the soul's awareness of the majesty and greatness of the divine presence and consequently of its own poverty, resulting in a deep experience of purgation; the chapter concludes with section 6: "Wherefore, because the soul is purified in this furnace and is like the gold in the crucible, as says the Wise Man, it is conscious of this complete undoing of itself in its very substance, together with the direst poverty, wherein it is, as it were, coming to an end, as may be seen by that which David says of himself in this respect, in these words: Save me, Lord (he cries to God), for the waters have come in even unto my soul; I am made fast in the mire of the depth and there is no place where I can stand; I came to the depth of the sea and the tempest overwhelmed me; I laboured crying, my throat has become hoarse, mine eyes have failed whilst I hope in my God. Here God greatly humbles the soul in order that He may afterwards greatly exalt it; and if He ordained not that these feelings should be quickly lulled to sleep when they arise within the soul, it would die in a very few days; but at intervals there occur times when it is not conscious of their greatest intensity. At times, however, they are so keen that the soul seems to be seeing hell and perdition opened. Of such are they that in truth go down alive into hell, for here on earth they are purged in the same manner as there, since this purgation is that which would have to be accomplished there. And thus the soul that passes through this either enters not that place at all, or tarries there but for a very short time; for one hour of purgation here is more profitable than are many there" (Peers, ed. and trans., *Complete Works of Saint John of the Cross*, 1:409–12). (Text reads: "vii.")

526.   "From what has been said we shall be able to see how this dark night of loving fire, as it purges in the darkness, so also in the darkness enkindles the soul. We shall likewise be able to see that, even as spirits are purged in the next life with dark material fire, so in this life they are purged and cleansed with the dark spiritual fire of love. The

pain of the souls in purgatory (read *Treatise on Purgatory*, pp. 20–21:[527] equal to {the} pain of hell); (2) their pain is without guilt: it is the pain of remorse at offending His love; (3) they have no *return on self*; their pain is *not reflective* (read pp.17–18[528]); (4) they are truly happy (p. 18[529]); (5) their perfect willingness to suffer;[530] (6) their advice to us (read p. 31[531]).

---

difference is that in the next life they are cleansed with fire, while here below they are cleansed and illumined with love only" (*Dark Night*, II.12.1).

527. "Because the souls in Purgatory are without the guilt of sin, there is no hindrance between them and God except their pain, which holds them back so that they cannot reach perfection. Clearly they see the grievousness of every least hindrance in their way, and see too that their instinct is hindered by a necessity of justice: thence is born a raging fire, like that of Hell save that guilt is lacking to it. Guilt it is which makes the will of the damned in Hell malignant, on whom God does not bestow His goodness and who remain therefore in desperate ill will opposed to the will of God.... Because the souls in Hell were found at the moment of death to have in them the will to sin, they bear the guilt throughout eternity, suffering not indeed the pains they merit but such pains as they endure, and these without end. But the souls in Purgatory bear only pain, for their guilt was wiped away at the moment of their death when they were found to be ill content with their sins and repentant for their offenses against divine goodness. Therefore their pain is finite and its time ever lessening" (cc. 3, 4).

528. "They cannot turn their thoughts back to themselves, nor can they say, 'Such sins I have committed for which I deserve to be here,' nor, 'I would that I had not committed them for then I would go now to Paradise,' nor, 'That one will leave sooner than I,' nor, 'I will leave sooner than he.' They can have neither of themselves nor of others any memory, whether of good or evil, whence they would have greater pain than they suffer ordinarily. So happy are they to be within God's ordinance, and that He should do all which pleases Him, as it pleases Him that in their greatest pain they cannot think of themselves.... Only once, as they pass from this life, do they see the cause of the Purgatory they endure; never again do they see it for in another sight of it there would be self" (c. 1).

529. "I believe no happiness can be found worthy to be compared with that of a soul in Purgatory except that of the saints in Paradise; and day by day this happiness grows as God flows into these souls, more and more as the hindrance to His entrance is consumed" (18–19 [c. 2]).

530. "As for will: never can the soul say these pains are pains, so contented are they with God's ordaining with which, in pure charity, their will is united" (18 [c. 2]); "The souls in Purgatory have wills accordant in all things with the will of God, who therefore sheds on them His goodness, and they, as far as their will goes, are happy and cleansed of all their sin" (22 [c. 5]).

531. "And so that blessed soul, seeing the aforesaid things by the divine light, said: 'I would fain send up a cry so loud that it would put fear in all men on the earth. I would say to them: "Wretches, why do you let yourselves be thus blinded by the world, you whose need is so great and grievous, as you will know at the moment of death and who make no provision for it whatsoever? You have all taken shelter beneath hope in God's mercy, which is, you say, very great, but you see not that this great goodness of

SAINT MARTIN (November 11, 1955)

St. Martin {is} Father and Patron of Monks. {His office is} a *monastic office*, {filled with} "existential theology"—the liturgy embodying monastic theology in a saint's life ({the} antiphons {are} from Sulpicius Severus' biography[532]).

1. First Vespers:[533] St. Martin's death {took place on} November 8, 397. The situation {was that} {Brictio}, a hostile and arrogant priest opposing him, "called Martin filthy and contemptible"[534] (later {Brictio} also {became} a saint). Martin is about to die; his disciples beg him to save them from the "*lupi rapaces.*"[535] Martin's prayer (second antiphon) {is}: "Lord, if I am still necessary to thy people . . . "[536] {The} third antiphon celebrates the perfection of his indifference (*apatheia*): "*nec labore victum, nec morte vincendum.*"[537] {The} fourth antiphon {relates} his triumph {as he is} received in {the} bosom of *Abraham*

God will judge you for having gone against the will of so good a Lord. His goodness should constrain you to do all His will, not give you hope in ill-doing, for His justice cannot fail but in one way or another must needs be fully satisfied. Cease to hug yourselves, saying: 'I will confess my sins and then receive plenary indulgence, and at that moment I shall be purged of all my sins and then shall be saved.' Think of the confession and the contrition needed for that plenary indulgence, so hardly come by that, if you knew, you would tremble in great fear, more sure you would never win it than that you ever could" '" (c. 15). Though the title of the chapter is "Reproaches which the souls in Purgatory make to people in the world," it seems clear from the context that the "blessed soul" is in fact actually Catherine herself.

532. The *Vita Martini* is found in Migne, *PL* 20, cols. 159A–176C, though the story of Brictio (erroneously named "Brictius" in all versions of the text) is in the author's *Dialogues*, 3.15 (Migne, *PL* 20, cols. 220C–221B). Merton also discusses Martin in *Cassian and the Fathers*, 137–38 and in Merton, *Pre-Benedictine Monasticism*, 13–17.

533. *Breviarium Cisterciense, Autumnalis*, 460.

534. This idea, but not these exact words, is found in the *Dialogues*: ". . . *plenus insaniae evomuit in Martinum mille convicia. . . . per inanes superstitiones et phantasmata visionum ridicula prorsus inter deliramenta senuisse*" (". . . full of madness, he spewed forth on Martin a thousand abuses. . . . [H]e had become senile with his inane superstitions and the absurd illusions of his visions which were completely nonsensical") (Migne, *PL* 20, cols. 220C, 221A).

535. "rapacious wolves" (first antiphon) (*Breviarium Cisterciense, Autumnalis*, 460).

536. "*Domine, si adhuc populo tuo sum necessarius*" (*Breviarium Cisterciense, Autumnalis*, 460).

537. "neither conquered by labor, nor to be conquered by death" (*Breviarium Cisterciense, Autumnalis*, 460).

(fatherhood): "*Laetus excipitur*"[538] (joy of the feast); "*Pauper et modicus, dives ingreditur.*"[539] {The} Magnificat {antiphon speaks of him as one} whose soul *possesses paradise* ({the} object of {the} monastic life), whence {comes the} exaltation of angels, saints and virgins: "*Mane nobiscum in aeternum*"[540]—everlasting peace and joy among the saints. The same idea is taken up in the invitatory: "*justus florebit in domo Domini plantatus.*"[541]

2. First Nocturn:[542] Martin {is} in the army. {He was} born in Hungary, son of a soldier, {and therefore} had to serve. At Amiens, {he} divides his cloak and gives half to a beggar. {In the} first antiphon, Martin, "*adhuc catechumenus*"[543] ({he} had been one for eight years) {hears the} words of Christ in {a} vision. {The} second antiphon {tells of} Martin's baptism as a result of this grace. {The} third antiphon {records} his refusal to Emperor Julian to fight the invading barbarians: "*Christi sum miles; pugnare non licet.*"[544] (Later {we learn} how he "fights" spiritually as a soldier of Christ. Now, a higher call, a higher service exempts him.) {In the} fourth antiphon, accused of cowardice, he offers to face the enemy unarmed. {The} fifth antiphon {presents} Martin as bishop: the three angels {are} sent to protect him against pagans whose shrine he was to destroy. {The} sixth, seventh, eighth {and} ninth antiphons {relate} some of his miraculous cures and their effects. {In the} tenth antiphon, {the} devil appeared as Christ, but richly dressed, and Martin saw through the vision, knowing Christ would always manifest Himself in poverty. {The} eleventh antiphon {tells of a} ball of fire during Mass (after another sharing of clothes). See {the} Magnificat antiphon of second vespers.[545]

---

538. "joyfully he is welcomed" (*Breviarium Cisterciense, Autumnalis*, 460).

539. "poor and unassuming, he enters [heaven] a rich man" (*Breviarium Cisterciense, Autumnalis*, 460, which reads: "... *modicus, coelum dives ...*").

540. "Remain with us forever" (*Breviarium Cisterciense, Autumnalis*, 460).

541. "the just man will flourish, planted in the house of the Lord" (*Breviarium Cisterciense, Autumnalis*, 460).

542. First through sixth antiphons (*Breviarium Cisterciense, Autumnalis*, 461); second nocturn: seventh through twelfth antiphons (*Breviarium Cisterciense, Autumnalis*, 462–63).

543. "still a catechumen" (*Breviarium Cisterciense, Autumnalis*, 461).

544. "I am a soldier of Christ; it is not permitted [for me] to fight" (*Breviarium Cisterciense, Autumnalis*, 461, which reads: "*Christi enim sum miles; pugnare mihi non licet*").

545. "*O beatum Pontificem, qui totis visceribus diligebat Christum Regem, et non formidabat imperii principatum! o sanctissima anima, quam etsi gladius persecutoris non abstulit, palmam tamen martyrii non amisit!*" ("O blessed pontiff, who loved

Summary: {Martin reached} perfection of prayer and poverty, {the} saint {as} a sign of God.

FEAST OF ALL THE SAINTS OF THE ORDER (November 13)

First Vespers:[546] the antiphons: *"fulgebunt justi"*[547] {is} appropriate for the season of forest fires! Just as a fire driven by a high wind runs wildly through the dry reeds, so the glory of God will be manifested in His saints. *Gaudent in coelis*:[548] first of all, this antiphon is associated with the martyrs, but adapted for confessors by the change of one phrase: *pro ejus amore saeculum spreverunt*[549] suggests the traditional teaching of the Church that the renunciation of the monk is a martyrdom, a death in witness to the Risen Christ. But it must be a real and total and whole-hearted renunciation. For His love we despise the world; we follow in His footsteps on the way of the Cross and we shall exult with Him forever, after the example of the great monastic saints. The Desert Fathers remain models of contempt for the world. *Beati eritis cum vos oderint homines*:[550] we have not come to the monastery to be popular and respected, but to be forgotten and even despised by the world. For this is correlative to our own contempt for worldly things (which does not however imply contempt for the souls of people who live in the world. These we love with a deep compassion, all the more so as we realize that we are sinners as they are, and all have a common need for salvation.) If we are estranged from the world and its ways, we will necessarily not be understood by the world, and will be treated with suspicion and contempt by it. But our reward is very great in heaven. *O quam gloriosum est regnum*:[551] it is a *kingdom* we are going to, in which we will be at home, rejoicing and

---

Christ the King with all your being, and did not fear the power of the empire! O most holy soul, even if the sword of the persecutor did not take away your life, the palm of martyrdom was not lost!") (*Breviarium Cisterciense, Autumnalis*, 468).

546. *Breviarium Cisterciense, Autumnalis*, 468–70.

547. "the just will shine" (*Breviarium Cisterciense, Autumnalis*, 468).

548. "they rejoice in heaven" (second antiphon) (*Breviarium Cisterciense, Autumnalis*, 469).

549. "they rejected the world out of love for Him" (*Breviarium Cisterciense, Autumnalis*, 469).

550. "Blessed will you be when men hate you" (Luke 6:22) (third antiphon) (*Breviarium Cisterciense, Autumnalis*, 469).

551. "O how glorious is the Kingdom" (fourth antiphon) (*Breviarium Cisterciense, Autumnalis*, 469).

sharing the liberty of Christ the King, kings, as it were, with Him. Our white habit reminds us of our future glory with Him, if we are faithful to Him and trust in His mercy and cooperate with His grace as did the monastic saints. The *capitulum* suggests that the monks are Christ's special favorites: "*Ecce ego et pueri mei quos dedit mihi Dominus.*"[552] Think of all these favored ones, the known and unknown monastic saints of all orders, and those that belonged to no order; for instance, one who comes to mind is St. Sequanus. {Recall} St. Cuthbert of Lindisfarne; the monks of St. Columban; those of Ireland; the Desert Fathers; the followers of St. Benedict; Cistercians; Carthusians; Camaldolese; Valombrosans; monks of Mount Athos, etc., etc. *The hymn*[553] hails not only the cenobites, but those who lived in solitude; all in common are to be praised above all because they withstood the assaults of hell in all its forms. They despised wealth and riches, and the luxury of the world, together with its dignities. All these they trod under foot, together with the pleasures of the flesh. They were content with simple and frugal foods, drank water from the spring, slept on the ground—the asceticism of the monastic saints. To be true monks, we have to be men of mortification and penance. Their solitude was not merely a place of recreation; they lived among snakes and wild beasts, and were not terrified by dreadful apparitions of the devil. But above all, they were men of prayer and contemplation, and far from mortal things their souls rose beyond the stars and joined the angels in contemplation. The grace we ask for in the collect is to "lead better lives,"[554] {to} be truer monks, inspired by the examples of so many monastic saints.

Feast of the Dedication of the Church (November 15)

First Vespers (the hymn and the lighting of the candles): the hymn *Urbs Jerusalem,*[555] and the lighted candles placed at the spots where the walls were anointed, remind us of the fact that our church is an image of

---

552. "Behold I and my children whom the Lord has given me" (Isa 8:18) (capitulum) (*Breviarium Cisterciense, Autumnalis,* 469).

553. "*Avete, solitudinis*" (*Breviarium Cisterciense, Autumnalis,* 469).

554. "*Concede, quaesumus, omnipotens Deus: ut ad meliorem vitam sanctorum tuorum exempla nos provocent, quatenus, quorum solemnia agimus, etiam actus imitemur*" ("Grant, almighty God, we pray, that the example of Your saints may spur us to a better life, and just as we celebrate their feasts, may we imitate their actions") (*Breviarium Cisterciense, Autumnalis,* 475).

555. "City of Jerusalem" (*Breviarium Cisterciense,* 146*).

the heavenly Jerusalem, the City of Peace. To say that this is "our feast" is not to say that the rest of the Church is excluded, but that the whole Church is present and celebrates with us on this day. In a sense, on this day we are the "whole Christ," for Christ, as it were, comes and makes our church His "station" for the celebration of the feast, just as the Holy Father used to celebrate Mass at different churches of Rome on different days in Lent, etc. The lighted candles remind us of the gates of the heavenly city, each one marked with the name of an apostle, because through the apostles we come into the Mystical Christ, and each gate is an apostle and also each gate is Christ. Jesus and the apostles {are} present among us, not in the material building so much as in the community itself.

{The} lessons[556] {focus on}: *hope*—if we appreciate our vocation, if we appreciate our opportunity to help one another come to God—we are "gates of heaven, apostles, Christ,"[557] to one another; *union*—but this function is exercised by Christ in us only if we live in truly fraternal union: realize that by being kind and humble with a brother we are helping to save his soul and save his vocation; if we are being rough with him, we may endanger his vocation; we should not seek or demand that others be nice to us, just seek to be nice to them, to give them peace—then Jesus truly lives and acts in us; *peace*—based on gratitude for all the graces Jesus has bestowed on us, through the community, through our present companions, their prayers, their example, their love, and through the Fathers who founded Gethsemani and kept it going—a treasury of graces on which we draw. Today is a feast of all the saints of Gethsemani—visit them in the cemetery, and recognize how much we owe to them, without being able to know it clearly in this life.

The GOSPEL:[558]

    a) contrast the lofty mystical tone of the epistle[559] and the apparent simplicity of the gospel. Yet in reality it is the gospel that reaches the greater mystical heights. For there is no greater mysticism than that by which we are united, in our ordinary life, with the

---

556. 2 Para [2 Chr] 7:1–7 (*Breviarium Cisterciense*, 151–52*).

557. The gate of heaven seen by Jacob at Bethel (Gen 28:17) (responsory, capitulum; responsory, fifth lesson) (*Breviarium Cisterciense*, 146*, 157*) is identified with the gate of the New Jerusalem marked with the names of the apostles and of the Lamb (cf. Apoc [Rev] 21:14) (responsory: fifth lesson) (*Breviarium Cisterciense*, 156*).

558. Luke 19:1–10 (*Breviarium Cisterciense*, 160–61*; *Missale Romanum*, (41); *Missale Cisterciense*, 34*).

559. Apoc [Rev] 21:2–5 (*Missale Romanum*, (40); *Missale Cisterciense*, 33*).

Word Incarnate, Who has come to be one of us in that life. It is by Him that we come to the Father, not by ascending, somehow, out of our ordinary life to find the Father beyond the stars, for this is impossible.

b) The gospel {was a} wonderful choice of the early Fathers who composed this office; who would have thought of Zacchaeus as providing the perfect gospel for the feast? One can imagine rather Jansenistic minds turning spontaneously to the cleansing of the Temple. But actually, this gospel contains infinite riches and graces that could be found in no other text.

c) The key to the text {is} "*Hodie in domo tua oportet me manere.*"[560] Note that here it is not merely "My house" or "My Father's house" but "*thy* house." Jesus comes to dwell in our house, and that is what makes it the Father's house. "*Hodie*" {is at once} the Feast of the Dedication, the present moment, {and} the short day of our earthly life. "*Domus tua*" {is both} the poor churches we build {and} our own poor souls. "*Oportet*" {means that} Jesus manifests the Father's will; He has been told by the Father to stay with Zacchaeus rather than with anyone else—and to stay with *us*.

d) Zacchaeus: first, he is *rich* (the Pharisees were poor), then he is a despised publican, and he was a little unprepossessing Jew; but "*he wanted to see Jesus*"[561]—Who He was. This simple desire to see the Person he had heard about may not have been totally free of "natural motives." How important above all {it is} to seek the Person of Jesus—to see *Him*—to really find out Who He is: the wonderful, God-given instinct to want to *see*, to know, to get close to someone "Who is coming," to verify by recognition the truth of what one has been told, to see one's hopes *even surpassed*. St. Ambrose[562] applies this to the Gentiles, just following the natural law, and seems to give them the advantage over the Jews and their complicated ceremonies and precepts; what is the value of these if we do not desire to *see Jesus*? *Zacchaeus took himself as he was* {and} was not afraid to accept the

---

560. "Today I must stay at your house" (Luke 19:5).

561. Luke 19:3.

562. *In Lucam*, bk. 8 (ninth lesson) (*Breviarium Cisterciense*, 159*).

fact of his lowly stature, and simply climbed a tree, *admitting he could not see any other way.* {Then comes} *the wonderful reward*: Jesus looks up, calls him by name, and says He is coming to dinner. *He hastened to come down and received Him rejoicing*, not caring what people might say.

e) {Note} *the various reactions*:

1) *Omnes*:[563] everybody, all the Jews, etc., criticized Jesus, and of course Zacchaeus. Jesus had gone to stay with a sinner.

2) *Stans autem Zacchaeus*:[564] his gesture is lavish, perhaps even a little vulgar; some might criticize him for ostentatiousness—not at all. Again he is admitting a public sin, and repairing it with interest. {Note the} complete abandon with which he *lays himself open to all claims* without question. He has become totally a new man, and yet he is the same Zacchaeus, fully responsible for the "old man," yet not troubled with that responsibility.

3) Jesus {says}, "*Hodie salus domui huic facta est.*"[565] The Fathers wanted us to understand that this meant *us*; we are the house of Zacchaeus. We can be and are Zacchaeus if we have his dispositions. *He too is a son of Abraham*, and remember how Abraham also received God and entertained Him. We are reminded here not only of the faith of Abraham but also of his hospitality.

Finally, the beautiful conclusion: "*The Son of Man came to seek and to save that which was lost.*"[566] What was lost previously belonged to Him. We belong to Him by right. He comes to claim His own, and does so, as we sit down to table with Him, and our brethren, in the Eucharistic banquet.

THE DEDICATION OF THE CHURCH (II)

1. Some thoughts from the liturgy (n.b. *Urbs Jerusalem*:[567] {the} marriage of God and man in purity of heart):

563. "all" (Luke 19:7).

564. "However Zacchaeus, standing" (Luke 19:8).

565. "Today salvation has happened to this house" (Luke 19:9).

566. Luke 19:10.

567. *Breviarium Cisterciense*, 146*.

a) Magnificat antiphon: *Pax aeterna ab aeterno Patre huic domui*[568] ({note the} wrong punctuation in {the} *Breviary*[569]); *Pax perennis, Verbum Patris, sit pax huic domui; Pacem pius Consolator huic praestet domui.*[570] {Note the} special beauty of this antiphon (not in {the} *Roman Breviary*) for vespers: {the} solemnity of {its} repetition; {the} commentary on Christ's words. {The} three Divine Persons bring peace upon the House of God—peace from the Father, peace given by the Holy Spirit, peace which is the Son: *Ipse est Pax nostra.*[571]

b) *Locus iste a Deo factus est inaestimabile sacramentum*[572] (again, {the} comma {is} in {the} wrong place in {the} *St. Andrew's Missal*[573]—God has made the place a "sacrament"). The church is a "sacrament," a mystery, an efficacious sign of the union of God and man.

c) Oration of the actual day of dedication: "O God, Who invisibly containest all things and supportest them [one word, "*contines*," includes these ideas] and yet for the salvation of mankind dost *visibly show the signs of Thy power* [God {is} invisibly present everywhere, {but with a} special presence in visible signs, present in {the} sanctifying action of mystery] glorify [*illustra*] this temple with the might of Thy indwelling [[{note the} significance of the lighting of the candles, a solemn and sacred ceremony, at the places where the walls were anointed with chrism (Christ)] that all who come to pray here may receive consolation from Thee in whatever trial they cry out to Thee."[574]

---

568. "Eternal peace to this house from the eternal Father" (*Breviarium Cisterciense*, 147*).

569. There is a comma after "*Patre*," linking the phrase "*huic domui*" to the following phrase, "*pax perennis.*" (Merton evidently regards this phrase as a vocative, parallel to "*Verbum Patris*," which follows [see following note], but as it is not capitalized in the *Breviary* it may simply be intended as a parallel to the initial "*pax aeterna*").

570. "Everlasting Peace, Word of the Father, let peace be upon this house, gracious Consoler, grant peace to this house" (*Breviarium Cisterciense*, 147*).

571. "He Himself is our peace" (Eph 2:14).

572. "This place has been made an inestimable sacrament by God" (gradual) (*Missale Romanum*, (40); *Missale Cisterciense*, 33*).

573. "This place was made by God, a priceless mystery . . . " (i.e. no comma needed after "God") (4.349).

574. "*Deus, qui invisibiliter omnia contines, et tamen pro salute generis humani*

d) {The} postcommunion gives the spiritual meaning of the mystery: the church, a "sacrament," unites us together in prayer, worship and charity. The sacred signs of the liturgy illuminate our minds with faith and unite us in charity; through the efficacy of the liturgy, we are led to "realize"—in two senses—the mystery: (1) the mystery is made real in us—what is symbolized is effected; (2) we become conscious of this spiritual reality that takes place. "O God, Who from living and chosen stones dost prepare an eternal habitation for Thy Majesty, grant that what profits the Church in her material building may be developed in spiritual growth"[575]—in other words, that the building may be "completed" by a corresponding spiritual building of the Body of Christ.

2. *St. Bernard's First Dedication Sermon*[576] (a few main ideas): from the beginning of the sermon, St. Bernard shifts the emphasis from the building of stones to the building of souls—the Clairvaux community. (The building is holy because of you.) In this sermon, inspired by the rites of dedication, he contemplates what they signify, the action of the sanctifying Spirit in the souls of his monks.

(1) To prove this, he says their virtues and their efforts, their good desires, are proof of the Holy Spirit living and working in them, building them into a Church. When he says this is *your feast*, he means it is not only the feast of your church, but of your dedication as a living temple to God. *Vos dedicati estis Domino, vos assumpsit et elegit in proprios*[577] (519).

(2) Then he says, the ceremonies of the dedication, performed by the bishop, have their effect on everyone who prays in the church, not only on those present at the time, but also on all who ever come

---

signa tuae potentiae visibiliter ostendis: templum hoc potentia tuae inhabitationis illustra, et concede; ut omnes, qui huc deprecaturi conveniunt, ex quacumque tribulatione ad te clamaverint, consolationis tuas beneficia consequantur" (*Missale Romanum*, (40); *Missale Cisterciense*, 33*).

575. "*Deus, qui de vivis et electis lapidibus aeternum majestati tuae praeparas habitaculum: auxiliare populo tuo supplicanti; ut, quod Ecclesiae tuae corporalibus proficit spatiis, spiritualibus amplificetur augmentis*" (*Missale Romanum*, (41); *Missale Cisterciense*, 34*).

576. Migne, *PL* 183, cols. 517D–521D.

577. "You have been dedicated to the Lord; He has taken you up and chosen you as His own" (Migne, *PL* 183, col. 519D, which reads: "... *elegit et assumpsit* ...").

there, especially the monks of the community. What the bishop did then, Christ, the *Pontifex futurorum bonorum*,[578] invisibly does each day in us (520). {In the} aspersion, he makes us humble and purifies us by penance and compunction, washes us with salt water—tears of penance mixed with the salt of wisdom, writes His law in our hearts, making them tractable and docile, and throwing out the devil. He anoints us with chrism in the sign of the Cross—{the} cross for penance, chrism for the consolation of charity; outsiders see the cross, but not the chrism, and they flee. But our penance, says St. Bernard,[579] is joyous, because our cross is anointed with the grace of the Spirit Who helps us. Then He places His light to shine in our lives and edify the world.

(3) *We look forward to the final and perfect dedication in the end of time.* In preparation for that day we must live together in charity, because *disjuncta ligna et lapides domum non faciunt.*[580] In heaven, the blessed form a perfect house of God, (a) perfectly united together not only by love but by knowledge, so that there are no suspicions or misunderstandings; (b) perfectly united to God, knowing Him and loving Him; (c) all the "stones" of the house are the council chamber of the Trinity, and they are witnesses of all His judgements (*vos sedebitis super sedes duodecim judicantes duodecim tribus Israel*[581]). The more intimate their union with essential charity, the more powerful the bonds of love that unite them to one another. {In} our common life, God {is} not just a means to unite us with one another. We come to help one another find God—which implies a certain solitude—and the more we are united to Him, the better we are united to one another. *Dissensions* in community {arise} in proportion as we are not contemplatives, not united to God, and thus merely desire others to be united to ourselves! *Perfecte adhaerentes ei beati spiritus, cum eo pariter et in eo penetrant universa.*[582]

578. "the pontiff of future goods."

579. Migne, *PL* 183, col. 520D.

580. "disconnected pieces of wood and stones do not make a home" (Migne, *PL* 183, col. 521A, which reads: ". . . *disjuncta nimirum ligna* . . .").

581. "You will sit upon twelve thrones judging the twelve tribes of Israel" (Matt 19:28).

582. "The blessed in spirit, perfectly united to Him, penetrate all things equally through Him and with Him" (Migne, *PL* 183, col. 521D).

(4) *We must desire to reach this consummation*, {which is an} extension of the Incarnation; {the} mystery of Christ explains all this.

THE FEAST OF OUR LADY'S PRESENTATION (November 21)

Maria Regula Monachorum:[583] Mary, as the first religious, is the Queen and Mother of each religious. Our vocation is from her; our whole life and perfection depend, in fact, on how closely we reproduce in our own religious life her gift of herself to God. This in turn depends on how close we are to Mary by love and confidence. We have come to the monastery to give ourselves to God. Sooner or later we must find that we cannot truly give ourselves to God without the special help of Mary, and that one of the greatest graces of the religious life is the grace to abandon our life, our body, {our} soul, all our gifts and actions and merits, our past, present and future, into the hands of Our Lady. Read *Eccli.* 21:24–31;[584] *Proverbs* 8:14–19 and 32–36.[585] All these passages show that to do the will

---

583. "Mary the rule of monks" (Ambrose Autpert, "*Sermo in Laudibus Beatae Mariae*," in Winandy, *Ambroise Autpert*, 94; a longer version of this sermon on the Nativity of the Virgin, erroneously attributed to Alcuin, a contemporary of Ambrose, is found in *PL* 101, cols. 1300–1308 [see Winandy, *Ambroise Autpert*, 85]). In his essay "The Humanity of Christ in Monastic Prayer," Merton identifies Ambrose as the abbot of the Monastery of St. Vincent on the Volturno and a spiritual heir of St. Gregory the Great, and calls him "a Benedictine master of the eighth century who is less well known than he deserves to be" (Merton, *Monastic Journey*, 104).

584. "Learning to the prudent is as an ornament of gold, and like a bracelet upon his right arm. The foot of a fool is soon in his neighbour's house: but a man of experience will be abashed at the person of the mighty. A fool will peep through the window into the house: but he that is well taught will stand without. It is the folly of a man to hearken at the door: and a wise man will be grieved with the disgrace. The lips of the unwise will be telling foolish things: but the words of the wise shall be weighed in a balance. The heart of fools is in their mouth: and the mouth of wise men is in their heart. While the ungodly curseth the devil, he curseth his own soul. The talebearer shall defile his own soul, and shall be hated by all: and he that shall abide with him shall be hateful: the silent and wise man shall be honoured."

585. "Counsel and equity is mine, prudence is mine, strength is mine. By me kings reign, and lawgivers decree just things, By me princes rule, and the mighty decree justice. I love them that love me: and they that in the morning early watch for me, shall find me. With me are riches and glory, glorious riches and justice. For my fruit is better than gold and the precious stone, and my blossoms than choice silver. I walk in the way of justice, in the midst of the paths of judgment . . . . Now therefore, ye children, hear me: Blessed are they that keep my ways. Hear instruction and be wise, and refuse it not. Blessed is the man that heareth me, and that watcheth daily at my gates, and waiteth at the posts of my doors. He that shall find me, shall find life, and shall have

of God perfectly we must be united perfectly with Mary, who is the Seat of His Wisdom.

The religious life {is} a state of perfection in which men and women consecrate their whole selves and their whole lives to God by vows, the observance of which assures that everything they do exteriorly will be, as it were, the "sacrament" (exterior sign) of an interior growth in charity, a renewal of their gift of themselves to God. The purpose of each one of the vows is to remove the obstacles to perfect charity and enable us to devote all our thoughts and all the strength of our love to God. Thus *chastity* delivers us from immersion in the desires and cares that are associated with the procreation of children, from the special distractions aroused by the strongest and most disturbing of the bodily instincts, and one which is very liable to make a really interior life impossible. *Poverty* delivers us from the desire of material things and from the "cares of the world," as well as from cares about our own life, health and future. *Obedience* {is} the vow which is most essential to the religious state, and *without which there is no religious life*; {it} places our judgement and will in the hands of another, so that, renouncing the freedom and the right to "lead our own life," as St. Benedict says, we "desire to be under a superior."[586] Obedience not only makes us do the will of another, but makes us love the renunciation of our own will and prefer to do the will of another; but this we do, not inertly and mechanically, but by a *renewed act of choice*, a new consecration of our freedom to God—for we retain our freedom and consecrate it to God by using it according to the will of another. In point of fact, this is the most difficult of the religious vows and gets more difficult as time goes on.

Life of Faith: the religious life does not consist merely in the exterior observance of the vows and the *Rule*. These are not ends in themselves, but means to an end—the total subjection of our body and soul, mind and will, to the Holy Spirit, by love. The perfect religious is one who in everything does the will of God, seen only in the light of faith, for no other reason than to please God. This is the life of true charity. The imperfect religious is one who has other motives than those of faith and of the love of God. He obeys because it is expedient, or because he likes the superior, or because he agrees with the command given—it suits him; it

---

salvation from the Lord: But he that shall sin against me, shall hurt his own soul. All that hate me love death."

586. "*abbatem sibi praeesse desiderant*" ("they desire to have an abbot over them") (*Rule*, c. 5) (McCann, ed. and trans., *Rule of St. Benedict*, 34).

corresponds to his own ideas. With such motives obedience will tend to be imperfect, or even no obedience at all. It *cannot be enough* for us to do things just because they are good in themselves. The religious does not bind himself to do what is merely good in itself, but the *precise good willed for him by God*—a totally different story! Not living by faith, the imperfect fail to see the real point of the religious life, which is *to give ourselves up entirely to God's good pleasure* and find all our joy in pleasing Him alone.

Mary as the Perfect Religious: we know of the virginity, poverty and obedience of Mary. How about her interior perfection? Father Thomas Philippe[587] tells us:

1) *Mary's was a completely unique perfection of obedience to the Divine good pleasure.* Her vocation itself was unique. God had a unique law for her alone, known to no other, never promulgated before; it was made known to her from moment to moment, and she had to receive it with blind and perfect faith. She had to adapt herself to ever new commands and counsels; her life was a constant ascent, {with} no repetitions on the same level, no routines—everything {was} new. Her life was always varying with the new and unexpected manifestations of God's will.

2) This was impossible without an altogether supreme fidelity of a kind unknown to the rest of us. As a consequence, Father Thomas Philippe remarks, "She never had any conceptions of sanctity, for everything in her was always changing." {She had} no prejudice in favor of a preconceived notion of what she "wanted to be."

3) Mary has as her mission now to form the members of the Mystical Christ after the model of her own perfection (*N.B.* for each of us this means something different—in all it means reproducing her faith, her docility, her obedience to God—how? by obeying *her*).

Mary and Our Perfection:

1) It goes without saying that we must first of all imitate Our Lady *by loving our religious vocation with its obligations and its sacrifices.* {We} must at all costs avoid equivocation. It is not so bad to lead a natural life in the world, but it is very bad to lead a natural and selfish life in the cloister—and it is not hard to do so! We must really

587. See above, Part II, n. 118.

want the deprivations consequent on our vows, and especially the *renunciation of our own will.*

2) But she asks more than this. She wants us to have the same kind of docility and perfection as her own. She wants us to *renounce completely* the conduct of our own lives according to our tastes, prejudices, opinions and natural predispositions. *She wants us to be completely guided by her.* This, however, is a special grace, a special favor, reserved for little ones, who will be completely satisfied with this one thing alone, pleasing her as our Mother, and abandoning ourselves entirely to her.

3) What does this involve?

   a) In order to know most perfectly, in all its details, the will of God, we place our life, all our thoughts and actions, *under her immediate control.* We become *completely docile to her good pleasure.*

   b) *We no longer act in order to attain our own personal ends.* If we really know what this means, we will see that it is extremely difficult to do this consistently for a lifetime. It *does not* mean acting to please a human superior, acting for the common good, for the success of a common project which we see and appreciate. It means much more: acting to please God whom we do not see, acting to fulfill His plan which we do not understand in its fullness. To act without a personal or natural end in view is to act in some sense in the void, and *it gives a sense of void which is often unbearable.* It is only made bearable when it is filled by love—love of God and of Mary. *We no longer seek our own satisfaction in anything,* even in spiritual things (but indeed we *find* great peace in everything). *We no longer act on our own preferences,* our own choice of *what is more perfect, or more expedient* or more profitable. *We no longer weigh in the balance perfect and imperfect,* more or less spiritual, more or less difficult, more or less meritorious. We do not decide and make our choices on the basis of our own standard of values, our own appreciations, our reading, our "system," our background.

   c) Our only standard and guide is *what is more pleasing to our Mother, here and now,* not more pleasing *in itself,* but according to the circumstances. *This means:* (1) giving preference first of all to our ordinary obligations; (2) giving preference to God's *signified will*; (3) fully accepting His good pleasure in events, situations, etc., taking things exactly as they come to hand; (4) asking our Mother to show us what she wants, and then following what is simplest, most obvious, and most reasonable in the situation, guided by faith and grace.

More about this docility:

a) It means first of all being very little, and in a sense, unambitious, accepting our weakness and limitations without fuss—not pusillanimity, however! We will be asked to face difficult and even impossible things, and must not refuse. Only do not worry about it beforehand. St. Louis de Montfort says it means being like Jacob who preferred to stay at home with his mother, and did not go out except to do her will.[588] It means to love what is more obscure and retired, to prefer what is hidden and interior, and not to engage in exterior or showy or extraordinary things, except on a clear indication of Mary's good pleasure, never out of personal ambition.

b) It means desiring in general what is more ordinary and less spectacular.

c) Mary is *most exacting* in the matter of obedience. She is "inexorable" on this point (Fr. T. P.). She will pass over many other things, but not this one. She does not mind our mistakes—she corrects them herself. She does not mind dangers—she will protect us in them. She does not mind our weakness—her power will supply. She does not worry about our faults, provided we are resolved to take whatever steps she will suggest

---

588. "As to Jacob, the younger son, he was of a feeble constitution, meek and peaceful. He lived for the most part at home, in order to gain the good graces of his mother Rebecca, whom he loved tenderly. If he went abroad, it was not of his own will, or through any confidence in his own skill, but to obey his mother. He loved and honored his mother. It was on this account that he kept at home. He was never so happy as when watching her. He avoided everything which could displease her, and did everything which he thought would please her; and this increased the love which Rebecca already had for him. He was subject in all things to his dear mother. He obeyed her entirely in all matters—promptly, without delaying, and lovingly, without complaining. At the least indication of her will, the little Jacob ran and worked; and he believed, without questioning, everything she said to him. . . . Such also is the conduct which the predestinate daily observe. . . . The predestinate tenderly love and truly honor our Blessed Lady as their good Mother and Mistress. They love her not only in word but in truth. They honor her not only outwardly but in the depths of their hearts. They avoid, like Jacob, everything which can displease her; and they practise with fervor whatever they think will make them find favor with her" (St. Louis-Marie Grignion de Montfort, *True Devotion to Mary*, 140–43).

and *not* try to get ahead of her with our own plans. *Why the insistence on obedience?* Mary realizes the *urgent need* for us to follow her blindly step by step, in order to escape our spiritual enemies and get to God. Lot was slow to believe the angels when they told him he must get out of Sodom as quickly as possible. People escaping through the iron curtain {must give} blind obedience to their guides; especially children—a false step may ruin everything. Obedience to her is sufficient to offset all our other failings, for if we are united to her, her prudence, wisdom, love, purity, humility, etc. are shared by us, become our own. Hence, in the matter of obedience, she is a "terror," because really *she* must do the work, and we must consent and follow.

d) But HOW?

(1) Mary will indeed guide us personally and directly, as our Mother. We simply do the signified will of God; accept (or try to accept) all His good pleasure, and *ask Mary at every moment to guide us.* If we trust in her and listen with childlike docility, we will *certainly know what is her will for us,* and it will be in fact most perfect for us. Note that it will not necessarily be most exalted or lofty in itself. We are not required to do all the greatest works of perfection, *but only those which accord with our state.*

(2) To be thus subject to Mary implies a very special grace of God for which we *must ask.*

(3) Then we keep *our hearts wide open,* cast out our own desires and preconceptions, and *believe firmly* in Our Lady's love for us, her power to intervene in our lives and show us what to do (of course, consult directors and superiors whenever it is helpful).

(4) Do the simplest and most ordinary things, what best fit our circumstances, as *children* of Mary; be most *childlike* and *go on trusting.*

(5) The *effects* {will be} peace, simplicity, *less trouble, fewer sufferings* (maybe), obscurity, giving up a thousand cares; above all, {the} greater glory of God, and union with Him!!

Additional Materials

The Opening of the Liturgical Year

God our Creator intends to sanctify everything He has made. He intends to manifest Himself in His world. This manifestation is to be not only natural, fleshly (in the vestiges of His wisdom seen in all created things) but also spiritual and divine. In other words, God not only saw, from the beginning, that all created things were "good,"[1] but He also intended them to be *holy*, that is to say, sanctified by a consecration that would transfigure them in His own light. For this it was necessary that man, the high priest of creation, should consecrate the universe to God by the action of his own spirit united to the Spirit of God and consecrated to God.

Man fell, and with him fell creation. God sent His Son into the world to redeem man and to elevate the fallen world, with Him, and to perfect the work of sanctification, the manifestation of the divine glory in the cosmos, the work which man had failed to accomplish in Adam. This is the work of Christ, the Lord and Redeemer of man, the Head of the Human Race, the King of the New Creation. We live in the Kingdom of Christ, the new world, consecrated to God, the Messianic Kingdom, the New Jerusalem. The history of the Kingdom is working itself out, but in the mystery of faith, hidden from the wise of this world ({see} 1 Cor. {1:19–21}[2]) and the final day of its manifestation is reserved for the future—the end of time.

Time, which is now enclosed between the two advents of Christ— His first coming in humility and obscurity, and His second coming in majesty and power—has been claimed by God for His own. Time is to be sanctified like everything else, by the presence and the action of Christ.

---

1. Gen 1:3, 10, 12, 18, 21, 25, 31.

2. Chapter and verse left blank in typescript; reading adopted from "Time and the Liturgy," the revised version of this material in Merton, *Seasons of Celebration*, 48.

The Redemption is not simply a past historical fact with a juridical effect on individual souls. It is an ever-present reality, living and efficacious, penetrating to the inmost depths of our soul by the word of salvation and the mystery of faith. The Redemption is Christ Himself, "Who of God is made to us wisdom and justice and sanctification and redemption" (1 Cor. 1:30), living and sharing His divine life with His elect. To be redeemed is not merely to be absolved of guilt before God; it is also to live in Christ, to be born again of water and the Holy Spirit,[3] to be in Him a new creature, to live in the Spirit. To say that the Redemption is an ever-present spiritual reality is to say that Christ has laid hold upon time and sanctified it, giving it a sacramental character, that is to say, making it an efficacious sign of our union with God in Him. So "time" is a medium which makes the fact of Redemption present to all men.

Christ has given a special meaning and power to the cycle of the seasons, which of themselves are "good" and by their very nature have a capacity to signify our life in God: for the seasons express the rhythm of natural life. They are the systole and diastole of the natural life of our globe. Jesus has made this ebb and flow of light and darkness, activity and rest, birth and death, the sign of a higher life, a life which we live in Him, a life which knows no decline, and a day which does not fall into darkness. It is the "day of the Lord,"[4] which dawns for us anew each morning, the day of Easter, the *Pascha Domini*,[5] the day of eternity, shining upon us in time.

For fallen man, the cycle of seasons, the wheel of time itself, is only a spiritual prison. Each new spring brings a temporary hope. Autumn and winter destroy that hope with their ever-returning reminder of death. For man living only in the flesh, only on the level of his nature, for man living without God, the great realities of human love and fertility are without issue. We are begotten by parents who disappear from the face of the earth and are forgotten. In our turn, we grow, become strong, bring forth sons, and then we too fail and die and are forgotten. Our sons in their turn will pass through the same cycle, which ends inexorably in death and in oblivion. It is as if the whole of nature were striving upwards, but striving in vain. Generation after generation she kindles the flames of countless human spirits, capable of an eternal destiny, souls that have insatiable aspirations for love, for wisdom, for joy in God. The flames leap up for a

---

3. John 3:5.

4. 2 Thess 2:2; 2 Pet 3:10.

5. "the Passover of the Lord" (Lev 23:5; Num 28:16; Deut 16:1).

brief moment, then die down and are extinguished. They are followed by others. None of them can reach up into eternity. The cycle of the seasons reminds us, by this perpetual renewal and perpetual death, that death is the end of all. The universe which came into being will some day grow cold, perhaps, and die. What will remain?

The modern city man, the "crowd man," is something more than fallen. He lives not only below the level of grace, but below the level of nature—below his own humanity. No longer in contact with the created world, or with himself, out of touch with the reality of nature, he lives in the world of falsity and illusion, the world of fictions with which modern man has surrounded himself. In such a world, man's life is no longer even a seasonal cycle. It is a linear *flight* into nothingness, a flight from reality and from God, without purpose and without objective, except to keep moving, to keep from having to face reality. To live in Christ we must first break away from this linear flight into nothingness and recover the rhythm and order of man's real nature. Before we can become gods we must first be men.

For man in Christ, the cycle of the seasons is something entirely new. It has become a *cycle of salvation*. The year is not just another year; it is the *Year of the Lord*—a year in which the passage of time itself brings us not only the natural renewal of spring and the fruitfulness of an earthly summer, but also the spiritual and interior fruitfulness of grace. The life of the flesh which ebbs and flows like the seasons and tends always to its last decline is elevated and supplanted by a life of the spirit which knows no decrease, which always grows in those who live with Christ in the liturgical year. "For though the outward man is corrupted, yet the inward man is renewed day by day . . . . For we know if our earthly house of this habitation be dissolved that we have a building of God, a house not made with hands, eternal in heaven" (2 Cor. 4:16, 5:1).

The Word of God having entered into time by His Incarnation, His birth of a Virgin Mother, has changed the cycle of the seasons from an imprisonment to a liberation. The Church prays God, at Christmas, that "the new birth of Thy only-begotten Son may set us free, whom the old bondage detains under the yoke of sin"—"*ut nos Unigeniti tui nova per carnem nativitas liberet, quos sub peccati jugo vetusta servitus tenet.*"[6] The liturgy makes the very passage of time sanctify our lives, for each new season renews an aspect of the great Mystery of Christ living and present

---

6. Collect: third Mass of Christmas (*Missale Romanum*, 18; *Missale Cisterciense*, 18); vespers collect: Christmas (*Breviarium Cisterciense, Pars Hiemalis*, 236).

in His Church. Each new season shows us some new way in which we live in Him, in which He acts in the world. Each new feast draws our attention to the great truth of His presence in the midst of us, and shows us a different view of His action in the world, now in his mysteries, and again in His saints, now in His sacraments, and again in the hallowed building of His churches, in His altars, and in the relics of His saints.

The liturgical cycle renews our redemption in Christ, delivers us from the servitude of sin and from the corruption of a fleshly mode of being, which in this time of struggle and preparation tends to assert itself in our lives. The liturgical cycle shows us that though we are caught in a struggle between flesh and spirit, though we are indeed the "fighting Church"—the Church militant—yet the victory is already ours. We possess the grace of Christ, Who alone can deliver us from the "body of this death."[7] He Who is in us is stronger than the world. He has "overcome the world."[8] In the cycle of the holy year, the Church rhythmically breathes the life-giving atmosphere of the Spirit, and her bloodstream is cleansed of the elements of death. She lives in Christ, and with Him praises the Father.

And so, while the cycle of time is a prison without escape for the natural man, living in the flesh and so doomed to disappear with all the rest of his world that passes away, and while time is for the man of our cities only a linear flight from God, for the believer who lives in Christ each new day renews his participation in the mystery of Christ. Each day is a new dawn of that *lumen Christi*[9] which knows no setting.

* * * * * * *

The liturgical year renews the mysteries of our redemption each day in the Mass. It renews our participation in particular mysteries of the life of Christ. It teaches us the ways of the saints and renews our union with them in the charity of the Spirit. It is a year of *salvation*, but also a year of *enlightenment* and of *transformation*. The mysteries of the liturgical cycle not only bring to our souls new outpourings of the salvific waters of grace; they also enlighten our minds with insights into the ways of God, ever ancient and ever new. They teach us more of Christ; they show us

---

7. Rom 7:24.

8. John 16:33.

9. "light of Christ" (versicle sung in the procession with the paschal candle on Holy Saturday) (*Missale Romanum*, 190; *Missale Cisterciense*, 164).

more of the meaning of our life in Him; they make us grow in Him; they transform us in Him. Indeed, the liturgy is the great school of Christian living and the great transforming force which reshapes our souls and our characters in the likeness of Christ.

Dom Odo Casel[10] has compared the liturgical year to a ring which the Church, the Virgin Bride of Christ, triumphantly displays as the sign of her union with the Incarnate Word. This holy ring is the gift of Christ to His Church as a pledge of His love and of His fidelity to His promises. The "cycle" or "circle" of the liturgy, which eternally returns to its beginning, is a symbol of the unity of God who is eternally the same yet ever new. More than that, however, the liturgical "ring" of feasts is a symbol of that first "cycle" of actions by which Christ redeemed the world—the "ring" created by His descent into time, His life, death, resurrection and ascension into heaven restoring all things, in Himself, to the Father. "The Father Himself loveth you because you have loved me and have believed that I came forth from the Father. I came forth from the Father and am come into the world: again, I leave the world and I go to the Father" (Jn. 16:28). These words of St. John show us that the Church's belief in Christ is *not a mere static assent to His historical existence, but a dynamic participation in the great cycle of actions which manifest in the world the love of the Father for the ones He has called to union with Himself, in His beloved Son.* It is not simply that we are "saved," and the Father remits the debt contracted by our sins, but that we are *loved* by the Father, and loved by Him in so far as we believe that He has sent His Son, and has called Him back into heaven and given all power into His hands.

In the liturgical year, the Church sees and acclaims this action of the Father who so loved the world that He gave His only-begotten Son[11] for the salvation of men. It is a dialogue between mankind and the Father, in which the Father manifests Himself in His Word, and in which the Church, filled with the Spirit of the Father and the Son, praises and magnifies the glory of the Father. To enter into the liturgical cycle is to participate in the great work of redemption effected by the Son. "Liturgy" is "common work"—a sacred work in which the Church cooperates with the divine Redeemer in reliving His mysteries and applying their fruits to all mankind.

---

10. Odo Casel, OSB, Introduction to Loehr, *L'Année de Seigneur*, 1.25–26; see (in English) Löhr, *Mass through the Year*, 1.xv; also found in the earlier version of this work: Loehr, *Year of Our Lord*, xxi–xxii.

11. John 3:16.

It is quite clear that the Church does not regard the liturgy as a mere source of aesthetic satisfaction, or as an expression of Christian culture. Nor is it merely a way in which the Christian society becomes formally aware of its existence and its relationship to God, in order to praise Him. It is a *work* in which the Church collaborates with the Divine Redeemer, renewing on her altars the sacred mysteries which are the life and salvation of man, uttering again the life-giving words that are capable of saving and transforming our souls, blessing again the sick and the possessed, and preaching His Gospel to the poor. In the liturgy, then, the Church would have us realize that we meet the same Christ Who went about everywhere doing good, and Who is still present in the midst of us wherever two or three are gathered together in His Name.[12] And we meet Him by sharing in His life and His Redemption. We meet Christ in order to *be* Christ, and with Him save the world.

* * * * * * *

In order to understand the full meaning of the liturgy, we have to grasp the liturgical conception of time. The Christian "present" of the liturgy has something of the character of eternity, in which all reality is present at once. The past and the future are therefore made present in the mysteries of the liturgy. In the Advent mystery, the Church not only relives the longing of the prophets and the patriarchs for the Redeemer, not only prays to God for the grace of a "new nativity" at Christmas, but also anticipates the coming of Christ at the Last Day. In every liturgical mystery the Church embraces the whole history of man's salvation, while concentrating her attention, for the time being, on one particular phase of that history.

At Christmas, we celebrate the coming of God into the world. We look especially at His birth at Bethlehem and see how that birth reveals to us the infinite mercy of God. But at the same moment we return to the very beginning of all, to the generation of the Word in the bosom of the Father {which} is also present to us, and we go forward to the end of all, when, having come again into the world at the Last Judgement, and taken all things to Himself, and made all things new, we ourselves will share, in heaven, in His eternal birth and hear the voice of the Father saying to us, in Him: "This day have I begotten thee!"[13]

12. Matt 18:20.
13. Ps 2:7; Acts 13:33.

In every liturgical mystery we have this telescoping of time and eternity, of the universal and the personal, what is common to all ages, what is above and beyond all time, and what is most particular and most immediate to our own time and place where we celebrate the liturgy. Christ in His infinite greatness embraces all things, the divine and the human, the spiritual and the material, the old and the new, the great and the small, and in the liturgy He makes Himself all things to all men[14] and becomes all in all.[15]

The works which Christ accomplished in time remain complete, unique and perfect in eternity, and the liturgical mysteries make these works present to us each time they are celebrated. Not only that, they incorporate us in His mysteries and renew their effect in time and in space. By the liturgy, while remaining in time, we enter into the great celebration that takes place before the throne of the Lamb in heaven, in eternity. The liturgical year takes the passage of time and elevates it to the level of eternity. Time is "baptized" and sanctified by the infusion of the divine light hidden in the liturgical mysteries, a light which flows forth to penetrate our lives and our actions and to fill them with the presence of the Lord Christ, the *Kyrios Christos*.

In each new liturgical feast we celebrate Christ Himself, not just the various things which He did, or the exploits of His saints. At Christmas, we celebrate Christ, living and present to us in mystery, and commune with the divine mercy that He manifests by His birth. At the Epiphany, we celebrate Christ as present among us, diffusing upon the world the light and glory of the Father and making known the Father's plan for the salvation of the gentiles. At Septuagesima we return to the creation of the world, in the Word, Who is present with us: we consider man's flight from God into the darkness of sin. We share with Christ the labors and sufferings of His public life in Lent; we enter into His Passion. In Holy Week, Christ is present in the midst of His Church as the Lamb slain before the beginning of the world,[16] as the Servant of Yahweh whose sufferings were foretold by Isaias and Jeremias, as the Christ Who is crucified even today in His holy Church. At Easter, He is present among us as risen and triumphant, and shedding upon us the light of eternal peace. At Pentecost, He is present among us as the founder of His Church and the Giver of the Paraclete.

14. 1 Cor 9:22.
15. 1 Cor 15:28.
16. Rev 13:8.

In all these liturgical seasons, as Dom Guéranger says,

> Christ Himself is the source as well as the object of the liturgy. Hence the ecclesiastical year is neither more nor less than *the manifestation of Jesus Christ* in His mysteries, in the Church and in the faithful soul. It is the divine cycle, in which appear all the works of God, each in its turn. . . . If, every year, the Church renews her youth as that of the eagle, she does so {because} by means of the cycle of the liturgy, she is visited by her divine Spouse, who supplies all her wants. (*Liturgical Year*, vol. i, p. 9–10)[17]

Pope Pius XII has canonized these teachings in the succinct formulas of *Mediator Dei*: "Throughout the entire year, the Mass and the Divine Office center especially around the Person of Jesus Christ."[18] "Whilst the sacred Liturgy calls to mind the mysteries of Jesus Christ, it strives to make all believers take their part in them so that the divine Head of the Mystical Body may live in all the members with the fulness of His holiness. Let the souls of Christians be like altars on each of which a different phase of the Sacrifice of the High Priest, comes to life again."[19] "Hence the Liturgical Year . . . is not a cold and lifeless representation of the events of the past, or a bare and simple record of a former age, *it is rather Christ Himself Who is ever living in His Church*."[20]

✳ ✳ ✳ ✳ ✳ ✳ ✳

The liturgy is the most direct way to union with Christ. It is the expression of the Church's consciousness that she is the Bride of Christ. It is the manifestation of her life in and with Christ. It is the evidence of her mystical life, which she has received from God, in Christ, by the Holy Spirit. The liturgy, indeed, is the fountainhead of all true Christian mysticism. It is the contemplation of the Spouse, given to her in the Holy Spirit Who alone knows all the deep things of God. The liturgy is inspired by that

---

17. Guéranger, *Liturgical Year*, which reads: "It is therefore Jesus Christ Himself who is . . . liturgy; and hence . . . year, which we have undertaken to explain in this work, is neither . . . Christ and His mysteries, . . . does so because by . . ." (italics added).

18. Pius XII, *Mediator Dei*, 53 (#151).

19. Pius XII, *Mediator Dei*, 53–54 (#152), which reads: "While . . . Sacrifice, offered by . . ."

20. Pius XII, *Mediator Dei*, 57 (#165), which reads: ". . . simple and bare . . . age. It . . ." (italics added).

"*sensus Christi*"[21]—the mind of Christ—which is hers alone. We must see that through the liturgy we enter into eternity, we ascend to Christ, or rather eternity enters into our lives, and we become aware of the Christ Who has descended into our souls. Our prayer-life must be nourished by the liturgy, formed by it. But the liturgical spirit leaves full scope to Christian liberty: *Ubi Spiritus Domini ibi libertas.*[22] The liturgy is not slavery to fashion and to passing modes. It is life and prayer and contemplation in Christ, and everyone can and must make use of it in his own way, though always according to the spirit of the Church. Each one must participate in a full, mature and free manner—which means to say that he must give what is his own to the liturgy, not submerge himself in it and lose his personality in a corporate act without contributing anything to it or receiving from it anything that is his own. The liturgy is the *common interior prayer* of the members of Christ expressed in open and public worship which manifests their union in charity and their participation in His sacred mysteries. As such, it is, in the words of St. Pius X, the source of all genuine Christian spirituality.[23] It is the prayer and praise of the Bride of Christ, the Church, and if we are one with her, then we too will be united, as she is, with the Divine Bridegroom.

November 25, 1955

⌒

Advent: "Redeeming the time"[24] (St. Paul)—read Ephesians 5:7–21.[25] {At the} beginning of {the} liturgical year, meditate on {the} "sacramental"

---

21. "mind of Christ" (1 Cor 2:16).

22. "Where the Spirit of the Lord is, there is liberty" (2 Cor 3:17).

23. Pope Pius X, Motu Proprio *Tra le Sollecitudini* (November 22, 1903): "les fidèles se réunissent précisément pour puiser cet esprit à sa source première et indispensable: la participation active aux mystères sacro-saints et à la prière publique et solennelle de l'Eglise" ("The faithful are united precisely in order to draw this spirit from its original and indispensable source: the active participation in the sacred mysteries and the solemn public prayer of the Church") (*Liturgie: Les Enseignements Pontificaux*, 175 [#220]).

24. Eph 5:16.

25. "Be ye not therefore partakers with them. For you were heretofore darkness, but now light in the Lord. Walk then as children of the light. For the fruit of the light is in all goodness, and justice, and truth; Proving what is well pleasing to God: And have no fellowship with the unfruitful works of darkness, but rather reprove them. For the things that are done by them in secret, it is a shame even to speak of. But all things that are reproved, are made manifest by the light; for all that is made manifest is light. Wherefore he saith: Rise thou that sleepest, and arise from the dead: and Christ shall

quality which has been given to time by the liturgy. Time {is} a mystery—the measurement of change resulting from interrelated successive movements. {The} liturgy takes time as it appears to us; liturgy {is the} wedding of time and eternity, the eternal realities {as} present to us temporally and successively. {We note the} prison of time for the pagan, the cycle of the seasons, {and the} meaningless "flight" of {the} modern pagan below {the} level of nature. For the Church, {the} cycle of the seasons = {the} cycle of salvation, {a process of} spiritual growth and faithfulness which *remains* ({cf.} 2 Cor. 4:16–5:1: spiritual growth in grace and union with Christ {and} *treasure in heaven*[26]): how? by the *Incarnation*: "*nova per carnem nativitas liberet*";[27] {He is} a man (temporal) Who is *God* (eternal). Each year {is} a *year of salvation*: {we are} "saved" by the feasts and mysteries that recur in time. {There is a} *dynamic participation* in the mysteries of Christ. {The} "work" of the liturgy {is} God's *work of salvation, in which we share*—liturgical life, sanctifying the year, {a} manifestation, {a} "witness" of {the} Church's life, in and with Christ. Before the Incarnation, "all was enclosed under sin":[28] n.b. {the} power of {the} "tempter," {the} "adversary," {still} obscure in {the} Old Testament, {but} revealed by Jesus {as} "the enemy." {This is the} mystery of sin and Law, from which there was *not yet* Redemption ({the} saints of {the} Old Law {were} saved by hope, but could not enter heaven). *Now* Redemption has come—we have but to accept it: *consentire salvari est.*[29] {We need to} stress {the} theme of *consent*—that is our present Advent. {The} first Advent {focuses on} hope ({the} promise)—deliverance from captivity to Satan; {the} second Advent {on} consent (merit)—deliverance from {the} molestations of sin, {with} perfection etc. *to come*; {the} third Advent {on} fulfillment

---

enlighten thee. See therefore, brethren, how you walk circumspectly: not as unwise, But as wise: redeeming the time, because the days are evil. Wherefore become not unwise, but understanding what is the will of God. And be not drunk with wine, wherein is luxury; but ye filled with the holy Spirit, Speaking to yourselves in psalms, and hymns, and spiritual canticles, singing and making melody in your hearts to the Lord; Giving thanks always for all things, in the name of our Lord Jesus Christ, to God and the Father: Being subject one to another, in the fear of Christ."

26. Matt 19:21; Mark 10:21; Luke 18:22.

27. "May the new birth in the flesh set free" (collect, third Mass of Christmas) (*Missale Romanum*, 18; *Missale Cisterciense*, 18); (collect, vespers, lauds: Christmas) (*Breviarium Cisterciense, Hiemalis*, 236, 255).

28. Gal 3:22.

29. "to consent is to be saved" (St. Bernard, *De Gratia et Libero Arbitrio*, c. 1 [Migne, *PL* 182, col. 1002B]).

(reward)—God {as} All in all. Hence our Advent has something in common with that of the prophets: they look forward to {the} second *and* third {of these}. ({Note the} readings {of the} first nocturn[30] here.)

~

Isaias (from Guillet, *Thèmes Bibliques*):[31]

1. Isaias {is} the "prophet of justice"[32] (cf. Amos and Michaeas): {note} his condemnation of social injustice (5:7; 10:2; 5:23) {and} His {(i.e. God's)} demand for justice in His people ({c.} 1); {note} His "process" against His people (3:14; 5:3, etc.; cf. Os. 2:4). Justice {is} the characteristic of the Messianic Kingdom (9:5–6, etc.; 1:26; 11:4; 28:17; 16:5 etc.; 32:1, 16; 33:5). Justice = peace in {the} Messianic Kingdom (9:6; 1:26; 54:13–14). The Justice of the Messias is not merely human but based on the *fidelity of God*, which condemns {the} infidelity of Israel (cf. Mic. 6; Is. 5:16, 33:5); {it} is the work of God's mercy (Mic. 7:8–9, 20 etc.). {On page} 58, {the} justice of {the} Messianic Kingdom {is} described: it is established by {the} Spirit of God (11:2; 28:6; 1:25–26) *after a terrible and purifying trial* (1:25–26; Amos 1:3–11, 16, 3:14, 5:18; Osee 4:1, 8:13, 9:7–9, etc.; Mic. 1:2–4 etc.; Mal. 3:2), which makes the purity of divine mercy shine forth over {the} humbled pride of man (Jer. 5). {It is} *totally new*, {a} complete transformation (43:19, 45:23–25, 54:12). {The} justice of God shines forth in Sion transformed (4:3–5, 1:25–27) (62: "La sainteté de Dieu se révèle en établissant dans Jérusalem la justice"[33]). When the justice of Yahweh shines forth in Jerusalem, it will do so *in her fidelity* (because of the *fidelity of the Messias* [11:5] and {the} mercy of Yahweh [54:10]). FAITH {is} the key—by it, and it alone, we attach ourselves to the just God and stand in His strength (7:9, 28:16); {the} fulfillment in {the} New Testament (Guillet, p. 86f.) {comes} in *Jesus*, objectively, {and} in grace, subjectively. Yahweh uses *human instruments* to do His work: (1) pagan, like Cyrus (45); (2) holy: the Servant. {On} p. 68, {the} liberation

30. It is not clear which day Merton may be referring to here, or if he is referring to the first nocturn readings for Advent generally, which are selected sequentially from Isaiah and do correspond roughly to the pattern of development Merton has just presented (*Breviarium Cisterciense, Hiemalis*, 177–227).

31. Guillet, *Thèmes Bibliques*, 57–74. In his journal entry for November 12, 1957, Merton calls Guillet's book "fantastically rich and useful" and adds: "Every line has something in it you do not want to miss. Opens up new roads in the Old Testament" (Merton, *Search for Solitude*, 135).

32. Guillet, *Thèmes Bibliques*, 57.

33. "The holiness of God is revealed in establishing justice in Jerusalem."

of Israel {is considered the} supreme manifestation of {the} justice of Yahweh (51:22, 54:17; cf. 49:4–6, 32:17); in God, justice = salvation (45 and 46); in man, justice = seeking Yahweh (51; cf. 58), preparing His coming (56:1, 59:14; cf. Ps. 103 [Guillet, p. 83]).

◦

Advent Readings from Isaias:

1. The prophets (nabis) were chosen by God to utter His special messages, in full consciousness of what they were doing: cf. {the} vocation of Jeremias (1:4–10), Isaias (6), Amos (7:15), Jonas; and {their} *mission—to* the People of Israel (also *against* the Gentiles and *to* the whole world). "Le prophète est un homme qui a une expérience immédiate de Dieu, qui a reçu la révélation de sa sainteté et de ses volontés, qui juge le présent et voit l'avenir à la lumière de Dieu, qui est envoyé par Dieu pour rappeler aux hommes des exigences et les ramener dans la voie de son obéissance et de son amour."[34] {This is} a phenomenon *peculiar to Israel* and one of the special modes of Divine Providence in guiding the Chosen People.

2. The prophetic message (a) always contains a teaching of immediate importance for the hearers; (b) often foretells consequences of ignoring or heeding this teaching; (c) sometimes looks to the last days; (d) very often has an *ulterior meaning* beyond the awareness of {the} prophet himself, concerned with the immediate issue; (e) the Church is concerned with their prophecies of {the} *Kingdom of God* most of all, and the greatest messianic prophet is Isaias.

3. *Moses* {is} *the first of the prophets* (Nm. 12:6–8; Dt. 34:10–12), *Jesus the "last"* (John {the} Baptist {is} the last prophet of {the} Old Testament: Mt. 11:9). {The} prophets all stand for *monotheism—against* idolatry {and for the} *universality* of Yahweh's reign; {for} *morality—interior* sanctity against legal formalism: "truly seeking God";[35] {for} *messianism—*and {the} salvation of the "remnant" (Is. 37:31–32) from which a new people will rise (READ ISAIAS 1[36]).

34. "The prophet is a person who has an immediate experience of God, who has received the revelation of His holiness and of His will, who judges the present and sees the future in the light of God, who is sent by God to remind people of demands and to bring them back to the way of His obedience and His love" (*Sainte Bible*, 973).

35. Cf. "*si revera Deum quaerit*" ("if he truly seeks God") (*Rule*, c. 58) (McCann, ed. and trans., *Rule of St. Benedict*, 130).

36. "Therefore saith the Lord the God of hosts, the mighty one of Israel: Ah! I will comfort myself over my adversaries: and I will be revenged of my enemies. And I will turn my hand to thee, and I will clean purge away thy dross, and I will take away all thy tin. And I will restore thy judges as they were before, and thy counsellors as of old."

4. *Advent {is} the season of prophecy*: READ DANIEL 7:[37] {the} Kingdom of God {is} ruled over by the "*anointed—Christ—Messias*"; rejected by His own, but their Savior (Is. 42:1–7 etc.).

∽

Isaias—Advent

1. *Catholic Biblical Commentary*:[38] even independent of {the} question of authorship, it is clear that Isaias falls into three sections, addressed

---

After this thou shalt be called the city of the just, a faithful city. Sion shall be redeemed in judgment, and they shall bring her back in justice. And he shall destroy the wicked, and the sinners together: and they that have forsaken the Lord, shall be consumed" (Isa 1:24–28).

37. "I beheld therefore in the vision of the night, and lo, one like the son of man came with the clouds of heaven, and he came even to the Ancient of days: and they presented him before him. And he gave him power, and glory, and a kingdom: and all peoples, tribes and tongues shall serve him: his power is an everlasting power that shall not be taken away: and his kingdom that shall not be destroyed. My spirit trembled, I Daniel was affrighted at these things, and the visions of my head troubled me. I went near to one of them that stood by, and asked the truth of him concerning all these things, and he told me the interpretation of the words, and instructed me: These four great beasts are four kingdoms, which shall arise out of the earth. But the saints of the most high God shall take the kingdom: and they shall possess the kingdom for ever and ever. After this I would diligently learn concerning the fourth beast, which was very different from all, and exceeding terrible: his teeth and claws were of iron: he devoured and broke in pieces, and the rest he stamped upon with his feet: And concerning the ten horns that he had on his head: and concerning the other that came up, before which three horns fell: and of that horn that had eyes, and a mouth speaking great things, and was greater than the rest. I beheld, and lo, that horn made war against the saints, and prevailed over them, Till the Ancient of days came and gave judgment to the saints of the most High, and the time came, and the saints obtained the kingdom. And thus he said: The fourth beast shall be the fourth kingdom upon earth, which shall be greater than all the kingdoms, and shall devour the whole earth, and shall tread it down, and break it in pieces. And the ten horns of the same kingdom, shall be ten kings: and another shall rise up after them, and he shall be mightier than the former, and he shall bring down three kings. And he shall speak words against the High One, and shall crush the saints of the most High: and he shall think himself able to change times and laws, and they shall be delivered into his hand until a time, and times, and half a time. And judgment shall sit, that his power may be taken away, and be broken in pieces, and perish even to the end. And that the kingdom, and power, and the greatness of the kingdom, under the whole heaven, may be given to the people of the saints of the most High: whose kingdom is an everlasting kingdom, and all kings shall serve him, and shall obey him. Hitherto is the end of the word. I Daniel was much troubled with my thoughts, and my countenance was changed in me: but I kept the word in my heart" (Dan 7:13–28).

38. Power, "Isaias," 539.

to three distinct audiences: (1) chapters 1–39: addressed to Jews of {the} eighth-century BC; (2) chapters 40–55: addressed to Jews of Babylon just before the return; (3) chapters 56–66: addressed to Jews after {the} return, about 520 BC. {The} CBC clings still to unity of authorship,[39] but the book is a post-exilic redaction with interpolations. {The} *Bible {de} Jerusalem*[40] attributes to different authors (disciples) {the} *Apocalypse of Isaias* (24–27); {the} *Book of Consolation* (differences of content, style, etc., {the} evident gap of 200 years); the decision of {the} *Biblical Commission*[41] (1908)—it was a warning, but since that time evidence has grown and more and more Catholic scholars incline to {the} *probability* of diverse authorship. Chapters 56–66 {are seen as} *a collection by diverse authors.*

2. *The Book of the Emmanuel* (ch. 6–12)—{there is a} close connection of Isaias' prophecies and doctrine with the historical background ({cf.} 4 Kings 16; 2 Par. 28): (a) *wealth and luxury* of {the} Jews at {the} expense of {the} poor; exterior religiosity without soul; {the} paganism of Achaz ({cf.} Michaeas 7); (b) *The Assyrian menace*—Assyria {as the} instrument of Yahweh (10:5ff.); (c) The *Syro-Ephraimite* war: (1) *The Inaugural Vision*: {the} threat of destruction and promise of {a} remnant (6—all); (2) {the} *first warning to Achaz, to cling to Yahweh* (7:1–9); (3) {the} PROMISE OF EMMANUEL (7:10–25) (4) {the} waters of Siloe (8:5–8); (5) a child is born to us (8:24—9:6).

3. The reign of the Messias as predicted in Isaias 1; Isaias the prophet of justice. *Outline: Book of Emmanuel*: 6: Vision—introduction; 7–8: prophecies of deliverance if faithful to Yahweh; 9: The Deliverer (1–6) (Assyrian invasion); 10: Fall of Assyria; 11: Messianic Kingdom; 12: Hymn of Thanksgiving.

4. *The Book of Consolation*

～

Isaias: Book of the Emmanuel
{Chapter} 6: King Ozias (Azarias in official lists), a good king, got leprosy and was replaced by Joatham (752); Achaz came to {the} throne in 742; Ozias died in {the} reign of Achaz, in 734 (?). {The} vision of Yahweh on a throne as *the true King*, {surrounded by} Seraphim, fiery

---

39. Power, "Isaias," 541.

40. *Sainte Bible,* 977–78.

41. Pontifical Biblical Commission, *De Libri Isaiae,* 613–14.

beings, {reveals} (a) {the} holiness of God; (b) Isaias' free acceptance of his mission; (c) {the} doctrine of the remnant (READ 8–13[42]).

{Chapter} 7: {The} politics of Isaias and those of Achaz—Achaz {is a} coward {and an} opportunist, {who} trusts in Assyria {and is therefore} against {the} anti-Assyrian Syro-Ephraimite bloc—these have beaten him before; Isaias {counsels} trust in God's promises to *David*—hence {the} prophecy of Emmanuel from {the} House of David (note {the} vast widening of perspectives); {he} *offers a sign*—any miracle—{but} Achaz hypocritically refuses to ask {for} a sign. Verse 2 {speaks of the} fear of the Jews; 3—Shear Yashub (a remnant will return); 4—"tails of firebrands"—they are "burnt out"; 14–18—{the} *Emmanuel Prophecy*: (a) almah {means a} young girl of marriageable age, never used of {a} married woman (critics vary—{it} probably means "girl"); (b) Emmanuel: God with us. {Verse} 15 {mentions} butter and honey—{there are} arguments: does this mean a prosperous age, {or a} lean year, {at the} time of his coming? In reality {it} means he shall have wisdom and judgement from birth, {reflecting the} custom of rubbing honey on {a} baby's lips (cf. {the} salt of baptism); {he is to be} *the supremely wise king*. {Verses} 17–25 {foretell} the invasion, {a} chastisement for unbelief, {the} fall of {the} House of David when Nechao defeats Josias (third after Ezechias), killed at *Megiddo* (609); Nineveh fell {in} 612. Chapter 8: the son of Isaias: MAHER-SHALAL-HASH-BAZ (deliverance from invasion) ({note the} primitive names); read 1–4: SHEAR YASHUB (remnant) and 16–22[43] (16: I bury this witness in the heart of my disciples) (note {also} 6–8).

42. "And I heard the voice of the Lord, saying: Whom shall I send? and who shall go for us? And I said: Lo, here am I, send me. And he said: Go, and thou shalt say to this people: Hearing, hear, and understand not: and see the vision, and know it not. Blind the heart of this people, and make their ears heavy, and shut their eyes: lest they see with their eyes, and hear with their ears, and understand with their heart and be converted and I heal them. And I said: How long, O Lord? And he said: Until the cities be wasted without inhabitant, and the houses without man, and the land shall be left desolate. And the Lord shall remove men far away, and she shall be multiplied that was left in the midst of the earth. And there shall be still a tithing therein, and she shall turn, and shall be made a shew as a turpentine tree, and as an oak that spreadeth its branches: that which shall stand therein, shall be a holy seed."

43. "And the Lord said to me: Take thee a great book, and write in it with a man's pen. Take away the spoils with speed, quickly take the prey. And I took unto me faithful witnesses, Urias the priest, and Zacharias the son of Barachias. And I went to the prophetess, and she conceived, and bore a son. And the Lord said to me: Call his name, Hasten to take away the spoils: Make haste to take away the prey. For before the child know to call his father and his mother, the strength of Damascus, and the spoils of

Chapter 9 (prose introduction): *Christmas: first nocturn*—first lesson and canticle,[44] *third nocturn*—first canticle[45]): formerly He has troubled the land of Zabulon and Naphthali, but in the latter days He will glorify the way to the sea beyond Jordan, where Galilee looks to the Gentiles. {In the context of the} Assyrian conquest (732) {and the} deportation {is the} prophecy of the coming of the Messias in Galilee. "*A child is born to us*" (READ 2–7[46]): 3: Thou *hast* increased the joy—Thou has made exultation great; 4: rod of their shoulder (beatings)—*In die Madian*[47] (Judges 7–8:[48] Oreb, Zeb, Zebee—Salmana—Ps. 82[49]); 5: *No more war*; 6–7 ({n.b.} importance of the *names* here): (a) Government on his shoulder—royal power; (b) the wonderful counsellor, a counsellor of wonderful things:

Samaria shall be taken away before the king of the Assyrians. . . . Bind up the testimony, seal the law among my disciples. And I will wait for the Lord, who hath hid his face from the house of Jacob, and I will look for him. Behold I and my children, whom the Lord hath given me for a sign, and for a wonder in Israel from the Lord of hosts, who dwelleth in mount Sion. And when they shall say to you: Seek of pythons, and of diviners, who mutter in their enchantments: should not the people seek of their God, for the living of the dead? To the law rather, and to the testimony. And if they speak not according to this word, they shall not have the morning light. And they shall pass by it, they shall fall, and be hungry: and when they shall be hungry, they will be angry, and curse their king, and their God, and look upwards. And they shall look to the earth, and behold trouble and darkness, weakness and distress, and a mist following them, and they cannot fly away from their distress."

44. Isa 8:23–9:2; Isa 9:1–3 (*Breviarium Cisterciense, Hiemalis*, 241).

45. Isa 9:1–6 (*Breviarium Cisterciense, Hiemalis*, 249–50).

46. "The people that walked in darkness, have seen a great light: to them that dwelt in the region of the shadow of death, light is risen. Thou hast multiplied the nation, and hast not increased the joy. They shall rejoice before thee, as they that rejoice in the harvest, as conquerors rejoice after taking a prey, when they divide the spoils. For the yoke of their burden, and the rod of their shoulder, and the sceptre of their oppressor thou hast overcome, as in the day of Madian. For every violent taking of spoils, with tumult, and garment mingled with blood, shall be burnt, and be fuel for the fire. For a Child is born to us, and a son is given to us, and the government is upon his shoulder: and his name shall be called, Wonderful, Counsellor, God the Mighty, the Father of the world to come, the Prince of Peace. His empire shall be multiplied, and there shall be no end of peace: he shall sit upon the throne of David, and upon his kingdom; to establish it and strengthen it with judgment and with justice, from henceforth and for ever: the zeal of the Lord of hosts will perform this."

47. "On the day of Midian" (Isa 9:3).

48. These chapters narrate the victory of Gideon and the Israelites over the Midianites.

49. "Make their princes like Oreb, and Zeb, and Zebee, and Salmana" (Ps 82[83]:12) (the defeated Midianite leaders).

wisdom, judgement, justice, telling us what to do; (c) God the mighty—
the Messias is {a} divine person with divine prerogatives; (d) Father forever (of His kingdom there shall be no end); (e) Prince of Peace—peace {is}
a characteristic of {the} Messianic Kingdom. Assyria is God's instrument
(read 10:12–19[50]); deliverance (read 10:24–27[51]); the Messianic Kingdom

50. "The Syrians from the east, and the Philistines from the west: and they shall
devour Israel with open mouth. For all this his indignation is not turned away, but his
hand is stretched out still. And the people are not returned to him who hath struck
them, and have not sought after the Lord of hosts. And the Lord shall destroy out of
Israel the head and the tail, him that bendeth down, and him that holdeth back, in one
day. The aged and honourable, he is the head: and the prophet that teacheth lies, he is
the tail. And they that call this people blessed, shall cause them to err: and they that
are called blessed, shall be thrown down headlong. Therefore the Lord shall have no
joy in their young men: neither shall he have mercy on their fatherless, and widows:
for every one is a hypocrite and wicked, and every mouth hath spoken folly. For all this
his indignation is not turned away, but his hand is stretched out still. For wickedness is
kindled as a fire, it shall devour the brier and the thorn: and shall kindle in the thicket
of the forest, and it shall be wrapped up in smoke ascending on high. By the wrath of
the Lord of hosts the land is troubled, and the people shall be as fuel for the fire: no
man shall spare his brother."

51. "Therefore, thus saith the Lord the God of hosts: O my people that dwellest in
Sion, be not afraid of the Assyrian: he shall strike thee with his rod, and he shall lift up
his staff over thee in the way of Egypt. For yet a little and a very little while, and my
indignation shall cease, and my wrath shall be upon their wickedness. And the Lord
of hosts shall raise up a scourge against him, according to the slaughter of Madian in
the rock of Oreb, and his rod over the sea, and he shall lift it up in the way of Egypt.
And it shall come to pass in that day, that his burden shall be taken away from off thy
shoulder, and his yoke from off thy neck, and the yoke shall putrify at the presence of
the oil."

(read 11:1–12[52]). Finale: chapter 12 (Monday lauds[53]).

～

Advent Readings {for the} First Sunday—emphasize "orchestration" {and} "choral effect." First nocturn:[54] Isaias 1; responsory 1: Psalms,[55] etc.; responsory 2: Daniel 7:13; responsories, 3, 4: Luke;[56] n.b. responsory 8: *"mitte quem missurus es"*[57] (cf. Exod. 4:13); responsories of {the} third nocturn {are} from {the} Book of Consolations.[58]

～

52. "And there shall come forth a rod out of the root of Jesse, and a flower shall rise up out of his root. And the spirit of the Lord shall rest upon him: the spirit of wisdom, and of understanding, the spirit of counsel, and of fortitude, the spirit of knowledge, and of godliness. And he shall be filled with the spirit of the fear of the Lord. He shall not judge according to the sight of the eyes, nor reprove according to the hearing of the ears. But he shall judge the poor with justice, and shall reprove with equity for the meek of the earth: and he shall strike the earth with the rod of his mouth, and with the breath of his lips he shall slay the wicked. And justice shall be the girdle of his loins: and faith the girdle of his reins. The wolf shall dwell with the lamb: and the leopard shall lie down with the kid: the calf and the lion, and the sheep shall abide together, and a little child shall lead them. The calf and the bear shall feed: their young ones shall rest together: and the lion shall eat straw like the ox. And the sucking child shall play on the hole of the asp: and the weaned child shall thrust his hand into the den of the basilisk. They shall not hurt, nor shall they kill in all my holy mountain, for the earth is filled with knowledge of the Lord, as the covering waters of the sea. In that day the root of Jesse, who standeth for an ensign of the people, him the Gentiles shall beseech, and his sepulchre shall be glorious. And it shall come to pass in that day, that the Lord shall set his hand the second time to possess the remnant of his people, which shall be left from the Assyrians, and from Egypt, and from Phetros, and from Ethiopia, and from Elam, and from Sennaar, and from Emath, and from the islands of the sea. And he shall set up a standard unto the nations, and shall assemble the fugitives of Israel, and shall gather together the dispersed of Juda from the four quarters of the earth."

53. *Breviarium Cisterciense, Hiemalis,* 58.

54. *Breviarium Cisterciense, Hiemalis,* 177–78.

55. Ps 79[80]:1, 3–4; Ps 23[24]:7; Matt 11:3; Ps 48[49]:2.

56. Luke 1:26–27, 30–32; 1:28, 35, 34.

57. "send whom You will send" (*Breviarium Cisterciense, Hiemalis,* 180).

58. The reference is actually to the canticles of the third nocturn (Isa 40:10–17; Isa 42:10–16; Isa 49:7–13) rather than to the responsories, which are not from the Book of Consolation (Isa 40–55) (*Breviarium Cisterciense, Hiemalis,* 180–82).

~

Third Sunday {of} Advent

{The} invitatory: *nescitis horam*[59]—but we know when Christmas comes. To be prepared for Christmas and other feasts is to be prepared for the unknown coming. Why unknown? {It} depends *entirely* on God's good pleasure.

{The} epistle[60] {focuses on} dispositions for "Advent"—to be ready at all times:

a) Joy *in the Lord, semper . . . iterum dico.*[61] {This is} not worldly joy, in feelings; {it is} in the will, {the} *heroism* of true hope. We are very poor in this respect!! Hope {is} the virtue of our age, precisely because of the world's despair, {its} hope in itself.

b) Moderation;

c) Lack of solitude; constant prayer {and} thanksgiving;

d) Peace of God above all understanding surrounds and guards our hearts; {note the} supreme importance of this peace which we cannot "touch" and can barely sense: *exsuperat omnem sensum.*[62]

~

Christmas

1. What is the specific grace of Christmas? *Puer natus est nobis:* The Child is born for us.[63] *To receive this Child* is the grace of Christmas.

---

59. "You do not know the hour" (Matt 25:13) (*Breviarium Cisterciense, Hiemalis,* 202).

60. Phil 4:4–7 (*Missale Romanum,* 5; *Missale Cisterciense,* 5).

61. "always . . . Again I say" (Phil 4:4).

62. "it surpasses all understanding" (Phil 4:7).

63. Isa 9:5 (introit: third Mass of Christmas) (*Missale Romanum,* 18; *Missale Cisterciense,* 18).

2. Who is this Child? *Lumen—splendor Patris* (hymn, vespers;[64] *collect: Midnight Mass;*[65] collect: *dawn Mass*[66]); *Rex*[67] ({the} dawn Mass stresses kingship) (epistle, third Mass;[68] gradual, third Mass[69]).

3. *How do we receive Him?* (a) *faith*: open your eyes—*Hoc in nostro resplendeat opere, quod per fidem fulget in mente* (collect, dawn Mass[70]); (b) *simplicity*: cast away complications of human grandeur (read {the} gospel of Midnight Mass[71]): (c) *Per haec sacrosancta commercia*[72] (read {the} secret {of} Midnight Mass[73] and {the} secret {of the} dawn Mass[74]).

64. "Light—splendor of the Father" ("*Christe Redemptor omnium*," l. 5) (*Breviarium Cisterciense, Hiemalis*, 235).

65. "*Deus, qui hanc sacratissimam noctem veri luminis fecisti illustratione clarescere; da, quaesumus; ut, cujus lucis mysteria in terra cognovimus, ejus quoque gaudiis in caelo perfruamur*" ("God, Who made this most holy night to shine forth with brightness of the true light, grant we beg that we may enjoy His happiness in heaven, the mystery of Whose light we have known on earth") (*Missale Romanum*, 15; *Missale Cisterciense*, 15).

66. "*Da nobis, quaesumus, omnipotens Deus: ut, qui nova incarnati Verbi tui luce perfundimur; hoc in nostro resplendeat opere, quod per fidem fulget in mente*" ("Grant us, we beg, almighty God, that we who are bathed in the new light of the Word made flesh, may show forth in our actions that which by faith shines in our minds") (*Missale Romanum*, 17; *Missale Cisterciense*, 17).

67. "King" (Ps 92[93]:1) (introit: dawn Mass) (*Missale Romanum*, 17; *Missale Cisterciense*, 17, which read: "*Dominus regnat*" ["The Lord reigns"]).

68. Heb 1:1–12 (*Missale Romanum*, 18–19; *Missale Cisterciense*, 18).

69. Ps 97[98]:3, 4, 2 (*Missale Romanum*, 19; *Missale Cisterciense*, 18).

70. "May this show forth in our actions that which by faith shines in our minds" (*Missale Romanum*, 17; *Missale Cisterciense*, 17).

71. Luke 2:1–14 (*Missale Romanum*, 16; *Missale Cisterciense*, 16).

72. "through this holy interchange."

73. "*Accepta tibi sit, Domine, quaesumus, hodiernae festivitatis oblatio: ut, tua gratia largiente, per haec sacrosancta commercia, in illius inveniamur forma, in quo tecum est nostra substantia*" ("May the offering of this day's celebration be acceptable to You, Lord, so that by Your generous grace we may be found through this holy interchange in the form of Him through Whom our substance is with You") (*Missale Romanum*, 16; *Missale Cisterciense*, 16).

74. "*Munera nostra, quaesumus, Domine, Nativitatis hodiernae mysteriis apta proveniant, et pacem nobis semper infundant: ut, sicut homo genitus idem refulsit et Deus, sic nobis haec terrena substantia conferat, quod divinum est*" ("May our gifts, we beg, Lord, prove to be appropriate for the mysteries of this day's birth, and always bestow peace on us, that as the One born as man also shone forth as God, so may this earthly substance bestow on us what is divine") (*Missale Romanum*, 18; *Missale Cisterciense*, 17).

4. *When do we receive Him?* in the sacred mysteries.

5. *What is the effect of our receiving Him?* {*The*} *Holy Spirit* {*is*} *given in renewal of life and liberation: Nova per carnem nativitas liberet* (*collect, day Mass*[75]) (*epistle,*[76] *postcommunion,*[77] *dawn Mass*); *In illius inveniamur forma in quo tecum est nostra substantia* (secret, Midnight Mass[78]); *Dignis conversationibus ad ejus mereamur pervenire consortium* (postcommunion, Midnight Mass[79]).

Summary: {we are given} grace to be children and sons with the True Son of God, {through the} HOLY SPIRIT IN OUR HEARTS CRYING ABBA FATHER,[80] {in a} spirit of fraternal love (1 John 4:2–14).

∽

THE LIGHT OF CHRIST IN HIS CHURCH
(Epiphany—conference on authority, direction, etc.)

Surge illuminare Jerusalem.[81] Epiphany themes are those of Christmas with a different modality. Both celebrate the appearance of God in the world, as Light of the world, as King and Savior. Christmas emphasizes the fact of His coming in human flesh. Epiphany focuses rather on the consequences of His coming, the effect of His power and light in the world, the response of the Church called to union with His light and His love. In a word, Epiphany focuses more on the presence of Christ in His Church as Savior and King—His light radiating out upon the world in His Church, His divine power drawing souls to Him from the ends of the

---

75. "May the new birth in the flesh set free" (*Missale Romanum*, 18; *Missale Cisterciense*, 18).

76. Titus 3:4–7 (*Missale Romanum*, 17; *Missale Cisterciense*, 17).

77. "*Hujus nos, Domine, sacramenti semper novitas natalis instauret: cujus nativitas singularis humanam repulit vetustatem*" ("May the newness of this sacrament, Lord, always restore us, on the nativity of the One Whose unique birth has driven away the old human state") (*Missale Romanum*, 18; *Missale Cisterciense*, 18).

78. "may we be found in the form of Him through Whom our substance is with You " (*Missale Romanum*, 16; *Missale Cisterciense*, 16).

79. "through fitting transformations may we become worthy to enter into fellowship with Him" (*Missale Romanum*, 17; *Missale Cisterciense*, 16).

80. Rom 8:15; Gal 3:6.

81. "Arise, shine, Jerusalem" (Isa 60:1) (capitulum, vespers: Epiphany) (*Breviarium Cisterciense, Hiemalis*, 349).

earth to be members of the Church His Bride, His action enlightening and forming them through His Church, and the Church's response of faith, adoration and love—finally the consequent union of Christ and His Church, the nuptials of God and man in the mystical Christ.

Epiphany explicitly celebrates the *sacrament of illumination*, baptism, as we shall see in another conference perhaps. In a word, in the Epiphany liturgy we find Christ in the mystery of the Church, the Savior Who redeems and sanctifies men through His Church, the king Who rules them through His Church, the Teacher Who enlightens them through the teaching authority of the Church and through the hidden action of the Holy Spirit in souls. Jerusalem—the Church—arises {and} is enlightened by her light that has come. Let us consider Christ's action in His Church, especially how His light comes to us through His Church, and most particularly how He acts upon us and enlightens us through the ministers He has chosen to be our guides.

Life-giving action of Jesus in His Church: Jesus came to give us a share in His own divine life. He does so by sending into our hearts the Holy Spirit. The Spirit descends upon us at baptism, making us sons of God in Christ, and we are pleasing to the Father, united to Him in His beloved Son. Living in us by His Spirit, Jesus communicates Himself to us and moves us with the sentiments and thoughts of His own Sacred Heart, transforming us in His likeness. All the actions of Jesus in the Church tend to diffuse and increase His life in souls, to bring them more and more under the sway of His life-giving action through His Spirit in their hearts. The sacraments are the chief channels of this life-giving action, for they are instruments for the direct communication of grace.

Authority of Jesus in His Church: Jesus rules visibly in His Vicar, who possesses all the authority of the Christ, on earth, and who shares that authority with the hierarchy and priests. All authoritative actions of the hierarchy flow from the authority of Christ. This authority establishes a *supernatural bond* between souls and Jesus, through the hierarchy. It is necessary for the union of souls with God in the mystical Christ, and its supreme end is the sanctification of souls, their transformation in Christ, and their perfect union with the Father. The divine authority in the Church embraces man in his entirety, in all the reaches of his life, private and social. It plunges even into the depths of his conscience, imposing *obligations* which cannot be evaded. It is not a mere external disciplinary power; it demands internal assent, and it can impose obligations which we are no longer free to disavow. It can overrule our most intimate choices, and exact submission. But this submission is to God, not to man, and its purpose is our liberation from slavery, not our subjection to an arbitrary human authority. The purpose of all this authority is still only to liberate our souls and bring them fully into the light of the truth which "'makes us free."[82] Corresponding to this power given by God to His human representatives, is a *divine guarantee* that their God-given authority is not a mere arbitrary exercise of human power. The pope has infallible authority in doctrine and the hierarchy is divinely assisted in the exercise of its rule. "I am with you all days, even to the consummation of the world" (Matt. 28:20). The authority of the Church is the divine authority of Jesus visibly exercised in the society of the saints (Colomer[83]).

Enlightenment of souls by Jesus in His Church: Jesus enlightens us not merely by teaching us truths and doctrines through the medium of His representatives. Above all we must understand that the light that Jesus gives us is His own Truth, His own Holy Spirit, and Himself in and with the Spirit. In receiving as our gift from God the divine Spirit, we receive into our hearts the very substance of divine life and divine truth. The Holy Spirit is not merely a passive "object" deposited in our hearts. He is Pure Act—Life, Light, Love. He lives and works in His Church in two ways:

a) Exteriorly, guiding and directing human instruments who will teach and preach the word of God, who will govern and guide souls. This exterior action is twofold: (1) ministerial (hierarchical)—popes, bishops, priests and their coworkers; (2) charismatic—independent of the established framework, {through} "free gifts" of the Spirit to preach and spread the word, {which} can be and is given to ministers of the word, and also to others who have no ministerial function. It is said that *all* have some charism, {a} gift to reach some souls. The exterior action of the enlightening Spirit is seen in preaching, writing, liturgy, art, etc. The liturgy is the "embodiment of the faith of the Church in visible acts"[84] and rites, in "visible mysteries,"[85] and

82. See John 8:32.

83. Colomer, *Catholic Church*, which reads: "The authority of the Church, then, is the same divine and eminent authority of Jesus, visibly exercised in the society of the saints."

84. Source unidentified.

85. "*Praesta nobis, quaesumus, omnipotens et misericors Deus: ut, quae visibilibus mysteriis sumenda percepimus, invisibili consequamur effectu*" (postcommunion: Ascension [*Missale Romanum*, 396; *Missale Cisterciense*, 257]) ("Grant us, we beseech

taking part in these we are moved by the Spirit to show forth the truth and light of God even though we may not be fully conscious of the fact; so too in preaching and writing {as well as in} *prayer*. By our prayer and penance we are instruments of the Holy Spirit secretly bringing light to other souls. Here the exterior and interior action of the Spirit are united.

b) *Interiorly*, by all manner of graces and gifts of the Holy Spirit, {Who} *heals* souls in sin and makes them capable of receiving light; *purifies* them to receive it; *sanctifies* them to be able to bear it; *instructs* them that they may grow in it; *enkindles* them to love the light; *moves* them to put into effect His teaching, and this in turn makes them more capable of seeing and loving the light; *strengthens* them to grow in capacity for holy action and contemplation; *anoints* them with divine graces that prepare them for transformation; *transforms* and *unites* them in the light.

The Spiritual Director: a most important agent in this work of the Holy Spirit is the *Spiritual Father*, in whom are united the *power of authority*, the *life-giving action* of the priesthood and ministry of the sacraments, the *sanctifying* and *teaching* power of the Spirit. As a manifestation of His great love and care for souls, God places all these powers and gifts in the instrument He chooses to cooperate with the action of His Divine Spirit in their souls. In the Spiritual Father, God gently adapts and tempers and adjusts all His divine power and light and love and grace to the needs and circumstances of the soul. The Spiritual Father is in the place of God to the soul, not only in the sense that God will support his decisions, but also in the sense that all the power and love and light and truth and wisdom and sanctity of God are concentrated in him, to guide the soul. He is the instrument God has chosen in His all-wise Providence to lead the soul to sanctity, to *filter through* to him the light and power and wisdom of God. Providence selects instruments purposely with this in view, in order that God may reach the soul in a way that will not trouble and upset and disconcert it, but will effectively and as it were naturally and sweetly and easily guide it on towards sanctity. The director is, in all

---

Thee, O almighty and merciful Lord, that what we have received as our nourishment in visible Mysteries we may enjoy in its invisible effect": translation as found in Merton, *Bread in the Wilderness*, 79, in which the third chapter of Part III, "*Sacramenta Scripturarum*," is titled "Visible Mysteries" [79–84], and is focused on participation in the Eucharist as a sharing in the redemptive death and resurrection of Christ).

truth, Jesus for the soul. He is a "sacrament," a "mystery" of Christ, in whom the Holy Spirit acts in a very special manner for our sanctification.

Who is the director: what has been said above is only fully true if there exists in the fullest sense a bond of spiritual sonship between the subject and the director, that is to say, if the director is really the *Father*, spiritual and charismatic, of the subject. It often happens that a subject cannot find a director, or that having a director, the charismatic bond does not exist except in an inchoate manner, as the director lacks the capacity to understand and penetrate the soul, and his decisions do not have the proper effect, do not inspire confidence, etc. Or it happens that the soul, moved too much by nature, and the director likewise dominated by nature, there grows up a false bond, which is not spiritual and charismatic, and which ends with bad effects in the soul due to *misdirection*. How does it happen that God allows a soul to be without a director, or to find a bad director? These are questions which it is hard to answer and perhaps presumptuous to raise. It is sufficient to say that God allows causes to be followed by their normal effects. Where there is a warped or false spirit, where directors themselves are malformed, He allows them to communicate some of their malformation to others. But he also protects the soul against bad directors, and the reason why one cannot find a director is perhaps that for many reasons one is better off without one, or that one does not deserve to find one (motives for seeking one being wrong—{an} overestimation of one's own spirituality and importance, etc.).

The canonical director: the spiritual director, in the ordinary sense of the word, is a guide, usually a priest, who is freely chosen by the subject, after adequate prayer and consultation, one who then takes upon himself, on the basis of a quasi-contract, the guidance of the soul. But in certain situations, for instance {the} novitiate, the Church places a Father and director over the subject. The Father Master in the novitiate is the ordinary director of the novices. He has a *juridical* function to help them decide their vocation, to select or reject them, to form them for their religious life. In this situation, the Holy Spirit guarantees special lights and graces to the Father Master, in order that he may fulfill his functions. It is explicitly stated (canon 561, n. 1[86]) that the Master of Novices

86. See Abbo and Hannan, *Sacred Canons*, 1:579: "The master of novices alone possesses the right and duty of supervising the training of the novices and only to him belongs the government of the novitiate; no one else, therefore, may intervene in these matters, under any pretext whatsoever, except those superiors to whom the

alone has the right and the obligation to watch over the formation of the novices and to run the novitiate, so that no one else is allowed in any way to interfere with him in these functions, except superiors and visitors (superiors—{i.e. the} abbot). The novices therefore do not (as do the professed) choose for themselves a director among the confessors. The only way in which a confessor enters in authoritatively to the question of a novice's vocation is when there is something in the internal forum that makes the novice unfit for profession; the confessor then can and must tell him to leave. (What is the internal forum? *intra et extra sacramentum*.[87]) But the confessor is not the director or spiritual father of the novice, although of course in practice he may exercise a great influence for the good and contribute to the novice's spiritual formation (which he will do best if he works along the same lines as the Father Master). The Father Master's position is not only juridical but also *charismatic*. (What is charismatic? What is juridical?) *He has a very special grace of state to select vocations and to guide them towards the goal of their vocation*. This is true even when perhaps there may be a lack of spontaneous human sympathy between the novice and the Father Master. Even though the Father Master may not perfectly understand the novice in everything, he will have *grace* to *guide* and *form* him. But of course here too there can be lacks and limitations!

∾

THE CHAPTER OF FAULTS: it is true that the chapter of faults is a very important observance and that much depends on it. Regularity is important. Observance is important. The *Rule* must be kept in order that we may attain the end for which we have come to the community life—union with God in peace, charity, prayer. Fraternal correction is an obligation of charity, and so a proclamation of a brother is a charitable reminder of some oversight or failing, the correction of which will be profitable to his soul and to the community at large. Hence the aim of a proclamation is to *help*, to *do good*. A wise proclamation will therefore always be judged in the light of this end. By proclaiming such a one, for such a fault, in such a way, will I really help him, will I really do good? Or will I be a scandal

---

constitutions entrust this authority and except the visitators. In reference, however, to matters affecting the house at large, the master of novices and the novices are subject to the governing authority of the local superior." For the original Latin see Gasparri, *Codex Iuris Canonici*, 190.

87. "within and outside the sacrament [of penance]."

to him, and will I do harm? We should always assume, unless there is evidence to the contrary: (1) that our brother is willing to be corrected and that he wants to be proclaimed for faults, because a good religious is glad to be proclaimed; (2) that even if we make an error of judgement, or if our proclamation is not perfect, it will be understood in good part and our good intentions will be appreciated; (3) that those who proclaim us mean well and sincerely wish our good, and are not acting out of personal spite, etc. However, much harm can be done when the chapter of faults is badly conducted and when the spirit becomes too human. Here are some of the drawbacks:

1. {a} tendency to lose {a} sense of proportion and perspective; we become hypnotized by the little exterior faults we wish to correct in others, and they become magnified beyond all proportion.

2. {a} tendency of unconscious personal and natural weaknesses to creep into our "zeal" for the *Rule*; we may have {a} pure intention, but there may indeed be unconscious spite and animosity against certain ones, and this will quite easily appear in the proclamation— it may be sensed by the other one. This is of course unavoidable, but it must be taken into account.

3. a wrong spirit, a spirit of "punishment," of "exacting justice," of "correcting abuses," may come to dominate our minds; charity cannot survive if, in the chapter of faults, we have set up our own judgement onto a pedestal and make it our god. From this flows false zeal, which disturbs peace, leads to interminable interior arguments over nothing, increases bad feeling, shuts the soul up in itself etc., hardens it against others. Thus community spirit is destroyed. In such circumstances, one proclaims in chapter uniquely in order to assert {one's} own will and judgement and impose them on others, including superiors, {using} proclamations to force {the} superior to see things my way.

Hence, some practical norms:

1. *simple and objective* proclamations: (a) {a} plain statement of {the} fault, in simplest terms; (b) accusation only for faults clearly based on {the} *Rule*, {the} usages, {the} known will of {the} superior; (c) to avoid as far as possible misunderstandings.

2. *charitable* proclamations: (a) feel kind towards the person proclaimed; do not be obsessed by a hostile image of him—if you are, don't proclaim; (b) {use a} kind tone etc., based on {a} kind attitude toward the person, not merely "put on"; (c) amusing proclamations do not achieve the right result.

3. *selfless* proclamations: (a) not {a} desire to impose my own will or interpretation of the *Rule*; (b) if I am annoyed at the way the superior handles the proclamation, then I am probably motivated by self-love; (c) not {to} be scandalized if the one proclaimed happens to commit the same fault over again; (d) not {to} proclaim, of course, for faults committed against myself; (e) not {to} proclaim because a brother does something I do not like, or in a way I do not like, or in order to make him do what I like.

The novitiate chapter of faults {is}, in part, a training ground. The proclamations may be taken apart and analyzed and criticized, so do not be upset if this happens. {With regard to} novitiate customs, this {is} the proper place for proclamations on these points, but {it} should not be a seed-ground for innumerable new "rules."

∿

Sexagesima

1. Epistle:[88] {the} lesson of {the} epistle {is that the} apostolic life means great sufferings and great graces. But what Paul glories in most of all is *in his infirmities*, and not either in his sufferings or his graces. Man must be content with his own nothingness to be an instrument of God. We make ourselves unhappy by struggling with our nothingness, as if it ought not to be (*see* {the} collect:[89] those who are weakest in themselves become instruments of God for {the}

88. 2 Cor 11:19–12:9 (*Missale Romanum*, 59; *Missale Cisterciense*, 49).

89. "*Deus, qui conspicis, quia ex nulla nostra actione confidimus: concede propitius; ut contra adversa omnia, Doctoris gentium protectione muniamur*" ("God, Who see that we trust in no action of our own, graciously grant that we may be defended against all adversities by the protection of the teacher of the Gentiles") (*Missale Romanum*, 58; *Missale Cisterciense*, 49).

protection of others—cf. St. Thérèse); {see also} *the antiphons—note {the} antiphon*[90] *and capitulum*[91] *of none,* how they go together.

2. Gospel:[92] the sower (Matt. 13—*vobis datum est nosse:*[93] preaching in parables; Christ sees parables in things because they are *there*; we too can find our own parables). {Note the} significance of the fact that the word of God is compared to *seed* that must bear fruit. {For an} introduction, {see} Isaias 55: {the} first part {focuses on the} gratuity of salvation (cf. Septuagesima[94]); *read* ISAIAH 55:[95] comment especially on vv. 8–11: My *thoughts {are} not your thoughts . . .* so shall my word be. {The} transcendence of God demands a free

---

90. "*Si vere, fratres, divites esse cupitis, veras divitias amate*" ("If you truly desire to be rich, brothers, love true riches") (*Breviarium Cisterciense, Hiemalis,* 448).

91. "*Libenter igitur gloriabor in infirmitatibus meis, ut inhabitet in me virtus Christi*" ("Freely, therefore, I will glory in my weaknesses, so that the power of Christ may dwell in me" [2 Cor 12:9]) (*Breviarium Cisterciense, Hiemalis,* 448).

92. Luke 8:4–15 (*Missale Romanum,* 59–60; *Missale Cisterciense,* 50).

93. "To you it is given to know" (Matt 13:11; Luke 8:10).

94. The reference is presumably to the gospel, the parable of the workers in the vineyard (Matt 20:1–16) (*Missale Romanum,* 57–58; *Missale Cisterciense,* 48).

95. "All you that thirst, come to the waters: and you that have no money make haste, buy, and eat: come ye, buy wine and milk without money, and without any price. Why do you spend money for that which is not bread, and your labour for that which doth not satisfy you? Hearken diligently to me, and eat that which is good, and your soul shall be delighted in fatness. Incline your ear and come to me: hear and your soul shall live, and I will make an everlasting covenant with you, the faithful mercies of David. Behold I have given him for a witness to the people, for a leader and a master to the Gentiles. Behold thou shalt call a nation, which thou knewest not: and the nations that knew not thee shall run to thee, because of the Lord thy God, and for the Holy One of Israel, for he hath glorified thee. Seek ye the Lord, while he may be found: call upon him, while he is near. Let the wicked forsake his way, and the unjust man his thoughts, and let him return to the Lord, and he will have mercy on him, and to our God: for he is bountiful to forgive. For my thoughts are not your thoughts: nor your ways my ways, saith the Lord. For as the heavens are exalted above the earth, so are my ways exalted above your ways, and my thoughts above your thoughts. And as the rain and the snow come down from heaven, and return no more thither, but soak the earth, and water it, and make it to spring, and give seed to the sower, and bread to the eater: So shall my word be, which shall go forth from my mouth: it shall not return to me void, but it shall do whatsoever I please, and shall prosper in the things for which I sent it. For you shall go out with joy, and be led forth with peace: the mountains and the hills shall sing praise before you, and all the trees of the country shall clap their hands. Instead of the shrub, shall come up the fir tree, and instead of the nettle, shall come up the myrtle tree: and the Lord shall be named for an everlasting sign, that shall not be taken away."

gift. His Word is His gift. (*Read* Rom. 10:1–17:[96] cf. {the} Old Law and {the} New Law of *faith*, which "comes by hearing"; *read* John 1:9–14:[97] everyone who "believes in His Name"[98] is the son of God, and He lives in them). {The different seeds are these}: 1—those who do not understand; 2—those who understand only, but have no love; how does the word take root? {the} necessity of *fortitude* in faith (see {and} READ Matt. 7:19–27[99]—*hear the words and do them*—cf.

96. "Brethren, the will of my heart, indeed, and my prayer to God, is for them unto salvation. For I bear them witness, that they have a zeal of God, but not according to knowledge. For they, not knowing the justice of God, and seeking to establish their own, have not submitted themselves to the justice of God. For the end of the law is Christ, unto justice to every one that believeth. For Moses wrote, that the justice which is of the law, the man that shall do it, shall live by it. But the justice which is of faith, speaketh thus: Say not in thy heart, Who shall ascend into heaven? that is, to bring Christ down; Or who shall descend into the deep? that is, to bring up Christ again from the dead. But what saith the scripture? The word is nigh thee, even in thy mouth, and in thy heart. This is the word of faith, which we preach. For if thou confess with thy mouth the Lord Jesus, and believe in thy heart that God hath raised him up from the dead, thou shalt be saved. For, with the heart, we believe unto justice; but, with the mouth, confession is made unto salvation. For the scripture saith: Whosoever believeth in him, shall not be confounded. For there is no distinction of the Jew and the Greek: for the same is Lord over all, rich unto all that call upon him. For whosoever shall call upon the name of the Lord, shall be saved. How then shall they call on him, in whom they have not believed? Or how shall they believe him, of whom they have not heard? And how shall they hear, without a preacher? And how shall they preach unless they be sent, as it is written: How beautiful are the feet of them that preach the gospel of peace, of them that bring glad tidings of good things! But all do not obey the gospel. For Isaias saith: Lord, who hath believed our report? Faith then cometh by hearing; and hearing by the word of Christ."

97. "That was the true light, which enlighteneth every man that cometh into this world. He was in the world, and the world was made by him, and the world knew him not. He came unto his own, and his own received him not. But as many as received him, he gave them power to be made the sons of God, to them that believe in his name. Who are born, not of blood, nor of the will of the flesh, nor of the will of man, but of God. And the Word was made flesh, and dwelt among us, (and we saw his glory, the glory as it were of the only begotten of the Father,) full of grace and truth."

98. John 1:12.

99. "Every tree that bringeth not forth good fruit, shall be cut down, and shall be cast into the fire. Wherefore by their fruits you shall know them. Not every one that saith to me, Lord, Lord, shall enter into the kingdom of heaven: but he that doth the will of my Father who is in heaven, he shall enter into the kingdom of heaven. Many will say to me in that day: Lord, Lord, have not we prophesied in thy name, and cast out devils in thy name, and done many miracles in thy name? And then will I profess unto them, I never knew you: depart from me, you that work iniquity. Every one therefore that heareth these my words, and doth them, shall be likened to a wise man that

Gandhi); 3—those who let the word be smothered (cf. also {the} Sermon on {the} Mount: *No man can serve two masters*;[100] Jesus inveighs against care for useless things—READ Matt 6:24–34[101]); 4—those who receive the Word and bring forth fruit *in patience*: *In patientia vestra possidebitis animas vestras.*[102]

∽

LENT: {in the} Ash Wednesday gospel,[103] Jesus teaches us purity of intention. The Lenten fast must be *spiritual* as well as *bodily*. The keynote {is that} a spiritual fast is one that is not carried out to be seen or appreciated by men. Jesus makes clear that a willful sadness about the Lenten fast would give it this human and natural character: "They disfigure their faces *that they may appear to men* to fast."[104] Sadness {is} used therefore as a sign, as a trademark of {the} human spirit (but not the only one: *any* emotion can become {a} means of attracting human applause). Whose attention are you trying to attract? A fast or observance that is aimed

---

built his house upon a rock, And the rain fell, and the floods came, and the winds blew, and they beat upon that house, and it fell not, for it was founded on a rock. And every one that heareth these my words, and doth them not, shall be like a foolish man that built his house upon the sand, And the rain fell, and the floods came, and the winds blew, and they beat upon that house, and it fell, and great was the fall thereof."

100. Matt 6:24.

101. "No man can serve two masters. For either he will hate the one, and love the other: or he will sustain the one, and despise the other. You cannot serve God and mammon. Therefore I say to you, be not solicitous for your life, what you shall eat, nor for your body, what you shall put on. Is not the life more than the meat: and the body more than the raiment? Behold the birds of the air, for they neither sow, nor do they reap, nor gather into barns: and your heavenly Father feedeth them. Are not you of much more value than they? And which of you by taking thought, can add to his stature one cubit? And for raiment why are you solicitous? Consider the lilies of the field, how they grow: they labour not, neither do they spin. But I say to you, that not even Solomon in all his glory was arrayed as one of these. And if the grass of the field, which is to day, and to morrow is cast into the oven, God doth so clothe: how much more you, O ye of little faith? Be not solicitous therefore, saying, What shall we eat: or what shall we drink, or wherewith shall we be clothed? For after all these things do the heathens seek. For your Father knoweth that you have need of all these things. Seek ye therefore first the kingdom of God, and his justice, and all these things shall be added unto you. Be not therefore solicitous for to morrow; for the morrow will be solicitous for itself. Sufficient for the day is the evil thereof."

102. "In your patience you will possess your souls" (Luke 21:19).

103. Matt 6:16–21 (*Missale Romanum*, 65; *Missale Cisterciense*, 55).

104. Matt 6:16.

at pleasing men is satisfied with human recognition—not necessarily honor, but just the sense of security that goes with recognition by one's fellows, acceptance by them, their approval. It is true that the Lenten fast has a social character and that we help one another by good example and the inspiration of fervor. But Christ asks of us the contagious fervor of a joy that looks beyond this world (where moth and rust corrupt the treasures of men[105]) to heaven. {The} Lenten mentality of the ancient Church {was symbolized by} "anointing the head"—the spirit, the intention—with the remembrance of Christ's Easter victory. Lent {is the} *ver sacrum*[106]—spring in {the} order of grace—cf. some ideas from Hermann Franke: *Lent and Easter*:

1. The Church endows Lent with a festive character, calling it a solemnity and a *solemne jejunium*[107] (cf. the Lenten preface: *Qui corporali jejunio vitia comprimis, mentem elevas, virtutem largiris et praemia*[108]). To be liberated from vice, to have our spirits lifted up by this liberation, to receive the gift of virtue and to taste even its reward in the assurance of merit in a pure heart—these make of Lent a joyful season, in the midst of struggle and penance. Lent {is} a time of hope.

2. The real significance of Lent is that it is a time in which the Church renews her baptismal life, returns to the springs of her spiritual youth, beginning over again so to speak with the catechumens being prepared for the *Easter illumination*.

3. Hence important elements in the Lenten spirit are: (a) baptismal consciousness[109] ({a} sense that by baptism we rise to a new life in Christ); (b) *desire of spiritual renewal*—union with Jesus in the battle between light and darkness, {an} eagerness for combat (Franke, 76); (c) fasting prepares for illumination and is itself a *food of the spirit*[110]—fasting enables us to penetrate the rich mysteries which the Church places before us, especially to learn, "My meat is to do the will of Him that sent Me";[111]

---

105. Matt 6:19.

106. "sacred spring."

107. "solemn fast" (collect: Saturday after Ash Wednesday) (*Missale Romanum*, 69; *Missale Cisterciense*, 59); see Franke, *Lent and Easter*, 11.

108. "Who by this bodily fast restrain vices, raise up the mind, bestow virtue and its rewards" (*Missale Romanum*, 311; *Missale Cisterciense*, 211).

109. See Franke, *Lent and Easter*, 14–16, 25.

110. See Franke, *Lent and Easter*, 79–80, 82.

111. John 4:34 (see Franke, *Lent and Easter*, 83).

(d) eagerness to join in the Easter nuptial banquet of the Lamb;[112] (e) {a} sense of the beauty of the Church, the Bride of Christ, renewing her splendor and virginal loveliness by the Lenten fast.[113]

~

Lent {is} "the most ancient, the richest in mysteries and in many ways the most interesting of all the liturgical seasons" (Cabrol[114]). {The} liturgical texts {are} determined by various factors: (1) {a} time of penance (cf. Old Testament lessons from {the} prophets); (2) preparation for baptism—scrutinies of catechumens—in Monday, Wednesday and Friday Masses, usually referred to (gospels etc. showing election of the Gentiles—Laetare Sunday,[115] etc.); (3) time of particular penance (Ash Wednesday; raising of Lazarus; Good Shepherd).

Lenten Masses (Trethowan[116]): {the} first Sunday[117] retains its classical form; {the} second Sunday[118] {is taken} from Ember Saturday—Moses and Elias—who fasted—{are} seen with Christ (transfigured); {the} second week gospels {focus on the} struggle between light and darkness; {the} third week {looks at} Christ the healer, the strong one; n.b. mid-Lent: *salus populi*;[119] Saturday[120]—Susanna: Mass for penitents. Laetare {Sunday is a} spring feast, {with} rejoicing of {the} Church over her catechumens. {In} Passiontide, the Passion {is central}.

~

JESUS IN THE LENTEN GOSPELS: when the Church fasts in Lent, it is to make Jesus Himself the nourishment of our spirits. In the word of God

112. See Franke, *Lent and Easter*, 85.

113. See Franke, *Lent and Easter*, 92–93.

114. "la plus ancienne, la plus riche, et à bien des points de vue, la plus intéressante des saisons liturgiques" (Cabrol, *Le Livre de la Prière Antique*, 245).

115. The reference here would seem to be rather to the epistle (Gal 4:22–31) than to the gospel (John 6:1–15) (*Missale Romanum*, 110; *Missale Cisterciense*, 89).

116. Trethowan, *Christ in the Liturgy*, 84–85.

117. *Missale Romanum*, 71–72; *Missale Cisterciense*, 60–62.

118. *Missale Romanum*, 84–85; *Missale Cisterciense*, 73–75.

119. "[I am] the salvation of the people" (introit, Thursday of the third week of Lent) (*Missale Romanum*, 103; *Missale Cisterciense*, 92).

120. Dan 13:1–9, 15–17, 19–30, 33–62 (epistle) (*Missale Romanum*, 107–108; *Missale Cisterciense*, 96–98).

we look upon the Word of God, the Living Bread sent down from heaven[121] to be the life of our souls. The Lenten Masses place our minds in an intimate contact with Jesus through the Gospels, which bring us to the altar and to the Eucharist with minds filled with the divine light that is given us in Christ. We receive into our hearts Him Whom we have heard teaching us and Whom we have contemplated as our divine example and exemplar in the Gospel texts. Who is He? What is the picture of Jesus, the record of His teaching which the Church gives us in these Lenten Masses, in order to transform our lives in His light and in the power of His grace?

1. *The First Sunday of Lent:*[122] here we see Jesus wrestling with evil—a preliminary struggle, that prepares for the opening of His public life and foreshadows the battle in Gethsemani and on the Cross. *He appears already as Victor.* The calm confidence with which He refuses to give away anything of His mission or of His integrity to the tempter shows Him already as the Conqueror of the devil who does not know Who Jesus is.

(1) Jesus is {the} One Who has come from God, and is led by the Spirit of God into the desert to fight the one whom He has come to fight. It is the battle of Light against darkness, of Reality against unreality, of Being against nothingness—but a nothingness that has a will with which to resist Truth and Being.

(2) Jesus fasts, although it is not necessary for His purification. It is necessary to sanctify our fasts. But His fasting weakens Him at least to the extent that He feels hunger (*esuriit*[123])—that is to say He not only felt hungry but he felt the weakness that comes from being without food.

(3) In this state of "weakness" He is approached by the devil. He is able to be tempted in the sense that the suggestions of evil are allowed to reach Him. Let us realize that Jesus takes on our weakness, our helplessness. He is never closer to us in this valley of tears than when we are weak and helpless and realize our helplessness before our enemies and abandon our own stratagems and plans simply in order to do His will. Then truly He resists temptation and conquers in our own hearts.

---

121. See John 6:33, 41, 50, 59.

122. Matt 4:1–11 (*Missale Romanum*, 72; *Missale Cisterciense*, 61).

123. Matt 4:2.

(4) The temptations center on the fact of His identity: "*Si Filius Dei es
. . .*"[124] The heart of this whole matter is the great question, "Who
are You?" Here in these temptations and in His fasting and solitude,
Jesus appears to us as Monk. It is the monastic Christ, the Christ of
the desert, our own particular aspect of Christ, that here appears
on this great Sunday. He becomes our teacher and model in these
temptations, for we are called to share in His temptations as well
as in His solitude and austerity. So too we are tempted in the same
way, and the temptation arises over the fact of our identity: "If you
are a saint . . ." "If you are a contemplative . . ." "If you are so good,
why don't you . . ." The devil as an angel of light provokes us to do
inordinate things in order to prove to ourselves and to him that we
are the person he has subtly suggested that we ought to think we are.

(5) The first temptation is to a false autonomy, a wrong independence
in the use of God's gifts—the subtle degeneration of spiritual
strength into magic power. The strength of the spirit comes from
perfect union with the Truth of God, the total submission of our
self to His Reality, so that we are "*in spiritu et veritate.*"[125] The power
of magic comes from the independent use of some supposed god-
like force inherent in ourselves or in things. "Command that these
stones be made bread"[126]—Jesus had the power to do this and the
right to do it. The evil spirit was not telling Jesus to do something
He could not do—He later multiplied loaves, etc. But he was sug-
gesting an *arbitrary act of power*, for which there was no reason
and no cause—merely for the sake of asserting His own identity, a
miracle for the sake of self-assertion and self-satisfaction. How many
temptations in monastic life are after all merely temptations to "assert myself," to "demand my rights," to show them "they can't do
this to me." (Note—there is more to it than being, or not being, a
doormat.) Jesus ignores the challenge because He is above it. If He
had accepted this challenge, He would have hardly been the Son of
God—so too if He accepted the challenge of the Jews: "If thou art
the Son of God, come down from the Cross."[127] Jesus replies that
man lives not by bread alone but by the will of God. Bread without

124. "If You are the Son of God . . ." (Matt 4:3, 6; Luke 4:3, 9).
125. "in spirit and in truth" (John 4:24).
126. Matt 4:3.
127. Matt 27:40.

the will of God feeds us for death. The will of God is life, and the nourishment of our true being is received only when we are attentive to every expression of God's mind and of His will. The will of God is our true sanctity.

(6) The second temptation is again an arbitrary act of power for the sake of self-assertion and self-glorification—*a presumptuous act of self-display* in the midst of the Holy City—and in particular an *assertion of invulnerability,* of being immune to the forces which harm other men, of *not being subject to the same laws as other men.* Jesus knew that His mission was precisely to prove Himself the Son of God not by any such display of magic power and invulnerability, but by *the full and total acceptance of man's ordinary condition,* the acceptance of death, weakness, shame, dishonor, opprobrium. And what would be proved by His resurrection was the love of God for Him and for all men in Him, not only the fact that He Himself is the King and Victor with divine power to lay down His life and take it up again. Jesus merely replies, "Thou shalt not tempt the Lord thy God."[128] Note: the angels do in fact come and minister to Him after the temptation is over. He allows Himself to be cared for by messengers of His Father.

(7) The third temptation {is} to power and possession—the devil shows all the kingdoms of the world and their glory. In other words he is promising that Christ can become a worldly king with worldly glory, and can receive all this at the hands of Satan if He will. The terrible thing about this is that it is in a certain sense true. Christ, the faithful servant of God, doing only the will of God, was bound to meet with the hatred and opposition of the world, and could only be King through crucifixion. Worldly glory and acceptance by the world were Satan's to give. So in refusing this offer, Christ was in fact accepting the Cross and renouncing the glory of the world. He was renouncing success and accepting apparent failure, by all worldly standards. For what? *for the adoration of God, for the recognition of the supreme dominion of God.* By His Cross, Jesus won back the power over all things: all power is given to Him because of His victory on the Cross. Because He became obedient unto death, every knee must bow to Him, even those under the earth. It was not so before His victory. So Jesus gives us the answer to our own

128. Matt 4:7.

temptations—in all of them there is only one solution: to adore God and to serve Him alone.

The Transfiguration gospel[129] (ember Saturday and second Sunday): this gospel again raises the question of the identity of Jesus: (a) His glorified being, {with} Moses and Elias speaking to Him—He is therefore the center of God's great plan for Israel; Peter seems here to put Him on a level with Moses and Elias. (b) The voice of the Father: *This is my Beloved Son.*[130] The identity of the Son as Son is not known unless we know of the Father. All through the Lenten gospels Jesus will be telling us that He is the Son sent by the Father. If He shows Himself full of the divine glory in this gospel, it is in order that we may know that He is the Son in Whom the Father manifests Himself. The Father is "well pleased"[131] in the Son— that is to say, He completely endorses the actions of the Son; they are the Father's will; they are the actions of the Father in the Son. Contrast the temptation of the devil urging Jesus to perform actions in His own name and by His own power, independently of the Father. The devil does not understand that to be a Son of God is to do the will of the Father. He thinks of divine sonship only as *power*—power for oneself.

2. *Jesus as Teacher*:

a) Preliminary to Lent—Ash Wednesday and the two following days—these Masses, later in composition, concentrate above all on teaching us how to fast and how to understand Lent. Jesus Himself teaches us His own view of penance and good works, and how they are to be done. *Ash Wednesday*:[132] "When you fast, be not as the hypocrites, sad . . ."[133] Jesus gives a clear statement of his values, and they reflect His own Being and His own mission. He teaches not only that we must be absolutely sincere and pure in intention (He Himself is the truth, the pure light of the Father), but that our hearts must be where eternal values are—in heaven, *with the Father.* Note that from the very first, the *teaching of Jesus goes direct to the Father.* This is of absolute and central

129. Matt 17:1–9 (*Missale Romanum*, 83, 85; *Missale Cisterciense*, 74).
130. Matt 17:5.
131. Matt 17:5.
132. Matt 6:16–21 (*Missale Romanum*, 65; *Missale Cisterciense*, 55).
133. Matt 6:16.

importance and must never be forgotten. If we fast and do good works, they are for the "Father who sees in secret"[134] and Who has reserved to Himself the right to reward us with ineffable gifts.

Friday after Ash Wednesday[135] {teaches} the same lessons again: (a) Jesus contrasts His own teaching with what has gone before: "you have heard it said . . . but *I say to you*."[136] He presents Himself then as the Master sent from God. Later on He will tell them He is the only Master: *unus est Magister vester, Christus*[137] (second Tuesday). (b) His teaching is a spiritual revolution, discarding all that they have known before, elevating it to a sublime level—to love enemies, to bless those that do evil to us. (c) Again the emphasis {is} on pure intention, sincerity, hiddenness, truth. (d) Above all, the doctrine is again *centered on the Father*. Why heroic charity? "That you may be the children of your Father who is in heaven."[138] Why be more perfect than the Gentiles? because we are bound to be *perfect as our heavenly Father is perfect*. Jesus Himself is the reflection of the Father's truth, and wishes us to be identified with the Father as He is Himself.

Thursday after Ash Wednesday, the gospel of the centurion,[139] in which the faith of the pagan centurion acknowledges Jesus as Supreme Lord, teaches us Who Jesus in fact is. He is the Son of God, to Whom all power has been given in heaven and on earth. Our life depends on faith in Him. He is our salvation. All things are in His hands. Faith {means} personal adherence to Jesus with all our powers, {as a} consequence of our acknowledgement of His divine Filiation.

Saturday after Ash Wednesday[140] {teaches} the same lesson in a different way. Jesus {is} walking on the sea, and the disciples {are} still not aware Who He really is, in spite of the miracle of the loaves that has just taken place. He is truly the Son of God.

---

134. Matt 6:4, 6, 18.

135. Matt 5:43–6:4 (*Missale Romanum*, 68–69; *Missale Cisterciense*, 58).

136. Matt 5:21, 27, 33, 38, 43.

137. "One is your Master, the Christ" (Matt 23:10) (*Missale Romanum*, 88; *Missale Cisterciense*, 77).

138. Matt 5:45.

139. Matt 8:5–13 (*Missale Romanum*, 67; *Missale Cisterciense*, 56–57).

140. Mark 6:47–56 (*Missale Romanum*, 70; *Missale Cisterciense*, 59).

b) *The teaching of Jesus*: the Lenten gospels do not cover the territory of a systematic presentation of all the doctrine taught by Jesus. They touch on a few salient points of His teaching, but for the most part they concentrate more and more on His Divine Person. However the *gospel of the first Monday* of Lent[141] (the Last Judgement) is of primary importance: (a) It shows definitely that Jesus, the Lord of life and death, will come to judge the living and the dead, seated upon the throne of His majesty and all the angels with Him; (b) Hence his teaching is all *ultimately eschatological*— it is all referred in the last analysis to a future event which will close history and show the full meaning of all that has so far happened in mystery; (c) Here Jesus manifests not only His own historical person but the existence of the Mystical Christ, the whole Christ. This is necessary for understanding the true identity of the Redeemer, with Whom we are to become one by charity; (d) Again, this is the result of the Father's plan, and terminates in the Father. Those who are united to Him in charity are the "*blessed of My Father*."[142] Commanded by the Father, Jesus calls to Himself those whom the Father has given Him. They will be united to the Father in Him. (e) This union with Jesus is "the kingdom prepared [by the Father] from the beginning of the world."[143] (f) But a more striking revelation of Jesus {is found in His words}: "I was hungry and you gave Me to eat . . ."[144] "When you did it to one of these My least brethren you did it to Me."[145] Jesus is then present in His members, and to know Him and love Him in them is to be united to Him truly and perfectly by charity. This is the very heart of His message. It is the Gospel, the mystery preached by St. Paul. All the teachings of Lent are to be seen in the light of this great fundamental gospel which is one of the cornerstones of the Lenten liturgy. The gospel of the first Monday is balanced by that of the Ember Saturday and the second Sunday, the gospel of the Transfiguration, showing Jesus as He is now, in glory. On the *eschatological primacy of charity* is based Christ's rejection of the

---

141. Matt 25:31–46 (*Missale Romanum*, 73–74; *Missale Cisterciense*, 63).

142. Matt 25:34.

143. Matt 25:34.

144. Matt 25:35.

145. Matt 25:40.

doctrine of the Pharisees. His teaching on *humility* is inseparable from this.

Second Tuesday:[146] we are not to be like the Pharisees—they bind heavy and insupportable burdens ({a} false and human notion of perfection, consisting in absolute commands and prohibitions based entirely on human custom and tradition—things which are insupportable to man and which destroy his true being. They make themselves masters and even gods. Jesus again tells us to lift our eyes to heaven—we have only one Father, Who is in heaven, and only one Master, Christ. To be sons of our Father and disciples of our Master, we must be humble; we must serve one another, abase ourselves before one another in simple charity. He that is the greatest among you shall be the servant,[147] and whosoever shall exalt himself shall be humbled, and he that shall humble himself shall be exalted.

On the *second Wednesday*,[148] He begins to reveal His own humiliation and abjection in the Passion in which He is to be delivered up to His enemies and to the Gentiles and put to an ignominious death. At the same time, the sons of Zebedee ask for the first places in the Kingdom, and He tells them that this is not the way—the princes of the Gentiles exercise power over them. "But it shall not be so among you—whosoever will be the greater among you, let him be your minister; and he that will be first among you shall be your servant. Even as the Son of Man is not come to be ministered unto, but to minister and to give His life a redemption for many."[149]

On *Ember Wednesday*,[150] after revealing Himself as greater than Jonas, greater than Solomon, Jesus asserts that those who do the will of His heavenly Father are united to Him as His brother, mother and sister. Again, this includes in itself all the essence of His teaching: He is the one sent by the Father, to bring men to the Father. He is sent to teach the Father's will, in which is all wisdom. He teaches this wisdom by accomplishing the Father's

---

146. Matt 23:1–12 (*Missale Romanum*, 87–88; *Missale Cisterciense*, 77).

147. Matt 20:26, 23:11; Mark 10:43; Luke 22:26.

148. Matt 20:17–28 (*Missale Romanum*, 89; *Missale Cisterciense*, 79).

149. Matt 20:26–28.

150. Matt 12:38–50 (*Missale Romanum*, 76–77; *Missale Cisterciense*, 66).

will Himself. All who do the Father's will as He does are united, with Him, to the Father. All the other lessons that are taught here and there in the Lenten gospels are to be seen in relation to this central teaching—for instance, the value of poverty and suffering (the gospel of Lazarus the beggar—second Thursday[151]). Note however that the purpose of the Lazarus parable is not primarily to teach a moral lesson, here in the liturgy—it is inserted above all for its reference to the Easter mystery: "If they hear not Moses and the prophets, neither will they believe if one rise again from the dead."[152] The primary purpose of the gospel is to awaken faith in the Resurrection, and only in the light of the Easter mystery do the poverty and suffering of Lazarus gain their full meaning.

3. *Special manifestations of the identity of Jesus in the gospels of the second week*: the gospels of the second week of Lent concentrate upon the conflict between Jesus and the Pharisees, the battle of light and darkness. The light came into the world, and His own received Him not.[153] In the battle with darkness and human pride, Jesus reveals His full stature as the Son of God, as the Way, the Truth and the Life.[154] These gospels bring out the Person of Jesus by contrast with the Pharisees, in declarations in which He tells them that He is not as they are. {The} *second Monday*[155] {includes} a series of provoking and mysterious statements, which the Pharisees do not understand. Jesus deliberately challenges and scandalizes them. "Where I go you cannot come"[156] meets with complete incomprehension. Yet {note the} importance of this—the *pascha Christi*[157]—Christ passing through the world, gathering to Himself His elect, taking them out of this world to the Father. It is supremely important to know where He comes from and where He is going, and how we are to follow Him. If we do not know, we shall "die in our sins" and be lost. *Vos de deorsum estis, ego de supernis sum. Vos de mundo hoc estis, ego non sum de hoc mundo.*[158] After

151. Luke 16:19–31 (*Missale Romanum*, 90–91; *Missale Cisterciense*, 80).

152. Luke 16:31.

153. John 1:11.

154. John 14:6.

155. John 8:21–29 (*Missale Romanum*, 86; *Missale Cisterciense*, 76).

156. John 8:21.

157. "the Passover of Christ."

158. "You are from below; I am from above. You are of this world; I am not of this world" (John 8:23).

telling them that He comes from above, He offers them again a challenge, which is in reality an invitation, a plea: "believe in me." *"If you do not believe that I am He, you shall die in your sin."*[159] They are stirred by this, and they ask Him: *Tu quis es?*[160] His answer {is} enigmatic: *Principium qui et loquor vobis . . .*[161] In order to identify Himself more fully, He says He is *the One sent by the Father* to utter what the Father has revealed to Him. "He that sent me is true and the things I have heard of Him, the same I speak in the world."[162] But they do not understand, says John, that He called God His Father. Finally, Jesus declares that His full identity as the One sent by the Father and the One perfectly united to the Father will be manifested by His crucifixion, in which He perfectly fulfills the Father's will. WHEN YOU SHALL HAVE LIFTED UP THE SON OF MAN, then shall you know that I am He and that I DO NOTHING OF MYSELF, BUT AS THE FATHER HATH TAUGHT ME, THESE THINGS I SPEAK: AND HE THAT SENT ME IS WITH ME, AND HE HATH NOT LEFT ME ALONE: FOR I DO ALWAYS THE THINGS THAT PLEASE HIM.[163] In a word, He is saying what He will say later to the apostles at the Last Supper: "He that seeth me seeth the Father also."[164] {This is} a deeper and more perfect statement of the identity of the Son: He Who is ever united to the Father by Whom He is generated. In the second Tuesday He reveals Himself again, as we have seen, in His humility, which is opposed to the pride of the Pharisees; they have to teach their own doctrine in order to receive for themselves glory from men. But there is only one Master and only one Father, and among them if they would be close to God they must minister to one another. The truth manifests itself in humility and only the humble can receive it (cf. as we have seen above the gospel of the second Wednesday: the sons of Zebedee). {The} *second {Friday}*[165] {is} the parable of the wicked vine-dressers, who kill the messengers of the owner. (The Son {is} sent by the Father—to hate the Son is to hate the Father.) The conflict reaches an acute point when Jesus reveals that He is the stone rejected by the builders which is to be used as the true cornerstone. The Pharisees prepare to

159. John 8:24.

160. "Who are you?" (John 8:25).

161. "The beginning, who also speaks to you" (John 8:25).

162. John 8:26.

163. John 8:28–29.

164. John 14:9.

165. Matt 21:33–46 (text reads: "Thursday") (*Missale Romanum*, 92–93; *Missale Cisterciense*, 82).

kill Him. This idea of *rejection by the wise of this world* is most important. The light shines in darkness and the darkness does not comprehend it.[166] It is not enough that we desire "truth"—everyone does that. We must accept truth on its own conditions. We must accept God on His own terms, and human wisdom tends of itself to reject Him. {On the} *second Saturday*,[167] {the gospel shows that} and yet God is always ready to receive man back. This gospel is not part of a "conflict sequence"; it was inserted to give comfort to the public penitents and to comfort us all; after the shattering lessons which we have learned, we need this comfort to recognize that God is a loving Father waiting to receive us back to Him. All that is necessary is our humility and our sincere desire for the truth, our earnest resolve to do His will and to fit into the place determined for us by His love.

4. *The character of the Christ*:

a) He is the *Strong One* (*agios ischyros*)[168] Who comes with the power of God to dislodge the power of the evil spirits who hold the world in thrall. Again the Sunday gospel has the character of triumph: {on the} first Sunday,[169] Jesus triumphs over the devil in the desert; {the} second Sunday {is} the Transfiguration;[170] {on the} third Sunday,[171] He is the Stronger One who comes to cast out the devil, and He says, with all certitude and definiteness, that He has come to bring blessedness to those who hear His word and keep it.

b) He is the Judge of the living and the dead, Who will reward us according to our charity. He comes with authority to cleanse the temple and cast out the money-changers from "His Father's house"[172] (first Tuesday;[173] fourth Monday[174]).

---

166. John 1:5.

167. Luke 15:11–32 (*Missale Romanum*, 95; *Missale Cisterciense*, 84–85).

168. Good Friday: Improperia, chorus (*Missale Romanum*, 184; *Missale Cisterciense*, 158).

169. Matt 4:1–11 (*Missale Romanum*, 72; *Missale Cisterciense*, 61).

170. Matt 17:1–9 (*Missale Romanum*, 83–84; *Missale Cisterciense*, 74).

171. Luke 11:14–28 (*Missale Romanum*, 96–97; *Missale Cisterciense*, 86–87).

172. John 2:16.

173. Matt 21:10–17 (*Missale Romanum*, 75; *Missale Cisterciense*, 64–65).

174. John 2:13–25 (*Missale Romanum*, 112; *Missale Cisterciense*, 102).

c) As the Master of life and death, He is the healer of all sicknesses
{and} has power to bring life and health to all (miracles: first
Friday,[175] {third} Thursday,[176] etc.).

{d)} As the Lord and Master of material creation, He walks on the
sea, calms the storm (Saturday after Ash Wednesday[177]). He miraculously multiplies loaves and fishes (Laetare Sunday:[178] this
gospel refers figuratively to the Eucharist).

e) He is the One Who cannot be harmed without His own permission—third Monday[179]—in His own city, Nazareth, the citizens
become incensed when He presents Himself as a prophet Who
knows He is rejected in advance—they try to throw Him over a
cliff and he passes through the midst of them and goes His way.

f) Above all He manifests His divine power as the *Victor over
death*—fourth Monday[180] {is} another "conflict gospel" in which
He challenges the Pharisees; they ask Him for a sign, and He
says, "destroy this temple [of my Body] and I will raise it again
in three days."[181] But above all He proves His power over death
by raising the son of the widow of Naim and his friend Lazarus
(fourth Thursday;[182] fourth Friday[183]).

g) Finally, He is the LIGHT OF THE WORLD. Because His doctrine is
not His own but the Father's (fourth Tuesday[184]), He is the One
who gives sight to the man born blind (fourth Wednesday[185]).
Finally, He declares (fourth Saturday[186]), "I AM THE LIGHT OF
THE WORLD. HE THAT FOLLOWETH ME WALKETH NOT IN

175. John 5:1–15 (*Missale Romanum*, 79–80; *Missale Cisterciense*, 69).

176. Luke 4:38–44 (text reads "second") (*Missale Romanum*, 103; *Missale Cisterciense*, 93).

177. Mark 6:47–56 (*Missale Romanum*, 70; *Missale Cisterciense*, 59).

178. John 6:1–15 (*Missale Romanum*, 110; *Missale Cisterciense*, 100).

179. Luke 4:23–30 (*Missale Romanum*, 99; *Missale Cisterciense*, 89).

180. John 2:13–25 (*Missale Romanum*, 112; *Missale Cisterciense*, 102).

181. John 2:19.

182. Luke 7:11–16 (*Missale Romanum*, 118; *Missale Cisterciense*, 108).

183. John 11:1–45 (*Missale Romanum*, 119–20; *Missale Cisterciense*, 109–10).

184. John 7:14–31 (*Missale Romanum*, 113–14; *Missale Cisterciense*, 103–104).

185. John 9:1–38 (*Missale Romanum*, 116–17; *Missale Cisterciense*, 105–106).

186. John 8:12–20 (*Missale Romanum*, 122; *Missale Cisterciense*, 111).

DARKNESS BUT HE SHALL HAVE THE LIGHT OF LIFE."[187] My judgement is true because I am not alone, but I and the Father that sent me . . . and the Father that sent Me giveth testimony of Me.[188]

h) In the beautiful gospel of the Samaritan woman (third Friday[189]), He reveals Himself explicitly as the Messias and the *Savior of the world.*

5. *The personality of Jesus:* everywhere in the Lenten gospels we find the human traits of the God–Man which are all significant revelations of God in Christ His Son—His tenderness and compassion (for the widow of Naim, for Lazarus—his human affections for His friends), His simplicity and kindness with the Samaritan woman, a gospel which shows how He wills to share all the conditions and limitations of human nature, to be really one with those whom He has chosen as His brothers. All the warm human traits of Jesus express this great truth, that the love of God has willed to descend among us in our own humanity and dwell among us as one of ourselves, truly our Brother. This is one of the greatest truths which the Gospel teaches about Jesus and this we must learn above all, that His love has sought to identify Him with us, and to be like us in everything, and all He asks is that our faith respond with a simplicity and a totality corresponding to His own.

∾

First Sunday {*of*} *Lent*: {the} epistle[190] {has a} special appropriateness for Lent. {Note} how the Church understands this epistle in this Mass:

1. *Not to receive* {*the*} *grace of God in vain:* Lent is a time of grace (*tempus acceptabile—dies salutis*[191]); grace will come and we must be disposed to receive it.

2. *Nemini dantes ullam offensionem:*[192] an overall prescription to be meek, not to hurt others, not to fight back when our will is balked (cf. {the} epistle {for} Friday[193]).

187. John 8:12.

188. John 8:16, 18.

189. John 4:5–42 (*Missale Romanum*, 105–106; *Missale Cisterciense*, 94–95).

190. 2 Cor 6:1–10 (*Missale Romanum*, 71; *Missale Cisterciense*, 60–61).

191. "the acceptable time, the day of salvation" (2 Cor 6:2).

192. "not giving any offense to anyone" (2 Cor 6:3).

193. Ezek 18:20–28 (*Missale Romanum*, 79; *Missale Cisterciense*, 68–69).

3. *Fiunt Dei ministros:*[194] Lent {is} a time above all to learn how to be servants of God.

(a) *In multa patientia:*[195] Lent {is} *a time of trial.* {There are} different trials: doing without things; our liberty impeded; frustration; opposition; hard work (*in laboribus*[196]). {See} St. Gregory on temptation (third nocturn[197]): *suggestione, delectatione, consensione.*[198]

(b) *In virtute Dei:*[199] knowledge given by God in silence and peace: longanimity, a special gift; *in suavitate, in Spiritu Sancto*[200]—Lent is also a time of *consolation.*

(c) *in all events* and *circumstances,* whether praised or blamed: *seductores et veraces, ignoti et cogniti.*[201]

(d) {the} *paradoxes of* {the} *spiritual life:* what is a paradox? *quasi morientes et vere vivimus;*[202] *nihil habentes et omnia possidentes.*[203]

⁓

Epistle[204] of today:[205] judgement—openness: manifestation of conscience; sacramental confession: accusations? past sins? Knowledge of motives: "getting it out" (breaking up blockage). Father must experience vicariously what is cooking—*empathy.* Daniel {is a} model of prayer: (1) who he is; (2) who we are—sinners; (3) our need (of {the] CHURCH); (4) why He should answer—not our "justifications,"[206] His name in us. Gospel (end):[207] comment.

194. "they become God's ministers" (2 Cor 6:4).

195. "in much patience" (2 Cor 6:4).

196. "in labors" (2 Cor 6:5).

197. *Homilia 16 in Evangelium* (*Breviarium Cisterciense, Pars Vernalis,* 178–80).

198. "by suggestion, by enjoyment, by consent" (twelfth lesson) (*Breviarium Cisterciense, Vernalis,* 179, which reads: ". . . *consensu*").

199. "in the power of God" (2 Cor 6:7).

200. "in sweetness, in the Holy Spirit" (2 Cor 6:6).

201. "deceivers and truthful, unknown and well-known" (2 Cor 6:8).

202. "as dying yet truly we live" (2 Cor 6:9).

203. "having nothing and possessing all" (2 Cor 6:10).

204. Dan 9:15–19 (*Missale Romanum,* 85–86; *Missale Cisterciense,* 75–76).

205. Monday, second week of Lent.

206. Dan 9:18.

207. John 8:21–29 (*Missale Romanum,* 86; *Missale Cisterciense,* 76).

∽

The Mystery of the Cross in the Rule of St. Benedict: St. Benedict does not explicitly mention the Cross in his *Rule*.

1. However at the end of the Prologue in which he gives a summary of his whole doctrine, he says that the life of the monk is an *education*, in the school of Divine Service, in which Jesus Himself is our Master, and we learn by *sharing in His Passion*: *constituenda est ergo nobis* schola Dominici servitii.[208] In this school there are "somewhat hard"[209] things, but they are necessary and love will make them easy, and if we love, we will *joyfully persevere*: *ut ab ipsius numquam Magisterio discedentes; in ejus doctrina usque ad mortem in monasterio perseverantes*; PASSIONIBUS CHRISTI PER PATIENTIAM PARTICIPEMUR; *ut et regni ejus mereamur esse consortes*:[210] (1) in the hard things of our life we are being instructed by a loving Master; (2) that is why we came here; (3) we are not just being taught speculative truths—we are being *formed*; (4) in all these things we are *united to Christ in His Passion*; (5) and will share His glory.

2. In particular, what "hard things" (*dura et aspera*[211]) give us a share in the Passion? (a) {the} third degree of humility: *Pro* Dei amore[212]—to obey in all things, imitating Christ—*obediens ad mortem*[213]—an explicit reference to His Passion; (b) {the} fourth degree of humility, {with its} emphasis on all that is *hard* and *contrary*, on special patience in undeserved trials—*propter te morte tota die afficimur*[214]—{an} indirect allusion to the Passion; (c) {the} seventh degree of humility, to believe oneself inferior to all, "a worm and

208. "Therefore we must establish a school of the Lord's service" (McCann, ed. and trans., *Rule of St. Benedict*, 12, which reads: ". . . *dominici schola servitii*") .

209. "*paululum restrictius*" (McCann, ed. and trans., *Rule of St. Benedict*, 12).

210. "so that, never withdrawing from His rule, remaining faithful to His teaching even to death, we will share through patience in the sufferings of Christ, so that we may be found worthy to be sharers in His Kingdom" (McCann, ed. and trans., *Rule of St. Benedict*, 12).

211. "hard and bitter things" (c. 58) (McCann, ed. and trans., *Rule of St. Benedict*, 130).

212. "for the love of God" (c. 7) (McCann, ed. and trans., *Rule of St. Benedict*, 42).

213. "obedient unto death" (Phil 2:8) (McCann, ed. and trans., *Rule of St. Benedict*, 42).

214. "For Your sake we are being put to death all day" (Ps 43[44]:23; Rom 8:36) (McCann, ed. and trans., *Rule of St. Benedict*, 42, which reads: ". . . *afficimur tota die*").

no man"[215]—{an} allusion to a psalm whose spiritual sense refers to Christ crucified.

3. The purpose {is} that we may not be proud of our good works but "*operantem in se Dominum magnificant*."[216]

4. {Note} the miracle {when} the sign of the cross breaks the goblet of poison (third responsory[217]): "*ac si pro signo lapidem dedisset*";[218] and the man of God understood it was a "drink of death which could not bear the SIGN OF LIFE."[219] {The} sign of the Cross {is the} sign of *Life*. The Risen Lord lives in us because He died for us. He lives in us in proportion as our "old man"[220] is put to death by His Spirit. For this we are monks.

∾

In the Holy Week liturgy we unite ourselves to the sacrifice of the Son of God as to the supreme act of worship. {An} instinct to worship {is} linked with the sense of the Holy and with the sense of *right*—placing ourselves in our true relationship to the rest of creation. *Holy Thursday* {marks} the offering of the divine Victim before His immolation. Jesus could have said Mass every day of His life if He had wanted to, {thus there is a} special significance of this offering *before* the event. We are all invited to participate *in this particular way* in a loving family repast. The liturgy brings this out most clearly {on} Holy Thursday evening—the Lord's Supper.

∾

---

215. "*vermis et non homo*" (Ps 21[22]:7) (McCann, ed. and trans., *Rule of St. Benedict*, 44).

216. "they glorify the Lord working in them" (Prologue) (McCann, ed. and trans., *Rule of St. Benedict*, 10).

217. "*Inito consilio venenum vino miscuere: quo oblato ex more ad benedicendum Patri, vir Dei signum Crucis edidit, et vas pestiferi potus ita confractum est*" ("After the plan had been made to mix poison with the wine, it was given as usual to the Father to be blessed; the man of God made the sign of the Cross, and the cup of tainted liquid was thus broken") (*Breviarium Cisterciense, Vernalis*, 450).

218. "as if for a sign he had given a stone" (*Breviarium Cisterciense, Vernalis*, 450).

219. "*potum mortis . . . quod portare non potuit signum vitae*" (third versicle) (*Breviarium Cisterciense, Vernalis*, 450).

220. Rom 6:6.

Passion Sunday

    1. Passiontide {marks} the Victory of Christ (*qualiter Redemptor orbis immolatus vicerit*[221]). *Vexilla Crucis prodeunt.*[222] {Note} the hymns: *Fulget crucis mysterium;*[223] *Regnavit a ligno Deus;*[224] *O Crux ave spes unica;*[225] *Et medelam ferret inde / Hostis unde laeserat.*[226] {It is a time of} mystical and sacramental participation in the Passion and Victory of Christ: our *eyes see* the salvation sent by God—in mystery.

    2. Daniel (epistle of Tuesday[227]) {is} a type of Christ {and of} His victory.

    3. *The struggle against evil*:

a) {Here is the} tremendous mystery of the Word made flesh in the midst of men and rejected by them, rejected by the holy, {and} the savagery with which the holy ones hounded Him to death. Pharisees have much in common with Trappists. Would we receive Him if He came thus unexpectedly today? An easy answer {can be found}: whatsoever you have done to the least of these My brethren.[228]

b) {There must be a} *struggle against the evil in ourselves: Commune consortium crucis Christi*[229] (St. Leo). "Certain and secure is our hope of promised beatitude, where there is participation in the Lord's Passion."[230] All have to bear the cross. Even when we are not asked to suffer martyrdom, we face the same enemy within ourselves and *more dangerously* ({a} fifth column). *We are very sick when we give in to all our desires and satisfy our own will*

---

221. "as the sacrificed Redeemer of the world conquered" ("*Pange Lingua*," ll. 5–6) (vigils hymn) (*Breviarium Cisterciense, Vernalis*, 239).

222. "The standards of the Cross advance" (vespers hymn) (actually "*Vexilla Regis* [of the King]") (*Breviarium Cisterciense, Vernalis*, 248).

223. "the mystery of the Cross shines forth" ("*Vexilla Regis*," l. 2).

224. "God reigns from the tree" ("*Vexilla Regis*," l. 12).

225. "Hail, O Cross, only hope" ("*Vexilla Regis*," l. 21).

226. "that He might bring healing there / Where the enemy had wounded" ("*Pange Lingua*," ll. 17–18).

227. Dan 14:27–42 (*Missale Romanum*, 127–28; *Missale Cisterciense*, 117).

228. Matt 25:40.

229. "a common participation in the Cross of Christ" (*Sermo 9 de Quadragesima*) (fifth lesson) (*Breviarium Cisterciense, Vernalis*, 242).

230. "*Certa atque secura est expectatio promissae beatitudinis, ubi est participatio Dominicae Passionis*" (fifth lesson) (*Breviarium Cisterciense, Vernalis*, 242).

in everything. {See} St. Gregory (third nocturn[231]): a proof that we belong to God {is} to have heard His words—if we *do what He says.* {See the} value of Trappist life from this viewpoint. {The} epistle[232] {looks at the} Old and New Laws—go on to {the} Law—Sinai. {The} *Passion fulfills all the Old Law and transfigures it, elevating it in Christ.* N.B. Jesus {was} crucified as *a violator of the Law*—{a sign of the} depth of the problem!

≈

Palm Sunday: there is a time for sadness and lamentation—{the} sin of pagans {is to be} "without affection" (Rom. 1[233] and St. Bernard: second nocturn, Feast of {the} Seven Dolors[234]). {There is} a time for tears. {It is} ridiculous, in view of the bitterness of life, the suffering, the injustice, to say that we must be *always* laughing. Our Christian life {is} predominantly joy, BUT God Himself came to earth in order to taste sadness and suffering in redeeming us (read Hebrews[235]). *The key* {to a} valid and Christian sadness is sadness *suffered with another*, not just sadness closed up within itself ({N.B.} our wrong forms of sadness—sulking, separateness, taking our own little troubles as greater than any others, nursing our own grievances and wars, and seeking comfort from others for nothing. The solution {is} seeing the greater sufferings of others, the sufferings of all mankind, and suffering with them—*suffering in Christ*).

{This is the message of} *The Lamentations*, {written at the time of the Babylonian} Captivity (580 BC), {when} the city of God {was} deserted because of {the} sins of the priests and the people. SIN {is} the great source of suffering. If there were no sin there would be no suffering, but conversely, suffering liberates from sin.

---

231. *Homilia 18 in Evangelia* (*Breviarium Cisterciense, Vernalis*, 244–45).

232. Heb 9:11–15 (*Missale Romanum*, 123–24; *Missale Cisterciense*, 114).

233. Rom 1:31.

234. Sermon on the Twelve Stars (*Breviarium Cisterciense, Vernalis*, 483–84).

235. "Who in the days of his flesh, with a strong cry and tears, offering up prayers and supplications to him that was able to save him from death, was heard for his reverence. And whereas indeed he was the Son of God, he learned obedience by the things which he suffered: And being consummated, he became, to all that obey him, the cause of eternal salvation" (Heb 5:7–9).

LAMENTATIONS 1: READ 2–7:[236] *Viae Sion lugent.*[237] Note {the} *restraint,* {the} understatement, {which} increases {the} force of great sorrow; {note the} majestic dignity of sorrow, {and} note {the} lack of resentment, {the} true humility. {These mark the} sufferings of Christ and {the} sufferings of His Church. Do we feel that our enemies are at fault or {are} we? READ 8–11:[238] *Jerusalem peccavit*[239]. . . . READ 12–14:[240] *O vos omnes*[241]—{see the} application to Christ (cf. {the} Servant of Yahweh—again {a} model of restraint in sorrow—we *do not know* true sorrow); a vintage—*quid? Posuit me desolatam;*[242] {note} the *burning anger*

236. "Weeping she hath wept in the night, and her tears are on her cheeks: there is none to comfort her among all them that were dear to her: all her friends have despised her, and are become her enemies. Juda hath removed her dwelling place because of her affliction, and the greatness of her bondage: she hath dwelt among the nations, and she hath found no rest: all her persecutors have taken her in the midst of straits. The ways of Sion mourn, because there are none that come to the solemn feast: all her gates are broken down: her priests sigh: her virgins are in affliction, and she is oppressed with bitterness. Her adversaries are become her lords, her enemies are enriched: because the Lord hath spoken against her for the multitude of her iniquities: her children are led into captivity: before the face of the oppressor. And from the daughter of Sion all her beauty is departed: her princes are become like rams that find no pastures: and they are gone away without strength before the face of the pursuer. Jerusalem hath remembered the days of her affliction, and prevarication of all her desirable things which she had from the days of old, when her people fell in the enemy's hand, and there was no helper: the enemies have seen her, and have mocked at her sabbaths."

237. "The ways of Sion mourn" (Lam 1:4).

238. "Jerusalem hath grievously sinned, therefore is she become unstable: all that honoured her have despised her, because they have seen her shame: but she sighed and turned backward. Her filthiness is on her feet, and she hath not remembered her end: she is wonderfully cast down, not having a comforter: behold, O Lord, my affliction, because the enemy is lifted up. The enemy hath put out his hand to all her desirable things: for she hath seen the Gentiles enter into her sanctuary, of whom thou gavest commandment that they should not enter into thy church. All her people sigh, they seek bread: they have given all their precious things for food to relieve the soul: see, O Lord, and consider, for I am become vile."

239. "Jerusalem hath sinned" (Lam 1:8).

240. "O all ye that pass by the way, attend, and see if there be any sorrow like to my sorrow: for he hath made a vintage of me, as the Lord spoke in the day of his fierce anger. From above he hath sent fire into my bones, and hath chastised me: he hath spread a net for my feet, he hath turned me back: he hath made me desolate, wasted with sorrow all the day long. The yoke of my iniquities hath watched: they are folded together in his hand, and put upon my neck: my strength is weakened: the Lord hath delivered me into a hand out of which I am not able to rise."

241. "O all ye" (Lam 1:12).

242. "He has made me desolate" (Lam 1:13).

of Yahweh—fire in my bones—the yoke of my sins: "I cannot bear it."
READ 2:1–10.[243] Sorrow for Christ: if we love Him, {we} must compassionate *His* sufferings ({the} meaning of our sufferings only comes *after* this—some try to "suffer" before compassionating with Christ). {We must have} sorrow for our sins which caused His sufferings, sorrow at the contrast between His love and our sins, {at} what He suffers for us without even consulting us about it!

{See the} suffering of Jesus in the Garden: He *wants* {the} comfort of {the} apostles but does not get it. {Here is the} mystery, that he wants our compassion, {and the} greater mystery that we do not give it. Every character in {the} Passion represents some of us—at best we are "the apostles." In the future He will ask this compassion of us, unexpectedly. If we think of it now, we will be more ready.

{See the} suffering of Jesus before His judges: *Circumdederunt me viri mendaces*[244] (cf. in Psalms). {It is the} same today, and always, the lies

---

243. "How hath the Lord covered with obscurity the daughter of Sion in his wrath! how hath he cast down from heaven to the earth the glorious one of Israel, and hath not remembered his footstool in the day of his anger! The Lord hath cast down headlong, and hath not spared, all that was beautiful in Jacob: he hath destroyed in his wrath the strong holds of the virgin of Juda, and brought them down to the ground: he hath made the kingdom unclean, and the princes thereof. He hath broken in his fierce anger all the horn of Israel: he hath drawn back his right hand from before the enemy: and he hath kindled in Jacob as it were a flaming fire devouring round about. He hath bent his bow as an enemy, he hath fixed his right hand as an adversary: and he hath killed all that was fair to behold in the tabernacle of the daughter of Sion, he hath poured out his indignation like fire. The Lord is become as an enemy: he hath cast down Israel headlong, he hath overthrown all the walls thereof: he hath destroyed his strong holds, and hath multiplied in the daughter of Juda the afflicted, both men and women. And he hath destroyed his tent as a garden, he hath thrown down his tabernacle: the Lord hath caused feasts and sabbaths to be forgotten in Sion: and hath delivered up king and priest to reproach, and to the indignation of his wrath. The Lord hath cast off his altar, he hath cursed his sanctuary: he hath delivered the walls of the towers thereof into the hand of the enemy: they have made a noise in the house of the Lord, as in the day of a solemn feast. The Lord hath purposed to destroy the wall of the daughter of Sion: he hath stretched out his line, and hath not withdrawn his hand from destroying: and the bulwark hath mourned, and the wall hath been destroyed together. Her gates are sunk into the ground: he hath destroyed, and broken her bars: her king and her princes are among the Gentiles: the law is no more, and her prophets have found no vision from the Lord. The ancients of the daughter of Sion sit upon the ground, they have held their peace: they have sprinkled their heads with dust, they are girded with haircloth, the virgins of Jerusalem hang down their heads to the ground."

244. "Lying men surround me" (Responsory, Vespers, Saturday of Fifth Week of Lent) (*Breviarium Cisterciense, Vernalis*, 260).

and hypocrisy of man. We also have all this in us, but our tears can open the way to faith.

{See the} sufferings of Jesus on the Cross, {the} absolute rejection by His people, {the} dereliction, forsaken by His Father (read ch. 3:1 to about 21;[245] fruit: 3:28[246]—*silence of the penitent*).

~

Easter Monday: Paschal Time:

1. *Introduxit vos*:[247] what is the land flowing with milk and honey? the Kingdom, *life in Christ*. All the realities of salvation are given, but not manifested, even in {the} present life—given where? in the sacraments. {The} Eucharist is above all where we taste "milk and honey."[248] {The} contemplative monastic life is a land flowing with milk and honey in the sense that we should be privileged to have a *greater realization*, {an} obscure possession of God, {to} realize {the} value of darkness (*O vere beata nox*[249]). But we need {the} mentality of our Fathers for this. {See the} first collect: *Perfectam libertatem*

245. "I am the man that see my poverty by the rod of his indignation. He hath led me, and brought me into darkness, and not into light. Only against me he hath turned, and turned again his hand all the day. My skin and my flesh he hath made old, he hath broken my bones. He hath built round about me, and he hath compassed me with gall and labour. He hath set me in dark places as those that are dead for ever. He hath built against me round about, that I may not get out: he hath made my fetters heavy. Yea, and when I cry, and entreat, he hath shut out my prayer. He hath shut up my ways with square stones, he hath turned my paths upside down. He is become to me as a bear lying in wait: as a lion in secret places. He hath turned aside my paths, and hath broken me in pieces, he hath made me desolate. He hath bent his bow, and set me as a mark for his arrows. He hath shot into my reins the daughters of his quiver. I am made a derision to all my people, their song all the day long. He hath filled me with bitterness, he hath inebriated me with wormwood. And he hath broken my teeth one by one, he hath fed me with ashes. And my soul is removed far off from peace, I have forgotten good things. And I said: My end and my hope is perished from the Lord. Remember my poverty, and transgression, the wormwood, and the gall. I will be mindful and remember, and my soul shall languish within me. These things I shall think over in my heart, therefore will I hope."

246. "He shall sit solitary, and hold his peace: because he hath taken it up upon himself."

247. "He has led you into [a land of milk and honey]" (Exod 13:5) (introit) (*Missale Romanum*, 345; *Missale Cisterciense*, 236).

248. Exod 33:3.

249. "O truly blessed night" (Easter vigil: Exultet) (*Missale Romanum*, 195; *Missale Cisterciense*, 168).

consequi mereatur[250]—{we} must be free from fears, doubts, hesitations, divisions and attachments to realize our new life.

2. The gospel of Easter Monday:[251] {note} the genuine humanness of the scene—{it} could not have been invented—{and} the *mysteriousness* of Our Lord's risen life—{the} interpenetration of these two {is} the life of the Kingdom (n.b. {an} *even more intimate interpenetration* {comes} *after Pentecost*). *Nos autem sperabamus:*[252] the sin of despair, from shattered human hopes. They let their hopes be shattered by what should have been the source of hope. Their lack of simplicity {is evident in their} failure to believe the women. Why? *O stulti et tardi corde ad credendum*[253]—whence this foolishness and sloth (cf. the "fool" of {the] sapiential books[254]). NONNE OPORTUIT[255]—this too we must realize; *mane nobiscum*[256]—and the "breaking of the bread."[257] *Nonne cor nostrum ardens erat*[258]—our heart burning within us as a sign of grace and love, but only one sign: n.b. in today's gospel and tomorrow's,[259] Jesus *opens their minds to the Scriptures.*

3. The Divine Mercy: what is the greatest and most characteristic attribute of God? His mercy, His goodness in action. "In every work of God *there appears, as its ultimate root, God's mercy*" (I, q. 21, a. {4}).[260] God is pure generosity, pure giving. All things are good because by loving them He makes them good. "It is more proper to

---

250. "May we merit to reach perfect freedom" (collect) (*Missale Romanum*, 345; *Missale Cisterciense*, 236; *Breviarium Cisterciense, Vernalis*, 316).

251. Luke 24:13–35 (*Missale Romanum*, 345–46; *Missale Cisterciense*, 237).

252. "We were hoping" (Luke 24:21).

253. "O foolish ones, and slow of heart to believe" (Luke 24:25).

254. E.g. "The fear of the lord is the beginning of wisdom. Fools despise wisdom and instruction" (Prov 1:7); "The fool foldeth his hands together, and eateth his own flesh, saying: Better is a handful with rest, than both hands full with labour, and vexation of mind" (Eccl 4:5–6); see also Prov 12:16; 14:7–9, 16; 15:2, 14; 17:24; 18:2, 6, 7; 28:26; 29:9, 11; Eccl. 10:11–15.

255. "Was it not necessary" (Luke 24:26).

256. "Remain with us" (Luke 24:29).

257. Luke 24:35.

258. "Was not our heart burning" (Luke 24:32).

259. Luke 24:36–47 (*Missale Romanum*, 347–48; *Missale Cisterciense*, 238–39).

260. St. Thomas Aquinas, *Summa Theologiae, Prima Secundae*, q. 113, a. 9: "*Et sic in quolibet opera Dei apparet misericordia quantum ad primam radicem ejus*" (Aquinas, *Opera Omnia*, 1.98) (text reads: "a. 3").

God to have mercy and to spare than to punish" (II–II, q. 21, a. 2).[261] God's mercy is the attribute proper to Him as supreme over all other beings, because they cannot be compared with Him or exist on the same level with Him. His punishing them is really no indication of His "power"; {it is} not commensurate with it. *His mercy is.* Hence He wills to have mercy but not to punish. "The omnipotence of God shows itself above all in pardoning and having mercy *because to remit sins at will is the mark of supreme power,* for if one is bound by a higher law he does not have this power" (I, {q. 25}, a. 3, ad 3).[262] "To pardon men and have pity on them is a greater work than the creation of the world" (I–II, q. 113, a. 9).[263] In the alleluia,[264] we exult in the special revelation of the divine greatness *through His mercy,* a revelation that could not be had in any other way. *The postcommunion* {is the} same as Easter Day, one of the most beautiful in all the liturgy. God's pardon and love {are received} in the gift of His Holy Spirit, in Whom we are one! *Tua facias pietate concordes*[265] (n.b. this {is} a grace of Easter). Also READ {the} gospel of Low Sunday,[266] down to *"quorum retinueretis retenta sunt"*[267]—{the} giving of power to absolve from sins. *The sacraments* {are} *remedies and channels of mercy.*

261. *"magis proprium est Deo misereri et parcere, quam punire"* (Aquinas, *Opera Omnia,* 3.78).

262. *"Dei omnipotentia ostenditur maxime in parcendo et miserando, quia per hoc ostenditur Deum habere summam potestatem quod libere peccata dimittit; ejus enim qui superioris legi astringitur, non est libere peccata condonare"* (Aquinas, *Opera Omnia,* 1:112–13) (text reads: "q. 21").

263. *"majus opus est ut ex impio justus fiat, quam creare caelum et terram"* ("It is greater to make a just man from an impious one than to create heaven and earth") (Aquinas, *Opera Omnia,* 2:454, citing St. Augustine, *Tractatus 72 in Joannem,* n. 3 [Migne, *PL* 35, col. 1823], which expresses this idea at greater length); the opening phrase is based on the collect from the tenth Sunday after Pentecost, which is quoted by Aquinas immediately before this statement, and which begins: *"Deus qui omnipotentiam tuam parcendo maxime et miserando manifestas"* ("God, Who show Your goodness above all in pardoning and being merciful").

264. Luke 24:32 (*Missale Cisterciense,* 237; the alleluia in the Roman Rite is Matt 28:2 [*Missale Romanum,* 345]).

265. "May You make us of one heart through Your kindness" (postommunion) (*Missale Romanum,* 346; *Missale Cisterciense,* 238).

266. John 20:19–31 (*Missale Romanum,* 357–58; *Missale Cisterciense,* 246).

267. "whose [sins] you shall retain have been retained" (John 20:23).

～

Low Sunday {emphasizes} faith:

a) {the} epistle:[268] "*Omne quod natum est ex Deo vincit mundum.*"[269]
*What does it mean to overcome the world? liberty from concupiscence
and pride,* from slavery to temporal things, human respect, *one's
own self-love. What does it mean to be born of God?* to receive Christ,
have Him living in us, to be sons of God in Christ. *Haec est victoria
quae vincit mundum—fides nostra.*[270] What is faith? more than mere
assent to revealed propositions; {it includes} intellectual assent, yes,
but {it is} dangerous to leave it at that, {the} danger of a spiritual life
that is all, or mostly, "in the mind." *Faith* {is} *the surrender of our
whole being to Christ: obedientia fidei*[271]—I believe Christ is the Son
of God, and I surrender myself to Him *in all things* as a consequence.

b) {the} gospel[272] {is the} story of St. Thomas: (1) he makes this complete surrender, at last: "My Lord and my God!"[273] (2) *but his faith
lacks simplicity.* {There is a} twofold lesson of {the} gospel: indirectly,
{it} gives {the} strongest motives of credibility. But to have motives
of credibility is something else than having faith. We have enough
motives of credibility in the Gospel itself. *We must be content to
accept the Word of God from other men*—and with simplicity. St.
Thomas {is} reproved because what he accepted from Jesus Himself
he should have accepted from the apostles.

c) {the} first nocturn[274] {focuses on} the risen life: *Si consurrexistis cum
Christo:*[275] (1) our life is hidden with Christ in God;[276] (2) {the}
consequences {are}: mortification of our visible and earthly "self," in
passions and in *speech*; especially *avoid lying* or all insincerity ({cf.
the} connection with {the} Resurrection and {the} Mystical Body);

---

268. 1 John 5:4–10 (*Missale Romanum*, 357; *Missale Cisterciense*, 245–46).

269. "All that is born of God overcomes the world" (1 John 5:4).

270. "this is the victory that overcomes the world: our faith" (1 John 5:4).

271. "the obedience of faith" (Rom 1:5).

272. John 20:19–31 (*Missale Romanum*, 357–58; *Missale Cisterciense*, 246).

273. John 20:28.

274. Col 3:1–17 (*Breviarium Cisterciense, Vernalis*, 318–20).

275. "If you have risen with Christ" (Col 3:1) (first lesson) (*Breviarium Cisterciense, Vernalis*, 318).

276. Col 3:3.

mercy and patience—another consequence; *super omnia caritatem habete—vinculum perfectionis*;[277] {the} consequences of this {are} joy; {the} Word of God "dwells abundantly in our hearts";[278] hymns and spiritual canticles;[279] "all in the Name of Jesus Christ Our Lord."[280]

∽

Third Sunday after Easter: {note the} special beauty of the Mass, {filled with} Easter joy; {there is a} "release," liberation in the desert itself. {The} *gospel*[281] and {the} *Apocalypse*: what book do we read in {the} first nocturn?[282] What is it all about? {We can see} today's gospel as a key to the Apocalypse. Read John 16:19–22:[283] these verses contain in another form the whole content of the Apocalypse—the *whole time of waiting* between {the} Ascension and {the} Last Judgement. {Note the} characteristic pattern: (a) the world shall rejoice and you shall be sad;[284] (b) you shall see Me again and your sorrow will turn into joy;[285] (c) your joy no man shall take from you.[286] {In the Apocalypse we find}: c. 1: {the} general prologue; c. 2–3: particular instructions to (all) churches (v.g. c. 2:8–10—the pattern realized here); c. 4: prologue to the main revelations—heaven opened, etc.; c. 5–11: the seven plagues (seven seals); cf.

277. "Above all these things, have charity, the bond of perfection" (Col 3:14) (fourth lesson) (*Breviarium Cisterciense, Vernalis*, 319, which reads: "... *omnia autem haec caritatem habete quid est vinculum* ...").

278. Col 3:15 (fourth lesson) (*Breviarium Cisterciense, Vernalis*, 319).

279. Col 3:16.

280. Col 3:17 (fourth lesson) (*Breviarium Cisterciense, Vernalis*, 320).

281. John 16:16–22 (*Missale Romanum*, 361; *Missale Cisterciense*, 249).

282. Apoc [Rev] 1:1–11 (*Breviarium Cisterciense, Vernalis*, 336–37).

283. "And Jesus knew that they had a mind to ask him; and he said to them: Of this do you inquire among yourselves, because I said: A little while, and you shall not see me; and again a little while, and you shall see me? Amen, amen I say to you, that you shall lament and weep, but the world shall rejoice; and you shall be made sorrowful, but your sorrow shall be turned into joy. A woman, when she is in labour, hath sorrow, because her hour is come; but when she hath brought forth the child, she remembereth no more the anguish, for joy that a man is born into the world. So also you now indeed have sorrow; but I will see you again, and your heart shall rejoice; and your joy no man shall take from you."

284. John 16:20.

285. John 16:22.

286. John 16:22.

again 16 (seven vials) (read 11, *in toto*,[287] as {an} example of {the} above pattern; read {22}:12–17,[288] the epilogue, and comment: He who hath

287. "And there was given me a reed like unto a rod: and it was said to me: Arise, and measure the temple of God, and the altar and them that adore therein. But the court, which is without the temple, cast out, and measure it not: because it is given unto the Gentiles, and the holy city they shall tread under foot two and forty months: And I will give unto my two witnesses, and they shall prophesy a thousand two hundred sixty days, clothed in sackcloth. These are the two olive trees, and the two candlesticks, that stand before the Lord of the earth. And if any man will hurt them, fire shall come out of their mouths, and shall devour their enemies. And if any man will hurt them, in this manner must he be slain. These have power to shut heaven, that it rain not in the days of their prophecy: and they have power over waters to turn them into blood, and to strike the earth with all plagues as often as they will. And when they shall have finished their testimony, the beast that ascendeth out of the abyss, shall make war against them, and shall overcome them, and kill them. And their bodies shall lie in the streets of the great city, which is called spiritually, Sodom and Egypt, where their Lord also was crucified. And they of the tribes, and peoples, and tongues, and nations, shall see their bodies for three days and a half: and they shall not suffer their bodies to be laid in sepulchres. And they that dwell upon the earth shall rejoice over them, and make merry: and shall send gifts one to another, because these two prophets tormented them that dwelt upon the earth. And after three days and a half, the spirit of life from God entered into them. And they stood upon their feet, and great fear fell upon them that saw them. And they heard a great voice from heaven, saying to them: Come up hither. And they went up to heaven in a cloud: and their enemies saw them. And at that hour there was made a great earthquake, and the tenth part of the city fell: and there were slain in the earthquake names of men seven thousand: and the rest were cast into a fear, and gave glory to the God of heaven. The second woe is past: and behold the third woe will come quickly. And the seventh angel sounded the trumpet: and there were great voices in heaven, saying: The kingdom of this world is become our Lord's and his Christ's, and he shall reign for ever and ever. Amen. And the four and twenty ancients, who sit on their seats in the sight of God, fell on their faces and adored God, saying: We give thee thanks, O Lord God Almighty, who art, and who wast, and who art to come: because thou hast taken to thee thy great power, and thou hast reigned. And the nations were angry, and thy wrath is come, and the time of the dead, that they should be judged, and that thou shouldest render reward to thy servants the prophets and the saints, and to them that fear thy name, little and great, and shouldest destroy them who have corrupted the earth. And the temple of God was opened in heaven: and the ark of his testament was seen in his temple, and there were lightnings, and voices, and an earthquake, and great hail."

288. "Behold, I come quickly; and my reward is with me, to render to every man according to his works. I am Alpha and Omega, the first and the last, the beginning and the end. Blessed are they that wash their robes in the blood of the Lamb: that they may have a right to the tree of life, and may enter in by the gates into the city. Without are dogs, and sorcerers, and unchaste, and murderers, and servers of idols, and every one that loveth and maketh a lie. I Jesus have sent my angel to testify to you these things in the churches. I am the root and stock of David, the bright and morning star. And the spirit and the bride say: Come. And he that heareth, let him say: Come. And

ears to hear let him hear what the Spirit says; *the Spirit and the Bride say
"come"* (explain)—liberation, joy, certainty {are found} in the soul that
has perfectly the mind of the Church and hears the Holy Spirit.

～

Eros and Agape

Eros (Cupid) {symbolizes}: (1) animal love; (2) {the} highest kind of
natural love—*desire* that begins in us and craves perfection and highest
union with God, even aspires to {the} "highest kind of disinterested love."

Agape {is}: (1) entirely from God—{it is} divine selflessness, all-
giving; (2) {it} descends to us—unless it is given to us we *cannot* know
it. Read 1 John 4:7-14:[289] he that loveth not, knoweth not God—God
is charity; God has *shown His charity by sending His Son*, that *we may
live by Him*; 10: In this is charity, not as though we had loved God, BUT
GOD HAS FIRST LOVED US, and send His Son (without Jesus, the agape
{is} impossible to us); if God has so loved us we also ought to love one
another; no one has seen God at any time (against pagan contemplation);
if we love one another, He abideth in us—and He is *seen* in us ({note the}
importance {of this passage} in St. Bernard!![290]); {cf. also} John 17:20:

he that thirsteth, let him come: and he that will, let him take the water of life, freely"
(text reads: "21").

289. "Dearly beloved, let us love one another, for charity is of God. And every one
that loveth, is born of God, and knoweth God. He that loveth not, knoweth not God:
for God is charity. By this hath the charity of God appeared towards us, because God
hath sent his only begotten Son into the world, that we may live by him. In this is charity: not as though we had loved God, but because he hath first loved us, and sent his
Son to be a propitiation for our sins. My dearest, if God hath so loved us; we also ought
to love one another. No man hath seen God at any time. If we love one another, God
abideth in us, and his charity is perfected in us. In this we know that we abide in him,
and he in us: because he hath given us of his spirit. And we have seen, and do testify,
that the Father hath sent his Son to be the Saviour of the world."

290. See Gilson, *Mystical Theology of St. Bernard*, 22–25, where 1 John 4:8-20 is
seen as providing St. Bernard with a "rich, complete and condensed synthesis" (21) of
the scriptural teaching on love; according to Gilson, this "doctrinal 'bloc' . . . passed
practically as it stood, with all its essential articulations, into the mystical theology
of St. Bernard" and "may be said to be felt throughout like that of a solid rock that
sustains the whole edifice" (24). In the *De Diligendo Deo*, Bernard's starting point for
loving God is that God first loved us: "*quia ipse prior dilexit nos*" (c. 1.1 [Migne, *PL*
182, col. 975B]; cf. 1 John 4:10, 19), and he repeats these words in chapter 6, sum-
marizing his argument thus far: "*Hic primum vide, quo modo, imo quam sine modo a
nobis Deus amari meruerit; qui (ut paucis quod dictum est repetam) prior ipse dilexit
nos*" ("See here first how God merits to be loved—without limit—for (repeating in
few words what has been said) He Himself loved us first" [c. 6.16 (Migne, *PL*, 182, col.

that they may be all one as Thou in Me and I in Thee . . . *that the world may know that Thou has sent Me.* The Cross must always be seen as the manifestation of the divine agape, not merely as an implicit *reproach to our guilt* or *challenge to our weakness.*

∾

Thoughts on Grace: {in} the formation of conscience and the Gospel teaching of grace, {there are} important differences if we think of ourselves as "virtuous without Christ" or "sinners saved by Christ." In temptation and sin:

   a. if I am "virtuous without Christ,"

   (1) my aim {is} to reach Him from Whom I am separated, and reach Him by my own virtuous acts;

   (2) the procedure {is that} when "I" am tempted, there is a division between the virtuous "I" and the "lower self" which is tempted—I do not say, "The evil I will not, that I do,"[291] but *the evil I will not, I do not do*; the evil desire, the sin, is there, but it is not "I" who do it;

   (3) the result {is that} unacknowledged sin is able to abound—all I have to do is keep saying "it is not a sin"; "I have not offended God," and the virtuous self is intact. But this is *not true*—{the} result {is} disaster.

   b. if I am a sinner saved by Christ,

   (1) my aim {is} to bring all my sins to Jesus, that He may destroy them; I want *everything to come out*; He does not want me to sin but He wants my sins; I want to face them; I must acknowledge them;

   (2) when I am tempted, it is "I" that am drawn to evil, I that would will evil—but the evil is killed by Christ in whom I am buried; the evil is mine, but it is inactive, and I look to Him alone

---

983D)]); see also the use of 1 John 4:8 ("God is love") and 4:18 ("Perfect love drives out fear") later in the treatise (12.35 [Migne, *PL*, 182, col. 996B]; 14.38 [Migne, *PL*, 182, col. 993A]).

   291. Rom 7:19.

{and} no longer fear; let the evil remain, it is inactive! "*Sufficit tibi gratia mea.*"[292]

(3) the result {is that} grace abounds and sin is not able to abound; the festering sore dries up ({a} comparison {to} the bandaged wound).

∼

St. Mark[293]

1. {The} litany, {based on the} *Robigalia*, {has} nothing to do with St. Mark; {it} existed before the feast; {it had been instituted} to protect crops from Robigo—{it} *should be outside*. Note {the} difference of our litany:[294] {it is} shorter, {with} our own proper saints (Lutgarde);[295] why {are} certain other saints in our litany (v.g. Sts. Edmund, Malachy, Louis[296])? {These are} "places" where saints' names come up.

2. The epistle (and first nocturn[297]): READ {the} epistle,[298] then Ezech. 2:1–2:[299] {the} theophany of Ezechiel (Jews had to be thirty years

292. "My grace is sufficient for you" (2 Cor 12:9).

293. April 25.

294. *Missale Cisterciense*, 174.

295. Along with St. Lutgarde (on whom, see Merton, *What Are These Wounds?*), the Cistercian litany includes Sts. Benedict, Bernard, Robert, Alberic and Stephen [Harding].

296. Sts. Edmund of Abingdon, Malachy of Armagh and Louis of France were all closely associated with the early Cistercians: Edmund (1175–1240), Archbishop of Canterbury, is buried at the Cistercian Abbey of Pontigny; Malachy (1094–1148), was a friend of St. Bernard, who wrote his life, and he died and was buried at Clairvaux (see Merton, *Valley of Wormwood*, 391–96); King Louis IX (1214–1270) was a friend and patron of the Order.

297. Ezek 1:1–13 (*Breviarium Cisterciense, Vernalis*, 508–509).

298. Ezek 1:10–14: "And as for the likeness of their faces: there was the face of a man, and the face of a lion on the right side of all the four: and the face of an ox, on the left side of all the four: and the face of an eagle over all the four. And their faces, and their wings were stretched upward: two wings of every one were joined, and two covered their bodies: And every one of them went straight forward: whither the impulse of the spirit was to go, thither they went: and they turned not when they went. And as for the likeness of the living creatures, their appearance was like that of burning coals of fire, and like the appearance of lamps. This was the vision running to and fro in the midst of the living creatures, a bright fire, and lightning going forth from the fire. And the living creatures ran and returned like flashes of lightning" (*Missale Romanum*, 554; *Missale Cisterciense*, 403–404).

299. "This was the vision of the likeness of the glory of the Lord. And I saw, and I

old before reading this); why {is it} used in this feast? (for {an} *evangelist*, {in} *paschal time—not* {for the} Feast of Luke or St. John, {but it} *is* in Matthew, Mark). Identify the four beasts? {Note the} connection with {the} shekinah (Ezech. 2:1–2). What is a cherub? cf. Ezech. 10:20: he understands that they are cherubim. When was this vision seen? (read 11:15–25:[300] {the} Shekinah in Jerusalem "points to" captivity).

⌖

St. Thomas Aquinas[301] {is marked by} clarity, universality, breadth of view. {We pray} to be informed with {the} spirit of St. Thomas. {The} epistle[302] {stresses the} great value of wisdom, greater than all other earthly goods; all other goods come with it. How? without our knowing, {through} His sharing of wisdom. Wisdom {is} the light of Christ, knowing the "highest cause," judging all in a divine way, by charity, which unites us to God. {Note the} *humility* of St. Thomas—and {his} *simplicity*.

⌖

---

fell upon my face, and I heard the voice of one that spoke. And he said to me: Son of man, stand upon thy feet, and I will speak to thee. And the spirit entered into me after that he spoke to me, and he set me upon my feet: and I heard him speaking to me."

300. "Son of man, thy brethren, thy brethren, thy kinsmen, and all the house of Israel, all they to whom the inhabitants of Jerusalem have said: Get ye far from the Lord, the land is given in possession to us. Therefore thus saith the Lord God: Because I have removed them far off among the Gentiles, and because I have scattered them among the countries: I will be to them a little sanctuary in the countries whither they are come. Therefore speak to them: Thus saith the Lord God: I will gather you from among the peoples, and assemble you out of the countries wherein you are scattered, and I will give you the land of Israel. And they shall go in thither, and shall take away all the scandals, and all the abominations thereof from thence. And I will give them one heart, and will put a new spirit in their bowels: and I will take away the stony heart out of their flesh, and will give them a heart of flesh: That they may walk in my commandments, and keep my judgments, and do them: and that they may be my people, and I may be their God. But as for them whose heart walketh after their scandals and abominations, I will lay their way upon their head, saith the Lord God. And the cherubims lifted up their wings, and the wheels with them: and the glory of the God of Israel was over them. And the glory of the Lord went up from the midst of the city, and stood over the mount that is on the east side of the city. And the spirit lifted me up, and brought me into Chaldea, to them of the captivity, in vision, by the spirit of God: and the vision which I had seen was taken up from me. And I spoke to them of the captivity all the words of the Lord which he had shewn me."

301. March 7.

302. Wis 7:7–14 (*Missale Romanum*, 521; *Missale Cisterciense*, 382).

St. Bernard's Dedication Sermons—Sermo 1:[303]

1. {The} Feast of Dedication is *our* feast: *we should not blush* to celebrate it (518–519: *sancta est etiam propter corpora*[304]); {one} must
   understand: {there is} nothing to celebrate in the stones. God {is}
   marvelous in His saints, in heaven and on earth (519).

2. {He} proves {the} holiness of Clairvaux by {the} action of {the} Holy
   Spirit in souls (519C).

3. We are dedicated: *vos dedicati estis—vos elegit et assumpsit*[305] (519D);
   He possesses us; we possess Him. For the ceremonies of dedication
   benefit not only those who were present but all who shall pray in
   that church (520A).

4. The ceremonies: in all, *the ceremonies* are spiritually fulfilled (520B).

5. Ceremonies (continued): the *"unctio"*[306] gives grace to {the} heart,
   and our light shines before men (520).

6. *Benedictionem expectamus in fine*[307] (eschatology): to complete {the}
   grace of sanctification (521); *domus non manufacta in coelis:*[308]
   UNITAS: to make us a house of God: *disjuncta ligna et lapides domum non faciunt*[309] (a) but if He dwell in us, *ineffabiliter beatificat
   inhabitans gloria majestatis*[310] (521); (b) the souls are witnesses to
   the counsels and mysteries of the Trinity: *tanto plus vident {. . .}
   tanto plus diligunt*[311] (521).

7. *Duplex gluten—plenae cognitionis, perfectae dilectionis*[312] (521CD);
   TRANSLATE: *tanto siquidem majori ad se invicem* etc.; *cum eo*

---

303. Migne, *PL* 183, cols. 517D–521D.

304. "it is also holy because of our bodies" (Migne, *PL* 183, col. 519A).

305. "you are dedicated—he chose you and raised you up."

306. "anointing" (Migne, *PL* 183, col. 520B, which reads: *"inunctio"*).

307. "We await a blessing at the end."

308. "a home in heaven not made with hands" (Migne, *PL* 183, col. 521A, which
reads: *"domum transibimus non manufactam aeternam in coelis"* ["we shall pass over
to . . . an eternal . . ."]).

309. "disconnected pieces of wood and stones do not make a home" (Migne, PL
183, col. 521A, which reads: *"disjuncta nimirum ligna . . ."*) (Migne, PL 183, col. 521B).

310. "The indwelling glory of His majesty blesses indescribably."

311. "So much the more they see, so much the more they love."

312. "a double adhesive: of full knowledge, of perfect love" (*"duplici glutino"* in
original).

penetrant universa[313] (521C). *The lesson: si pervenire desideras, concupiscat et deficiat anima tua in atria Domini.*[314]

~

All Saints: ({This is} "our" feast {according to} St. Bernard.[315]) What is a saint? one who has many virtues? one who is united to God? There is *only one saint* in heaven—*tu solus sanctus.*[316] To be united to Him is sanctity. We are united to Him by charity. It is possible to have many virtues and not be a saint because it is possible to have "virtues" without charity (1 Cor. 13). (Note {the} connection {of} All Saints and Christ the King: {the} introit of Christ {the} King[317] is from {the} epistle of {the} Vigil of All Saints;[318] {note also the} connection with {the} Ascension.)

1. *Catechism {of the Council of} Trent: Prophetae planius et apertius de Ecclesia quam de Christo locuti sunt.*[319] {This is} a sentence full of meaning. Christ came to unite the Church to Himself, to prolong His Incarnation in the Church; {therefore the} closer our union with {the} Church, {the} closer our union with Christ—hence {the} primacy of {the} sacraments and {the} liturgy. (Here *comment on {the}*

---

313. "*Tanto siquidem majori ad se invicem dilectione copulantur, quanto ipsi charitati, quae Deus est, viciniores assistunt. Sed nec ulla separare eos ab invicem suspicio potest, ubi nihil omnino quod in altero sit, alterum latere patitur penetrans omnia radius veritatis. Quoniam adhuc qui adhaeret Deo, unus spiritus est cum eo nihil dubium est quin perfecte adhaerentes ei beati spiritus cum eo pariter et in eo penetrent universa*" ("Indeed by the degree of deeper love that they are united to one another, to the very same degree of the love which is God do they draw their neighbors. But no suspicion can divide them from one another, when the ray of truth penetrating all things allows nothing at all that is in one to be unknown to the other. For because the one who cleaves to God is one spirit with Him, there is no doubt that the blessed in spirit, perfectly united to Him, penetrate all things equally through Him and with Him").

314. "If you desire to arrive [at this home], let your soul aspire and withdraw to the house of the Lord" (Migne, *PL* 183, col. 521D).

315. *In Festo Omnium Sanctorum Sermo* 5 (n. 1): "*Festiva nobis est dies*" ("This is a feast day for us") (Migne, *PL* 183, col. 475C).

316. "You alone are holy" (Gloria) (*Missale Romanum*, 229; *Missale Cisterciense*, 180).

317. Apoc [Rev] 5:12 (*Missale Romanum*, 770).

318. Apoc [Rev] 5:6–12 (*Missale Romanum*, 776; *Missale Cisterciense*, 549).

319. "The prophets spoke more plainly and openly about the Church than about Christ" (*Catechismus ex Decreto Concilii Tridentini*, 73 [I. x.1: "*De Nono Articulo*"]).

end of {the} epistle:[320] {the} end in view {is the} glorious Church, {a} manifestation of {the} mystery of God: {the} *way* {is} the beatitude.) {Here we see the} importance of believing in {the} mystery of the Church. {The} Holy Spirit, {the} Sanctifier, has given us {the} Church, and acts on us only in {the} Church; only in and through {the} Church are we in contact with Jesus—hence {the} importance of objectivity.

2. *Liturgy of the Feast:* {see the} responsory of vespers,[321] and {the} twelfth responsory of {the} nocturn:[322] *Beata vere mater Ecclesia, quam sic honor divinae dignitationis illuminat. Beata vere*—truly blessed: the only true blessedness and happiness are from God; *Mater Ecclesiae*—*Mother* Church, Mother of life and grace—but we must be united to her to receive it; {the} monk {is} in {the} very heart and center of her motherly action; *Honor divinae dignationis illuminat*—the glory of the saints, from the condescending gaze of God, which illuminates and transfigures {the} Church ({in the} light seen in the Transfiguration of Christ). {It} *follows* the bloody victory of the martyrs {and} the unbloody victory of the confessors {through the} Cross {and through} suffering: *per crucem ad lucem.*[323] The monk, who embraces the Cross, truly joys in {the} glory of all the saints. This feast reminds us that our sufferings were not worthy to be reckoned with the glory that is to come, that by them we come to {the} full glory of {the} Christian life in heaven.

---

320. Apoc [Rev] 7:2–12 (*Missale Romanum*, 778–79; *Missale Cisterciense*, 550–51).

321. "*Beata vere mater Ecclesia, quam sic honor divinae dignationis illuminat, quam victoriosorum gloriosus Martyrum sanguis exornat, Quam inviolatae confessionis candida induit virginitas*" ("Truly blessed Mother Church, whom the honor of divine dignity so illuminates, whom the glorious blood of the martyrs adorns, whom the pure virginity of unharmed profession clothes") (*Breviarium Cisterciense, Pars Autumnalis,* 426).

322. "*Beati estis Sancti Dei omnes, qui meruistis consortes fieri coelestium virtutum, et perfrui aeternae claritatis gloria: Ideoque precamur, ut memores nostri intercedere dignemini pro nobis ad Dominum Deum nostrum*" ("Blessed are you, all saints of God, who have deserved to become the companions of the heavenly powers, and to enjoy the glory of eternal light: therefore we pray that you might be mindful of us and deign to intercede on our behalf to the Lord our God") (*Breviarium Cisterciense, Autumnalis,* 439).

323. "through the cross to the light."

3. *Participation in the blessedness of God*: {see} St. Augustine on {the}
sonus epulantis;[324] {the} Community of the Divine Persons {is}
shared with us in Christ (read 1 John 1:1–7,[325] {especially} the end:

324. "the sound of one feasting" (Ps 41[42]:5); see Augustine, *Enarrationes in Psalmos*, 117.22 (v. 27) (Migne, *PL* 37, col. 1500): "Deus Dominus, et illuxit nobis. *Dominus ille qui venit in nomine Domini, quem reprobaverunt aedificantes, et factus est in caput angeli* (Matth. xxi, 9, 42); *mediator ille Dei et hominum homo Christus Jesus* (I Tim. ii, 5). *Deus est, aequalis est Patri et illuxit nobis, ut quod credidimus intelligeremus, et vobis nondum intelligentibus, sed jam credentibus, enuntiaremus. Ut autem et vos intelligatis,* Constituite diem festum in confrequentationibus, usque ad cornua altaris: *id est, usque ad interiorem domum Dei, de qua vos benediximus, ubi sunt altaris excelsa.* Constituite diem festum, *non tepide ad segniter, sed* in confrequentationibus. *Ipsa est enim vox ex-sultationis, soni festivitatem celebrantis, ambulantium in loco* tabernaculi admirabilis usque ad domum Dei. *Si enim est ibi spirituale sacrificium sempiternum sacrificium laudis, et sacerdos sempiternus est, et altare sempiternum pacata mens ipsa justorum. Hoc apertius dicimus, fratres: quicumque Deum Verbum intelligere volunt, non eis suf-ficiat caro, quod propter eos Verbum factum est, ut lacte nutrirentur; nec in terra sufficiat iste dies festus quo agnus occisus est: sed constituatur in confrequentationibus, quousque perveniatur, exaltatis a Domino mentibus nostris, usque ad ejus divinitatem interiorem, qui nobis exteriorem humanitatem lacte nutriendis praebere dignatus est*" ("The Lord is God and has shone upon us. He is the Lord Who comes in the name of the Lord, Whom the builders rejected and Who has become the cornerstone [Matt 21:9, 42]; He is the mediator between God and men, the man Christ Jesus [1 Tim 2:5]. He is God, equal to the Father, and He shines upon us so that we might understand what we have believed, and so that we might proclaim to you who do not yet understand but already believe. So that you might also understand, establish a festal day in assemblies, up to the horns of the altar, that is, up to the inner house of God, from which we have blessed you, where the heights of the altar are. Establish a festal day not lukewarmly or sluggishly, but for assemblies. For it is the very voice of exultation, of the sound of celebration, of those who walk in the place of the wondrous tabernacle up to the very house of God. For if the spiritual sacrifice there is the everlasting sacrifice of praise, both the priest is everlasting, and the everlasting altar is the very mind of the just, now at peace. We say this more plainly, brothers: whoever wishes to understand God the Word, for them the flesh which the Word became for their sake so as to nourish them by milk, does not suffice; nor is that earthly festal day enough on which the lamb is slain: but let a festival be established for assemblies until that point is reached when our minds have been raised up by the Lord all the way to His inmost divinity, Who deigned to offer to us His outer humanity to nourish us as by milk").

325. "That which was from the beginning, which we have heard, which we have seen with our eyes, which we have looked upon, and our hands have handled, of the word of life: For the life was manifested; and we have seen and do bear witness, and declare unto you the life eternal, which was with the Father, and hath appeared to us: That which we have seen and have heard, we declare unto you, that you also may have fellowship with us, and our fellowship may be with the Father, and with his Son Jesus Christ. And these things we write to you, that you may rejoice, and your joy may be full. And this is the declaration which we have heard from him, and declare unto you: That God is light, and in him there is no darkness. If we say that we have fellowship

that which we have heard, seen, handled, Life eternal that was with the Father hath appeared. That which we have seen we declare (the saints speak—{the} prophets, evangelists, etc.) *That you may have fellowship with us and our fellowship may be with the Father*; that you may rejoice. The way {is the} God {Who} is light—if we walk in darkness {we have} no fellowship; {v.} 7: *If we walk in the light* we have fellowship and the blood of Jesus Christ has cleansed us from our sins.

4. The light is charity, forgiving as we have been forgiven, loving as He has loved us: *ut unum sint*[326] (John 17): {this is} our Cistercian vocation.

∾

THE IMMACULATE CONCEPTION: the purpose of every liturgical feast is to give glory to God, to praise Him and magnify Him in admiration at what His mysteries reveal of His infinite goodness. In all the feasts of Our Lady and of the saints we ultimately magnify and extol the greatness of God; we contemplate God in them; we praise the great work of God in them. All the works of grace are manifestations of the mystery of Christ, and Christ Himself is the great manifestation of the Father. The Immaculate Conception is most intimately connected with the mystery of our Incarnation and Redemption, and in it we see a peculiar evidence of the divine goodness and love. Mary is enriched with the fullness of every grace, so as to be Mother of the Redeemer and to bring Jesus to us. The great power of the redemptive sacrifice of Jesus is shown by the fact that without any difficulty it extends to whatever object God pleases, whether before or after the historical act itself. The Immaculate Conception is a pledge of God's will to restore us all to the original purity and blessedness He intended to give us all in and through Adam. We can truly *rejoice with* Mary, for her Immaculate Heart is a Mother's heart and she is Mediatrix of all grace; she wills to share her blessedness with us—hence

---

with him, and walk in darkness, we lie, and do not the truth. But if we walk in the light, as he also is in the light, we have fellowship one with another, and the blood of Jesus Christ his Son cleanseth us from all sin."

326. "that all may be one" (John 17:21).

{the} liturgical texts showing how the primary object of the feast is the glory of God in His "great work" in Mary (*Fecit mihi magna*[327]).

A right attitude: hence from the very first, we must not enter into the joy of this feast with sentiments of obsessive guilt because of *our* sins; we must not let a barrier of mistrust separate us from our Mother, as if this feast had nothing to do with us. She indeed is pure, but we . . . No, the first thing of all is that the Immaculate Conception is *a pledge of our own purification and sanctification by the all-powerful merits of the Cross of Jesus*. The Immaculate Conception is the first great testimony to the power of the Cross. Instead of holding back with incomprehension and diffidence, we should enter fully into the joy of this feast with our Mother, for the same power that kept her free from every stain of sin has also sanctified us in baptism, in penance, in religious profession, and draws us always after her to "run in the odor of her ointments."[328] To apprehend the sweetness of this odor we must love the beauty of our Lady's Immaculate Heart. The office everywhere calls our attention to the beauty and the love of Mary's whole person—TOTA *pulchra es*[329]—there is nothing in her which is not good and holy and worthy of love, and able to inspire confidence and joy and happiness in her children. We must not spoil this feast by a *wrong mentality*. Unfortunately this wrong mentality can easily be contracted by a superficial or wrong idea of the theology of the Immaculate Conception. Theology loses its meaning when great truths are studied *without perspective* and out of context. The Immaculate Conception loses very much of its meaning when it is taken out of the proper context, when we fail to see it in the perspective of the Incarnation, when we forget that Mary is the Mother of Jesus the Savior and our Mother, when we forget that her sanctity is essentially the same kind of sanctity (purity of charity, by the grace of the Spirit of Jesus) as God wills for us also, when we forget that Mary *is a woman and a mother*, and that Jesus is truly her Son, and that what He received from her was a true human nature with a body of *flesh*. The Immaculate Conception is only part of the great mystery of Mary's divine motherhood. Let us avoid at all costs an unconsciously docetist and manichaean attitude toward the Immaculate Conception. Jesus, the Word Incarnate, has willed to be the

---

327. "He has done great things for me" (Luke 1:49).

328. Song 1:3.

329. "You are completely beautiful" (first antiphon) (*Breviarium Cisterciense, Hiemalis*, 489).

King and Head of a sanctified material creation. Our bodies are elevated to the level of spirit by the work of grace. Mary is not a pure spirit—that is precisely the meaning of the Immaculate Conception.

How do we get this wrong attitude? In brief, we can easily develop a wrong mentality if we consider this the feast merely of Mary's "conception" and not rather of her whole person. What we celebrate is not just the conception of Mary but *Mary who was immaculately conceived*. Let us not forget the simple fact that the expression "Immaculate Conception" is a figure of speech, a periphrasis, technically called *metonymy* (the use of the effect for the cause, or the cause for the effect—or the use of an idea connected with a thing in order to express the thing itself). A common metonymy {would be that} we say we read "Shakespeare," when in fact we read the plays of Shakespeare. Another metonymy {is to speak of} "the Holy See" (*sedes*) (cf. synecdoche, in which we use the part for the whole or the whole for the part: "he is a good *soul*"; "all *hands* on deck"). Our use of the term "Immaculate Conception" can be either of these, either metonymy or synecdoche. So just as when we say "the *hired help*" we mean the man who is hired to help and not just the help he gives, so when we say "the Immaculate Conception" we mean Mary who was immaculately conceived, and not just the conception that brought her into being. Our Lady herself made this quite clear at Lourdes where she said, "I am the Immaculate Conception." So if we forget the fact that this is a metonymy or synecdoche, we will be likely to go astray. Remember that this is the feast of Our Lady, immaculately conceived and full of every grace from God, most pleasing to God, beautiful in His eyes and in the eyes of men, most loving towards all men, powerful to aid her children, *because of the fact that she was immaculately conceived and thus was able to become the Mother of God*, etc. In a word what we celebrate here is *all the results, fruits and consequences of the Immaculate Conception*, including the riches of grace which Mary gained all through her life, and even implicitly the Assumption and Coronation in heaven in so far as these follow from the Immaculate Conception. More precisely we look at all these fruits in their cause—hence the use of the metonymy here. If we get off to a bad start, forgetting this is a special kind of phrase, we then take the *next wrong step*. We define "conception" and define "immaculate," link the two terms together, and consider them more or less in reference to the person of Mary, but more in the abstract than in the concrete. Thus we become focused on two things *other than* Mary and much less beautiful: (a) conception: the physiological process by which, through the union of organic elements, a new living animal comes into existence, in this case a human organism; (b) immaculate: the absence of sin. Hence we have a weird combination—first a kind of vague physiological concept which we cannot allow to take shape too definitely in our mind, and then a negation, the absence of sin. But a negation inevitably calls to mind its positive counterpart, and we remember in fact that the instrument by which original sin is transmitted is human seed. With this, we more or less inevitably conclude to a totally wrong idea, that sexual generation is itself evil and the root of evil. But since the Immaculate Conception was without evil, then we unconsciously come to think of Mary's generation as somehow abnormal and inhuman, a kind of synthetic process, something that might take place in a laboratory—like the discovery of a new plastic, or some other substance. Remember we do not consciously formulate these blasphemies, but there is nevertheless in our mind a whole series of such notions if we allow our thought to get off on the wrong track. For inevitably, what we then find is not divine truth but a hazy conglomeration of images and associations belonging to our own curious civilization—I need only point to the storehouse of images from which we can draw out material: for instance the modern obsession about sanitariness and cleanliness and germlessness—antiseptics, everything wrapped in cellophane, the fear of every form of dirt, the fear of human contacts, the fear of things touched by another—already the ideas have become pathological, and they become more and more so as we proceed further. We must certainly avoid looking at the Immaculate Conception in this morbid and unhealthy way. If we do not avoid this error, the great feast will be an occasion for a display of emotional immaturity and sickly sentimentality, not of true devotion and love for Our Lady.

Correctives—a few points from theology:

1. How is original sin contracted? and where? Original sin inheres *in the soul*, like all sin. It is a spiritual thing, not a bodily defilement. How does it infect the soul? The seed is the instrumental cause of the transmission of original sin. The organism formed by this seed receives into itself a soul, which contracts original sin by the fact that it is the form of a substance tainted with sin. (If you make a statue out of tar, the statue is made of tar—the form informs a tar statue, not one of marble.) BUT why is human seed the instrumental cause for the transmission of sin? because *originally it was intended to be the instrumental cause for the transmission of justice.*

God simply intended that by propagation, in the ordinary way, the descendents of Adam should receive human nature with all the qualities attached to it. By propagation, had Adam not fallen, we would have received all the gifts and prerogatives that were his. In Mary's case, normal human conception was then not the cause of the transmission of sin, but by the grace of God and by His special gift, it did not merely become the *occasion* of the imparting of grace, but acted instrumentally according to the original plan of God. The conception of Mary was then a holy and sacramental act, a great mystery. The spiritual difference from all other such acts is of course immense, but in every other respect it was a perfectly normal and ordinary human conception.

2. As a result, the human person of the Blessed Virgin is integrally and perfectly human in every respect. Her vocation was to be a mother, and she was therefore endowed with everything needed to fulfill that vocation. At the same time, she was called to be a Virgin—her vocation to consecrated virginity was in fact inseparable from the Immaculate Conception. There was no other possibility. In the Immaculate Conception we see, *in causa, in radice,*[330] the great mystery of Virginity–Motherhood which was what St. Bernard and the Fathers most loved to contemplate and praise in Our Lady. In Our Lady there is all the warmth and tenderness of a human mother's love and far more besides. We do her a great dishonor and we also blaspheme God unconsciously if we think of our Mother as a frigid and remote and unfeeling being, an iceberg with no need to love anyone and no interest in those who have such feelings. Mary *needs to love her children* not by reason of the compulsion of passion but because of the infinite power of grace. The imperious power of natural instinct makes every mother (at least every normal mother) love her children with a love that is often blind and unreasonable. There is nothing blind and unreasonable in Mary, but her love is all the more powerful and more imperious because it is commanded by the grace of God and moved directly by His Spirit. It is God's own love in her. It is impossible for Mary not to love us, just as it is impossible for her not to love God. It is impossible for her not to love us with an ardent and strong and total love, far greater than any love we

---

330. "in its cause, in its root."

have ever known or been able to imagine. All this is the result of the Immaculate Conception.

3. Absence of the effects of original sin, none of the *wounds* inflicted by original sin: the soul of fallen man {is} unconsciously fixed on our *unreal value* (untruth) which *it wants to be real*—by an arbitrary act of will: "as gods."[331] {The} only solution {is} to conform our mind and will to actuality, what is willed by God. In Our Lady's will, there is not and cannot be any *malice*, no conscious or unconscious movements of selfishness and their results, no hidden vindictiveness, no tyrannical demands, no bitterness, no possibility of hate masking under apparent love. In Our Lady's intelligence there is {not} and cannot be any *ignorance*, yet {there is} perfect simplicity—so many things that we know that are useless she did not have to know; she could do better without them. Hence {there was} ignorance of sin, but a correspondingly greater knowledge of sinners. {There is} perfect truth in Mary's thought and will, fixed purely on God, on WHAT IS, but not voluminous knowledge which can be ignorance in the sight of God. In Our Lady's irascible appetite {there was} no *weakness*, no fear, no pettiness, no defects in obedience to grace etc., no irritability, no impatience. In her concupiscible appetite {there was} *no concupiscence*, no *disorder* in her thoughts and emotions—hence her emotions {were} pure and perfect. {There is} no defect in her most pure body. At the same time we do not have to imagine her with a most extraordinary physique and beauty of form. She was a perfectly ordinary person, outstanding by her *spiritual* beauty. She has very wisely left us no likeness of herself—*all* representations of her are permissible, provided only they are *sacred*. We are not limited to any particular type or race, etc. Everything in her {is} balanced, harmonious, beautiful, peaceful, holy, full of love and goodness.

4. In short, the best way to conceive the Immaculate Conception is to really understand the words of the angel: the angel's salutation was positive, not negative. He did not say, "Hail, free of sin, free of evil desires, free of wickedness, etc. Hail O thou with no defects"—but "Hail *full of grace*," and not only that but "*The Lord is with thee.*" In Mary, then, we see not only a perfect human being, with all that a human person was supposed to have by God, with all the wonderful

331. Gen 3:5.

goodness that God wished to give to a human nature, but also God Himself is with her, and God Himself loves this great work of His love and takes His pleasure in her heart and becomes man of her pure flesh. Above all, the beauty of Mary and her glory comes from the fact *that God's will is done perfectly and without obstacle in her.* The grace we most seek in this feast is that His will may be done in us as it is in her (read St. John {of the} Cross: *Ascent*—page 76–77,[332] 96–97).

~

Immaculate Conception—points from the liturgy: in this feast, as in the Canticle of Canticles, we see a certain amount of dramatic dialogue. We celebrate the Immaculate Conception as a wedding feast, in which we participate. God, intending to wed human nature in Mary, first weds her pure soul which He endows with every possible gift of His grace. We are present at the wedding: God, the Divine Bridegroom, speaks to Mary; she in turn speaks to Him and to us, and we, for our part, speak mostly to her.

332. "God communicates Himself most to that soul that has progressed farthest in love; namely, that has its will in closest conformity with the will of God. And the soul that has attained complete conformity and likeness of will is totally united and transformed in God supernaturally.... And it is this that Saint John desired to explain when he said: *Qui non ex sanguinibus, neque ex voluntate carnis, neque ex voluntate viri, sed ex Deo nati sunt.* As though he had said: He gave power to be sons of God—that is, to be transformed in God—only to those who are born not of blood—that is, not of natural constitution and temperament—neither of the will of the flesh—that is, of the free will of natural capacity and ability—still less of the will of man—wherein is included every way and manner of judging and comprehending with the understanding. He gave power to none of these to become sons of God, but only to those that are born of God—that is, to those who, being born again through grace, and dying first of all to everything that is of the old man, are raised above themselves to the supernatural, and receive from God this rebirth and adoption, which transcends all that can be imagined" (*Ascent of Mount Carmel*, II.v.4,5 [Peers, ed. and trans., *Complete Works of Saint John of the Cross* [1953], 1:76–77]; it should be noted that this is not the 1946 edition generally used by Merton [in which the same material is found on pages 80–81]; in neither edition is there relevant material found on pages 96–97, which may perhaps be an inadvertently erroneous repetition of the same reference, with "9" mistakenly substituted for "7"). Noteworthy here in particular is the relevance of the quotation from John 1:13 to the Feast of the Immaculate Conception.

1. {For} *our part,* we have the antiphons of vespers,[333] in which we praise Mary's beauty: *Tota pulchra es,*[334] etc.; and we ask her to draw us after her.

2. Mary then speaks in the capitulum: "The Lord has possessed me from the beginning";[335] then she sings her Magnificat in the responsory.[336]

3. We again come in with the hymn,[337] the versicle,[338] and join Mary in her Magnificat—it is now ours as well as hers. She takes the antiphon: "*Beatam me dicent.*"[339]

4. {In} the antiphons of the first nocturn,[340] we declare the mysteries we see revealed, speaking rather to one another than to the Lord or to Mary.

5. {In} the responsories, (1) we speak to Mary: *Ne timeas, invenisti gratiam;*[341] (2) Mary {speaks} to us: *Transite ad me;*[342] (3) Here the Lord speaks for the first time: *Electa mea candida;* {. . .} *Veni de Libano Sponsa.*[343] He speaks again in the ninth responsory (*Hortus conclusus*[344]) and in the Benedictus antiphon.[345] Otherwise we do most of the talking.

❧

333. *Breviarium Cisterciense, Hiemalis,* 489.

334. "You are completely beautiful" (first antiphon).

335. "*Dominus possedit me in initio*" (Prov 8:22) (*Breviarium Cisterciense, Hiemalis,* 489).

336. Luke 1:46, 49 (*Breviarium Cisterciense, Hiemalis,* 490).

337. "*Ave maris stella*" ("Hail, Star of the Sea") (*Breviarium Cisterciense,* 174*).

338. "*Immaculata Conceptio est hodie sanctae Mariae Virginis*" ("Today is the Immaculate Conception of the Blessed Virgin Mary") (*Breviarium Cisterciense, Hiemalis,* 490).

339. "They will call me blessed" (Luke 1:48) (*Breviarium Cisterciense, Hiemalis,* 490).

340. *Breviarium Cisterciense, Hiemalis,* 490–91.

341. "Do not fear, you have found favor" (Luke 1:30) (first responsory) (*Breviarium Cisterciense, Hiemalis,* 491, which reads: "*Ne timeas, Maria, invenisti gratiam*").

342. "Come over to me" (Eccli [Sir] 24:18) (second responsory) (*Breviarium Cisterciense, Hiemalis,* 492).

343. "My shining chosen one; come from Lebanon, my spouse" (Song 4:8) (third responsory) (*Breviarium Cisterciense, Hiemalis,* 492).

344. "an enclosed garden" (Song 4:12) (*Breviarium Cisterciense, Hiemalis,* 496).

345. Gen 3:15 (*Breviarium Cisterciense, Hiemalis,* 498).

Feast of the Immaculate Conception—some themes from the office. This is a rich office and at the same time very easy to understand.

1. *First vespers*: in all four antiphons[346] the Church cries out in praise of Mary and ends with a prayer. The first contains the whole teaching of the feast: Tota pulchra es . . . *macula originalis non est in te*[347] (in {the} background {is} God speaking to Mary as His spouse). {She is} all fair, all full of grace, {with} no sin, no imperfection, no self-will, nothing contrary to God's love. Yet {she is} perfectly human—avoid {the} danger of {the} Immaculate Conception turning Mary into a problem of theological algebra—"quantitative" sanctity. {Note the} meaning of {the} white garment: "innocence through victory" (Vonier[348]). Her beauty and her radiance {are} spreading the light of God by reason of her divine motherhood (*vestimentum suum*[349]). *Tu gloria Jerusalem*:[350] Mary the new Judith is the glory of the Church, the one member of the Church who is perfect, and who is the instrument for the salvation of all the others, for by her total self-renunciation in her *"fiat,"*[351] {her} perfect obedience to God's will, she brought the Savior into the world; this obedience was able to be perfect because there was no self-will in her. *Trahe nos*:[352] draw us after thee, in love and purity of heart and dedication of ourselves to God, {with} perfect correspondence to love, in simplicity. {In the} *capitulum*,[353] Mary speaks; all the glory belongs to God; she is the fruit of His eternal plan. Before all things He saw her "playing in the world" (epistle[354]) because of Jesus. {The} responsory[355] (*Magnificat*) {allows us to} join in Mary's Magnificat—a special aspect of

---

346. *Breviarium Cisterciense, Hiemalis*, 489.

347. "You are completely beautiful . . . There is no original stain in you" (first antiphon).

348. "The metaphor of the white garment belongs to the New Testament, and its meaning is this: innocence through victory: the elect are in white garments because they overcame" (Vonier, *Victory of Christ* [1934], c. 20: "The Victory of the Christian" [Vonier, *Collected Works*, 1.323]).

349. "your garment" (second antiphon).

350. "You are the glory of Jerusalem" (third antiphon).

351. "Let it be done" (Luke 1:38).

352. "Draw us" (Song 1:3) (fourth antiphon).

353. Prov 8:22–24 (*Breviarium Cisterciense, Hiemalis*, 489).

354. Prov 8:22–35 (*Missale Romanum*, 468–69; *Missale Cisterciense*, 333–34).

355. Luke 1:48–49 (*Breviarium Cisterciense, Hiemalis*, 490).

monastic prayer. {In the} *versicle*,[356] we proclaim that she crushed the serpent's head. {The} *oration*[357] {reveals the} theology of the feast. {The} Immaculate Conception (a) had for its purpose to prepare a worthy Mother for the Redeemer; (b) was effected through *the foreseen merits of His Passion.* Unless we see the Feast of the Immaculate Conception as a celebration of the victory of Christ over sin and death and the devil, we cannot understand it; Mary without Jesus is nothing; {the} Immaculate Conception without the Cross is less than nothing, a pure illusion; (c) by her intercession we can be preserved from all sin. Summary: *trust in Mary and faith in her power,* plus *great hatred of sin,* and *great admiration for the wisdom of God's love*—these are the graces of the feast.

2. First nocturn—lessons:[358] SIN:

a) The snake says to the woman, WHY *did God command you? Doubt* {is} the beginning of sin, doubt of the wisdom and justice of God, doubt of God in His will; Eve simply repeats the precept and the sanction.

b) {The} devil denies the sanction: (a) "you shall not die"[359] (note they are already immortal if they obey God—all he promises is that *they can disobey* without losing anything); {he} makes a promise: (b) "your eyes shall be opened—you shall be as Gods"[360] (they are already "gods"); {he} promises an *experience* of evil, as though it were a good—{this is} emptiness, falsity, lies.

c) Eve then, assenting to this proposition, is *fascinated by the beauty of the tree.* By listening to doubt and to false promise,

356. "*Quae serpentis caput virgineo pede contrivit*" ("who crushed the serpent's head with her virginal foot") (*Breviarium Cisterciense, Hiemalis,* 490).

357. "*Deus, qui per immaculatam Virginis Conceptionem dignum Filio tuo habitaculum praeparasti: quaesumus; ut, qui ex morte ejusdem Filii tui praevisa, eam ab omni labe praeservasti, nos quoque mundos ejus intercessione ad te pervenire concedas*" ("God, Who prepared a worthy dwelling place for Your Son through the Immaculate Conception of the Virgin, we ask that as You preserved her from every fall through the foreseen death of Your Son, You may also allow us to reach You cleansed through her intercession") (*Missale Romanum,* 468; *Missale Cisterciense,* 333); (collect: vespers, lauds) (*Breviarium Cisterciense, Hiemalis,* 490, 498–99).

358. Gen 3:1–15 (*Breviarium Cisterciense, Hiemalis,* 491–92).

359. Gen 3:4.

360. Gen 3:5.

she had acquired a taste, an inclination, to disobey, and *she did not resist the inclination*—with what simplicity she reaches out and takes the fruit.

d) But then, they fear God—{there is} guilt. They hide when they hear His voice, as He comes to walk with them in Paradise.

e) God calls Adam and questions him, {revealing} their shame and their excuses.

f) God then curses the serpent and promises a woman who shall crush the serpent's head. In Mary there is none of this sin—no doubting God, no hesitation in rejecting falsity, no appetite for what is not. She is the one human being who is perfectly *true*. The rest of us are all false, and depend on her to come to the light of truth and to liberty and friendship with God, depend on her to resist the inclinations we have inherited from Adam. One of these inclinations is *angelism*, {an} attraction to false purity, {a} form of pride and self-exaltation, a tree "beautiful to look at,"[361] our "angelic" image of ourselves. Act not according to a false preconception of our own about interior purity, but {in} simple acceptance of the will of God.

~

MARY AND THE PRIEST: some points for meditation from Fr. Paul Philippe: "The Blessed Virgin and the Priesthood":

1. {With regard to} Mary, our vocation, {both} religious {and} priestly, {is} in her hands. Mary, the Mother of the High Priest in and from Whom we receive our priesthood, is therefore the Mother of all priests.

2. She became our Mother by the *fiat*[362] of the Incarnation and by her compassion on Calvary, meriting there all the graces of our religious and priestly lives.

3. On Calvary she did not know this explicitly herself, but she knew it in a general and confused way, and was united with her divine Son Who knew and saw all this clearly, so that in a way she saw and knew all this in Him. In any case she sees and knows us clearly now

361. Gen 3:6.
362. "Let it be done" (Luke 1:38).

in heaven, and sees every need for grace etc. *"It is she who has asked conjointly with Our Lord, that we be priests. . . .*Divine Love in its designs for eternity has decreed that we should be called to the Priesthood *by virtue of the merits of Christ and those of His Mother and in answer to their common prayer"* (p. 14[363]). *"It is she who even now is ceaselessly asking for all the graces we need to persevere in the love of Christ and of souls, to walk in the narrow way of perfection so often contrary to our inclinations, to carry out with zeal our ministry, and to celebrate each Mass with more fervour than the preceding one."*[364]

Take these points individually:

a) to persevere, against great obstacles, perhaps; these {are} allowed {in order} to increase our faith and trust: we do not have to worry about {the} future—trust honors her.

b) to overcome ourselves and walk in the way of perfection—without her we will yield to our inclinations; {the} priest who ignores this {is} left to himself!

c) zeal in ministry—true supernatural zeal, not natural: natural zeal hinders the action of Mary; for Trappists, she gains abandonment and peace with whatever God gives.

d) {as for saying} each Mass with more fervor, if we approach this in the natural way we will fail, {from} straining, self-consciousness, anxiety. Mary will take care of our priestly zeal and make this simple. What is meant by "more fervor than the preceding"? Do we know? greater purity of love; emptiness of self; simplicity.

4. She does this not only for our sakes, but because without the priest there is no Mass, no sacraments; paganism {becomes} almost inevitable. Yet note Mary's action for instance in Japan, keeping up a fervent Catholic life in Christians for three centuries without priests, after {the} departure of St. Francis Xavier—helped by the Japanese martyrs: she obtained for them the grace of martyrdom. *She knows the graces we need, the ones we cannot understand or ask for.* How wise to leave our lives in her hands and trust everything to her, letting her choose. This does not mean quietism; it means accepting

---

363. Text reads: ". . . His Holy Mother in answer . . ." (italics added).
364. Philippe, *Blessed Virgin and the Priesthood*, 14 (italics added).

our lives as they are in fact arranged by Divine Providence, knowing that there is indeed a plan and a purpose which we cannot see, and that this is the *best* plan and purpose for us, watched over by her maternal heart.

Second Meditation: let us enter into the mystery of Jesus' love for us on the Cross—in this mystery Mary has a necessary part. Jesus could have redeemed us without dying on the Cross, but He willed to die on the Cross and leave us the Most Blessed Eucharist in order that we might have a most evident proof of His love for us, that we might be able to *see and appreciate* His love, that we might be able to receive Him Who is Love within our own hearts by communion, in which we are united to His love and His sacrifice. In dying for us, in leaving us the Blessed Sacrament, Jesus has proved His infinite love for us by giving Himself in a divine manner.

2. Mary's part in this: (a) Mary gave Jesus His body, making this perfect gift of Himself to us possible; {she} gave Him His human heart, His character, His way of loving as man; (b) Mary cooperated in the priestly act by which He redeemed us, by her loving compassion; (c) Mary was necessary to Jesus in the Passion—He willed to have her consolation, her compassion, her understanding, her sharing with Him His great act of love for men. She shared His solitude, and she alone could; thus she shared His divine gift of penetrating into the inmost hearts of all. She entered with Him into the solitude of every human heart. {There was a} mutual compenetration of the hearts of Jesus and Mary on Calvary—the suffering of ONE HEART and ONE SOUL, whereby Mary too becomes one heart and one soul with everyone who enters into the Passion of Christ Jesus. Thus Jesus deigned to *need* Mary in His suffering and sacrifice. The priest is another Jesus, and what Mary is to Jesus she is also to the priest (M. Claret de la Touche[365]). She is our Mother especially as priests; she forms in us a priestly heart like that of her Son.

3. We are priests above all in order to offer Mass, the re-presentation of the Passion. In the Mass, we are living instruments of Jesus, the High Priest, hence called to an indescribable intimacy with Him.

---

365. Mother Louise Marguerite Claret de la Touche (1868–1915), quoted in Philippe, *Blessed Virgin and the Priesthood*, 37.

Through Mary we are led to this intimacy with Jesus in our Mass. Mary's intimate union with Jesus on Calvary is continued and re-produced in the Mass—how? by her union with the priest celebrat-ing. The priest may not think of this, but Mary does, and she unites herself with him. "From Heaven and in the Beatific Vision, she sees and acts conjointly with the Christ–Priest who lives and acts in His Priest" (p. 49). The mystery of Mary's co-redemption continues daily in Mass. If Jesus needed her, we do much more!

4. The priest at Mass is united with Jesus' love for Mary, Mary's love for Jesus, and the love of both for all men. The priest *profits specially* by the invisible help of Mary, standing at his side. The union which begins at the altar should continue throughout the day. Unlike the layman, says Paul Philippe,[366] the priest by his character shares in the love of Jesus the High Priest for Mary His Mother. St. John Eudes compares the love of the priest of Mary and their union to an espousal.[367] (Read Louis de Montfort, p. 54.[368])]

---

366. Philippe, *Blessed Virgin and the Priesthood*, 51–52.

367. See Philippe, *Blessed Virgin and the Priesthood*, 52–53.

368. "The Most Blessed Virgin . . . gives herself entirely and ineffably to him who gives her all of himself. She submerges him in the abyss of her graces. As the conse-crated person belongs wholly to Mary, Mary also belongs wholly to him, so that one may say of this perfect servant and child of Mary what St. John the Evangelist says of himself, 'Accepit eam discipulus in sua'" (John 19:27: "The disciple received her into his home") (quoted in Philippe, *Blessed Virgin and the Priesthood*, 54).

APPENDIX A—VERSIONS OF THE TEXT

TL (I:46–47)

66–68   FORTY HOURS
          TMb/c (see SEPTUAGESIMA [I])
          TL (I:48–49)

68–70   ASH WEDNESDAY [I]
          TMb/c (2 typed pp.—Ash Wed. [1]–2)
          TL (I:50–51)

70–72   *Ash Wednesday* (II):
          TMb/c (1 typed p.)
          TL (I:52)

72–73   FIRST SUNDAY OF LENT
          TMb/c (1 typed p.)
          TL (I:53)

73–74   SECOND SUNDAY OF LENT
          TMb/c (1 typed p.)
          TL (I:54)

75–76   WEDNESDAY OF THE FOURTH WEEK OF LENT
          TMc (1 typed p.)

76–88   PASSIONTIDE
          TMb/c (8 typed pp.—Passiontide [1]–8)
          TL (I:55–62)

88–89   WEDNESDAY IN HOLY WEEK
          TMa (1 typed p.—Holy Week)
          TMb/c (1 typed p.)
          TL (I:63–64)

89–94   THE EASTER MYSTERY
          TMb/c (4 typed pp.—Easter m. [1]–4)
          TL (I:65–68)

94–97   HOLY WEEK (A Brief Outline)
          TMb/c (8 typed pp.—Holy Week [1]–8—combined with
             THE LAST THREE DAYS OF HOLY WEEK)
          TL (I:69–70)

97–102 THE LAST THREE DAYS OF HOLY WEEK
          TMb/c (see HOLY WEEK (A Brief Outline))
          TL (I:71–77)

102–9   *Holy Saturday*
          TMb/c (1 typed p.)
          TL (I:78–79)

109–10 EASTER SEASON
          TMb/c (1 typed p.)
          TL (I:80)

110–12 EASTER THEMES
          TMb/c (1 typed p.)
          TL (I:81)

150–51   TENTH SUNDAY AFTER PENTECOST
        TMb (1 typed p.)
        TL (I:109)

151–53   SEPTEMBER EMBER DAYS
        TMb (2 typed pp.—September Ember Days [1]–2)
        TL (I:111–12)

153   EIGHTEENTH SUNDAY AFTER PENTECOST
        TMb/c (1 typed p.)
        TL (I:113)

154   NINETEENTH SUNDAY AFTER PENTECOST
        TMb/c (1 typed p.)
        TL (I:114)

154–56   TWENTY-FIRST SUNDAY AFTER PENTECOST
        TMb (1 handwritten p.)
        TL (I:115–16)

156–57   THE LAST SUNDAY AFTER PENTECOST
        TMa (1 handwritten p.)
        TMb/c (1 typed p.)
        TL (I:116)

~

162–65   THE MYSTERY OF MARY AND THE CHURCH
        TMa (2 typed pp.—Mary and Ch [1]–2)
        TMb/c (3 typed pp.—Mary and Church [1]–2)
        TL (II:1–3)

165–69   ST. BERNARD'S SERMONS FOR THE FEAST OF ST. ANDREW
        TMa (2 typed & 2 handwritten pp.—St B F of Andrew [1]–2)
        TMb/c (4 typed pp.—St. B. F. St. Andrew [1]–2)
        TL (II:4–7)

169–74   THE PRIEST IN THE MONASTERY—
FEAST OF ST. THOMAS THE APOSTLE
        TMa (3 typed pp.—priest [1]–3)
        TMb/c (3 typed pp.—priest [1]–3)
        TL (II:8–11)

174–79   CANDLEMAS
        TMb/c (3 typed pp.—Candlemas [1]–3)
        TL (II:12–14)

179–82   SAINT AILRED—*Cistercian Life in His Time*
        TMb/c (2 typed pp.—Ailred [1]–2)
        TL (II:15–16)

182–86   THE FEAST OF SAINT JOSEPH
        TMb/c (3 typed pp.—St. Joseph [1]–3)
        TL (II:17–19)

186–89   FEAST OF OUR HOLY FATHER SAINT BENEDICT
        TMb (2 typed pp.—St. Benedict [1]–2)
        TL (II:20–21)

APPENDIX B—TEXTUAL NOTES

Additions and Alterations in TMa

4   wills,] *followed by cancelled* Hearts
     humble] *added below and marked for insertion*

5   In the epistle, . . . darkness," etc.] *added on line*
     patriarchs and prophets.] *followed by x'd out* But we do not
     level.] *preceded by x'd out* most

6   subjects of meditation and as] *typed interlined and marked for
     insertion*
     veniet] *followed by x'd out* (Mag 1st st
     for the . . . salvation] *added on line*

7   The fruit . . . at Christmas] *interlined*

9   Read . . . white as snow] *added on line*
     Whose presence is judgement] *added on line*
     awaken attention, . . . in the liturgy.] *typed opposite page*
     awaken . . . realize.] *interlined*
     He speaks . . . liturgy.] *added on line*

9–10 joy . . . union with God.] *typed opposite page*

11   form the profound . . . liturgy] *interlined and marked for insertion*
     2.] *followed by x'd out* The Epistles
     (gospel . . . Sunday)] *added on line*
     testimony before] *interlined above cancelled* witness to

12   John as an individual] *added in left margin*
     a voice . . . hear] *added on line*
     The Jews . . . alteration.] *added on line*
     Note: John . . . than he.] *opposite page*
     our whole] *followed by x'd out* universe

13   question] *followed by x'd out* his earlier
     He asks . . . a Precursor.] *added on line*
     destroyed] *preceded by x'd out* ruin
     This makes] *preceded by x'd out* puts hi
     Then Jesus . . . prophet.] *added in lower margin*

16   *Dominus . . . is near.*] *added on line*
     he sees Him "closer"] *added on line*

17   message] *interlined with a caret above cancelled* whole
      certainly feel] *preceded by x'd out* indeed
18   must be] *preceded by x'd out* would
      irresistibly] *preceded by x'd out* powerfully in heaven
19   Note . . . nothing.] *added in left margin*
      cf. Wisdom] *added on line*
22   Our times . . . vocation.] *added on line*
23   Let the light] *preceded by x'd out* We beg that
      disciples. He] He *typed interlined above x'd out* and
      pardon] *preceded by x'd out* peace
24   Where . . . Sacrament!] *added in lower margin preceded by*
        cancelled Read Isaias
      1.] *added in left margin*
      First of all, . . . He is.] *interlined*
      He manifests . . . mystery)] *added in left margin*
      Admire . . . participate.] *opposite page*
25   And the Word] *preceded by x'd out* . . . He was in the world, and the
        world was made by Him, and the world knew Him not
      But "He . . . not."] *added on line*
      useless . . . learned.] *opposite page*
      this . . . mystery] *added in left margin*
      learned.] *followed by cancelled* The
      the Incarnate] *preceded by x'd out* Him
25–26 *Sed* necessarium . . . *credat*] *interlined*
26   (not just any faith)] *added on line*
      (in the Christmas liturgy)] *added on line*
      (the unity . . . God)] *added on line*
      est ex] *preceded by x'd out* ex
      in no sense . . . divinity] *added on line*
      man just . . . sin] *added on line*
      humana] *preceded by x'd out* carne subsistens
      the heart . . . Mystery] *added on line*
      True contemplation . . . Man.] *added in lower margin*
      this great] *preceded by x'd out* our faith in
      Man, not only to be] *followed by x'd out* the human Word and a
        human nature subsisting in one Person
27   blood,] *preceded by x'd out* flesh
      2.] *added in left margin*
      Yahweh] *preceded by x'd out* God
28   The Word] *typed interlined above x'd out* Jesus
29   3.] *added in left margin*
      permeates] *preceded by x'd out* it
30   CONCLUSION: . . . the monastic life.] *added at foot of page*
      "*Dies sanctificatus*"] *interlined*

come.] *followed by x'd out* The day of s

30–31   But now . . . est.] *added on line*

31   realities] *altered from* reality *followed by x'd out* is pr

this simple] *preceded by x'd out* it cann

the introit] *preceded by x'd out* there

which differ] *followed by x'd out* with

32   Read {the} gospel] *added in left margin*

33   Dominus] *preceded by x'd out* decor

theologically,] *followed by x'd out* reflecting that

takes note] *preceded by x'd out* dec wonder

This Mass] *preceded by x'd out* It is

33–34   or rather . . . Head.] *added on line*

34   her hands] *followed by x'd out* at

"sanctified] *preceded by x'd out* day

35   the mystery] *preceded by x'd out* whose

rejoice in celebrating] *typed interlined above x'd out* celebrate

37   It is a . . . Life.] *added on line*

contemplation . . . connection] *added in left margin and marked for*
    insertion to replace cancelled it

love of] *preceded by x'd out* contact

"that they] *preceded by x'd out* of His wisdom by

filled] *followed by x'd out* unto

38   Jesus, for] *preceded by x'd out* the

most necessary] *preceded by x'd out* main

readiness] *interlined below cancelled* dispositions

to love] to *interlined*

to wonder] *added on line following cancelled* admire.

Body] *preceded by x'd out* Word of God

while we are] *interlined below cancelled* being

empty] *added in left margin and marked for insertion to replace*
    cancelled purify

39   three modes . . . triumphant.] *added in left margin and marked for*
    insertion

grace of] *followed by x'd out* Jesus

40   cf. *introit*: . . . admirabilis" etc.] *typed in upper right margin and*
    marked for insertion

Admiration . . . to God.] *opposite page*

witness to] *followed by cancelled* what

outpouring] *preceded by x'd out* inpouring of love and outpo

41   firm . . . of Mary] *interlined*

42   that help] *followed by x'd out* us to

or to express . . . faith] *added on line*

43   Conclusion: . . . peace.] *added in lower margin*

49   saw then] *preceded by cancelled* have seen

50   *a new theme*] *added in left margin*
89   His bruises] His *typed interlined above x'd out* our
            rebellions.] *preceded by x'd out* iniquities
            Let us ... hearts.] *opposite page*
113   monastic habit] monastic *typed interlined*
141   "not ... days"] *altered from* not ... days
            children of the world] *interlined below cancelled* seculars.
142   3.] *followed by x'd out* Sunday has acquired an individuality
            It is ... to man.] *added on line*
            not the same] *added on line*
            Sabbath ... for the Sabbath] *added on line after* liberty. *and marked*
               for insertion
            for them ... the Sabbath] *interlined with a caret*
            by showing ... in Him.] *interlined*
            Hebrews 4:3–11] Hebrews 4:3
143   Lord's Day. ... 20:19–23] *added in left margin*
            etc.: ... tone.] *interlined*
            tone] *preceded by cancelled* Easter
            freedom ... "things"] *interlined with a caret*
            Our "conversatio ... good.] *added in lower margin*
            (cf. St. John 20)] *added on line*
144   shine] *followed by x'd out* burn forever
            light of ... day of grace] *added on line*
            day in which ... to you."] *interlined*
            the day on ... in Him] *added on line*
            Let *Him* ... rejoice in it] *added in left margin*
145   thus light ... Church] *added on line*
            sadness] *followed by x'd out* as a sin
            strictly a Gospel] a *interlined with a caret*
            fetter the spirit] *followed by x'd out* that
146   Lord's Day, ... to be] *added on line*
            beauty of] *followed by x'd out* family
            Ida ... eternity] *interlined*
162   the Christian outlook] *preceded by x'd out* Christianity
163   PERSONALLY] *followed by x'd out* TOOK PLACE
            understood] *interlined above cancelled* completely and perfectly
               realized
            achieves] *followed by x'd out* in
164   practically no] *preceded by x'd out* little
            taken to] *preceded by x'd out* used to
165   or bear] or *typed interlined above x'd out* and
            desire and love] *followed by x'd out* even at the
166   movements] *interlined before cancelled* attractions
            followers of Christ] *followed by x'd out* as

explaining] *followed by x'd out* on

167   However, . . . confidence.] *opposite page*

consideration of] *interlined with a caret*

168   Obedience] *interlined above cancelled* Justice

coin is] *preceded by cancelled* both

169   courage.] *followed by cancelled* The four corners of the Cross of St
Andrew

                A demonio meridiano / pride + self-satisfaction

                A sagitta volante in die / *false security, flattery,*
temptations + [ ]

                Against Timor nocturnus / fear of penance

                Against Sagitta volante in die / insult and bad treatment
by others

A negotio . . . tenebris] *interlined above cancelled* A sagitta volante
in die

(also . . . Apostle)] *added on line*

169–70 *The power . . . path to God.*] *opposite page*

170   is constantly] *preceded by x'd out* remains in contact with

himself and in] *interlined with a caret*

When we see] *preceded by x'd out* It is

It brings . . . conflict.] *added on line*

2] *added in left margin*

As a religious, . . . pleasing Him.] *added in left margin and*
continued interlined

171   He must be . . . the Good Shepherd.] *opposite page*

put him] *preceded by x'd out* give him

active life,] *followed by x'd out* in the

Here too . . . trust.] *added on line*

172   ordained] *preceded by x'd out* supposed to make the

sacrifice of] *followed by x'd out* the Cross

He must be . . . others.] *added in left margin*

minor orders,] *followed by x'd out* and

195   FEAST OF THE SEVEN DOLORS] *added in upper margin*

196   participation] *preceded by x'd out* action on Calvary

197   Note the elements] *preceded by x'd out* The death on Calvary which
strictly In the separation of Jesus' soul from His Body

Jesus' soul] *preceded by x'd out* Jesus' soul separated from His Body

moment] *followed by x'd out* He

possession] *followed by x'd out* finally

leaving me to] *followed by x'd out* take

cared for] *followed by x'd out* the

198   Therefore she . . . body.] *added in left margin and marked for*
insertion

207   mystery] *typed in left margin before x'd out* action

208	is the great] *preceded by x'd out* has so
	desert] *followed by x'd out* – in the
	John is . . . light.] *added on line*
	"He shall . . . birth"] *interlined*
	(introit: vigil)] *added in left margin*
	St. Ambrose . . . 'common good.'"] *added in left margin*
211	exceeding] *typed interlined and marked for insertion*
	Lord")] *followed by x'd out* and
	Et tu] *followed by x'd out* propheta
212	cf. {the} whole . . . religion"] *interlined above cancelled* (cf. central
	doctrine] *followed by cancelled* Further, they were taught directly
	by God the Master of all
217	*and canticles*] *interlined above cancelled* of 1st n.
219	laud] *preceded by x'd out* go into the question who the
220	That comes] *preceded by x'd out* Search for
	ornaments] *followed by x'd out* His charity
221	fervor,] *followed by x'd out* resist
222	*Multae . . . none*] *interlined*
	Read . . . here] *added in left margin*
223	not because . . . herself] *interlined and marked for insertion*
	the sinner] *typed interlined and marked for insertion*
224	vouchsafed] *followed by x'd out* to
	her tears] *preceded by x'd out* the
	but we . . . by Mary] *added on line*
	it is by] *preceded by x'd out* 1st verse
225	seeks her] *followed by x'd out* in
226	consolation] *followed by x'd out* it is no
232	king came] came *altered from* comes
	opened] *altered from* opens
	on very intimate] *preceded by x'd out* closely
233	and inheritance] *interlined below and marked for insertion*
	often] *interlined with a caret*
237	The actual . . . Malachy] *added in left margin*
238	typical . . . verse] *added on line*
	antiphons] *followed by cancelled* + Responsories
	Church of Cîteaux] Church *interlined above cancelled* house
243	Jesus] *typed in left margin before x'd out* It
	fired to the] *preceded by x'd out* of the
	before He] *preceded by x'd out* in His infancy as St Bernardine expl
244	the creation] *preceded by x'd out* all the
246	initiate] *preceded by x'd out* bring
	magniloquent] *preceded by x'd out* grandiose
247	Greek liturgy . . . every day.] *added in lower margin*
251	prayer, but] *followed by x'd out* is

252   beads] *followed by x'd out* in common
       either . . . lectio] *added on line*
       Unless a] a *interlined with a caret following x'd out* a person has
       daily] *typed interlined and marked for insertion*
       usually right] *preceded by x'd out* right that one should
       each case] *preceded by x'd out* this now
       out of love] *followed by x'd out* and not
       the merit of] *preceded by x'd out* her merits and
       mysteries] *followed by x'd out* and
       obedience] *followed by cancelled* and

253   with intense concentration] *added in left margin and marked for
          insertion*
       The song . . . itself] *added in lower margin*
       of prayer] *added in upper margin and marked for insertion*
       aura of love] love *interlined above cancelled* prayer
       the grace] *preceded by x'd out* her
       motherly] *interlined below cancelled* loving
       While we are] *preceded by x'd out* The Rosary is essentially very
          simple
       mysterious] *preceded by x'd out* mysteries and
       they attract] *preceded by x'd out* it attracts and
       and the Person . . . divine] *added on line*
       through and with] *preceded by x'd out* in His mysteries
       the greatest] *preceded by x'd out* a gre
       expressing] *followed by cancelled* that
       devoutly] *preceded by x'd out* meditate simply on these mysteries

254   *The Rosary and Contemplation*] *added in left margin*
       to learn] *preceded by x'd out* prepare the way fo
       to most . . . rosary] *typed interlined above x'd out* the rosary
       this prayer] *followed by x'd out* Rhythm
       a special] *interlined below cancelled* its

255   *affectu*] *preceded by x'd out intellectu*
       has loyally] *preceded by x'd out* cannot
       Meditation on the Mysteries] *interlined*
       for some] *preceded by x'd out* from
       should never] should *interlined above cancelled* will

256   Each one] *preceded by x'd out* It means
       clothe] *preceded by x'd out* receive this
       kind of joy] *preceded by x'd out* joy
       communicating] *preceded by x'd out* the members of the

257   and united] *preceded by x'd out* the fulfil
       understanding] *preceded by x'd out* vision
       the mental] *preceded by x'd out* its psychological consequences and
          effects

brutality] *preceded by x'd out* cruelty of
As Jesus] *preceded by x'd out* In t
Mary's sacrifice] *preceded by x'd out* Mary with
Mary's heart] *preceded by x'd out* in the absence of Jesus

259   vision] *followed by x'd out* with G
They love us *in . . . in* Him] *added on line*
Good inspirations . . . our regard.] *added on line*
(Feast of St. Michael)] *added on line*
In this . . . God's will] *added in left margin*
cooperating] *preceded by cancelled* united

260   some good angels] *interlined with a caret above cancelled* they
human being] *preceded by x'd out* man had

260–61 They act . . . motorcycle] *added in left margin*

261   *Raccolta: . . . completion*] *opposite page*
Why is . . . ourselves.] *opposite page*
flesh of] *followed by cancelled* God
fed not by] *followed by cancelled* our
souls] *interlined below x'd out* soul
confident] *preceded by x'd out* happy
especially . . . get there] *added on line*

262   lies in] *followed by x'd out* the f
Note the . . . of spirits.] *added in left margin and marked for insertion*
Incarnate] *preceded by x'd out* Word
note . . . melody] *added on line*
Votis, . . . hearts] *added on line*

263   St. Gregory] *preceded by x'd out* the theories of
explains] *preceded by x'd out* about
names and] *preceded by x'd out* nine choirs
The tone . . . gentle.] *added in lower margin*
read Daniel 7:9–18] *added in left margin*

264   Read] *added in left margin followed by* Zach I.9–17
8–17] 17 *added above cancelled* 16
vision] *followed by cancelled* life
Read] *added in left margin followed by* Dan 8:15–19
to Daniel] *followed by cancelled* cf. also
Read] *added in left margin followed by* Dan 9:21–27

265   mystery of the] *interlined*
Read] *added in left margin followed by* Dan. 10:9–21

267   Thus we . . . struggle.] *interlined*

268   What are . . . sacrifice.] *added on line*
However, . . . agitation] *added in left margin*
Note that . . . *demands.*] *added in left margin*
destroy] *preceded by x'd out* ruin the spiritual

269	Note . . . sensitivity] *added in lower margin*
	as our founder] *added on line*
	it comes] *followed by cancelled* very much
	whatever] *preceded by cancelled* that
270	and seeking] seeking *interlined with a caret*
	rest] *preceded by x'd out* seek what is natural
	illusions] *interlined below cancelled* figments
	Love means . . . pleases Him] *added on line*
	field] *preceded by x'd out* soil of
271	e) Finally, . . . peace.] *added in left margin*
276	overflows in] *interlined above cancelled* consists in
	in us] *added on line*
277	And what is . . . infinite God.] *added on line*
	(common of martyrs)] *added on line*
	theme is] *followed by x'd out* God
	to us . . . intelligam] *added on line*
	read *Wisdom* 1:5ff.] *added in left margin*
278	placed] *preceded by x'd out* given
	READ] *preceded by* Read Wisdom 1:12 to end *added in left margin*
	Read 2:12 . . . end] *added in left margin*
279	Desire . . . will of God] *added on line*
280	whole life.] *followed by x'd out* The canticle ends here
	Indeed the "fire" . . . of God] *added in left margin*
	there is only] *preceded by x'd out* The sain
	complete] *interlined below cancelled* make
	journey after] *preceded by cancelled* same
	their love.] *followed by x'd out* Everything else is
281	cannot be too] can *interlined above cancelled* must
	sense?)] ? *added on line*
	in purgatory accept] *preceded by x'd out* of
	(apply . . . poor souls)] *added on line*
282	same is clear] is *interlined above cancelled* seems
282–84	"When the divine . . . p. 31] *added in lower margin*
284	truly happy] *preceded by cancelled* perfectly un
285	"called Martin . . . a saint] *interlined and marked for insertion*
286	some of] *preceded by cancelled* His
288	Valombrosans] *followed by x'd out* Down to the
	mortal things] *followed by x'd out* that
291	(n.b. *Urbs* . . . heart)] *added on line*
292	solemnity . . . words] *added in right margin and marked for insertion*
	Oration] *preceded by x'd out* Postcommunion
	"contines,"] *altered from* contines
293	(The building . . . you.)] *added on line*

1] *added in left margin*
2] *added in left margin*
294   3] *added in left margin*
The more intimate . . . to ourselves!] *opposite page*
not just] *preceded by cancelled* just
295   (4) We must . . . all this.] *added in lower margin*
Read . . . 32–36] *added in upper margin and marked for insertion*
295–96 All these . . . Wisdom.] *interlined*
296   assures] *preceded by cancelled* keeps them in a state of perfection
instincts, and] *followed by cancelled* the
life,"] *followed by cancelled* and
we] *interlined above cancelled* makes us
297   It *cannot* . . . story!] *opposite page*
and counsels] *interlined with a caret*
298   If we . . . of Mary.] *opposite page*
lifetime.] *followed by cancelled* Indeed it is imposible
We do not . . . background.] *interlined*
299   *will*] *followed by cancelled* first of all
300   *Why the* . . . everything.] *opposite page*
If we trust . . . *state*.] *opposite page*
To be . . . to Mary] *interlined above cancelled* This
above all, . . . Him!!] *added in left margin*
301   God our] *preceded by cancelled* In the
made] *interlined above cancelled* created
This] *altered from* this *preceded by cancelled* But
to perfect] *preceded by x'd out* again
The history] *preceded by x'd out* But the glory and
hidden] *preceded by x'd out* It is still hidden
302   of God] *preceded by x'd out* is
giving it] *preceded by x'd out* making it a
So "time" . . . all men.] *added on line*
given . . . power to] *interlined with a caret above cancelled* laid hold of
cycle] *preceded by x'd out* natural
express] *preceded by x'd out* are the cycle rhyt
activity] *preceded by x'd out* life and death,
no decline] *preceded by x'd out* a birth
cycle of] *preceded by x'd out* seasons themselves offer
spiritual] *added in upper margin and marked for insertion*
prison] *followed by cancelled* for his spirit.
Our sons] *interlined with a caret above cancelled* They
and in] *added on line*
upwards,] *followed by x'd out* without success
insatiable] *preceded by x'd out* infinite
The flames] The *altered from* the *preceded by* and

303   then die] then *interlined above cancelled* and
grow cold] *preceded by x'd out* lose
The modern . . . be men.] *opposite page*
nothingness] *preceded by cancelled* the
something entirely new] *interlined above cancelled* completely
  changed
of grace] *followed by x'd out* and
flesh which] *followed by x'd out* ebb flows with the dying year
ebbs] *followed by x'd out* in the spring
dissolved] *followed by x'd out* we
The Word of God] *typed interlined above x'd out* Christ
an imprisonment] *preceded by x'd out* a prison to

304   shows us] *followed by x'd out* how
mysteries,] *followed by x'd out* now in His saints
His churches] *preceded by x'd out* the C
mode of being] *interlined and marked for insertion to replace
  cancelled* life
in this] *preceded by x'd out* also tends to
time of] *preceded by x'd out* interregnum
though we] *preceded by x'd out* they
"fighting Church"] *altered from* fighting Church
is a prison] *preceded by x'd out* for the
new dawn] *interlined before cancelled* rebirth
our union] *preceded by x'd out* our bond of
insights] *preceded by cancelled* new

305   souls] *preceded by x'd out* lives in the
for the ones] ones *altered from* one
called Him] *preceded by x'd out* raised

306   an expression] *preceded by x'd out* a means of and
society] *followed by x'd out* be takes
renewing] *followed by x'd out* and reliving the livin mysteries holy
  mysteries
uttering] *preceded by x'd out* teaching again the lessons of
that are capable] that *added in left margin to replace x'd out* with
  which He instruct
sick] *preceded by x'd out* poor and the
has something] *preceded by x'd out* is
not only re-lives] *preceded by x'd out* not only longs for
particular] *preceded by x'd out* aspect of aspect
at Bethlehem] *preceded by x'd out* in time
return to] *preceded by x'd out* consider
to the generation] to *interlined with a caret to replace cancelled* and
  followed by x'd out contemp
having come] *preceded by x'd out* after the I

307 works which] works *interlined above cancelled* things
   works present] works *interlined and marked for insertion to replace*
    cancelled things
   presence] *altered from* present
   new liturgical] *followed by x'd out* celebration it is rather Christ
    Himself that
   Epiphany, we] *followed by x'd out* come
   gentiles] *followed by x'd out* In Lent
   as the Servant]] *preceded by x'd out* yet
308 youth as] *followed by x'd out* the eagle
   Pope . . . Church."] *opposite page*
   canonized] *preceded by cancelled* succinctly
   a former] *preceded by cancelled* the
   The liturgy is inspired] *interlined and marked for insertion to*
    replace cancelled It is moved
309 participate] *followed by x'd out* full
   spirituality.] *followed by x'd out* It is the
   read Ephesians 5:7–21.] *added on line*
310 spiritual growth in . . . heaven] *added in right margin*
   liturgical life, . . . year] *added in right margin*
   obscure . . . enemy."] *added in right margin*
311 totally . . . 45:23–25] *added in left margin*
   fulfillment . . . subjectively] *added in lower margin and marked for*
    insertion
312 "Le prophète . . . amour."] *following* is Isaias. *and marked for*
    transposition
314 (1908)] *interlined*
   4 Kings 16; 2 Par. 28] *added in right margin*
   3. The reign . . . of justice.] *following* 12: Hymn of Thanksgiving
    and marked for transposition
316 Christmas] *followed by cancelled* II Noct.
   way to] to *interlined above cancelled* of
   Jordan,] *followed by cancelled* the
   Oreb] *interlined with a caret*
   importance . . . here] *added in left margin*
319 What is] *preceded by cancelled* Read Isaias
321 modality] *followed by x'd out* Christmas shows
322 shall see] *preceded by x'd out* see
   another conference] *preceded by x'd out* the
   through the hidden] *preceded by x'd out* the
   instruments] *preceded by x'd out* direct
   authoritative] *preceded by x'd out* actions of
   impose] *preceded by x'd out* make dema
323 and exact] *preceded by x'd out* in a the

guide souls.] *followed by x'd out* b) Interiorly, enbling souls to
    absorb the truth and receive it

324   able to] *preceded by x'd out* equal to
His teaching] *typed interlined and marked for insertion*
cooperate] *preceded by x'd out* bring the
In the Spiritual] *preceded by x'd out* The director is the immediate
    source o

325   But he also] *preceded by x'd out* or He protects
326   What is the internal . . . *sacramentum*] *added in left margin*
What is charismatic? . . . juridical?] *added in left margin*
oversight] *preceded by x'd out* minor

331   of {the} human . . . applause] *added on line*
332   Lent . . . *ver sacrum*] *added in left margin*
spring . . . grace] *interlined*
eagerness . . . 76] *added in left margin*
especially . . . sent Me"] *added in left margin*

333   word of God] *preceded by x'd out* divine
334   place] *typed interlined above x'd out* bring
minds in] in *altered from* into *by x'ing out*
prepares] *preceded by x'd out* opens His public life
It is necessary . . . fasts.] *interlined*
Let us realize . . . hearts.] *opposite page*

335   Jesus to do] Jesus *typed in left margin following x'd out* him
How many . . . doormat.] *opposite page*
hardly] *preceded by x'd out* proved

336   The will . . . sanctity] *interlined*
divine power] *preceded by x'd out* super
Note: the angels . . . His Father.] *interlined*

337   The Transfiguration . . . oneself.] *opposite page*
view of] *followed by x'd out* the

338   right to] *preceded by x'd out* reward
(second Tuesday)] *added on line*
consequence . . . Filiation] *added on line*

339   one of] *preceded by x'd out* the l
is then] *preceded by x'd out* it the
The gospel of the first . . . glory.] *opposite page*
Ember] *preceded by cancelled* 1st Saturday
glory.] *followed by cancelled* And it relates His glory to His passion,
    because Moses + Elias are speaking to Him of that which is to
    come.

340   commands] *preceded by x'd out* dos and dont commands and
341   3] *added in left margin*
challenges] *preceded by x'd out* provokes

342   perfectly] *preceded by x'd out* will draw all

by Whom] *preceded by x'd out* from Whom He procedes [*sic*]
(The Son . . . the Father.)] *added on line*
reaches] *followed by x'd out* it

344   miraculously] *preceded by x'd out* distributes br
Tuesday] *typed interlined above x'd out* Wednesday

345   woman] *followed by x'd out* His humanity
grace will come] *preceded by cancelled* ways of [winning] grow—
our hearts will
an overall] *preceded by cancelled* a [   ]

346   St. Gregory . . . *consensione.*] *added in left margin*
(c) . . . blamed] *added in left margin*
seductores . . . et cogniti] *following paradoxes and marked for
transposition*
Epistle] *preceded by uncancelled* Move up [G D.]

347   Jesus] *interlined above cancelled* God

351   2–7] *interlined above cancelled* 4–5
a . . . *desolatam*] *added in left margin*

352   2:1–10] *added on line following cancelled* 20–27

354   realize] *preceded by cancelled* in d
n.b. in . . . *Scriptures*] *added in left margin*

359   importance . . . St. Bernard!!] *added in left margin*

364   "our" feast . . . 1 Cor. 13] *added in upper margin*
Note . . . Ascension.] *added in left margin*

365   end in view . . . beatitude] *added on line*
in heaven.] *followed by cancelled* Our eyes on the end in view
Epistle of the Mass—the end Gospel—the means

368   liturgical . . . *magna*] *added in left margin*
The Immaculate Conception is the first] The Immaculate
Conception *interlined with a caret above cancelled* It
taken out] *preceded by x'd out* separated
is a woman] *preceded by x'd out* was a woman
The Immaculate . . . motherhood.] *added on line*

369   can easily develop] *added in upper margin and marked for insertion
to replace cancelled* have
not just the] *followed by x'd out* phenomenon act of concep
effect] *interlined above cancelled* part
cause] *interlined above cancelled* whole
cause] *interlined above cancelled* whole
effect] *interlined above cancelled* part
Another . . . *sedes*] *added on line*
"all *hands* on deck"] *added on line*
So just as] *followed by x'd out* we say
where she said] *interlined with a caret*
be likely to] *added on line*

370   organism] *preceded by x'd out* animal
           of sin.] *followed by x'd out* A negative
           sexual] *preceded by x'd out* the se
           already the ideas] *preceded by x'd out* if we follow this any further
           a display] *preceded by x'd out* neurotic anxiety

371   did not merely] *preceded by x'd out* become the occasion for the
           is integrally] in [*sic*] *typed interlined above x'd out* was
           need to love] need to love thought of
           It is impossible for her] *followed by x'd out* to
           total] *preceded by x'd out* powerful love

372   none of . . . original sin] *added on line*
           soul of fallen . . . by God.] *added in left margin*
           perfect truth . . . of God.] *added on line*
           no irritability, no impatience] *added on line*
           no *disorder* . . . perfect.] *added on line*
           At the same . . . race, etc.] *opposite page*
           permissible] *preceded by cancelled* adequate
           goodness] *preceded by x'd out* delight

373   Above all, . . . 96–97] *added in lower margin*
           see a certain] *preceded by x'd out* have a little dramatic
           mostly to her.] *followed by x'd out* 1 – The voice of God 1. – Our
             part

375   avoid] *preceded by cancelled* not

376   Unless . . . illusion] *added in left margin and marked for insertion*
           Eve simply] *preceded by cancelled* B)
           By listening] *preceded by cancelled with sinful*

377   for meditation] *added in left margin*
           Mary, our vocation, . . . hands] *added in upper margin*

378   against great . . . honors her.] *added on line*
           for Trappists, . . . gives.] *interlined*
           simplicity.] *added on line*

379   Jesus' love] *preceded by x'd out* of
           gave Him His . . . as man] *added on line*
           She is our . . . of her Son.] *interlined*

380   Through Mary . . . our Mass.] *added on line*
           The mystery of . . . p. 54.] *added in lower margin*

Additions and Alterations in TMb

4   and taste] and *added on line*
           But this . . . through the liturgy.] *added in upper margin and*
             marked for insertion to replace cancelled etc.
           own. It takes] It *interlined with a caret*
           beyond ourselves.] *followed by cancelled* Yet
           of the liturgy, and this] of *added on line following cancelled* of the

thought and love in

The liturgy elevates] The liturgy *interlined below cancelled* it

a desire which . . . and Redeemer.] *added on line*

It sees Him] It *added in left margin*

the creatures] *preceded by cancelled* we,

5   Love burns . . . the darkness.] *added on line*

6   established. . . . reign!] *added on line following cancelled* satisfied

7   all that impedes] *added in left margin to replace cancelled* from

there shall be] *interlined below and marked for insertion*

words . . . thrilled] *interlined below and marked for insertion*

descended, You] You *added on line following cancelled* thou

came] *altered from* camest

Your great] Your *interlined above cancelled* thy

pray You] You *added in right margin to replace cancelled* Thee

8   *Aspiciens*] *altered from* Aspicienes

furnish] *added in left margin to replace cancelled* contain

11   thoughts] *altered from* thought

their chance.] *followed by cancelled* This is not what concerns us
now.

12   we get a] *interlined with a caret*

16   Isaias is] is *interlined with a caret*

foretells] *interlined with a caret*

18   brings . . . surrounds us] *interlined below and marked for insertion*

the bright] the *interlined above cancelled* a

adoration] *preceded by cancelled* and

22   treasury] *interlined above cancelled* springs

24   Christmas is the great] is *interlined above cancelled* –

25   and kindness] *preceded by cancelled* of God

by the citizens] by *interlined below cancelled* of

26   penetrate] *followed by cancelled* into

27   Savior . . . that] *preceded by cancelled* Lord."

down] *interlined above cancelled* to us

30   Who unites] *followed by cancelled* our

41   at the nativity] at *interlined below cancelled* of

increase] *interlined above cancelled* infusion

(introit: third Mass)] *interlined below* (communion: midnight
Mass) *added on line and cancelled*

43   11] *preceded by cancelled* 9

44   subtle aggression] *preceded by illegible cancelled line*

45   Distinguish . . . aggression] *opposite page*

impatience, . . . coldness.] *added in left margin and marked for
insertion*

basic principle . . . than that.] *opposite page followed by uncancelled*
a healthy

toward God.] *followed by cancelled* The destruction of idols sets us
   out on a new road

47 much] *interlined above cancelled* Most

brothers of] *interlined above cancelled* sons with

49 as the light] light *interlined above cancelled* eyes

secondary] *added on line following cancelled* embroidered

Cana] *followed by cancelled* The hymn is late – also the Benedictus
   antiphon and introduces a note of confusion. Is not as merry as it
   sounds.

of Christmas.] *followed by cancelled* The Vesper is repeated.

Light] *added in right margin and marked for insertion to replace
   cancelled* star

fulfillment] *added in left margin and marked for insertion to replace
   x'd out* are

Testament!] *followed by cancelled* Note how the liturgy constantly
   builds up. The Old Testament and New companion and
   comparison.

50 Jews, . . . His glory.] *added on line*

are moved] *followed by cancelled* and kingdoms all (Herod's place
   in the office) God

All nations] *preceded by x'd out* God is

our feet.] *followed by cancelled* He presents you His treasure and
   soon wings [*sic;* the Kings *in TMa*] of the nations are fattend [*sic;*
   gathered *in TMa*] together with the Sons of Abraham

Epiphany in] in *altered from* is

tried us] us *added in left margin and marked for insertion*

51 the peace] *preceded by cancelled* Hear

adore the Lord] Lord *added on line*

those who ardently thirst] *added on line*

and can never satisfy them] *added on line*

54 "epiphany"] *interlined below and marked for insertion*

the "epiphany."] *added on line following cancelled* it.

56 Note: the Greeks . . . *Transfiguration*] *interlined*

57 on the Cross.] *followed by cancelled* So in the Idiomeles of Sext,
   Great Hours, Byz. Lit.—Jesus says to the Baptist

Jesus says to the] *added in upper margin and marked for insertion*

(in the *Idiomeles* . . . Liturgy)] *added in upper margin and marked
   for insertion*

60 Easter Mystery] *preceded by cancelled* great

God's wisdom] wisdom *interlined and marked for insertion to
   replace cancelled* goodness

The whole . . . (SOPHIA).] *added on line*

66 useless] *interlined above cancelled* Unless

70 II] *added on line*

71   poignant] *interlined with a caret*
        Compunction is the] *added in left margin and marked for insertion*
        absorb] *altered from* absorbing *preceded by cancelled* by
        his repentance] his *interlined above cancelled* their
72   truly] *interlined with a caret*
        here below] *interlined with a caret*
74   (especially superiors)] *added on line*
        read today in chapter] *added on line*
83   at the altar,] *interlined below cancelled* in him
84   same victim] same *interlined below and marked for insertion*
        but in . . . manner.] *interlined below and marked for insertion*
85   of the Scriptures] *followed by cancelled* and for that matter
          of the liturgy.
88   cf. . . . Wednesday, Holy Week] *added in upper margin*
94   us, in the mystery] *followed by x'd out* to
97   come prepared, . . . in chapter] have been [*altered to* come *in TL*]
          prepared, . . . in chapter *added on line*
        #251] *interlined below and marked for insertion*
97–98   Love one . . . of Christ.] *added in lower margin*
98   4:00] 4 *interlined above cancelled* 5
99   tierce] *followed by cancelled* and interval of about 45 minutes.
        at 11:00 . . . communion] *interlined*
        long] *interlined above cancelled* usual
        about two . . . reading] *added on line*
102   In order that . . . for Masses.] *opposite page*
        more fruitfully] *interlined with a caret*
        fire of] fire *interlined above cancelled* light
        Meanwhile, . . . creation.] *added on line*
108   "Christ the unconquered . . . follows Jesus."] *altered from* Christ the
          unconquered . . . follows Jesus.
        purgatory] *followed by cancelled* again
110   "My Lord and my God."] *added on line*
112   tunc] *altered from* tum
113   heart of the] *interlined with a caret*
        monastic] *interlined below and marked for insertion*
        repeat] *added on line following cancelled* reflect
        unless God intervenes.] *added on line*
        Dantès] *interlined below cancelled* Santes
116   victory of God.] *followed by cancelled* The Preface of Paschal Time
          and of Pentecost (cf. Flicoteaux.)
119   All creatures] creatures *interlined below cancelled* things
120   We need] *added in lower margin and marked for insertion to*
          replace cancelled but
122   Berdyaev] *altered from* Berdaeyev

131   sharers] *altered from* shares
142   *Sunday . . . Easter*] *altered from* Sunday . . . Easter
        They are] *interlined below and marked for insertion*
144   opposed] *altered from* opp
        to the] *interlined below and marked for insertion*
145   time] *interlined below cancelled* place
        psalms on Sunday.] St. Benedict, however, permits labor for those
            who cannot read or meditate—therefore as a recreation, as a
            mitigation.
146   "almsgiving"] *altered from* almsgiving
        or Reverend Father] *added on line*
        at least.] *followed by cancelled* stations, longer time for them
149   from vain] from *interlined below cancelled* of
        see . . . "Ecclesiastes"] *added on line*
150   temptations, or] *followed by cancelled* otherwise
        throws . . . meaning of] *interlined above cancelled* as a commentary on
152   back upon] upon *interlined below cancelled* to
166   be distressed by] *added in lower margin and marked for insertion*
            to replace cancelled feel
        at first!] ! *added to replace cancelled* :
171   and seek . . . lost sheep] *added on line*
166   of England.] *followed by cancelled* We will see about his writings
            later.
185   Today . . . his own!] *added on line following cancelled* How he is in
            his own!
212   compassion . . . imperfections)] *added on line*
229   light of a glorified body] *interlined below cancelled* lumen gloriae
240   (1958)] *added in upper margin*
        Because Jesus . . . Clairvaux.] *interlined*
        the Galapagos] *preceded by x'd out* Travellers in a desert
        for us] *preceded by x'd out* St Benedict—St Bernard is our
            interpreter of St Benedict
        helps us] *preceded by x'd out* brings this water to us.
241   not be . . . perfect love] *added on line*
        (1) timor . . . malitiam!"] *added in left margin*
242   praise God with] *followed by x'd out* joy
        50:12–19] *preceded by x'd out* 12
243   1. St. Bernardine] *followed by cancelled* Just a few points—
247   concrete?] *altered from* concrete.
        "placed end to end,"] *altered from* placed end to end,
        integration . . . of Christ] *added on line*
        we look . . . results] *typed interlined*
247–48 with our minds . . . new humility.] *typed after* dependence on Mary
            and marked for transposition

247   Mary holds] holds *altered from* hold
249   12] 2 *interlined above cancelled* 5
273   *proficiendo*] *preceded by cancelled* celebrando proficere et
       each feast] each *interlined above cancelled* this
274   Incarnate] *interlined with a caret*
275   to give] *followed by cancelled* way
291   II] *interlined following cancelled* 1955
295   THE FEAST] *preceded by cancelled* NOTES FOR
       OUR LADY'S] *interlined above cancelled* THE
       PRESENTATION] *followed by cancelled* 1956

Readings adopted from TMa

12   John as an individual] *added in left margin*
      voice] voice
      already come] already come
13   him but for] him, for
19   cf. Wisdom] *omitted*
24   *manifests*] manifests
      fact] fact
      salvation by love] salvation and love
27   meet Him!] meet Him.
      His own Person,] His Person,
30   His sacred] The sacred
      faith . . . of faith.] faith in the sacraments.
      bringing the gift] bring the gift
      life, denouncing] life. We must go forth in faith, denouncing
      level and above] level above
      Our monastic] The monastic
      coming] coming
      receiving] receiving
      "*Dies sanctificatus*"] *omitted*
30–31   But now . . . *est.*] *omitted*
32   Read {the} gospel] *omitted*
33   *Dominus*] Deus
      whole . . . formal] *omitted*
33–34   or rather . . . Head.] *omitted*
34   with the first alleluia] with first alleluia
      light—in all] light—in all
      other light] other lights
35   Thy Word] the Word
      we who rejoice] we rejoice
36   *The transformation . . . moral.*] The transformation . . . moral.
38   *with the Church*] to the Church
      to *love*] love

	of Christmas night] of the Christmas night
39	"nativity of light,"] nativity light
	Especially] Secret, Dawn Mass: Especially
40	Divine" (secret: dawn Mass).] Divine."
	calling . . . the God] calling . . . the God
42	ineffably] ineffable
	wonderful new] wonderful and new
43	for Christmas!)] for Christmas)
48	has a cosmic] has a cosmic
	1] omitted
	Dominus—Salvator . . .—apparuit.] Dominus Salvator noster hodie mundo apparuit.
	in the vigilance] interior silence
49	dominates] permeates
	the Magi—their] the Magi—their
	2. The Psalms of Vigils] The Psalms of the Vigil
	their Star.] the star.
	saw then] saw then
	see now] see now
	in power] in heaven
	magnificence] magnificence
	fire] trees
50	sitting] speaking
	(meditative and solemn)] (meditative and)
	of His city] of this city
	which stands firm] nations stand firm
	crowns] thrones
	and to Whom . . . singing] and to know you are praying
	"Come and . . . the Lord,"] and come and . . . the Lord
	a new theme] omitted
	their power] their powers
51	justice] favors
	those who love] those that love
	Epiphany of Love] Epiphany of Love
	listen] bother
	read Isaias . . . half] omitted
88	as weakness] as a weakness
89	Let us . . . hearts.] omitted
142	Lord's Day] Lord's Day
	Sabbath . . . for the Sabbath] Sabbath . . . for the Sabbath
	man, not man] man and not man
143	Lord's Day] omitted
144	Let Him] Let Him
146	let Him . . . to be.] "let Him . . . to be."

as the virtue] as a virtue
for a long] for long
Ida of Léau] *omitted*
essence] exercise

147   *The City of God*] *City of God*
156   *read Daniel 9:26–27*] read Daniel 9:26–27
the profanation of the temple] profanation of temple
The presence . . . everywhere] The presence . . . everywhere
utter . . . situation] utter . . . situation

157   *order of*] order in
163   too is without] is too, without
164   in her communion] in the communion
168   should be by] should by
If we . . . analyze] If we . . . analyze
If we obey . . . interiorly] If we obey . . . interiorly
the theme of the] theme of
The very fact] *The fact*
for the gift] for the *gift*

170   especially *obedient*] specially *obedient*
171   *often . . . tempted*] often . . . tempted
172   theology, indeed,] theology, and indeed,
174   They must be "valiant] They must be zealous for their duties and
     be "valiant

197   then feels] feels then
208   a feast of renunciation] feast of renunciation
a burning] the burning

209   cf. the Visitation] cf. Visitation
epistle of the vigil] epistle of the vigil

211   makes for really] makes really
212   before God the] before the
not vain] not vain

213   (*curiositas*)] *omitted*
vexatio malitiae] *vexatio*

216   what is a confessor?] *omitted*
220   *reality and*] *reality of*
against *useless*] *against useless*

222   of none] none
224   service] services
243   Her Immaculate Heart] *Her Immaculate Heart*
244   as dogma] as a dogma
252   while we walk] walk *altered to* walking
253   *No one . . . Hail Mary*] No one . . . Hail Mary
"sings" itself] "sings" for itself
motherly] *omitted*

Who love us] Who love us

255   are more ... Of course we] *omitted*

259   *in God*] in God

(Feast of St. Michael)] (St. Michael)

260–61 They act ... motorcycle] *omitted*

261   *Raccolta: ... completion*] *omitted*

focusing] forming

help us get] help us to get

262   bring our] bring out

spirits.] spirits!

264   the thousands] thousands

the prophet] a prophet

of angels with] of the angels with

place] places

with angels] with the angels

266   *desires*] desires

desire] desire

will of God] will of God

Tobias 3] Tobias 3

267   brief ... of Tobias] *omitted*

268   *our share*] our *share*

of our peace] of the peace

269   *suspiciousness*] suspiciousness

270   Some ... Bonilla] *Some ... Bonilla*

278   *rebellion ... will*] rebellion ... will

Read] Read

despair] despair

283   also 436] *omitted*

284   the pain of remorse] pain of remorse

285   November 11, 1955] *omitted*

lupi] *lupes*

apatheia] *omitted*

Abraham] Abraham

(fatherhood)] *omitted*

286   idea] *omitted*

"fights"] fights

Martin as bishop] *omitted*

287   saint] sent

kingdom] kingdom

289   clearly] closely

Gospel] Gospel

290   this office] the office

thy house] thy house

our own poor] our poor

rich] rich

see *Him*] see Him
to *see*,] to see,
one has] we have
Gentiles, just] Gentiles' past
see Jesus?] see Jesus?

291   *admitting*] admitting
lays . . . claims] lays . . . claims
"The Son . . . lost."] "The Son . . . lost."
(n.b. *Urbs . . .* heart)] *added on line; omitted*

292   solemnity . . . words] *omitted; added in right margin and marked for insertion*

293   2] *omitted*

294   for penance] of penance
We look . . . of time.] We look . . . of time.
Dissensions] Dissensions

295   *Eccli.*] Eccli.
Proverbs] Proverbs

296   their gift] the gift

297   *to give . . . pleasure*] to give . . . pleasure
Mary's was . . . pleasure.] Mary's was . . . pleasure.
at all costs] at all cost

298   *completely . . . pleasure.*] completely . . . pleasure.
preferences] preference
what is . . . expedient] what is . . . expedient
This means] This means

300   *ask Mary . . . guide us.*] ask Mary . . . guide us.
our hearts wide open,] our hearts wide open,
less . . . sufferings] less . . . sufferings
Him!!] Him.

Readings adopted from TMb

4   and taste.] taste, etc.
sentimental] *sentimental*
sober and *sincere*] sober, sincere

5   *introit*] introit

6   *perfecto" (Magnificat*] perfecto" (Ant. *Mag.*
before the First] *before First*
Sunday of Advent] *Sunday Advent*

7   as a thief] like a thief
Distinguish the] Distinguish
the mere] mere
He is present] *He is present*
God comes unexpectedly] God came unexpectedly
reign] reign

8   *Magnificat . . . is taken*] *Nomen* Domini venit de longinquo (Mag
      antiphon, taken
      Israel?] *followed by* Note the uncertainty—distance, fog,
      awakening, questioning, sentries shivering on the wall—the
      monks at their night office are these sentries—super muros
      tuos Jerusalem constitui custodes.
      3) *The Vigils:*] *added*
      Lessons of . . . Isaias 1:] Read Isaias 1—(Lessons of 1st nocturn)

9   are the princes] are prince
      Read . . . white as snow] read on to 18—sins as scarlet shall be
      made white as snow
      JOHN THE BAPTIST] JOHN BAPTIST
      a) *Second . . . introit*] a) Introit 2nd Sun
      in the liturgy.] in liturgy.
      "*Alleluia*"] Allel. 2nd Sun
      offertory] Offertory 2 Sun
      communio] Communio 2 Sun

10   *vesper*] Vespers
      sing praises to] sing praise to
      b) *Third . . . introit*] b) Introit 3rd Sunday

11   also . . . this Third] 1st antiphon Vespers of 3 Sun
      cf. responsory . . . Sunday:] Resp. 10, 3 sun—
      profound . . . liturgy] profound mystical content of the liturgy
      Precursor, St. John the Baptist] Precursor St John Bapt
      2. *St. John the Baptist:*] St John Baptist

12   of solemnity] of the solemnity
      He . . . claim] John does not claim
      Then they] John's baptism *added in left margin*
      the witness . . . John] the witness and judgement of John
      Note:] Note:
      first tremendous lesson] first tremendous lesson
      proclaims (John 1:26):] proclaims:
      but there . . . of you] *In the midst of you there stands one*
      like the Jews] like Jews
      (John 1:15] *John* 1:15
      John declares] Declares
      3. *The Gospel*] Gospel
      the problem] the "problem"

13   Note that John] Note he
17   whole world.] whole people.
23   John 20:1–2,] *John* 20:1–2,
24   Aggaeus] *Aggaeus*
      Isaias] *Isaias*
      (a mystery)] (mystery)

	are so many] and so many
25	only the fact] only fact
	this is part] this part
	in our hearts] in hearts
	with ourselves] with themselves
	Gloriae?" (Psalm 23).] *gloriae?"*
26	(Athanasian Creed)] *added*
	this is the heart] the heart
	means to penetrate] to penetrate
27	Christ Jesus our Savior] Christ Jesus
	St. John's Gospel] St. John
	forth ye] ye forth
28	at {the} end] end
	Ephesians] *Ephesians*
	Genesis] *Genesis*
29	Ephesians 5] *Ephes. 5*
30	and the spirit] and spirit
39	may shine forth] may show forth
41	epistle: Midnight Mass] epistle: Midnight
	firm . . . abandonment] firm . . . abandonment
	introit: third Mass] introit: third
42	Read] Conclusion: Read
	4:2ff.–14] 4:2ff to 14
50	refuge] refuge—but again the great storm.
	Psalm 46] 46
	Psalm 65] 65—Again same themes
	Psalm 71] 71
51	*Psalm 85*] 85
	poor] poor and thirsty
88	WEDNESDAY OF HOLY WEEK] Holy Week
142–43	difference between . . . created things.] *added*
143	READ] *added*
	a)] *
144	b)] **
156	THE LAST . . . PENTECOST] *The Last . . . Pentecost*
157	the heavens] heaven
162	LOVE] love
	given us] given to us
163	*holy.*] holy.
164	Pentecost is the feast] Pentecost the feast
	The Church also] Church also
	Conclusions] Conclusions
165	and our strength] and to our strength
166	those who . . . rivers] those in the rivers

	n. 4] n. 5
167	LOVE] Love
	the consideration] consideration
169	put into effect] put it into effect
	desire the strength] desire strength
169	Pride and self-complacency] Pride, self-complacency
170	alas!] alas
	must be especially] should be especially
171	*His charity*] His charity
195	*The Mystery . . . Compassion*] THE MYSTERY . . . COMPASSION
196	*Subjective redemption*] Subjective redemption
	objective redemption] objective redemption
	argument] argument
	Mary's Share in Calvary] Mary's Share in Calvary
197	Father, seems] Father, seemed
199	April 29] *added on line*
	inspiration] inspiration
202	Read Romans] *Read Romans*
	bless and thank God] thank God and bless Him
204	({as} if {a} forest fire)] (forest fire)
209	God chooses] God who chooses
	helpless and reserves] helpless, reserves
211	*The hymn for lauds*] The hymn for lauds
	wonder and admiration] *wonder admiration*
212	ourselves with security] ourselves security
	for the vigil] *for vigil*
	because they stand] for they stand
	What do they teach us?] What do they teach us?
213	simple] A simple
224	vigils] matins
	anointing them] anointing it
237	joy and optimism] joy—optimism
	upon the earth] upon the people
238	rather artless] even rather artless
243	came forth from] came from
244	date, September 8] date, 8 September
245	The year begins . . . 1.] (Year begins . . . 1)
247	the Roman] Roman
261	*Bread of Angels*] Bread of Angels
262	*the hymn*] the hymn
263	*Tobias*] Tobias
264	churches are the] churches the
269	64, 65,] 65, 64,
278	this was the philosophy] this the philosophy

279   not to be too] not be too
280   10:17] 10, verse 17
281   the whole difference] whole difference
       in a place of peace] in peace
       that they are suffering] of their suffering
285   SAINT MARTIN] *St Martin*
286   saints and virgins] saints, virgins
       The same] Same
       is taken up] taken up
       the invitatory] *invitatory*
       Now, a higher] A higher
       face the enemy] face enemy
       tenth antiphon] tenth
       eleventh antiphon] eleventh
       of second] second
287   FEAST . . . ORDER] Feast . . . Order
288   mind is St.] mind like St.
289   The GOSPEL] *Feast of the Dedication of the Church. II.* The GOSPEL
       it is the gospel . . . heights.] it is in the gospel that the greater
          mystical heights are reached.
290   by Him that] by this that
       build] build!
       Zacchaeus took] *He took*
291   *the various reactions*] the various reactions
       abandon] trust
       that responsibility] the responsibility
       CHURCH] CHURCH (1955)
293   (a few main ideas)] (a few of the main ideas)
       from the . . . sermon] From the beginning
       building is holy] building holy
294   (520)] *added*
296   religious is one who has] religious has
297   poverty and obedience] poverty, obedience
299   our life, all our thoughts] our lives, our thoughts
       of God and of] of God, of
       Mary. *We no*] Mary. We *no*
       profitable. *We no*] profitable. We *no*
299   to hand] from His hand
       it beforehand.] them beforehand.
300   *Why the . . . obedience?*] Why this . . . obedience?
       If we] 2) If we
       best fit] best fits
       be most *childlike*] be most childlike
       cares] cares!

Readings adopted from TL

1–3	TABLE OF . . . Last Sunday after Pentecost] *added*
62	disturbed] *interlined above cancelled* growing
66	(cf. Vonier)] *added on line*
70	effects] *altered from* effect
	the ashes] *preceded by cancelled* of
	are a] *interlined with a caret*
	sacramental!] ! *interlined*
	of the blessing)] *added on line*
72	salubre] *altered from* salubra
76	"about"] *altered from* about
95	liturgy] *interlined below and marked for insertion*
97	come] *interlined above cancelled* have been
	mandatum)] *followed by cancelled* 1. Morning—No Mass *de Beata* after Night Office—Interval—about an hour after frustulum Chapter will be fairly long.
	1.] *added in left margin before cancelled* 2. Tierce and
	of {the} Poor] *followed by cancelled* at [illegible time]
98	guest house.] *followed by cancelled* 3. Work—about two hours and a quarter. 4. Interval—one hour; then *Sext*, dinner etc. 5. After dinner—interval is ten minutes longer; then *None*, followed by Lenten reading. 6. No work in the afternoon. After *None*, Lenten reading. *Then an interval of one hour.*
	2.] *added in left margin before cancelled* 7.
	MANDATUM] *followed by cancelled* Wash feet well after Lenten reading. (*The one time annually when it is prescribed!*) *Do not rise* when Reverend Father and the other foot washers enter. Reverend Father washes twelve person's [*sic*] feet, including the *first two choir novices on each side.* (Try to keep feet hidden while removing and putting on shoes and sox). Afterwards do not rise when they enter but rise with Father Prior as the washers bow before abbatial seat.
	Mass of] *preceded by cancelled* 8
	evening Mass] *interlined with a caret*
	at the very . . . instituted!] *added on line*
99	of the feet] *followed by cancelled* (Collation, Compline, retire.)
	(afternoon)] *added on line*
105	quite a] *interlined below and marked for insertion*
109	We must] *added in left margin*
110	Our bad . . . weakness.] *added on line*
121	stability of God] *followed by cancelled* suggested
150	He is also . . . other people] *added on line*
151	"under . . . God."] *altered from* under . . . God.
159–61	LITURGICAL . . . Perfect Religious] *added*

163	Augustine)] *followed by cancelled* Ephesians
175	protection] *altered from* protections
182	(March 19)] *added on line*
195	(Friday in Passion Week)] *added on line*
203	(Day of Recollection: May)] *added on line*
207	(June 24)] *added on line*
212	(June 29)] *added on line*
213	(July 2)] *added on line*
216	I] *added on line*
	(July 16)] *added on line*
218	II] *interlined*
	(July 16)] *added on line*
222	(July 22)] *added on line*
228	(August 6)] *added on line*
234	(August 15)] *added on line*
237	(August 20)] *added on line*
243	(The sermon . . . ideas.)] *added in lower margin*
	(August 21)] *added on line*
244	(September 8)] *added on line*
288	(November 15)] *added on line*

BIBLIOGRAPHY

Abbo, John A., and Jerome D. Hannan, *The Sacred Canons: A Concise Presentation of the Current Disciplinary Norms of the Church*, 2 vols. St. Louis: Herder, 1952.

Abbott, Walter M., gen. ed. *The Documents of Vatican II*. New York: Guild, 1966.

Acta Sanctorum. 68 vols. Antwerp: Société des Bollandistes, 1643–1940.

Berdiaev, Nicolas. *Le Sens de la Création: Un Essai de Justification de l'Homme*. Translated by Julien Cain. Textes et études philosophiques. Bruges: Desclée de Brouwer, 1955.

Biver, Paul. *Père Lamy: Apostle and Mystic*. Translated by John O'Connor. London: Burns, Oates and Washbourne, 1937.

Bouyer, Louis. *The Paschal Mystery: Meditations on the Last Three Days of Holy Week*. Translated by Mary Benoit, RSM. Chicago: Regnery, 1950.

Breviarium Cisterciense Reformatum. 4 vols. Westmalle, Belgium: Ex Typis Cisterciensibus, 1951.

Butler, Cuthbert, OSB. *Benedictine Monachism*. London: Longmans, Green, 1919.

Cabrol, Fernand, OSB. *Le Livre de la Prière Antique*. 5th ed. Tours: Mame et Fils, 1919.

Catechism of the Council of Trent for Parish Priests. Translated by John A. McHugh, OP and Charles J. Callan, OP. 2nd ed. New York: Wagner, 1934.

Catechismus ex Decreto Concilii Tridentini ad Parochos. Ratisbon: Manz, 1866.

Catherine of Genoa, Saint. *Treatise on Purgatory; The Dialogue*. Translated by Charlotte Balfour and Helen Douglas Irvine. New York: Sheed & Ward, 1946.

Cicero, Marcus Tullius. *De Natura Deorum; Academica*. Translated by H. Rackham. Loeb Classical Library. New York: Putnam, 1933.

Colomer, Luis. *The Catholic Church, the Mystical Body of Christ*. Translated by Palmer L. Rockey, 2 vols. Paterson, NJ: St. Anthony Guild, 1952, 1956.

Daniel, Walter. *The Life of Ailred of Riveaulx*. Edited and Translated by F. M. Powicke. New York: Nelson, 1950.

Denzinger, Heinrich, and Clement Bannwart, SJ, eds. *Enchiridion Symbolorum Definitionum et Declarationum de Rebus Fidei et Morum*. 12th ed. Freiburg: Herder, 1913.

Dickens, Charles. *David Copperfield*. 1850. Reprint, New York: Penguin, 2004.

Dumas, Alexandre. *The Count of Monte Cristo*. 1844–45. Reprint, New York: Modern Library, 1996.

Kleist, James A., trans. *The Epistles of St. Clement of Rome and St. Ignatius of Antioch*. 3rd imprint. Ancient Christian Writers 1. Westminster, MD: Newman, 1949.

Flicoteaux, Emmanuel, OSB. *Le Triomphe de Pâques: La Cinquantaine Pascale*. L'Esprit liturgique 6. Paris: Cerf, 1952.

Franke, Hermann. *Lent and Easter: The Church's Spring.* Translated by Benedictines of St. John's Abbey. Westminster, MD: Newman, 1955.

Gaillard, Jean. "Dimanche." In *Dictionnaire de Spiritualité Ascétique et Mystique*, edited by Marcel Viller, SJ, et al., 3:948–82. 17 vols. Paris: Beauchesne, 1932–1995.

Garrigou-Lagrange, Reginald, OP. *The Mother of the Saviour and Our Interior Life.* Translated by Bernard J. Kelly, CSSp. St. Louis: Herder, 1957.

Gasparri, Petrus Cardinalis, ed. *Codex Iuris Canonici.* New York: Kenedy, 1918.

Gilson, Étienne. *The Mystical Theology of St. Bernard.* Translated by A. H. C. Downes. New York: Sheed & Ward, 1940.

Guardini, Romano. *The Living God.* Translated by Stanley Godman; and *The Rosary of Our Lady.* Translated by H. Von Schuecking. The Inner Life Series. New York: Longmans, Green, 1957.

———. *The Lord.* Translated by Elinor Castendyk Briefs. Chicago: Regnery, 1954.

———. *Les Signes Sacrés.* Translated by Antoine Giroudet. Paris: Spes, 1938.

Guéranger, Prosper, OSB. *The Liturgical Year.* Translated by Laurence Shepherd, OSB. 15 vols. Westminster, MD: Newman, 1948–1949.

Guillet, Jacques. *Thèmes Bibliques: Études sur l'Expression et le Développement de la Révelation.* Theologie 18. Paris: Aubier, 1954.

Hamman, Adalbert, ed. *Patrologiae Latinae, Supplementum.* 5 vols. Paris: Garnier, 1958–1974.

Jones, Alexander. "Matthew." In *A Catholic Commentary on Holy Scripture*, edited by Bernard Orchard, OSB, et al., 851–904. New York: Nelson, 1953.

Kennedy, John S. *Light on the Mountain: The Story of La Salette.* New York: McMullen, 1953.

Konrad of Eberbach. *Exordium Magnum Cisterciense.* Edited by Bruno Griesser. Series scriptorum S. Ordinis Cisterciensis 2. Rome: Cistercienses, 1961.

Lambing, Andrew. *The Sacramentals of the Holy Catholic Church.* New York: Benziger, 1892.

Laurentin, René. *Initiation Théologique.* 4 vols. Paris: Cerf, 1954.

Lefebvre, Gaspar, OSB. *Saint Andrew Daily Missal.* 4 vols. St. Paul: Lohmann, 1947.

[Lehodey, Vital, OCSO] *A Spiritual Directory for Religious.* Translated from the Original French Text "*Directoire Spirituel à l'Usage des Cisterciens de la Stricte Observance*" by a Priest of New Melleray Abbey, Peosta, Iowa. Trappist, KY: Abbey of Our Lady of Gethsemani, 1946.

La Liturgie: Les Enseignements Pontificaux, Présentation et Tables par les Moines de Solesmes. Paris: Desclée, 1954.

Loehr, Aemeliana, OSB. *L'Année de Seigneur: Le Mystère du Christ au Cours de l'Année Liturgique*, 2 vols. Bruges: Beyaert, 1946.

———. *The Mass through the Year.* Translated by I. T. Hale. 2 vols. Westminster, MD: Newman, 1958–1959.

———. *The Year of Our Lord: The Mystery of Christ in the Liturgical Year.* Translated by a Monk of Saint Benedict. New York: Kenedy, 1937.

McCann, Justin, OSB, ed. and trans. *The Rule of St. Benedict in Latin and English.* Orchard Books Series. London: Burns, Oates, 1952.

Mercenier, E. *La Prière des Églises de Rite Byzantin.* 2 vols. in 3 bks. Chevetogne, Belgium: Monastère de Chevetogne, 1937–1953.

Mersch, Emile, SJ. *The Whole Christ: The Historical Development of the Doctrine of the Mystical Body in Scripture and Tradition.* Translated by John R. Kelly, SJ. Milwaukee: Bruce, 1938.

Merton, Thomas. "The Advent Mystery." *Worship* 38 (December 1963) 17–25.

———. *The Ascent to Truth.* New York: Harcourt, Brace, 1951.

———. "Ash Wednesday." *Worship* 33 (February 1959) 165–70.

———. *Bread in the Wilderness.* New York: New Directions, 1953.

———. *Cassian and the Fathers: Initiation into the Monastic Tradition,* edited by Patrick F. O'Connell. Monastic Wisdom 1. Kalamazoo, MI: Cistercian, 2005.

———. *Charter, Customs, and Constitutions of the Cistercians: Initiation into the Monastic Tradition 7.* Edited by Patrick F. O'Connell. Monastic Wisdom 41. Collegeville, MN: Cistercian, 2015.

———. "Christian Worship and Social Reform." *The Merton Seasonal* 34/4 (Winter 2009) 3–11.

———. *The Christmas Sermons of Bl. Guerric of Igny.* Translated by Sr. Rose of Lima. Gethsemani, KY: Abbey of Gethsemani, 1959.

———. "Church and Bishop in St. Ignatius of Antioch." *Worship* 37 (January 1963) 110–20.

———. *Cistercian Fathers and Forefathers: Essays and Conferences,* edited by Patrick F. O'Connell. Hyde Park, NY: New City, 2018.

———. *The Cistercian Fathers and Their Monastic Theology: Initiation into the Monastic Tradition 8.* Edited by Patrick F. O'Connell. Monastic Wisdom 42. Collegeville, MN: Cistercian, 2016.

———. *The Climate of Monastic Prayer.* Cistercian Studies 1. Washington, DC: Cistercian, 1969.

———. *Conjectures of a Guilty Bystander.* Garden City, NY: Doubleday, 1966.

———. *Contemplative Prayer.* New York: Herder & Herder, 1969.

———. *Dancing in the Water of Life: Seeking Peace in the Hermitage. Journals, vol. 5: 1963–1965,* edited by Robert E. Daggy. San Francisco: HarperCollins, 1997.

———. *Early Essays: 1947–1952.* Edited with an introduction by Patrick F. O'Connell. Cistercian Studies 266. Collegeville, MN: Cistercian, 2015.

———. "Easter: The New Life." *Worship* 33 (April 1959) 276–84.

———. *Entering the Silence: Becoming a Monk & Writer. Journals, vol. 2: 1941–1952,* edited by Jonathan Montaldo. San Francisco: HarperCollins, 1996.

———. "The Good News of the Nativity." *The Bible Today* 21 (December 1965) 1367–75.

———. "A Homily on Light and the Virgin Mary." *Worship* 37 (October 1963) 572–80.

———. *In the Valley of Wormwood: Cistercian Blessed and Saints of the Golden Age,* edited by Patrick Hart, OCSO. Cistercian Studies 233. Collegeville, MN: Cistercian, 2013.

———. *An Introduction to Christian Mysticism: Initiation into the Monastic Tradition 3.* Edited by Patrick F. O'Connell. Monastic Wisdom 13. Kalamazoo, MI: Cistercian, 2008.

———. *The Last of the Fathers: Saint Bernard of Clairvaux and the Encyclical Letter, Doctor Mellifluus.* New York: Harcourt, Brace, 1954.

———. *Learning to Love. Journals, vol. 6: 1966–1967,* edited by Christine M. Bochen. San Francisco: HarperCollins, 1997.

———. *The Life of the Vows: Initiation into the Monastic Tradition 6*. Edited by Patrick F. O'Connell. Monastic Wisdom 30. Collegeville, MN: Cistercian, 2012.

———. "Liturgical Renewal: The Open Approach." *The Critic* 33 (December 1964) 10–15.

———. "Liturgy and Spiritual Personalism." *Worship* 34 (October 1960) 494–507.

———. *Love and Living*. Edited by Naomi Burton Stone and Br. Patrick Hart. New York: Farrar, Straus & Giroux, 1979.

———. *Medieval Cistercian History: Initiation into the Monastic Tradition 9*. Edited by Patrick F. O'Connell, Monastic Wisdom 43. Collegeville, MN: Cistercian, 2019.

———. *A Monastic Introduction to Sacred Scripture*. Edited by Patrick F. O'Connell. Novitiate Conferences on Scripture and Liturgy 1. Eugene, OR: Cascade, 2020.

———. *The Monastic Journey*. Edited by Brother Patrick Hart. Mission, KS: Sheed, Andrews & McMeel, 1977.

———. *Monastic Observances: Initiation into the Monastic Tradition 5*. Edited by Patrick F. O'Connell. Monastic Wisdom 25. Collegeville, MN: Cistercian, 2010.

———. *Mystics and Zen Masters*. New York: Farrar, Straus & Giroux, 1967.

———. "The Name of the Lord." *Worship* 38 (February 1964) 142–51.

———. *Nativity Kerygma*. Trappist, KY: Abbey of Gethsemani, 1958.

———. "Nativity Kerygma." *Worship* 34 (December 1959) 2–9.

———. *New Seeds of Contemplation*. New York: New Directions, 1961.

———. *Notes on Genesis and Exodus*. Edited by Patrick F. O'Connor. Novitiate Conferences on Scripture and Liturgy 2. Eugene, OR: Cascade, 2021.

———. *Pre-Benedictine Monasticism: Initiation into the Monastic Tradition 2*. Edited by Patrick F. O'Connell. Monastic Wisdom 9. Kalamazoo, MI: Cistercian, 2006.

———. *Raids on the Unspeakable*. New York: New Directions, 1966.

———. *The Road to Joy: The Letters of Thomas Merton to New and Old Friends*. Selected and edited by Robert E. Daggy. New York: Farrar, Straus & Giroux, 1989.

———. *The Rule of Saint Benedict: Initiation into the Monastic Tradition 4*. Edited by Patrick F. O'Connell. Monastic Wisdom 19. Collegeville, MN: Cistercian, 2009.

———. *Run to the Mountain: The Story of a Vocation. Journals, vol. 1: 1939–1941*. Edited by Patrick Hart. San Francisco: HarperCollins, 1995.

———. "Le Sacrement de l'Avent dans la Spiritualité de Saint Bernard." *Dieu Vivant* 23 (1953) 23–43.

———. "The Scandal, Perspectives and Lessons of *Ecclesiastes*." *Monastic Orientation*, Series VI (Dec. 1954–Oct. 1955), 47–56. In *Collected Essays*, vol. 17 (24-volume bound set of published and unpublished materials assembled at the Abbey of Gethsemani and available both there and at the Thomas Merton Center, Bellarmine University, Louisville, Kentucky).

———. *The School of Charity: The Letters of Thomas Merton on Religious Renewal and Spiritual Direction*. Selected and edited by Patrick Hart. New York: Farrar, Straus & Giroux, 1990.

———. *A Search for Solitude: Pursuing the Monk's True Life. Journals, vol. 3: 1952–1960*. Edited by Lawrence S. Cunningham. San Francisco: HarperCollins, 1996.

———. *Seasons of Celebration*. New York: Farrar, Straus & Giroux, 1965.

———. *Seeds of Contemplation*. New York: New Directions, 1949.

———. *Seeds of Destruction*. New York: Farrar, Straus & Giroux, 1964.

———. "Self-Denial and the Christian." *Commonweal* 51 (31 March 1950) 649–53.

———. *The Sign of Jonas*. New York: Harcourt, Brace, 1953.

———. *Silence in Heaven: A Book on the Monastic Life*. New York: Crowell, 1956.

———. *Solitude and Togetherness*. Audiobook. 11 CD set. CD 9: "Silence and Purity of Heart." Chevy Chase, MD: Now You Know Media, 2012.

———. *The Springs of Contemplation: A Retreat at the Abbey of Gethsemani*. Edited by Jane Marie Richardson, SL. New York: Farrar, Straus & Giroux, 1992.

———. "Time and the Liturgy." *Worship* 31 (December 1956) 2–10.

———. "The Time of the End Is the Time of No Room." *Motive* 26 (December 1965) 4–9.

———. *Turning toward the World: The Pivotal Years. Journals, vol. 4: 1960–1963*. Edited by Victor A. Kramer. San Francisco: HarperCollins, 1996.

———. *What Are These Wounds? The Life of a Cistercian Mystic, Saint Lutgarde of Aywières*. Milwaukee: Bruce, 1950.

———, trans. *Wisdom of the Desert: Sayings from the Desert Fathers of the Fourth Century*. New York: New Directions, 1960.

———. *Witness to Freedom: The Letters of Thomas Merton in Times of Crisis*. Selected and edited by William H. Shannon. New York: Farrar, Straus & Giroux, 1994.

Merton, Thomas, and Robert Lax. *The Letters of Thomas Merton and Robert Lax: When Prophecy Still Had a Voice*. Edited by Arthur W. Biddle. Lexington: University Press of Kentucky, 2001.

Migne, J.-P., ed. *Patrologiae Cursus Completus, Series Latina [PL]*. 221 vols. Paris: Garnier, 1844–1865.

———, ed. *Patrologiae Cursus Completus, Series Graeca [PG]*. 161 vols. Paris: Garnier, 1857–1866.

Missale Cisterciense: Reformatum juxta Decretum Sacrorum Rituum Congregationis Diei 3 Julii 1869. Westmalle, Belgium: Ex Typographia Ordinis Cist. Strict. Obs., 1951.

Missale Romanum: Ex Decreto Sacrosancti Concilii Tridentini Restitutum: S. Pii V, Pontificis Maximi, Jussu Editum: Aliorum Pontificum Cura Recognitum: a Pio X Reformatum et Benedicti XV Auctoritate Vulgatum. 4th ed. New York: Benziger, 1944.

Montfort, Louis-Marie Grignion de,, Saint. *True Devotion to Mary*. Translated by Frederick William Faber. Bay Shore, NY: Montfort, 1956.

Nomasticon Cisterciense, seu Antiquiores Ordinis Cisterciensis Constitutiones A.R.P.D. Juliano Paris . . . Editio Nova, ed. Hugo Séjalon. Solesmes: E Typographeo Sancti Petri, 1892.

Nugent, Robert, SDS. *Thomas Merton & Thérèse Lentfoehr: The Story of a Friendship*. Staten Island, NY: St Pauls, 2012.

O'Connell, Patrick F. "The First Cistercian and the Greatest Trappist: Thomas Merton's Poems on John the Baptist." *The Merton Annual* 26 (2013) 107–39.

———. "Mary." *The Thomas Merton Encyclopedia* by William H. Shannon, Christine M. Bochen, and Patrick F. O'Connell, 285–87. Maryknoll, NY: Orbis, 2002.

———. "Thomas Merton's *Silence in Heaven* and *The Silent Life*: The Evolution of a Contested Text." *American Benedictine Review* 67/3 (September 2016) 266–93.

O'Malley, John W. *Catholic History for Today's Church: How Our Past Illuminates Our Present*. Lanham, MD: Rowman & Littlefield, 2015.

Parsch, Pius. *The Church's Year of Grace*. Translated by Daniel F. Coogan et al. 5 vols. Popular Liturgical Library. Collegeville, MN: Liturgical, 1953–1959.

Pax Animae: A Short Treatise, Declaring How Necessary the Tranquillity and Peace of the Soul Is, and How It May Be Obtained, by St. Peter Alcantara, From an Old English

Translation of 1665, ed. Jerome Vaughan, OSB. 2nd ed. London: Burns & Oates, 1876.

Peers, E. Allison, ed. and trans. *The Complete Works of Saint John of the Cross.* 3 vols. Westminster, MD: Newman, 1949.

———, ed. and trans. *The Complete Works of Saint John of the Cross.* 3 vols. 3rd ed. Westminster, MD: Newman, 1953.

———, ed. and trans. *The Complete Works of Saint Teresa of Jesus.* 3 vols. New York: Sheed & Ward, 1946.

Philippe, Paul, OP. *The Blessed Virgin and the Priesthood.* Translated by Dorothy Cole. Chicago: Regnery, 1955.

Pius XII, Pope. *Encyclical Letter of His Holiness Pius XII on the Sacred Liturgy: Mediator Dei* (Vatican Library Translation). Translated by Shawn G. Sheehan. Washington, DC: National Catholic Welfare Conference, 1948.

———. *Munificentissimus Deus—The definition by His Holiness, Pope Pius XII, of the dogma that Mary, the Virgin Mother of God, was assumed, body and soul, into the glory of heaven.* Translated by Joseph C. Fenton. Washington, DC: National Catholic Welfare Conference, [1951].

Pontifical Biblical Commission. *Ex Commissione de Re Biblica, De Libri Isaiae Indole et Auctore. Acta Sanctae Sedis* 41 [1908] 613–14.

Pontificale Romanum Summorum Pontificum Jussu Editum a Benedicto XIV et Leone XIII, Pontificibus Maximis Recognitum et Castigatum. Taurini: Marietti, 1941.

Power, E., SJ. "Isaias." In *A Catholic Commentary on Holy Scripture*, edited by Bernard Orchard, OSB, 539–73. New York: Nelson, 1953.

The Raccolta: Or, A Manual of Indulgences, Prayers, and Devotions Enriched with Indulgences. Issued by the Sacred Penitentiary Apostolic. New York: Benziger, 1952.

Regulations of the Order of Cistercians of the Strict Observance Published by the General Chapter of 1926. Dublin: Gill, 1927.

Rituale Parvum Cisterciense e Fontibus Authenticis Excerptum. Roscrea, Ireland: Typis Cisterciensibus, 1944.

La Sainte Bible traduite en français sous la direction de l'École Biblique de Jérusalem. Paris: Cerf, 1956.

Scheeben, Matthias. *Mariology.* Translated by T. L. M. J. Geukers. 2 vols. St. Louis: Herder, 1946–47.

———. *The Mysteries of Christianity.* Translated by Cyril Vollert, SJ. St. Louis: Herder, 1946.

Schroeder, H. J., trans. *Canons and Decrees of the Council of Trent: Original Text with English Translation.* St. Louis: Herder, 1941.

Shakespeare, William. *Romeo and Juliet*, ed. J. A. Bryant, Jr. New York: Signet Classic, 1998.

Stolz, Anselme, OSB. *L'Ascèse Chrétienne.* Chevetogne: Editions de Bénédictins d'Amay, 1948.

Thomas à Kempis. *The Imitation of Christ.* Edited by Thomas S. Kepler. World Devotional Classics. Cleveland: World, 1952.

Thomas Aquinas, Saint. *Sancti Thomae Aquinatis Doctoris Angelici Ordinis Praedicatorum Opera Omnia, secundum Impressionem Petri Fiaccadori Parmae 1852–1873 Photolithographice Reimpressa.* 25 vols. New York: Misurgia, 1948.

Trethowan, Illtyd, OSB. *Christ in the Liturgy.* New York: Sheed & Ward, 1952.

Van Houtryve, Idesbald. *Benedictine Peace*. Translated by Leonard J. Doyle. Westminster, MD: Newman, 1950.

Vonier, Anscar, OSB. *The Collected Works of Abbot Vonier*. 3 vols. Rev. ed. Westminster, MD: Newman, 1952–1953.

Waddell, Chrysogonus, OCSO, ed. and trans. *Narrative and Legislative Texts from Early Cîteaux*. Studia et Documenta 9. Cîteaux: Commentarii Cistercienses, 1999.

Ware, Kallistos. "How Do We Enter the Heart, and What Do We Find When We Enter?" In *Merton & Hesychasm: The Prayer of the Heart*, edited by Bernadette Dieker and Jonathan Montaldo, 3–16. The Fons Vitae Thomas Merton Series. Louisville: Fons Vitae, 2003.

Winandy, Jacques. *Ambroise Autpert: Moine et Théologien*. Tradition monastique; collection de spiritualité monastique. Paris: Plon, 1953.

SCRIPTURAL INDEX

1

∽

New Testament

GENERAL INDEX

191–92, 304, destruction of, 120, drink of, 348, elements of, 304, hour of, 175, love of, 278, 296, moment of, 284, of body, 107, of soul, 59, 107, pact with, 278, passage through, lviii, 280, penalty of, 59, perpetual, xlii, 303, prince of, 59, punishment of, 59, reminder of, xlii, 302, salvation from, 7, shadow of, 23, 193, 316, shameful, 278, sign of, xxxvi, 165, sin as cause of, 58, slaves of, 113, to law, lx, to sin, lx, tree of, 165, tyranny of, 22, 60, victory over, xxxi, xlvi, lviii, 57, 76–77, 144, 376, victory through, 145, waters of, 63, 71

debt, 113, 305, for sin, 113, 222
debtors, 222
decay, sign of, xlii
deceitful, 277
deceitfulness, 278
deceivers, 346
deception, 188
decline, 302
dedication, final, 294, perfect, 294
dedication of church, ceremonies of, 293, day of, 292, feast of, xiii, xxxv, xli, 288–95, 363–64, rites of, 293
deer, 106, 136
defeat(s), 148, virtue of, 109
defect(s), 372, in obedience, 372
defection, 205
deficiency, in holiness, 223
defilement, bodily, 370
degeneration, 335
degradation, utter, 109
degrees, of spiritual life, 74
deity, archaic, 123, Manichean, 146
deliberation, 87
delight, 167, wooded, 181
deliverance, 310, 314, 317
delusion, lvi, 203

demands, 139, 203, irate, 139, tyrannical, 372, unformulated, 268
demon, noonday, 169
Denzinger, Heinrich, 59, 260
dependence, 186, complete, 258
deportation, 316
deprivation(s), 186, 298
dereliction, 353
derision, 353
desecration, 156
desert(s), xxiii, lxiii, 20, 48, 50, 64, 72, 117, 119, 151, 208, 334–35, 343, 357
desire(s), xxi, 4–7, 9, 21, 171, 216, 223, 271, 273, 296, 300, 326, 349, 359, anxious, xxv, 15, ardent, 6, 165, 168, 226, deep, 248, evil, 360, 372, fervent, 168, for truth, 343, good, 293, heavenly, 102, 106, 136, humble, 4, intensity of, 188, loving, 4, man of, lxiii, 265–66, objects of, 239, purity of, 188, secular, 35, spiritual, 70, to please, 16, worldly, 35, 39
desks, 98
desolation, 156, 170, 265, abomination of, 156, 265
despair, 139, 221, 278, 319, sin of, 354
despairing, hope of, 246
destiny, eternal, 302
destitute, lvii
destruction, xxxvi, 4, 18, 117, 165, 278–79, deliverance from 240, of nature, 276, of sin, 87, of world, 157, poison of, 278, threat of, 314, tree of, 165
detachment, 149, 248, 268, from persons, 202, from self, 202, from things, 202, scientific, lxxv
detraction, 276, 278, statute on, 74
development, human, xliii, social, lxxiii, spiritual, xliii

of eternal life, 249, to David,
315
propagation, 371
prophecy, xxviii, 26, 133, 358,
eschatological, 265,
fulfillment of, 85, 94, 265,
messianic, 265, scriptural,
85, season of, 313, three
dimensions of, 5–6
prophet(s), 5–6, 12, 25, 30, 33, 74,
89, 93, 95, 130, 132, 134,
153, 178, 184, 209, 222,
257, 263, 265, 311–12,
333, 341, 352, 358, 364,
367, awareness of, 312,
credentials of, 210, desire of,
xxvii, false, 149, 156, 317,
greatest of, 208, longing of,
18, 306, message of, 312,
mission of, 312, mouth of,
210, of servant songs, 88,
vision of, 264, vocation of,
210, 312, words of, 235
proportion, 276, sense of, 327
propositions, assent to, 356,
revealed, 356
proselytes, 130
Proserpine (Persephone), 175
protection, 175, angelic, 260, of
monastic life, 202
proud, 258
proverbs, maxims of, 91
providence, 147–48, divine, 119,
182, 184, 210, 259, 312,
379, mystery of, 133, 147,
particular, 260
prudence, 166, 180, 295, path of, 20,
worldly, 202
prudent, 295
Prudentius, 230
psalms, xxxvi, 213, 310, in English,
li, love for, li
psalter, 99, Latin, liii, Vulgate, l
psychology, religious, lxxvi
publican, 150
punishment, 59, 89, 108, 113,
281, of damned, 281, of

purgatory, 281, spirit of, 327,
terrible, 281
purgation, 283, interior, 176
purgatory, 108–9, 280–85, as place
of peace, 281, punishments
of, 281, souls in, 282, 284–85
purification, xlvi, 38, 41, 65–66, 281,
368, interior, 16, outward,
83, period of, 76
purity, false, 377, interior, 377,
lovers of, 246, of charity,
273, 368, of love, 378, of
monastic tradition, 273,
original, 367, passive, 244,
static, 244
purpose, 379
pusillanimity, 221, 299
python(s), 17, 316

qualities, mediocre, 171
Quenon, Paul, vii–viii, lxxix, 92
quiet, 101, monastic, 200
quietism, 167, 378
Quinquagesima, xx, 65–66

rabbi, title of, 187
race, human, 105, 133, 205, 228,
257, particular, 372
racism, lxxii
Rages, 266
Raguel, 266
raiment, 331
rain, 50, 106, 110, 123, 214, 329,
331, 358
rainbow, 240
ram(s), 8, 233, 351
ransom, 193
Raphael, Archangel, 263, 266–67
rapidity, 280
rashes, 53
ratification, of Son's sacrifice, 103
reading(s), 258, 298, different, 146,
Lenten, 99, light, 145–46,
liturgical, xlix, spiritual, 99,
146, vernacular, xlix
reality, 12, 306, 334, acceptance of,
170, eternal, 310, facing, xlii,
303, flight from, xlii, 303,

Printed in the USA
CPSIA information can be obtained
at www.ICGtesting.com
LVHW092041271223
767549LV00004B/55